The
HUMAN PERSON

An Approach to an Integral Theory
of Personality

By

MAGDA B. ARNOLD
ASSOCIATE PROFESSOR OF PSYCHOLOGY
LOYOLA UNIVERSITY, CHICAGO

and

JOHN A. GASSON, S. J.
PROFESSOR OF PSYCHOLOGY
SPRING HILL COLLEGE

IN COLLABORATION WITH

CHARLES A. CURRAN   ALEXANDER A. SCHNEIDERS

VINCENT V. HERR, S.J.   WALTER SMET, S.J.

FRANK J. KOBLER   LOUIS B. SNIDER, S.J.

NOËL MAILLOUX, O.P.   ANNETTE WALTERS, C.S.J.

THE RONALD PRESS COMPANY ✦ NEW YORK

Library of Congress Catalog Card Number: 54–6960

PRINTED IN THE UNITED STATES OF AMERICA

PREFACE

IN THIS volume a group of Catholic psychologists have attempted to formulate an integrated theory of personality based on a Christian conception of human nature. They first examine the basic assumptions and principles of scientific theories in general and of theories of personality in particular. Following a survey of present-day views, a theory of personality is developed which includes human values yet rests on a valid scientific basis and can be tested experimentally. In this theory the related factors of learning and emotion are given their proper place in personality integration, thus providing an important theoretical contribution in these two areas. Finally, this personalistic conception of man is shown to provide the theoretical foundation for a psychotherapy which respects Christian concepts and values. A discussion of the role of religion in focusing personality integration concludes the book.

This book, with its emphasis on the place of values in modern psychology, addresses itself to professional psychologists as well as serious students, to all who are interested in a comprehensive study of man. It is a primary text for courses in personality. As supplementary reading, it will be found useful in courses in Theory and Systems, Learning, Emotion, and Psychotherapy.

The papers given at the Workshop in Personality at Barat College in June, 1951, are the basis of this volume, although some of the papers have been developed by the contributors beyond the limits set in the symposium. At the workshop ample discussion was allowed for each paper. But the discussion was sometimes diffuse, raising certain issues and leaving out others, and taking for granted many points that needed to be made explicit to a wider audience. In editing the papers, it was found desirable to reduce such discussion to the essentials, to clarify the issues raised, and to supply needed background material. This we did in the sections headed "Comment."

iii

Through these "Comments" we hope to achieve an integrated whole instead of a collection of individual papers and to preserve the remarkable spirit of harmony and unity of purpose which characterized the discussions. These "Comments" are presented in two forms. For those papers where brief comments suffice, they appear as the final section of the chapter. There were other papers, however, which seemed to require more extensive treatment because they represent critical surveys of some field of psychology or advocate a particular type of approach. For these we have supplied an additional chapter to provide for a positive treatment of the issues raised. While the individual authors are responsible only for the opinions expressed in their chapters, as editors we are responsible for writing the comments and expanding some of them into separate chapters.

The conference at Barat College chose personality as the center of discussion because the greatest need for an integral theory is bound to be felt in the area which deals directly with the proper subject matter of psychology, the human person. At the same time, it was necessary to discuss the whole problem of theory building, not only in psychology but in science in general. In examining the fundamentals of theory, it also seemed advisable to provide auxiliary information whenever necessary, even though that meant occasional excursions into the physical sciences, philosophy, ethics, and asceticism. We believe that it is necessary to set a theory of personality against the whole background of the disciplines which deal with the properly human conduct of man, not merely to relate the science of personality to the other positive sciences. If our attempt is even modestly successful, it should provide a theoretical foundation to support an expanding scientific structure. It should be at least a small step toward breaking down that departmentalization of knowledge which has been deplored for so long.

We should like to express our gratitude and appreciation to Professor Gordon W. Allport for his genial criticism, timely suggestions, and gracious encouragement; and to Dr. Gardner Murphy for his kindly consideration in pointing out some important lacunae and suggesting how they could be filled. We are also indebted to Professor Sir Ronald A. Fisher, Cambridge, England, and to Messrs. Oliver and Boyd Ltd., Edinburgh, for permission to reprint the extract from their book *Statistical Methods for Research Workers.*

In particular it is our grateful duty to express our appreciation and thanks to Barat College for affording us not only a place to meet but also the facilities for carrying out our work. The editors are particularly grateful to Mother Margaret Burke, R.S.C.J., and Mother Joan Arnold, R.S.C.J., for recording and transcribing the proceedings. Each one of the participants feels that the hospitality of Barat College was a major factor in the results that were achieved. Not only was each one of us stimulated to work long and arduously but everyone enjoyed the experience of a most rewarding fellowship. Each of us found new meaning in the sentiment expressed by St. Augustine: Ubi amatur non laboratur, et si laboratur, labor amatur.

Cambridge, Mass.   Magda B. Arnold
Spring Hill, Alabama   John A. Gasson, S. J.
February, 1954

CONTENTS

PART I

The Science of Psychology

PART II

Personality Structure

PART III

Personality Integration

PART IV

Psychotherapy and Self-Integration

PART V

Self-Integration Through Religion

PART I

THE SCIENCE OF PSYCHOLOGY

Chapter 1

BASIC ASSUMPTIONS IN PSYCHOLOGY *

By Magda B. Arnold

When we try to evaluate a scientific theory, we have to examine the evidence upon which it rests. But the evidence is not something naturally "given"; it represents rather an answer to some particular question the scientist has put to nature. The way he puts his question will depend on his basic assumptions concerning the nature of his object of investigation and the nature of reality. These prior assumptions will determine the way the problem is set for investigation, the method of investigation itself, and, of course, the final interpretation. Such assumptions or principles are rarely stated in psychology because they are usually taken over from other sciences. They are applied to psychology without examination because the whole scientific climate of our day is such that the scientist tends to forget that his assumptions are not the result of his scientific investigation but the basis of it. In spite of this general neglect, however, these basic assumptions or principles have to be examined and justified before we can decide whether or not the theory which stems from them is valid. There is bound to be resistance to such an examination of basic principles because they cannot be arrived at by scientific method or experiment. Being prior to scientific investigation, they are necessarily speculative or *meta*physical; they belong to the field of philosophy.

But philosophy has been a bogeyman for psychologists ever since psychology became a science. To be called an armchair

* When an author is merely mentioned in the text, reference numbers have been omitted for greater ease in reading. The author's name and chief publication will be found listed alphabetically at the end of each chapter. When any author is quoted, the quotation carries the page reference and also the number referring to this list at the end of each chapter.

philosopher is still a deadly insult, in spite of the fact that the exact sciences have made the armchair respectable again, for the modern revolution in physical science is a product of the study rather than the laboratory. Psychology still suffers from its early struggles to become a science and has not yet outgrown the aggressive and belligerent spirit it developed in its attempt to free itself from its philosophical heritage.

Basic Assumptions in Science

In Physics. Every scientist assumes that the objects he investigates are real, not imaginary, and that everything he investigates is the effect of some cause. He also assumes that he can come to know these cause-effect relationships and that he must submit to the laws of logic in doing so. So far, these assumptions are universally valid for scientific investigation in psychology as well as in physics. But there is another assumption, accepted as a working principle to escape unnecessary controversy, which belongs in a different category. It is the assumption that the scientist can investigate what is, without reference to its ultimate nature, origin, or destiny. This working principle is entirely defensible in experimental physics and chemistry, but begins to be doubtful in biology and is definitely harmful in psychology.

I have advisedly said such scientific agnosticism is defensible only in *experimental* physics, for as soon as the physicist begins to be interested in theory, he inevitably begins to speculate on the ultimate nature of the physical object he is dealing with, on its place in nature, on the beginning and end of the physical universe; in other words, he relinquishes his working principle, leaves physics, and breaks into a wider and more abstract field, engaging in philosophical speculation rather than making first-order scientific inferences. Examples can be found in the works of Sir James Jeans, Sir Arthur Eddington, and Albert Einstein.

In Biology. In biology, the experimentalist has a much narrower field of immunity to theory. He cannot help being interested in the origin of life, nor can he help trying to attack this particular problem with the tools of his science. His method of attack will depend, however, on his basic assumptions as to the ultimate nature of living things, assumptions which he has taken from philosophy, whether he knows it or not. If he assumes that only matter exists, then life must be a special development from inorganic matter; therefore, the biologist and biochemist will try to discover and produce a chemical compound which will exhibit characteristics of life. If, on the other hand, he were convinced that life is a unique form of matter, representing a different level of organization, then he would spend his time investigating the differences between living and nonliving things, would attack, for instance, the problem of growth, tissue repair, and aging, not as if it were a problem in chemistry, but a living process with further laws of its own which ought to be discovered and applied.

To illustrate by an example: Medical science has concentrated for years on discovering more and more powerful biocides in combating disease, on the assumption that the invading germs and bacteria must be removed, and that the only possible way to remove the invading germ is to kill it. The analogy with a machine is obvious. If a foreign body interferes with its functioning, that foreign body must be removed before the machine can resume its proper operation. At the same time, it is well known that the living body has defences of its own which the machine does not possess; and such knowledge is utilized to some extent, for example, in vaccination which induces the formation of antibodies in such abundance that sometimes immunity is conferred for life, a result which surely could not be obtained by using even the most powerful of "wonder drugs." In addition, it is known that there are many and sometimes dangerous side effects of these drugs. For this reason, the efforts of medical research are directed towards improving their selectivity so that cell life will be protected while the invading life will be destroyed.

But it would at least be worth trying to explore the other avenue (which would seem the logical one) on the alternative assumption of the nature of life, namely, that of finding means of supporting the body's own reaction against pathological processes. Perhaps it is for that very reason—that the body is looked upon as a machine which must be adjusted from the outside—that cancer research has so far made such slow progress. For cancer is a proliferative process in which there is no invader from outside that could be removed. The difficulty is rather that cells are multiplied haphazardly, having seemingly escaped the body's organizing plan.

In Psychology. As we go from biology to psychology we notice that we can hardly avoid the questions of origin and purpose in dealing with our subject matter, man. What man is and where he is going cannot lightly be dismissed. Were we to restrict ourselves to the working principle of the exact sciences, our field of investigation would contract intolerably. It is no accident that this working principle was introduced into psychology at a time when the only interest of psychologists was the observation of static "elements of consciousness." Studies in sensation, rote memory, just noticeable differences, remain valid whatever the nature of man is thought to be.

But the situation changes radically when psychologists begin to study man in his daily living. Now we are dealing with human beings in their human activities, with men and women who love and hate, who know and act, who have purposes and aims, who are held legally responsible for their actions, and who can be declared insane and confined to mental hospitals if they can exercise such responsibility no longer. Now it becomes vitally necessary to know whether man's nature is such that he *can* know (differently from animals), that he can fashion purposes or even *a* purpose in life (as no animal can), and that he can be held responsible for his actions (as animals are not).

To raise this question at all might seem folly. Surely every psychologist has to admit these human characteristics as facts of his own experience, even though he might not admit his subjects' reports. But it is a curious fact that psychologists have insisted again and again that human beings differ from animals only quantitatively and not qualitatively. As a result, they have increasingly avoided terms which could imply a qualitative difference; so reasoning has become problem solving, desires become drives or needs, willing turns into striving. One is almost forced to conclude that experiential evidence is not respectable in psychology or that there is a prior assumption that man and animal have like natures.

Such a prior judgment will influence our scientific description; it will also influence the experiments we devise. If we equate reasoning with problem solving or trial-and-error learning, we shall set up learning situations in which a solution by reasoning is not possible, such as mazes and mechanical puzzles, and then conclude with satisfaction that there is no essential difference in the performance of apes and men.

Finally, every experiment is expected to contribute to eventual prediction and control of the subject matter—in our case, of human beings. Therefore we must face the question: In whose favor are we going to exercise that control? Every psychologist would answer that such control must be used for the benefit of man himself, an answer which does not follow from his scientific investigations but from a prior conviction of the value and dignity of man. That answer raises further questions: Where is man's true benefit? In unhindered "living out" of his drives, in their restraint for the sake of society, or in a self-perfection in which his every action is subordinated to his final goal? It is apparent that any one of these answers really implies a definite view of the ultimate nature of man, his origin, and his destiny.

It has been said that such questions can safely be left to the philosopher and the moralist because the psychologist or social scientist merely contributes his findings; he merely states what man can do and how his actions affect him and his fellow-men. The moralist or politician will then translate these findings into action, will apply them; in this way the scientist provides the principles, and the practical man applies them. But we have seen the spectacle of psychologists and other social scientists being called in by government agencies to help them *decide on action*. In their turn, these scientists have claimed to be able to make a contribution to what *ought to be done*, forgetting that science only provides factual evidence, only finds out *what is*, and not what *ought to be*. Without realizing it, every social scientist arrives at his conclusion of what ought to be done by interpreting his facts on the basis of prior philosophical assumptions which are always implied, but never stated explicitly.

This is true not only in the field of social action, but also in the fields of education and psychotherapy. To guide individuals as well as groups, we have to know what is the essential nature of man and his destiny, and science cannot tell us that. In practice, however, every educator and every psychotherapist needs a model toward which a human being should aim or should be led, whether he calls it the mature man, or the well-adjusted man, or the responsible man; if science cannot provide it, every educator or therapist will have to supply such a norm from his own convictions. And these he never examines because he mistakenly believes them to have the authority of science.

Personality Theories

It could be asked : Cannot the therapist draw upon personality theories which will admittedly be based upon philosophical assumptions, examine them, and harmonize them with the available evidence in the field, so that a workable model or norm for the human being could be chosen? Unfortunately, just as his colleagues in the exact sciences, many a theorist in psychology is under the illusion that he is keeping to his working principle of leaving philosophy and metaphysics aside when in fact he is entering those fields by offering explanations as to the nature, origin, and destiny of man. (To say that man has no discernible destiny except the life he makes for himself here and now is dealing with the question of man's destiny, too.) As a result of this illusion (that he is making a scientific pronouncement when in fact he is dealing with metaphysics), he does not state his assumptions as such, but implies that they are scientific conclusions. Thus he holds to a strict determinism, based on the conviction that human life is continuous with animal life and inorganic things. Hence even the new laws that may be necessary are merely an extension of the same mechanical laws that apply all along the line. The eminent *Gestalt* psychologist, Kurt Koffka, for example, said that a typist learns to type in the same way that a wire "learns" to be bent. And if much is made of "dynamic" principles, they are dynamic only in the sense that the principle according to which a machine functions is dynamic. All too often, human purposes are considered "elaborations" of tissue needs, responsibility is reduced to successful socialization or a strong superego; art, religion, science itself, become the accidental excrescences of unconscious forces, biological drives, whose primary aim is inhibited.

A man may say he paints because he is intrigued by color and design; that he enlisted in a national crisis because it was his duty; that he chose a friend for an important post because that friend had the best qualifications for it. Many a psychologist knows better; he knows that in every case what the man did was not done because it was right or even because he wanted to do it; it was done only because the man's temperament, upbringing, environment, cultural milieu determined it. He almost prides himself on this interpretation, perhaps in the belief that he has achieved the same extension of knowledge that the physicist has provided for us when he informs us that this solid table is but a cloud of discrete whirling electrons which occupy an inconceivably small proportion of the space of the table. Yet the table *did* provide what evidence there was for the physicist's deductions, whereas the human being, the subject matter of the psychologist, is *not allowed* to contribute his evidence, namely, his experience of the way in which he functions. It is true that the table cannot talk, but the human being can and does, and he tells the psychologist that he has aims and purposes, that he thinks, that he can make deductions, can reason, that he can decide for or against any given action. If we take the psychologist's convictions seriously (which on his own showing also must be determined in ways he does not suspect) why should we not take our subject's convictions seriously too? It is true that the human being does not know by inspection or experience what his heart or liver or stomach looks like, so that we have to trust to external observation. But the human being does know what he is going to do; therefore, he can predict his action in a way which no external observation can equal; yet we refuse to let him, who is our scientific material, speak for himself.

Moreover, if we insist that human behavior is the result of internal and external agents in such a way that the deliberate choice of the human being is itself determined beforehand, then the choice becomes merely the outward expression of causes over which man has no control. Then any man who believes he can choose freely, rather than being compelled to choose in a causally determined way, must suffer from a persistent delusion which is no less a delusion for being universal. How such a cosmic delusion could have come about or what purpose it could serve (for purpose is allowed to evolution, though not to human beings) no one has explained as yet. A psychologist's conviction that he can avoid philosophy thus leads him to mistake philosophical assumptions for scientific conclusions in the light of which he is forced to disregard the evidence provided by his subject matter and look upon his human material almost as though it had a structural flaw. In what other science do men approach their subject matter with the conviction that it is not as it acts?

There are other possibilities of delusion, too. If a psychologist is convinced that he does not and need not have any metaphysical assumptions, he must assume that such a feat is possible for other human beings, too. Those who claim the necessity of a philosophy of life or a religious conviction must seem to him to give in to subjective needs which preclude an objective orientation to reality. But surely, if his assumption is valid, a religous conviction is not merely an amiable weakness; any man who believes something exists, when in fact it does not, suffers from a hallucination or a delusion. Therefore, if a man believes in God and Heaven, and God does not exist, then that man suffers from a delusion or at best is a victim of wishful thinking. If God does exist, that man is a realist and the unbeliever is deluded. To diagnose a delusion in either case we must know whether God is.

Thus the question of God's existence, which includes the question of the ultimate origin, nature, and destiny of man, cannot be completely avoided in psychology as long as the diagnosis of delusion and hallucination falls within its province. It is a curious fact that those psychologists who take religion seriously at all do so almost apologetically, discussing "religious experience" as a psychological fact, yet ignoring the conclusion that religious experience without objective foundation can only be a delusion; such a position is held by Jung and by Allport. On the other hand, those psychologists (for example Leuba and Kubie), who regard religion as an outworn superstition of former ages, invoke science in support of their disbelief.

If, then, the question of the nature, origin, and destiny of man has to be faced and we recognize that the answer will decisively influence our scientific research and theory, we had better investigate the alternatives open to us. The problem, obviously, requires not a scientific but a philosophical method of inquiry, and the alternative we choose will provide the basic assumptions for our scientific research.

Alternatives

Physical Naturalism. The first alternative is provided by the philosophy of physical naturalism and is the one commonly chosen by psychologists: Man is the latest product of an evolutionary process which started from inorganic matter and ended with the human being; thus nature is continuous. Therefore, strict deterministic causality holds throughout the realm of nature and everything in man must be explicable by the same physical and chemical laws that hold for inanimate objects. Man's actions are determined by a combination of external and internal forces in the same way that every natural object is; he is molded by his social environment and develops into a mature human being if his needs are integrated with social demands; he lives his life in a continuous attempt to adjust and to get the satisfaction compatible with the demands made upon him in his life situation. This answer leaves out any account of the origin of inorganic matter and ignores the puzzling appearance of human convictions of freedom, responsibility, and purpose.

Other alternatives have been tried one by one and found wanting. Idealism was superseded by critical idealism, which produced a latent but lasting distrust in man's ability to know reality even though Kant's position was never openly acknowledged by psychologists. On the other hand, dualism, in the form of psychophysical parallelism, has held sway in psychology until very recently, yet it has never offered a solution for our pressing problems.

Critical Idealism. The critical idealist starts with the assumption that a generalization distorts reality. What is known in a generalization is not objective reality, individual reality, or total reality. What is known is some aspect or similarity common to all cases of the same class. In this way the generalization is really something the mind makes; it is not a given reality. What is given is a sensation complex which is interpreted in a concept. The individual events are not things but mental fictions. Hence they are called *facts* (facta), things made by the mind. If the facts of science are not *given in experience* but *made out of experience*, what these facts mean will depend upon the particular laws which the mind follows in constructing them (Cf. Planck, 18, pp. 43–83).

Theorists in science frequently speak of universes of discourse and modes of correspondence because the way in which these concepts are related to one another in a system is similar to the way in which materials are manipulated according to the rules of a game. An example would be the hands in poker. They are not natural combinations. The relationship of the single cards in the hand to one another and of one hand to another, is significant only under the rules of the game. The hands do not have a natural "value," but one derived from poker rules. From this point of view, the causal relationships between scientific data —the scientific "values" which result from the scientist's evaluation of his data—are considered to be mental fictions (constructs) as much as, if not more than, the "facts" the scientist deals with. If this be so, then his structure of causal relations which forms an explanation of the facts is a mental fiction worked out by the mind and the mind alone. Significance is attributed to this structure only if some similarity, usually functional, can be found between this mental structure which is the science and the mass of sensation complexes which is the experience of reality.

Psychophysical Parallelism. If critical idealism has caused the loss of reality, dualism in the form of psychophysical parallelism has produced results no less unfortunate: it has created a permanent split between one kind of reality and another, between psychological and physical facts.

The ideal of science has always been to unify not only the knowledge of the objects of science, but to unify the domain of science itself. It has been difficult to unify the field of psychology because human activities obviously cannot be put into one homogeneous class. The failure of psychophysical parallelism to establish a homogeneous domain in psychology and its failure to account consistently for the continuity of psychological facts with the facts of the natural sciences makes it as unsatisfactory as critical idealism. Psychophysical parallelism implies not only duality but separate duality, so that laws referring to one branch will not apply to the other. No wonder that dualism in this form has failed, for as long as man is split into two different and opposed entities we shall never put Humpty-Dumpty together again. As long as the scientist is preoccupied with concepts stemming from atomistic monism, the human being will never be unified. No matter how we put separate and distinct things together, the bond which unites them will remain external so that we shall always have two things and not one. We can string pearls, but we make a string of pearls, not a single jewel.

The notion that a unit can be single *and* complex can seldom be found in contemporary scientific literature. Complexity is generally thought of as the result of addition. As a matter of fact, complexity (or at least our awareness of complexity) is always the result of division or differentiation. If we assume that man is a compound unit to begin with, we can find multiple aspects distinct from one another in concept, but they are the integral parts of the single compound unit. Parts are never antecedent to the whole but are the product of breaking up the whole.

Personalistic View. This is precisely the point of view taken by our alternative basic assumption, the hierarchical view of nature and the personalistic view of man.[1] According to this alternative, there is an essential difference between the inorganic and the organic, and between animal and human being. They represent different levels of organization, are informed by different principles of organization, and form a hierarchy from the inorganic to man, in which each level has specific laws of function over and above the laws which hold for the next lower level of organization. The plant is subject to the gravitational pull, but also has a tendency to counteract it. The animal has in addition the ability to move from place to place, to escape an unfavorable environment, while the human being has also the ability to change the environment according to his plans. As judged by this activity which is essentially different from that of plants and animals, man must have a principle of organization which is also different.

This principle of organization accounts for his actions, whether physical, biological, or psychological. It is different from the actions but not opposed to them: on the contrary, it "informs" them, that is to say it gives them their characteristically human form. Man is thus a compound unit, made up of the principle of organization and the material organized. Whenever he acts, he acts as a whole. He can act on different levels, the physical, the biological, the rational; if he slips and falls, he is subject to the gravitational pull as any other object is; he grows and reproduces, as does any living thing; but he reasons, discovers the laws of nature, and reflects about himself as no other living thing can. His falling off a roof, his growth and reproduction are the activities of a man; they are not activities to which reason must be added to make them such: but only rational and volitional acts are human activities, properly speaking.

Thus the human being is an irreducible unit who has some activities in common with animals, plants, and inanimate things. But even in such activities he functions as a human being, represents a different level of organization and therefore a different

---

[1] The term "personalistic" is used here as an antonym of "mechanistic" or "robotic." Naturally, we agree with the Personalist philosophy or psychology in this usage.

organizing principle, and must be studied and explained on his own level rather than by analogy with a lower level.

According to the hierarchical concept of nature, the universe as we know it must have had a beginning, no matter how far back in time; and that beginning must be the creative act of One who had no beginning. The same creative act resulted in the development of life. The human being is one form of life—a creature who can know himself and his Creator, toward whom he tends as the goal of his specifically human capacities. And finally, the human being can and does choose whether or not he will strive for this goal or instead choose some other goal. This answer *does* include and justify our conviction of freedom, responsibility, and purpose.

Now the question will be raised: But is such an alternative scientific? And the answer must be, of course, that it is no more scientific than the assumption of physical naturalism, for both answers are given prior to scientific investigation. If that is so, surely there must be a way in which the validity of either of the rival assumptions could be tested by the scientist? There is, and it is a way which ought to be entirely congenial to the empiricist.

Because basic assumptions determine the approach to scientific investigation and its method, and because scientific results are interpreted in the light of their basic assumptions, the final conclusion will be a combination of prior assumption and experimental fact. Psychology as a science enjoys an advantage no other natural science possesses: the observer is always one of the objects he is observing. Experimental fact cannot contradict our own experience, for it is our experience which registers the observation. Experimental controls will refine our observation and expand it. Contradiction comes in only when deductions are made on the basis of an assumption which demands it. If the basic assumptions of the nature of man are correct, and the experimental evidence is combined with such a true view, then the end result, our conclusion, should give us a picture of the human being which may extend our experience but cannot contradict it. We should expect psychology to give us a more detailed picture of human functioning than our individual experience presents, a better knowledge of the conditions which facilitate or hinder it. Psychology cannot discover principles of human functioning contradictory to our experience, however, for in this science we have the unique privilege of being on the inside, so to speak, able to provide a check on its results. In psychology there is thus the possibility of an empirical verification of scientific generalizations from the inside, which ought to be gratifying to a scientist.

In addition, of course, basic assumptions can be judged on their inclusiveness, their ability to provide explanations for all the problems with which we are faced.

Problems and Conclusions

Now what are some of the scientific results? I shall mention only a few, and among them I shall touch upon more controversial issues, so that there will be an opportunity to compare generalizations based on either set of assumptions: physical naturalism and strict deterministic explanations or the hierarchical view of nature and personalistic view of man.

Human Choice and Decision. In the area of choice it has been shown by Ach and his pupils that the act of decision is different from the act of carrying out that decision. The latter may be emotionally toned, the former is not.

On deterministic premises, the act of decision could be interpreted as the felt overbalancing of one set of determining forces over another set. But we can always distinguish something that *happens to us* from something *we do*. Ach's subjects were convinced that the act of decision was something *they did*.

Learning and Intention. It has been repeatedly demonstrated that learning and remembering depend on the intention to learn, also called the "will to learn," or set (16).

The deterministic interpretation insists that even basic assumptions (like any other "set") are acquired by learning, but this interpretation disregards the very results of Meumann's investigation, namely, that set or intention is necessary before any learning can occur. It seems more in keeping with the results to say that the human being can *decide* to learn in a given situation or *refuse* to learn—that is, he exhibits freedom of choice.

Conditioning: We know from Razran's experiments that adult conditioning is different from conditioning in animals or small children in several significant respects:

a) The formation of the conditioned reflex itself depends on the subject's attitude; he may deliberately associate the unconditioned and conditioned stimulus, and in that case the "conditioning" is immediate and stable. Or he may decide the experimenter is trying to deceive him, and so he develops inhibitory responses (less salivation to conditioned stimulus than in the control period). Finally, he may adopt the attitude, "I won't do anything I am not told to do," and he does not develop conditioned responses, but inhibitory responses do not develop either.

b) In adult human beings conditioned responses do not become extinct (unconditioned). Once an adult has associated two stimuli as belonging together, reinforcement is not needed any more and only a change in his attitude (namely, the decision that the two stimuli do not belong together after all) can break the conditioning.

Razran concludes from these facts and from the results of conditioning experiments in animals and children that there has been an evolutionary advance in the process of conditioning from amoeba to human adult; this advance remains in animals and children on the quantitative level; it is merely an increase in the speed of conditioning. But in children after about four years of age a new form of the conditioning process appears which is the one found in his experiments with adults. At that time there appears, he says, a

. . . twofold control: first, ability to prevent and stop conditioned reflex formations that are incongruous with the individual's set of symbolic reactions . . . second, the capacity to reinstate, by means of symbols, conditioned responses unaided and undiminished, or to wrest control and gain functional independence from conditioning stimuli (21, p. 120).

Razran refuses to see in this new control anything essentially different from previous conditioning, and insists that such control proceeds "ultimately according to the same principles of interdependence, conditioning, and dominance" as are operative in animal conditioning. He supposes this new control system to be "mechanical and summative in structure but emergent and suprasummative in function" (21, p. 120).

Thus Razran subordinates his experimental results to his mechanistic assumptions. He had to recognize the control the human being exercises over the connections he makes, but claims that this control is the result of emergent evolution. If there is an emergence in evolution, however, that must mean a break in the orderly chain of cause accounting for effect; it is impossible that a cause should produce of itself an effect greater than itself, therefore that emergence, that "plus" in organization, must emerge from somewhere outside the causal chain. If that is so, then emergent evolution postulates the interference of a *Deus ex machina* at each evolutionary step, while the hierarchical conception postulates only one God and one creative act.

But even granted the "emergence" of this new control system, Razran still contradicts himself, for he says that its emergent structure is mechanical without specifying how a nonmechanical way of functioning can "emerge" from a mechanical structure, even on the principle of emergent evolution. In this way he accomplishes the difficult feat of remaining a mechanist while willing to deal with nonmechanical phenomena (as long as they are only functional) in a nonmechanical way.

Again, the alternative set of assumptions seems much better fitted to explain the experimental results. If the personalistic concept of man is correct, we would expect that the human being can form connections or not, that here as everywhere else he has freedom of choice. More than that, his decision is the important causal factor in the chain of events that starts from it. According to his decision he will become conditioned, and this conditioning will last unless he revokes his decision. Or, if he decides that conditioned and unconditioned stimulus are not connected, he will never develop the conditioned response, no matter how often the stimuli are presented.

Unconscious Determinants. Perhaps the most widely accepted arguments against self-determination have been marshalled by Freud, who pointed out that his technique of free association uncovers unconscious determinants in all human actions. In a lecture on the use of free association in dream analysis, he says:

I have already taken the liberty of pointing out that in each one of you there is a deep-rooted belief in psychic freedom and volition, a belief which is absolutely unscientific, and which must capitulate before the claims of a determinism that controls even the psychic life (8, p. 84).

True, the psychic determinism Freud affirms here is a determination of associations. But he makes the connection with volition precisely because for him the emotional determination of associations is at the same time proof of the causal determination of actions (i.e., determination by efficient causes). In another statement he explains how that psychic determinism can be reconciled with the feeling of choice of which all of us are aware in our normal waking life:

As is known, many persons argue against the assumption of an absolute psychic determinism by referring to an intense feeling of conviction that there is a free will. This feeling of conviction exists, but is not incompatible with the belief in determinism. Like all normal feelings, it must be justified by something. But, so far as I can observe, it does not manifest itself in weighty and important decisions; on these occasions, one has much more the feeling of a *psychic compulsion* and gladly falls back upon it. (Compare Luther's "Here I stand, I cannot do anything else.") On the other hand, it is in trivial and indifferent decisions that one feels sure that he acted of his own free will, and *without any motives*. From our analysis we therefore need not contest the right of the feeling of conviction that there is a free will. If we distinguish conscious from unconscious motivation, we are then informed by the feeling of conviction that the conscious motivation does not extend over all our motor resolutions. Minima non curat praetor. What is thus left free from the one side receives its motive from the other side, from the unconscious, and the determinism in the psychic realm is thus carried out uninterruptedly (4, pp. 161–62. Italics mine).

Freud seems to contend that whenever we know the motive for our decision, we feel a psychic compulsion, not freedom; and when we are conscious of freedom of choice, we know of no motive for our decision though the motive exists—in the unconscious.

Now the first question is: When there is a conscious motive, does it always result in a feeling of compulsion? And conversely, when there is a feeling of compulsion, is there always a conscious motive? The term "psychic compulsion" is obviously used by Freud with a meaning different from the ordinary dictionary definition: "an impulse or feeling of being irresistibly driven toward the performance of some irrational action." The psychic compulsion under which Luther acted was different in kind and not only in degree from psychic compulsion as ordinarily understood. Luther declared that it was logical necessity that compelled him to take his stand and to persist in it. Luther knew that he could act contrary to his judgment. But if he were to act in conformity with it, there would be nothing else he could do. Logic did not drive him to *action*. His compulsion was the conviction of a logical necessity, not action forced on him either from within or without. The only inner constraint he felt was the constraint to assent to what was represented as true.

Now the "psychic compulsion" as ordinarily understood refers to a drivenness to external action in spite of all logic and reason, and contrary to it. Thus an important decision carries with it a conviction of *logical* inevitability, a psychic compulsion carries with it the feeling of being compelled to *act*, no matter how one struggles against it. For the normal person, both an important and unimportant decision carry the feeling that it is within his discretion to choose either one of the available alternatives for action. In the extreme feeling of compulsion which we call a compulsion neurosis, there is an impulse toward external action to which there seems no alternative. There is no awareness of the source of compulsion, therefore no conscious motivation. The action to which the neurotic feels compelled takes on an importance out of all proportion with actuality, a fact which he recognizes but cannot alter. He feels that action is necessary and that this is the only action that is possible.

In the case of logical conviction, there is a *necessity for judgment*, which is antecedent to the decision for action. What is compelled is the *assent of the mind*, not a decision for action. In the case of a compulsion, what is compelled is not only the overt action but the *decision to act* as well. We can answer our first question, then, by saying that a *conscious (rational) motive* brings with it a necessity for judgment, not for action. There is correspondingly a feeling of logical conviction, but not of compulsion to action. Conversely, when there is a feeling of compulsion to action, as in the case of the compulsion neurotic, there is no conscious motive.

Secondly, we may ask: Is it true, as Freud says, that a feeling of freedom of choice (which we often have in trivial matters) means that the motives, the determiners of action, are unconscious? Conversely, does unconscious motivation always result in a feeling of freedom? Let us look at the evidence from psychoanalytic investigations to which Freud refers. There are, first, various actions of normal persons which have been shown to be the effect of unconscious causes, such as disturbed acts ("Fehlleistungen") like slips of the tongue or pen, symptomatic acts (meaningless gestures) and inhibitions (forgetting of names). Then there is the clinical observation that many actions for which the neurotic can give no reason are found to be the result of unconscious desires. He washes his hands all day because he is unconsciously afraid of infection which is threatened by his own sexual desires; he drinks to excess because he wants to escape responsibility. Furthermore, even rational actions of normal persons, which they think they have decided upon freely, are found to be influenced by their unconscious desires. However, they can only be said to be so *influenced*, not determined; Zilboorg, for instance, points out that the discovery of an unconscious motive for any action does not make the (conscious) motive invalid (26, p. 118).

Thus the only real evidence for unconscious determination of human actions comes either from disturbed and symptomatic acts and inhibitions, all of which by definition are not intended, therefore not free, or from neurotic compulsion which is not felt as free action. The patient suffering from a compulsion neurosis can give no reason for his actions but will say: "I had to do it," "Something made me do it," implying that he is not responsible for it. The normal person will say: "I did it because I wanted to do it," implying that *he* made the decision and is responsible for it though there may be no conscious motive (as in a trivial act). We see, then, that an action without conscious motives may be accompanied either by a feeling of freedom (in the normal) or by a feeling of compulsion (in the neurotic). Where unconscious motivation can actually be demonstrated, there is never a feeling of freedom, but either the conviction of lack of intention, therefore *lack of freedom* (as in disturbed acts), or a *feeling of compulsion*. Freud to the contrary, the available evidence does not prove that a decision we feel to be free is unconsciously determined, nor does it prove that unconscious motivation, when it exists, is accompanied by a feeling of freedom.

In treating a conviction of logical necessity as a feeling of compulsion, and in equating conscious and unconscious motives, Freud really asserts that a rational motive acts as if it were an efficient cause operating prior to the event; and that this motive wins out in a given event because it was connected with the stronger desire, possessed the stronger instinctual roots. Once Freud identifies motives (conscious and unconscious) with efficient causes, the only kind of determination he can admit is a determination of the person's decision by forces outside the act of decision itself. For that reason, Freud contrasts determinism with the only opposite he can conceive, and that is being uncaused. In establishing strict psychic determinism he meant to establish the fact that events necessarily have causes. He hoped to find antecedent factors that would be in the strict sense of the term the efficient cause of the event in question. Since he was dealing with psychological events, the antecedent factor had to be on the psychological plane—the instinct-driven motive.

At the same time, Freud himself recognized that these causes or motives as perceived by us do not allow us to predict the subsequent event:

So long as we trace the development from its final stage backwards, the connection appears continuous, and we feel we have gained an insight which is completely satisfactory and even exhaustive. But if we proceed the reverse way, if we start from the premises inferred from the analysis and try to follow these up to the final result, then we no longer get the impression of an inevitable sequence of events which could not be otherwise determined. We notice at once that there might have been another result and that we might have been just as well able to understand and explain the latter. . . . We never know beforehand which of the determining factors will prove the weaker or the stronger. *We only say at the end that those which succeeded must have been the stronger.* Hence it is always possible by analysis to recognize the causation with certainty, whereas a prediction of it by synthesis is uncertain (9, pp. 226–27. Italics mine).

Yet if there had been another result, we could with equal certainty conclude that the other motive had been stronger. Is it not possible, then, that our analysis ex post facto also has not uncovered the decisive element of the causal chain? In fact, the well-known "overdetermination" of dream or symptom may be an indication that our analysis traces back not a chain of necessary cause-effect relations but various chains of associations, all of them leading back to the same emotion-laden events, which are motives but not decisive.

Moreover, Freud recognizes that there is no proof that any given decision was forced by a determining factor as there would be if we could predict it. But, like other determinists, he takes the fact of a given decision as proof of its determination by past extrinsic causes. He certainly does not admit, still less support, the other alternative, namely that *the decision itself* reinforces either the one or the other set of influencing (not determining) factors. Yet, in the absence of other proof, the conviction that one set of determining factors (efficient causes) must have been stronger than a rival set is simply the expression of a *philosophy* of determinism, and not a scientific inference or explanation.

The only way out of the impasse of overdetermination and unpredictability would be to admit that the person can act rationally in such a way that he can make a decision on the basis of evidence, and set up motives for himself which are guides to action; and that he does so because he has judged such action to be suitable, not because he was told to act this way in childhood, or because the present situation imposes such action according to the "reality principle." By refusing to admit this alternative, Freud is forced to postulate causality of a peculiar type: The same traumatic experience can produce opposite effects (rejection by the mother results in compulsive desire for love in one person, in a rejection of love in another), and one effect can be a disguise for another.

Conversely, the same reaction may be traced back to opposite causes (one anthropologist may hold the theory of a matriarchal form of original society because of his hatred of the patriarchal power of his own father; another may hold a matriarchal theory in an attempt to restore the early domination of his later devalued mother (7, Vol. II, p. 9). If one and the same cause can have two opposite effects, or the same effect can have two opposite causes, then either causal dependence cannot be demonstrated at all because there are too many factors, or there is some factor which inclines the human reaction either in the one or the other direction, regardless of the supposedly causal event in the past. In either case, the claim of complete causal dependence of actions on unconscious motives to be uncovered by free association has no basis in fact.

Personality Development. The same insufficiency of deterministic explanations is found in the area of personality development. Anne Roe * has recently pointed out that none of the "determinants" usually given as the cause of maladjustment really determines. She says:

> No one who has worked with normal adults can have failed to have noted that almost every combination of circumstances which has been cited as an excuse for one disability or another can be found in the histories of normals (23, p. 341).

Yet there are many supposedly scientific papers, she says, which assume without further ado that childhood events or family circumstances are in themselves a sufficient cause for maladjustment.

* Quotions from *Feelings and Emotions: The Mooseheart Symposium*, edited by M. L. Reymert, copyright 1950, by permission of McGraw-Hill Book Company, Inc.

In every such case, that has been done—not on the basis of sufficient evidence, but on the basis of a prior assumption of mechanistic determination.

Another statement by Anne Roe supports this claim :

After twenty years spent in research, most of it with normal adults, I have come to the conclusion that maladjustment is never inevitable and that it is not unrealistic to think that a man is capable of being responsible for himself. It is true that this responsibility may take the form of responsibility for seeking help when it is needed, but that is only a form of it (23, p. 341).

Psychotherapy. It is well known in psychotherapy that nothing can be done for the patient unless he wants to get well, even at the price of temporary pain and discomfort; and this determination to get well cannot be predicted from his past history. In accepting his freedom of choice to want or not to want to pay the price of getting well, we do not equate his decision with "uncaused" but with "self-caused" behavior; and we accept the fact of choice as an additional but deciding factor, together with factors of desire for comfort, esteem, approval, with habits, cultural influences, hereditary predispositions, etc. Thus we do not relinquish the possibility of prediction (e.g., of success of therapy) but we introduce the missing factor without which prediction becomes impossible.

With a change of assumptions in which we grant to man his freedom of choice, we shall be able to treat the human person clinically as we are wont to treat him socially and legally : as responsible for his actions. To quote Anne Roe again :

It seems to me that in the praiseworthy effort to relieve people of unnecessary guilt feelings and to remove the stigma from mental disorder which for so long prevented any adequate treatment, we have gone too far [in assuming the almost mechanical determination that is usually implicit]. We have, in effect, taken from man personal responsibility for his own integration and maturity. Have you thought of the philosophical and political implications of this insistence on the blamelessness of man for his mental and emotional disorders? (23, p. 341).

If we follow Anne Roe, then this change of assumptions is not only more in accord with clinical facts, but also has constructive philosophical and political implications, while the assumption of determinism has implications which would make an accident of political freedom and destroy social living which is based upon a sense of responsibility.

From Rogers' careful work in nondirective therapy we may quote some of the changes in the person which have been observed in successful therapy, and which therefore are connected with more normal functioning. The person tends:

to perceive his abilities and characteristics with more objectivity and with greater comfort;

to perceive all aspects of self and self-in-relationship with less emotion and more objectivity;

to perceive himself as more independent and more able to cope with life problems;

to perceive himself as more able to be spontaneous and genuine;

to perceive himself as the evaluator of experience, rather than regarding himself as existing in a world where the values are inherent in and attached to the objects of his perception;

to perceive himself as more integrated, less divided (24, p. 139).

It seems, therefore, according to these studies, that the more normal a person is, the more he feels he can act reasonably, objectively, and the more he feels himself active, spontaneous, integrated; the opposite was true before therapy. If that is so, these results can again be understood and interpreted better in the light of the personalistic concept of man. It is the normal man whom we could expect to have control over himself and his environment, because in him there is a proper ordering of his proper human functions: where that control breaks down we would expect some difficulty, some interference with normal functioning, for in that case the proper human order of functioning is lost. For the determinist, on the other hand, these results are very nearly unintelligible, for nondirective counseling can hardly provide enough external motive power to change the person's attitude, seeing that the counselor does nothing but reflect the client's feelings. Perhaps it is this felt threat to de-

terministic thinking that makes nondirective counseling so unacceptable to the majority of psychologists.

It is heartening that in the field of personality study voices
have been raised in protest against mechanistic assumptions of
psychological theorists. Allport says:

> In taking stock of the situation I observe how many of us seem so
> stupefied by admiration of physical science that we believe psychology
> in order to succeed need only imitate the models, postulates, methods,
> and language of physical science. . . . While we righteously scorn
> what one of us has called "the subjective, anthropomorphic hocus
> pocus of mentalism" we would consider a colleague emotional and
> mystical should he dare speak of the "objective, mechanomorphic
> hocus pocus of physicalism" (2, p. 182).

> The machine model in psychology had its origin not in clinical or
> social experience, but rather in adulation of the technological success
> of the physical sciences. . . . Besides the mechanical model, there
> are two other currently popular paradigms in psychology that are, in
> my opinion, only slightly less inept in guiding significant research or
> theory concerning the foundations of social morality. I refer to the
> phylogenetic model and to the infant mind (2, p. 183).

> The models we have been following lack the long range orientation
> which is the essence of morality. Infant and rodent have immediate
> goals and indulge in anticipatory goal-reaction, but have no directive
> schemata. . . . By contrast . . . the essence of moral behavior is of
> this sort. It presupposes long range purposes whose directions precede
> their specifications (2, p. 188).

It may be pertinent to point out (as many observers have
done), that a personalistic concept of man is surely more appropriate for the study of man than a mechanomorphic one, however appropriate a mechanistic explanation may be for the study
of mechanisms.

Determinism and Teleology in Science

And now we are ready to deal with the curious and persistent
conviction of psychologists that a mechanistic deterministic
philosophy in some way is more "scientific" than any other, that
in fact it supplies the only possible postulates for a scientist. To

show that such a conviction exists, a few quotations will suffice, though they could be multiplied indefinitely.

The first quotation is from Snygg and Combs, who are non-directive counselors, and who in practice recognize the growing self-awareness and self-determination of the client:

> As a *science*, phenomenological psychology must accept determinism because prediction and control are only possible in a field where behavior is lawful and caused. As a *method*, it also recognizes that the behaver often feels that he has a choice of behavior even though none exists in reality, since he always chooses the one which is pertinent to his phenomenal field at the instant of action (25, p. 25, footnote. Italics mine).

Snygg and Combs assume that psychology must presuppose determinism because prediction and control would be impossible without it. Yet we have seen that the deterministic account does not allow prediction—either because there is a factor persistently missing from the explanation, or because the profusion of causal factors never can be completely known.

In the second part of their statement, Snygg and Combs concede that their method recognizes a feeling of free choice, but deny all validity to it. They say that the behaver feels he has a choice though there is none, "since he always chooses *the one which is pertinent to his phenomenal field* at the instant of action." Now this could mean "the choice he is *aware* he is making." No other choice is possible because *this* is the choice he has made. If this is what is meant, then it confuses determination which *follows* choice with determination which *precedes* it. If the authors mean by "pertinent" that the choice is the only one the behaver could possibly make at this instant, they are simply saying that a man feels he has a choice because he always chooses as he must choose—which is like saying that a man feels warm because it is always cold. This, of course, is not logical proof but belongs in the category of affirmation. The authors merely affirm that the deterministic hypothesis must be chosen because it must be chosen because it must be chosen—in the way Gertrude Stein affirms that a rose is a rose is a rose.

Another quotation from a recent textbook, Prothro and Teska:

> Any living organism is passive unless it is being stimulated or is in a state of disequilibrium from previous stimulation.
>
> In order to conceive of the world of living organisms as anything other than a chaos, we must assume that activity is a response to stimuli, either past or present.
>
> All so-called "spontaneous" activity has its origins; but because of the complexity of the human organism and the almost countless number of stimuli in its environment to which it can react, the causes are often hard to determine (20, p. 72).

Thus the author considers that we cannot conceive of order unless we equate living beings with nonliving things; they must both be passive. This can never be proved for human beings but has to be assumed.

It is obvious that such an assumption is not arrived at *after* evidence has been collected, but before. If before, it is not scientific but expresses rather the philosophy of the scientist. The generalizations which will follow can be predicted from this sample: whenever the evidence is unclear, the inference will be that the stimuli are there, but we can never know all of them. And the evidence *for* the assumption can never be clear in human beings, else the author would not admit that "the causes are hard to determine." But evidence *against* this prior assumption (such as the statement of a man that he tried to remember his wife's birthday because he wanted to, not because of any given stimulus) will not be accepted because of the prior deterministic conviction.

It would take us too far to trace in detail the historical development of this conviction that a mechanistic-deterministic philosophy in some way is more scientific than any other. Suffice it to say that it dates back at least to the positivism of Comte, who said that science is not interested in the notion of final causes. Hence, scientists say they must accept the dictum that science explains the "how" of things and leaves it to philosophy to explain the "why" and "what" of nature. In explaining how things happen, however, science cannot do without assumptions about the nature of the thing it investigates, as was discussed earlier; and such assumptions are answers to "why" questions. At this point, even in answering the "why" of existence, the scientist somehow tries to exclude final causes and so avoids purpose or design in every form as explanatory principles.

This distrust of final causes was justified in Comte's time; in that day everything had for centuries been explained as the result of final causes. As McDougall said:

> It was asked: Is the solar system, are volcanic eruptions, lightning, and the flow of rivers purposive? The question meant: Are these things designed, constructed, or set in action, as our machines are, in order to serve some purpose? . . . The same question was asked of the structures and processes of the animal body. And for a long time science accepted the positive answer, regarded the animal body as a machine cunningly designed to realize the purpose of its Designer and Creator. Then came the Darwinian theory: and science saw that it was no longer necessary to regard the structure of each animal species as the product of a designing creator and said: The structure and movements of the animal body are not teleological or purposive (15, p. 284).

In passing, it is interesting to note that Darwin merely substituted evolution as purposive agent: the human smile, he says, is the remnant of the animal snarl which served to frighten potential attackers and has now degenerated because there is no more need to frighten enemies. Also, modern biology is using the term "purpose" again in describing functional systems. Cannon, for instance, in his book, *The Wisdom of the Body*, describes in great detail the various mechanisms in the body which have the purpose of maintaining a homeostatic balance. Thus purpose is allowed to the body but not to man.

Today the attempt is made to reduce evolution itself to mechanical causation where natural selection is the causal agent, as Reichenbach does in his recent book (22). It is perhaps instructive to make clear just what is involved in this attempt. Reichenbach tries to show how purposiveness may be inferred from a strictly causal sequence:

A man who sees for the first time the pebbles on a beach might very well conceive the idea that they were deposited according to a certain plan. Close to the ocean, partly covered by the water, there lie the larger pebbles, followed a little further up by the smaller ones, which in turn are followed by layers of sand, first consisting of coarse grains and eventually changing into the fine-grained sand of the upper parts of the beach. It looks as though someone has cleaned up the beach, neatly assorting pebbles and sand according to size. We know that it is unnecessary to assume such an anthropomorphic interpretation; the water transports the pebbles and casts the lighter ones farther up the beach, thus automatically assorting them as to size. It is true, the individual impacts by the waves follow the irregular pattern of chance; and nobody could predict the place where a certain pebble will finally be deposited. But there is a selection at work; whenever a larger and a small rock are transported by the same wave, the smaller one will be carried a little farther. Chance in combination with selection produces order (22, p. 196).

When he invokes the principles of chance and selection to explain order and arrangement, the scientist refers to the properties of the natural objects as explaining this order, which is the result of an interchange of energy or action between them. If one were to ask why this body has these properties, the scientist would reply that the question is "meaningless," the body simply has them and we discover them by observing how it acts. It is right here that we uncover one of the hidden assumptions of natural science.

Clearly, an explanation of order from the properties of bodies supposes that there is some relationship between the result that is order and the properties of these bodies. Unless that relationship were constant, the observer would never be able to discover the properties of a body from the way it acts; in any given case of observation the body might just happen to act that way, and that action might have no connection with its properties. The scientist could hardly account for constancy and uniformity by referring to the properties of natural bodies, if the relationship between results and properties were never apparent.

Our philosopher might object that constancy and uniformity are imposed on the event by the observer's interpretation—but the observer surely does not impose these characteristics arbi-

trarily. If he did, it would be just as meaningful to say that there
was no order in the arrangement of pebbles on the beach as to
say that there was order—or to say that the heavier pebbles
were deposited after the lighter ones, when the water receded
after having carried the heavier pebbles far up the beach and
then back again. If observation established the fact that the
heavier pebbles were deposited first, observation ought to establish the fact that heavy bodies are deposited first in every case.
Our scientific philosopher does not tell us why the properties
of bodies are such that in these conditions the heavy body is
always deposited first. It cannot "just happen." Hence, there
ought to be some account of the relationships between the properties of the body and the results produced. Such an account is
given by natural teleology, which is thus complementary to the
causal explanation of the scientist.

Today there is no danger any more of substituting final
causes for efficient causes; and science can investigate efficient
causes only. We certainly do not want to go back, as Etienne
Gilson says,

> . . . to the good old times when fishes had fins because they had
> been made to swim. Now it may well be true that fishes have been
> made to swim, but when we know it we know just as much about
> fishes as we know about airplanes when we know that they are made
> to fly. If they had not been made to fly, there would be no airplanes,
> since to be flying-machines is their very definition: but it takes us at
> least two sciences, aerodynamics and mechanics, in order to know how
> they do fly. A final cause has posited an existence whose science
> alone can posit the laws (10, p. 132).

While final causes cannot substitute for efficient causes, efficient causes also cannot do duty for final causes. Efficient
causes are the only causes which can be investigated by the
methods of science in a closed physical system: The ground is
wet because it has rained; the drop of mercury coheres because
of its surface tension. But there is no reason to assume that none
but efficient causes can exist because only efficient causes are
investigated in physics. To insist that only efficient causes could
have produced the system itself is to make a serious mistake. The
scientist can only ask: "What causes produce the effects observed

within the system?" "How do they produce such effects?" And: "How is the system interrelated?" As soon as such inter-relation is discovered, however, it will reveal finalities or tele-ologies. Teleology does not of itself imply that some extrinsic factor is *immediately* at work in the event; but since the event is not self-explanatory, there must be some reference to a factor which will complete our understanding of it—unless, of course, we are content to regress indefinitely. The modern objection (Reichenbach, 22) that there need not have been a first event because there is no difficulty in conceiving of an infinite series in either direction is based on a misunderstanding. Though we can deal with infinite series mathematically, we need an explana-tion of the *existence* of the series, and only a cause outside the series itself could bring it into existence.

Final causes, then, cannot be altogether avoided even in physics; but when the psychologist takes over the physicist's antipathy to final causes and is influenced by it in dealing with human behavior where final causes (purposes) are the rule, then this antipathy will lead him to an outright rejection of factual evidence. When a human purpose becomes the effect of prior efficient causes which are called motives, motives again the effect of physiological drives, they the effect of the function of certain organ systems, etc., etc., such reduction is possible only in complete disregard of the principle that no effect can be greater than its cause, a principle which is scientifically quite irre-proachable.

In this way, a healthy reaction against the use of final causes as scientific explanation in the exact sciences led to the refusal to admit final causes even where they are the only intelligible explanation—in human behavior. When purpose is again ad-mitted in biology, though in a restricted way, with evolution or nature as the purposive agent, one almost begins to suspect that there would be no resistance to teleology as long as purpose could be thought to "emerge" in some unspecified way from causal determinants, as long as purpose itself could be explained mechanically.

But to reduce the purposiveness of nature or evolution to mechanical causation, as Reichenbach does, is no solution either.

Natural selection may account for the persistence of chance variations but it does not account for the bewildering number of chance variations, all tending in the same direction, which must have occurred during evolutionary history. The vertebrate eye, for instance, could hardly have developed in one small step. But the many changes necessary before it became functional could hardly have been useful at the time. Only when it finally became functional could it have been of advantage to the animal and so perpetuated by natural selection.

Nor is the evidence convincing which supports the theory of chance mutations which could produce a decisive change in one leap. All the instances of artificial mutation reported so far show variations *within a given level* of organization. Artificial radiation may produce dramatic changes in successive generations of drosophila : some flies have no wings, some have wings of different shape or color. But there is no instance on record where radiation or any other manipulation of a species which has no wings would produce offspring with wings. That a progression from a lower to a higher level of organization should happen even once and should then be repeated over and over again *by chance* really contradicts our notions of randomness.[2] Observe, for instance, the progressively more and more effective organization of the nervous system from protoplasmic transmission in sponges to a nerve net in coelenterates, to the ventral nerve cord in annelids, to the spinal cord with specialized brain segments in vertebrates, and the further range of brain evolution postulated from chordates to mammals.

Can we really credit the notion that this apparently systematic progression should be the result of chance variations which persistently happened in the same direction, and persistently happened not only by adding new structures, but by re-

[2] Cf. Goldstein: "The question of evolution is usually seen as a development from the lower to the higher creatures. An actual genetic emergence of the latter from the former is assumed. . . . In principle . . . it remains implausible how the 'more perfect' should arise from the 'less perfect' . . . The fundamental thought which mature observation impressed upon us, and which we adopted as an orienting principle, is that the less perfect becomes intelligible as a variation and aberration of the 'perfect,' but not the opposite" (11, p. 494).

organizing the organism in the process? If chance has such a powerful cumulative and directional effect, then our notions of randomness and probability are seriously in need of revision. We can only assume that the scientists who refuse to acknowledge that such directionality implies purposiveness know that such an admission would logically lead to a further one, which they believe to be "unscientific" if not "mystical."

As Gilson says,

Why should those eminently rational beings, the scientists, deliberately prefer to the simple notions of design, or purposiveness in nature, the arbitrary notions of blind force, chance, emergence, sudden variation, and similar ones? Simply because they much prefer a complete absence of intelligibility to the presence of a non-scientific intelligibility.

Unintelligible as they are, these arbitrary notions are at least homogeneous with a chain of mechanical interpretations (10, p. 130).

But as we have seen, mechanical interpretations are adequate only in the experimental sciences which deal with inanimate objects; the fact that these sciences were historically the first-comers should not have influenced the unbiased student of nature to extend interpretations from material to which they are adapted to material to which they are not. In very fact, we are still inclined to admit only those explanations as scientific which have been hallowed by their efficacy in the sciences in which they were first used—an interesting "cultural lag" which has lasted far too long.

To sum up our investigation of the scientist's seemingly incurable conviction that a mechanistic-deterministic philosophy is more "scientific" we could say that the scientist still labors under the mistaken notion that mechanical interpretations are scientific per se just because they have been found adequate in Newtonian physics; more than that, they therefore must be the only adequate answers not only in science but in philosophy.

In particular, when a psychologist deludes himself in accepting this conviction, his delusion is more dangerous even than that of the biologist. In deluding himself, he does violence to his subject matter, falsifies his results, and, worst of all, deludes human beings into thinking they need not exercise their freedom of choice because they have none.

Once we begin to realize that the alternative assumption of freedom of choice, creation, and the eternal destiny of man are not only equally as tenable as the mechanistic assumptions, but even more reasonable for a scientist, we can begin to review the factual evidence in every field of psychology and see where it leads, if interpreted in the light of our alternative assumptions. In this way we shall do a service not only to the science of psychology but to confused, harassed, unhappy modern man, who dares not believe in common sense unless it has the stamp of scientific approval.

COMMENT

Mechanism and Determinism

The preceding paper has discussed the objections to strict determinism in psychology. Now it may be objected that there is a difference between mechanistic and nonmechanistic (dynamic) systems; while there is determinism in a dynamic system, it is often believed to be a determinism appropriate to human behavior. Moreover, the fact that most modern theoretical physicists have long since abandoned mechanism as a basic postulate in physics makes it doubly desirable to discuss in what sense a system of acting factors can be fully determined yet not mechanistic. By the same token, it would be helpful to understand how an explanation may allow for nothing but rigid determinism and yet not be mechanistic in principle.

We must distinguish clearly what is the core principle of mechanism. The essence of mechanism, as we understand it, is not that it denies that bodies are active but that it denies that bodies are *changeable* (qualitatively). Hence any change that happens in the elements of a system will be a change in relative position and nothing else. In such a system the only effect produced by any given cause is a change in location (position in space) of the body acted upon. It is an axiom that such effects are *necessary* effects; the acting causes have no discretion over what the effect will be.

Dynamic systems as contrasted with mechanical systems are either (1) systems of *forces* rather than of acting bodies, or (2) systems of bodies that undergo true internal qualitative change. In the first case, the same mechanistic principles prevail but they are applied to *forces* (which *may* be qualitatively different). In the second case, qualitative changes are admitted but the effects produced in the system are just as determined and just as dependent on antecedent causes. At present most explanations of the activity of natural bodies are dynamic in the first sense. But even if a dynamic explanation admits real qualitative differences in natural bodies, natural science requires that their activity be necessarily and constantly the same, and predictable. Modern quantum mechanics and the principle of uncertainty enunciated by Heisenberg strike directly at this requirement.

The principle of indeterminacy can be understood in one of two ways: (1) that a given event is not determined, i.e., that it has no determinate state, or no cause, or is not a constant effect of the same cause, or may proceed from causes of a different or opposite nature; or (2) the event has a cause and is determinate in itself but observers are in principle unable to arrive at such knowledge and determination. These meanings are the result of modern speculations in the philosophy of physics and are not relevant to our topic. For this reason, we will not use the term "indeterminism" in our discussion of self-determination. Least of all do we want to rest our case for self-determination in human action on Heisenberg's principle of indeterminacy.

Freedom and Determinism

An acting cause which is not antecedently determined to a course of action is said to be free. The terms "free" and "freedom" are used in a great variety of meanings. Freedom in the widest sense is the immunity of anything from anything. Thus students speak of free days, that is, days on which they are immune from school. Physicists speak of a freely falling body, of a body whose fall is not interfered with. School children get free lunches, that is, lunches for which they do not have to pay.

Freedom in a more restricted sense is the immunity of an agent from some impediment. This is usually understood to be of two kinds, often referred to in contemporary discussions as "freedom from" and "freedom to." More technically, they are called *freedom of spontaneous action* and *freedom of independence.* Freedom of spontaneous action is the immunity of an agent from external necessity or physical force. By physical force we mean a force by which an agent is compelled to act against his conscious inclinations, or is restrained from an action to which he is consciously inclined. In this sense wild animals are free, caged animals are deprived of freedom. Actions that are spontaneous in this way may be very rigidly determined. The animal seeks food because it is driven by hunger. But both hunger and the seeking are internal qualitative states necessarily resulting from the action of some cause. The seeking implies a goal-directedness or purposiveness. However, we must distinguish a purpose which is merely *accomplished* by the agent from a purpose which is also *intended* by the agent. In the case of an animal's activity caused by the hunger drive, the purposes (nutrition and tissue repair) are accomplished by the animal but not intended or set by him; they are inherent in animal nature (which was not designed by the animal). In such activity, when the necessary conditions for action are present the animal has to act and in a way which is determined by these conditions.

In contrast to this freedom of spontaneity is the *freedom of independence.* This is the immunity of an agent from the law of a superior or from obligation. Man enjoys this freedom only to a limited extent, namely in those actions which are neither positively prescribed or explicitly forbidden by a law. This is the freedom we speak of when we talk about "academic freedom," or "political liberty," or "freedom of speech." In all these we enjoy certain immunities, but these immunities are not unlimited or absolute. This freedom is neither primary nor basic but is founded on *freedom in the strictest sense.*

Freedom in the strictest sense, or at least freedom in the restricted sense in which we use the term, is *freedom of choice.* We are accustomed to speak of it as the power of self-determination. Psychologists, on the basis of both common experience and controlled observation, can recognize in self-determination *the ability we have to settle the issue between conflicting motives by the active interposition of the ego.* In our discussion, whenever and wherever we use the terms "freedom," "free," or "self-determination," we will mean this ability and only this. A conflict of motives consists in the fact that an impulsive inclination toward one of the alternatives contends with an impulsive inclination toward the other alternative. (By *motive* we mean an object or a course of action intellectually judged to be *good*, that is, suitable, desirable, useful, effective, etc.; or *evil*, that is, unsuitable, undesirable, dangerous, etc. Let it be noticed that our use of the term "motive" is not the same as is the general practice among psychologists. We use it in a much more restricted sense and it is in this restricted sense that it will universally appear in our discussion. We do not object to the use psychologists make of the terms "motive" and "motivation" as referring to physiological drives; we wish merely to state that this is not our usage.)

This conflict arises immediately when a judgment is made which proposes the pros and cons of the choice. The motive (in the sense we use the term) is no *motive* unless it actually moves, namely to an impulsive natural inclination toward that object. The relative strength of the two contending impulsive inclinations may differ considerably. What we insist upon just here is the important fact that prior to free choice there occur impulsive inclinations to both alternatives which are independent of the ego-in-action and prior to its decision. The crux of the matter with respect to self-determination is whether this conflict of motives is universally and necessarily settled by that motive which exerts the stronger pull. In experiments by Prum, Michotte, and Wells (Cf. Gruender, 12, pp. 416–17) it was found that a choice between equally motivated alternatives was the most interesting and frequent case observed. Under these conditions, the subject extricated himself from the predicament by an active interposition of the ego and had a most lively experience that it was *by the ego-in-action* that one of the hitherto equal motives was strengthened and the choice was made. It was not the strengthened motive which determined the choice— the subject had no new motive—but it was the choice which strengthened the motive by eliminating the alternative. When the choice was made in favor of the hitherto stronger motive (in cases where the alternatives were not equal) the experience of the ego-in-action could be described by saying: "I yield to the stronger attraction." The purely intellectual judgment, "this is more attractive," and the experience, "I yield to the stronger attraction," are two very different things. The judgment is a matter of objective evidence and is forced on the ego, while the experience "I yield" includes the experience of the ego-in-action.

From what has been said so far we can see that self-determination by no means implies either uncaused action or unmotivated action or unpredictable action. All choices are caused but they are caused by the chooser. All choices are motivated (in fact, where there are alternatives there is a plethora of motives) but the motives are the alternatives as they are apprehended as suitable or unsuitable, desirable or undesirable. Choices are even predictable, but only in cases where the customary reaction of the chooser to motives is adequately known. It is quite true that we cannot describe self-determined activity in terms of causes that are entirely outside the person making the choice, nor can we account for it in terms of necessary connections between the person and the action which the environment exercises upon him. Both these factors are involved in every choice but these are not the factors that determine what the choice will be. Free choice always has a cause but it is important to remember that there are various types of causes. The chooser is the efficient cause (or producer) of the act of choosing, the motives are the final causes (or incentives) of the activity of choosing. The external environment may contain both types of causes, and influence both the chooser and the choosing by varying the motive force of the motives. Since the concept of causality is important for science, particularly psychology, we will discuss this matter at some length.

The Concept of Causality

Our whole concept of the causality implied in a mechanistic or organismic deterministic system needs clarification. First of all, we need a concept of causality that will include every known type of cause-and-effect relationship, otherwise it is impossible for us to understand the relationships which our investigations discover.

Bridgman, in his *Reflections of a Physicist*, seems to have lost confidence in human reason in this area, or at least he has put limits to the extent to which things can be understood by us. This, of course, is tantamount to a denial of the principle of intelligibility. Unless we work on this principle we stultify ourselves from the very beginning. If we doubt that the same is the same or that being is being, we delude ourselves in thinking that we know anything at all. If we do know anything at all, we know that we cannot affirm and deny the same thing in the same statement. If we do make an assertion that denies itself we are talking and thinking nonsense.

If, then, we go by the principle of intelligibility, we know that whatever is or is known can give a comprehensive account of itself, maybe not to our mind but to some mind. And as far as our minds go, our knowledge of anything can lead us to some understandable explanation, even though it be not comprehensive. Our examination of any object will show us that an intelligible account of it can be found in the object itself or in something outside it. Whatever is, and whatever it is, has a sufficient reason for being, and for being what it is. If we wish to understand the thing completely we should know all the reasons it has for being. It is in trying so to broaden our knowledge of things that we come to find the various kinds of *causes*.

If we begin with some phenomenon that begins to be, it is quite clear that this phenomenon does not explain itself. If it could, then at least it would not explain why it *began* to be. Anything that *begins* to be has the reason for its existence *outside* itself. This is what we mean by the principle of causality. Note how different this concept is from the principle of "causality" that is discussed by the theoretical physicists and the positive scientists in general. It has been the fashion since the time of Kant to assert that Hume destroyed the principle of causality and that Kant restored it to science. What Kant restored was a figment of the imagination, or rather, in the process of restoring what the learned world thought Hume had destroyed, Kant made of causality merely a way in which the mind is geared to think. We need not be surprised if the modern physicist has thrown the sand of quantum mechanics into these gears. By so doing, however, he has not banished the principle of causality from science, he has but shown that Kantian notions are not adequate in formulating the explanations which the infinitesimally small of the physical world give of themselves. The principle of causality in its simplest form means only that whatever begins to be receives existence from the action of something not itself. Whatever it is that gives existence to the newly existing thing is called a cause. Because its causality is expressed in action, it is technically called an *efficient cause,* to distinguish it from other causes which this same newly begun thing also has.

The acting cause is not the only account that can be given of this thing that begins to be. The thing that begins is something, and something distinctive in itself and different from both the acting cause and other things that are. Though it began to be, it did not come from sheer nothing. It was the product of a change rather than the result of strict creation. Even artistic creations and mathematical formulae are modifications of existing materials.[3] The materials are simply the stuff out of which the new thing is made, which stuff has been informed by a new principle of organization or of order. The stuff is called the *material cause*; the inner principle of specification is the *formal cause.*

What the thing is made of and what makes it to be itself are elements of the explanation a thing can give of itself. This account that it gives of itself makes it impossible for it to be just anything you please or anything *else* you please. The acting cause, when it acted, produced not just anything but this definite thing. It must, then, have been somehow ordained or oriented to doing just this when it acted. It is unthinkable that anything you please produces just anything you please; definite causes are pointed somehow toward definite effects. Acting causes, moreover, act in time. It follows that an acting cause cannot just produce anything you please but is pointed toward producing something definite. This determination brings us to order, and order brings us to foreordination.

[3] To say that the equations of the theorist in physics are modifications of already existing materials seems to go counter to recently published accounts of creative thinking in the sciences, for instance in the works of Hadamard, Pfister, Cannon, and others. All we mean is that the inventor does not start from sheer nothing: Einstein already had the symbols that sorted themselves into the equations expressing the General Theory; Kekulé had the images of the dancing atoms that formed the models which he formulated in his equations; Cannon had the elements that sorted themselves in the hunch which he called the Emergency Theory.

Thus the principle of sufficient reason, which is the same as the principle of intelligibility, not only establishes the principle of causality, as we showed, but it also uncovers the principle of *finality*. This terrifying principle means that when an action takes place something definite is produced; when a cause acts, the effect is something definite.

Some causes are not only active but also intelligent; these can determine for themselves what to make, and can use the proper materials to make it. Of these we can say that they set purposes for themselves. Other acting causes are without intelligence—they can only do what they do when they do it; of these we say that what they do is determined either by the sort of thing they are or by the use other causes may make of them.

Types of Causality in Science

It seems that the physicist has always assumed that he deals exclusively with efficient causes (or what we have identified as efficient causes) and their effects. He sometimes even denies that he is at all concerned with final causes or any of the other three classes of causes which Aristotle has laid down. It is true, of course, that the physicist is dealing with forces or energies. In mechanics, for instance, he speaks of mass in action, of forces which initiate change of velocity, motion, acceleration; of potential or kinetic energy. In thermodynamics he has elaborated statistically a whole science which describes the effects of heat and how they are produced, and explains them as effects of heat in action, i.e., as an efficient cause. He has a treatise on optics where the laws are set up which determine the propagation of electromagnetic energy either as visible light or as invisible radiation. In electricity and electromagnetism he deals with energies and the effects of these energies, how they are modified, and how they modify material bodies. He says he can give an adequate explanation of his world in terms of these energies; there are even some who say that they can give a complete explanation of the universe in these terms. But we must remember that the physicist, in his researches and his experiments, is always working on the principle of *constancy*. He knows that the stuff he uses is going to produce a certain effect and no other—and that means in fact working on the principle of *finality*. His knowledge of the material he works with may be indeterminate, but he knows that when he discovers what it can do, it will always do that under the appropriate conditions. He knows that the relationship between some particular object which he observes in action, and the action in this particular object, is necessary and determined. He has no particular concern with the material composition of the bodies or the masses which he observes; he takes for granted that the particular body he is working with is made up of something, but he is primarily interested not in its chemical composition but its physical activities.

Components and molecular or atomic structure are the domain of the chemist. The chemist determines for himself what are the particular elements which go into a reaction to form certain compounds. The chemist is not concerned with the ultimate composition or the ultimate principles which will explain *how* material substances react or *why* they should react in chemical composition; the chemist *is* concerned with material and formal causes because he knows that the elements are qualitatively different. He tries to express this qualitative difference in terms of number, e.g., atomic weight or atomic number. Since he can express it quantitatively he supposes that this expression is an explanation of the inner reality of the thing. But there must be some ultimate reason why hydrogen has only one electron, though it may have one or two neutrons in the nucleus, and why helium has two electrons. There must be some ultimate reason why a body with two electrons is chemically inert. To say that helium is inert because it has two electrons, and that the inertness of helium explains why its outer shell is complete, is not giving any real explanation at all. There must be some ultimate reason why two electrons complete the first shell, eight complete the next shell, and eight more complete the third shell. The chemist as a chemist is not particularly concerned with this ultimate explanation, though he is concerned with the fact that iron, for instance, is a substance that has definite properties, different from aluminum, which is a substance that has other properties of its own. He works with qualitative differences, and it is only because he assumes qualitative differences that he can make progress. Of course, it is the fashion among chemists at the present time to explain chemical reactions in quantitative or strictly numerical terms. It is the fashion for chemists to assume that since molecules can be broken up into atoms and atoms can be broken up into electrons and protons, and since nuclei can be broken up into protons and neutrons and there are also the peculiar particles called mesons, perhaps the whole universe is an aggregate made up of electrons and protons and other particles. It can be shown, however, that a very substantial change takes place when a molecule is broken up into its atoms, and another substantial change occurs when the atom is split—as is evidenced by the change that took place when the atom bomb was dropped on Nagasaki.

The chemist deals with material causes only in the sense that elements go to make up compounds and the molecules in the compound go to make up the molar mass. The chemist is concerned with the stuff of which chemical elements and compounds are made; he is also interested in the different properties exhibited by all these elements and compounds. He may say that he is interested only in chemical processes as chemical processes, but he cannot possibly understand these unless he assumes first of all that it is the elements and compounds that are active in the reaction (they act as producing causes) and that his function is only to see that the conditions are supplied under which the reaction occurs.

While the chemist does not deal with material, formal, and final causes explicitly, he has to admit them as first principles which have been established elsewhere, in the philosophy of nature, no matter how much modern physicists may deny it.

Similarly the biologist, in his experiments, discovers constant and uniform ways in which living cells act under certain conditions. He knows, of course, that biochemistry in the organism is different from laboratory chemistry. He knows that there is something at work in the organism which he has not yet been able to introduce into the laboratory reaction, but he is more interested in finding out how that something works than what that something might be in itself. He assumes some principle of organization which does account for the difference between biochemistry in the living body and biochemistry in the laboratory; that is, he assumes a formal cause. He is also interested in the chemical composition of the products of living chemistry. He may even try to reproduce them in his biochemical laboratory; he assumes material causes because he knows he cannot make anything out of nothing.

The psychologist takes the human person as he finds him and studies the way the person acts, that is, he accepts the person as an acting cause. The psychologist is interested in activities of the human being. He supposes, of course, that it is the *human being* who is acting and not a robot that is moved by external forces. He works on the principle that formal causes exist, whatever he may call them. He supposes that the human being is a *human* being, though for purposes of systematizing knowledge he may classify him as a dynamic physical system, as a physiological organism, or as a complicated set of chemical reactions. But the psychologist interested in personality is not satisfied merely to split up the human being into various categories; he wants to know him as a single unit working under definite conditions and producing definite results. These results may be human activities themselves or the effects of such activities on himself or on his environment.

The psychologist takes the human being as he finds him and tries to discover the unique factors that account for the pattern of activities which characterize this individual in his uniqueness. He is not particularly interested in finding out how much a person is like a piece of iron, nor is he particularly interested in discovering his likeness to a white rat, but he is very much interested in discovering how a human person is different from a piece of iron and a white rat. He is interested in distinctly human activities. He may try to explain them in terms which are applicable in the same way to a piece of iron or to a white rat, but he very soon realizes that he has not *explained* a human person, he has merely equated him with an object or an animal. It is our contention that the psychologist, if he assumes from the beginning that the human person is only an intelligent *mammal,* will discover at the end of his researches that he has described a mammal and failed to describe an intelligent one. If, however, he assumes that the human individual is an *intelligent* mammal and tries to discover wherein this intelligence lies, he may at the end of his researches have come to understand a human being as a human being. That is briefly the import of Allport's insistence on a proper model for our psychological research.

The psychologist knows that the human being, when he does something, always does something definite; that is to say, the psychologist works on the principle of constancy, which is another way of saying finality. He knows, too, that the human being has some discretion in the matter and can set goals for himself. Because the human being sets up purposes for himself in a way which is distinctive of human beings, the principle of constancy must be modified. But to assume that this distinctive characteristic is not distinctive is to frustrate the very purpose the psychologist has set for himself.

In summary: the psychologist in the field of personality research either explicitly or implicitly assumes that the human being is the efficient cause of his activity, whatever other efficient causes that activity may have. He takes for granted that the human being is made up of a certain *kind of stuff* which is *organized in a distinctive way*—in other words, that the human being has a material and a formal cause and that his distinctive characteristic is to be found in the formal cause which distinguishes him as a human being from everything else, no matter how similar the basic stuff may be out of which he and everything else are made.

Finally, the psychologist expects that the human being will act in a human way, that he has purposes (or final causes) which are either inherent in his nature or set up by himself. Unless these assumptions are made in psychology, the most painstaking research can do no more than provide data for physiology or biology or ecology but it cannot explain the properly human activity of human beings (including the activity of experimenting and theorizing).

REFERENCES

1. ACH, NARZISS. 1910. *Ueber den Willensakt und das Temperament.* Leipzig: Quelle & Meyer.
2. ALLPORT, GORDON W. 1947. Scientific models and human morals. *Psychol. Rev.* 1947, 54, 182–92.
3. ———. 1950. *The individual and his religion. A psychological interpretation.* New York: The Macmillan Co.
4. BRILL, A. A. (ed.) 1938. *The basic writings of Sigmund Freud.* New York: Modern Library, Inc.
5. CANNON, WALTER B. 1939. *The wisdom of the body.* New York: W. W. Norton & Co., Inc.
6. ———. 1945. *The way of an investigator: A scientist's experiences in medical research.* New York: W. W. Norton & Co., Inc.

7. DEUTSCH, HELENE. 1945. *The psychology of women.* 2 vols. New York: Grune & Stratton, Inc.
8. FREUD, SIGMUND. 1920. *A general introduction to psychoanalysis.* London: Boni & Liveright.
9. ———. 1934. Psychogenesis of a case of homosexuality in a woman. In: *Collected papers,* Vol. II, No. 18. (1920). London: Hogarth Press, Ltd.
10. GILSON, ETIENNE. 1941. *God and philosophy.* New Haven: Yale University Press.
11. GOLDSTEIN, KURT. 1939. *The organism.* New York: American Book Co.
12. GRUENDER, HUBERT. 1932. *Experimental psychology.* Milwaukee: Bruce Publishing Co.
13. HADAMARD, J. 1945. *The psychology of invention in the mathematical field.* Princeton: Princeton University Press.
14. KUBIE, LAWRENCE S. 1950. *Practical and theoretical aspects of psychoanalysis.* New York: International Universities Press.
15. McDOUGALL, WILLIAM. 1926. Men or robots? In: *Psychologies of 1925.* (Ed.) CARL MURCHISON. Worcester, Mass.: Clark University Press.
16. MEUMANN, ERNST. 1912. Beobachtungen über differenzierte Einstellung bei Gedächtnisversuchen. *Z pädag. Psychol.,* 1912, **13**, 456–63.
17. PFISTER, OSKAR. 1917. *The psychoanalytic method.* Trans. Chas. R. Payne. London: Kegan Paul.
18. PLANCK, MAX. 1936. *Philosophy of physics.* New York: W. W. Norton & Co., Inc.
19. POINCARÉ, HENRI. 1921. *The foundations of science.* Trans. G. B. Halstead. New York: Science Press.
20. PROTHRO, E. TERRY, and TESKA, P. T. 1950. *Psychology: A bisocial study of behavior.* Boston: Ginn & Co.
21. RAZRAN, GREGORY H. S. 1935. Conditioned responses: An experimental study and a theoretical analysis. *Arch. Psychol.*. 1935, **28**, No. 191, 1–124.
22. REICHENBACH, HANS. 1951. *The rise of scientific philosophy.* Berkeley: University of California Press.
23. ROE, ANNE. 1950. The use of clinical diagnostic techniques in research with normals. In: *Feelings and emotions: The Mooseheart Symposium.* (Ed.) MARTIN L. REYMERT. New York: McGraw-Hill Book Co., Inc.
24. ROGERS, CARL R. 1951. *Client-centered therapy.* Boston: Houghton Mifflin Co.
25. SNYGG, DONALD, and COMBS, ARTHUR W. 1949. *Individual behavior.* New York: Harper & Bros.
26. ZILBOORG, GREGORY. 1951. *Freud: His exploration of the mind of man.* New York: Chas. Scribner's Sons.

Chapter 2

THE CONCEPT OF "THEORY" IN SCIENCE AND IN PSYCHOLOGY

By JOHN A. GASSON, S. J.

ANYONE WHO has tried to trace the semantic fortunes of the term "theory" in the last half century has found an innumerable [1] multitude of meanings which are bound to lead to confusion.[2]

Theory in Science

At the risk of being thought naïve, we will begin with some of the Greek progenitors of the term as the point of departure for our exploration of the meaning of theory in present-day science and psychology. However, apart from a word or two about Plato and Aristotle, our discussion will embrace only what has been thought of theory in the last fifty years, and even within that period we shall concentrate on the highlights. About Plato we need only say that for him theorizing means a flight into the empyrean to contemplate the Ideas. Actually it is a process of remembering what the soul knew before the body overwhelmed it at birth and rendered the knowledge unconscious. The flight to the Ideas is the Platonic Dialectic, a mode of formal and formalized discourse according to strict rules which brings the mind from the world of things to the world of Ideas and back again. Explanation in Plato's sense is the exposition of the degree to which things of sense participate in the Ideas.

---

[1] The term is used designedly. To number a multitude there is required a unit that can be applied as a measure unequivocally. Number and multitude are not synonymous.

[2] If *theory* has had such a checkered semantic career, think of what has happened to *cause* and *reason* or even to innocuous *is*, as for instance at the hands of the late Count Korzybski.

49

Aristotle, however, worked out a fairly complete scheme of science and method. It has become the fashion among theorists in science to contrast Aristotelian concepts and methods with Galilean methods, and to ascribe the scientific progress of the last four centuries to the overthrow of Aristotelian principles in the Copernican and Galilean revolution. But that is an over-simplification of the history of science (see *Appendix*, page 70). Aristotle describes two types of explanations, just as there are two types of demonstrations. The one is an explanation that establishes the fact, the other shows why the fact is so and cannot be otherwise. This second type of explanation (δι–ότι) leads to true science, for it reveals the causes of the fact.

This compressed statement of Aristotle's philosophy of science merits some expansion, but we will simply put it this way: A science is a body of *demonstratedly* true and certain conclusions derived from *true and certain* principles. The principles of a science cannot be demonstrated in that science; but they can be established in some other science that reaches deeper to the roots of reality. The basic Science of Reality (First Philosophy) establishes the principles that make the things of science intelligible to us in a real sense, even though it does not provide the first principles for the different positive sciences. Science is primarily an acquired habit of mind that enables a thinking person to *understand* the objects that belong to the field of a particular science (e.g., chemistry, mathematics, philosophy), to *relate* them one to the other by demonstrating necessary connections, and finally to *unify* them by a single principle of order which will embrace all objects belonging to a specific field. The habit of science, then, is different both in function and object from wisdom, understanding, prudence, method, art (technique), though these also are necessary equipment for the scientist. A theory as Aristotle conceives it is an insight into the relation between all the objects of a field of knowledge, couched in a statement expressing that relation.[3]

[3] Anyone who desires a fuller exposition of Aristotle's philosophy of science is referred to Maritain, (31), *Distinguer pour unir*. For interpretations of this philosophy the reader is referred to the current flood of books and articles on the philosophy of science.

Aristotle's theory of science is not much accepted among theorists of science these days. This is not surprising since even the nineteenth-century theorists, with their naïve faith in the omnipotence of scientific method and Newton's laws, are at present of no more than historical interest. Pearson's *Grammar* no longer gives paradigms appropriate for present-day inflections. This state of opinion has been fifty years a-growing. Stemming from the works of such men as Mach, Poincaré, Duhem, Ostwald, there came at the turn of the century a growing disenchantment with the old mechanics as the physics and the metaphysics of nature. A vigorous group of "energetists" arose who energetically explained how mechanics "explained" nothing. Indeed, Mach insisted that "explanations" are the bane of science; that mechanism had broken down because it resorted to "metaphysics," to going beyond the sense data to transphenomenal "causes," "reasons," and such. Physics found mechanical explanations no longer valid. Nay more, science had better recognize that its laws and theories are but economical *descriptions* of what goes on as our sense experience gives it to us. If the description applies to all objects of a class under defined circumstances, the description is a law; to try to know *why* they act as they do is to succumb to illusion (28, Introduction, and 26, pp. 338–43).

One family of mechanists, the atomists among the chemists, did not quite go along with this trend. Too much had happened in chemistry since Dalton's day to allow them to think that atoms and molecules were not *real*. Avogadro had counted them. Canizzaro had confirmed the count. True, Ostwald had made his sensational blast, "Die Ueberwindung des wissenschaftlichen Materialismus," at Lübeck in 1895. Had Aristotle been present at that distinguished gathering of German physicists and physicians, he would have cheered (at least silently, out of deference to the solemnity of the company) at one passage in that famous discourse:

The atomistic concept pretends, for instance, that iron and oxygen —even if all their sensible properties have disappeared in rust—are nonetheless present in a new substance in which they would just now have assumed entirely new properties. We have been so accustomed to this idea that it becomes difficult to see its strangeness, even its absurdity. But if we reflect that all we know about a substance comes from our knowledge of its properties, we see that an assertion which claims that there is still a determined substance but without a single one of its properties, is not far from sheer nonsense (34, p. 558).

There was more to it than Ostwald's quarrel with "metaphysics" and "explanations"; he had touched on a sore spot, a real problem, and on their atomistic premises the chemists could not explain it. The problem was how the emergence of a single new substance could be explained by the simple addition of several substances already in existence, or in more general terms, how the phenomenon of chemical change could be "reduced" to mere addition or subtraction. However, ten thousand difficulties never made a doubt. Even Ostwald, in his "conversion" in 1909, relegated the problem to the future and a hope. To date, that hope has not been fulfilled. Every new advance in atomic physics raises more problems than it solves. New phenomena are predicted; the phenomena are found and expose the inconsistencies in the theory on the basis of which they were predicted. Quantum phenomena are a sore trial to the theorist; electrons are nowhere in the atom and where they are, they— like the famous soldier—are riding off in all directions. They are neither particles nor waves nor even wavicles; they are at best symbols in an equation.[4]

Moreover, the wonderful success of thermodynamics in building up a systematically articulated body of conclusions by deduction from a few relatively simple general principles, without recourse to transphenomenal "explanations," gave encouragement to the belief that a natural science could be constructed which would be independent of any consideration of the *nature* of the elements; the *relations* between them are revealed by science, predicted and verified in a systematic way. A science

[4] It is extremely interesting to note the very recent conceptions about the structure of matter that have stemmed from the inconsistencies which are continually cropping up in the mathematical development of quantum theory and the experimental verification of predictions. The concept of *virtual* photons, protons, electrons, is becoming a commonplace. Morse's article, "Physics and Radiation" (32), will be amazingly enlightening if read in conjunction with Hoenen's *Philosophy of Inorganic Nature* (18).

of this sort would, of course, begin with experimental observations, generalize the observations into laws, account for laws with hypotheses, develop hypotheses by mathematical or logical deductions into predictions of unobserved phenomena, and then verify the predictions by experiments designed specifically to test the predictions.

Duhem, who did not despise metaphysics as did Mach, but ignored it as quite irrelevant to physics, had high hopes of building a science of nature that was complete and autonomous, independent of any philosophy, but in itself an adequate philosophy of nature. We must not suppose that Duhem was *ignorant* of metaphysics. He was well acquainted with it. He was, however, positivistically oriented and therefore inclined to look upon the philosopher as "cabin'd, cribb'd, confined" to his ivory tower.[5] Duhem believed that metaphysics is totally a priori and deductive. For him, science had to do with matters of fact, and matters of fact are *found*, not deduced. He claimed that science as a body of knowledge must be built by discovering what is and classifying our knowledge as we classify the things we come to know. But classification, whether of ideas or things, presupposes a fairly complete knowledge, otherwise our classifications are merely tentative. Duhem foresaw science as a complete and perfect theory (classification); modern scientists hope for no more than a continued rearrangement of items and classes (Cf. Conant, 10).

How much progress has been made from this orientation of theory structure can be gauged by the brilliant results of thermodynamic research and the experimental triumphs stemming, for example, from Gibbs's theory of phases. Brilliant as has been the career of thermodynamics, not all theorists are fully content with it as an account of the "what" in "what goes on." The present-day positivists, refined in the crucible of fifty years, renounce any hope of describing *reality*, and look for meaning only in the rules formally laid down for correspondence between

[5] One might remark that the current repudiation by scientists of ivory towers (which originally and poetically were either an adornment or a secure guard) is a remnant of the adolescent iconoclasm of the positivists, who for all their dissembling all come from Missouri.

names and symbols, symbols and sensation complexes. For them, the *formal* relations between symbols are the source of wisdom, knowledge, understanding. These are the men of the Vienna Circle, the unified scientists for whom theorizing is an exercise in "creative imagination," and invention of a theory is a "free creation of the mind."

Thus we see that in the evolution of the concept of theory in the past few decades there has been revolution, convolution, and involution to such an extent that science has become a quest without a grail, a voyage without a goal, a game without a victory.[6]

Types of Theory

However, in all this variety of ideas and opinions we can discern certain family features which divide them off into three fairly well-defined groups. The first family we call the family of *explicatory theories* (Aristotle, Newton). These are centered on the notion that theory is an explanation in the persistently traditional sense of the word. The second family we call the family of *classificatory theories* (Duhem, Poincaré). These center around the concept that theory should attempt no more than to express in a mathematical equation as simply as possible a group of experimental laws. Science is a body of knowledge classifying phenomena as cases under these laws. The third family we call the family of *symbolic theories* (quantum theory, Vienna Circle). These center around the notion that science is a hypothetico-deductive system of mental constructs which symbolizes reality in some way. Theory in such a system is developed purely by mathematics and symbolic logic.

Explicatory Theories. An explicatory theory is a simple expression of a necessary relation existing between all the objects of a field of knowledge. This relation is the source or foundation of all the contingent relationships that might occur between the objects of the field. A theoretical statement is based on or ex-

---

[6] An interesting and instructive amplification of this sentiment can be found in Conant, *Science and Common Sense* (10). See also Pratt, *The Logic of Modern Psychology* (41).

presses a small number of auxiliary suppositions, which are the result of immediate inference from experimental observations. These statements are most accurately expressed in quantitative terms. The basic propositions of the theory are to be developed by mathematical or logical deductions and the conclusions drawn from this development must be verified by suitable experimentation. Since the relationships expressed by the formulations in the theory are causal in the strict (not in the Kantian or positivistic) sense of the term, even though they may be expressed in a mathematical equation, the explanation which they represent is an explanation in the Aristotelian sense, for the mathematical deductions are strict demonstrations (δι–ότι). Since the explanation given is proposed as a real and a true (not merely a correct) explanation, recourse to experimental confirmation is required.

Though none of the expositors of the "classical" explanatory theories ever expressed himself quite this way, at base experiment is necessary because mathematical deduction can only give relations that are *potentially* unique, though it does give *necessary* connections (relations that flow from the nature of quantitative being as such). For instance, Einstein in the mathematical development of the theory of relativity came to the equation $e = mc^2$, which stated the quantitative relationship between energy and mass, if mass were convertible into energy. The equation did not predict that the conversion could be effected; but *if it actually happened*, the equation predicted that this would *necessarily* be the quantitative relationship (necessary from the very nature of quantity and extension as such). Experiment proved that the conversion actually did happen and the equation was verified. Moreover, logic can give necessary connections (relations that flow from the factual data or from the nature of the elements) but it cannot arrive at a *unique* nexus.[7] For ex-

[7] Cf. the following passage quoted by Caldin from Sir Edmund Whittaker, *The Beginning and End of the World* (Riddell Lectures, Oxford, 1942), p. 17, and quoted here by permission of Oxford University Press, publishers:

It happens very often that different physical systems are represented by identical mathematical descriptions. For example, the vibrations of a membrane which has the shape of an ellipse can be calculated by means of a differential equation known as Mathieu's equation: but this same equation is also arrived at when we study the dynamics of a circus performer, who holds

ample, any strictly logical dialectical argument can establish *formal* connections between events: if it is raining, the river bank is wet; if the river overflows, the bank is wet; if an animal has emerged from the river, the bank is wet; if water leaks from a tank on the bank, the bank is wet, etc. Logic will not establish which of these events has actually occurred. Actual observation must decide what *actually* occurred if it is given that the bank is wet. Hence an actual and necessary connection can be found only by inference *and* actual experience or experiment. Lest misunderstanding occur, it must be emphasized that the logic mentioned is not the formal logic of the logisticians (though that is not excluded); and the uniqueness does not wear its full mathematical panoply.

Classificatory Theories. Classificatory theories can best be described in the words of Duhem:

A theory of physics is not an explanation. It is a system of mathematical propositions deduced from a small number of principles the aim of which is to represent as simply, as completely, and as exactly as possible a group of experimental laws. Experimental verifications are not the bases of theory; they are its culmination (12, p. 24).

The aim of the theory, then, is classification of phenomena as cases under a law. The theory of relativity is just such a theory. The mathematical expression of the theory is deduced from two simple principles: First, the principle of relativity of uniform motion—a principle which found at least *negative* confirmation in the Michelson-Morley experiments; and secondly, the principle of the invariance of the velocity of light. These principles were developed mathematically by the use of a Riemannian metric to yield the simplest covariant law of space-time. The equations that contain the principles are said to be "free creations of the mind."

---

an assistant balanced on a pole while he himself stands on a spherical ball rolling on the ground. If now we imagine an observer who discovers that the future course of a certain phenomenon can be predicted by Mathieu's equation, but who is unable for some reason to perceive the system which generates the phenomenon, then evidently he would be unable to tell whether the system in question is an elliptic membrane or a variety artiste (8, p. 207).

How they happen, not one of the theorists has been able to establish intelligibly. Hadamard (17) has written an extended treatise on this subject recently, called *The Psychology of Invention in the Mathematical Field*. There have been other accounts of greater or less merit but not one of them touches adequately on the basic problem: Whence does the mind or imagination (for most theorists mind and imagination are synonymous) have the power to create out of *sheer nothing* the symbols that represent reality, however that reality is to be understood? To do this simple little stunt the imagination must be not merely mathematically infinite but metaphysically and actually so.

Mathematical theorists cannot account for the equations by induction from experience because the equations generalize the data and induction can give no more than a sum of particulars. The equations establish universal relationships; experience can report only the singular. The equations are perfectly exact; sense data never report objects that are exact nor can they report the inexact object exactly. It is precisely these epistemic considerations (assumptions) which have led to the systematic agnosticism that goes by the name of *operationalism*, as it began the century in Poincaré's conventionalism.

Symbolic Theories. Logical positivists are satisfied that they have demonstrated that classical explicatory theories have been wrecked one by one on the rocks of epistemology. Explicatory theories presuppose at least a moderate realism. In them, the things of science are *things*. The positivist epistemology makes the things of science (scientific facts) not things but conceptual constructs. For this reason, logical positivists say that classical explanations are of little value because they are based on an incorrect epistemology. Of course, we must bear in mind that the classical explanations they refer to are theories in physics based on Newtonian physics and Kantian epistemology. The physics, they say, is not comprehensive enough, the epistemology is incorrect.

But strange to say, if Kant's meaning of knowledge is carried to its logical conclusion it will be found that scientific facts turn out to be mental fictions—which is exactly their status in logical positivism. Kantian forms and categories would ultimately require that what is called a fact be merely an interpretation which the mind puts on the sensory complex so as to fit it into a priori frames of reference. Except for the basis of Newtonian physics, what the positivists say about the construction of theories or the interpretation of reality sounds very much like Kantian formulations. Their "auxiliary concepts" are symbols of scientific facts; the "facts" are symbols of state variables; state variables are symbols of objects, whatever these objects may be in themselves.

Logical positivists loudly abjure Kant with all his forms and categories, and appeal to Einstein and Minkowski who, they proclaim, dispatched Kant's epistemology when they destroyed Newton's absolute space and time. But they go even further in a distrust of the mind in the role they assign to the observational value of a state variable and to experimental verification. The positivist repudiates idealism, yet remains a cryptoidealist all the same. His theories are "free creations of the mind" because they cannot be constructed by induction from sense data; there is nothing that corresponds to the concept but a measuring operation. Meaningfulness is found by reference to time. Quantum mechanics is the palmary example of such symbolic theories. It makes no pretense of having its equations represent *what is*; it pretends only to express in an accurate way *what is thought*, and is satisfied so long as it is expressed systematically according to a definite conceptual scheme.

Nevertheless, the explanatory theorists, the conventionalists, and the logisticians were all to a great extent at one in the general method of systematization of their knowledge. Except for some of the more advanced operationalists (who reluctantly have forsworn the law of contradiction) they all conformed their thinking to the laws of two-valued logic. The variety in the three families of theories we have described is to be laid mostly to the initial assumptions regarding the nature of the world and the nature of science. But there is a type of theory, or more properly a way of theorizing, that is very different. It gives rise to different theories even where the basic assumptions are the same. This way of theorizing is based on the indeterminately valued logic of dialectical systems.

The Dialectical Method. The logic of dialectical systems is more flexible and imposes few if any controls on thought. Dialectical systems tend to "arrange all forms of knowledge in an order according to the sequence of their development" (McKeon, 30, p. 662), and use dialectics as a formal logic and experimental methodology. Thus dialectical modes of thought are inclined to identify a developmental or genetic kind of logic with metaphysics, just as they identify operation with understanding. As McKeon remarks:

Dialectic is a method of fact and process in which thing and thought are inextricably intermingled and in which formal and linguistic systems are posterior and relatively unimportant (30, p. 679).

Thus opposites can substitute for one another, contradictions cease to be fatal to thinking because they can be resolved on a different level, thought can be "converted" into fact. For the dialectically oriented theorist the interplay between theory and practice (the theoretical and the practical or experimental) is more important than the consistency of the system itself. The dialectician reads into the terms that describe the world meanings of his own, in most cases remote from common usage. It is by this means that he comes in science to his "first unification of fact" or his original hypothesis. This hypothesis does not conform to reality but melts away when confronted with opposite facts. Scientific progress occurs because the stimulus of the original unification is strong enough to clasp discordant facts into another resynthesis. All of us these days are familiar with dialectical scientific theories that go to extremes; science in the U.S.S.R. is the best example.

Theory in Psychology

From what has been said so far, one can surmise how complicated the situation can become when an attempt is made to apply these diverse concepts of theory to psychology. Quite apart from the debate whether psychology can be called a science at all, the patent diversity of the scientific objects in psychology from those in physics and chemistry makes it difficult to apply to psychology the scheme of theory construction proposed for the positive sciences. That may be the reason why some theorists in psychology, seemingly without being aware of it, have relied upon a kind of dialectical logic in ordering the chaos of clinical data. This reliance on dialectic may explain why certain theorists are curiously indifferent to strict logical consistency or the objective validity of their theoretical systems. Kris, an important modern theorist, points out that some psychoanalytic propositions are unverifiable—for example, the intense aggression of earliest infancy resulting in self-punitive tendencies. Kris * continues:

> Psychoanalysis as a science cannot, I believe, directly deal with these propositions; moreover, their value for the formation of other empirical propositions can be seriously questioned. Their place in Freud's thinking, however, and their immense stimulating effect, is a matter of great concern to those interested in the history of ideas (25, p. 338).

For the ordinary scientist, it would be a serious matter if the very foundation of his explanatory system were not verifiable and could not be used in formulating valid new hypotheses. But the dialectical thinker seems to value them for their stimulating effect, and so uses them even though they should be neither true nor verifiable. And the clinician who uses the dialectical method is convinced that practical therapeutic action will make up for any insufficiency of theory, or rather, that theory cannot be thought apart from action. It is this feature of psychoanalytic thinking which has not been sufficiently appreciated by psychologists who have tried to find experimental verification for psychoanalytic concepts.

In a comparison of Freudian psychoanalysis with classical academic psychology, Kardiner criticizes the scientific procedure and results of psychoanalytic theorizing as follows:

> Once we have our explanations, what criteria can we establish to validate them? First, it can be verified on different subjects. This

* By permission from *Psychological theory, contemporary readings*, edited by Melvin H. Marx. Reprinted from same chapter in S. Hook and M. R. Kronvitz (eds.), *Freedom and experience*. Copyright 1947, Cornell University Press, Ithaca.

form of validation will hardly be very convincing because by this time we have a closed system derived from certain recurrent clinical facts, and as long as those clinical facts remain constant, the explanation will be considered valid. This is the type of proof that has largely been used in psychoanalysis as a form of validating explanations. In actual practice, however, it is a form of begging the question. This kind of demonstration establishes not the validity of the explanation but only the constancy of the facts upon which it is based.

A second method of validating a psychoanalytic explanation derives from the fact that these explanations were considered to be useful implements for effecting changes in the organization of personality. There, the explanation which effects therapeutic success is thereby validated. This is decidedly an unwarranted conclusion and an exceedingly untrustworthy criterion. Too many unknown factors enter into therapeutic success to be used as a check on the validity of any explanation. In fact, some therapeutic procedures are effective without any explanations whatsoever. Furthermore, it is a well established fact that dynamic explanations useful in mobilizing one individual to change will not do so in another. And finally, therapeutic success on similar types of cases can be achieved by explanation systems that have nothing in common.

The only real check on the validity of an explanation is an operational one (23, pp. 243–44).

But Kardiner fails to detect that the leap from alleged therapeutic success to a universal explanation is characteristic of dialectical systems. It might even be said that his recourse to an operational check can be no more productive of verification than the therapeutic one because his own theory of method is based unwittingly on the dialectical mode of reasoning. He adopts the concept of an "action syndrome" in which "the drive can be assumed axiomatically to exist." By this means he is confident that psychoanalysis can become a science. He continues:

The merits of our particular theory depend on two factors: (1) It is an operational tool, a guide to action; (2) its operational effectiveness depends on the assumption that no facts exist other than those we have recognized (23, p. 252).

In the first place, Kardiner's reliance on an "operational tool as a guide for action" reminds us how close the operationalist comes to the dialectic identification of action and thought, when for so many of them the operation is the definition of the thing. Only in the dialectical method can the identification of action, thought, and thing bear the fruit of understanding. Secondly, the assumption that no facts exist, other than the ones the scientist recognizes, can mean that the operations are not significant until all the facts are known. But surely no scientist will say that at any moment all the facts relevant to a given state of affairs are known or recognized. If the assumption means anything it must contain some way of including not only the unknown facts but also of reconciling all the contrary facts. This can be done easily enough by the dialectical method, but it is doubtful whether it is a good check on the validity of an explanation.

The use of a dialectic of the sort we have described emancipates the thinker from the classical laws of thought. With such a method and in such a system there is ample room for "creativity." Many new and "progressive" concepts may emerge; but in such a system the thinker is always in danger of losing contact with reality. There is good reason to believe that many dialectical thinkers leave reality at their first step, when they choose which facts they will recognize. It is important for the theorist to remind himself that creation is not the business of man's mind except perhaps in art. In all other areas his business is to produce.

The application of a theory of science to the data of science is no less difficult in academic psychology. Cantril reflects the current confusion among theoretical psychologists in his recent review of psychology in the past five decades, at least as he tries to isolate certain trends. For some time now, he tells us, there has been a dissatisfaction with the atomism of Wundt. Since then, there has been a trend toward "wholes," which trend has become very much more pronounced in the last twenty years. There has been a persistent attempt to establish a homogeneity of domain in psychology and to make that domain continuous with the rest of nature. Psychologists no longer concern themselves with "absolutes" and the resulting dichotomies, as had "traditional" psychology.

At present, Cantril says, dichotomies are being merged; psychology is discovering that "subjective" and "objective" no longer have much meaning, that psychology deals not with objective or stimulus situations but with events in the organism for which the objective situation does not give an adequate account. Similarly, the old controversy between nature and nurture is a meaningless squabble, as Cantril puts it, because Nature and Nurture are really the same thing: Freud, McDougall, and Malinowski have proved that, especially Malinowski. Man is his environment—his social environment. Cantril complains that there is still an elementarism remaining; psychologists still think of entities acting in or reacting to a field—and that is not scientific. The trend is now to an ultra-subjectivism (unreality) and "transactions." Shorn of the involved terminology with which transactionism is usually clothed, this could mean that psychology is laboriously striving to discover from the enormous mass of undigested "clinical" data, first, that the human being is a *unit*; secondly, that he is subject to real *change*.

Transactionism, as proposed by Dewey, is none too clear about the fundamental nature of "transactions," nor does it stipulate the parties engaged in the transactions. As a starting point for psychological theory it has little to offer that is new or solid. A theory must begin somewhere with something. Transactionism is still uncertain on the basic issues. True, most present-day theories in psychology break down on the basic issues, but at least some of them do take a stand.

What are the basic issues? To begin with, there is the problem of law in psychology. Law implies uniformity and constancy. Where can we find a firm basis for uniformity in psychology? The perennial problem of the difference between the psychic and the physical still plagues us, and no homogeneity thus far proposed will do. We can, of course, with Boring accept a psychophysical parallelism, make it a salt-and-sugar mixture, and hope that future research will change it into something really homogeneous. That is really admitting defeat but dodging the obloquy.

The other theorists assume a homogeneity but get wrecked on the issue of dimensionality: Can we find a set of dimensions that are univocal in all cases, as are *L,M,T*, (Length, Mass, Time) in physics? Can they be used properly in all cases of our subject matter? When the measurements are made, what shall we do with the results? Some theorists make quality, intensity, extensity, and protensity the dimensions of consciousness, but then bog down on the problem of making the measurements refer to consciousness and not to something else. (It is not only possible but customary to define *red* in terms of Ångströms, but does that measure a sensation?) Nafe, for instance, approaches the matter by reducing all "felt experience" to patterns of pressure, and then suggests measuring the movement of nonnervous tissue in the vicinity of the active neuron. But if sensations as well as feelings and emotions are simply different patterns of pressure, how are we going to distinguish these different dimensions of experience by mapping pressure patterns somewhere in the body?

To achieve homogeneity of domain by establishing a correlation of variables inside the physiological process works well enough in some cases, but what about processes that do not have a specific physiological correlate or have one for which it is not possible to obtain unique results? The logical positivists would avoid all these difficulties by banishing any consideration of the content of our statements in psychology, and by concentrating on a *syntactical* language for our assertions. The language of physics is to be taken as a base, and our psychological language is to be constructed exclusively according to form. Logical syntax will insure generality, completeness, and rigor (Cf. Jørgenson, 22, pp. 79–81). This prospect does not appeal much to most of us. If we begin by emptying out the baby from the bath, what have we to bathe, even if we have all the water we need?

It is not my purpose to go into any account of *Gestalt* psychology and the theoretical development it has received in recent years. This much can be said, however: The older generation of *Gestalt* psychologists still hope for real explanations. Their younger colleagues tend more and more toward the symbolic character of mathematical theories though their point of attack still remains "wholes" and "whole properties": their statements express the functional relations between them. It is quite true that their principles can be applied univocally only to the perceptual field and even in that field can be shown to be of insufficient generality; but they do attempt to show that these principles operate in whole areas as well as in whole elements in these areas.

That the *Gestalt* psychologists also are blocked by the problem of dimensionality can be seen clearly enough in those theorists who occupy themselves so assiduously with the problems of psychological dimensions (e.g., Lewin). One of the principal motives which led Lewin to adopt topology as a mathematics (or a mode of measurement) of personality was the fact that topological spaces are not metricized. He believed that he would be able to define part-whole relationships and part-part functional changes with an unmetricized geometry. It is true that such a theory in geometry is absolutely general in a mathematical sense. But without a metric neither the theory nor the geometry is of any value in a real situation.

Perhaps the most assiduous among recent theorists are the neobehaviorists, Tolman and Hull. Their ideal is to establish laws which, after the pattern of the laws of physics, are statements of invariant function variables. The simplest statement is $R(f)S$. This simplicity is impossible, however, basically because in the living organism, and a fortiori in the human being, no unique function can be determined, whatever be the value assigned to R or S and whichever of them is taken as the independent variable. Hence Tolman, for instance, interpolates inferred intervening variables which are either undemonstrated or, more likely, undemonstrable. He postulates two classes of S variables and three classes of functions. To handle all these adequately in a mathematical framework requires a mathematics which as yet has not been developed. But apart from the technical difficulties of a mathematical nature the whole theory fails to take into account the peculiar kind of indeterminacy that is proper to the organism and the indeterminacy that is proper to the human being.

In dynamic systems, as physicists are insisting more and more, the laws of dynamics are determinately applicable only if the systems are completely closed. But biological systems—organisms—are open systems; their laws have not yet been fully *determined* (discovered). Human organisms are purposive to a greater degree and on a higher level than nonhuman organisms and their dynamics must include that function which determines that a set of acting factors may or may not result in a definite event. Whatever intervening variables are used, they all must be expressions of dynamism in the organism. At best, these can be measured only as instantaneous states. Instantaneous states, in principle, are static or stopped processes. When values are assigned to the inferred variables, what is expressed is something other than the dynamism sought for. Even if the values found did express process as process, they would be inapplicable to the human organism where the variables involve qualitative changes that do not include a time factor or continuity.

Without exception, the equations Hull sets up or derives contain variables that depend on time or are integrations of continuous functions between parameters. For example, *drive strength* may be measured by the number of hours of food privation, and *action potential oscillation* by the integral from minus infinity to sigma of the probability function (20, pp. 344–45). However, there are events in the human being which do not depend on time though they happen in time: for example, the extinction of a conditioned response immediately the human subject makes up his mind to it; the failure to condition even over a long period when the human subject refuses to become conditioned (see our discussion on conditioning, page 17 f.). One could hardly conceive consent or refusal as the limit of an integral function or even of an integrodifferential function.

Hull's attempt to bend the physicalism of the Vienna Circle to the analysis of molar masses of behavior labors under at least two initial inconsistencies: All analysis of a molar mass is in principle inexact because it is molar; to bridge the gaps, hypothetical entities must be assumed which are in principle unobservable. Again the basic issue of dimensionality is not adequately met. For Hull it might be not so much the problem of quantizing (as it is for Tolman) but of defining not merely the *kind* of behavior but the behavior itself. In dimensional analysis in physics the general equations involve L,M,T—length, mass, time. The kind of units used for actual measurement may be as arbitrary or as whimsical as one pleases, but the dimension itself is strictly defined. It is either a length or a mass or a time, or some other variable that can be related to them. In psychology, however, it is not at all clear just what the dimensions are which are used by Hull. Not all psychologists agree that behavior can be defined by S,R,V—stimulus, response, intervening variable. In physics, the meaning of L is accepted by all; in psychology, the meaning of S is challenged by many. Moreover, the units chosen by Hull are not true units. At least, as meaures of intensity they conform only to the simplest form of ordinal scale because we have no assurance that the interval between steps is equal. If such an assurance be claimed it is only on an assumption which the theory may not be strong enough to support—a matter of which Hull himself was well aware (20, p. 322).

Conclusion

What, then, are we to do? If we assume (as no doubt we safely can) that psychology can be a scientific discipline, can we proceed to theorize? And if we do, what kind of theory will we construct and how shall we go about it? Where are we going to start, since we must start somewhere? Somewhere relatively close to our goal—if we have a goal—rather than a long way back?

To begin with, the theory will have to be *truly* scientific. Let us take that to mean that it will deal with real things, not merely with "free creations of the mind." Next, that it will give *explanations* of the way things *change*; finally, that the explanations, while not pretending to reach to ultimates, must be comprehensive, that is, must explain all the phenomena the theory is constructed to include. Put succinctly, we are looking for a theory which will express what is and how it changes in terms of a few simple hypotheses. The implications of these hypotheses should be capable of being unfolded by logic or mathematics or both, to account for what actually happens. The theory itself must be consistent not only with the facts observed but also with principles established in other sciences and disciplines.

Hence we assume moderate direct realism as our epistemological base. This excludes from the start the meaning given the term "knowledge" by most contemporary theorists both in physics and in philosophy. It also excludes all theories that are at best classificatory (taxonomic) or symbolic. We shall not exclude either their classifications or their symbols, but we strive to assign a real correlate to the symbol. If this correlation fails or leads to anomalies or antinomies, we shall consider that our theory is defective and not that things are unintelligible. This, of course, means that in addition to the principle of moderate realism we assume also the principle of intelligibility. That is, we take for granted that real things are and that they can be understood without involving contradiction. If they are not so understandable, they are simply *nonsense*, like Ostwald's substances that remain the same but possess entirely different properties.

Moreover, we take for granted that classical mechanism, no matter how sophisticatedly proposed or how precisely developed, simply will not work in psychology just as it does not work in physics or chemistry. That it does not work in physics is amply attested by the whole development of the atomic theory (see *Appendix*, page 71). We assume, furthermore, that the domain of psychology is continuous with the domain of the natural sciences; but more important than homogeneity, is the qualitative heterogeneity which differentiates these domains and the elements contained in each. The subject matter of psychology is not merely (or at all) numerable atoms or elements or even relations; it is *qualities*, for activities are qualities of the human organism. These qualities can be expressed mathematically; they even *must* be, so that psychology can proceed accurately and exactly, but they must be quantified *properly*, else the whole structure will be sheer fiction or symbol. We assume that the unity which underlies this qualitative heterogeneity is original, not derivative. That is, the varying qualities may be distinct in a unit, but the unit is not an aggregate of qualities. Hence the unit is not an isomorphism in a field nor an identity or contiguity of elements or relations that are distinct entities in themselves.

Our frame of reference also implies that there are substantially discontinuous natures in the organic world; that animals differ in *kind*, not merely in degree of organization, from humans. The time-honored distinctions *generic* and *specific* have their value because they are taxonomic, but that is not the only value they have and biology is not their only field of application. In chemistry, for instance, the problem whether molar masses, molecules, atoms, nuclei, are units or sheer aggregates is not a *scientific* question; but the assumption that molecules or atoms are mere aggregates has sent nuclear physicists searching for forces which hold the nucleus together—as if a unit needed something outside itself to make it one! Human organisms are *generically* continuous with the brutes and that not merely in a taxonomic sense, but they are just as different specifically (and that not in the taxonomic sense) from the *genus animale* as humans are different among themselves. Biologists in their specialized terminology can be taxed with the present usage which equates "to be differentiated" with "to be different only in degree." Differentiation supposes a comparison as to degree but does not make a difference in kind. Hence the statement that man is a more highly differentiated mammal implies that the difference is one of degree only, not of kind.

All these assumptions we have stated are ultimates, and these we find not in the science of psychology but outside it. But unless we assume the right ultimates neither our data nor our methods will be of any avail for an understanding of the phenomena we presume to study in psychology. Most of the theorists in psychology are unwilling to accept any ultimates or absolutes, except of course those that each one of them unwittingly puts at the base of this same unwillingness. If "this world is all a fleeting show for man's illusion given," [8] then science is sheer amusement, disciplines are new games, and theories are new rules for games. We hope that our science will be more than just a game.

In brief, then, a theory in psychology should be real, simple, unified, comprehensive, capable of development, and verifiable in experience. It postulates certain ultimates from the philosophy of nature and the philosophy of man, or at least does not presume to establish such ultimates or contradict them. It is designed not only to describe what happens, but even more to explain why what happens could not possibly have happened in any other way.

APPENDIX

It is not our purpose to enter into any detailed discussion of the meaning and implications of the so-called Copernican (or Galilean) revolution. Nevertheless, there are several generally held misconceptions which it would be well for us to examine. It is generally believed that science was held in thrall for centuries by Aristotle's concept of nature and his scientific method; that progress in science became possible only after Galileo introduced the experimental method and scientists returned to an atomistic concept of nature; and that it was the atomism of the "ancient Greek philosophers" which was the fruitful mother of modern and contemporary scientific progress—and Galilean modes of thought were its midwives.

Born, for instance, in his synoptic article on the progress of physics in the last fifty years, written for the *Scientific American* in September 1950, proclaims that the first half of the twentieth century marked the triumph of atomistics. That he meant the atomism of Democritus is clear from his reference to "the ancients."

---

[8] Russell puts the same idea more prosaically in his famous remark about mathematics, to the effect that in mathematics we don't know what we are talking about nor whether what we say is true (42, p. 84). Whitehead, Werkmeister, Reichenbach, Blanshard, and Cassirer are voluminous. They elaborate their thought painstakingly and with great insight, for which they are to be reverenced and emulated. Yet the fact remains that no baker's skill will avail to make bread if sawdust is used instead of flour.

This linking of Dalton's atomic theory with the atomism of the Greeks is a widespread myth.

A little reflection would have shown that the particles of physics today bear not the slightest family resemblance to the atoms of Democritus. The assumption is altogether too simple that the atoms of Dalton are the atoms of Democritus *redivivi*. Two thousand years of history should not be telescoped so conveniently, leaving unanswered such questions as: Why did it take so long for the Galilean principles to flower into Dalton's atomic theory? The particles of Democritus had been waiting for two thousand years and more. It was not until 1808 that Dalton enunciated his theory. Galileo had dropped his weights off the tower many years before that. Descartes had refurbished the mechanicism of Democritus and mathematicized it some two hundred years before Dalton. How come this pregnant concept had such an unseemly period of gestation? If the ancient Greeks (Parmenides, Democritus, Leucippus) had been the progenitors of 1950 atomistics, why do the atoms of modern science bear so little resemblance to their putative forbears?

The principles of atomism had been applied to chemistry for two centuries before Dalton without any notable progress. It was only after he propounded two hypotheses that contradicted classical atomism that any progress was made. These hypotheses were: (1) Atoms of the *same element* all have the same properties, particularly weight; the atoms of diverse elements have diverse properties. Hence the molecules of a compound have a constant composition and properties proper to the compound. The molecules of the same compound all have the same properties. (2) In the composition of one molecule of a compound only *a few atoms* of one element join with *a few atoms* of other elements. This is a far cry from the atoms of Democritus, all of which have the same properties but differ only in size, shape, and velocity of motion. Dalton's postulates demanded: (*a*) that all the atoms had to be small; (*b*) that only certain compositions were possible; (*c*) that masses of the atoms were limited to a few species (up until now only 98 have been discovered; atomism postulates an infinite number); (*d*) that the number of atoms in a molecule of a compound be strictly determined (not indeterminate).

These demands are not met by the atoms of Democritus. The "ancient Greeks" taught that the atoms were of all sizes; that the various kinds of aggregates had to be infinite in number since the proportion of atoms varying in size and shape was continuously variable, for they could make no distinction between what is a true chemical compound and a simple mixture. From atomistic principles there can be no assignable reason why chemical compounds are not all simple mixtures.

On the other hand, the doctrine of the "minima naturalia" (Cf. QQ DD De Potentia Q 4 art. 1 ad 5) which was a commonplace among thirteenth-century philosophers who followed Aristotle, would allow, if not require, these four demands. We can upbraid them, if we like, for not having developed a physics and a mathematics that would have made these principles fruitful—just as we can blame Fresnel for not having developed wave mechanics in his time—but we should be sure what we blame them for.

COMMENT

Quantification of Qualities

Perhaps the main problem in a theory of human personality is to develop ways and means of quantifying the psychological phenomena which have been demonstrated and investigated experimentally. This is important not only for the proper isolation of "elements" (human activities) but also for experimental investigation.

The subject matter of scientific psychology is human activities. All activities are qualities, but there is a difference between activities of the person and the actions of material bodies. Ever since Locke, there has been a peculiar misunderstanding of the term "quality." It has been treated as if it were some kind of substantial entity. What we mean by quality is a way of being, an internal state of a given thing, which from the inside makes it to be thus and so. To give an example: A warm body has the quality of heat; the filament of a burning light has the quality of radiation; the free-falling body has velocity. Heat, radiation, velocity, are included in what we mean by qualities. When they produce effects on other bodies, these qualities are also actions. There is nothing particularly recondite in the statement that the subject matter of physics is either the actions or the qualities of bodies.

When we treat the subject matter of psychology scientifically, we must remember that human activities also are qualities, though not in the sense that sensation, for instance, is said to have a quality. Since activities are qualities and as such are subject to intensification and remission, they are amenable to comparison and measurement. The most accurate way in which we can determine relationships between them is quantitatively. When we relate qualities to number in a suitable way, we are quantifying qualities.

When we assign a number to a quality, we answer the question: How much of that quality is there here? One way to find an answer would be to determine the geometric quantity of the body possessing the quality. To find out how much heat there is in an amount of water, we could say, since there is a gallon of water, there is a gallon of heat. Obviously, this would hardly do (though we could measure how much red there is on the side of a house by measuring the area of the house). In asking how much of a quality there is, what we want to know is not so much its volume but its *strength*.

The intensity of a quality is measured not by growth in the quality but by change. If we want to measure the strength of any quality, we must observe its effects and not the quality in itself. If we want to know how strong our muscles are, we measure the amount of work they do. In the same way, we measure the intensity of heat in a thermometer by the amount of expansion produced in the mercury thread.

If, on the other hand, we conceive the intensity of a quality as if it were an aggregate of units of intensity, as if greater intensities were achieved merely by addition, we contradict the very notion of intensity. The point perhaps could be clarified by an example: If we charge a small sphere electrically, and transfer the charge to a large sphere, the charge will be found spread uniformly over the whole surface of the large sphere. But in any portion of that sphere the intensity of the charge will be different from the intensity that could have been found on a corresponding equal area of the small sphere. The whole charge is distributed over the large sphere just as the whole charge was distributed over the small sphere, but the intensity of that charge differs. If we thought of the intensity or density of an electric charge as an aggregate of unit charges, then a unit charge which would behave in exactly the same way could not be distributed over a large sphere. But the very notion of intensity of charge seems to exclude this limitation.

We can measure the intensity of a quality in one or all of three ways: First, by determining the extent to which it produces a change in some *other* body; secondly, by discovering the *number* of other bodies in which this change takes place; thirdly, by determining the *number of changes* wrought by this quality in other bodies.

In all three cases measurement is essentially an operation by which we assign to the changes that occur a place on the number continuum. The place to be assigned and the means used to discover it will depend on the amount of information our observations give us. We must know what is the relation of the observed change to other changes of the same class and what is the relation of the quality we are measuring to the changes we observe.

When we try to determine the extent to which a quality produces a change in another body, for instance, we may discover that this change is found only in some parts of the other body in one instance, and in different parts in other instances. If we have no more information than that there are changes and that they are different, we cannot establish any priority among them. So we can establish at best a *nominal scale,* giving the number *one* to one group of parts and number *two* to any other group and so on, because in such a scale the order of the number continuum has no relevance to the order of the changes and we have no information which could establish this relevance.

If we have information that indicates that the changes observed are comparable to one another as greater and less (e.g., the end point of the thread of mercury in a thermometer under the influence of varying applications of heat) we are able to establish an *ordinal scale*. If we have no information that will show the minimum or maximum extent of the change, we may set minimum and maximum points arbitrarily and assign numbers according to the *order* of the number continuum; but because our information does not give us the size of the interval we can use the numbers in the continuum only according to their ordinal but not their cardinal value. Should we have information which not only indicates a lowest or highest point in the range of intensity but also makes clear that the intervals in the changes observed are constant and equal, we can establish an *interval scale*. The numbers assigned in such a scale are not only more significant, but they can be operated upon mathematically to generate true information about the quality, which observation will not give.

It is outside the scope of this comment to enter upon a full discussion of the theory of measurement. The simplified (and obviously inadequate) description of the principles of scaling given above will do for our present purpose. The reader is referred to Huntington (21) and to Kendall (24) for a proper discussion of this subject. But it is clear from this simple presentation that these considerations are basic to theory as well as to experimental practice in psychology. It is unfortunate that designers of experiments sometimes pay more attention to mathematical and statistical theory than to the relevance of certain mathematical operations to the data to be evaluated. An analysis of the methods to be used to gather data and the proper appraisal of whether or not these data are amenable to refined mathematical treatment would be more fruitful than the application of high mathematics to intractable psychological data. To illustrate our point let us see how these considerations could be applied in a somewhat complex psychological investigation.

Suppose a psychologist is faced with the problem of trying to understand, analyze, and predict a man's ego control and devise ways and means to make it more effective. Ego control, let us say, is defined as a capacity for making an adequate adjustment in a variety of different situations. That is to say, a man with adequate ego control is not coerced in the situation either by persuasion or emotion, but can do what is objectively required.

To quantify a quality like ego control we must first examine the various possible ways in which it can be demonstrated. Suppose a carpenter has to do a rush job and finds he has mislaid a tool he urgently needs for it. Now he can either procure a substitute tool and finish the job, or he may become angry, and start to swear, but after a while he may look for the tool and find it; or he may become so completely disorganized that he will not even be able to look for the tool effectively. In the first case, he remains in control of the situation. In the second, he loses control of his temper but remains in control of himself sufficiently to do what is required. In the third instance, he loses control completely. This example will show us not only the meaning of ego control but will also provide a suggestion for measuring it.

Ego control, as an activity, is a quality in the person. To measure it, we have to quantify its intensity. In the first instance, there was no loss of ego control, hence we can say that ego control is at relative maximum. In the second case, there was a temporary loss of ego control, and we can say that ego control here is between maximum and minimum. In the third case, there was complete loss of ego control as far as this particular situation is concerned, therefore for our purposes ego control here is at minimum.

To test the degree of ego control of a given person, we could now set up an experiment which uses situations similar to our example above. A task is set and well started and then our subject is faced with an obstacle, a frustration, to which he can react in various ways. According to our discussion, we measure an activity by its effects, first on the situation, secondly on the person himself. The effects on the situation can be observed and measured. How many ways of overcoming the obstacles has the subject discovered? How many does he try? Does he use the most effective of all those he has found? How long is the task interrupted? Among effects on himself, we could measure his loudness of voice, the vocabulary he uses when he sees himself frustrated, aimless movements, degree of muscular tension, attempts at self-justification, etc.

But for our purpose there are some drawbacks to such an experiment. We do not know whether the person would react with the same degree of ego control in other situations, and it is impossible to subject him to too many frustration experiments. Frustrations in social situations, important though they are, could be reproduced in the laboratory only to a limited extent without serious harm to him. For this reason it would be preferable to have an experimental situation which would provide information on the way in which the person reacts to many varying types of frustration.

For this purpose, the TAT (Thematic Apperception Test), MAPS (Make-a-Picture-Story Test), or a similar storytelling test could be used profitably; but in using it, we have to decide on one of two alternatives. Either the test itself could be used as a sample situation, or we examine the product of the test, the TAT stories, for evidence of ego-control. If we take the person's reaction to the TAT situation itself as a sample of his ego control, we would have to determine whether he tells a coherent story, how many times he repeats himself, whether he shows signs of malaise or embarrassment. That procedure would restrict us unduly, for most persons do have the minimum of ego control which is required in such a situation, and the differences that could be observed are very small. Moreover, there is an interfering factor here which is not ego control, in fact, which works in the opposite direction. This factor is creative imagination or verbal facility, whatever we may want to call it. Anyone who has great facility in storytelling would find this particular situation not frustrating but exhilarating.

If the person's way of attacking the TAT situation cannot be taken as an indication of ego control, we must look for instances of ego control in his stories. The assumption underlying all projective techniques is that everyone will necessarily deal with any situation in the way that is characteristic for him. If he talks about people and social situations, he will let his characters act in a way that is conceivable to him. If they trangress his own moral code, there will be an indication of it in the story, either by a disapproving remark or by the just punishment that will follow such a transgression. In every story, then, the person in some way talks about himself and his convictions. If we can strip the story of its incidentals and find the core that applies to the storyteller, we shall have a record of many situations which manifest ego control in many different ways.[9]

After listing and analyzing these situations, we can establish an ordinal scale of ego control. First of all, we have to judge whether a given situation (story) portrays ego control or not. Our subject may tell a story of a fishing trip, for instance (Card 16), where the fisherman has a good catch and returns home after a good day's work. In this story there is no challenge to the hero's ego control,

[9] The problem of creative imagination as reflecting the life situation of the individual will be more fully dealt with in Chapter 14. An exposition of the method of TAT analysis here referred to will be found in a previous publication (1).

therefore we cannot judge what it would be under adverse circumstances. Under normally favorable circumstances we must assume everyone to have sufficient ego control for the occasion, therefore our variable can only be judged under difficult circumstances. If, however, there were many stories of favorable circumstances with no difficulties in sight, it would be for the psychologist to decide on internal evidence whether that is an indication of escape daydreaming or an indication that ego control is not a problem to this particular person. Since the situations portrayed in the TAT for the most part elicit stories of conflictful or frustrating problems, there should be evidence of ego control in abundance.

To establish the ordinal scale, we take situations which portray control, and then find the percentage of instances in which the challenge was met successfully (e.g., five successes out of ten ego control stories would give us a percentage of 50). We now rank the individuals in the group according to the percentage of success.

If we could make the assumption that ego control is normally distributed we could assign the standard deviation found in an unselected sample as a unit which would determine the size of the intervals, and so could transform our ordinal scale into an interval scale. But this assumption cannot be made, for we know that ego control is the result of deliberate choice and discipline which cannot without proof be assumed to be distributed normally in the population. Until we can determine the relative size of the rank differences on other grounds, we shall have to be content with an ordinal scale for measuring ego control.

The dimensions of ego control as discussed here would be:

> *intensity*—ego control in very difficult situations
> *extensity*—ego control in a wide variety of situations

In this way, it is possible to quantify a quality (or activity) by observing and measuring its effects in the situation and in the person; the stories told in the TAT represent not only effects in the situation but also in the person, for he can only tell what he can conceive, and his conception of the possibilities of a situation are the effects of his past actions. But it is necessary to insist that such quantification presupposes that we start with the quality we intend to quantify, that we first demonstrate its existence in some concrete instances, and then begin to measure its effects. The usual procedure in a complex situation like the TAT is to search for ego control by counting the "needs" or "presses" in the TAT story, or by trying to measure the "attitudes" which conceivably might go to make up ego control—for instance, attitudes of superiority, dominance, cooperation, or the like. This will not result in quantification of a quality but in the kind of atomization we referred to in the beginning of our discussion. To start to quantify by taking the quality as a whole is not only correct according to theoretical principles but is essential for experimental success.[10]

REFERENCES

1. ARNOLD, MAGDA B. 1949. A demonstration analysis of the TAT in a clinical setting. *J. abnorm. soc. Psychol.*, 1949, **44**, 97–111.
2. BELL, E. T. 1945. *The development of mathematics*, 2d ed. New York: McGraw-Hill Book Co., Inc.
3. BORING, EDWIN G. 1946. Mind and mechanism. *Amer. J. Psychol.*, 1946, **54**, 173–92.
4. BORN, MAX. 1950. Physics. *Scientific American*, 1950, **183**, 28–31.
5. BRIDGMAN, P. W. 1936. *The nature of physical theory.* Princeton: Princeton University Press.
6. ———. 1950. *Reflections of a physicist.* New York: Philosophical Library.
7. BRUNSWIK, EGON. 1951. Three papers in: *Psychological theory*, (ed.) MELVIN H. MARX. New York: The Macmillan Co.
8. CALDIN, C. F. 1950. Science and philosophy. *Brit. J. Phil. Sci.*, 1950, **1**, 196–210.
9. CANTRIL, HADLEY. 1950. Psychology. *Scientific American*, 1950, **183**, 79–86.
10. CONANT, JAMES B. 1951. *Science and common sense.* New Haven: Yale University Press.
11. DUHEM, PIERRE. 1903. *Evolution de la mécanique.* Paris: Joanin.
12. ———. 1906. *La théorie physique.* Paris: Chevalier et Rivière.
13. ———. 1909. *Etudes sur Leonard de Vinci*, 2e ser. Paris: A. Hermann et fils.
14. ———. 1913–1917. *Système du monde*, 5 vols. Paris: A. Hermann et fils.
15. FRESNEL, AUGUSTIN JEAN. 1821. *Mémoire sur la diffraction de la lumière.* Mémoires de la Académie Royale, 1821/2, vol. 5.
16. GIBBS, JOSIAH W. 1948. *On the equilibrium of heterogeneous substances.* Vol. I, pp. 55–354. In: *The collected works of J. Willard Gibbs.* New Haven: Yale University Press.
17. HADAMARD, J. 1945. *Essay on the psychology of invention in the mathematical field.* Princeton: Princeton University Press.
18. HOENEN, P. 1949. *Filosofia della natura inorganica.* Brescia: "La Scuola."

[10] Chapter 7 attempts to reduce these principles to practice.

80 THE HUMAN PERSON

19. HULL, CLARK. 1940. *Mathematico-deductive theory of rote learning.* New Haven: Yale University Press.
20. ———. 1943. *Principles of behavior.* New York: Appleton-Century-Crofts, Inc.
21. HUNTINGTON, C. V. 1942. *The continuum and other types of serial order.* Cambridge: Harvard University Press.
22. JØRGENSEN, JØRGEN. 1951. *The development of logical positivism.* International encyclopedia of unified science, vol. II, no. 9. Chicago: University of Chicago Press.
23. KARDINER, A. 1941. Psychoanalysis and psychology. *Phil. Sci.,* 1941, **8**, 233–54.
24. KENDALL, M. G. 1948. *Rank correlation methods.* London: Chas. Griffin & Co.
25. KRIS, ERNST. 1951. Psychoanalytic propositions. In: *Psychological theory contemporary readings.* (ed.) MELVIN H. MARX. Reprinted from same chapter in: *Freedom and experience.* (eds.) S. HOOK & M. R. KONVITZ. Copyright 1947, Cornell University Press, Ithaca. New York: The Macmillan Co.
26. MACH, ERNST. 1893. *The science of mechanics.* Chicago: Open Court Publishing Co.
27. ———. 1895. *Popular scientific lectures.* Chicago: Open Court Publishing Co.
28. ———. 1914. *Analysis of sensations and the relation of the physical to the psychical.* Chicago: Open Court Publishing Co.
29. ———. 1926. *Principles of physical optics.* New York: E. P. Dutton & Co.
30. MCKEON, RICHARD. 1951. Philosophy and method. *J. Phil.,* 1951, **48**, 653–82.
31. MARITAIN, JACQUES. 1934. *Distinguer pour unir.* (2e ed.) Paris: Desclée de Brouwer et Cie.
32. MORSE, PHILLIP. 1951. Physics and radiation. *Amer. Scientist,* 1951, **38**, 390–98.
33. NAFE, PAUL. 1942. Towards quantification in psychology. *Psychol. Rev.,* 1942, **49**, 1–18.
34. OSTWALD, WILHELM. 1895. Die Ueberwindung des wissenschaftlichen Materialismus. *Naturwissenschaftliche Rundschau,* 1895, 567–72.
35. ———. 1902. *Vorlesung über Naturphilosophie.* Leipzig.
36. ———. 1914. *Auguste Comte: Der Mann und sein Werk.* Leipzig.
37. PAULING, LINUS. 1947. *General Chemistry.* San Francisco: W. H. Freeman & Co.
38. POINCARÉ, HENRI. 1906. *La science et l'hypothèse.* Paris: Flammarion.
39. ———. 1913. *La valeur de la science.* Paris: Flammarion.
40. ———. 1934. *Science et méthode.* Paris: Flammarion, 1934.
41. PRATT, CARROLL C. 1948. *The logic of modern psychology.* New York: The Macmillan Co.
42. RUSSELL, BERTRAND. 1901. Recent works on the principles of mathemathics. *The International Monthly,* 1901, **4**, 84.
43. TOLMAN, E. C. 1932. *Purposive behavior in animals and men.* New York: Appleton-Century-Crofts, Inc.

Chapter 3

EXISTENTIALISM AND SCIENTIFIC SYSTEMATIZATION

By W. Smet, S. J.

THE PRECEDING papers have raised some questions which should be discussed before we attempt any formulation of personality theory. First, the terms current in psychological circles imply an attempt on the part of the psychologist to put a screen between human reality and himself. When we talk, for instance, of correlation matrices and factors, of scientific models, classifications, and a conceptual framework, of fields and field forces, does it not seem as if we were afraid to expose ourselves to the reality of the human being, as if we needed a scientifically objective armory to defend ourselves?

In the second place, I have the impression that we have accepted without question the very doubtful assumption that the present scientific structure of psychology must not be questioned. We seem to have limited our task to finding new hypotheses, concepts, and systems that will give a more adequate explanation of scientific facts than the systems now in vogue, but all these attempts stop short of questioning the validity of scientific systematization itself. Could it not be that the system-building itself is at fault, quite apart from the particular systems which have been constructed so far?

Finally, I would like to raise the question how a return from an exclusively secularistic orientation to a Christian orientation could be achieved, whether by the introduction of some new "model," or by the use of a conceptual framework (such as the Thomistic) which will emphasize the dependence of man on his Creator—or should there perhaps be a much more fundamental reorientation in the *basic attitudes* of those psychologists who call themselves Christian? Should not such a reorientation consist in approaching the human person in a different way, in following Christ's example by treating the human being as a person, a brother, and a fellow-creature? In other words, should not the "I-Thou" relationship be made the basis of psychology?

The Existentialist Versus the Essentialist Approach.[1] Probably everyone is willing to admit that our philosophy of life is often influenced by our basic approach to life. Among many possible attitudes to reality, we can distinguish a "subjectivistic" and an "objectivistic" approach, recently renamed "existentialist" and "essentialist." To avoid any misunderstanding it should be noted that a subjectivistic approach (especially as applied to the existentialist approach) must not be confused with *subjectivism*, which is an error concerning reality, in which the person takes nothing to be real but his own experiences; external reality is then reduced to a mere fiction. The subjectivistic approach rather implies a special quality of some events; there are realities which cannot be objectified and studied from the outside without losing their distinguishing characteristics.

In any group we find persons who are more inclined to one or the other approach, whose basic attitude is either that of the existentialist or that of the essentialist. The objectivist or essentialist is identified without much difficulty. He tackles problems with assurance because he approaches them and knows them from the point of view of norms, essences, principles. He feels at home in that aspect of reality which can be expressed by clearly defined concepts or quantitative measurement. His task in the quest for truth is to define the experiences of others and to make them communicable, so that others can come to

---

[1] An "existentialist approach" as used here means a personal experiential approach. It is a way of knowing which yields affective knowledge as distinct from abstract knowledge (see Comment, page 91 ff.). As used here, it is a method of knowing the world and not a system of knowledge about it. Hence it should not be confused with the philosophical system of existentialism, which has chosen this as the *only* approach to reality, while Dr. Smet insists (next page) that both the subjective and the objective approach, the existentialist and essentialist way of knowing, belong together.—*The Editors*.

some common agreement; this agreement can then be formulated and systematized.

The subjectivist or existentialist, on the other hand, feels safe and happy in the realm of concrete, vital experience. He is not much interested in formulations and systems but rather in coming to know the concrete thing intimately and immediately. For him reality must be experienced in its immediacy to be known fully, and not explained or defined. He judges reality more by connaturality than by reason. The objectivist's theoretical arguments seem meaningless to him, and he is, therefore, defenseless. His major task in our culture is to make us aware of the dynamic and vital aspects of reality, and most of all the person and personal relationships. The essentialist expresses reality and communicates it to others by *definition*; the existentialist, on the contrary, tries to evoke it by *description*.

These two attitudes toward reality do not exclude each other. Rather they should converge and complete each other because they belong together. It is only when they are isolated from each other and one or the other is taken to be the *only* expression of reality that they run the danger of becoming false and worthless. Both existentialism and essentialism are valid approaches to reality, provided they are used side by side and not in isolation.

However, since they are opposites, antagonism is inevitable. In fact, we even have to admit that the influence of the objectivist will always dominate in our culture because of his particular personality type. His way of approaching reality is characterized by active conquest and domination. His appetite for systematization and unification is insatiable. He simply cannot let the subjectivist be. The existentialist, on the other hand, is at a disadvantage precisely because of his basic attitude. He will not impose his frame of reference, his point of view, upon reality because it is essential for him to respect the integrity of the real and to submit himself to its impact.

In philosophy the essentialists have reigned for many centuries. In religion the conflict has always been latent. The same is true for education and politics, though there is undoubtedly a strong tendency toward more subjectivity since the last century. But the battleground par excellence is really psychology. The objectivist stresses psychology as an exact science which must develop an adequate conceptual system. The more psychology becomes interested in the whole person, however, the more will the need be felt for a serious consideration of the subjectivistic approach.

Implications for a Christian Reorientation. We must take into account both these approaches in a Christian reorientation of psychology because the acceptance of the whole truth, in this case the whole human reality, is a prerequisite for such a reorientation. Instead of relying exclusively (or too exclusively) on an objectivistic science, we have to accept courageously and honestly the challenge imposed upon us by reality, and to solve the antinomy of existentialism and essentialism in a constructive way.

To guard against possible misunderstanding I wish to emphasize that existentialism is stressed in this paper only because there is greater need for it. But I am not advocating existentialism as being more in line with a Christian philosophy. As mentioned before, existentialism and essentialism must be complementaries; they become disloyal to the truth as soon as either the one or the other claims to be the whole truth. The consistently Christian attitude is, therefore, to accept both as necessarily complementary in the study of the human person.

When we assume that the mathematical and logical structure of psychology is to be accepted unquestioningly, we may actually prevent a reorientation of psychology on a Christian basis. Once such an objectivistic science is accepted, no room seems to be left for any other attitude toward the human person than that which constantly seeks to reduce human relationships to objective and quantifiable factors. This does not mean that we should discard scientific psychology. For practical reasons we cannot do without it. As soon as we attempt to study the human person at all, we have to study him from the outside. But I do claim that a concentration on the scientific study of man will not give us knowledge about him that will be adequate from a Christian point of view. Only when we become aware of the deficiencies of the objectivistic approach itself, and when we begin to concentrate on the psychological knowledge derived from the Christian experience of ourselves in relation with our fellow man, shall we reach our goal.

Practical Application. Some practical applications will illustrate these considerations. In the first place, we must, in our assumptions for a psychology on a Christian basis, make a clear statement concerning the ethical obligations of the psychologist not only as a member of a profession, but also as a scientist. We are beginning to recognize the need for such a statement; this recognition can be seen in the proposal of the American Psychological Association (1) for ethical standards for psychologists.

Second, there should be an emphasis on the basic attitude of the psychologist to the person, in his scientific research as well as in psychotherapy. Instead of concentrating on the *requirements* of our science in studying personality, we ought to emphasize the *attitude* the psychologist ought to adopt to do justice to the human relationship in which he is involved. Instead of methods and concepts useful in studying the human subject, let us emphasize and investigate the ideal conditions for the direct experience of the human person. In this way we shall draw upon a source of psychological knowledge untapped heretofore.

Perhaps an illustration will clarify my point. Psychoanalysts are sometimes suspected of bad faith in their description of human nature. But let us not be unfair; their personality theory is an accurate enough systematization of their clinical experience. But—and this applies to nearly all of us at one time or another—the other person will act in the way we expect him to act. If a psychologist expects his client to behave as if he were the playball of impersonal forces, buffeted by id-impulses, and acts toward him as if he were, then his client will respond according to expectation. If we perceive personality only in quantifiable dimensions, there is a good chance that we shall observe only what we are looking for and the person will never reveal himself to us in his uniqueness as a human individual. Only if we try to approach the other person honestly in such a way that an "I-Thou" relationship becomes possible will he reveal himself to us as a person. It is our personalistic attitude, it is our understanding love and our faith in him that will awaken in the other the "person" kept hidden in him because of our previous lack of respect and trust.

When we come to experience fully and to actualize the basic Christian attitude to the universe and to the person in ourselves, then and then only will the right model and the right conceptual framework for psychology present themselves. We shall discover that most of our previous difficulties were due to the fact that we had moved too far away from the person or that we looked at him through the screens of our conceptualized notions. It is always amusing to see people start at the wrong end, and that really seems to be the trouble with psychology today. Perhaps psychologists should go back to the kindergarten for a while to relearn how it feels to approach another as a human being. Perhaps also we can explain why we find it so difficult to reform psychology—we have developed too much mind and too little heart.

At any rate, let us examine our own attitudes before we start blaming psychology for some of its mistakes. Do we really wish to know more about the human person, and to come closer to him? Or do we find that we are actually more interested in scientific methodology, in experimental design, in diagnosis, in systematization? Are we willing to submit ourselves to the vigilant self-training which is required before we can become more person-centered in our approach to others? To which do we attach more importance in our own training and in that of our students: the accumulation of scientific knowledge, or our own psychological and spiritual development—and with it the improvement of our interpersonal relationships?

Finally, this whole question is also relevant in our relations with other psychologists. To reach our goal, a reorientation of psychology, is it enough to make an inventory of the materialistic assumptions that underlie modern psychology and to show logically and experimentally how other assumptions give a better explanation of all the facts? I doubt such facile optimism. Let us not forget that one of the reasons why mechanistic and biological models are preferred and tenaciously defended is precisely that they are much more easily tested within the structure of modern scientific psychology than the Christian conception of man. It would be preferable by far, it seems to me, to support the existentialist emphasis in modern psychology, for by bringing the psychologist closer to a direct experience of the human being, and by giving him the example of a really personalistic attitude, many theoretical differences would disappear by themselves.

At the present time, the emphasis upon the existentialist point of view is important because it seems to be a real opening in a hitherto completely objectivistic and mechanistic structure. If we refuse to use it, we may miss our chance of reorienting psychology toward what we know from our Christian experience is the living reality of the person. It seems to me that we have come upon the scene as Catholic psychologists at a moment when the basic postulate of deterministic science itself is being questioned, when there is no longer any agreement on the concept of scientific theory, briefly at the very moment when the epistemological chaos is nearly destroying the concept of science itself, almost without hope of salvation. But out of that crisis— which will affect the sciences of man more than any others—will come some other still undefined conception of science, though we cannot as yet predict the form it will take. If there is any chance that this new notion of science will be closer to the truth, that it will portray reality more adequately, we must take sides now. If we do not, we may miss the chance altogether and suffer shipwreck along with the conception of science we are trying to remodel.

Others around us are already taking the lead in a new direction—especially the nondirective group with Rogers, and the proponents of phenomenological (and existentialist) psychology in Europe. Let us not lag behind refusing our help and merely looking on until the new approach goes astray like all the rest. Perhaps the reason why we prefer to stick to the conventional scientific and objectivistic approach is only the fear that, secure enough in psychology to claim our place, we are not yet secure enough to go our own way.

COMMENT

Existentialism as a Critique of Scientific Method

We are all agreed that science does not embrace the whole of reality, that we want to know the human being differently and more immediately than the science of psychology allows us to do. We are all agreed also that we want to find the human person in psychology. But how will the existentialist approach help us do that?

The basic problem in understanding anything, including the human person, is how we come to know; in addition, the problem in science is how we communicate that knowledge. We come to know by abstracting the essential meaning of the object; that is, we form a concept. We communicate by passing on that concept, and the judgment based on it, to someone else. There are two ideas implicit in the term "communication." First there is the term "communis," and then the term "unio." In communication by conceptualization and by definition there is a common basis, for the concept we use is referred to the same object by everyone. Precisely because we abstract from the incidentals of perception and restrict ourselves to the universal concept, that concept will be understood by everyone in the same way, it will arouse the same ideas, the same judgment. There is, therefore, a genuine union between those who communicate, on the common basis of the definition and the concept. The existentialist, however, communicates by evocation. That must mean that he describes and alludes to the single unique situation; but in that case he can never be sure that what is evoked in the hearer is what the speaker wishes to evoke, for there is no common basis unless the speaker can refer to common experience rather than to the unique event.

Perhaps it would be more correct to say that the two approaches are distinguished not so much by the fact that one deals with concepts and the other does not, as by the fact that they represent different stages in conceptualization. Evocation also needs concepts and will use concepts that not only describe the situation but also describe the speaker's *feelings in the situation*. The difference is, then, not in conceptualization as such but in taking the speaker's relation to the situation and his attitude in it into account in the existentialist approach, while the objectivistic approach disregards everything but the objective situation.

Perhaps an example will make the point clearer. A very brilliant student consistently failed in analysis of clinical material, whether he had to deal with a full-length life history or with projective material. He was well aware of his shortcomings and explained that he had the same difficulty in his personal relationships. He never knew how a given situation would affect his friends, was never sure how they would take his remarks, was completely unable to account for their reactions to him or to anybody else. He admitted that he had been puzzled about this for a long time; so he tried to improve his personal relationships by a more and more detailed analysis of the other person's words and actions. He treated them as he would treat a problem in logic, always on a strictly objective plane—and his conclusions always proved to be wrong, his predictions of the behavior of others were always off the mark. It had never occurred to him that he could have an immediate emotional participation in the other person's concerns, he never asked himself: "How would *I* feel, what would *I* do if I were in his shoes?" Now it seems that the experimentalist tends to develop this very attitude in his dealings with his subjects. In fact, he appears to consider it a virtue, the virtue of objectivity which has to be carefully tended. He forgets that objectivity is a virtue in interpreting his data, but that his data will be falsified at the source if he treats the human being as an object and not as a person in collecting data.

In psychology, then, an existential approach would mean that the psychologist himself, the experimenter or clinician, always has to be considered part of the situation. He can never be eliminated, nor can he eliminate himself no matter what scientific controls he uses. Natural science assumes tacitly that objective scientific method will eliminate the observer as a person or, at the very least, will make him interchangeable with any other observer. It is also assumed that the process of knowing (or measuring) does not change the object. As a consequence of the latter assumption, the notion has developed that measuring or observing can be depended on to show the object as it is: thus, what cannot be measured in physics cannot exist. In this way, the notion of simultaneity was tested and found wanting; because two events could not be *demonstrated* or *measured* simultaneously, it is held that the notion itself is "meaningless." Much later, it was decided in very much the same way that the electron has either position or velocity but not both, simply because the two cannot be *measured* at the same time. Such logic might make us assert that the human being possesses either the function of speaking or that of singing but not both because they cannot be observed at the same time. When physicists come to see what psychologists have had to realize long ago—namely, that the process of observing and measuring can and often does change the object, or at least fixates its appearance at a given point in time, they will cease equating the object *as it is* with its appearance during the time of observation or measurement.

The existentialist approach is a timely reminder to psychologists not only that the assumptions of physical science are inadequate for a science of man, but that the scientific method itself is in need of revision when applied to psychology. Both assumptions implicit in scientific method, that the observer can be eliminated (preferably by substituting a recorded pointer reading), and that the process of observing or measuring does not change the object, are invalid in psychology.

We know that the observer can never be eliminated because the observer is our most sensitive measuring instrument. We have come to see that personality ratings can be vastly improved and a high degree of agreement can be reached if trained clinicians are used as judges instead of college freshmen. We are also becoming aware of the fact that the experimenter himself has to be carefully trained, not in applying the proper controls to the subject or to the situation, but in refining his own capacities as a psychological observer. This demand is met, for example, in the experimental or diagnostic field by the careful training of the Rorschach expert, who himself becomes a highly refined measuring instrument, and in the clinical field in the training of the nondirective counselor, who becomes a highly sensitive indicator of the client's psychological growth.

The importance of the psychologist in the testing situation is further realized by the demand that the Binet tester establish rapport because otherwise the test will not show the real ability of the person tested and will therefore not be valid. We have come a long way from the belief that the only way to be scientific is to be so "objective" as to become a robot in an experimental situation in which not only instructions and external conditions but the experimenter himself must be strictly standardized. Today we know that standard instructions will not insure equal understanding on the part of the subjects and that a wooden and mechanized manner is not the approach that will motivate them to do their best.

Moreover, we have known for a long time that the process of knowing, observing, and measuring does change the object of our investigation. We know that mental tests cannot be repeated without precautions because they have changed the person taking them; we know that diagnostic projective techniques may sometimes produce considerable insight, which amounts to a change in the person's life situation; we have learned to take into account the effects of transference and countertransference; we have also learned that transference is not inherent in the therapeutic process but is the result of a specific technique and varies with the therapist (2).

But these things have been known and dealt with in a practical way without becoming incorporated into a systematized body of knowledge within which these insights could be explored and developed. That the human relationship between psychologist and client, whether in the laboratory or the clinic, must be conceptualized before it can become communicable, before it can be examined, developed, and improved, is a truism which even the existentialist cannot deny. Is not the existentialist conceptualizing his experience even though he does it by "evoking" rather than by defining? How else could he communicate his concern over the lack of such a relationship to anybody else? What the subjectivist is insisting on in a science is a knowledge of the human subject in a person-to-person relationship, because the human being—unlike physical objects—can never successfully be studied in isolation.

If the existentialist refuses to admit conceptualization at all because he thinks it would destroy immediate experience, he is under a misapprehension as to the nature of knowledge. *Experience* of a thing is concerned with the individual thing as it is in all its wealth of detail, and is essentially enjoying it or suffering from it. But *understanding* abstracts from the incidentals to grasp the essentials, to see the relations this thing has with other things. It aims at the truth of the thing as it is in itself, and not as it is a source of enjoyment or suffering.

To give a simple example: If we want to explain to an apprentice mechanic what an automobile is and how it works, we shall concentrate on the necessary and indispensable parts, on the motor and its connection with wheels and steering gear, but we shall leave out of our explanation a description of the seating arrangement and various gadgets that distinguish the individual car but are not essential for all cars. If we want him to have the experience of an automobile, he has to ride in it. Of course we agree that no amount of description and knowledge of function will substitute for that experience. In fact, this experience, this enjoyment, cannot be communicated at all except by giving another the same experience, and even then his experience will be different from mine. But this experience, whether of an object or a person, is on the level of sensory apprehension and will not of itself lead to understanding, that is, to rational knowledge.

To lead to such knowledge this experience has to be conceptualized. Only when it is abstracted and grasped in a concept can we communicate it to others so that they, too, become aware of it—not in its accidental or accessory elements but in the very core of that reality, its essence. In abstracting from accidentals, we do not destroy reality. We know that we have only a part of reality, but it is the part which is essential for knowledge as well as for the communication of knowledge. By means of concepts we can see the reality of the object more and more adequately, we penetrate its meaning, we come to know it in relation to more and more other things: we can understand it and explain it.

In our clinical practice, we need not only conceptual knowledge but also experience. To communicate the truth of things, we have to use concepts; but sometimes it is necessary to communicate another kind of knowledge which used to be called "veritas vitae." When a child or adult has always been frightened, has never had the experience of being loved and accepted, then no amount of conceptual knowledge about affectionate human relationships will convince him. He needs a corrective experience. In the therapeutic situation he will find someone who accepts him, who loves him and is willing to work together with him until he can reorganize his life. Such an experience of a human relationship surely is the communication of a truth, but it is *veritas vitae* and not *veritas*. Both objective truth and such truth about living, which we might call subjective, are real and are the object of knowledge, but they are not on the same level of knowledge. The one refers to truth in the abstract, the reality of things as they are in themselves; the other refers to my relationship with the reality of things. It is a knowledge which will affect my emotions and therefore my actual immediate living.

The clinical psychologist, then, needs *veritas* as well as *veritas vitae*. The client seeks experimental knowledge, *veritas vitae*, but often will realize during therapy that he cannot live rightly and at peace with himself until he has come to penetrate more deeply into the truth of things; only when he does will he be able to relate himself rightly to the universe of things and people. The psychologist must be able to give him the corrective experience of living rightly by providing the right human relationship. But he must also be capable of pointing out the way, at least, to the truth about things.

When he trains other psychologists, he must conceptualize all his knowledge, even his knowledge of the corrective experience conveyed in person-to-person relationships. If knowledge has to be passed on to others as a science presupposes, there must be a search for uniformities, for laws, for ways in which the essentials of that situation could be expressed and conveyed to the neophyte.

As a science, therefore, psychology must provide laws and directives which will apply to both levels of knowledge, else it would not be science. But when this science is applied in the psychologist's own clinical or experimental situation, it will take on the character of an art. The psychologist has to acquire the art of dealing with human beings in such a way that the human relationship in which he is involved will be one which liberates, enhances, and perfects the other. The clinician, at his best, will then exemplify in his human relationship to his client what human relationships are meant to be—a sharing of goodness which will both heal and perfect.

Persuasion and Demonstration

Dr. Smet's remark that demonstration alone will not result in conviction is obviously correct. Any psychologist is well aware of the fact that conflicting opinions cannot be reconciled by a logical proof or a demonstration of fact. Rigidity is not the exclusive property of the neurotic—it is present in all of us. In those things which do not concern us much, we are willing enough to examine factual evidence. But there are some truths that have implications for our daily living. Because they concern us so deeply, we refuse to admit that they are open to demonstration and proof. Basic assumptions obviously belong in this category. Scientists or not, we have accepted one view and we refuse to listen to any evidence to the contrary; we cannot bear that a rival view should claim a hearing. We think the other belief must be deluded, a wish fulfilment. But if one view is a wish fulfilment, why not the other? If God and heaven are projections based on unconscious mechanisms, couldn't the view that this is the only world that concerns us be wish fulfilment, too? If the one belief is an escape, could not the other be an escape, too? To be sure, it would be an escape from different threats, but could be an escape all the same. If it should occur to us at some point that perhaps our own belief is not the only possible one, that there might be reasons (not unconscious motives) for the alternative convictions, then and only then shall we be ready to examine the evidence.

But it is more than doubtful whether the experience of a genuine person-to-person relationship will *necessarily* produce such a readiness to examine an alternative set of assumptions about human nature. It is conceivable that for a time some persons may find a great deal of comfort in the thought that the only warmth and love in the universe is the warmth of human love and sympathy. In that case, a warm counseling relationship could be established which would not in the least lead the counselor to a different view of man's position in the universe. The counselor may find eventually that giving affection is possible only as long as somebody gives it to him in return. He may be fortunate for a long time, until he almost thinks his store of affection is inexhaustible. And he can become intoxicated by this seemingly inexhaustible giving until he feels himself godlike. Thus the immediate person-to-person relationship, no matter how warm, no matter how real, does not of itself produce a view of man as a creature dependent on his Creator, therefore could not be counted on to effect a revolution in the scientist's outlook.

Furthermore, the psychologist as a scientist has the obligation to search for the truth as best he can and to present what he has found, whether or not the scientific world is ready to accept it. That holds good not only for isolated facts or theories but also for an alternative synthesis such as has been advocated here. It is a curious fact that the synthesis of Thomas Aquinas was an anomaly in his time. St. Thomas used the material available in his day to unify it, against violent opposition from friend and foe alike. His synthesis was not accepted by his contemporaries nor even by his successors, for some centuries, but eventually it proved to be the guide through a maze of conflicting views and theories that grew up in disregard of the unification he had achieved. His example should encourage us today at least to strive for a synthesis, especially in the area of psychology. Again, as in his time, an extraordinary amount of material is available; whether some kind of synthesis will be possible, no matter how modest in extent, remains to be seen.

Ethical Standards for Psychologists

The psychologist not only has the same obligation as other scientists to search for the truth of things disinterestedly and to communicate that truth to others. He has an additional obligation which stems from the fact that he alone among scientists is a member of the class of life he studies. Therefore he has an obligation as a human being to his subjects, who are his fellows, to maintain a human relationship with them—which is precisely the point emphasized by the existentialist.

This double obligation has certain practical consequences. As a scientist, the psychologist intends to search for truth. As a human being who is aware of his relationship to his Creator, he knows that what is true must ultimately lead to God who is Truth. Therefore, any trifling with truth, any attempt to divorce science from human concerns, to cultivate science for science's sake, any indulgence of idle curiosity, runs counter to his obligation as a scientist and a human being, and hence is morally wrong. That does not mean that practical problems should be favored over speculative or theoretical ones but rather that the problem we attack should be significant and not trivial, and should be aimed at enlarging our comprehension rather than at collecting more and more minute facts. It also means that the scientist's work should be seen *sub specie aeternitatis*, in its relationship to the larger whole. Any attempt to isolate an area and refuse to see it also in relation to the total pattern, to isolate the human being, for instance, in such a way that we see him as an animal and disregard his human functions, contradicts the obligation of the psychologist toward his subject matter.

The psychologist's obligation toward other human beings consists in treating them as persons and refraining from using procedures which invade their privacy, offend their human dignity or will hurt them in their conduct as human beings. If science is the search for truth, that truth is sought *for the use of human beings*. The only justification there is for encroaching upon the life of another human being is the hope that what he reveals will contribute either to his welfare or to the welfare of others. That means first of all that we must be sure that our study is based upon assumptions which will lead to the truth and therefore contribute to man's welfare.

A taxonomic study of the sex life of human beings, for instance, is based on the palpably wrong assumption that sex in the human being is an exclusively physiological function which can be studied taxonomically and will reveal scientific laws of physiological functioning to replace moral laws of human conduct. It cannot be assumed that what human beings actually do is what they ought to do according to the demands of their own human nature (Cf. page 115 ff.). Perhaps it would not occur to a taxonomist but should occur to a psychologist that the assumption which equates what is with what ought to be in human conduct, and equates human nature with animal nature, is contradicted by the very fact that human beings wrestle with the problem of morals, that they are painfully torn between what they want to do and what they ought to do. The animals a taxonomist ordinarily deals with never suffer from pangs of conscience! Even if human scruples are reduced to the influence of bigoted social customs, could such customs ever arise in animals? If not, why did they arise in man?

In clinical situations, there would seem to be an additional obligation, that of seeing that therapy does not achieve its aim at the expense of the patient's moral standards. It can happen, of course, that these standards are themselves a product of neurosis or maladjustment; but before assuming that they are abnormal, they will have to be judged first in the light of what is adequate conduct for a human being, not on the basis of some supposedly "realistic" notion of what would be right for human beings if they were animals. On the contrary, in many cases the patient will find himself able after therapy to come up to standards he himself found impossibly exacting before. Provided his standards are objectively adequate, this is the result we would expect, for therapy should make it possible to function in an integrated way, subordinating wants to rational goals.

REFERENCES

1. AMERICAN PSYCHOLOGICAL ASSOCIATION, COMMITTEE ON ETHICAL STANDARDS FOR PSYCHOLOGY. 1951. Ethical standards in clinical and consulting relationships. Section 3, Part I. *Amer. Psychol.,* 1951, **6**, 57-64; Parts II-V, *Amer. Psychol.,* 1951, **6**, 145-66.
2. ROGERS, CARL R. 1951. *Client-centered therapy.* Boston: Houghton Mifflin Co.

PART II

PERSONALITY STRUCTURE

Chapter 4

CONTEMPORARY PERSONALITY THEORY

By Sister Annette Walters, C. S. J.

A SUPERFICIAL scrutiny of the various theories of personality currently popular among psychologists might lead us to conclude that all is chaos in what is undoubtedly the most important area of modern psychology. Not only do the proponents of the different schools of thought use different concepts and different language, but they also use the same terms with different meanings. Yet as Allport has pointed out:

> The existence of many schools of psychology is not . . . an evil. It is rather a demonstration of the richness of mind. Each competent surveyor has his own point of departure, and maps out as much of the territory as he is competent to explore. His sense of boundaries and connection . . . is his own, and may serve admirably for the map *he* is preparing. The penalty of undertaking the systematic study of mental science is the necessity of learning many maps by heart. No two are drawn from the same point of view, nor have they the same objectives in mind. Often they do not even overlap one another's territory (1, p. 564).

Some Changing Emphases in Personality Theory

Since 1937, when Allport published this statement, tremendous strides have been made in all areas of psychological research, including that of personality. As a result, it is clear today that the personality theories of most schools have something in common, in contrast to the situation that existed a decade or more ago. In the early days of personality study it was inevitable that different schools of thought should arise. The field was so vast and so little of it had been explored that no one person could possibly get a vision of the whole. Each psychologist formulated his own goals and mapped out the particular area he was going to explore. In doing so he was often oblivious to the work of others in the field. Today, however, in most areas of psychology this situation is changing. As psychologists become more cognizant of what their colleagues are thinking and doing, the boundaries that separate schools are gradually breaking down. Established facts and methods, once the exclusive property of distinct schools, have become a part of psychology as a whole, now that they have stood the test of time. Schools of psychology are becoming relatively unimportant, with the possible exception of schools that have developed distinct and more or less sacrosanct theories of personality, such as the Freudian school. Even here, a really thorough study will show that all schools have something in common. Already we can discern some powerful trends toward unification of theory.

The chief drawback to unification of personality theory at this time is not so much disagreement about observable fact as disagreement concerning the *nature of man* and the *nature of truth*. Psychologists with positivistic leanings, of course, do not recognize that their disagreements are primarily philosophical in nature; they apparently believe that their theories are the logical result of scientific research. A few of them have even made some rather extreme statements about the implications of personality research for the good life. Instances in point are Cantril's proposals for a new "scientific morality" and Sutich's proposed code of ethics for psychologists, based almost entirely upon protocols collected from nondirective therapeutic interviews. A short time ago, at a meeting of psychologists in the Midwest, a new Ph.D. claimed that the research of nondirective therapists had proved beyond a doubt that a democratic form of government was the only kind consistent with human dignity!

In the light of such confusion, it is refreshing to find Karen Horney specifically recognizing that psychotherapy is based upon our notion of what constitutes the good, and of our point of view regarding man's essential nature. The following long quotation from Horney does not imply agreement with her idea of man's nature and of his goal in life. It is used because she has raised a very important question, and because her statements highlight the changing emphases in personality theory today. The opening chapter of her book, *Neurosis and Human Growth*, is entitled "A Morality of Evolution." In this chapter she points out that the trend in neurotic development (which is the subject matter of her book) involves

. . . a fundamental problem of morality—that of man's desire, drive, or religious obligation to attain perfection. No serious student concerned with man's development will doubt the undesirability of pride or arrogance, or that of the drive for perfection when pride is the motivating force. But there is a wide divergence of opinion about the desirability or necessity of a disciplinary inner control system for the sake of insuring moral conduct. Granted that these inner dictates have a cramping effect upon man's spontaneity, should we not, in accordance with the Christian injunction ("Be ye perfect . . .") strive for perfection? Would it not be hazardous, indeed ruinous, to man's moral and social life to dispense with such dictates? (7, p. 14).

Horney then goes on to show that the goal which we set for human growth (which she equates with morality) depends upon "different interpretations of essential human nature." Furthermore, she says,

. . . superimposed checks and controls cannot be relinquished by anyone who believes—in whatever terms—that man is by nature sinful or ridden by primitive instincts (Freud). The goal of morality must then be the taming or overcoming of the *status naturae* and not its development.

The goal must be different for those who believe that there is inherent in human nature both something essentially "good" and something "bad," sinful, or destructive. It will center upon the insurance of the eventual victory of the inherent good, as refined, or reinforced by such elements as faith, reason, will, or grace in accordance with the particular dominating religious or ethical concept. Here the emphasis is not exclusively upon combating and suppressing evil, since there is also a positive program. Yet the positive program rests either upon supernatural aids of some sort or upon a strenuous ideal of reason or will, which in itself suggests the use of prohibitive and checking inner dictates.

Lastly, the problem of morality is again different when we believe that inherent in man are evolutionary forces, which urge him to realize his given potentialities. This belief does not mean that man is essentially good—which would pre-suppose a given knowledge of what is good or bad. It means that man, by his very nature and of his own accord, strives toward self-realization, and that his set of values evolves from such striving. Apparently he cannot, for example, develop his full potentialities unless he is truthful to himself; unless he is active and productive; unless he relates himself to others in a spirit of mutuality . . .

We thus arrive at a *morality of evolution,* in which the criterion for what we cultivate or reject in ourselves lies in the question: Is a particular attitude or drive conducive or destructive to my human growth? (7, p. 15).

Notice that Horney consistently avoids stating what is good or bad in terms of an objective norm. The criterion of normality is a purely subjective one which the client evolves for himself. Horney's method of therapy proceeds from this assumption. I have quoted Horney because she has clearly brought out into the open the fact that therapy and therapeutic techniques grow out of our conception of man and what constitutes the perfection of his personality, conceptions which go beyond science and philosophy and into the realm of religion.

Another of the newer emphases in personality theory is the attempt to relate it to ethics. I think we can truthfully say that most responsible professional psychologists and psychiatrists today see an intimate relationship between personality theory and ethics. Sometimes they simply state the fact that there is a relationship without stating where this notion comes from. In a recent issue of the *American Psychologist,* for instance, the following statement appears in the report of the APA Committee on Ethical Standards for Psychology:

The problems which people bring when they seek the help of a clinical or consulting psychologist often have ethical implications. Whether the client is assisted in choosing an occupation or in reworking the basic pattern and texture of his life, he must make choices that have ethical meanings for him. Furthermore, the psychologist's ethical standards and his professional techniques are inseparable. The attitudes, values, and ethical concepts of the psychologist are expressed in his clinical relationships and very directly influence the directions taken by his client (2, p. 145).

Let me cite two more examples to make my point clear. The late Paul Schilder entitled the last chapter of his book, *Goals and Desires of Man*, "Morals." In this chapter he writes:

> Psychology has been considered a descriptive science. It is supposed to find out the actual facts and procedures, but it is also supposed to be separated from ethics. . . . But this fails to recognize that the unit of psychological experience includes action. . . . An idea, a thought, a dream, indicates goals and by its very existence changes motive action. There is no difference between psychology and ethics (11, p. 267).

Next let me illustrate a trend toward the construction of an ethical system based on scientific method alone. I quote from Cantril:

> When that portion of the "world stuff" we know as "man" emerged with its capacity to use concepts, to manipulate symbols, to communicate over a distance, and to write its own history, then it also acquired the capacity to plan its own social and economic life for the future. It therefore acquired unique responsibility.
>
> A system of ethics, a code of morality, is not something based on *a priori* generalizations, on casual speculations, or wish-fulfillments. It means that social scientists have a major responsibility in searching for the laws of the moral world just as physical scientists have searched for the laws of the physical world (5, pp. 365–66).

Sources of a Theory of Personality

The psychologist who addresses himself seriously to the construction of a theory of personality must not content himself with mastering the subject matter of his own field of specialization; he must of necessity cross the borderline of many disciplines other than his own. As McClelland says in the preface to his book, *Personality*, "to do the job well requires a knowledge of practically all of present-day psychology, since all that psychologists know is needed to conceptualize adequately the single personality" (9, p. 11). McClelland goes on to say:

Consider for a moment what a psychologist ought to know before he ventures to speak with any authority about personality. To begin with, he must be thoroughly grounded in the basic principles of psychology, in learning theory, for instance, where he should be able to deduce a theorem from Hull's postulates, draw one of Tolman's "balloons" properly, master the facts on conditioning and learning, and so forth. He should know the tremendous literature on psychological paper-and-pencil tests from the Bernreuter Personality Inventory to the Minnesota Multiphasic Test. Ultimately this should lead him to the intricacies of factor analysis so that he can understand the contributions of men like Cattell and Guilford. After he has spent a year or so on this he ought to take up anthropology, and travel, mentally at least, through the South Seas with Margaret Mead and Malinowski, to Alor with DuBois, to the Southwest with Kluckhohn and Leighton. After studying culture and personality in books, he should of course spend a year or two in the field, after which he will be ready for psychoanalysis. For who can understand the Old Masters like Freud without three to seven years of "didactic" therapy? Perhaps by choosing one's analyst carefully, some of the views of the neo-Freudians like Horney, Fromm, and Alexander can be learned in the process. To save a little time, our hypothetical well-educated student of personality could take a summer off to attend a Rorschach Institute so that he can make a stab at understanding the some eight hundred studies of personality made with this instrument. But even this is only a beginning. What about the Thematic Apperception Test and its intricate interpretations? How about some of the ancient techniques, like hypnosis, or some more modern ones like non-directive interviewing? Surely he should know these. And if he is to be really educated he should have read the "great books" and should be familiar with the history of culture of Western civilization. How else will he be able to understand the depth and complexities, the richness and variety of human personality? (9, p. xii).

Unfortunately for the Christian psychologist, McClelland's view of the situation is an understatement. The challenge presented to the Christian psychologist is even greater; it is that of developing a theory of personality which does no violence to the established facts of experimental and clinical psychology, which is socially and culturally oriented, and which is at the same time consonant with sound principles of philosophy—particularly those principles concerned with the nature of man and of truth. But even this is not enough. I would go further and insist that the Christian psychologist equip himself with a deep understanding of theology—especially the theology of grace and of the Mystical Body of Christ. I am not suggesting, of course, that we confuse science, philosophy, and theology. Nor do I mean that we psychologists can or should become professional philosophers and theologians. But if we are going to work in the field of personality theory we must see it as a whole.

Science and philosophy study the natural man only; they give us no understanding of how man's nature is refined and elevated by supernatural grace. Scientific and philosophical studies of interpersonal and intergroup relations, for instance, give us one kind of valuable information about man as a social animal, but they do not yield the depth of penetration into human solidarity that we derive from an understanding of the Mystical Body of Christ. The academic psychologist can perhaps ignore this fact, in so far as he is not dealing with real people in life situations. The psychologist applying his training and knowledge, and especially the psychotherapist, needs a theory of personality that embraces the whole of reality as it influences his client's adjustment and growth. When we deal with human beings, baptized in Christ, the natural man is a pure abstraction. With the infusion of supernatural grace, all man's life, including his feelings, emotions, attitudes, thoughts, and actions, are raised to a new plane. It is not enough for us to effect a synthesis between scientific psychology and philosophical psychology, as, for example, by reconciling scientific studies of human choice with a philosophy of free will. We must also take into account what Paul Claudel has called the "mystery of God moving a human will to move freely." The basic problem of developing a theory of personality acceptable to Christians is to allow room for the working of grace. In constructing this theory, however, we will have to draw upon all the relevant knowledge provided by the natural and social sciences, by clinical research and experience, as well as by philosophy and theology.

Christian Principles and Personality Theory

The New Determinism and Human Freedom. It used to be fashionable to speak of heredity and environment as the two factors that influenced human development. Then field theory came in and we spoke of the interaction of the two. Later still, the organism itself was recognized as a factor in its own growth.[1] Today psychologists recognize that the whole organism plays a role in its own development. Yet in abandoning the older idea of determinism, they have not brought the idea of human freedom into their formulations. Lecky, for instance, while condemning the mechanistic determinism of the older school, says specifically that

. . . it must be understood that our intention in opposing this belief is to emphasize not the idea of freedom, but the idea of self-activity. The conception of free will, even as a possibility, betrays a preoccupation with anything save real individuals (8, p. 16, footnote).

We are all familiar, I suppose, with the rectangle Woodworth uses to illustrate the relative influence of heredity and environment upon human development. One of my colleagues has suggested that we use a solid instead, and let one dimension stand for heredity, another for environment, and still another for free choice. The relative importance of each of the three factors may vary from one person to another. But all three factors play a part in the development of every human personality. We must, however, be more explicit in our recognition of the interaction of heredity, environment, and man's free choice in the develop-

---

[1] This view is well expressed by Lecky:
Conforming to the rigid determination of the nineteenth century, the older forms of scientific psychology were committed to a causal program in which behavior was determined solely by two sets of factors, environment and heredity. Thus we were given to consider opposing theories of environmentally determined habits and natively determined instincts similar to the doctrines of epigenesis and preformation in early biology. In recent modifications of psychological and biological theory, however, the organism itself is beginning to appear as to some extent its own determiner. There is a coherence in the behavior of any single organism which argues against an explanation in terms of chance combinations of determiners, and points to an organized dynamic system which tends toward self-determination (8, p. 3).

ment of his personality. It is very misleading, I believe, to discuss at length as most of our textbooks do the role of heredity and environment, and then to add, as it were, an afterthought that, of course, people are not the slaves of heredity and environment; they have the power to "make themselves" freely. We must show concretely how human freedom operates by illustrating its role in individual life histories.

Every clinical psychologist is haunted by the specter of determinism. He can predict with a high degree of accuracy what his client will do. I have known Catholic psychologists and psychiatrists to have their first real doubts about the faith when they found in their clinical practice that determinism does operate in the lives of their clients. They have not been taught, unfortunately, to distinguish different levels of personality. I propose that in working out a statement concerning the interaction of heredity, environment, and human freedom, we distinguish at the same time the different levels of personality. We must raise and answer the question: How deep is depth psychology? If we were to accept the theories of Freud or Jung, for instance, I think we would have to say that in the very depths of human personality there is no freedom.

Levels of Human Personality. Most psychologists distinguish different levels of personality in the sense that they do not equate the external manifestations of personality with the inner world of meaning. Even factor analysts, such as Cattell, distinguish between surface traits and source traits. Projective testers distinguish between the relatively unchanging structure of the personality and changing mental content and behavior. They claim that we understand a person only when we know the *meaning* of his behavior. Meaning is on a different level from overt behavior. Some psychologists assume that we can reach the depths of personality only with the specialized tools of our profession. Our diagnostic instruments do, we know, enable us to understand the "structure" of a given personality—how flexible or rigid it is in adjusting to new situations. They show us how the person characteristically perceives his world, and we are consequently able to predict with some degree of accuracy how our client will react in the future. We get significant clues to the unconscious as well as to the conscious motivation of the person we have tested. In short, we are able to penetrate depths of personality which are closed to those who do not have access to our specialized tools of diagnosis.

Is there not, nevertheless, a center of personality that is not accessible to the psychologist? Surely, the Christian must admit that there is. The inmost core of personality, that which involves man's relation to God, will always remain his own secret. Unless he chooses to reveal it, or unless, as in the case of some great saints, God chooses to make it known, we can never know how a man stands before his God. A psychologist cannot with all the tools at his disposal—inventories, situation tests, Rorschach, the Thematic Appreciation Test, hypnosis, or dream analysis—ever form an accurate judgment as to his client's relation to God. Hence, he cannot predict either that the man will or will not save his soul. The determinism that operates on a superficial level, or even at the deeper levels recognized by the so-called depth psychologists, fades out completely in the inmost core of the human personality. Ought we not as Christian psychologists bring into our formulations of a theory of personality an explicit statement to this effect?

Human temperament and behavior, we know, are profoundly influenced by biochemical, physical, and environmental stimuli; certain aspects of personality are, I believe, determined to a considerable extent by such factors. These temperamental characteristics and overt behavior are open to direct observation. The inner act of will, however, cannot be observed by others; it can only be inferred. Furthermore, in dealing with a given concrete case, we need to be aware of the "mystery of God moving a human will to move freely." Depth psychology, no matter how deep, does not transcend the natural order. Environmental stimuli do not determine the inner act of willing however much they may affect the way in which the decisions of the will find outward expression.

The fundamental moral decisions are made in the inmost depths of the soul, and it is at this level that the effects of right or wrong choices are first experienced. Temperamental characteristics and external behavior are affected last of all. Thus it can happen that a person genuinely turns to God and resolves to do God's will. Yet the superficial habits of impatience, petty vanity, or hastiness of temper may still be observed in him. He may, for all we know, be a saint. We commit the logical error of overgeneralization or the sin of rash judgment if we judge the inner worth of a person on the basis of the characteristics we observe in him, either through casual observation or with our diagnostic tools. I propose, then, that in our theory of personality we recognize our limitations as psychologists and state explicitly that there is more to the depths of personality than meets the eye or tickles the ear of even the most paternal psychoanalyst! [2]

The Goal of Human Growth (Norms of Adjustment). Implicit in much of current personality theory is the idea that the good is always relative and is subjectively determined. Current emphasis on the "meaning" of the life situation or the "private world" tends to highlight this view. Therapy directed to helping a person as he is may also be guided by such a philosophy. For the Christian, the problem of adjustment can never be that of merely accepting himself as he is. The goal for the Christian is to bring his subjective values into harmony with objective good. He must adjust to the whole of reality—the outside world, the world of objective truth and value, and God's will for him.

The implicit denial of objectively worth-while goals is the secret, I believe, of much of the opposition of Christian scholars to modern psychology. In a crude form it was present in Freud. In a more subtle and perhaps more dangerous form it is found in Horney, Fromm, and other neo-Freudians. It is explicit in Cantril's formulation of a scientific morality. It is basic to the proposed code of ethics for psychologists published several years ago by Sutich. It finds support in Margaret Mead's anthropological studies, especially in her book, *Male and Female.* It is, I think, one of the important reasons for the opposition of many Catholics to Rogers' nondirective therapy.

[2] An excellent study of this problem is found in Beirnaert (3), *Does sanctification depend on psychic structure?*

Psychological literature commonly presents two goals of satisfactory adjustment: (1) the satisfaction felt or expressed by the individual as to the adjustment he is making, and (2) the degree to which the individual's behavior conforms to the expectations of society. Neither of these goals is based upon an objective or absolute criterion of what constitutes the "good." Neither of them is enough for the Christian. The Christian goal is to become "another Christ," and in the pursuit of this goal everything that does not help or which positively hinders its attainment must be ruthlessly jettisoned. What he likes or what other people like about him matters only secondarily. Furthermore, the Christian must view the problems of life not as obstacles to be eliminated as easily or as quickly as possible, but as crosses to be borne in union with Christ for a time as long as God wills. His goal of adjustment can never be safety or security or comfort. The measure of his stature as a Christian is the degree of his participation in the sufferings of Christ—the agony in the garden as well as the crucifixion on Calvary. His own likes and dislikes and the mediocre values of his social group cannot slake his thirst for the ultimate objective Good, which is God. Adjustment on the natural plane alone, therefore, is never sufficient for a Christian. His practical judgments, the decisions of his everyday life, must be based not only upon reason, but upon reason operating under the influence of the inspirations of grace.

Interpersonal and Intergroup Relations. Another problem, and one which I shall merely touch upon at this time, is that of human solidarity. All schools stress the importance of interpersonal and intergroup relationships in the development of personality. Typically, I believe, the philosophical assumptions underlying the discussion of love and friendship and their role in personality development are such that a Christian cannot accept them. As an illustration I would like to quote several significant passages from Symonds' popular textbook, *The Dynamics of Human Adjustment.*

Love . . . grows out of the envy of another person who is older, stronger, more beautiful, or more competent. . . . There are two

methods for maintaining self-respect: one by the road of achievement, the other through love of another person (13, p. 532).

Love is in a sense a momentary thing and represents the values
existing at the moment. What is valuable today may lose its value
tomorrow. . . (13, p. 536).

Narcissism is basic in mother love. Children who were once part
of the mother, continue to occupy her hopes and fears. She becomes
devoted to them because it is through their development that she is
able to realize her own goals and aspirations (13, p. 535).

It was Plato, I believe, who said that love grows out of a
sense of poverty and need. Both Aristotle and St. Thomas
Aquinas rejected Plato's idea. If I understand St. Thomas correctly, love is the result not of poverty but of wealth. A person
has a real desire to communicate *the goodness he possesses*.
It is the property of goodness to diffuse itself. This philosophical
notion ought to be made more explicit as it relates to interpersonal and intergroup relationships.

Legitimacy of Generalizations from Animal Studies. Lastly,
we need an explicit statement showing the limitations of animal
research as a basis for personality theory, and particularly as
it relates to studies of social life. The study of rats in competition for food may tell us how much punishment the animal will
take before it overrides his hunger drive, but such findings
have limited relevance for human psychology. In some respects,
of course, the rats do resemble a crowd of children around a
picnic table when the food is giving out. But that is not the
whole story. During the depression of the thirties, children as
young as ten years of age were observed to go without lunch
rather than stand in a line leading to free lunches for children
whose families were on relief. The desire for prestige, the urge
to protect their families from the social stigma of being less
capable of providing for their children than other families, were
powerful enough in some children to make them go hungry. Yet
so far as I know, no proud and independent white rat ever
refuses to take food pellets paid for out of the state budget for
university research! The essential differences between man and
other animals are so great that studies of psychological significance for personality theory must be made on man alone.

Scientific Models

The basic question which arises when we set up models is : In building a theory of personality satisfactory to Christians, where shall we look for a model? All theories springing from what are properly called "schools" of psychology have received their inspiration from the natural sciences, either physics or biology. Are these models, however, adequate for psychology? I believe that they are not. Scientific psychology is different from all other sciences and hence must be its own model. Any other approach will end in a blind alley. The human person as such eludes all systems based on natural science models, no matter how subtle or internally consistent these systems may be.

This is certainly true for *Gestalt* psychology, and its offshoot, topology. It is even more true of the sophisticated brands of behaviorism, such as the systems of Hull, Skinner, and Tolman. It is amusing to find Tolman (14) combining principles derived from research on rats with Freudian principles of motivation. Had Tolman restricted his research to work with rats, he would not have had to compromise on scientific principles in this unseemly fashion. It is amusing, too, to find such a sociologist as Davis trying to find a theory of motivation to account for the different kinds of learning in different social classes. In his *Children of Bondage* (6), for instance, he devotes a whole chapter to the learning theory of Hull. Later the data are interpreted in the familiar frustration-aggression postulates which have been popularized by Dollard. The final interpretations are made without any reference to Hull's theorems, which were carefully presented in one of the earlier chapters, ostensibly as a theoretical basis for interpreting the findings of the study. The reason is that Hull's system, like the other systems based upon physical or biological models, is incapable of offering an interpretation of individual personalities.

In conclusion, I suggest that a science of personality acceptable to Christians must be a science in the broad sense of the term, and must not be limited to data provided by what is commonly known in the natural sciences as the scientific method.

Every natural science that deals with man must of necessity be a science of a part of man only. An adequate theory of the whole personality will be based upon a recognition of this fact. We must start with the notion that psychology is different from every other science, and it must develop its own vocabulary, its own concepts, and its own methods. We must avoid borrowing terms from the natural sciences, such as "vectors," "fields of force," "tension systems," "homeostasis," and perhaps even "dynamics." I say this though I am aware of strong trends toward the unification of theory in all the sciences. A science must first exist in its own right before it can be unified. If psychological theory is to be integrated with scientific theory in general, its subject matter must be capable of systematic presentation, its data must be internally consistent, and it must have a theoretical foundation peculiarly its own in terms of which all its data can be interpreted. If this happy condition is ever realized in psychology, then I am confident that a workable theory of personality will be just around the corner.

COMMENT

The Question of Scientific Morality

The preceding paper emphasizes the need for an objective standard of human conduct. Since the present preoccupation of clinical psychologists with the possibility of a "scientific morality" makes the discussion of this topic particularly timely, we propose to discuss in some detail how such an objective standard of right and wrong action could be discovered.

The essential problem facing us is to discover not only what individuals actually do but what they ought to do. The oughtness in this case is based on the recognition, strictly within the psychologist's province, that not everything we do is necessarily what we should do to function as proper human beings. Now our problem is to see whether this proper human functioning can be discovered by the method of natural science, by observation and inference.

The positive sciences can establish only what things *do*. To discover what things *should* do or what they *ought* to do, we must assume that the way things act is also the way they ought to act.

Such an assumption is fully justified when we are dealing with physical objects. As we saw in the preceding chapters, the nature of things is determined toward certain effects or ends. What inanimate objects do and the results achieved thereby are not something they choose for themselves but something imposed upon them by their nature. Similarly what the animal does and the results achieved in the total pattern of activity are rigidly determined by the specific nature of each animal. The human being, however, much as he is subject to the same laws as the rest of the things of nature in those activities which he has in common with them, has the capacity not only to bend his activities to his own uses but also to shape his ends, rough-hewn however they may be by nature, age, or circumstances. That does not mean that the human being is undetermined. As everything in nature, the human being also is basically designed toward an end, the perfection of his proper human nature. Because of his capacity to determine himself, he must consciously and of set purpose implement this basic determination, or suffer disintegration, disruption, or frustration on one level or another. When he implements it, he acts as he ought to act, but he is free to act contrary to this basic design. He must observe the law of gravitation to survive, but he may step out across the void if he likes. He may observe dietary laws to maintain his health or choose to live on claret and cigars. He may be guided by the rules of mental hygiene or despise them to go mad. He may respect his neighbor's goods or court a term in jail for robbery. He must attain what a human being is made for or wind up as a plain damned fool. As a result of human self-determination, actually observed human behavior will not always be an example of the way human beings ought to behave, and cannot be taken as the basis of observation from which to develop the laws of what man ought to do, that is, the laws of *moral science*.

Since the actions of human beings must be directed to their final end by their own choice, the moral law is no more than a pattern which will indicate how human actions must be coordinated and directed so that this purpose may be achieved. Since this pattern must be actively and deliberately achieved by the person in his actions, the necessity implied by the moral law is a moral necessity, while the necessity implied by physical laws, as shown in our discussion of the principle of constancy or finality, is a physical and antecedent necessity.

If the human being has to achieve his final purpose by his actions, he will achieve it particularly by actions which are distinctively human. Moral perfection, therefore, will be found essentially in his judgments and particularly in his choices, because it is these which distinguish the human being from the animal. For the same reason, morality will ultimately be found in his acts of choice informed by knowledge and not in overt actions. Overt actions are no more than the expression of the pattern which he has decided upon; they receive their moral characteristics from the person's intention, from the direction in which his will is aimed, because actions are chosen for the particular purposes the individual sets up for himself.

To derive oughtness or moral law from human actions, we must examine them not as we find them concretely in actual human conduct, but as they are when they achieve the results which human acts are meant to achieve. All activity is toward something, is aimed toward an end, as we have seen in our discussion of finality. That end or purpose sets the agent in action in a particular way. Thus the purpose or final cause is first in intention and last in execution. Every human act is either a doing or a making; to account for it we have to start with its purpose or intention, the end it is meant to achieve. This purpose may be chosen explicitly in every single instance, but the individual purposes of these actions must be so ordered and related one to the other that the whole sequence of human actions as they constitute human life will lead the person to that end for which he as a human being is designed.

The beginning of moral science, then, must be found in establishing the final end or ultimate purpose of human existence, not merely for the individual but for every human being as a human being. As will be discussed in more detail in our theory of personality, an examination of the capacity of the human being to know and love is bound to show that the only goal which can adequately satisfy the human desire for knowledge and love is ultimate goodness, that is, God. Nowhere in nature do we find that there is an affinity or a desire for which there is no possible satisfaction in the world as it exists. Plants need sunshine and water, and both are available, although at any given time or in any given region plants may suffer for want of either or both. Animals need food, they strive for it, and they find it in nature, though in any particular area they may suffer from lack of it. Men need God, they have a desire for love which nothing but Love in person can satisfy; on the same principle, this must be a world which contains the satisfaction of this striving and that consists in the perfect love and possession of God.

Since that perfect possession of God cannot be had in this life, we must find some relatively ultimate purpose for human beings here and now. The end of human existence in this life is so to order our human activities that they will help us to achieve our final destiny, the perfect possession of God in knowledge and in love. Actions which will lead directly to that end are good actions—that is, they are *morally* good, and actions which will deflect a person from that end are morally bad. Since by far the greater number of our human activities are directly concerned with the circumstances of everyday rather than with our final end, we need some standard which will enable us to judge in every concrete case whether this particular action will lead to the possession of God or not.

What standard can we set up to indicate what kind of action will intrinsically be oriented toward the achievement of our final purpose, and what kind of action is so constituted that it will obstruct us in our striving or deflect us from our final end? We can judge these actions in the same way we judge actions in physical nature. Since the way physical objects act is the way they ought to act, we can discover how the individual object ought to act by examining its activities *as they are expressions of its nature*. From the manifestation of the nature of an object in its actions, we can form some idea of what this nature demands. We know that human nature is different from animal nature—it is a rational nature. When an activity satisfies the demands of this rational nature, we can be sure that it will lead us to the end for which the rational nature was designed. We say, therefore, that those human actions are morally good which fulfill the demands of human nature.

We know, too, that human nature, whether conceived abstractly or concretely, is not isolated. We know that man is contingent, that he came into being from some cause which can ultimately be traced back to the first cause, God. God created the human being, either immediately or through some intermediate process. Since he was created by God and is dependent upon Him, he has a relationship to God. Moreover, the human being is not a simple spiritual substance but a composite. In the physical order he is made up of matter and spirit, which are substantial principles essentially related to each other. Thus man, who is a compound of material and spiritual elements, which we call body and soul, finds himself related not only to God, his creator, but also to his component parts, that is to his body and to his soul, and to himself as a whole. He himself as he is in concrete reality exists in an environment, particularly a social environment. That means that he is also related to other persons and to the physical world in which he finds himself. Since he has a rational nature and is related to God, to himself, and to his social and physical environment, he must satisfy the demands of his rational nature in these relationships and must also satisfy the demands these relationships make upon him. The degree of perfection with which these demands are met in any action is the criterion of its moral goodness.

The basic relationship of man to God is one of dependence. Any act, therefore, which indicates that the individual either denies this dependence or is trying to escape from it, is morally bad, whether it is an inner act of choice or is also expressed in overt action. Any act which not only indicates but acknowledges his dependence upon God is morally good. Hence we say that worship of God is intrinsically good, blasphemy is intrinsically evil.

With respect to man's relationship to himself, the first demand which man as he exists makes upon himself is the demand for continuing existence. Any action which tends directly toward the destruction of his own life is morally bad, even though that action be only an inner act of the will. Therefore we say that suicide is morally bad. Any action which in any way destroys the integrity of the body, even though it will not end in the destruction of life, is intrinsically evil because the body as part of man demands that it be kept integral and healthy. So mutilation of the body in greater or less degree is intrinsically evil. Any action which tends toward the preservation of the person, on the other hand, is morally good.

Human nature adequately conceived also requires that the diverse powers of the human being be used for their purposes, and that in achieving their aim the human being achieve his own self-actuation. Therefore, none of the human powers must be diverted from achieving its primary aim. The generative power, for instance, must not be used by the human being in such a way that its very exercise frustrates the purpose inherent in it. That is not merely a misuse but an abuse, a positive distortion of the generative power: to use a power *merely* for the satisfaction which can be found in its exercise is a distorted use of that power. This principle is universally acknowledged in the case of eating, when the practice of the old Romans is condemned. They wanted the pleasure of eating but prevented the food from being digested. So, too, speech was given to us to express our thoughts, but if we use it in such a way that what it expresses is not what we think, and we know it is not, we are using this capacity in a way which goes directly counter to human integrity.

Furthermore, any activity which goes counter to what could be called the integrity of the soul is morally bad. Any activity which directly impairs a man's capacity to think and think correctly, to love and love what is good, is intrinsically evil. For instance, to force one's thinking into a "party line" is going counter to the integrity of the mind; to make one's love life a series of promiscuous sex adventures goes counter to the integrity of human love. Striving to attach one's self to evil precisely because it is evil, as in such practices as devil worship, black magic, or spiritism, would go counter to the integrity of the human spirit.

With respect to man's relationship to his environment, there are certain social relationships that must be maintained. These should be characterized by justice, loyalty, and fidelity. A rational nature demands of its very self that the rights of others be respected, that another's proper functioning is not interfered with, that one man help (and not hinder) another to achieve his final end. Social relationships are primarily to be found in the family, in the community—whether it be the civic, national, or international community—and in religious societies which have been established to help men find the goal of their striving.

Now human nature demands that the individual so order his activities in domestic society that the necessary character of this society be preserved. From an examination of domestic society we know that it must be both one and permanent. Any action, therefore, which would destroy either the *unity* or the *permanence* of domestic society is intrinsically wrong. For the perfection of the inner unity of the family there will be required mutual love of the members of the family for one another, and mutual support and protection. This is not the satisfaction of mere animal instincts but the requirement of human nature as such, endowed as it is with intelligence and will, which is designed to enter into such social relations in this fundamental form of human society on a human level. These relations constitute the matter of what is conjugal, parental, and filial *piety*.

If the family is to be the proper permanent or stable base upon which the beginning and developing life of the individual may be built, it must have external security. This security must be founded not only on the availability of food, clothing, shelter, and the like, but fundamentally on the capacity and the right of individuals to provide these necessities for themselves and for those who are dependent upon them. It is upon this attribute of human nature that those rights are founded that are called "unalienable" in our Declaration of Independence; it is upon this attribute that the right of private property is founded. To ensure his life, a man must be able *to own*. To ensure the effectiveness of ownership for life, liberty, and happiness, a man must be secure in his rights. To be secure in his rights he must join forces with others to protect himself and them in the enjoyment of his and their possessions and of the fruits they yield.

He must band together with others because it is only in the group and with it that he will be able to achieve the full realization of his human capacities. If it is natural, therefore, to live and work in cooperation with others, it is the requirement of human nature to provide for the needs of the group—to look to the *common welfare*—and that not in opposition to individual needs and requirements, but so as to reconcile individual needs to the common welfare so that both are adequately provided for. Hence the individual may be called upon to put his life in danger, for instance, in the cause of common defense. To defend his own interests as well as the interests of other workingmen, he may be required to form labor unions. In all this he must so act that what he acquires for himself is not at the unjust expense of any other, whether colleague, employer, governing body, or social group as a whole. This is what his nature requires of him as a human being.

Justice, then, as a norm or rule for human action is not merely a matter of self-restriction, a giving way when confronted by another more able to commandeer the means for subsistence and progress. It is a respect for the right each has from his human nature to free access to these means. Rights are not free gifts from some dominative authority, arbitrarily given and as arbitrarily to be taken away. Rights are the moral powers the human being has, to implement and actualize his potentialities without restriction. But human nature itself sets limits to this freedom by the very relationships it establishes between a man and his neighbors.

A man is free to speak his mind on anything, but he does wrong if he says what is wrong or harmful or false, for his neighbor has a right to truth. Truth is sacred; opinions are worth only as much as the reasons that justify them; error has no juridical standing at all. The workman is free to offer his labor to anyone he pleases, in union with his fellow craftsmen or by himself, but it would be wrong for him to bargain individually if this bargaining would jeopardize the suitable position the union has gained—just as it would be wrong for him to skimp his work and not give an honest day's work for a decent day's pay. The employer is free to hire whom he wills, but he must look to his workmen's psychological and moral needs as well as his money earnings. The citizen is free, within the laws of this country, at any rate, to work out his salvation as suits him best, but he would be wrong to abdicate to the government the complete control of his economic, intellectual, and moral destinies—just as it would be wrong for the administration to refuse to safeguard individual freedom. Nations are politically free and sovereign, but their sovereignty is no justification for aggrandizement at the expense of weaker nations any more than a man's physical strength is justification for unjust aggression upon his neighbor.

This will suffice to point out the possibility of inferring an objective standard of oughtness or morality from the demands of human nature properly conceived. Since every individual human being has a *human* nature (different from animal nature), he will be subject to the same demands as all other human beings. Since this human nature remains essentially the same in different historical periods and in different cultures, these demands will likewise remain the same. In consequence, this objective standard of oughtness constitutes an *absolute*, binding for every human being, though different times and different customs may make it either easier or more difficult to meet its demands. It is important to realize that these demands are not imposed from the outside by an alien force but are imposed *by our own nature* and are designed to result in its self-perfection.

But it is abundantly clear that this is not psychology. All these considerations come from another science (or, if there is doubt about giving the name "science" to any discipline that is not hypothetico-deductivo-empirico-physical, let's call it simply a discipline). Psychology has to do with human actions not as they are morals but as they are functions. The psychologist knows what the conditions are for effective learning just as an engineer can compute the relations between the dimensions of the girders of a bridge and the load that the bridge can stand. Learning that conforms to these conditions will be *good* learning in the same way that a bridge built according to the specifications of the engineer will be a *good* bridge. The psychologist can and does say: "The mother's emotional demands on the child ought to be moderated." "Proper form and color contrast ought to be used in advertisements." "X foot-candles ought to be adequate illumination to distinguish men from trees walking." But the engineer does not presume to find in his art the norms which will determine whether his bridge is a boon or a boondoggle. Neither should the psychologist presume to find in his science good morals as well as good psychology.

This matter will be treated in a later chapter (see Chapter 13), but it seems advisable here to draw attention to the limitations of our science. Psychology is not a panacea for all human ills, nor can it fulfill the messianic hopes of those enthusiasts who are persuaded that sheer psychological knowledge will not only find an

answer for every man's problem but also lead him out of want
and fear and strife into a state of bliss everlasting.[3] The engineer
can afford to neglect all considerations beyond the principles of
physics and the conditions of the site for his bridge because his
bridge will be a good bridge whether it is a boondoggle or the answer to a crying need. But the psychologist cannot be sure that the
human being will be good or that his society will be ideal if only
his psychological functions are in order. To determine what makes
a man a good man needs considerations beyond the empirical laws
which can be discovered by the psychologist.

The science of psychology does not provide any criteria which
would allow us to decide which of these wider considerations will
give us an objective moral norm and which are irrelevant. Neither
is it possible to derive such criteria from psychological hypotheses,
either by deduction or by experimental verification. What positive
science can do is to say *what is* or *what is happening*. As a positive
science, it can go no farther than that. If in spite of its limitations
it does go beyond them, it does so only with the proviso that it
borrows or appropriates from another domain. Thus physics formu-
lates laws that describe Young's Modulus, for instance, but only on
the proviso that there is a constancy or connectivity in the nature of
physical bodies (Cf. Bridgman, 4, pp. 211 ff.). But the law of
constancy is not a law of physics. It is prior to and beyond physics.
We blush to say it is a meta-physical matter (to use a mode of expression dear to the General Semantics enthusiast). The law of constancy will not be deduced either by mathematics or by logic unless
it is already contained in the premises of the deduction. Neither
will it be verified experimentally because it is the very foundation,
epistemologically, of experimental verification. Positive science
can map its own field and locate its objects therein and be sure that
where they are is also where they must be, and that they will be
there provided it is antecedently necessary that they be there. But
if " 'taint necessarily so," then positive science loses control of the
past as well as the future and becomes confused about the present
(Cf. Bridgman, *loc. cit.*).

[3] Witness the spate of books in the past half-decade on psychology and the
world crisis.

In artifacts standards may be set up to which the products must conform or be rejected. What would be said of the inspectors whose job it is to exercise "quality control" over the product, if they varied the standards to conform to the actual state of the products, justifying this procedure by the principle that standards which are not in accord with the actual state of things are of no use?—that what the products ought to be is to be found in what they actually are? Now the life of the individual human being may in a real sense be called his "artifact." He may make the various actions that comprise it conform to any standard he devises for himself or accepts from the social milieu in which he lives. He may direct his actions to a goal that maximizes altruistic service and minimizes selfish indulgence to any degree conceivable, with or without conflict, frustration, and inner pain. He may assert his *independence* of all laws and be overwhelmed by the sheer weight of social and political pressures; he may restrict his own freedom to mere *spontaneity*, to become the plaything of the inner and outer compulsions of physics and physiology; he may recognize and assume (as well as reject) his *responsibility* for every deliberate thought, word, and deed. But in any and every case, willy-nilly, he carries within himself the sanction of his success or failure as a human being, namely the achievement of complete happiness or the loss of it for good and all.

REFERENCES

1. ALLPORT, GORDON W. 1937. *Personality: A psychological interpretation.* New York: Henry Holt & Co.

2. AMERICAN PSYCHOLOGICAL ASSOCIATION, COMMITTEE ON ETHICAL STANDARDS FOR PSYCHOLOGY. 1951. Ethical standards in clinical and consulting relationships. *American Psychologist,* Section 3, Part I, 6, 57–64; Parts II–V, 6, 145–66.

3. BEIRNAERT, LOUIS. 1951. Does sanctification depend on psychic structure? *Cross Currents,* 1951, No. 2, 39–43.

4. BRIDGMAN, P. W. 1927. *The logic of modern physics.* New York: The Macmillan Co.

5. CANTRIL, HADLEY. 1949. Toward a scientific morality. *J. Psychol.,* 1949, 27, 365–66.

6. DAVIS, ALLISON, and DOLLARD, JOHN. 1940. *Children of bondage; the personality development of Negro youth in the urban South.* Washington, D. C.: American Council on Education.

7. HORNEY, KAREN. 1950. *Neurosis and human growth. The struggle toward self-realization.* New York: W. W. Norton & Co., Inc.
8. LECKY, PRESCOTT. 1945. *Self-consistency. A theory of personality.* New York: Island Press.
9. McCLELLAND, DAVID C. 1951. *Personality.* New York: William Sloane Associates.
10. MEAD, MARGARET. 1949. *Male and female: a study of the sexes in a changing world.* New York: Wm. Morrow & Co., Inc.
11. SCHILDER, PAUL. 1942. *Goals and desires of man: a psychological survey of life.* New York: Columbia University Press.
12. SUTICH, A. 1944. Toward a professional code for psychological consultants. *J. abnorm. soc. Psychol.,* 1944, **39**, 329–50.
13. SYMONDS, PERCIVAL. 1946. *The dynamics of human adjustment.* New York: Appleton-Century-Crofts, Inc.
14. TOLMAN, E. C. 1942. *Drives toward war.* New York: Appleton-Century-Crofts, Inc.

Chapter 5

PERSONALITY THEORIES BASED ON PHYSICAL AND BIOLOGICAL MODELS

By JOHN A. GASSON, S. J.

IN THE previous chapter it was pointed out that the models which have been developed in psychology so far have not been satisfactory. Physical and biological models (in Allport's terms, the model of the robot, the rat, and the infant mind) have not been successful for the description of human behavior. They have led psychologists (from Titchener to Koffka, Skinner, and Hull) to use jargon which no longer describes human beings in recognizable form and then, making a virtue out of necessity, to proclaim that science must not use the language of common sense. This kind of "deanthropomorphizing," which has been considered the hallmark of the scientist, sends us after a veritable will-o'-the-wisp. When the psychologist takes to equating human action with the action of bodies in the physical universe, it is either because he really believes that they are alike or, more likely, because he believes that quantification will be facilitated if he can use available mathematical equations which accurately describe the actions of material bodies. When he has thus divested his scientific expressions of any likeness to common human experience, he believes that he will be truly objective.

But in psychology such a procedure indicates a curious inversion of thinking. No doubt there is virtue in excluding undue anthropomorphism. We falsify facts if we judge the experience of animals by what we would experience if we were in that particular situation. We would be guilty of anthropomorphism if we read our emotions into the actions of physical bodies. But refusing to judge objects or animals by analogy with our experience is one thing, and refusing to use our experience in interpreting the actions and experiences of human beings (including our own), in favor of an analogy with physical movement, is an entirely different matter.

This inversion of thinking becomes even more inexplicable when we remember that our ideas of action and change arise genetically out of our own experience of *action within ourselves*.[1] It takes only a little reflection to understand that our experiential knowledge of reality comes genetically from what we do with the things we perceive. The baby handles everything he can find and puts everything into his mouth. As he grows older, his knowledge of things grows by doing, by manipulating everything he sees in many different ways. It is this doing which we come to recognize as *action*. We generally pay little attention to the fact that this doing is something *we* do and not just something that happens, or something that external reality does to us. This characteristic, that we initiate action, is so much part of our activity that we take it entirely for granted and attribute it, unwittingly, to action as action.

When we apply the notion of *action* to objects in the external world, we are more or less aware that it should be modified in some way, that it should only be used as an analogy. All too often, however, the scientist implicitly retains the idea that action starts in the acting body (as it does in his own action), but he never pays attention to this kind of "anthropomorphism." Even in treating moving systems in a strictly mechanistic way, he never thinks of accounting for the *origin* of motion in the

[1] An interesting confirmation of this statement can be found in an experimental report by Michotte, who found that colored rectangles when moved along a slot at varying speed "caused certain specific impressions" (in the observer) e.g., the impression "that an object A *goes toward* an object B," "that A *pursues* B," "that A *joins* B and *unites itself* to it," "that A *bumps* B," "that A *chases* or *repels* B," "that A *distorts* B by exerting pressure on it," "that A *pulls* B," "that A *goes to find* B and *take it away*," "that A *pushes* B with follow-up" (18, pp. 114–15. Michotte's italics).* He concludes that these interpretations (which are curiously consistent from one observer to the other) are given because the speed and direction of his own movements which accompany these various emotions and attitudes are similar to the speed and direction of movement of the observed rectangles.

* By permission from *Feelings and Emotions: The Mooseheart Symposium,* edited by M. L. Reymert. Copyright 1950 by McGraw-Hill Book Company, Inc.

system—because he unwittingly assumes that motion starts in what is moving. In drawing an analogy between vital actions and actions of physical bodies, he must assign similarities and differences—that is the very essence of analogy. But because this implicit notion is concealed in the analogy, he confuses the point of similarity (that bodies move) with the point of difference (that living bodies originate motion and physical bodies do not). So action as we know it in physical objects is taken as the primary analogue without any realization of this unconscious distortion.

Now when the psychologist wants to become strictly "objective" he draws another analogy between the actions of physical bodies, which he considers primary, and human action. But this time the distortion is reversed: the notion which was illegitimately concealed in physical action (that motion starts in what is moving) is now discarded from human action where it belongs. Human actions in which other bodies are moved are compared to mechanical action and found identical; thus the properly human characteristic of originating action is forgotten entirely, and even actions which are not analogous to mechanical motions (looking, speaking, thinking) are explained by mechanical principles. By this kind of double distortion the psychologist proposes to avoid "mysticism" and "superstition" in his science. Yet he, more than anyone else, ought to see how pernicious this distortion is, for he ought to know better than anybody that human beings are not the same as inorganic things. He knows that they do not behave in the same way and that no amount of mathematical treatment will make them identical. In human beings we are dealing with vital action, action that can be understood by us directly, intuitively, or (to use a modern term) "by empathy." [2]

It would seem to be a betrayal of man's innate capacity for arriving at an understanding of reality to distort reality in an attempt to achieve rigor and objectivity. This distortion may not be fatal in physics, for the distorted elements are not particularly

[2] The very fact that psychologists had to coin a new term to signify this direct understanding of human action by another human being is an interesting illustration of our thesis.

relevant to the problems involved : the physicist finds his physical systems in motion and accounts for changes within the system; the origin of the motion is not particularly relevant. What is important in psychology, however, is not the energy exchange between person and environment, but the fact that the human being can initiate characteristic human activities and carry them on irrespective of any effects they may have on the environment (e.g., doing mental arithmetic or solving a crossword puzzle without a pencil).

On this distorted analogy are based the physical and biological models which have been so extensively used in theory-building in psychology, as, for instance, in the attempt to use dynamics to emphasize the developmental nature of psychological activity.

Physical Models

Dynamics. First of all, the concept of dynamics as used in physics cannot validly be applied to human motivation because of the wide difference in the components of the "systems." In physics we deal with separate particles—even the dynamics of chemical change in the molecule, or radiation in the atom, is worked out as the mutual interchange of energy between separate particles. When the number of particles involved is greater than four, only probability theory and statistics are adequate to deal with the mathematical complexities encountered. If we try to build a psychodynamics as we do a thermodynamics or hydrodynamics, we are forced to do one of two things : We must either assume that the person is a system of particles in a field in exactly the same way as the bodies of physics, and that means resurrecting the old atomistic mechanism (the ghost of which modern physics has laid for good and all), or we must find correlates in the person for the particles and forces that are the elements of physical dynamic systems but which behave in an entirely different way. In either case, we are confronted with the problem of defining accurately what it is we are talking about and what exactly we mean by what we say about it.

Some psychologists, beguiled by the positivistic conception of science, believe it is safer to talk about what we do with the things of science rather than to talk about the things themselves. Thus Tolman, Stevens, Hull (Cf. Marx, 17, and "Symposium on operationism," 20), for instance, as well as many others, are agreed that operational definitions are the only definitions that are valid. Definition here is used to mean a description of what we do with some object so that we can come to measure it. Length is defined by the operations we use to measure a long object. The formula $f = ma$ is called a definition because it describes how we divide or combine certain quantities to obtain a quantity which describes what we call "force." This arbitrary use of the term "definition" implies that the nature of the object is what our measurements or manipulations *make it to be.* The physicist here is oblivious of the fact that in measuring length he has decided beforehand with what instrument to measure it; on the basis of what judgment or "definition" does he arrive at such a decision?

It is easy enough in physics to take such a prior decision for granted; length is "obviously" measured by a yardstick, weight by scales. But if a new way of dealing with an object has to be found, e.g., in measuring the rate of radiation, for which common sense has no immediate solution, the physicist will carefully investigate how the object acts—that is, what is its nature —so that he can measure those actions. Therefore the nature of the object must be such that only a particular operation will measure it. The operation of measuring, then, indicates something about the nature of the object, but we must know that nature at least approximately before we can measure it. Hence a *knowledge of the object* (which is attained by abstraction and expressed in concepts and definitions) is *prior* to measurement or quantitative statement.

This arbitrary and unrealistic use of a traditional term (definition) in operationism might be more easily tolerated were it not that so many other terms acquire arbitrary and therefore misleading meanings. What we would ordinarily call a definition is by the positivists termed "determination," as, for instance, in the statement, "force is determined by the structure of the field." "Determine" here means what needs to be thought to have a clear and distinct idea or concept. With regard to the strange word "structure" (it is strange to ears not accustomed to the esoteric language of the modern theoretical physicist), it means *vectors* in space at any point *and acceleration* at any point in a field, a field being a complex of systems, and system a complex of moving particles or waves, or perhaps just a complex of motions.

When these notions are brought into psychology, they should be translatable into less restricted language if they are to make ordinary sense. If "structure" means anything at all in psychology, it must mean that characteristic which makes perceptible the unity of a complex. The psychologists who have made the most extensive use of this term, Titchener and his disciples earlier, and more recently the psychoanalysts, give little evidence that they are aware that the term "structure" has a meaning other than architectural.

It would be well for all psychologists to ponder what Bergmann says about reducing psychological concepts to the particles of physics:

No good purpose, either methodological or epistemological, is served by construing any psychological concept in analogy to the elementary particles of physics. . . . If the analogy is pressed too hard it is either unnecessary or misleading. If it is intended to insure the existence of other minds, the idea being that I know of your data as I know of particles, then we have seen that this can be achieved much more simply. Thus the analogy is for this purpose unnecessary. If it is meant to suggest a direct or functional similarity between brain states on the one hand and the microstructure of all matter, whether brain or stones, on the other, then it is clearly misleading. . . . I cannot, of course, here go through a list of all psychological concepts in order to prove that there is not a single one among them that cannot be satisfactorily construed as a defined concept, i.e., without use of those elaborate technics. . . .

To say that it is not *necessary* to construe our subjects' conscious contents or, if you please, their unconscious wishes as we construe the particles of physics is one thing. To say that it *cannot* be done is another. I see no reason why it could not be done; and I am sure that if it is done carefully one can avoid the confusions that beset the careless way of talking about this possibility. But, I repeat, there is no question, either methodological or epistemological, about a psychological concept that cannot be answered without this complicated exercise. And I would also argue that we do not understand any such question fully, if we do not, among all the possible answers, recognize the one which is the simplest (5, pp. 109–10. Bergmann's italics).

Homeostasis. There are psychologists who try to construe psychological concepts in terms of the interaction of the particles or masses of physics. Those who have a predilection for mechanical models find a unifying concept in *homeostasis*. Now that concept fits very well in geology and geophysics because the interaction between the crust of the earth and the underlying sphere constitutes a passive reactive system in the gravitational field of the earth, but thus to describe the active forces in a human person belies the notions basic to the concept.

Action or change in a physical body is never initiated in the body which changes; the change is induced by some other body acting upon it. A body at rest is moved by another body in motion; a body at a lower temperature is heated by a body at a higher temperature; an electron moving from one orbit to another does so under the influence of some factor outside the electron itself. If a system is in equilibrium, it will remain so until the equilibrium is disturbed from the outside. Even if tensions are introduced into the system, the tensions arise not from the state of the system as it is in equilibrium, but from the accumulation of energy in some part of the system against the inertia and friction of the component particles. The redress of balance in an inertial or gravitational system is a reactive one, not a purely active one.

In living systems there are, of course, reactive activities; but what is distinctive of living reactions is the fact that vital action cannot be accounted for fully merely in terms of the energy input on the part of the stimulus.[3] If, then, we treat psychologi-

[3] Recent experiments on photosynthesis offer an interesting confirmation of this. Warburg and Luttgens reached the striking conclusion that the chloride ion is a coenzyme essential for photochemical reaction and photosynthesis. Arnon and Whatley, in a series of experiments to test these conclusions, discovered that these results were confirmed in vitro, but in vivo the chloride ion did not function in that way. Evidently, in the intact green cell photosynthesis occurs without participation of either chloride or bromide (2, p. 554).

cal activities merely as cases of homeostatic dynamics, we shall find ourselves making psychology a part of physics instead of constructing a dynamic psychology. *Psychological* dynamics would require a self-initiated change in the state of the system; the introduction of tension states is not sufficient to give the system the activo-active character which psychological states require.

If physical terms are to be useful in psychology, the implications of sheer mechanicism will have to be purged from them; but not all the concepts of physics are amenable to such purification. "Homeostasis" is such a term which resists all our efforts. As has been said above, homeostasis reduces all human activities to the status of passive reactive systems. When tensions are introduced to account for the initiation of activity, the question arises : Whence comes the accumulation of energy that accounts for the activity which restores the balance? For example, a man goes into the dining room for lunch—that is an action which is to redress the imbalance produced by hunger contractions in the stomach; the hunger contractions are a reaction to the imbalance brought about by muscular activity; the muscular activity was in answer to some disturbance of equilibrium brought about by some factor in the environment, etc., etc. Now all these are expenditures of energy, hence no one of them nor all of them together will account for the accumulation of energy. Hunger contractions do not give a man the energy to go to the dining room; the tissue depletion that brought on hunger contractions does not give the stomach the energy to contract; the disturbance of equilibrium that brought about muscular activity does not supply the energy for it; or even if the imbalance did produce the energy needed for its redress, the reaction goes much beyond the energy that might be supplied by the preceding imbalance. The lion may go on a hunting expedition stimulated by hunger contractions, but these surely do not supply the vast amount of energy expended in the course of the lion's hunting. Unless we somehow get outside the homeostatic system, there will not be any activity at all.

Moreover, the whole theory of homeostasis is based on the assumption that every phenomenon that is observed in a person after environmental interference is an adaptive reaction. If however, the person as a homeostatic system always automatically selects the reaction that makes for survival, how are we to account for the host of nonsurvival reactions which are just as well known in physiology as in psychology? Some types of environmental interference seem to result in a vicious circle effect against which the organism cannot set up an efficient reaction. Thus hemorrhage leads to lowered blood pressure, which is reacted to by sympathetic excitation; this results in greater permeability of the capillaries, which in turn reduces the circulating blood volume with a resultant fall in blood pressure until the patient dies in shock (Cf. Gellhorn, 10, p. 263). Quite clearly, there must be something not contained in sheer homeostasis that accounts for a systemic blocking and reversal of the circular reaction in the patient who recovers spontaneously; if not present, it must be supplied from the outside, e.g., by blood transfusion to restore the plasma volume to normal.

When we consider more complicated activities, those which have a predominance of psychological components, for instance, the insufficiency of the concept of homeostasis is much more evident. For example, an anxious person may experience intense fear—which produces rather massive physiological effects. Even though the original situation is no longer dangerous, these physiological effects themselves become fear-producing (the person notices his racing heart and suspects heart disease) ; as the fear increases, so do the physiological effects, until our patient develops a full-blown heart neurosis. Sheer homeostasis will never cut into this circular reaction. The patient may, in the course of the circular reaction, decide to resign himself to heart disease, and stops worrying. The vicious circle will stop, too, and the neurosis does not develop—but homeostasis cannot account for this way of cutting into the circle. Or the circle may be broken by psychotherapy which reduces the fear, but here again the effectiveness of therapy is not the result of a sheer redress of balance in an unbalanced system.

Thus any account of psychological activity in terms of sheer physical systems is unsatisfactory because the precise point which is of most importance is left unexplained. What psychology has

to explain is not how the human being is like a robot, but precisely how the human being is *not* like a robot. Unless we concentrate on this difference we shall find at the end of our quest
the human being as lifeless, scattered, and inert as the bodies of
Newton's universe.

Topology. Psychologists in general now are abandoning this
purely mechanistic approach and attack the problem differently.
They try to find correlates in the person for the particles and
forces that are the elements of a strictly dynamic system. One
of the more captivating formulations of this type is that of Lewin
and his school. The blending of field theory and analysis situs
to describe the dynamic interaction of elements within the human
personality gives a most charming appearance of accuracy and
systematic rigor. However, upon examination this initial impression tends to disappear. The more one studies these essays
into applied topology, and the more one gets below the surface
shine of words, the clearer it becomes that the psychologist has
been beguiled into thinking that what Einstein did for physics
with Riemannian geometry, a psychologist can do for psychology
with topology.

Thus far the topology of the psychological theorist from
Lewin on has hardly been on a professional level. Brown (7)
warns his readers against mathematical naïveté with respect to
Jordan's theorem. But he himself does not escape naïveté if he
believes that in his paper he is theorizing topologically about
psychology. The topology of the field theorists is of the simplest;
what emerges is not a theory on a topological model but a catalog of figures of speech using topological words which can be
used as tropes in speaking of psychological phenomena.

The term "life space," for instance, is used as a construct to
account for the psychological situation at a given moment. Now
what can life space mean for the plain ordinary psychologist
whose mind is not encumbered with the intricacies of relativity
theory and quantum mechanics? Life means activity and change.
If activity and change are going to be in a space and that space is
to be a real location, what could that space be? It could be the
volume enclosed by the person's skin. Quite clearly that is not

what Lewin means by life space. Life space could mean the interval between birth and death. This, too, is not what Lewin means. Life space may mean that portion of the physical space of the universe within which the individual may find himself at any moment in the interval between birth and death. It does not seem that this is the space that Lewin refers to.

Now these are the only three real spaces within which a human being passes his life. If the life space is something different from any or all of these, then the term must be some kind of abstraction. If it is an abstraction, the phrase is at best a figure of speech. Now a figure of speech is apt if there is some point of similarity between what is expressed by it and the reality to which it refers. If there is no point of similarity (and there is not, for we saw above that "life space" does not refer to any real spaces), then the term is a sheer symbol and the psychological reality to which it refers must itself be an abstraction or a sheer symbol. It would seem, then, that Lewin's psychological topology is an excursion into symbolism. Now symbols are significant only if they mean something. What can the symbol "life space" symbolize?

A clue might be found in the scientific orientation of a man like Lewin, who was basically a mathematician. It can be summarized in Wittgenstein's (23) first three statements and their implications (Cf. our discussion, pages 57–59):

Die Welt ist alles was der Fall ist. 1.
Die Welt ist die Gesamtheit der Tatsachen, nicht der Dinge. 1.1
Denn, die Gesamtheit der Tatsachen bestimmt, was der Fall ist, und auch, was nicht der Fall ist. 1.12

The world is everything that is the case. 1.
The world is the totality of facts, not things. 1.1
For the totality of facts determines what is the case and also all that is not the case. 1.12

From this we can gather that what makes up the individual's universe is what he knows to be the case, that is, whatever has significance for him. Life space, then, as a symbol, would refer to the sphere of an individual's self-reference or his sphere of significance.

As is clear, these phrases are figures of speech also. They are not concepts, for "significance" and "self-reference" are relations, and relations are not things, but neither are they "Tatsachen." Relations are founded in qualities of things; they are not themselves qualities or properties of things. The relation of significance is necessarily founded in an act of knowledge. But an act of knowledge is not amenable to geometrization. When we speak of a *sphere of significance*, we are much more in the realm of figures of speech. Significance is not subject to intensification or remission, except in so far as the act of knowledge which founds the significance is subject to intensification or remission. But the activity of knowing is more or less intense only with reference to the greater or smaller multitude of objects which it encompasses, or the extent to which it penetrates into the inner nature of the object that is known.

It will be objected, of course, that all this is irrelevant since topology deals with abstract spaces and that "life space" should be understood as a quasi-abstract space. One can, of course, admire the hardihood of a psychologist who launches out into topology, but it is to be feared that few if any are equipped for the voyage. Bell,* a man whose opinion is not lightly to be dismissed, has this to say of topology and mathematicians :

> Experts in topology claim that their methods render complicated situations in analysis spatially intuitive; and to judge by the results they obtain with apparent ease in some of the most intricate problems of modern dynamics, they must be right. But to less gifted mathematicians, by nature condemned to trudge through every step of a logical argument in order to credit its conclusion, topology must remain an untravelled highway. . . . One thing seems certain: to think topologically, the thinker must begin young. The cradle with its enchained teething rings may be a little too early; but the education of a prospective topologist should not in any case be deferred beyond the third year (4, p. 453).

If this be true of mathematicians what could be said of psychologists who venture to use topology for a "simple" explanation of everyday events in the lives of everyday people?

* By permission from E. T. Bell, *The Development of Mathematics.* Copyright 1945, McGraw-Hill Book Company, Inc.

If to the trivialities [4] of topology which have so far found their way into psychology there are added the vectors of field theory, the situation becomes thoroughly confused. Not all topological spaces remain invariant under all transformations. It is a complex problem to determine which transformation can be made in which spaces. To which of the abstract spaces, then, are we going to liken "life space"? And when the psychological event is tailored to suit the properties of that space (for no matter how much we close our eyes to the fact, that is what must be done in topological modeling), how much of the psychological factor will be left to remain invariant under the transformations?

If we waive all these considerations, together with such problems as the metricization of abstract spaces and the whole problem of dimensionality in geometry (which we have not mentioned but which are problems fundamental to the theory), there still remains the question: What profit will it be for psychology to topologize and vector? Analysis situs is hardly calculated to give the simplest answers regarding methods in theory-building, or the nature of the relations existing between the human being, his behavior, and the goals he seeks to reach. It cannot account for change or distortion in a region or domain. Its principal concern is connectedness and part-whole relationships. It does not deal with wholes as wholes but only as wholes are numerable. Numerability necessarily implies some kind of division—but division destroys a whole. If we make a whole an aggregate of parts, totality becomes merely an extrinsic denomination. The concept of whole is prior to the concept of parts, for parts both genetically and logically arise only in the processs of division. Herein lies, we believe, the reason for the intractability of topology for psychological purposes.

Psychoanalysis ("Dynamic" psychology). Finally, the concepts of dynamics are inapplicable to psychology because the sources of activity are treated differently in the two fields. However much the geometries of space are adapted to psychological events and however much dynamic concepts from physics are

[4] The designation is a mathematical term borrowed from Professor Everett Larguier, S. J., a professional topologist, who in a private communication gave a sympathetic appraisal of topological theory in psychology.

refashioned to represent functional relationships between elements in behavior, the basic problem eludes description and solution. The basic problem in psychodynamics is to account for the *origin* of behavior. Physics *finds* its systems in motion; it does not account for the motion in a system. Geometry deals only with instantaneous states. When physics and geometry are wed and the combination is used mathematically to account for a dynamic system, either motion disappears or position dissolves. Thus motion and position can never be made to appear in the same experimental arrangement; whatever device we might use to account for both of them in our mathematical description, what we account for is motion that is already in the system and not the origin of the motion.

If psychology is studied from a dynamic point of view, it is not the process itself that is of principal concern but the origin of the process. Freud, for example, was not satisfied to discover the symptoms of disturbed or aberrant behavior; he was concerned with etiology. He called his formulations and theories dynamic precisely because he meant to account for the *origin* of psychological or pathological processes. He developed his whole notion of instincts as the sources out of which these processes arise so as to account for the existence of various behavior patterns. The whole panoply of defense mechanisms was introduced to account for the particularization of these diverse modes of action; as the basic instinctual drives are diversified by various modes of defense, there will arise diverse types of behavior. Because Freud's concept of cause was confused and inadequate, he did not always arrive at the real origins of aberrant behavior. The scientific atmosphere of mechanicism in which he had been educated was biased toward the conception that all action phenomena were purely mechanical in nature. Thus it was that in more than one case Freud arrived at origins that were not causes in themselves but were related to the phenomena in question at most by chance or *per accidens*. For true dynamism in psychology we need not only a system of acting factors, but also factors that are of such a nature that they do not merely react to external stimulation but can initiate action on their own.

In fact, Freud's system should be termed an inertial system rather than a dynamic one. Alexander's systematization of the principles of psychoanalysis seems to bear this out. The two basic laws on which the system is built, the principle of stability and the law of inertia, are simply transliterations of Newton's first two laws of motion. The third law, that of surplus energy, merely energizes the machine but does not account for any vectors (1, pp. 33–44).

Cybernetics. An active factor in at least one of its aspects, the steering toward a goal, is claimed to have been incorporated in the newest model of man with which science has presented us: the feed-back or servo-mechanism. Its originator, Norbert Wiener, claims that modern electronic servo-mechanisms are purposive, that is, they can be set toward a goal and then can adjust themselves to changing circumstances by means of signals from the goal (negative feed-back). Therefore they are purposive though determined, as human beings are in his opinion, and can serve as adequate models for human behavior. Wiener points out that previous mechanical models of man have been inadequate because organisms are purposive while mechanisms were not. But servo-mechanisms can be called purposive in the same sense as organisms, for they not only have a goal but they can also adjust to changing conditions in its pursuit.

Since the servo-mechanism is the latest of a long line of physical models and promises to occupy the psychologist's imagination for at least some time, it might be profitable to discuss it at some length. Purpose in servo-mechanisms consists, first, of a prior set which is built into the machine: data are punched in and the conditions for choice (yes/no) are prescribed by the design of the mechanism itself. Such purpose, therefore, is always external to the machine. Secondly, the servo-mechanism is designed so as to execute that external purpose exactly as prescribed, though that execution is modified by feed-back information from the goal.

With human beings, on the other hand, the intention is always intrinsic, the goal is set by the human being himself—or, at least, the goal which is inherent in his nature has to be implemented by him. Secondly, the execution of this purpose, though modified by information from the goal (comparable to but not identical with a feed-back mechanism), is also modified by internal direction. And finally, the execution is not prescribed from outside the human being but chosen by himself. The human being has a set or intention which is intrinsic rather than extrinsic because there always is a possiblity of choice or change, while the machine has no choice of response once it has been built and the data have been punched in. In the machine, the execution of the "purpose" is directly prescribed by the initial design; errors will happen only if the relay tubes are defective. In the human being, there is a selection of the way in which his purpose will be executed and there can be error both in the selection and the execution—but such an error cannot be the result of defects in the neuronal circuit, for an error can be detected and corrected immediately though no replacement of defective neurons can have taken place.

The one analogy which does seem to hold is the modification of the movement toward the goal by feed-back information. Both the self-propelled missile and the person throwing darts improve their aim, the one by receiving information of the course of the target, the other by seeing the location of the hit. There is evidence, however, that at least in human coordinated movements there is a factor of internal direction which consists in the gradual refinement of aim, and happens even if no feed-back information is available; in fact, feed-back information seems to interfere. In an experiment in dart throwing, first Vandell and his associates and later Beattie found that "imaginary" practice was as effective as actual practice—if not more so—in improving scores. In imaginary practice, the subject was merely sitting in front of the dart board and imagined picking up the darts and throwing them, one after another, into the bull's-eye. In a later modification (E. Garver (9), unpublished research), it was found that scores improved during actual dart throwing when the subject was prevented from seeing the location of his hits, but aimed every time straight at the bull's-eye. These results would indicate that the improvement of internal direction is actually more important for a person's aim than the feed-back information, which in some cases may actually prove a hindrance.

Thus servo-mechanisms are comparable to human purposive behavior only in a narrowly restricted area, that of the mechanical execution of a purpose by means of feed-back information, which on the human level is only one factor in the execution of a purpose. True, feed-back enthusiasts are pointing out that there is another analogy between man and the machine in that the human brain as well as the machine has reverberating circuits which could be used for storing information. Not only that, but both seem to be able to transform particulars into universals, according to Northrop:

> Assume that an impulse from the eyes fires a neuron which is a member of a regenerative loop and that its impulse is the epistemic correlate of the introspected "idea" or "datum" *blue*. It follows from the character of a regenerative loop that this impulse will be transmitted continuously without ceasing around the loop, so long as the energy necessary to restore the neurons to a capacity to fire is maintained by metabolic activity. [Thus] . . . one has the form of the fact remaining constant over time through different particular events; one has universals (19, p. 413).

If universals were a kind of composite photograph, perhaps that would be their mechanism. Or if universals could be obtained by collating the largest number of common characteristics of different objects, then it might be possible to arrive at them in a mechanical way. Or, finally, if universals represented the common form of a wide range of transpositions, then it could be argued that there might be a scanning process which would reduce the variations to their common theme much like the process by which letters of any size or shape are translated into a basic sound for each letter of the alphabet, so that print can be translated into sound to facilitate reading for the blind. What makes a universal, however, is not that a single thing *occurs a number of times*, but that there is an *abstract feature* that is *common* to many things and belongs to each in unequivocally the same way. When we perceive it and recognize that it so belongs by finding it in many instances, we have a universal concept that is known as such. The first time we perceive such a feature we have a universal concept, but we do not know it as universal until we have made a comparison and applied the concept to many things. We know that this is *something*; this is *something moving*; this is a *man*. In these stages of recognition there is a gradual increase in knowledge. In each of these stages we know a common feature and recognize it as such because we have the notion that this experience is essentially like many other experiences, and this thing as *something* is essentially like many other *things*; this thing as *moving* is like *moving things*, and this thing we call a *man* is like other things called *men*. In the electronic computer, the "universals" are given to the machine together with a comparing unit which scans for likeness and difference. The human being can obtain universals from particulars only if he first *discovers* something common about this chair or this table or this man which determines their nature (over and above particular qualities of color or shape or size), and then discovers *that it is common* to many individuals singly and unequivocally.[5] Reflection on what we mean by a *common* noun, which is the sign of a universal concept, ought to make this clear. Remembering means not only having these

[5] That there really is a discovery involved can be gathered from the moving passage in which Helen Keller describes her first understanding that a word denotes a concept. She says:

Earlier in the day we had had a tussle over the words m-u-g and w-a-t-e-r. Miss Sullivan had tried to impress it upon me that "m-u-g" is mug and that "w-a-t-e-r" is water, but I persisted in confounding the two. . . . We walked down the path to the well-house. . . . Someone was drawing water and my teacher placed my hand under the spout. As the cool stream gushed over one hand she spelled into the other the word water. . . . Suddenly I felt a misty consciousness as of something forgotten—a thrill of returning thought; and somehow the mystery of language was revealed to me. I knew then that "w-a-t-e-r" meant the wonderful cool something that was flowing over my hand. . . . That living word awakened my soul, gave it light, hope, joy, set it free! . . . I left the well-house eager to learn. Everything had a name, and each name gave birth to a new thought (13, pp. 23–24).

What Helen Keller discovered was that the pattern spelled into her hand stood for that essential something that distinguishes water from anything else. She also discovered, and that was the reason for her joy, that everything she knew had something essential, and that this essential something had a name which she could learn and which other people knew, too.

categories at our disposal, but also selecting the appropriate one according to the needs of the moment.

Again, as in our discussion of purpose, the differences between man and machine are incomparably more striking and important than the similarities. In every case, it is the difference between self-directed behavior in the human and the execution of an external set in the machine. Therefore, the servo-mechanism can at most be expected to throw light on the mechanical routinized execution of a problem which in the human being can never be isolated from the nonmechanical self-determined intention. Taking the servo-mechanism as a model in psychology would help little toward a fuller knowledge of human purposive behavior and might very well be a stumbling block for further research because it favors exclusive attention to the least important aspect of human activity.

Biological Models

Physical models, then, together with the terminology of the physicist, have little to offer for psychology. It might even be said that physical models have to be discarded in favor of biological models, and that these might offer wide possibilities for the psychologist because they are based not on mechanical but on organismic factors. In an attempt to explore this possibility, we propose to discuss the personality theories of Lecky and Goldstein.

Lecky's Self-Consistency. For Lecky, there is no difficulty about the active character of the organism or its unitary structure. He says:

> The usual enunciation is that the organism acts because it is stimulated. We assume, on the contrary, that every organism, as long as it remains alive, is continuously active. . . . Life and activity are coexistent and inseparable. . . . A stimulus does not initiate activity, but merely tends to modify . . . the activity already in progress (14, p. 80).

This activity is directed toward the achievement of unity in the form of self-consistency. Lecky means by the striving toward self-consistency the attempt of the organism to organize values in such a way that they are felt to be consistent with one another. This striving is stimulated by the environment which presents a continuous series of new problems to be solved. Therefore conflict, which demands continual solution of problems, is the condition for achieving unity. The unity of the person is shown in the personality structure.

For Lecky, self-consistency is always the goal of living, but in organizing his values to achieve self-consistency, the individual will organize them around the conception he has of himself. Therefore self-definition is a focal point of personality structure. Once such a definition is accepted, the individual "endeavors to perfect himself in the part to which he has been assigned, and grows more and more unmanageable the more his behavior is condemned" (14, p. 107). In this way, self-consistency becomes strictly subjective; for Lecky, the neurotic personality structure is just as much the result of a striving for self-consistency as the normal personality. Moreover, there is a natural tendency in every individual to preserve his own organization of personality, be it normal or neurotic. Therefore resistance to therapy is interpreted as the individual's desire to maintain his personality, that is, he is trying to defend a scheme of life which the therapist is trying to change.

The aim of therapy, for Lecky, is a redefinition of the individual's concept of himself and the technique "consists in making the subject aware of his inconsistency" (p. 110). It is difficult, of course, to see how the individual could be inconsistent if self-consistency is subjective and there is no hint in the system that there is some objective standard to which any individual's approach to self-consistency could be compared. Lecky seems to assume that every person does all he can do under the circumstances, that self-consistency is a natural product of growth, just as the opening of the flower is the natural result of plant growth; circumstances can interfere so that a given individual's self-consistency will look like inconsistency to the observer, and will subjectively result in unhappiness as the outward sign that this solution leads to conflicting behavior patterns.

This conception of the human being is built after the model of biological growth where perfection will be reached if external and internal conditions are favorable. The person himself really has no voice in this process; though determined intrinsically, by his nature, he does not determine himself. But the fact remains that human beings do have purposes of their own which they do achieve, even purposes that involve the direction of their lives. Human beings patently can—and often do—persist in striving for incompatible goals which make inner harmony and integration (self-consistency) impossible. Moreover, the self-concept is not developed haphazardly, as Lecky implies, but can represent true knowledge of one's self. Nor is it unchangeable; though the person may resist having it changed for him, he himself can and does not only change his "definition" of himself but also the conception of a self-ideal toward which to strive.

Goldstein's Self-Actualization. Goldstein's concept of self-actualization is similarly biological. He also assumes that self-actualization is a natural process, inherent in organic nature. To actualize his potentialities, the individual develops preferred ways of acting, perceiving, evaluating; these preferences become behavior constants as they develop into durable habits. The closer these constants are to objectively demanded action, the more integrated, the better "centered" the individual will be. Self-actualization suffers restrictions, both from the physical and the social environment. The individual continually has to "come to terms" with his world. In encountering the restricting influence of other creatures, which means "impact, catastrophic reactions, antagonism, competition, and struggle between 'mind' and 'life,' " man develops his capacity for suffering the inevitable tension produced by the degree of self-actualization his nature is capable of achieving and the degree his world will allow him to achieve.

This suffering, according to Goldstein, "reveals the very highest form of life in the phenomenon of freedom." Self-actualization is not only restricted by others; it is also helped by others, says Goldstein, for everyone's behavior constants are in some way incomplete, onesided, faulty. Only by knowing and assimilating other ways of living can we supplement our own. Such complementary constants are the basis of justice and tolerance; only the realization that our own preferred ways of acting are as incomplete, as restricted as those of others, will prevent us from rigidity and dogmatism. In the interest of their striving for self-actualization, human beings will learn both to encroach upon others and to restrict themselves in favor of others, which is another important facet of human freedom.

Freedom or self-determination is restricted in Goldstein's system to voluntary self-restriction and voluntary encroachment upon the environment and to the endurance of the suffering inherent in the restriction of his potentialities, whether imposed by himself or by the environment. He does admit that man can oppose this natural process of self-actualization, but considers this a merely transitory phenomenon in the inevitable chain of action and reaction in which the natural impetus to self-actualization is bound to be successful unless catastrophe intervenes. Thus man becomes an animal with special difficulties in "centering," in maintaining the balance between his inherent striving toward self-actualization and the obstacles interposed not only by the environment but by himself.

Though such a highly developed biological model is a decided improvement on the physical model (among other reasons, because it allows a more humane language), it is still unsatisfactory. If human self-actualization is the natural unfolding of a process inherent in human beings as a species which differs from individual to individual only because there are differences within the species, then freedom is merely a tool of this natural process, and responsibility must be abrogated in accordance with the difficulties and limitations imposed by the environment. The more difficulties in the environment the greater will be the obstacles to integration, to proper centering, and the more likely will be a "catastrophic reaction" which will restrict the individual's possibilities still further. We are forced to the conclusion that the animal is in a happier state than the human being with regard to self-actualization because these difficulties of centering do not exist and it necessarily (without any internal opposition) becomes as perfect as its nature permits.

But we surely have the right to assume that the human being, who has a natural tendency toward self-actualization as well as the animal, is provided with tools for achieving it that are at least not less effective. If he was given mind as a tool to achieve the purpose of life, self-actualization, yet mind can oppose life, as Goldstein says, then there must be an additional factor which accounts for such failure. Normally, an additional tool would make for more efficient self-actualization. Only if man is free to use that tool as *he* chooses, either as a help toward his natural goal or as a help toward a rival goal of his own, will the possession of an additional instrument result in possible or actual opposition to his natural goal.

Thus freedom must be not only the freedom to restrict one's self and to suffer restriction, as Goldstein has it, but also the freedom not to do so. Then man is free to follow his natural goal, self-actualization, but also free to oppose it—and such freedom is not a transitory phenomenon but a condition of his being. Thus we see that a theory such as Goldstein's, if it is to reach consistent conclusions, will have to postulate man's capacity for positive intervention in his own affairs.

Combined Models

Thus physical and biological models by themselves do not provide the comprehensiveness in theoretical approach that psychologists are seeking. There is an increasing trend toward field theory concepts, especially among theorists using clinical data as their point of departure. They seem to believe that the use of field theory concepts will bring psychology abreast of the scientific times—just as in physics unified field theory has reconciled antinomies in theoretical physics. We saw above, however, that field theory (even when joined to topology) leaves too many psychological facts unaccounted for.[6] They fail, for instance, to provide laws which render the psychological "field" amenable

[6] Spence remarks, "Like so many of these field theorists, Lewin sets up a most attractive program for theory. Taken in conjunction with his interesting experiments, the illusion is neatly created that there is some connection between them" (17, p. 75, note).

to control and manipulation. Such deficiencies in comprehensiveness can probably be attributed to the fact that each different group of theorists is interested in a very different realm of psychological phenomena. It could be surmised that all theory would be more fruitful if the noncompetitive systems of theory were combined and articulated one into the other.

Such an attempt is to be found in Bronfenbrenner's contribution to a recent symposium on perception (6, chap. 8, pp. 206–58). The paper professes to give no more than a conceptual framework to support a fully articulated and developed theory of personality. Nevertheless, the concepts are sufficiently comprehensive to account for phenomena in all psychological realms. Bronfenbrenner's integrated theory is remarkable for its breadth of view, its depth of penetration, and its virtuosity of synthesis. To have accomplished so much so well within the limits necessarily imposed by the context of the symposium is an unusual achievement. His synthesis merits more extended study than we can devote to it here. What we shall attempt to do (borrowing from Bronfenbrenner's kit the same tool Bronfenbrenner borrowed from Freud) is to examine more closely some of the important concepts in Bronfenbrenner's framework to find their latent content. We are led to do this by the fact that in many instances he says what we ourselves would say; it is important for us to discover whether he means what we would mean by the terms he uses.

The concepts we propose to examine are (1) the unity of personality; (2) growth by differentiation and integration; (3) self-determination and the concept of will; (4) tolerance of unreality. We do not imply that these are the key concepts of Bronfenbrenner's framework. We merely say that the meaning he gives to these concepts will show with sufficient clarity the fundamental conceptual background of his synthesis. Perhaps the easiest and safest way to give a glimpse of the theoretical structure is to quote Bronfenbrenner's own summary:

Personality Structure

1. Personality is conceived as a hierarchical organization of psychical systems.

2. Psychical systems are dispositions to respond in a particular way to selected aspects of the psychical field.

3. The psychical system is an integrate involving conative, affective, and cognitive dimensions. The first two are intimately linked and represent the functional aspect of the system: the last contributes the structural framework.

4. The self-system or ego occupies a dominant position in the total hierarchy.

5. The ego is conceived both in terms of function (regulative-integrative-creative) and content (self-other).

6. The regulative-integrative-creative functions are made possible by a maturing capacity for abstraction and perceptual reorganization.

7. The self-other system is a perception of the self in relation to other selves.

8. The self-other system includes substructures which maintain a high level of abscission. In other words, the ego contains dispositional systems toward the self and toward the other which are not accessible to awareness.

Personality Development

1. From the outset, the human organism is conceived as a system. As such, it has the following properties:

a) It possesses boundaries which segregate it from the rest of the field and which are selectively permeable in both directions.

b) It functions as a unit—acts and is acted upon as such.

c) It maintains a dynamic equilibrium (i.e., it maintains a level of excitation) both within itself and with the external milieu.

2. From birth, the human organism manifests an active impulse to growth; that is, to extension, differentiation, and integration both within itself and in relation to the external milieu. This impulse is holistic and undifferentiated as to content. It has three aspects which are intimately intertwined.

a) *Conative:* an impulse to action, to utilization of maturing physiological organs and tissues (this is analogous to the activity drive of classical psychology).

b) *Affective:* an impulse to affective expression and investment of ever-widening dimensions of the organism and its milieu.

c) *Cognitive:* an impulse to utilize the capacity to abstraction, to organize experience in terms of concepts.

3. The conative-affective aspects precede the cognitive in both the order and rapidity of their development. Conative-affective impulse

activity is referred to as *experience*. The cognitive organization of experience is designated as *perception*.

4. The advent of perception marks the beginning of psychological (as distinguished from physiological) development. The conatively-affectively-cognitively organized impulse to activity (i.e., a dispositional organization) is designated as a psychical system.

5. Personality development involves the progressive expansion, differentiation, and integration of psychical systems.

6. Psychological growth is provoked and paced by physiological changes in the growing organism. This physiological development involves cumulative differentiation of affectively toned processes which require for their expression invasion and consequent emotional investment of ever widening dimensions of the environment—notably its interpersonal aspects.

7. The importance of the interpersonal field derives from the child's lengthy period of dependence on others for his comfort and survival. The interpersonal field thus becomes the principal context for the ever widening investment of affective impulses.

8. The reliance of the infant upon the mother for his affective integration, taken together with his capacity for learning, leads him to become reactive to changes in the affective organization of the mother—and later other persons—as such changes are manifested through muscle tensions, abortive movements, and other behavioral signs. Such experience of another's emotional state is designated as *empathy*.

9. With the development of perception, the objective condition of dependence on others becomes a psychological one, that is, the child begins to perceive others as they are related to his impulses and needs.

10. Personality development is a function of the degree and manner in which the biologically rooted affective impulses find expression in the interpersonal context into which they inevitably intrude.

11. The interpersonal field has two broad interrelated dimensions which may be distinguished as *structure* and *support*. The former refers to the boundaries, prescriptions, and proscriptions that are perceived in the life space of the developing person. The latter refers to the manner and degree to which dependence needs are met. Whether the impulse to conative-affective-cognitive expression appears externally as destructive or constructive depends on the dialectic balance between the forces of structure and support.

12. Personality development is a function of progressive expansion, differentiation, and integration of self-other relationships which

is paralleled by like processes within the intrapsychic self-other system. This osmotic-like isomorphic process takes place through the medium of empathy.

13. The forces determining personality structure exist only in the present. Hence personality change can be effected only through modification of the immediate psychological situation.

14. Optimal conditions for personality development involve tolerance for unreality and a gradual shift from firm to fluid structure of the interpersonal field.

15. The developmental process progresses through the creative restructuring of objective reality. To be effective, this creativity must encompass the sphere of reciprocal interpersonal relationships. Thus, the person moves from the receptive dependence of infancy to the creative interdependence and self-determination of mature adulthood (6, pp. 253–55).

This summary shows how and why a theory of personality can be at once the focus and the culmination of an inquiry into perception. The position taken by Bronfenbrenner is "that perception is the principal vehicle of the process of personality development" (6, p. 207). Only questions of motive force and direction of movement need to be added to arrive at core problems of psychology as a science. This is what Bronfenbrenner does try to do: the structural framework for his theory he finds in Lewin; the motive force and the direction of movement he finds in the work of the other four men whose ideas he integrates into a unified scheme: Freud, Rank, McDougall, and Sullivan.

Not everything he finds in the work of these five men is grist for his mill; in fact, he finds a sufficient number of points that are strikingly incompatible with a general theory or leave crucial questions unanswered. From the rest he gathers enough good grain for his purpose.

While reviewing Lewin's theoretical position Bronfenbrenner subjects him to a trenchant criticism. He brings out quite clearly that Lewin continually talks about psychic systems but always shies away from specifying their source or content (6, p. 214). Of the multiplicity of systems that may be presumed to exist in Lewin's exposition, the self-system is the only one that he identifies by name. And even of this one he never mentions the structure or content. Lewin evades the whole issue of what are the forces in the psychological field:

> We are told that there are systems of forces acting within and between the individual and his environment, but what these forces are, whence they come, and wither they impel remain unanswered questions. True, Lewin does speak of needs presumably of biological origin, which underlie the psychical systems and determine the forces of the psychological environment, particularly in the early years of life, but he never specifies psychical systems. He merely resorts to the now familiar formula: "By a process of development (which I cannot here discuss more fully) in the course of the first year of life a psychological environment is formed."

Finally one may argue that Lewin does offer directive principles for behavior in postulating that personality tends toward attainment of dynamic equilibrium, differentiation, and a happy medium between fluidity and rigidity. But what is it that is being equilibrated, differentiated, and stabilized? Or to put it bluntly, what is man? Lewin has given us a skeleton without flesh and blood, a moving skeleton perhaps—but still not a living human being. In a sense, in doing this, Lewin has achieved his ideal of a mathematical theory for psychology. His is a psychological calculus, complete with differentiation and integration, and with empty symbols as variables (6, p. 215).

The Unity of Personality. Despite this deficiency, Bronfenbrenner adopts the concepts and the framework of Lewin as the skeleton of his integrated theory. Personality structure is a hierarchical organization of psychical systems. A system is a disposition on the part of the person to respond in a particular way to selected aspects of the psychological field. The psychological field is an abstract space to which is ordered the social situation of the individual, precisely as it is perceived by the individual. Of the multitude of systems that may be engaged in any situation at any point of development, one system holds a dominating position and is relatively "strong" and enduring. This is the self-system. It is distinguishable by the rather high level of segregation from the rest of the psychic structure.

The adoption of a hierarchical organization is a distinct advance over the common atomization that hitherto has made human personality merely a congeries of acts or traits or factors, as far as the psychologist was concerned. Here is a theory that begins with the notion that personality is a unit, qualitatively heterogeneous but ordered and articulated. It would have been a longer step in advance had there been a hint in this hierarchical organization that there is an answer to the question Bronfenbrenner himself had put to Lewin : What is man? In the formulation, an important distinction is lost sight of or ignored. Personality is said to be an organization of psychical systems. But to equate personality with *dispositions* is to make it something *internal, inferred, not immediately observable.* Hence it is distinguishable from the observable personality which involves the actual activities, movements, and changes that occur. But to identify the self with one of the systems, or a group of dispositions, would be tantamount either to "reifying" each of the systems (for if one system or group of systems is a "thing" then each of the systems is a thing) ; or making the self completely actualistic in nature (i.e., making it a group of actions without an actor) as are the dynamic fields in physics. In the first case, personality loses unity and dissolves into atoms. In the second, the person gets lost in the organization of systems. The problem of unity must be faced, of course, and for sheer theoretical purposes no stricter unity need be demanded than a functional one, such as exists in the parts of a watch or an internal combustion engine or, for that matter, in a tuned electrical circuit. We must remember, however, that the theory applies to a *person.* As we pointed out earlier, psychic systems on the model of physical dynamic systems do not account for the person.

Growth by Differentiation and Integration. That Bronfenbrenner finds himself unwittingly in this dilemma is understandable enough when we reflect that he takes perception as the way in which the person structures his world and himself (6, p. 207, Note 4) and that development is a process of differentiation and integration like that found in biological organisms and physical systems (6, p. 207). If psychological development is an image of physical (biological) development then perception is psychological metabolism and differentiation is a stage in the onto-

genetic process. It seems essential to clarify this point so that
our own remarks not be misunderstood. It may be that we mistake Bronfenbrenner's meaning. If we do, then at least it will
be clear why we have done so. The usage of the terms "differentiation" and "integration" in psychological literature is am-
biguous because they are taken to describe biological and psychological functions indiscriminately. In biology, differentiation is
the emergence of a cell morphologically different from its parent,
and integration is the coalescence of such cells into tissues that
have a specific function. To confine the terms to this one meaning requires some justification, however, and to make this
biological meaning the fundamental and general meaning requires a better reason. How accurately psychological phenomena
can be described by biological terms is a matter of opinion, of
course. When we begin to investigate the fundamental nature
of psychological processes, it seems preferable not to use *meta-
phors* as if they were proper terms without making clear the
concepts which the terms are intended to convey. Context may
give a clue, but frequently enough such terms as "differentiation"
and "integration" will determine their context rather than vice
versa.

We venture to say that in the present instance it is the terms
that determine the context. In the final formulation of the theory
the dominant self-system has for its content self-other relationships. It functions as a unit to maintain a dynamic equilibrium.
This functioning is motivated by an active impulse to growth,
which is holistic and *undifferentiated*. Growth is a process
of differentiation and integration. These statements look clear
enough on the surface; it is what we would say ourselves—provided Bronfenbrenner means what we would mean by the same
terms. Does he? We think not. His orientation is Lewinian,
hence the system is *quasi*-physical, but the emphasis is on the
physical and not on the quasi. For the field theorist the *primary*
concept is always the physical dynamic system. We have already
discussed the implications of this attitude in an earlier part of
this chapter. Moreover, the system is *quasi*-biological; Lewin
expressly professes that his theory is rooted in biology. If that is
the case, then differentiation and integration are used as terms

from physics and biology. If they are biological terms, what are the implications?

Differentiation implies that the personality, and in particular the self-system, begins its career as a simple undifferentiated unit or cell. By a process of some sort of emergence the simple unit divides, changes its morphology in and by means of such "mitosis," and becomes, in its mature stage, something quite different from the initial stage, though retaining its identity throughout. This growth is provoked and paced by the physiological growth of the soma and is accomplished by the "assimilation" of the external reality in the psychological twin of feeding, which is perception.

But perception, even if we use the figure of feeding to describe it, functions in a different way from nutrition. It assimilates the environment, but its assimilation is by way of *form*, not by way of *matter*. In nutrition the food is changed into the substance of the feeder, losing its own identity in the process. In knowledge, the knower comes to possess some characteristic of the object without any change in the identity of either the knower or the known. Perception as a process depends on mature physiological structures in a healthy condition; but given the requisite conditions, it neither improves nor deteriorates as a function. If it is differentiated at all, it is differentiated in its contents. Knowledge as a function is differentiated *by the objects it reaches*, not by the representations *it constructs for itself* on the *occasion* of a sense impression.

Does the self-system (we will say nothing about personality as a whole or any of the other systems; the same considerations will apply to all) begin its career as an undifferentiated unit? Is it a bit of (psychological) protoplasm which through successive stages of morphological change reaches a definite and specialized identity? And if it does, what are the stages in its ontogenetic development? Such stages have been found and described in the biological evolution of the organism. They have not been found and have not been described in the (psychological) ontogenesis of the ego—except by extrapolation of the biological into the psychological sphere. There is no evidence that the ego is initially undifferentiated in this biological sense. The evidence that is adduced to support such a hypothesis is equivocal and can be used to support contrary if not contradictory interpretations. The ego *matures*, it is true, but no one has shown that this maturation is unequivocally *ontogenetic*. If the development of the self is ontogenetic it would have to begin with a germinal self and develop in the process of experience. In such a process, there would have to be some *function* which is developing in this manner. Now perception, the "vehicle of ego growth," could be that function; at any rate, it would be the most likely function according to the theory of perception to which Bronfenbrenner subscribes.

But surely perception is not a sort of general function that becomes differentiated into special functions like the mesenchymal cells which differentiate into connective tissue. Perception as a general term is the name of a class of capacities and their functioning; it is not the name of a generalized and undifferentiated capacity that develops into a class of specialized functions and activities. Neither is the conative-affective impulse a generalized, holistic, undifferentiated motive force that becomes differentiated in activity, as an exhalation becomes a whistle. There is no "reservoir of psychic energy" that differentiates into psychic systems. Given the requisite maturity, the infant eye will see a color properly from the beginning, though the infant may not be able to name it. His color sense will not improve by experience, though his verbal classification might. The child, given the *necessary* evidence, will make a correct judgment— for instance, the whole is bigger than any of its parts. Experience may improve the child's technique for finding the evidence, his ability for *assenting* to it will not improve. The baby will want what he sees from the time he is able to recognize it. His standards for evaluating what he sees may change; his wanting may increase or diminish as a result of changes in evaluation; but his wanting will not *improve* in function. Psychic functions are specialized from the very beginning. Dispositions to react to the environment in a specialized way are basic equipment for the human organism. We do not teach our eyes to see or our ears to hear, though we may teach ourselves what to look at or what to listen to. We do not teach our minds to understand the truth, though we may teach ourselves *what* is true and where to look for it. We do not teach our appetites how to love or hate or hope, though we may teach ourselves what to love or when to hate or where to hope. We do not "invest our environment with pleasure" and thereby learn how to enjoy it; we enjoy a pleasure-giving object and learn to seek it. The differentiation of psychic systems, if there is such differentiation, cannot be on the model of cell differentiation in biology; it is more on the model of the differentiation in the tools we use when we eat our dinner.

Integration also is used in its biological meaning. Physiologically speaking, integration implies the combination of diverse cells into a unity that is at least functional. The biologist is content to explain it by reference to metabolism and feeding which provide the material and energy for the process. When the psychologist likens perception to metabolism and feeding, and makes it the principal "vehicle" for growth, the functional unity achieved does not seem to be enough. The results of action and interaction between the person and his world will accrue to him willy-nilly; a natural process of integration, like the integration of organ systems, will *not* arrange the elements. What is implicit in psychological integration is that the elements are *properly* arranged. Bronfenbrenner recognizes this when he adopts the Rankian concept of self-determination as distinctive of the mature adult personality.

Determination and Will. Rank's contribution to the theory is the concept of will. Bronfenbrenner is careful to note that the term, even as Rank uses it, does not contain any implication that could be called unscientific (6, p. 232). Rank means by will a positive guiding organization and integration of self which creatively utilizes as well as inhibits and controls the instinctual drives. When this positive active force is added to the contents of the system, we have not only motive force but direction as well. The will, then, in the context of the theory, is a generalized impulse to integrated affective expression which is prior to growth and development and which determines what the integrated personality will be.

The prototype of the Rankian will is found in the Freudian ego; as the notion is developed by Rank and used by Bronfenbrenner, it presents certain characteristics that are not Freudian, which deserve consideration. We will examine only the characteristic of self-determination and the attribute of creativity. Rank maintains that the will itself arises as a resistance to compulsion. The compulsion may come from the outside (parental commands) or from the inside (the demands of the instincts). In any case, active willing is a resistance to these compulsions. The first level of willing is a generalized defense of the self against destruction in the conflict which is life. The second level of willing is found in the striving for a particular goal which the self sets itself to possess, from envy of and in competition with others. The highest level of willing is achieved when the self gives up comparisons, establishes its own standards, creates its own ideal, and works toward it.

The will itself goes through stages of development. On the first stage the individual accepts as his own what previously he had been forced to, either by external factors or internal drives. In this stage most of mankind are content to linger all their lives. There is no great opportunity for creativity but also not much of an occasion for conflict. On the second stage the individual wills as his own what is usually contrary to the early coercions. He feels that only that is *his own* which is contrary to someone else's will, or which is not anybody else's. Here of course there is opportunity for creativity, since this stage is one where conflict is constant. It is on this stage that neurotics remain once they have arrived there. The third and highest stage is reached when the individual has created an autonomous inner world for himself which bears no resemblance to outer reality because it is the result of the creative encroachment of the individual upon the external world. At this stage the will is completely autonomous and must seek satisfaction and release in the creation and projection of a world of its own. For Rank (and interpretatively for Bronfenbrenner) self-determination is equivalent to complete autonomy. This stage is achieved in the genius, or some other extraordinary individual. The ordinary normal individual reaches only that stage of growth where he accepts as his own the "slings and arrows of outrageous fortune." The neurotic is superior to the normal individual since he has reached the second stage, but he is unable or unwilling to attain the third.

It would seem, then, that the kind of self-determination that is the ordinary and normal endowment of the great mass of mankind is no self-determination at all. Hobson's choice is a choice if one wants to call it such, but one exhausts all one's courtesy giving it that name. Similarly, the neurotic choices of the second stage which may lead to genius or neurosis, as the case may be, do not of themselves determine the result—unless, of course, the choices are creative *because* they are *contrary* to accepted norms or real standards. In that case, creativity comes perilously close to mere contrariness.

The creative encroachment that leads to self-determination is the achievement of extremely few, it would seem, and these few all live in a world of their own. This is not very encouraging to the vast majority of human beings, ourselves included, who try to keep in touch with reality, both physical and social, and who try to determine life and action according to the reasonable requirements of both. Bronfenbrenner, of course, is inclined to the Rankian notion of creativity from the very theory of perception he accepts. For him, the creative individual must build his ego-ideal from factors which he not only chooses for himself but fabricates for himself. That is why he is so much taken with Lewin's "planes of unreality" and Rank's "illusions."

Tolerance for Unreality. Tolerance for unreality is considered one of the optimal conditions for personality growth in its shift to fluid structure in the interpersonal field. But what can "unreality" mean in the context of perception theory as it is presented? In principle, the theory holds that all perceptions are fabrications. Any exact correspondence between what perception fabricates and what actually is, apart from perception, is entirely *per accidens*. In the theory we find no criterion as to what is real and what is not. What is going to give us the "veridical" universe according to which we can calibrate our perceptions? Pointer readings on a galvanometer? Correlations in a statistical table? The experimenter's knowledge of what the distorted room *really* looks like? *Quis custodiet custodes?*

Zeal for "homogenizing" the domain of psychology and erasing the boundaries between the normal and abnormal has led to obscuring the difference in psychological efficacy between the real and the unreal. Just so, in the case of the theory of perception adopted by Bronfenbrenner, the "veridical" universe and utter paranoia are only asymptotic parameters of essentially the same perceptive process. If the "plane of unreality" is to be a dimension either of psychological structure or of the forces that influence development, what discriminates it as a dimension must be found in it and not in the process of perception. To lay dreams, fantasies, whims, reveries, ambitions, plans, delusions, hallucinations, illusions, and erroneous judgments along the same scale can be done, of course. But to say no more about their psychological effect than that they are all unreal, and as such must be taken into account, does not help very much to clarifiy them as "valences" or to understand their function in personality development. Quite apart from any judgment the perceiver may make, what is simply imagined because it is not present, though it exists, will surely have a different psychological effect from what is simply imaginary because it is impossible of actualization. Tolerance for unreality is necessary, to be sure, but tolerance for what kind of unreality? My believing in last summer's rain or next winter's snow is a tolerance of unreality (in Lewin's sense) but is it no better or worse for personality growth than believing in dehydrated water or solid postholes? If the kind of relation that exists between the planes of reality and unreality "is decisive of all creative behavior," surely that relation cannot be merely ease of passage from one to the other. What is necessary before this ease of passage will be of any avail psychologically is that the environmental situation be perceptible *as it is*. Otherwise there will be no plane of reality the person can go from or return to, and he will be forever imprisoned in the plane of unreality and wind up as a schizophrenic or paranoid.

We are well aware that our review of Bronfenbrenner's position cannot be definitive just as it was not comprehensive.

Bronfenbrenner himself warned us that he was giving but the bare bones of a conceptual framework. We have sketched some of the ground that produced his concepts. We know that these concepts will be refined and perfected in the course of Bronfenbrenner's program of research. We venture to predict that before the research is completed it will discover not only a human personality but a human person who in all the vicissitudes of life somehow is pointing toward a single goal, which he does not invent but discovers, in his concept of human destiny.

COMMENT

Whether or not the preceding criticism of current theories is acceptable, it is at best a negative undertaking. To provide a positive working out of the principles underlying this critique obviously goes beyond the limits of an editorial comment. The next chapter will provide such a positive theory of personality and strive to fulfill the requirements laid down in Chapter 2 and Chapter 4.

REFERENCES

1. ALEXANDER, FRANZ. 1948. *Fundamentals of psychoanalysis.* New York: W. W. Norton & Co., Inc.
2. ARNON, DANIEL I., and WHATLEY, F. R. 1949. Is chloride a co-enzyme of photogenesis? *Science,* 1949, **110,** 554–56.
3. BEATTIE, D. M. 1949. The effect of imaginary practice on the acquisition of a motor skill. Unpublished Master's thesis, University of Toronto.
4. BELL, E. T. 1945. *The development of mathematics.* New York: McGraw-Hill Book Co., Inc.
5. BERGMANN, GUSTAV. 1951. The logic of psychological concepts. *Phil. Sci.,* 1951, **18,** 93–110.
6. BLAKE, ROBERT R., and RAMSEY, GLENN V. (eds.), 1951. *Perception, An approach to personality.* New York: The Ronald Press Co.
7. BROWN, J. F. 1936. On the use of mathematics in psychological theory. *Psychometrika,* 1936, **1,** 77–90.
8. CANNON, WALTER B. 1939. *The wisdom of the body.* New York: W. W. Norton & Co., Inc.
9. GARVER, ENID. Unpublished research. Bryn Mawr College, Bryn Mawr, Pa.
10. GELLHORN, E. 1943. *Autonomic regulations.* New York: Interscience Publishers, Inc.
11. GOLDSTEIN, KURT. 1939. *The Organism.* New York: American Book Co.

12. GOLDSTEIN, KURT. 1940. *Human nature in the light of psychopathology.* Cambridge: Harvard University Press.
13. KELLER, HELEN. 1917. *The story of my life.* New York: Doubleday & Co., Inc.
14. LECKY, PRESCOTT. 1945. *Self-consistency.* New York: Island Press.
15. LEWIN, KURT. 1935. *A dynamic theory of personality.* New York: McGraw-Hill Book Co., Inc.
16. ————. 1936. *Principles of topological psychology.* New York: McGraw-Hill Book Co., Inc.
17. MARX, MELVIN HERMAN (ed.). 1951. *Psychological theory, contemporary readings.* Chapter by K. W. Spence, The nature of theory construction in contemporary psychology. Reprinted from *Psychol. Rev.,* 1944, **51,** 47–68. Copyright by American Psychological Association, Washington, D. C. New York: The Macmillan Co.
18. MICHOTTE, ALBERT E. 1950. The emotions regarded as functional connections. In: *Feelings and emotions: The Mooseheart Symposium.* (ed.) MARTIN L. REYMERT. New York: McGraw-Hill Book Co., Inc.
19. NORTHROP, F. S. C. 1948. The neurological and behavioristic psychological basis of the ordering of society by means of ideas. *Science,* 1948, **107,** 411–17.
20. Symposium on operationism. 1945. *Psychol. Rev.,* 1945, **52,** 241–94.
21. VANDELL, R. A., DAVIS, R. A., and CLUGSTON, H. A. 1943. The function of mental practice in the acquisition of motor skills. *J. gen. Psychol.,* 1943, **29,** 243–50.
22. WIENER, NORBERT. 1948. *Cybernetics, or control and communication in the animal and the machine.* New York: John Wiley & Sons.
23. WITTGENSTEIN, LUDWIG. 1933. *Tractatus Logico-Philosophicus.* New York: Harcourt, Brace & Co., Inc.

Chapter 6

PERSONALITY THEORY: A FORMULATION OF GENERAL PRINCIPLES

By J. A. GASSON, S. J.

IN OUR discussion of the concept of theory in science we concluded that a theory is an insight into the necessary relationships that exist between all the objects of a field of knowledge, couched in a statement that expresses that relationship. This insight is to be concerned with real things—not figments of the imagination or fictions of the mind, nor symbols in an equation, nor just words in a syntactical context. The statement is to express what is and how it changes, in a few hypotheses which are capable of being developed to account for what actually happens. These hypotheses are not to be chosen arbitrarily like the axioms of a hyperspatial geometry but are immediately inferred from experience, observation, or experiment as a tentative explanation that will "save the phenomena." The explanation will strive to include all the phenomena belonging to it, and only those. So a psychological theory will be neither a hyperphysics nor a hypomathematics but will deal with psychological events in a psychological way according to their psychological aspects.

Basic Postulates

Let us begin, then, by making explicit the concepts that comprise our basic systematic outlook—reveal our hidden assumptions, as they say. Our first postulate is that of epistemological realism, a moderate and immediate realism. We call it a postulate, not because it is arbitrarily or gratuitously assumed but because we can find it justified elsewhere and so need not establish its validity here. Nor do we take it as a premise from which we will draw conclusions. The "postulates" we list here will be used only as negative norms or guides in the understanding of our subject matter. We take our stand on an immediate realism because we do not wish to condemn ourselves to that sort of intellectual vegetarianism in the life of learning which the logical positivists so ardently recommend—especially since they insist that only their hydroponic diet is fit for consumption.

We take for granted that in dealing with personality we are dealing with something that is real and that can be discovered by us. Our knowledge is not something which is constructed purely and simply out of our own "creative minds." Neither is our world. We find our world; we do not make it. And the knowledge we gain in our discovery is valid only in so far as it reflects faithfully what we find. Truth is not primarily a matter of logic but a matter of conformity with what is. And knowledge which reflects truth, though it may be increased by logic, does not begin in it.

Our second fundamental postulate is that the person is an *original* unit; that is, a single undivided substance, distinct from other substantial units in the universe. Hence a human being is not an aggregate of heterogeneous substances (like the snakes and snails and puppy dogs' tails that little boys are made of) which are his physical components, nor is he merely a conglomerate of qualitative properties and actions. The psychological self is as much an undivided substantial unit as any transcendental Ego. What is of prime interest for the psychologist is not the substantiality of the self but its diverse activities. Thus the person, remaining single, undivided, and substantially the same in the midst of a static and dynamic heterogeneity of properties and states, is subject to variation which is qualitative and *accidental*. This term we use in a strictly technical sense. Thus a human being has arms and legs and head and skin and bones and blood and tears but we would not say that these parts together *constitute* the human being—as if these things were complete entities in their own right and the person only an aggregate of them. The human being is a whole which may be divided into these parts. In the same way, stature, temperament, wisdom, humor, sociability, introversion, and the like are attributes of a person, but it is the person who possesses them, not they which constitute the person.

Third, we maintain that the human person is different in kind from other living organisms, not merely more complicated or more highly differentiated. The complexity of the human organism is a *consequence* of humanness, because the human being is essentially on a higher level. We judge this superiority by the specific properties which show him to be able to rise above the passive determinability of bodies in physical nature and also above the determination of activities imposed upon the plant and brute animal by the environment. This does not mean that the human being is entirely emancipated from the laws of physics and biology (among others) but that the human being has degrees of freedom above the rest of the organic world, just as organisms have degrees of freedom above inanimate things.

We suppose, then, that there is an essential difference between spontaneity and self-determination. Spontaneity is completely compatible with rigid determinism. Goals, whether recognized as such or not, initiate spontaneous movement in the organism once they are known; given the perceived goal and the animal (without any other external intervening factors) the animal can no more hold itself from moving goalward than my watch can suspend itself in the air when I drop it. There is purposiveness in spontaneous activity, but that sort of purposiveness has different characteristics from the purposiveness of self-determination. In spontaneous activity the animal achieves a purpose which nature imposes upon him; in self-determined action the person sets the purpose for himself. In parenthesis it may be added that both spontaneity and self-determination imply a system of acting factors of such a nature that they do not merely *react* to external stimulation but can initiate action on their own. (The reaction meant here is, of course, the reaction mentioned in the third law of motion in mechanics. For this reason we prefer to speak of the *action* of living organisms consequent upon a stimulus rather than a *reaction to* a stimulus. Contemporary psychology has not as yet unloaded the burden of mechanism from the term "reaction.")

Lastly we assume that the lower orders of organization are present in higher organisms virtually but not actually or formally. The higher organism can achieve results which lower organisms achieve, but they need not operate in exactly the same way: the human being grows and nourishes himself, but the vegetative processes of growth and nourishment do not constitute a separate plant organism in the human being. This need not be taken to imply that the human being assimilates his food by thinking or simply willing it, but it does mean that the level at which the human being functions is to be judged not by the bottom but by the top grade of his activities. This principle of virtuality is the most efficacious way of correlating phenomena in human behavior with functions in lower-level organisms without running into antinomies and inconsistencies. It is a principle which is operative throughout all natural phenomena; at present it is a powerful tool for the physicist in explaining quantum phenomena hitherto unamenable to systematization.

Basic Definitions

Since our theory is to be comprehensive, designed to include all the phenomena of personality, the problem immediately arises as to what the real things are which we are going to try explaining. The unity of the person is made apparent by a distinctive configuration or constellation of activities which is proper to and characteristic of the individual and thus indicates his uniqueness and individuality. What is revealed by this distinctive pattern of activities is what we mean by the term "personality." This pattern which shows the personality in action implies an agent who acts in an organized way through his capacities, powers, and habits. Personality is the work of a person.

Since the object of our inquiry is the psychological organization of personality, physiological and physical factors are not our chief concern. This does not mean the the person's physiological activities or the physical effects of the environment do not affect his behavior, nor does it mean that his behavior is a segment of his total living, somehow split off from the rest of his activities and independent of them. It *does* mean that our primary concern is with psychology, so physical and physiological factors will concern us only in so far as they are also psychological experiences.

Psychologists are not all agreed as to what could be defined as psychological, particularly if it is to be distinguished from physical and physiological. We are all well aware of the manner in which early psychologists tended more and more to become purely physiological in the treatment and subject matter of what they called psychology. It seems advisable, therefore, to clarify the notion of what is psychological so as to eliminate some of the confusion that spontaneously arises whenever the term is used.

If a return to elementary semantics will be pardoned, we may use as our point of departure the root meaning of the term "psyche." Historically, *psychological* referred to those activities and characteristics which involved the soul, or that principle which differentiated living organisms from inanimate nature. Now the basic properties of living things enable them to perform such functions as nutrition and growth. Nutrition and growth are, however, principally in the domain of physiology, so that very soon even historically *psychological* as an adjective was restricted to those functions of living beings which are on a higher level than nutrition and growth, namely, the functions of sense perception, sensory feelings, emotion, and similar activities.

It is interesting to note that the activities of the living being, though originating within it and designed for its welfare and enhancement, are all in some way or another concerned with an object which is distinct from and often enough separate from it, and have for their term some kind of union and assimilation between the active living being and the object toward which this activity is directed. In nutrition, for example, the function is concerned with some material, food, that is to be taken in and assimilated by the organism. The formal function of nutrition is contained in the process of changing the substance of the food into the substance of the living being.

On a higher level this same concern with objects other than the active organism can be discerned. In the process of sense knowledge some *formal* characteristic or quality of the known object is brought in and assimilated by the knower in a distinctive way. In vision, for example, it is not the material of the visible object that is taken in or apprehended by the looker, but precisely that quality which renders the visible object visible (electromagnetic energy reflected or radiated at frequencies that lie within the range of the visible spectrum). So also, in emotional activity, particularly if it is largely on the sensory level, we find that there is a reaching out for some object which has already been united to the subject by means of a perceptual process. This reaching out is toward what is called affective union and tends toward a possession of the object complementary to that achieved in knowledge.

It would seem, then, that activities in which "the soul" is characteristically concerned always include some reference to or occupation with an object other than the active organism. Since occupation with the other in the process of nutrition is completely on the physical and physiological level, we can exclude it from what we propose to call the strictly psychological. The strictly psychological, then, will refer to the activities of knowing and wanting which are aimed toward the other. Hence *psychological*, in the proper sense of the term, means *having cognitive and affective aspects*.

Knowing and Wanting as Psychological Activities

When we speak of psychological activities, we refer primarily to cognitive and affective activities in the proper sense of the term, that is, knowing and wanting. There are, however, activities which are characteristic of the human being which are not themselves either knowing or wanting, but which are the outcome of knowledge and emotion. Implicit in affective union is the physical possession of what we know and want. Therefore external actions which lead to such possessions are psychological. Similarly, wanting or desiring is not only felt but expressed in look or posture; therefore, emotional expression is psychological.

To illustrate the connection between knowing, wanting, and external action, let us recall Kant's famous example of the difference between knowing and having twenty dollars. A man who knows about twenty dollars possesses them in a cognitive way, in imagination or memory. This mode of possession is quite different from having twenty dollars in his pocket. He may want twenty dollars, and that wanting includes wanting to have them in his pocket or at least available for use. He is affectively inclined, then, to acquire them so that they will be in his pocket. Some external action is required for that; but whatever it is, a day's work or merely cashing a check, this action has a psychological aspect because it is rooted in his previous cognitive and affective activity. *Behavior*, then, is psychological only in so far as it stems from previous cognitive or affective activity.

Cognitive union with the other can be achieved on several levels. It may involve only the act of sense knowledge without any complex organization of the cognitive experience. It may go further and involve not only meaning and organization but some sort of abstraction from sense data, and require conceptualization, judgment, and reasoning. It is important to point out that, in speaking of cognitive activity on the sensory level, we are not referring to sensation as it is ordinarily understood. Most psychologists would say that sensation is the assimilation of *sense data*; but surely that function of acquiring and assimilating sense data belongs to the external senses. There is, however, a sensory function which assimilates the *object* which gives rise to the complex of sense data. This function of assimilating sensory wholes does not belong to the external senses but is a sense function which uses external sensations as its primary data. We can call it the *integrating sense* because it assembles the separate sense qualities into a single object.

There is considerable evidence for such an inference. Hebb, for instance, points out that a figure on a background

. . . is seen as one, unified and distinct from its surroundings, by any normal person, by the congenitally blind on the first occurrence of vision following operation for cataract, by the normal rat, and apparently also at first vision by the rat that has been reared in darkness. The unity and distinctiveness of such figures from their background, then, is independent of experience, or "primitive" (11, pp. 19–20).

Moreover, such perception of shape seems actually to mean the primitive perception of an *object* rather than of a *design*. Lashley, for instance reports:

> It is almost impossible to train . . . [the rat] to jump to a single figure of less than 2 cm in diameter. . . . This great reluctance to jump to small figures is unexplained. . . . Much of the behavior of the rat with the jumping apparatus suggests that the figure is not a symbol indicating the correct card but is an *object upon which he jumps*. With solid figures most animals strike the center of the figure or claw at its upper margin, and the refusal to jump to small figures may be a result of this identification of the figure with the landing place (14, p. 171. Italics mine).

Thus we seemingly experience prior to all learning not isolated sensations but external objects.[1] In that case, William James's much quoted statement that the infant experiences nothing but a "buzzing, booming confusion" is seriously in need of revision. Indeed, if William James were right, how could it ever occur to the infant (and still less to the rat reared in darkness) that the various sensations he can distinguish, of color, hardness, roughness, pain, are evoked by one and the same thing?

Schilder, one of the few modern psychologists who have tackled this problem, suggests that the object is "constructed" by our movements toward it. He says:

> One may even go a step further and say that the sense datum does not exist without its motor responses and the motor response is common to all senses. . . . The intersensory connection is, therefore, to a great extent dependent on actual motility, or, still better, on action, and only this perpetual trial and error process determines the final unit of action. . . . This final unit of action is the object (23, p. 175).

We may legitimately ask how a motor response could ever be made before there is an object to respond to. Isolated sensations are not localized in external space. Vision alone gives us

[1] Cf. Gibson's recent statement: "There is overwhelming evidence to show that solid vision is primary and that plane vision is acquired only with training and by adopting a special attitude. The impression of a visual *world* may well prove to have a straightforward explanation; the impression of a visual *field,* however, is a very sophisticated kind of seeing and its explanation is far from being simple" (8, p. 405).

no more than patches of color; hearing, diffuse sounds; touch, a sensation at some spot on the body surface. To make any response in the direction of the object, there must first be a perception of an *object*, not of a series of isolated sensations.

For the sake of economy we can say that such integrative sensory functions are performed by the imagination. And by imagination we mean an internal sense which has among its functions the production of images of objects either present in sensory experience or apart from it. This sense function need not include either reminiscence or creative imagination because these involve higher level processes. It is true, of course, that we find imagination in the human being seldom if ever as a pure sense function.

In man, imaginative activity nearly always deals with images and meanings which are the result of reasoning and understanding. But in the brute animal we need not postulate anything beyond sheer associative recall and spontaneous revival of past events. For this reason, we classify imagination as a sensory function which uses external sensations to picture the object which evoked them here and now, and which again pictures the object known in the past when a present experience recalls it. Moreover, in the animal the cognitive union and the affective activity to which it leads (his knowing and wanting) are aimed at the relatively few natural goals toward which he is oriented and which he knows and wants only in their sensory aspects. After all, when the animal is not interfered with by man and subordinated to human use or whim, his activity centers around those objects which will provide him with physical survival and afford the propagation of the species.

The human being, however, even when he finds himself in rather straitened circumstances, looks to his environment to provide him with values other than physical and species survival. The environment of the human being offers not only objects but meanings which are above and beyond sheer physical nature. Human society, of course, is engaged in acquiring the means of livelihood and in propagating the race, but the activities which are characteristically human involve such things of the spirit as art, science, democracy, human welfare. For human beings, the cognitive union reaches those aspects of objects and persons in which the individual can find his own proper enhancement. The human being is interested in food but also in table manners. He is interested in a mate but also in friendship. He is interested in conviviality but also in social cooperation. The human being must possess a distinctive capacity for assimilating these nonmaterial aspects of his environment in a cognitive way. By the same token, he is impelled affectively to acquire these nonmaterial values for himself.

This affective relationship of man to his environment is of singular importance, for it originates and implements the outward actions by which he intends to achieve his general and his specific goal. The pattern of these outward actions, the striving they actualize, the affective impulses accompanying his striving, and the organized knowledge at the root of his wanting, comprise the psychological elements out of which the personality is formed. It is these psychological elements which we must examine and explain in a psychological theory of personality. More specifically, it is the active character of the sources of human behavior that must be accounted for in our theory. External activity (behavior) may be evoked by events in the environment, but what makes the individual behave in a distinctive pattern or in any kind of pattern at all can be understood only in terms of his knowing and wanting, which are antecedent to outward action though consequent upon the impact of man's environment. Any psychological theory of personality must account for the active character of man's relationship to his environment if it is to be a theory of human personality and a theory of personality dynamics.[2]

[2] It might be just as well to remark here that any resemblance between our conception of personality dynamics and Freudian or neo-Freudian concepts is purely coincidental. Quite apart from the terms used to name them, our concept of the driving forces of human personality is derived from ideas extant in psychology a millenium and a half before Freud. The theory of powers, the principle of finality, the theory of unconscious orexis, were propounded by Aristotle. We have developed the implications of Aristotle's unconscious orexis (the Scholastics called it *appetitus naturalis* as distinguished from *appetitus elicitus*) in conjunction with the principle of finality. That the results of this development account for phenomena which psychoanalysts have claimed as their discovery does in no way indicate an intellectual or genetic dependence on Freud.

The Active Character of Human Behavior

Impulse and Urge. If we analyze the concept of active power as we have been using it, we shall find that it contains implicitly a relationship between the person having the power and the object toward which it tends. This relationship becomes actual when the power functions. We express this relationship in the very definition of an active power, for in the definition of every function the term of the function is necessarily included. So we define the visual power as the capacity to see and we define the function of seeing as the cognitive assimilation of the color qualities of objects.

At this point it might be advisable to state what we mean by a power or capacity. Powers are not separate entities within us which function separately. They are the capacities we have of functioning in various ways with regard to various objects. The human being is substantially a unit, but he does not function immediately by his substance. His activities are not substances. He functions through powers that are properties of his substance, and these powers are specified by the activities they perform. The only way in which we can distinguish activities is by observing the properties of the objects at which the activity aims. We know the difference between seeing and hearing not by examining the functions themselves but by examining the properties of the objects which we reach by seeing and hearing. When an object is seen, it comes to us through the quality and pattern of color; when the same object is heard, it comes to us by vibrations which it sets up in the ear. It is the same object acting upon us, but it acts by different modalities of its energy. It does not produce the sensations but stimulates the person to produce sensations of seeing, hearing, smelling, tasting, etc.

There is, of course, a necessary hierarchy in the powers of the human being. Some activities are of a lower order, some are of a higher order. We know that the particular function which organizes our behavior and makes it something characteristically human is the capacity for intelligent free choice. Therefore, intelligently determined choice and decision are high level human functions and organize lower level functions. In using our intelligence, we depend on imagination to supply the material from which we abstract concepts. Our imagination does not and cannot function unless external sense experience first provides the material. Sensation and imagination and the affective experience connected with them are lower order psychological activities; but as psychological activities they are on a plane higher than the nutritive, reproductive, or reparatory capacities. Vegetative functions are superior to mere gravitational and inertial actions. Hence we have a gradation from gravitation which man has in common with all bodies, to growth and reproduction which he has in common with the smaller community of living bodies, to sensation, imagination, and affectivity which he has in common with the still smaller community of the animal kingdom, to reason and self-determination which only human beings possess.

It is a commonplace of metaphysics that all active powers have a natural inclination to go into activity when their object is present and the conditions are favorable. This inclination is not something added to these functions but is in their very nature, for it is related to their act and object. In the human being this natural inclination to action is not a passive orientation of his capacities to their proper objects but an impulse to action, capable of itself to move the person in a certain direction, though it may require some external stimulus to trigger it off. This bent toward action is found in all human capacities, cognitive and motor as well as appetitive functions, not only on the sensory but also on the intellectual level. If this native impulse to act were not present, these functions could never start moving at all.

This tendency can and sometimes does come into awareness. A little reflection will make clear to us that there is present in us, for instance, an impulse to focus on any object that comes into our field of vision. Moreover, we frequently find that there is not only an impulse to see but also a tendency to *look* for something to see; not only an impulse to hear, but also a tendency to *listen*. Though these two modalities are in themselves the same tendency, they deserve to be differentiated as modalities. When

the object of any function is present and activity is free and unhindered, the felt tendency of the function to go into action we
call *impulse*. When the object is not present, or when activity
is hampered or constrained, the inclination to action is felt more
intensely. When we enter a dark room, we not only look to see
but we peer into the darkness. Let us call this heightened impulse "urge."

The terms "impulse" and "urge" are not altogether satisfactory. They have been used in such a variety of contexts and
meanings (even in psychology) that our use may easily be misunderstood or misinterpreted. So far, our search for more appropriate terms has been fruitless. In Latin *nisus* would do nicely
for impulse; in fact it is the traditional term used to express the
appetitus naturalis of inanimate bodies; but a term to express the
heightened intensity of impulse is wanting. *Connisus*, as an intensive of *nisus*, would be apt but might distress the purists. *Impetus* is a poor second choice. Recourse to the Greek does not
help much. *Orexis* and *synorexis* would be a satisfactory pair,
but the one has long since been devoted to *elicited* appetite, and
the other is a neologism pure and simple. *Horme* and *hormesis*
suggested themselves; but *horme* has long since been taken out
of the public domain by McDougall and *hormesis* would be an
orphan without *horme*.

The concepts we wish to express have been very well described by McDougall:

> When we are suddenly incited to effort, when some tendency is
> suddenly brought into play, we feel, we say, an impulse to do this or
> that. And, if we find it impossible to take appropriate action, we
> nevertheless experience the working of the tendency as what we call
> *desire*; we contemplate the goal towards which we are impelled, the
> object towards which the tendency sets, and, in contemplating it, we
> are aware of the tendency towards it. These experiences of striving,
> of impulse, of desire, are experiences of activity common to, and in-
> dicative of, the strong working of all tendencies.
>   . . . It is when for any reason we are compelled to postpone or
> suspend action that the aroused tendency asserts itself most clearly in
> consciousness. In such cases we use a number of words to express it;
> we say we long, or crave, we wish for, or have an appetite for, or

an inclination, or urge, or impulse towards, that goal towards which we tend (17, p. 117).

We finally chose the terms "impulse" and "urge" because *impulse* carries the meaning of "simple incitement to action," while *urge* can denote an intense impulsion because of its meaning of "impelling strongly or urgently." *Urge* seems a better choice than *drive* (which also carries the meaning of strong impulsion) because it implies vital action. "Drive" has consistently been used in psychology whenever the impulsion was meant to imply mechanical action.

Self-Actuation. Impulse and urge account for the innate motive power in single functions. In addition, some factor is needed which will account for the organization or integration of these activities to form some recognizable unit or pattern. This organizing factor, of course, is also active and must, therefore, be a specification or specialization of the same native tendencies which we have called impulse and urge. In the human person, as we know from experience and observation, the active powers do not operate in a unified and harmonious way if they are left to themselves. If there is a pattern, we know that the distinctive characteristics of that pattern have been arranged by the individual himself. In clinical practice we often meet patients whose lives seem to be lived almost entirely at random. We can find some segmental patterns, for their individual actions are not completely isolated, but these segments do not form a rational whole because in them the single powers are left to follow their natural bent regardless of any total pattern. Randomness can be excluded only if a single direction is given which orders all our activities (or the major part of them) and keeps them from being at cross purposes. In the human being it is the person himself who sets this direction and achieves this harmony. The instrument of such active direction is the will, which itself is activated by *impulse* and *urge*. Let us study this tendency now in its *natural* or *unconscious* dynamism.

We can discover the basic modes in which man by choice patterns his complex activities by observing the behavior of mankind as a whole. We shall find that the characteristic which distinguishes human behavior is the continuing striving to better one's self. This is not simply the basic orientation of being as being to achieve its own proper level of perfection, or rather, it is this basic orientation specified by the distinctive properties of the human being. Beings other than man have a definite limit, both in kind and in extent, to their potentialities and their possibilities of actuation. Man's perfectibility is indefinite in extent and embraces the capacity to actualize within himself, in his knowledge, the properties of all things. Thus there is in the human person not only the native bent to exercise his active functions; he is also capable of exercising these functions in an integrated and harmonious way so that he acts as a smoothly functioning unit. Hence there is a bipolar direction in impulse and urge: toward the outside, the tendency to assimilate all the qualities of the person's environment in an ordered and integrated way, and toward the inside a basic tendency to enrich the self so that it is continually pointed to perfection beyond the limits set by any present situation, and continually impelled to progress beyond these limits. This self-actuation implies not only the exercise of the person's inner active functions and capacities but also the appropriation of external reality as such.

The self-actuation we speak of here is clearly quite different from the self-actuation discussed by Rogers and Goldstein (see our discussion, page 147 ff.). For both these authors, self-actuation is essentially a natural unfolding, such as is found in other living things. For us it is a specific actuation of potentialities peculiar to the human being, which contains biological unfolding but goes beyond it. Self-actuation in this sense is peculiar not only to the human species but to the individual as well. (As is clear, our formulation is an extension and application of the theory of potency and act.)

Self-Actuation by Possession and Stabilization. Self-actuation, then, is achieved by the bipolar mode of action of impulse and urge: one movement toward *possession*, reaching out toward external reality to make one's own whatever may be valuable or desirable in it; the other, toward enhancement through that possession by stabilizing it and making certain of that stability, for momentary possession does not enrich the self. Hence psychological stabilization means not only possession but permanence of it. This permanence depends to a great extent on the social nature of human life. Our lives are not lived in isolation. From the first moments of our awareness, we come more and more to realize that we live in the midst of a social group. We cannot establish ourselves in secure possession of anything or anyone (not even of ourselves) until we are sure that the members of our social group will not only acknowledge our title to our possessions but respect it. From the subjective side psychological stabilization means establishing the self in and through what it possesses, for the building up of self is the term of acquisition and stabilization; if the psychological self, as it is enlarged by appropriation from the external environment, is labile, then the acquisition of these added qualities is neither rewarding nor permanent. The self can become stable only if it assimilates its possessions and so, becoming enhanced, it can add new ones to its integrated unity.

That the psychological self can only become stabilized by integrating each successive stage in its development so that it will form a firm basis to which new possessions can accrue may be illustrated by an analogy with tree grafting. In grafting, the new slip is not merely inserted into the bark which is the outer integument of the tree—the bark is penetrated and the slip is inserted into the outer layer of the wood of the tree, which is its latest growth. The self can be compared to a tree in so far as each successive year's growth is represented by the outermost layer of new wood, which in turn becomes the base for the new growth.

The comparison limps, of course, because the tree grows by changing what the environment offers into its own substance and matter, while the personality assimilates only the qualities of the environment in a psychological way, by means of knowing, wanting, understanding. But at least the comparison brings out an architectonic feature in the structure of the self as it grows psychologically. Until and unless the new acquisitions become firmly united and integrated into the self growing by appropriation, these new gains are labile and impermanent and may be lost or at least not utilized adequately. While the new gains remain labile the person, under stress of one kind or another, may revert to earlier and by now outworn modes of stabilization which will not give real vitality to what the self acquires. Grafting into the heartwood of the rootstock is never successful.

This reversion or regression to outworn modes of stabilization can be illustrated by a thousand and one examples in ordinary life as well as by innumerable instances drawn from clinical material. The progress made by a student in any science mirrors not only the general modalities of growth but may also illustrate reversions. A mathematics major may, for instance, progress satisfactorily through theory of equations, calculus, and differential equations, but his progress will be real only as far as he derives and understands the fundamental theorems. What he understands of each successive theorem serves as the base upon which his understanding of further derivations is built. Suppose now he comes to a difficulty in differential equations which he cannot solve because he has not fully understood .(assimilated) a theorem in calculus. To solve his problem he reverts to algebra. This may or may not be of help, but in any case it is not the effective or advanced way of procedure.

Self-Actuation in Doing, Making, Sharing. The actualization of the self, however, is achieved not only by receiving or acquiring from the external environment. The self not only reaches out to unite to itself all that reality offers but it also goes out in using the external world to change it for its own individual purposes. This going out reaches its highest plane when these changes give external expression to the self in its uniqueness, and thus give the peopled environment a share in the self. This outgoing is the dynamic root of the characteristic of the human being which we express by the phrase *homo faber*.

Surely such a distinctively human feature merits some attention from psychologists. It is not the *use* of the environment that is humanly distinctive, for all organisms must use the environment for survival as individuals or as a species. Nor is it peculiar to man that his use *changes* the environment, for feeding and burrowing and nest-building also change physical nature. What is distinctive of human doing and making is that the human being is *psychologically responsible* for what he makes. As Nuttin * puts it in a more general context: "Man intervenes intentionally in his own development in order to actualize higher potentialities . . . in other words, . . . man can know himself and reflect on what he is going to do, in order to *give* a meaning to a situation and his own activity" (22, p. 346. Nuttin's italics).

We should like to discuss this concept of psychological responsibility and contrast it with the notion of *man the doer* current in psychological literature.

In a recent book, Cantril attempts a theoretical formulation of human experience by giving a systematic account of *homo faber*. The broad view he takes of humanity, however, leads him to pay more attention to Man the Inventor over long sweeps of geological time than to Man the Maker during the waking hours of the solar day. For Cantril,† the humanity of man is found in his capacity "to sense value attributes in his experience and to seek an enhancement of these value attributes through participation in new situations. The standard of value attributes each person uses is influenced by his own unique biological and life history" (3, p. 40). Cantril believes that only by introducing these particular concepts will it be possible to give an intrinsically reasonable account of man's experience. He admits that his concepts look metaphysical today, but tomorrow's scientific progress will show them to be entirely acceptable.

For "objectivist" readers, Cantril's formulations must be not a little puzzling. What does he mean by "metaphysical," for instance? Whatever it is, it must be something unworthy of a true scientist. He ventures to be metaphysical and hopes that his concepts will become unmetaphysical in the course of time. Cantril's metaphysics are a little puzzling. Let us concentrate, for instance, on the "value attributes" which man "senses." Cantril subscribes to Whitehead's notion of value: "Value is the word I use for the intrinsic reality of an event"

---

* By permission from *Feelings and Emotions: The Mooseheart Symposium*, edited by M. L. Reymert. Copyright 1950, McGraw-Hill Book Company, Inc.

† Quotations from Hadley Cantril, *The "Why" of Man's Experience.* Copyright 1950. By permission of The Macmillan Company.

(24, p. 131). But for Whitehead the intrinsic reality of an event is intrinsic neither to reality nor to the event but to the experiencer to whom the event happens. Moreover, the event is not something that happens *to* an experiencer, it is something that happens *in* him. An event is the "grasping into unity of a pattern of aspects" (24, p. 174).

The capacity to "sense value attributes," then, really ought to read : "the capacity to sense the intrinsic reality of a grasping into unity of a pattern of aspects in experience." For what can "sensing" mean in this context? It surely does not mean looking at or listening to or touching something. It could not mean surmising or being vaguely aware of something, as when we have a "sense of familiarity" in a strange place or when meeting a stranger. Guessing surely is not the most perfect human act. Nor can it mean being sure that there is value in the situation being lived through. Perceptions like that too often die aborning—witness any teacher who has tried to sell the adventure of learning to a last period class on Friday afternoon. If any vibrant meaning is to "emerge" from "sense" it must surely connote not only clearness of perception and certainty of knowledge but also appreciation and the joy of personal possession. But such an interpretation would hardly fit Cantril's context.

When Cantril explains artifacts and their consequences, the scientific metaphysics he employs enables him to discover an engaging kind of *homo faber*. It is Man the Inventor that appears on the scene. The evolutionary development of that marvelous mechanism, the hand, permitted man to make his first tool. From this emerged man's capacity to inquire, think, and plan. This led to intellectualizing and abstracting and the formation of reliable judgments. This in turn brought about the ability to make value judgments. And from here the cycle starts over again : Value judgments increased man's ability to invent, his inventions made him better able to plan, etc. "Since early times man's conscious attempt to devise tools of one kind or another in order to carry out his purposes has accelerated its pace" (3, p. 42). Man's development, however, was not steady and gradual but occurred in leaps and bounds, each bound following upon the invention of some new great tool: the use of fire, smelting of metals, the wheel, the boat, and so on, down the history of man to the atom bomb. Each tool gave greater scope, greater scope brought new problems, new problems sharpened the intellect, the sharpened intellect invented another tool, and produced another sudden jump.

This telescoped history of mankind unfolds a marvelous panorama, following the approved practice of the archeologist and paleontologist as well as the accepted mode of the social and cultural anthropologist. We will not quarrel with it; but let us remember that "a thousand years are but a day" in their sight. Time vistas stretch into the dim past and cultural history is painstakingly trying to sharpen its vision. The cutural history of paleolithic man can be deciphered only in broad outline from the odds and ends he left buried in geological detritus. His psychological history is a matter of inferences, extrapolations, and speculations from the evidence of these "relics." A conclusion like that of Cantril, "The whole process of man's emergent development is therefore inextricably interwoven with man's inventions" (3, p. 44), should therefore be assessed with due caution.

Thus Cantril's contribution leaves us with our problem unsolved. We are investigating the concrete individual as he tries to make the most of himself in his daily living. We are looking for the dynamic roots from which invention springs; for the impetus that sends a man along his road to better himself, his environment, the human race. It is easy enough for Cantril to rest his case on "evolutionary development," "creative selection," and "emergence," but that is simply another way of saying: "It just happened that way. It happened; that's all." The "capacity to sense value attributes," distilled out of the terminology used to explain it, finally turns out to be the capacity of making a practical judgment, based on the guesses we make about a world which we have conjured up for ourselves (Cf. 3, pp. 164–77, especially p. 171).

As we said at the beginning of this section, the human person does not achieve actualization merely by coming upon something in the environment which is suitable for him, and appropriating it. He has an urge to look for what he needs; to seek it if it is not at hand; and to make it if what he finds is not fully suitable for his present needs and desires. "Creative selection" is not the cause of the "psychological responsibility" which characterizes the products of human invention, craft, and art; it is the result of it. The tendency to possess, reaching out to give being to what as yet is not, is at the root of man's creativity. The self "looks before and after," then produces what is not. The tendency to possession can find satisfaction by acquiring objects in the physical environment; but in a deeper sense it possesses as its very own that to which it has given being, that which it has made. On the level of knowledge, the tendency to possession can lead to acquiring a body of information; but how much more is that knowledge one's own that comes from one's own discovery and invention? On the plane of contact with others, the self may reach out to acquire a companion, friend, or spouse, but how much more is one's child one's very own?

And in the enhancement of the self that comes when the self possesses what it has made, there is found a deeper psychological stabilization. For now the very being of the self has been augmented, enlarged, even multiplied by what it has made. It now is a firmer, less labile self which becomes the base for further appropriation, further making. Knowledge is acquired by doing, as we see in Aristotle's example from geometry (Metaphysics, IX 1051).[3] He shows here how we learn a theorem by making the "construction" and in it see the truth of the theorem. Geometry becomes more our own as we use it to solve practical problems of mensuration or, in a more complicated and recondite way, when we use it as a model for theoretical constructions in

[3] By referring only to Aristotle in this connection we may seem to do scant justice to Dewey and many recent authors who have written well and extensively on learning by doing and knowing by doing. We do not mention them because these authors, particularly Dewey, do not mean by knowing and knowledge what we want to express by these terms. Dewey reserves the term "knowledge" almost exclusively to the *result of inquiry,* and "knowing" to the *process of inquiry,* where inquiry means experimenting in thought or fact to solve a problem. Our meaning is simpler; we mean by knowing that we make something our own by using our senses and our understanding. Knowing as something we do to ourselves fits our context better than knowing as something we do to the environment.

quantum physics. The same is true of any kind of knowledge. Upon the foundations thus established we build not only a greater knowledge of geometry but also of other branches of mathematics and other sciences.

When we have learned the basic skills in any kind of craft, we not only make what our skill permits but each craftsman "experiments" in methods, materials, design, thereby to become more skillful and more stable in his skill. In what, unhappily, has been called the *fine* arts, the artist is not content to acquire the skill and the style of the masters but he is ever "trying something new," something of his own. In our own time, this urge to novelty and originality has run riot to such an extent that basic skills are despised and the limitations of materials are disregarded. Some artists do not care to draw—they needs must produce "impressions" or "moods" or a "total experience." They could with profit sit at the feet of the little girl who explained what she did in her drawing lesson and said: "I think, and then I draw my think." Too often the modern artist looks and then paints his *look*, or he emotes and then paints, sculpts, models, or abstracts his emotion. He has the urge to make but he does not have anything to make; he is impelled to realize himself, but the self that emerges is but a ghost of himself.

This impulse to make, as it flowers into action, enhances and actualizes the self not only because thereby its single capacities are perfected by exercise and so become more easy and sure in their operation, but also because the whole self, in expressing itself by making, establishes itself in a wider and wider field. Coming into control of wider fields, the self acquires a higher degree of stability. Manual skills are perfections of motor functions. The ease and sureness with which a man works are also grounds for increased self-confidence and self-esteem. The making of things, whether it be a mud pie, a dress, a golden goblet, a poem, a song, or a new chemical compound, is a higher reach of self-actuation than mere acquisition. In making, what was an individual, intangible, and perhaps fleeting thought is made substantial and enduring. The self is made more real, its actual expression is multiplied, and by this multiplication it is enriched.

It would be an exaggeration to say that the "motive" for making is the sheer gain in self-esteem (even on the unconscious level). Self-esteem may be a by-product or a necessary consequence, but it cannot be the purpose of self-actualization. Maslow, for instance, finds that the people he calls "self-actualizers" are generally noted for possessing

> . . . a quality that could be called "humility" of a certain type. They are all quite well aware of their own worth, so that there is no humbleness of the cringing or of the designing and calculating type. They are equally aware of how little they know in comparison with what *could* be known and what *is* known by others. Because of this it is possible for them without pose to be honestly respectful and even humble before people who can teach them something which they do not know or who have a skill they do not possess. They give this honest respect to a carpenter who is a good carpenter; or for that matter to anybody who is a master of his own tools or his own craft (18, p. 27).

It would be a greater mistake to maintain that the motive is sheer sensual pleasure. This is a reduction of a complex phenomenon to a single principle as lazy as is the concept that human doing and making are reducible to reflex motor reactions to perception or a chance constellation of random movements.

Paradoxically enough, as the self is actualized in making and as the field of possession enlarges, simple possession for the self and by the self is no longer enough. As the self reaches out to give being to what it makes, it finds itself *sharing* its own being with what is made. In this sharing, the self experiences no privation but rather an enlargement and enhancement. The craftsman or artisan respects the products of his skill just as he respects the material he uses to make them. He makes them for his own or another's use, it is true, but nonetheless he cherishes them. And as he was *intellectually responsible* in their making so he is *intellectually responsible* in their use. If they for whom he works misuse what he has made, he feels misused himself.[4]

[4] Or let us say he did, before the modern industrial system dehumanized the craftsman and the artisan. They now work not to make things, but to make money. Gill remarks: "During many centuries of man's past in the ordinary business of making things, both the idea of making them well and

Man the maker respects the works of his hands, if they approach the idea that he has in his mind of what he wishes them to be. He respects them because what he makes is a *realization* (a bringing into thinghood) not only of an idea within the mind but also of a potentiality dormant and hidden, till now, within the self. His making need not mean *destruction*; his making changes materials, it does not destroy them—and judged in human terms the change can be always for the better. The artisan will be limited by the nature of his materials. If he is a responsible worker, he will not hope to gather grapes from thorns nor figs from thistles any more than he would expect to make a sow's ear from his silk purse. He will respect his materials and will put himself into them. If he wants to carve an infant out of stone, he will so carve that his idea of the infant will live in stone—in the stone he uses. He will not try to make the stone resemble flesh and blood. He will share his being with the stone as the stone can receive it. And as he, the artisan and maker, is of some human use, so will he impart his being only to what will be of some human use. His own perfection as well as the perfection of his work will be judged by the degree to which he puts his whole self, his soul, into it.

To reach this highest level of self-actuation there need be no conflict, either of man within himself or of man with his environment. He may be "straitened" until he conceive adequately what this externalization of himself is to be and give it substance and birth in his making. He may be hampered until he understands the nature of his materials and their capacities. But there need be no conflict. This fact seems to be clear when we consider the higher reaches of self-actuation in the acquisition of science and learning. *Bonum est diffusivum sui.* No matter how much knowledge a man may have or how little, no man is

---

the instinct for making them beautiful were united. But in the last 150 years, since the introduction of the factory system and the development of machinery, the idea that the workman was responsible for making things well, and that in the course of so doing he would naturally satisfy his sense of beauty, has disappeared in the trades which supply the necessaries of life. . . . So we have the designer who designs what he never makes and the worker who minds the machine which makes what he never designs" (9, pp. 96–97).

content until and unless he communicates it. He will be quite aware that he does not fully possess it until he knows he is capable of sharing it. From the waggy-tongued gossip to the most erudite scientist, we all feel that the perfection of knowing is in sharing our knowledge with others. And we all feel, too, that the most learned man is he who can communicate his knowledge not only to the small company of his peers but to any intelligent person. It would literally be preposterous to believe that the outcry of the scientific world against the imposition of security restrictions is merely a plea against bridling the satisfaction of idle curiosity. It is an outcry against being forbidden to complete our full possession of knowledge by sharing it.

In sharing its knowledge the self not only enriches another without suffering any privation, but in so doing it enriches itself—and this not merely by reciprocation, but from within, because shared knowledge becomes more fully our own. In the sphere of social living, possession and stabilization expand self-actuation by the perfection that is found in communicating the self to the other. Possession of a companion is fullest when each puts himself at the disposal of the other in the common experience. The self-stabilization that is inherent in having a friend is firmest when the possession which makes the friend *dimidium animae meae* reaches to the enhancement of this half even at the expense of the other half. How true this is in the relationship between spouses, no one who has lived a truly happy married life will deny. They who do deny it, never having lived that way, speak from ignorance.

Conflict is no more required to achieve human perfection in going out toward other persons than it is in relation to the physical environment. It is true that the human being finds in his dealings with others not only more opportunities for conflict but also stronger reasons moving him to it. In fact, it would seem that the very principle we have postulated as the basis of human action would inevitably lead to conflict. If the human being must actualize himself by appropriating to himself his external world and stabilizing himself in its possession, then it would seem that conflict between individuals striving for possession of the same external world is inevitable in any society. If the human being, as we contend, is basically (naturally and unconsciously) oriented towards the actuation of *self*, and towards the other *only* as the other provides the means to his self-actuation, then only one of two possible results would seem to follow. Either the other will be frustrated in his striving for actuation, or the self will be unable to attain its proper goal of perfection.

This inconsistency is only apparent, not real. As we saw above, the firmest and most enduring possession of the self in knowledge and love is in the giving of self. It is the perfection of the individual, to be achieved in giving and sharing, that is the natural base of society. In any social group, no matter whether it be natural or established purely by convention, whether it be permanent or temporary, for important purposes or unimportant ones, so long as it is truly human, it is only by the gift of self that each member can obtain, in and from the group, what none of the members singly possesses. Furthermore, in the dedication of self one makes for the common welfare, there will be found the surest and most stable condition for achieving the actuation of one's highest potentialities.

Each human being becomes a member of human society by being born into it, and that means being born into a family. The family is the first and fundamental social unit. And the family by nature is founded by love and in love. Whether such love is primarily biological or reaches a truly human level, its foundation is always *union*, not dissension; and least of all aggression. Society, like the family, does not grow from conflict among random groups of hostile human beings. On the truly human plane, the love that is the foundation of social life is the fruit of rational knowledge and deliberate choice. The possession of another by knowledge not only leaves the other in his own identity but enhances him. Love is the reciprocal of knowledge, for the knowing self is the improved self, and the known and loved other becomes the better part of the knower and lover who almost by sheer self-interest is drawn to enhance the beloved. Without love no human relationship can endure except by force or accident. Without love no family or state can be permanent. Without love human society is impossible.

Self-Actuation by Self-Direction. Self-actuation involves not merely the realization of the potentialities of any of our functions taken singly, nor their actualization in the organized tendencies toward possession and stabilization (which includes making and sharing), but also their working together toward a unified pattern of life. If the self in setting up a goal is motivated only by the tendency to acquisition inherent in its functions, that tendency in its concrete realization would give the activities of the person a single direction and bring about self-actuation. Were the self rigidly determined in its orientation to perfection as the lower organisms are, his tendency to possession would always move the person to what is suitable to him as a whole, and the actuation achieved would be truly enhancing. The human being, however, is not totally subject to the law of fixed natural necessity in the pattern which his life is to take. He must organize his activities and orient them by *deliberate* knowledge and intent.

It may easily come about (and, in fact, it generally does, taking mankind by and large) that what the individual perceives and understands as suitable for acquisition is only the pseudo-suitable. He may be in error or he may deceive himself as to what is properly suitable or what will contribute to his self-actuation. When that happens, his tendency to possession will move him away from, or at least not effectively toward, his proper goal of growth and development. On the other hand, if the tendency toward psychological stabilization is given free rein, a similar imbalance will ensue, because of an all-too-likely misunderstanding of what is the most secure way in which possessions may be retained. So it happens that the tendency to acquisition and the tendency toward stabilization fortify and implement the tendency to self-actuation but may also warp it. And as self-actuation progresses, it has a reciprocal influence on the tendencies to possession and psychological stabilization.

That self-actuation does in fact modify the tendencies to possession and stabilization is obvious, because the field in which the self can find what is suitable for further actuation will widen as the self is actuated. At the same time it will narrow, also, because the individual soon becomes aware that in this wide field with its numerous opportunities for possession, stabilization, and actuation there are too many objects offered. He can do only one thing at a time. He cannot have everything either simultaneously or even successively. He has at least this restriction that his capacity to possess here and now is always limited. As self-actuation grows in the field of possession, the tendency of the self to establish itself in the wider field becomes more intense. However, here again, just as in the field of increased possession where actuation was limited by sheer physical impossibility, in the field of psychological establishment actuation is restricted by the difficulty of bringing all these diverse elements into a rational pattern.

The psychological consequences of this expansion and restriction may be called "conflict" or "tension" or "repression." But whatever else these terms may mean—and psychologists have put many meanings into them that do not appear on the surface—there is no need to interpret them as anything more than modalities of impulse and urge on the higher level of psychological activity. Impulse becomes urge whenever there are difficulties or restrictions in the exercise of a single function as well as of an organized action tendency toward possession and stabilization. Impulse and urge as action tendencies do not come into awareness except at the end of acute and prolonged reflection. But the point to emphasize is not that this expansion and restriction of the field in which the basic motive forces find play is unconscious, or that the individual is unaware of the reason why he feels more strongly carried in one direction rather than in another, but that a *rational pattern* is required to achieve harmony in the play of these tendencies.[5]

The Self-Ideal

This rational pattern is not something that just happens. There is no antecedent physical or psychological necessity by

[5] See also Allport's recent statement: "The view of motivation that I am here proposing says that the important thing is the person's systematized design for living. This design—not his hypothetical instincts—is the dynamic force in his life" (1, p. 157).

which the self-actuation of an individual takes on a definite goal or direction. This feature of self-determination has not been adequately formulated in modern theories of personality, even by psychologists who insist on self-determination as the central factor in personality development. Rogers, for instance, insists that the person will not only recognize what ought to be done in any problem that confronts him but will also necessarily do it, provided only that a permissive atmosphere relieves him of the necessity of defending himself. Freud in his early formulations similarly assumed that insight, once achieved, will automatically produce a cure; but later experience led to the modified view that insight has to be supplemented by identification with the therapist which will provide the proper motive for the patient's change in behavior. Failures in therapy, therefore, are never laid at the patient's door but have to be explained by inadequacies of technique or of therapist, or by recourse to constitutional factors.

But these factors, though present, cannot account for all the failures. No matter how modest the therapist, he knows that there are cases where none of these factors, singly or combined, can account for his lack of success. The patient must be willing to pay the price if he is to get well, and for some patients the price seems to be too high. The price is his willingness to organize his life according to a rational pattern which will give direction to his life, regardless of difficulties and discomfort.

The human person must determine his goal and direction for himself progressively, not only in the over-all pattern of his life, but also in many smaller segments of his behavior. This direction or goal is the ideal of the perfect person as the individual conceives him. Needless to say, this self-ideal is not an idealized version of one's self, but it is human nature at its best incarnated in a concrete person. We strive not toward something but toward someone whose perfection we gradually make our own. In all human history there is only one man so perfect that even his enemies have to acknowledge him as such: Jesus Christ. Even in non-Christian cultures, the ideal human person is one who is and acts Christlike. For people who have no knowledge of such a historical person, the same qualities nevertheless appeal as ideal.[6]

Such an ideal, of course, implies some understanding of the ideal personality as a pattern on which to fashion one's life. Since understanding implies knowledge, there is always the danger that the individual either does not have sufficient information or that he has the wrong kind of information as to what the ideal personality should be. We can distinguish, then, at least two different kinds of self-ideal: one which emphasizes the *self*, that is, the self-ideal as the person actually conceives it, or *what he wants to be*. The other emphasizes the *ideal*, the human personality in its proper perfection as this individual is capable of achieving it, that is, *what this person ought to be*. That some sort of self-ideal is the term of every person's striving is clear not only from common experience but also from clinical observation. It is frequently not well or clearly formulated in the person's awareness, it may even escape accurate formulation when he tries to express it; but there is at least some kind of knowledge that what he *is* does or does not measure up to what he wants to be.

If we take the person as he is in the present, going toward his self-ideal, we must distinguish between his *self-concept*, that is *what he thinks himself to be* (though he may never have formulated his thinking) and *what he really is*. What I am and what I think I am, what I want to be and what I ought to be, may be

---

[6] In Chapter 4 (Comment) we have treated the norms or standards against which a person must measure himself to discover whether he is functioning well as a *human* being. We said there that these norms are not exclusively psychological, but are found when human nature is considered in all its aspects.

In Chapter 13 we shall show that these nonpsychological norms must be complemented by psychological norms which define well-ordered and effective psychological functioning and are only remotely concerned with *ultimate* results. A truly integral personality must be top grade according to both these standards.

In Chapter 19 we will deal at length with the personality of Christ as the term and motive for personality integration.

Let us say, then, that the self-ideal as it ought to be in the abstract is a transcendent, objective, absolute standard. In the concrete individual, it is that approximation to Christlikeness which the individual judges to be proper and possible for himself.

synonymous for a very few persons; but as a rule, there is a discrepancy between what I am and what I want to be, or even between what I am and what I think I am, and a further gap between what I want to be and what I ought to be.

The gap between what I am and what I think I am is usually made the center of psychotherapeutic efforts. Nondirective therapy, for instance, tries to reduce this gap by giving the person an opportunity of recognizing and accepting his organic perceptions and thus coming to a correct self-concept. Psychoanalysis also, by making the unconscious conscious, induces the patient to accept his strivings as well as his actions and thus brings him to a better knowledge of his own functioning. The discrepancy between self-concept and self-ideal likewise comes in for its share of attention, though in most cases in a negative way: if the distance between the person as he is and his self-ideal is too wide, most therapists consider it their duty to help the patient close the gap, preferably by lowering his exaggerated demands upon himself. But unless it is first shown that these demands *are* exaggerated by comparing them with the self-ideal as it ought to be for this person, the remedy may prove worse than the disease. If there is merely a gap between what I am and what I want to be, but I know myself as I really am, and what I want to be is the same as what I ought to be—though it may be a goal far distant on the horizon—then there may be continual striving and falling short, but there will be no inner disturbance, for my striving is always clearly directed toward what I ought to be. But if there is a gap between the self-ideal as it actually is and the self-ideal as it ought to be, then there will be a disturbance whether the goal is near or far distant. Perhaps an example will make this clear.

A man may be a petty tyrant though he may think he is simply saving others from their own stupidity and carelessness. What he wants to be is the center around which the small universe of his family, business, or other sphere of authority revolves. What he ought to be is not a tyrant, not even a benevolent one, but a good father or administrator. To consider himself masterful when he is simply arbitrary is self-deception. As long as it lasts, he will not even consider changing his ways.

When he acknowledges that he is a tyrant and not always benevolent, the distance between what he is and what he wants to be will increase, even though his self-ideal still remains to run other peoples' lives for them. But at least he has a starting point. There is still a basic cleavage, of course, between his self-ideal as it is and his self-ideal as it ought to be. This cleavage cannot be removed by reducing the distance between what he is and what he wants to be—say by being content to be tyrannical only in safe situations. Now as before there will be a possiblity of frustration and resistance. Only when his self-ideal is finally changed to what it ought to be and he is determined to become an intelligent and reasonable superior or father will his life at last become free from continual friction and emotional disturbance.

The closer the self-ideal as it is approximates the self-ideal as it ought to be, the more unified will be the actuation of the personality. Similarly, the more the self-concept approaches what the person really is, the more assurance will there be that he will take the right approach to the self-ideal. And finally, the shorter the distance between the self as it is at present and the self-ideal, the more integrated, the more humanly perfect will the person be. If I function in such a way that what I am is in line with what I want to be, and what I want to be is also what I ought to be, I shall be functioning smoothly, without hindrance or obstacle from within.

The self-ideal is the rational purpose implicit in the active integration and organization of personality. Integration is achieved when the activities of the person under the impetus of impulse and urge are first brought into being and then into pattern. The pattern is determined by the basic impulse toward self-actuation in possession, stabilization, making, and sharing, when it is directed toward a self-ideal. The integration will be effective and harmonious if the self-ideal as it is does not diverge from the self-ideal as it ought to be; and when the self-concept is not only correct but shows at least an orientation toward the self-ideal. The mode of self-integration can of course be influenced and modified by external factors but the core of integration will be found in the relationship of the self-ideal as it is to the self-ideal as it ought to be. If they converge, the personality will grow and the person will function well. If they diverge, the person will have recourse to a variety of modes of part integration, called mechanisms of defense, to achieve some measure of harmony. These mechanisms are not native to man; they are the result either of the lack of a rational pattern of self-organization or the overriding of whatever rational pattern there might be by the appetitive functions, which are usually strongly moved to follow their natural bent.

That there are personalities that are well organized points to the fact that human activities can be organized. Moreover, these human potentialities are not merely capable of being organized but contain an active tendency toward unity and integration; as they are realized in action singly and progressively, they unfold the tendency of the self to unified action. This native tendency to unification is not strong enough to accomplish harmony. Man must determinedly and deliberately organize and integrate himself. If he patterns his life toward a goal which diverges from the goal as it ought to be, he will go counter to this natural impulse toward unity and harmony—he will be subject to a psychological pulling apart. This pulling apart occurs not because he is trying to unite two or more incompatible *activities*, but because he is trying to unite (to himself) several incompatible *objects*: "No man can serve two masters." It is worthy of note also, that the more a person's activities and strivings are centered about the self as self, the less do they become amenable to effective integration and harmony, while the more they are concerned with outgoing and sharing, the more they are not only integrated but enhanced. "He that loses his life shall find it."

Personality Organization

Psychologists usually call the pattern or organization of the person's behavior the *structure* of his personality. The term "structure" here is used as an exact synonym for the term as used in modern physics, particularly by those psychologists who are trying to establish a "dynamic" orientation in psychology. However, the dynamic orientation as transferred from physics is not adequate in psychology, as we have shown before, since the person is active in a way different from activities of physical bodies. Therefore, if the notion of structure is to be significant at all in psychology, it must indicate something characteristically psychological.

Now the distinctly psychological feature in *structure* as applied to the human person is the fact that it constitutes a single active whole. Psychologically speaking, structure must mean that attribute which makes the uniqueness of the person perceptible to us. There is no satisfactory English word for this concept; as a matter of fact, there is no satisfactory word in the literature of psychology which would contain the implication we want in a term describing what we mean by psychological structure.[7]

It is this putting together, either in any particular situation or throughout man's whole life, which makes the whole complex a single unit. It is the foundation of the relationship which exists between the several activities constituting the complex. So structure in personality will be found in action. But because a man's actions are not all going on simultaneously, this structure is both their root and their fruit. The personality structure is not only the source out of which activities arise but it will also be a product of these activities. It will be well to remember also that the structure does not *constitute* the unity of personality, it merely reveals it. We can say, then, that the *structure* of personality is the way in which the activities and characteristics of a person are patterned to manifest the uniqueness of the individual. Thus in more technical terms, the structure is the formal cause of personality—and personality is the patterned totality of activities and powers.

Conflict As a Modality of Impulse and Urge

It is hard to find in current literature a psychological explanation of this putting together of elements in personality develop-

[7] We could give a new usage to the noun σύνταγμα, stressing the middle voice (what one has put together for one's self). However, there is no need of this new word if *structure* in personality is taken in this active, on-going sense.

ment which does not use conflict (and frustration) as its most fundamental concept. In fact, were we to believe our theorists we would come to the conclusion that conflict is the reason why there is any progress anywhere: If you desire a fine lawn, you continually cut the grass and roll it. If you wish for a thick hedge, you clip and clip and clip the shrubs. Gold is tried by fire; iron must be beaten before it can be wrought; St. Paul says even of God that He chastises every son He receives. From more scientific sources we hear that conflict is the law of nature and progress and perfection come as the result of combat.

We venture to be doubtful about all this. It does seem a queer kind of arrangement where a man comes to his perfection by breaking himself to pieces; a civilization comes to consummation by being done to death. Something does not ring true in this collection of contradictions. We would rather say that being as a being, and any being as a being, is by its very nature pointed to completion in the tranquillity of right order. At least for the human being, the achievement of his distinctively human perfection consists in coming to possess the rest of creation in a way which, far from destroying or damaging, rather enhances it—namely by knowledge and love. He would find attaining this end impossible if the *essential* condition for his earthly career were contention, struggle, combat, hostility, and destruction. If conflict is the essential condition of man, that is what it would seem to mean (Cf. Coker, 4).

It is a commonplace among psychologists that conflict is essential to psychological growth. According to Zilboorg's exposition of Freud, for instance, such conflict is inevitable:

The generic name he [Freud] gave to these forces [of the unconscious] was drives, instincts. "After long doubt," says Freud, "and vacillations we have decided to assume the existence of only two basic instincts. . . ." One of these instincts strives to bind, to unite things; the other seeks to break up and destroy. . . . Instincts never appear or never act in their pure form. They are antagonistic to each other and they become fused in most singular proportions and manners. Let Freud say it: "In biological functions the two basic instincts work against each other or combine with each other. Thus the act of eating is a destruction of an object with the final aim of incor-

porating it, and the sexual act is an act of aggression having as its
purpose the most intimate union. This interaction of the two basic
instincts with and against each other gives rise to the whole variega-
tion of the phenomena of life" (25, pp. 36–37).

And Zilboorg continues:

Freud gradually leads us to the inescapable conclusion that the
superego draws a great deal on our reservoir of aggressive drives, and
utilizes these not only to restrain the ego but even to act against the
ego itself; it may even kill the ego, which means it may even lead to
suicide. "You will note" says Freud in his letter to Einstein, "that
if and when this process (of turning one's aggression against one's
own self) proceeds with too great an energy, it might be proved
quite unhealthy for the person, whereas the turning of this aggression
unto the outside world might serve as a satisfactory and satisfying
release." Freud adds: "One must admit that these [aggressive, dan-
gerous] drives are closer to nature than our opposition to them" (25,
p. 96).

In these passages quoted above the notions: aggression, antagonism, destruction, killing, suicide, danger, seem to be used
in their dictionary meaning. In the term "aggression" the ordinary man usually finds overtones of hostility—analysts certainly put it into the term, as our quotations show. The object
of aggression is an enemy. The interaction between aggressor
and aggressee is combat, strife, warfare, in some form or another. Now it is true that on the psychological plane the environment resists man's conquest and constitutes the problems
in knowledge and technique which he must solve, not only to
maintain his identity and survive but to develop and progress
spiritually. But in that case, is *conflict* necessary? Why could
not the same results be achieved simply because the process of
assimilating the environment is *difficult*? Even if man's environment were chaotic and unordered to his use, there is no
need of conflict. On the social plane, there certainly is conflict
in the baldest and cruelest sense of the word, but is it necessary?
Is it even an efficacious means for progress? Even the Utopia
of the Marxist, whose whole social doctrine is rooted in class
struggle and world revolution of a bloody kind, is a state where
class struggle is ended and everyone works together with every-

one else in bliss ever increasing. The very notion of society connotes one mind, one heart, one effort toward a common goal.[8]

But, say the field theorists, individual personality growth can be achieved only as tensions are set up in psychic systems, and these tensions are a species of conflict. Goals, barriers, regressions, substitutions, etc., are the matrix out of which the personality grows. Now the tension or the conflict would have to be within the psychological field; so the combatants must be "dispositions to react in a specific way." For the sake of brevity, let us divide the systems that would be involved into two groups and call them higher and lower; the higher including rational, aesthetic, altruistic strivings, the lower having only sensory goals and strivings which fall short of more inclusive goals. If true conflict occurs, what would it be?

On the sensory plane, when there is opposition between two sensory goals, or when there is a sensory goal and a barrier blocking it, it does not seem necessary to postulate a true conflict. A barrier constitutes a difficulty. Difficulty *occasions* a heightening of impulse into urge and urge carries through, over, or around the barrier. If the barrier is too strong, motion toward the blocked goal stops; then there is regression or substitution; or there is merely a cessation of activity until another goal is perceived or the barrier weakens; or finally, the field of perception remains narrow, the blocked goal continues to attract, motion is ineffective, but the striving continues.[9] But it is not clear that this constitutes a psychological conflict.

[8] See also Allport's remark: "So obvious is the priority of affiliative groundwork that one must perform contortions in order to give equal footing to the alleged aggressive instincts. By some psychoanalysts the feat is achieved by assuming that eating, perhaps the most conspicuous of the infant's activities, is a destructive act—'oral aggression,' it is called. 'Our primordial ancestors,' writes one Freudian, 'were cannibals. We all enter life with the instinctive impulse to devour not only food, but also all frustrating objects. Before the infantile individual acquires the capacity to love, it is governed by a primitive hate relationship to its environment.' This statement precisely reverses the order of love and hate in ontogenetic development. Furthermore, it inverts the meaning of the act of feeding. When I devour roast beef it is not from hate but from love. Acts of incorporation into myself are, from my point of view, affiliative" (1, p. 152).

[9] Lewin's solution of this problem by the use of process differentials is hardly a solution. He says: "If one tries to deduce the dynamics of a process

When psychological conflict does arise, it occurs when a sensory and a rational goal are incompatible or when two rational goals are opposed. Thus the conflict comes in every instance from some inconsistency in choice. The person is either unable to choose or makes a choice unwillingly or regrets an irrevocable decision. In short, he wants to have his cake and eat it, too. There is, for instance, the simple matter of deciding whether to stay in bed late or get up so as to polish up a class lecture scheduled for the first period in the morning. This problem can become conflictful when no decision is made until the sheer lateness of the hour routs you out of bed to skimp your shave and rush to get to class only five minutes late. The situation is not serious, but what makes it a conflict is not so much the incompatibility of the objects as the desire for two different things which cannot be fitted into a reasonable scheme. Where higher goals are concerned (for instance, more time at home with the family or prolonged work in the laboratory to finish a difficult research program) conflict occurs not because these two goals oppose each other but because we want to do both at once. A man either cannot make up his mind which one to choose at a given moment, or he chooses one under pressure, or he chooses one quite reasonably but lets himself stay sorry for himself because he cannot have both. If the choice is Hobson's choice, the result is resentment—it shouldn't be called conflict.

Conflict, then, is a disturbance that arises when there is an inconsistency of rational choice. In that case, the conflict is clearly conscious. There is another kind of conflict (as we have seen in our discussion of the tendency to possession and stabilization) which is produced whenever the tendency of the human being to possess things and possess them permanently clashes with the limitations inherent in his nature. This conflict is un-

---

from the actual event, one is compelled to resort to process differentials" (15, pp. 32–33). But that is predicting after the event. By a neat bit of logical sleight-of-hand he shows that it is not the vectors that determine the dynamics but the dynamics that determine the vectors. Old-fashioned logicians would call that amphibology.

conscious but may become conscious; in fact, for fully integrated self-determination it is necessary that it do so. This conflict essentially consists in the incompatibility of the goal chosen by the person with the natural or rational order of things. The individual, for instance, may want to possess a given object permanently and wholly, yet reflection will show him that that is impossible. Or a man may try to amass a fortune so that he will never suffer want, yet he knows that a catastrophe might deprive him of all he has at any moment. In both cases, the goal pursued is incompatible with the order of nature; in both cases also, the person may come to know the source of his malaise in his choice of a goal which is incompatible with the order of things, and rectify his choice accordingly.

This conflict occurs with more serious consequences when the goal pursued is not a minor one but is represented by the person's self-ideal. If his self-ideal diverges from the self-ideal as it ought to be for him, there will be a psychological pulling apart, which represents an unconscious conflict. If the person has the wrong self-ideal he will necessarily not only be at cross purposes with the natural law but frequently enough also in opposition to human law. Even though he successfully maintain for himself the self-ideal chosen on the basis of private preference, he is in danger of legal or at least social punishment.

Even if the society he lives in has no punishment for actions which he permits himself even though they go against the natural law, there are at least natural consequences which he wants to avoid and of which he is afraid (for instance the loss of trust and affection that is the consequence of cruel and deceitful actions). He chooses an action and tries to evade the consequences, yet he is forced to suffer them. In this case also, the cause of the disturbance can be found by reflection and can be identified as the same incompatibility of chosen goal with the natural order. Whenever an individual tries to possess an impermanent object permanently, or to pursue a course of action without accepting its consequences, or to choose a pattern of life inimical to his human nature—in other words, whenever his goals are incompatible with the natural scheme of things, there will be symptoms of a psychological pulling apart, and frequently he will become aware of the unconscious conflict which these symptoms indicate.

To sum up: conscious conflict can be considered basically as an inconsistency of choice, unconscious conflict as a choice of goals which are incompatible with the order of things. When the conflict is conscious it will be found to be the result either of an inability to choose because the person is not willing to sacrifice the alternative goal, or it is the consequence of making a choice unwillingly and wanting the alternative, or finally, of regretting an irrevocable or necessary decision. When conflict is unconscious (though its symptoms of unhappiness, malaise, guilt feelings are clearly evident) its antecedent is either a choice of an end without choosing the necessary consequence or means (e.g., striving for power and wanting the love of one's puppets), or choosing a goal in accord with the tendencies toward possession and stabilization but without regard to inherent limitations (trying to make a fortune and keeping it untouched by catastrophe), or choosing a self-ideal which diverges from the self-ideal as it ought to be.

These conflicts, which are grounded in man's refusal to conform to a natural or rational order of things, we must clearly distinguish from the situation, also called conflict by many psychologists, in which the activities of the human being are merely made difficult: the conquest of the environment in which man wrests a livelihood from a meager soil or finds ways and means to overcome the extremes of climate; or the difficulties he encounters when he tries to impose a rational pattern upon his actions, when he attempts to subordinate his sensory to his rational goals. These difficulties of action do not constitute conflict; they are compensated for by the heightened impulse toward the goal which we have called urge. This upsurge of heightened energy will conquer the difficulties in his way as long as he is singlemindedly concentrating on the goal. Only when indecision enters, and the goal is desired but the difficulties are not accepted, then a real conflict develops, that is, a conflict which consists in the incompatibility of our choice with the natural order.

But the psychoanalyst will say that all this is a travesty on what he means by psychological conflict. What the psychoanalyst means by conflict is an event in the unconscious. The person never becomes aware of it except for the few remnants that remain after the battle. Frequently enough, anxiety or some irrational behavior is the only sign from which it can be inferred that there must have been a conflict. This appeal to the unconscious may be a convenient expedient to cloak our ignorance, or it may be based on solid factual evidence. To decide this question, let us examine what could be understood by the term "the unconscious."

The Unconscious

The notion of an unconscious from which impulses or images or ideas break into ordered conscious rational life has been so persistent in psychology (even before Freud raised it to the dignity of a scientific dogma) that it is imperative for any theory of personality to examine it, define it operationally, or otherwise come to terms with it. Miller's book on *Unconsciousness* has provided a survey of definitions and usages which make such an undertaking seem almost futile because of the superabundance of meanings which have been attributed to the term by writers in the field. It would seem advisable, then, to discuss systematically what such a notion could imply and to see whether these implications agree with the various usages of the term as reported by Miller.

We will not adopt the charming and urbane expedient used by Miller in a more recent paper (20), which enabled him to make penetrating remarks on the attributes of God. We will not start our discussion, as he does, from the psychology of ignorance, but rather from an analysis of knowledge. Everybody will agree that knowledge is a relationship between at least two —knower and known. There are some philosophers who seem to imply that knowledge is a relation between one, for they contend that knowledge and the knower are one; but for the ordinary run of people, a relationship implies at least more than one. A relationship not only implies at least two termini or subjects of the relationship, two things that are related, but also a foundation or basis for it; some quality, quantity, or determination the two have in common. For instance, fatherhood implies two persons and an activity, generation, which is found in both: the father producing, the son being produced. In knowledge there is the knower, the known, and the activity that establishes the relationships between them, namely the act of knowing. It is worthy of note that the act of knowing *is not one of the terms of the relationship* but is the basis of the relationship. It is also worth remembering that a relationship is not a thing nor a quality of a thing but is based on a quality or determination of the things that are related (Cf. our discussion, page 138).

Now when we use the term "conscious" we refer to some kind of knowing. Consciousness, then, implies a knowledge relationship, that is, it implies a subject knowing, something known, and an activity which establishes the relationship. We said it implies *knowledge*. It implies something more than the plain or garden variety of sensation and perception or even conceptualization. It is because these other implications have been lost sight of by psychologists that the term "consciousness" has been put to misuse. To find these implications, we shall have to go back to the roots of the word. Consciousness is derived from the Latin *conscius*, which is an adjective made up of *scius* from the root *sci* (know) and the combining form of the preposition *cum*. Now when *cum* is used as a prefix it has three functions: (*a*) to denote *together with*, e.g., colloquium, talking together with others; (*b*) to denote an *intensification*, e.g., concussion, a violent shaking; (*c*) to denote *completeness*, like the word complete itself, or conclude, confuse, consume, etc. So *con*scius could imply: (*a*) a knowing of one thing or event *together with* a knowing of something else; (*b*) a more *intense* kind of knowing; (*c*) a *completed* kind of knowledge. Or it could imply all three in the same act of knowledge.

In English *awareness* is used as a synonym for *consciousness*. The Anglo-Saxon root for the word is *gewaer*, an intensive of *waer,* which is a cognate of the Greek ὁϱᾶν (so see) and the Latin *vereri* (to fear). Hence in the Anglo-Saxon word there is the implication that when one is aware, one not only perceives but also interprets what one perceives. Let us see now whether in common usage these etymological nuances are present. The following expressions are common enough : *I am aware of the music that is playing; I am aware that I am listening to the music; I am aware of things past; I am aware that I am remembering things past; I am aware that I am afraid; I am aware that I am afraid to look; I am aware that I am afraid to look because I shall see blood; I am aware that I feel faint because I looked at blood flowing.* It is common enough also to take *I am aware that I am afraid* not to be the exact equivalent of *I am afraid.*

In all these statements involving awareness we find an implication of knowledge. I apprehend directly some object or event.[10] That is the direct content of my perception. But in every case I am also implicitly aware that I am the subject of this awareness; that this content is in me. It is here that the implication of togetherness is found. Together with the content that is known, which is what the act of knowing reaches directly and explicitly, there is the awareness of myself and the fact of my knowing, which is reached directly but implicitly. The objective reference may be very narrow ; I may be so "absorbed" in the object or event that other contents in my act of knowing are obscured and not attended to : for instance the self, the fact of knowing, other aspects of the event, can only become known by a kind of reflection and remission of the concentration on the "absorbing" content. This happens in emotional experiences where awareness is so riveted on the situation or the bodily changes that go along with it that the emotion increases uncontrolled. It is this concentration of attention that is implied in the *intensive* form. But to be aware of a known and not to be aware of that to which the known is related in such a relational activity is to be incompletely aware. To be implicitly aware of the self in the act of awareness completes the activity, or rather makes it a *complete* activity. Note that the awareness of self and of the fact of acting is *implicit.* When the self or the act of knowing becomes the ex-

[10] Note that we do not use the term "event" in the technical sense that Whitehead and other epistemologists have given it. We use it in the first meaning listed in the dictionary—a happening.

plicit content of awareness, we have reflection or introspection, not simple direct awareness of self or activity.

But our awareness is never confined to any single simple act of apprehension such as we analyzed above. Any state of awareness contains not only the explicit and implicit contents of simple apprehensions, like exteroceptive or proprioceptive sensations, but also the explicit contents of integrations from sense data into objects, concepts, meanings, judgments relating objects to one another and to the self, interpretations as well as emotional states and other experiences which are explicit contents. And it is the *explicit* contents to which our attention is drawn and to which our awareness refers. Consciousness or awareness is primarily an awareness of *explicit contents*.

What is not actually and formally included in the explicit contents is not fully in awareness. What is implicit in the contents (psychologically, not logically) may become explicit by simple reflection or introspection. Then it becomes fully and explicitly conscious. But it is only the self as acting and the fact of acting that becomes conscious that way. What the self is and what the nature of the activity is can become known and understood only by prolonged processes of reasoning which open up the logical as well as the psychological connections between the contents of the direct consciousness. Thus it may happen that some event, when perceived, will arouse some emotional experience within me; I may be aware that I have an emotion but be unable to say whether it is fear or disgust or aversion. The emotion is in itself differentiated but I am not able to differentiate it in my awareness.

So too, without prolonged and intricate reasoning and insight I may be unable to make explicit (i.e., to understand) the *connection* between various experiences which are explicit contents of consciousness, and so be unaware of their relation to one another. Explicit awareness and understanding of this connection come through judgment, reasoning, and insight. What is past in experience is implicit in the self, but it may require much reflection and investigation to make it explicitly known, and even more to render it useful for present needs. To sum up then : Normal full consciousness is a state wherein the person can perceive and interpret his surroundings, and in which the self and its past experience are fully available for use in the present.[11]

So then, what is *conscious* must indicate some psychological experience, something *lived through* of which we know; a *knowing* or a *wanting* or a *doing* or a *happening* in us of which we have direct knowledge and which we refer to ourselves. Such psychological experience, moreover, in itself or in its content, must be fully *available* to us here and now for the needs of the present moment. That we see and what we see must be available to us in a situation where we need to see it—a banana peel on the walk where our next step will land; that we remember and what we remember, when the situation calls for it—when the wife sends us to the store to buy the groceries; that we fear and what we fear, when fear is necessary so that we can protect ourselves— when we have offended a vengeful person; that we hurt and where we hurt—when we have suffered an injury. Furthermore, such availability for the needs of the present also implies that as means to fulfill these needs they must be *under our control.* We brush off a fly by a movement that is conscious, as contrasted with a choreic movement that is unwanted, not under the person's control, and which he is not aware of having initiated.

Conversely, what is unconscious can be: What is *not lived through*, that is, there is either no awareness that *anything* is going on, or there is no awareness of *what* is going on, be it *external event* or *human function*; an experience that is temporarily *not available to understanding* or *memory*; what is lived through is *not under our control*, is indeliberate and naturally determined. All these categories can be found in Miller's definitions (19) or rather, Miller's definitions can be ordered by means of these categories and subsumed under them.

No awareness that anything is going on:

This category indicates absence of awareness. It includes the following definitions (Miller's numbering):

2b. anesthetized, asleep—unresponsive to stimulation.

---

[11] This definition is substantially that of Moore (21, p. 9). Though we arrive at it in a different way, we wish to acknowledge our indebtedness to his work.

Unaware of external events:

The following definitions all indicate a lack of awareness of objects or situations.

2*a*. absent-minded—unresponsive to stimulation,
4. undiscriminating,
6. unsensing (criterion often surprise),
7. unnoticed or unattending,
14. ignoring.

Unaware of human functioning:

This category indicates a lack of awareness of the way in which the person functions.

16. unaware of discrimination.

Not available to understanding (but capable of it) :

8. insightless, not involving insight (criterion: learning curve rises gradually instead of suddenly),
11. unrecognizing (if a need can be satisfied but is not, the need is unrecognized),
13. unable to communicate; incommunicable; unable to describe or talk about.

Not available to memory (but capable of it) :

9. unremembering;
15*a*. psychoanalytic meaning: belonging to the unconscious, repressed, can be made available only by free association.

Not under our control:

5. conditioned, acting on basis of conditioning,
10. unlearned or inherited, instinctive,
12. involuntary (criterion: mediated by parts of the nervous system which are not under voluntary control),
15*b*. psychoanalytic meaning: belonging to the unconscious, not under voluntary control.

In addition, what is incapable of becoming aware, what is not lived through, not a psychological experience, cannot be said to be conscious, therefore must be *not conscious* (though not *un*conscious) ; this category accounts for the remaining two of Miller's definitions of unconscious as

1. inanimate or subhuman; incapable of discrimination,
3. not mental.

Our category *unaware of human functioning* requires elucidation. Actually, we are never aware of the way in which a given power works. The function as a function does not come into awareness. When we say we are aware that we see, we do not mean that we are aware of the actual nature of the function of seeing. What we are aware of is the object we see and the fact that we see it. When we want something, we are aware that we want it, but what the inner nature of this wanting is can be understood by us only after an intricate and prolonged process of reasoning.

When our muscles move, we are not aware that our *muscles* are moving, we may be aware only that our arms and legs and fingers are moving. We know that it is useless to try making the individual muscles move, for we are not aware of the way in which our individual muscles work together. We can come to a knowledge of that by a study of anatomy and physiology, but that is not necessary for movement; in fact, too much attention to the process is liable to interfere with smooth execution. We are conscious only of the intention or aim of movement; our consciousness of movement is the movement itself and not the process by which it is brought about. If we were immediately aware of our functions, there would not be so many contradictory theories on pitch perception, form and color perception, and all the other theories we find in physiological psychology.

Similarly, when the imagination works, it images objects. It does not image its own function. When we think, we are aware of the objects we are thinking about, but we are not aware of the nature of the process itself. Creative thinking, creative imagination, *as functions*, are unconscious. In fact, we are not immediately aware that we have an imagination, we are aware of images, and we denominate a certain activity as "imagining" or "imagination" because it produces images. We are aware of the images, and we conclude that we have an imagination. We are not even aware of ourselves except in so far as we are active.

The content of consciousness, then, consists of the objects we know (remember, imagine), the objects toward which we strive, either emotionally or volitionally, and the actions which concern them. Put differently, consciousness includes both the term and the product of psychological functions (we are aware not only of the banana we reach for but also of our reaching). And it would seem that the unconscious, then, should designate what is not included in the content of consciousness, namely the natural or connatural mode of action of our powers. Such functioning is unconscious, whether in the psychological or the vital sphere. We become aware of the products of the functioning of the single powers (objects known, wanted, remembered, imagined, the successive happenings in a dream or a story, body movements) ; we can also come to know how to control our functions as the means for satisfying our present needs—that is, we acquire control over our muscles which goes beyond the coordination achieved by moving toward objects. By reflection, we may learn to relax our muscles or even to control our heart beat. After we come to know by reflection that we can relax our muscles and how we do it, we become aware of the sensation of muscle relaxation ; in this way reflection extends our direct sensory awareness. The dynamic power of the unconscious, so dear to psychoanalysts, is accounted for in our scheme by the degree of impulsion (impulse and urge) activating the single functions ; we can become aware of it by observing the degree of attraction or interest which various objects have for us.

The bimodal action of impulse and urge toward the possession of objects, and toward actuation of the self in such possession, is likewise unconscious but can become known by reflection. Furthermore, we have seen that the single powers in their direction toward self-actuation have a basic tendency toward organization, which must be made effective by rational control and direction. Therefore, it stands to reason that we can become aware not only of the actual goal we strive for but also of the degree to which this self-ideal resembles the self-ideal as it ought to be. In other words, it must be possible for us to know where we are going and how far we have come. But because self-actuation implies self-love, it is difficult for us to know ourselves and our true progress without self-deception. Not only does self-love influence our reflection, but our knowledge of ourselves is impeded by the very fact that the degree of impulsion of our powers, their tendency toward possession and stabilization, that is, the nature of their working, can become known to us only by prolonged reflection. And that would have to precede our self-estimate. We make erroneous judgments, false estimates, without being aware of it. In spite of these difficulties, the very fact that our human perfection requires a self-knowledge which would enable us to progress seems to make it likely that there is some power or function in the human being which would supply the necessary unbiased information. On what can the self reflect to obtain that information?

If we reflect on the way in which we exercise our *will*, we shall not succed, because we properly choose only what we know. We do not spontaneously, at random, reach out for single objects or an ordered pattern of objects; we can choose only as far as these objects are *known* to us. We attain this knowledge conceptually or in judgments, whether speculative or practical. The functions of concept formation, reasoning, judging, are conscious as far as their content is concerned. We may not be aware that the meaning we attach to an object or an event is the fruit of long experience in various situations.

Things have meanings for us almost instantly when we perceive them. Yet this meaning has been acquired over a long period of time from many experiences with them. These experiences were not strictly intellectual operations; the whole organism took part in them. As these events acquire meaning, this long process of experience—of knowledge, emotion, movements—is telescoped into a single apprehension and a single judgment which give us the meaning of the object or event or situation. We acquire habitual modes of evaluating in this way, and these habitual modes will influence the direction we give to our activities in a particular situation. An examination of our particular modes of evaluating will require not only an examination of the content of our judgments and its meaning in intellectual operations, it will also require an investigation of these previous experiences which have given rise to these ways of evaluating.

If we want to discover the contents of the unconscious and its influence on behavior, we therefore shall not examine the acts of will directly but rather try to identify those factors which influence our decisions. These must be found in the antecedents of choosing, namely in intellectual evaluation and deliberation. Nor can we examine our judgments directly, for that requires a knowledge of the materials out of which the judging process arises. We have already seen that intellectual evaluation and judgment are the product of a long series of experiences which comprise not only the present perception and judgment but the material out of which these are drawn, namely sense experience, memory, imagination, and emotion.

If we could examine the emotions we would be fairly sure to gain a picture of the functioning of the total personality, because emotional states do involve the whole person. But emotion is judged as it is known in our awareness, and as long as we concentrate on the object of the emotion, we "emote" without knowing how we do it. And as soon as we concentrate on the emotion itself, all we are immediately aware of are the organic changes that go with it. We know that we are angry, but as soon as we start to introspect, the emotion of anger as such evaporates and we are left with various bodily sensations which cannot be used as an indication of the direction of our striving.

If not in emotion, we can only find the material for discovering our real striving in the imagination. It is the only function left. If we succeed in freeing imagination from the deliberate rational control which we exercise in our ordinary waking life, will it reveal anything about ourselves that is not available to reflective knowledge because of our unconscious prejudices and our self-love? Will our imagination give us a recognizable picture of what we are as a total person here and now, what we want to be, and how far what we want to be diverges from what we ought to be? Such use of the imagination seems plausible if we consider that the imagination was designed as an effective

instrument toward the organization and actuation of the person
in his quest for perfection. If we could examine the product of
the connatural functioning of the imagination, freed from the
interference or direction of rational and deliberate control, we
could perhaps find an imaginative picture of the person in his
life situation, of the way his activities are organized, the ideals
toward which he strives.

The usual way of investigating the working of the unconscious, introduced by Freud, is through free association in waking life and free associations to dreams. In psychoanalytic free
association, there is a deliberate effort to exclude rational control; in dreams, rational control is absent anyway. It will be
pointed out in Chapter 14 that free association investigates imaginative functioning in the form of memory; past events are
recalled by the force of emotional preoccupation which provides a
genetic picture of emotions but without any ordering of such
emotions according to significance to the person, according to
his rational pattern of life. It will also be pointed out in Chapter
14 that productive imagination, working spontaneously in
dreams and stories, will give a picture of the life situation of the
person, his goals, the means he chooses to reach them, and his
present status. Our preliminary investigations confirm that
productive imagination, when left to itself, produces a figurative
narration of the present life situation. It frequently presents us
with an image of the structured personality pattern in symbolic
terms, and with an image of the orientation of the pattern toward
what is suitable and perfective for this particular person. This
does seem to indicate that the imagination is an important instrument in helping the person to know and choose the means
to his goal of human perfection.

What, then, does investigation by these methods reveal about
unconscious conflict? What it is expected to reveal is not that
there are persons in whom there is a psychological pulling apart,
inner unrest, disturbance, and discomfort—we do not need to
use such means to discover that. What such an investigation
is expected to reveal is what the conflict is about and what are
its causes—*when there is a conflict.* Our findings will not give
us grounds for concluding that conflict is a *necessary* condition

for psychological growth, much less that it is a *cause* of development and integration.

That conflict is a necessary condition for growth would have to be established by logical deduction. But our analysis of the notion of the unconscious nowhere arrives at the idea that conflict (in the strict analytic acceptance of the term) is the inevitable outcome of any process or state that might be termed unconscious in any of the senses we discovered. It is only by *assuming* that conflict is there that we can interpret the so-called "remnants in the unconscious" as signs of its having existed. That we are not explicitly aware of the influence of our past experience on our present perceptions and actions need not rouse hostile factions within us against one another. If our perceptions are erroneous we may encounter difficulty or contradiction from reality but it does not follow that we always do.

The kind of unconscious that we called *unawareness of human functioning* is not the source of conflicts. Biological functioning is normally designed for inner harmony and peace (in the purely physiological sphere this state is called health and well-being). If psychological conflict arises out of physiological functioning it comes almost exclusively from a mistaken appraisal of the part such functioning plays in total living. In psychological functioning it is an error of evaluation that occasions an inconsistent or incorrect choice. But errors and false judgments are not per se effects of any function, conscious or unconscious.[12]

The same thing can be said of all the other categories of the unconscious that we examined. Impulses do lead us into trouble,

[12] What we mean to say here is that no psychological power or function performing normally is the cause of an error or false judgment and hence of a bad choice that leads to inner conflict. If vision, for example, is normal and working as it was designed to work, it does not result in hallucination. If hallucinations arise, some factor other than vision has interfered. Intellectual understanding, working unhindered, does not lead to a false appraisal of the objective situation. Neither love nor fear nor hope nor any other emotion is designed to determine judgment. Emotions are designed as instruments for reaching a goal, not for clouding the judgment. If they do cloud the judgment, it is an unfortunate accident. In the same way, errors are not the normal consequences of knowledge functions, they are unfortunate accidents.

but it is not because they are impulses or because they are un-conscious, it is because they impel us to goals that are incom-patible with one another. Unknown or wrongly known connec-tions between events in a person's experience may occasion trouble—and frequently they do—but in so far as they do they are not the means of growth or progress but the contrary. There are events and sources of activity within us that are firmly de-termined. We have no initial deliberate control over our sense impulses or our initial will impulses. These may incline us in directions counter to the requirements of our physical or social environment. We may find ourselves in an inner battle because of these inclinations. But it is not inevitable that our uncon-scious impulses will take us in the wrong direction or involve us in a war with ourselves or our environment. We can conclude that when conflict does arise it may be the occasion of psycho-logical growth if it is properly managed. If it is improperly managed, it may just as easily be the occasion of regression and disruption.

If these naturally determined springs of action were the cause of conflict, and conflict itself the condition for growth, human nature would be oddly designed. It would be a complex of formal contradictions. To us this is simply unintelligible. What we find in clinical investigation as well as in psychological ob-servation only entitles us to say that unconscious factors can lead to conflict and that conflict may be the occasion of psychological growth. To say that conflict is the cause or condition of progress is unwarranted.

So at the end we must conclude that even what is usually understood by "unconscious conflict" is the result of a person's divergence from his true self-ideal. By nature his naturally de-termined behavior is compatible with the objectives of his de-liberate good choices. That is to say, when any human function, even on the unconscious level, is allowed to proceed according to its natural design, it can be effective toward growth and progress. It is when wrong choices intervene that conflict arises. But the state of affairs brought on by bad choice can hardly be thought of as conducive to real progress.

Conclusion

In our attempt to present the principles and hypotheses which
are to form the skeleton of a theory of personality, we have tried
to keep the normal human being as the touchstone of our concepts. We have endeavored to work out a theory which is comprehensive and will apply to the behavior of ordinary human
beings who are psychologically well, though it also provides some
account of the behavior of persons who are psychologically not
well. Our primary hypothesis has been that powers and capacities of the human being are natively designed to work in
harmony and order to bring the person to that condition of development and self-realization that is proper to each single individual; second, that these powers are active in character and are
not merely components of a passive reactive system; and third,
that the human being is self-determined and must attain the
goal of perfect self-actualization by deliberate control and direction of himself and his activities.

We did not adopt these hypotheses arbitrarily. They are the
result of scientific observation, personal and historical, of human
beings in action. These hypotheses are nothing new or revolu-
tionary; they have been in the domain of learning for a long
time. We have essayed to form a unified general theory of
human personality upon these hypotheses, a theory which can account for human activities in the spheres of life that are characteristically human. Our theory applies to all kinds of human
affairs: economics, social living, science, art, religion; and to
eating, drinking, and making merry as well. It is a theory that
is easy to apply because human activity need not be distorted
by translation into the terms of the theory. Thus there was no
need to have recourse to any kind of dialectical method, either in
applying our inferences to observed data or in the systematic
development of the data themselves.

The test of any theory is, of course, its durability under experimental verification. Any scientific theory merits attention
only so far as it is amenable to investigation or even suggests a
design of experimental verification. We believe our concepts
will prove fruitful. The paper that follows indicates that our

theory is amenable to experimental or at least observational confirmation. That it needs elaboration and correction goes without saying. At any rate, we propose it as a possible junction where the way of the clinician and experimentalist can meet.

Summary of Major Theoretical Propositions

1. Psychologically, *personality is the patterned totality of human powers, activities, and habits, uniquely organized by the person in the active pursuit of his self-ideal, and revealed in his behavior.*

2. The capacities or powers of a human being are hierarchical and active in nature; upon presentation of their specific object, they are capable of initiating action.

3. The active nature of these powers *impels* or *urges* the person (when the necessary conditions are provided) not only to be active in pursuing their specific objectives but also to do so in an ordered and coordinated way. The function and nature of *impulse* and *urge* are unconscious, though they can become known by formal reflection and reasoning.

4. Human powers have a bimodal way of natural action: toward possession of external reality, and toward actuation of the self by stabilizing possessions; hence in their integrated action they constitute a natural tendency in the *person* toward possession and toward self-actuation in possession.

5. The prime factor in integrated action is the will, or the capacity of self-determined action. Like the other capacities it has a natural and unconscious way of acting. For fully integrated personality, there must be active and *deliberate* ordering not only of concrete actions but also of the total behavior pattern.

6. The rationale of this order is the self-ideal.

7. For proper integration, the self-ideal as it is must approximate closely the self-ideal as it ought to be for any given individual; if it does not, there will be internal disturbance which may be called conflict.

8. The externally perceptible organization of a person's activities, habits, and powers, as they go toward a self-ideal, is called the *personality structure*.

9. At the root of this structure (syntagma) there is *unity*, not conflict. Impulse, heightened to urge, makes it possible for the person to deal with difficulty, whether internal or external.

10. *Conflict* arises from inconsistent choice, or from incompatibility of the chosen goal with the natural order of things. This incompatibility may not be recognized, or it may be recognized but not connected with the disturbance. Only in this sense can psychological conflict be called *unconscious*.

11. *Unconscious*, when it is used as a characteristic of psychological processes, may mean any one of the following: (1) not the *explicit* content of an act of awareness; (2) not the *implicit* content of an act of awareness; (3) not *immediately* and *directly* available to understanding; (4) not available to understanding for *correct* judgments; (5) not available to memory; (6) not under voluntary control, indeliberate, and naturally determined.

12. When deliberate reflection is insufficient to provide the self-knowledge requisite for effective regulation and integration of action toward the proper self-ideal, an integral analysis of the imagination in its connatural mode of action will provide an accurate picture of the personality structure, the direction of striving, and the roots of conflict when conflict exists.

REFERENCES

1. ALLPORT, GORDON W. 1950. A psychological approach to the study of love and hate. In: *Explorations in altruistic love and behavior.* (Ed.) PITIRIM A. SOROKIN. Boston: The Beacon Press.
2. BRILL, A. A. (ed.). 1938. *The basic writings of Sigmund Freud.* New York: Modern Library, Inc.
3. CANTRIL, HADLEY. 1950. *The "Why" of man's experience.* New York: The Macmillan Co.
4. COKER, R. E. 1942. What are the fittest? *Scientific Monthly,* 1942, **55,** 487–94.
5. FREUD, SIGMUND. 1920. *A general introduction to psychoanalysis.* London: Boni & Liveright.
6. ———. 1920. *The ego and the id.* London: Hogarth Press.
7. ———. 1933. *New introductory lectures on psychoanalysis.* New York: W. W. Norton & Co., Inc.
8. GIBSON, JAMES J. 1951. What is a form? *Psychol. Rev.,* 1951, **58,** 403–12.
9. GILL, ERIC. 1944. *It all goes together.* New York: Devin-Adair Co.

10. GOLDSTEIN, KURT. 1940. *Human nature in the light of psychopathology.* Cambridge: Harvard University Press.
11. HEBB, D. O. 1949. *Organization of behavior. A neuro-psychological theory.* New York: John Wiley & Sons.
12. KARDINER, A. 1939. *The individual and his society.* New York: Columbia University Press.
13. ———. 1941. Psychoanalysis and psychology. *Phil. Sci.,* 1941, **8**, 233–54.
14. LASHLEY, K. S. 1938. The mechanism of vision. XV. Preliminary studies of the rat's capacity for detail vision. *J. Genet. Psychol.,* 1938, **18**, 123–93.
15. LEWIN, KURT. 1935. *A dynamic theory of personality.* New York: McGraw-Hill Book Co., Inc.
16. ———. 1942. Field theory and learning. National Society for Study in Education, 41st Yearbook, Part II, pp. 215–42. Bloomington, Ill.: Public School Publishing Co.
17. McDOUGALL, WILLIAM. 1933. *The energies of men.* New York: Chas. Scribner's Sons.
18. MASLOW, A. H. 1950. Self-actualizing people: a study of psychological health. In: *Personality, Symposium No. 1, April, 1950,* pp. 11–34. New York: Grune & Stratton, Inc.
19. MILLER, JAMES GRIER. 1942. *Unconsciousness.* New York: John Wiley & Sons.
20. ———. 1951. Unconscious processes and perception. In: *Perception: An approach to personality.* (Eds.) ROBERT B. BLAKE and GLENN V. RAMSEY. New York: The Ronald Press Co.
21. MOORE, T. V. 1939. *Cognitive psychology.* Philadelphia: J. B. Lippincott Co.
22. NUTTIN, JOSEF. 1950. Intimacy and shame in the dynamic structure of personality. In: *Feelings and emotions. Mooseheart Symposium.* (Ed.) MARTIN L. REYMERT. New York: McGraw-Hill Book Co., Inc.
23. SCHILDER, PAUL. 1942 *Mind: Perception and thought in their constructive aspects.* New York: Columbia University Press.
24. WHITEHEAD, ALFRED NORTH. 1925. *Science and the modern world.* New York: The Macmillan Co.
25. ZILBOORG, GREGORY. 1951. *Freud. His exploration of the mind of man.* New York: Chas. Scribner's Sons.

Chapter 7

A RESEARCH METHOD VALIDATING
SELF-DETERMINATION

By Louis B. Snider, S. J.

BEHIND THE research techniques and procedures of a science lies a frame of thinking within which the scientist works. The tools invented, their use, and the interpretation of their results will all be influenced to some degree by the scientist's preconceptions of his subject. Seldom has this been more evident than in the modern psychologist's empirical approach to the study of personality.

Scientific psychology grew up in an atmosphere of physical science. Its proponents were mostly men trained in physiology and biology; so interest centered primarily on the changes of the material organism. Its concept of man was modeled on the concept of anorganic matter; so research methods copied those of physics and chemistry. With an almost adolescent embarrassment for its "antiquated" antecedents, modern psychology repudiated philosophy as "unscientific," mind as "mystical," inherent powers or capacities as "figments of the imagination." Eager to attain the status of a science, modern psychology ventured beyond Descartes, the philosopher who set the stage for today's dogmatic materialism. He had divorced soul and body, leaving the body an inert statue. Modern psychology, taking a page from Spinoza, adopted a monistic philosophy and accounted for mental phenomena as just "another aspect of matter." Man thus became wholly inert, able only to receive and transmit the energy present in the environment. He seems to differ from a statue only by reason of distinguishable components of personality variously designated as traits, dynamics, systems, needs, fields of force, and so forth—all of which are described as we describe matter in motion. Since the first impetus and the later directional tendency of these components of personality come from outside the organism, the components themselves are essentially static and subject to the laws of mechanics both for their activity and their direction. In essence, therefore, the concept of personality is the same whether it is defined in terms of *S-R* bonds, *S-O-R* interchange, traits, Freud's "dynamics," Lewin's "fields of force," or Murray's "needs and press." A like mechanico-dynamic concept colors the thinking of *Gestalt* psychologists. The only unity in personality is accidental, brought about by the space-time framework within which an organism functions.

Over the course of the past thirty-five years a variety of devices have been invented and employed in the study of personality: rating scales, questionnaires, inventories, check lists, and the like. Usually the purpose of such studies has been to determine how a person stimulates others, how others stimulate him, or what "traits" he possesses. Research with these tools has been confined for the most part to correlational studies and to experimental designs using factor analysis. The result at times would appear to be more favorable to the refinement of statistics than to the accumulation of knowledge about human personality.

In more recent years the development of projective techniques, with their insistence on a holistic approach in clinical study, has held out a promise of improved research methodology. But most investigators, unlike most clinicians, have used the new tools in the old way, paying only lip service to the holistic approach. For example, they have treated isolated Rorschach symbols statistically as though these symbols represent unitary "traits," apparently unmindful of the fact that unless a scoring symbol stands for the same quality in every person tested, numerical values assigned are spurious. Yet every psychologist knows that, in the configuration of a Rorschach pattern, the quality represented by a scoring symbol varies with the number and kind of other symbols in the configuration. Many have noted this defect in Rorschach research methodology; few have sought a remedy.

The traditional use of the Thematic Apperception Test in research labors under the same defect in methodology. In their search for "variables," investigators have set up hypothetical constructs without due regard for what the subjects are actually saying about themselves in their stories. Too often the investigator analyzes story content in terms of preconceived notions based on a chosen personality theory. Thus analysis becomes confused with interpretation, and the investigator ends with numerical values of dubious psychological significance.

If TAT productions are atomized into a number of "variables" on the assumption that words, phrases, and sentences have discrete meanings which will reveal the individual's personality, the question of norms is inevitable. Murray recognized this need for norms in his approach to TAT analysis and gave the average total score of college males for each of the variables in his *Manual*. Stein lists "a distribution of common stories based on a study of 88 normal adult males." Eron, Rosenzweig, Rosenzweig and Fleming, Cox and Sargent, and Whitehouse have all done specific research in quest of norms. This preoccupation with norms indicates how tight is the grip of the nomothetic approach on research thinking in American psychology. Hartman has gone so far as to suggest that the psychometric approach of intelligence testing be made the model of personality study.

There are no "right" and "wrong" answers in the TAT. Each theme must be considered in relation to all the other themes if its individualized meaning is to be learned. Hence the same theme used by two different subjects will not of necessity have the same meaning for each. Thus isolated individual themes cannot be added to arrive at a "normal" theme. The important fact to be noted is *how* the subject reacts to a situation suggested by a TAT picture. Joel and Shapiro have stressed this important aspect in their "ego-function analysis." Arnold emphasizes the same aspect in her concentration on the role of the story outcome.

The research method proposed and demonstrated in this chapter grew out of Arnold's clinical method of TAT analysis. The basic assumptions and, as far as practicable, the procedures are the same. Since Arnold's method of analysis and interpretation differs radically in its rationale from methods which rely upon mechanico-dynamic theories of personality, it may be well to set down the basic assumptions upon which this TAT analysis is based.

1. Everything imagined must have been experienced previously in some way (in real life or in thought).
2. Each story with its stated outcome has a "moral," proposes a conviction (either a casual conviction or one strongly held; in the latter case, more than one story will express it).
3. When the stories are formulated as propositions, they will represent a statement of the person's philosophy of life.
4. This philosophy is a working philosophy, that is, it indicates how people are thought to act or how they should act; what actions are right, what actions are wrong; what will lead to success; what are the things to strive for.
5. Each story with its outcome contains an indication of *the way in which the person handles his impulses and emotions,* rather than an indication of the kind of emotions he has or their intensity.

   (Therefore, using "attitudes" or "themes" without reference to outcome of stories will give emotions without indicating whether they are the person's own emotions which he accepts or someone else's of whose conduct he disapproves. Neither will such procedure give any indication how the person's emotions influence his actions.) [1]

Through the use of creative imagination, the person reconstructs out of his own experience new combinations of images, selected purposefully, modified to fit the unity which he has in mind, and organized according to a plan. Thus there is an intrinsic purpose which controls the images and which implies intellectual evaluation in their selection. In telling a story in any detail, it is impossible not to give some indication of one's own convictions—whether the hero did the right thing or not and

[1] Private communication from Dr. Magda B. Arnold, April 1952. For a discussion of the assumptions underlying other TAT interpretations, see Lindzey (7).

whether he deserves his fate. It follows, therefore, that the imagination, if allowed to work freely, will give an unvarnished picture of the person's principles as applied to life situations.

However, free activity of the creative imagination does not mean free association. Rather, imagination is given full rein in the sense that it is not employed in the service of action. It sets up various situations and works through their complications. But since this operation is under conscious control, solutions will be found in accord with the principles which the person would apply to a similar situation in real life. It is this process which can be detected in a TAT analysis. Furthermore, since the unity of the person imparts unity to all the situations expressed in a TAT protocol, it is clear that the sequence of story outcomes will follow the person's system of principles used in self-actuation and self-direction. This unique set of principles is the person's philosophy of life; and from it can be found his hierarchy of values, his habitual dispositions toward modes of action, his proneness to emotional reactions or to reasonable control of self. This is the type of information, it would seem, which is required if the psychologist is to succeed in the prediction of human acts.[2]

Since the TAT stories can be stated in propositions which express the dispositional tendencies of the person for action in life situations, it is clear that the story *situations* (death of father, quarrel with sweetheart, etc.) are only part of the storyteller's intention. What he really thinks about the story events can only be inferred from the outcome. It is not enough to know that the hero runs away from home to avoid punishment. Is the evasion successful? Does the runaway make good or does he suffer? Does he return voluntarily or is he forced to return? It is the essential outcome of the story that gives the key to the narrator's thinking in the situation.

[2] Moral certitude in the prediction of human acts is possible if the person has developed the habit either of self-discipline (he acts according to reason) or the habit of self-gratification (he acts according to emotions). The TAT reveals the habitual tendency toward the one or the other if the test is used to ascertain a person's goals and the strength of his rational motivation for the achievement of those goals.

Arnold's method of TAT analysis was primarily designed for diagnosis and therapy. For personality research, the main problem is to quantify qualities in such a way that the investigator can draw comparisons between groups which are actually different in some psychological quality. How this may be done is demonstrated in the following investigation of the personality of high and low academic achievers in a high school for boys. Story elements are isolated according to objective criteria in such a way that the statistical measure of the difference between groups will mean a real psychological difference. These criteria are selected on the basis of thematic material as understood in Arnold's method of analysis. Thus in the present investigation *thematic material* means the full import of the story: what the story says, what the subject is thinking about a particular situation, and the final solution of a problem. Hence, the outcome of a story assumes a far greater importance in the present research method than it has heretofore enjoyed in those techniques which consider thematic material as story fragments or expressions of emotions.

Our problem was to find the reason for high or low academic achievement when the boys are of equal intelligence. With pairs of boys matched for intelligence and comparable in socioeconomic background, the difference in achievement should be reflected in their life goals as expressed in the TAT. Our procedure in selecting the groups of high and low achievers was as follows:

From a class of 122 senior high school boys, twenty pairs of subjects were selected on the basis of equal intelligence and differing academic achievement. At the time of entrance into high school the 122 pupils had a mean I.Q. of 122.84 (S.D.11.6) as measured by the Henmon Nelson Test, Form A. In the first semester of junior year, the mean raw score on the A.C.E. was 105.75 (S.D.16.6). The results of these two tests were averaged after converting the I.Q.'s of the Henmon Nelson and the raw scores of the A.C.E. into standard scores. Further selection was made from among the 122 students whose averaged standard scores for intelligence were between 50 and 72.5.

Differentiation of high and low achievers was made on the basis of actual success throughout six semesters of high school as measured by teachers' grades. An index of achievement was established by converting the average of each student's grades for six semesters into standard scores. In the calculation of these standard scores, the 122 members of the senior class were included. The difference between the standard scores of the grades and the standard scores of intelligence constituted an index of how far above or below expectancy each student was achieving. On the basis of this index, two groups were selected from among those students who had an average standard score above 50 for intelligence; one group showed academic achievement within the upper third of the class, the other within the lower third. The groups were paired as closely as possible for intelligence and differentiated as much as possible on the basis of achievement.

The data relating to intelligence, grades, and chronological age of the two groups are summarized in Table 1. The t test is used to measure the significance of the difference between group means. A t of 2.71 indicates a probability (P) of .01. At this level of confidence there is only one chance in a hundred that the difference between the two groups could have arisen by chance. A t of 1.69 indicates that there are 10 chances in 100 that this is merely a chance difference (P = .10). Therefore, a t much below 1.69, as indicated in Table 1 for intelligence and age, means that the two groups are substantially alike in these two respects. With regard to achievement, however, they are very well differentiated; in fact, there is no overlap in the scores.

Since many factors other than intelligence and personality may contribute to success or failure in the classroom, an effort was made to evaluate and control other variables which might influence individual success or failure. A school for boys was chosen on the assumption that it would yield a population relatively free from the distraction of sex in an adolescent classroom. This school emphasizes humanistic studies and selects its students from a large group of applicants on the basis of competitive examinations. Consequently, the students work in a traditional atmosphere of serious mental application. Many of them are

TABLE 1

MEANS, STANDARD DEVIATIONS, RANGES, AND MEASURES OF DIFFERENCES
FOR INTELLIGENCE, CLASS GRADES, AND CHRONOLOGICAL AGE OF TWENTY
HIGH AND TWENTY LOW ACHIEVING MALE HIGH SCHOOL SENIORS

	High Achievers (N 20)	Low Achievers (N 20)	t
Henmon Nelson			
Mean I.Q.	130.90	129.05	
Standard deviation	6.30	6.47	.848
Range	115 – 142	118 – 140	
ACE			
Mean percentile	95.25	95.10	
Standard deviation	3.96	3.40	.113
Range	86 – 99	88 – 99	
Combined intelligence rating			
Mean standard score	57.15	57.30	
Standard deviation	3.77	3.67	.118
Range	51.0 – 65.5	51.5 – 65.5	
Class grades for six semesters			
Mean grade	91.04	80.28	
Standard deviation	1.59	2.67	16.550
Range	88.9 – 95.1	73.8 – 82.0	
Standard scores for grades			
Mean standard score	63.70	44.35	
Standard deviation	2.83	4.07	17.763
Range	60 – 71	32 – 49	
Chronological age			
Mean age in months	208.50	210.60	
Standard deviation	3.43	5.21	1.402
Range in years	17–0 – 18–0	16–7 – 18–7	

preparing for professional fields. All the subjects in this investigation had attended the same high school for three full years and were midway through their senior year at the time of personality testing. Some variations, however, had occurred during the years of elementary schooling. The high achievers had attended an average of 1.85 elementary schools; the low achievers, an average of 2.30 elementary schools. The homes of two high achievers had been broken by the death of a parent.

The parents of two low achievers were separated. Another boy in this group had lost his mother through death. Two high achievers and four low achievers had no brothers or sisters. In general, the low achievers tended to come from smaller families than the high achievers. There is an average of three children in the homes of low achievers; four in the homes of high achievers. An examination of the birth order revealed no significant differences between the two groups. With one exception, all subjects were Catholic. Both parents were of the same religion in the case of all high achievers. Two instances of mixed religion were reported in the homes of low achievers. In each instance, the mother was Catholic and the father Protestant. The socioeconomic level of all families was upper middle class. When those extracurricular activities which consume an appreciable amount of time and attention were considered, it was found that students in both groups were about equally active in sports, dramatics, debating, and school publications.

Having selected the twenty high achievers and the twenty low achievers, the investigator administered the TAT individually, using Murray's directions for administration. An electrical recording was made of each set of stories to obtain a verbatim account of everything that the subjects said. Eleven cards were used: 1, 2, 4, 5, 6BM, 7BM, 8BM, 10, 12M, 14, 16. When the eleven stories were completed, the investigator said:

Now, without looking at any of these pictures again, make up a composite story in which you weave together as many of the pictures as you remember. You may change the character and the plot all you wish. Just weave as many of the pictures together as you can.

Thus each of the forty subjects told twelve stories in all, giving a total of 480 stories in the investigation—240 stories of high achievers and 240 stories of low achievers.

As a part of the initial exploratory stage of analyzing these stories, various parental, peer, and sibling situations were investigated for group differences. Statistical analyses were also made of situations in which the theme was death, anxiety, emotional relationships, parental interference with plans, rejection, dependence, hostility, and the like. The purpose of this approach was to test whether categories set up without reference to the outcomes of the stories would yield anything of statistical significance. *None of the results was significant.* Therefore, to avoid a trial-and-error approach to the solution of the problem—an approach which seems inherent in quantification of variables randomly selected on the basis of words, phrases, sentences, or concrete situations in TAT stories—the decision was made to set up a series of rational hypotheses about factors that might be expected to be associated with achievement, and then to test these hypotheses with empirical data derived from the TAT stories.

It could be argued that academic success depends chiefly upon rational self-determination, how the person actuates and directs himself. In particular, it could be said that

1. Academic success depends upon the clear perception of a rational goal.
2. Academic success also depends on strength of motivation. It will therefore be associated with a strong desire to achieve rational goals.
3. Academic success depends not only on the clear perception of a rational goal and the desire to reach it; it is also necessary to perceive and select the appropriate means to the chosen goal.

If our reasoning is correct, high achievers should give some evidence that they have rational goals, a strong desire to reach them (as indicated by a willingness to make sacrifices), and the realization that they must choose the appropriate means to their goal. They should, then, tell stories in which the characters follow rational goals and perceive them clearly; give up immediate wants for a greater end, or suffer failure for not doing so. Moreover, they should tell stories in which the characters choose rational means to reach their goal or are penalized for failing to do so.

To obtain empirical verification from the data of the TAT, we have classified thematic material associated with goal-striving in its various aspects. These classifications are made according to objective criteria. On the basis of the selected categories the differences between groups are tested by chi square (χ^2). The chi square test shows whether the obtained frequencies are greater than could be expected on the basis of chance alone. A chi square of 3.84 indicates that there are only five chances in a hundred that this difference in frequencies between the two groups is merely a chance difference. For the purpose of this study, we have accepted this .05 level of confidence (P) as the criterion of significance. Any level of confidence lower than .05 becomes increasingly significant.

Since we had a group matched for intelligence but did not analyze the matched pairs as such, the question arises why we did not do so. On a related problem Fisher says:

In cases in which each observation of one series corresponds in some respects to a particular observation of the second series, it is always legitimate to take the differences and test them . . . as a single sample; but it is not always desirable to do so. A more precise comparison is obtainable by this method only if the corresponding values of the two series are *positively correlated,* and only if they are *correlated to a sufficient extent* to counterbalance the loss of precision due to basing our estimate of variance upon fewer degrees of freedom * (Fisher, 5, p. 132).

We do not think that intelligence and thematic categories are very highly correlated. If they were, high achievers should show the same trends as low achievers in all thematic categories, for the two groups were matched for intelligence pair by pair. Since they show opposite trends there cannot be a high positive correlation. Hence we felt justified in treating the matched groups as unrelated in this respect.

The basis of the dichotomy between the two groups for chi square is the *presence or absence of the various categories of thematic material* as defined in the text. Thus in Table 2 the basis of the dichotomy is not successful versus unsuccessful adjustment as the headings might suggest, but the presence or absence of successful adjustment (first category), and the presence or absence of unsuccessful adjustment (second category). In fact, in these data, successful and unsuccessful adjustment and the other opposite categories are not mutually

* Reprinted from Fisher, *Statistical Methods for Research Workers,* published by Oliver and Boyd Ltd., Edinburgh, by permission of the author and publishers.

exclusive classes. Any high achiever may tell one or more stories with a theme characteristic for his group, but also one or more stories which fall into a category characteristic for low achievers. For instance, if among his twelve TAT stories there is even one story of successful adjustment after father's death, he is counted in this category. If in addition he tells even one story of giving up or failing after father's death, he is counted in the category of unsuccessful adjustment as well.

Since these pairs of opposed categories are related, it would not surprise us if there were a correlation between the occurrences of themes—presumably highly negative, as a glance at the numbers of high and low achievers in each category will indicate. Since we are not trying to construct a scoring system at this time but merely to demonstrate the differences between the two groups and the value of the categories for diagnostic purposes, we decided not to give a score to each occurrence or nonoccurrence and then add the scores to make an over-all comparison. We thought it more instructive to give the detailed information on the results for each category separately. The chi squares and their corresponding P values are therefore only appropriate for the particular category under consideration. The question of combining the chi square results for each pair of categories poses a difficult problem because of this admitted high correlation. We did not attempt it; rather, we take the position that the pairs of categories are replications of the same idea measured in two opposite ways.[3]

The appearance of thematic material in a single story seems sufficient to include a subject in the tested category, although this procedure does not account for differences of intensity as measured by repetition of themes. However, this defect does not seem to be a valid objection against this method since inspection of the data showed that failure to consider intensity lessens rather than increases the differences between groups. Thus any difference actually found with our method would be smaller than the true difference between the two groups. This is substantiated by the data of Table 4, which represents an approach to the measurement of intensity.

[3] We are grateful to Professor Frederick Mosteller of Harvard University for consultation and advice in this matter.

The results of the first analysis are tabulated in Table 2.

TABLE 2

DIFFERENTIATION OF TWENTY HIGH AND TWENTY LOW ACADEMIC
ACHIEVERS ON THE BASIS OF TAT STORIES WHICH EXPRESS THE HERO'S
REACTION TO SELECTED EMOTIONAL SITUATIONS

Thematic Material	High (N 20)	Low (N 20)	χ^2	P
A. *Reaction to catastrophe:*				
1. *Successful and unsuccessful adjustment* After death of father, the son goes own way successfully, perhaps providing for his mother;	5	0	3.657	.06
or he finds difficulty in breaking away from mother. He gives up his own ambition or suffers failure	0	5	3.657	.06
2. *Self-reliance and dependence* After death of a parent, the son shows self-reliance;	11	2	7.293	.01
or he shows emotional dependence	0	11	15.173	.0001
B. *Rational and emotional motivation:* Mother tries to restrain son by emotional demonstration, but he succeeds without suffering or loss;	9	2	4.389	.04
or he accedes to mother's emotional needs or suffers from emancipation	1	8	5.161	.02
C. *Presence and absence of reasonable dependence:* Wife (or girl) dissuades from wrongdoing; or husband (boy) goes own way and suffers dire consequences	7	0	6.234	.01
Wife (or girl) dissuades from wrongdoing or persuades to acceptable action	12	1	11.396	.001

Throughout this study, Yates's correction for continuity has been included in
the formula for χ^2. See McNemar, Quinn, *Psychological Statistics* (New York:
John Wiley & Sons, Inc., 1949, p. 207).

This Table has been constructed to show the way each pair of opposite tendencies in the thematic material differentiates high and low achievers. Since the samples studied are small, the consistency of these opposing tendencies is perhaps more revealing than the statistical values themselves. The various categories will now be discussed in detail.

Reaction to Catastrophe

Successful and Unsuccessful Adjustment. Successful adjustment was shown in stories in which the son, after his father's death, carries out his own plans for the future but makes thoughtful provision for his mother, if necessary. Unsuccessful adjustment is shown in stories in which the son, after the father's death, finds greater difficulty in breaking away from his mother to make his way in the world. He may give up his own ambitions or strike out for himself only to meet failure. It can be seen from Table 2 that successful adjustment occurs in stories told by five high achievers and by no low achievers, while unsuccessful adjustment is shown in stories told by five low achievers and by no high achiever.

According to Table 2, themes of successful and unsuccessful adjustment differentiate high and low achievers in the present study; but the difference fails to meet the criterion of significance which we have accepted. A similar analysis of themes in which a mother dies yielded no tendency toward a difference between groups.

Self-Reliance and Dependence. Death themes were further analyzed so as to estimate the degree of self-reliance and dependence in the subjects. If a subject met one of the following criteria, he was classified as self-reliant or dependent, respectively.

Criteria of *self-reliance*: After the death of a parent, a child

- a) Assumes responsibility and makes an adequate adjustment;
- b) Turns the catastrophe to a useful end by striving to eliminate the evil that brought about the parent's death;
- c) Follows a previously chosen career despite mother's emotional needs;

d) Looks upon a parent's death as a blessing in disguise— not as an escape from restrictions for himself but as freedom from pain, mental or physical, for another.

These criteria indicate a reasonable assumption of responsibility for one's own actions. On the other hand, the following criteria of dependence have in common an emotional dependence on another. This reliance on another is such that it reduces the story character's opportunities for success.

Criteria of *dependence*: after the death of a parent, a child

a) Makes an outward adjustment but suffers emotionally because of another;

b) Turns to another in grief. There is no mention of any adjustment other than the mutual consolation;

c) Turns to another for assistance in solving problems;

d) Commits suicide or meets some other drastic end because of the loss;

e) Gives up own ambitions or goals because he cannot bear the suffering of another;

f) Waits for another to make a decision about his freedom to pursue his own ambition.

From the data of Table 2, it appears that self-reliance, as expressed in the thematic material of the present study, is associated with high academic achievement. A still greater difference between groups emerges when high and low academic achievers are compared on the basis of our criteria for emotional dependence. This comparison suggests that emotional dependence is associated with low academic achievement.

Although a relatively small number of stories make up the matter of the above analysis, yet the selection of death themes for special treatment is justifiable on the grounds that approximately 60 per cent of the subjects gave stories of this type.

Rational and Emotional Motivation

From the statistical analysis of emotional dependence it seemed likely that thematic material expressing such dependence might appear also in stories that do not deal with death themes.

Stories were examined in which the emotions of another influence the actions of the character in the story, for instance, stories in which a parent or girl friend tries to control a boy's behavior through tears, pleas, recall of past sacrifices or favors. The stories were analyzed to find whether reason or emotion was the dominant influence in the character's decision. If a son, despite his mother's tears and pleas, follows a reasonable course of action and succeeds, reason is considered dominant. If he accedes to his mother's emotional appeal or tries reasonable action only to fail in his purpose or to suffer misfortune, emotion is considered as the dominating factor.

Stories in which reason controls behavior are told more frequently by high achievers; whereas stories in which emotions control behavior are told more frequently by low achievers. Thus the data support the findings of our analysis of death themes. High achievement is associated with stories of independence from emotional domination; low achievement is associated with stories of submission to emotional domination.

Presence and Absence of Reasonable Dependence

The role of reason in the personalities of high and low achievers was further investigated by an analysis of those stories in which a character relies on another's judgment. In such stories, it is not the other person who dominates the situation but rather the reasons presented by that other person. Thus for someone to agree to a reasonable request indicates his reasonableness. Reason rather than feeling constitutes the primary motive for action. Therefore a category, *reasonable dependence*, was set up by selecting stories in which submission to another's will was brought about by reason rather than by emotion: for instance, someone dissuades the hero from crime or violence, implying that crime or violence is not the reasonable solution; or someone persuades a character to a positively desirable action such as the assumption of his responsibilities, or assent to necessary surgery. In these stories, the hero's choice, influenced by a rational goal, leads him to cooperate with a reasonable woman.

From the data of Table 2, it may be seen that high achievement is associated with stories which portray the hero as amenable to dissuasion from a morally reprehensible or socially unacceptable act. The difference between high and low achievers becomes even more pronounced when to these stories of dissuasion from an unreasonable course of action are added stories of persuasion to a reasonable course of action, with or without moral implications.

We shall now try to bring out the psychological significance of the results shown in Table 2 and present, on the basis of our data, a psychological interpretation of the personality traits of our two groups.

Reactions to catastrophe, as designated in this study, must be taken in a limited sense. Many catastrophic situations may occur in the life of a man; but for the purpose of this investigation, we have chosen only death themes for analysis and interpretation. On the assumptions of our methodology, it seems safe to state that the narrator's reaction to such themes will be indicative of his basic reaction to most catastrophes. Moreover, the frequency with which death themes occur in adolescents' TAT stories offers a rich sample for the study of reaction to catastrophe.[4] However, despite these limitations and the failure of the thematic material to differentiate the two groups with statistical significance, the following interpretation of death themes seems to merit cautious acceptance.

When a catastrophe comes, high achievers seem to feel that they can assume responsibility and rearrange their lives with-

[4] Stories of a father's death emphasize the necessity for freedom from theoretical bias in the interpretation of the TAT. If an interpreter considers only the *fact* that an adolescent son narrates a story in which a father dies and a mother needs a son's care, under the influence of psychoanalytic theory the temptation might arise to interpret the situation as Oedipal. But the story as a whole usually says something entirely different: death of a father is a catastrophe which might endanger the son's plans and ambitions. A father's death suggests a loss of external or economic security for an adolescent. The Oedipal interpretation of the theme fails to differentiate the two groups in the present investigation. Our analysis supports the hypothesis of goal-striving. The only conclusion to be drawn from an Oedipal interpretation would be that there is a high incidence of Oedipus conflicts in this particular adolescent population—a conclusion scarcely supported by other unbiased evidence.

out emotional impediments. They manifest self-confidence. Persons of this kind may tend to glory in a challenge, seeing in it an opportunity to test their strength. But more important, it would seem, is the positive way in which high achievers meet a challenge and take action to overcome threats to their security. They focus their attention upon the threatening situation itself and not upon the damage it may do to them.

The personality picture of low achievers is almost diametrically the opposite. Rather than face catastrophe as a challenge to be met, they tend to focus attention upon the emotional turmoil generated by the situation. Thus they feel inadequate to the task of overcoming the catastrophe and give way to feelings and emotions which further impede successful adjustment. Though they may not openly admit feelings of inferiority, they show by their reactions a submission to adverse circumstances almost verging on fatalism. They are crippled for constructive action. Thus they lack the desire to put forth effort at the very time when effort is required. Their chief recourse, it appears, is to seek solace from another. Low achievers seem to look for security in dependence, perhaps in dependence upon a mother who represents for them love and affection. There is, as it were, an emotional rather than rational communication between parent and child in the stories, probably indicative of the low achievers' habitual social relationships. It might be expected that they respond to the emotions of others without much deliberation, and to their own emotions with impetuosity. In the sense that they tend to be dominated by emotions rather than to control them in accordance with reason, low achievers may be said to be less mature emotionally than high achievers. Since they are inclined to work on an emotional level, they may be somewhat deficient in a sense of responsibility. Fear, and possibly other negative motivation, may mean more to them than a positive goal to be attained by striving. Thus persistence suffers. This is suggested by TAT stories of emotional dependence in which low achievers show a readiness to abandon their own plans or to expect evil consequences should they strike out for themselves.

Rational and Emotional Motivation. The present investigation started from the hypothesis that academic achievement would be associated with rational motivation. Such motivation is on a conscious level. The person is moved to act by the goodness perceived in an object or experience. This goodness is present in the object whether or not it is recognized by the person; but the person is not affected by objective goodness unless he knows it. Therefore, two factors are necessary for a rational motive: the object or experience must be good in itself—practical, pleasurable, or befitting—and it must be known as good by the individual. That which is known as good, and consequently is desired, is called a *value.* An appreciated value which influences a person to act is a *motive.*[5] Values are relative since they derive their strength from the way the objective good is intellectually grasped by the individual; and therefore the strength of a motive depends more on the subjective meaning attached to a good than it does on the objective goodness itself. Furthermore, a person can change his values and does so in the activity called *deliberation.* In the last analysis, it is not the sheer strength of the motive that determines choice. Rather, the person determines his choice according to principles which are themselves generalized values. Thus self-determination is an activity initiated and carried out by a person, and not the activity of an organism running its course, determined by its past.

High achievers, according to our results, have established a hierarchy of values in which the good befitting a man takes precedence over the pleasurable, and a means is judged useful by reference to the befitting goal. Therefore, they function on a reasoned level. Not being compelled by their emotions, they appear to be less self-centered and more confident in their own ability to cope with problem situations. Since reason dominates their actions, it might be surmised that high achievers are more

[5] Modern American psychologists ordinarily stress a different concept of motivation. Relying on the biological sciences, they emphasize the role of drives, feelings, and emotions, when speaking of motivation. Much of that type of motivation is common to men and animals. Rational motivation is specifically human.

ready to assume responsibility than low achievers who are led by their emotions. The long range planning and adherence to adequate means directed toward a goal bespeak greater intellectual and emotional maturity than is to be found in low achievers.

Presence and Absence of Reasonable Dependence. High achievers appear to be more amenable than low achievers to arguments or persuasion *when the object of conviction or persuasion is to accomplish some (morally or socially) befitting end.* They are more ready to accept the reasons of another. Thus they are dependent not on another but on the reasons as presented by another.[6] Under reasonable persuasion, the heroes of their stories give up crime careers, stop hostilities, abandon irrational attitudes. Briefly, high achievers reach a better balance between dependence and independence than low achievers because reason controls the direction of their decisions.

Absence of themes in which the hero follows sound advice, suggestions, arguments, would seem to indicate that low achievers try to create the impression of complete independence. They seem to think that self-reliance means independence not only of people but of right reason as well, namely that it means doing what one wants to do rather than doing what one ought to do. This attitude might be expected to find expression in bluffing, stubbornness, refusal to cooperate—all of which militates against the readiness to learn which is of paramount importance in an academic situation.

[6] The thematic material designated as *reasonable dependence* in Table 2 not only contributes to an understanding of the personality of high achievers but serves as well to illustrate how the present method of analysis differs from the traditional ones. In Table 2, the stories classified as *reasonable dependence* revolve about acceptance of arguments or reasonable pleas of another. In the usual classification of variables, this kind of theme would probably be listed as submission, perhaps with the implication of dependence on a person. Taken in its whole context, however, the type of dependence indicated by the thematic material acquires a far richer meaning since it is based on a reasonable acceptance of ideas rather than upon an emotional "need." It is clear that this meaning would be lost in an atomization of the records into undifferentiated variables without regard for the specific nature of the dependence or the circumstances under which this expression of "submission" is evoked.

Goal-Directed Striving

All human activity begins with a goal. A man must know where he is going before he can advance. Even the person who walks about aimlessly, without a definite destination, has at least the vague goal of being some place other than his present location. He might be said to have a negative goal. He knows what he does not want, though he may not know what he wants.

The man with a definite goal in mind, however, may be expected to conform his actions to a pattern designed to accomplish that goal. He uses means as steppingstones to an end. If he acts reasonably, wanting his ultimate objective, he will select and choose more immediate objectives along the way until he reaches his final destination. It is this reasonable choice of lesser goals as means to a final objective that we call *prudence*, a virtue by which a person selects appropriate means to a suitable end. The objective value, therefore, of any means will be in direct proportion to its effectiveness in the accomplishment of the desired end. When the subjective value estimated by the person agrees with the objective value of the thing itself, a man may be said to be facing reality, at least so far as a particular goal is concerned. He must seek to conform his mind to the objective value of the extramental world and not seek to conform the extramental world to the subjective value with which he regards that world.

To investigate possible differences between high and low achievers in the way they perceive their goals and strive toward them, various categories of thematic material were set up which are summarized in Table 3.

Objectivity and Subjectivity. *Objectively valued goals* are recognized in those TAT stories in which a character goes out to attain a purpose, to accomplish a task, to win a reward. The emphasis is on the goal and not on the person's satisfaction in reaching it. The person may be said to be task-oriented. *Adequate measures* are means that are demanded by the objective situation. If a son stubbornly insists on going away to school because that is what *he* wants, regardless of the circumstances,

TABLE 3

DIFFERENTIATION OF TWENTY HIGH AND TWENTY LOW ACADEMIC ACHIEVERS
IN TERMS OF GOAL-DIRECTED STRIVING EXPRESSED IN TAT STORIES

Thematic Material	High (N 20)	Low (N 20)	χ^2	P
Objectivity and subjectivity				
Objectively valued goals with adequate means taken toward success	18	8	8.901	.003
Subjectively valued goals with emphasis on personal considerations	4	13	6.548	.01
Self-denial and self-centeredness				
Decision despite sacrifice	17	6	10.230	.002
Emotional decisions without suffering	7	14	3.331	.07
Modification and rigid adherence to plan				
Goals are modified in accordance with circumstances	13	4	6.548	.01
Rigid adherence to previous decision despite change in circumstances	4	12	5.104	.02

or because he desires to prove to his parents that they are wrong in hindering his education, the story does not fit into this category. Likewise, if the emphasis in the story is on the emotional strain of separating one's self from home, rather than on the positive pursuit of an ambition, the theme is not included in this category. A successful conclusion must be reached in the story through reasonable control of environment and through the adoption of means adequate to successful accomplishment. Thoughtful planning, in keeping with the limitations of reality, must be explicitly mentioned or clearly implied.

Subjectively valued goals. This category includes all thematic material which portrays the story character's desire to make a choice solely because of personal considerations. Advised or ordered to some course of action, he mulls over his own reasons, stubbornly resists or procrastinates unreasonably, develops arguments within himself for noncompliance, conforms to the will of another sullenly or not at all. He may resist pressure in a task because he has set his heart on something objectively less important, for instance, he slips away from his violin practice to play baseball. These stories depict the hero as self-oriented rather than task-oriented.

The term "subjectively valued" is used to indicate that attention is turned away from the objective value to be found in the goal and is focused more on the psychological reaction to it, as though that reaction and not the intellectual appreciation of a value were the total motive.[7] Therefore, this category provides a measure of egocentric motivation. Here the storyteller values personal factors above all other considerations. This is indicated clearly by the outcome of the story which is favorable to the hero despite his selfishness. If he is punished or fails in his purposes, the story is not counted in this category.

As may be seen in Table 3, the high and low achievers in this study are significantly differentiated in terms of thematic material expressive of objective and subjective values set upon goals. High achievers tend to tell stories in which the hero is task-oriented. Low achievers tend to tell stories in which the hero is self-oriented.

Self-Denial and Self-Centeredness. *Decision despite sacrifice.* Themes of this kind are characteristically those in which a man follows duty or some other reasoned motive with consequent loss or suffering to himself or to a loved one. This loss is not merely a temporary emotional strain. It includes such calamities as physical injury, death, loss of love. The primary goal may or may not be reached in these stories. The important aspect is

[7] Even motivation of this kind is rational, a fact frequently disregarded by modern psychologists. The emotions, feelings, attitudes, do not necessarily determine a person's decisions. The individual who submits to their influence is one who has set so high a value on self-gratification that he prefers to follow their inclinations rather than to oppose them at the sacrifice of comfort. This is analogous to saying that he prefers the pleasure principle dictated by the organism to the reality principle dictated by reason.

the hero's willingness to deny himself or make a sacrifice as a consequence of a reasonable decision. The hero struggles on despite hardships, making his farm a success because he does not want to leave the farm and accept an easier job in the city; or he sacrifices pleasure so that he can become a great musician through long and arduous hours of practice.

Emotional decisions. In this category we include stories in which the story character acts contrary to reason, fails to think through a situation, makes an impulsive decision. Forced to play the violin, for instance, he "bounces it off the wall and runs out." Also included are stories in which the narrator intrudes himself into the story to solve the hero's dilemma on a superficial (emotional) basis: "From the look in his eye, I would say that he leaves this girl and goes back to his wife." In these stories, the hero suffers nothing because of his decision. Should he change his mind after reflection, the story is not included in this classification because then the character is presumably acting on reasoned principles; for instance, a husband argues with his wife, walks out, but returns "after thinking it over."

The data of Table 3 show that a majority of high achievers tell at least one story in which a decision is made despite sacrifice; while relatively few of the low achievers narrate such stories. The difference between groups, when compared on the basis of this kind of thematic material, is statistically significant. On the other hand, low achievers seem somewhat more inclined than high achievers to tell stories in which the hero makes emotional decisions. However, the difference between groups, in terms of emotional decisions in stories, fails to meet our criterion for significance

Modification and Rigid Adherence to Plan. *Modification of plan in accordance with circumstances.* Thematic material selected for this category includes stories in which the main character changes his ambition or life's goal because of someone's death, financial failure, or other circumstances over which he has no control. As is evident from the nature of the theme, adaptability to circumstances and not vacillation of purpose is the criterion for inclusion in this category. Furthermore, modification of plans and not abandonment of plans is required.

Rigid adherence to previous decision. Despite circumstances which call for an adjustment of plans, the hero continues to strive for a previously selected goal. This type of behavior fails to take reality factors into account and suggests an inability or unwillingness to adapt one's self to environmental changes. Included in this category are stories of suicide after failure, insistence on revenge, refusal to repent or to heed advice, constant work without regard for family and friends, speeding without concern for warnings, premonitions, feverish activity. There is a close affinity between this type of story and that of purely subjective motivation. In both kinds of story the character does not or cannot weigh values objectively. The stories differ, however, in at least one respect: in stories of purely subjective motivation the character is in a quandary about all action and seeks motivation from his personal feelings; in stories of rigid adherence to a single purpose the character has already made a decision about one course of action and now refuses to change his course despite a proposal of an objectively superior goal. He insists, for instance, on playing ball to the exclusion of study. In this category, the outcome of the character's singlemindedness is without adversity despite his unreasonable attitude.

An analysis of TAT stories in which the hero either modifies his goals in accordance with circumstances or rigidly adheres to a preconceived plan reveals two statistically significant differences between our groups. Thematic material in which goals are modified seems to be associated with high achievement. Low achievers apparently prefer stories in which the hero rigidly adheres to previous decisions despite an adverse turn of circumstances.

Since the type of thematic material analyzed in Table 3 indicates a difference between high and low achievers in their intellectual, volitional, and emotional relation to objective goals, it was thought desirable to investigate whether these statistical differences would persist if "impurities" were eliminated from the calculations, that is, if those subjects were eliminated who

TABLE 4

DIFFERENTIATION OF TWENTY HIGH AND TWENTY LOW ACADEMIC ACHIEVERS ON THE BASIS OF TAT STORIES IN WHICH THE HERO'S MODE OF GOAL-STRIVING IS UNIFORM

Thematic Material	High (N 20)	Low (N 20)	χ^2	P
Objectively valued goals and adequate means, but *no* stories with subjectively valued goals	15	4	10.025	.002
Subjectively valued goals but *no* stories of objective goals and adequate means	1	9	6.533	.01
Decisions with sacrifice but *no* emotional decisions	11	2	7.293	.01
Emotional decisions but *no* decisions with sacrifice	0	10	10.800	.001
Modification of plan but *no* stories of rigid adherence to a goal	12	2	8.901	.003
Rigid adherence to a goal but *no* stories of modification of plan	3	10	4.103	.04

express clear objective goals in one story and strong subjectivity in another. Such an analysis, given in Table 4, may be looked upon as a measure of intensity.

A comparison of Tables 3 and 4 reveals that the differences between groups tend to be heightened when "pure types" are isolated. This is particularly true in the case of *emotional decisions.* In Table 3 it may be seen that seven high achievers recounted stories in which the problem was solved by an emotional decision. From Table 4, however, it appears that all these seven subjects also told stories in which decision led to sacrifice. It may be reasonable to suggest that even these high achievers, though they do occasionally give in to emotion, possess more mastery over their impulses and more readiness to follow an ideal at the cost of personal sacrifice than do the low achievers.

With respect to our category of *goal striving*, the following personality delineations seem warranted by empirical data:

High achievers appear to be more aware of the relationship between ends and means than low achievers. They see more clearly what they want and realize more fully the steps required for the attainment of their goals. Their recognition of objective values leads them to be decidedly task-oriented. One might expect the high achiever, once he has set his compass on a goal, to busy himself about the necessary means of arriving at his chosen destination and not to dissipate his energies with impatient efforts to hasten the day of accomplishment.

High achievers are more ready to make sacrifices. They realize that they cannot have everything and so in their decisions are prepared to forfeit an alternative goal. Confronted with a choice between two values, they recognize the impossibility of having both and willingly forego one for the sake of possessing the other. Thus they are free to make decisions and to avoid conflicts which, in an academic situation, might hinder concentration. While they set high values on their goals, high achievers are flexible and can direct their energies toward success in another pursuit if and when circumstances demand an alteration of plan. This suggests a greater capacity for the avoidance of frustration.

High achievers are more apt to decide a matter on the basis of objective evidence and objective value, controlling their impetuosity while they can evaluate the situation in terms of principles and ideals. This greater object-reference prior to decision enables them to reason more effectively about the adequacy of means, to deliberate more fully, and to choose more freely. In short, the high achiever lives more securely because he has learned to direct his life by reason.

Basically, then, the success of achievers in the present study would seem to be due, not to the presence or absence of feelings, emotions, attitudes, or other "structural elements" of personality, but to the way in which the achiever employs reason in his self-determination. His emotions, then, become "driving forces" toward the desired goal, aiding rather than distracting the person in the attainment of his goal.

Low achievers fix their attention on the subjective evaluation of the end in terms of personal satisfaction or gratification without due consideration for the objective value of the goal itself. They are primarily concerned with immediate results and impatient about delay. Reluctant to sacrifice a possible goal, they are more prone to conflict and consequent impairment of mental efficiency. They want to "have their cake and eat it." As a result, they suffer greater loss of security than do high achievers because they fail both in personal satisfaction and in the attainment of objective goals.

Evaluation of goals in terms of subjective gratification, without sufficient regard for objective values, leads the low achiever to an over-emphasis on the emotional value of a goal. Like a child, he can give as a reason for his desire only the unsatisfactory response, "Because I want to." This impetuosity may beget frustration. So he generates more physical than mental energy; and his physical energy is largely under the direction of emotional urges, uncontrolled or poorly controlled by reason.

Deficient in rational control, the low achiever plunges on toward a goal. He may overlook the proper means, fail in prudence, meet obstacles with rigidity. Perhaps he is unable to modify his plans because he has not worked out the possibilities in detail. He merely has a goal. He has not stopped to deliberate upon the particular means to that goal. His rigid adherence to a plan tends to maintain his subjective orientation: he wants a thing when he wants it—which in common language is called obstinacy, very different from productive perseverance.

In general, therefore, it might be said that the low achiever is more egocentric, less objective in his evaluation of purposes, more prone to conflict and frustration. He is inclined to work more on the sense level than on the intellectual level. His "driving force" is less controlled by reason than the "driving force" of the high achiever. In an academic setting, the low achiever finds more sacrifices required of him than he is willing to make. The consequence will be insufficient perseverance in his efforts toward academic success. He seeks self-gratification where the high achiever disciplines himself.

What has been said about the personalities of high and low achievers finds confirmation when other areas of TAT material are analyzed.

Stories of Daydreams and Chance Success

Stories in which the hero daydreams were analyzed to investigate in more detail the subject's attitude toward goals and motivation. Since daydreams of themselves need not be detrimental to productivity, they were also considered in relation to action. Various kinds of dreams were examined, for instance dreams of achievement, of suffering, of love, of pleasure, and of fear. Table 5 summarizes the material on stories of daydreaming.

TABLE 5

DIFFERENTIATION OF TWENTY HIGH AND TWENTY LOW ACADEMIC ACHIEVERS
ON THE BASIS OF TAT STORIES NARRATING DAYDREAMS OR CHANCE SUCCESS

Thematic Material	High (N 20)	Low (N 20)	χ^2	P
Daydreams:				
Daydreams of all kinds	11	19	6.533	.01
Daydreams of a suffering hero ..	1	9	6.533	.01
Daydreams of achievement	6	10	.938	.33
Daydreams of achievement followed by successful action	4	1	.914	.36
Daydreams of achievement not followed by successful action	2	9	4.389	.04
Stories of chance success:				
Stories in which success is won by chance, luck, a *deus ex machina,* or through unexpected aid from another	1	11	9.643	.002

Several significant differences between high and low achievers appear in the data of Table 5. It would seem that TAT stories of daydreams, and stories of daydreams about a suffering hero, are associated with low achievement. On the basis of stories relating daydreams of achievement as such, the two groups are not significantly differentiated; but when these stories are analyzed for subsequent action, a statistically reliable difference appears. Low achievers tell stories in which the hero rests content with his dream and makes little or no effort to act it out in reality.[8] TAT stories of daydreams, and stories of daydreams of the suffering-hero type, are associated with low achievement.

Somewhat similar to stories of daydreams about success are the stories in which the hero is actually successful, but not as a result of reasonable effort but by chance, a stroke of luck, a *deus ex machina*, or through unexpected aid from another. For instance, he gets an inheritance from a forgotten relative. These themes seem to tap a wishful element in the subject's personality, an element which may supplant the desire to succeed when he does not know the means to take toward a goal, or perhaps when he does not want to make the effort. It is as though he were saying: "I don't know how this situation can be met, but everything will turn out all right in the end. There is no need to work or to worry. If the worst comes, somebody will help." Psychologically, this kind of attitude seems to indicate dependence and an undeveloped sense of responsibility. More than half the low achievers and only one of the high achievers tell stories of this type; thus the difference between the two groups is statistically significant. This category should also be compared with our category, "objectively valued goals" (Table 3, and discussion), *where adequate means are taken* to reach the desired goal. Such stories are characteristically given by high achievers.

From the foregoing analysis it may be suggested that low achievers are more inclined to find satisfaction in daydreams. In line with what has been said about the motivation of low achievers, this tendency would appear to be the result of their desire for immediate satisfaction, their impulsive actions, and their refusal to sacrifice. Daydreams are immediately satisfying, especially if they are dissociated from physical or mental effort. Low achievers may daydream to escape disciplined action and to produce the immediate satisfaction which is the

---

[8] The thematic material for this category consists of stories in which no action followed the dream or in which the hero realized his dream's accomplishment without reference to any intervening activity, e.g., "The boy is sitting in class dreaming of the day he will be a great doctor. He becomes a doctor and discovers a cure for cancer."

primary goal of their desires. This substantiates the contention that they are less realistic in their ambitions and less inclined to exert effort toward an objective goal.

Daydreams about a suffering hero may be associated with feelings of self-pity as well as with guilt feelings. In an academic situation which calls for a reaching out toward an objective goal, low achievers are inefficient and ineffectual. Their concern with self-gratification reduces their scholastic success and leads to frustration of their desire for achievement. They compensate by fantasying success, which cushions them against the harshness of real failure. Moreover, since low achievers shun the sacrifice entailed in effort but do not want the pain involved in failure, their only recourse is to have both comfort and success by withdrawing from reality into fantasy where they can control events without paying the price of self-denial which is demanded by productive activity. If they recognize the necessity of pain as an alternative of their rejection of responsibility or as the price of inertia, they can mete out the pain in acceptable measure in their intrapunitive daydreams without loss of real comfort.

Frustration

Reasonable Management of Frustration. From our results so far, we can expect decided differences in the way in which high and low achievers meet frustrating situations. The high achiever, with his reasoned approach to thwarting persons, circumstances, and objects, would be expected to master the situation with less emotional disturbance. The low achiever, on the other hand, could be expected to react more emotionally in the same situation. Table 6 gives a detailed analysis of stories of frustration in which a person wants to reach a goal but is temporarily or permanently prevented from progress. The outcome of these stories was analyzed according to the following criterion: the hero is adequately motivated and he succeeds in his reasonable control of frustrating conditions. Every high achiever related at least one story which met this criterion but only seven low achievers told a story that met it. The only conclusion warranted by this difference is that successful manage-

TABLE 6

DIFFERENTIATION OF TWENTY HIGH AND TWENTY LOW ACADEMIC ACHIEVERS
ON THE BASIS OF TAT STORIES EXPRESSING REACTIONS
TO FRUSTRATING SITUATIONS

Thematic Material	High (N 20)	Low (N 20)	χ^2	P
Reasonable management of frustration:				
Hero exercises reasonable control, with adequate motivation, and succeeds in overcoming the obstacle	20	7	16.41	.0001
Hero exercises reasonable control, with adequate motivation, but the outcome of the story is not entirely favorable	8	2	3.333	.07
Hero cooperates with another to the benefit of both	9	1	6.533	.01
Hero enlists help of father and succeeds	13	3	8.438	.004
Escape from frustration:				
Fantasy with success	4	10	2.747	.10
Regression with success	0	4	2.500	.11
Projection with success	0	3	1.975	.16
Ignoring with success	0	4	2.500	.11
Either regression, projection, or ignoring	0	8	7.656	.01

ment of frustrating conditions in TAT stories is associated with high achievement.

Next we were interested in examining the stories of frustration in which the hero failed in his effort. The frustrating conditions either nullified his efforts or mitigated his success. More high achievers than low achievers told this type of story, but the difference escapes significance.

A difference of attitude toward cooperation in a frustrating situation was tested by selecting those stories in which the hero cooperates with another to the mutual benefit of both. This cooperation is in the nature of teamwork and does not imply dependence in the sense of subservience. The differentiation of groups tabulated in Table 6 suggests that stories of cooperation for the purpose of overcoming obstacles are associated with high achievement.

Of the high achievers' stories, 77 per cent centered on some frustrating situation while 70 per cent of the stories of low achievers were of this kind. In view of these data, we hesitate to accept the mere mention of a frustrating situation as indicative of frustration in the narrator.

The traditional method of TAT analysis was tested on the same data by isolating the usual "variables." Various areas of frustration, e.g., independence, security, and achievement, were analyzed independently of story outcomes. Thus *independence* was considered to be frustrated in stories where a character is pressed to do something against his will, or is restrained from doing something he desires. *Security* was subdivided into mental and physical security. If the character was worried, suffered loss of limb or body organ, was the victim of another's aggression, his physical security was considered to be jeopardized. Frustration of security in the home was categorized separately: members of the family are at odds in the story, someone is sick, has died, or divorce breaks up the family unit. Frustration of achievement was categorized from stories in which someone or something impedes success: friends call the hero to play and he fails an examination the next day; surgery is made doubly difficult for want of proper instruments; inferiority feelings prevent learning. *No significant differences between groups were revealed in any of these analyses.*

Similar barren results were produced by the analysis of various frustrating situations such as parental pressures, home status, financial loss, emotions or hostility of others, physical handicaps, and feelings of guilt or inferiority.

Escape from Frustration. Both groups told stories in which the hero meets frustrating situations with fantasy. There are more low than high achievers who told such stories but the difference between the groups is not statistically significant. Low achievers also narrate stories in which frustration is successfully met by regression, projection, and ignoring—all escape reactions.[9] Although none of these reactions taken singly occurred in enough stories of low achievers to constitute a statistically significant difference between groups, one or other of these reactions occurred in at least one story of eight low achievers. No high achiever narrated a story of this kind. Hence, when these three escape reactions are considered as a unit, a statistically significant difference between groups emerges; and thematic material of this kind seems to be associated with low achievement.

From the above analysis it would seem that high achievers have a greater capacity than low achievers for preventing real frustration by using reasonable means of overcoming the obstacle.

The tendency of high achievers to tell stories ending in failure or partial success seems to require interpretation, even though the difference between groups falls short of statistical reliability. Psychologically, such stories seem to be related to the stories of sacrifice and modification of plans which were discussed above.

A realistic view of success in any endeavor must recognize certain limitations, a price to be paid commensurate with the value of the goal. Perhaps the high achiever realizes this fact more fully than the low achiever, and his stories of failure reveal his inclination to be realistic in his expectation of limited good to be derived from his efforts. This is in keeping with his readiness to make sacrifices and with his greater realism as expressed in fewer stories of daydreams and his refusal to provide chance solutions to problems.

[9] Following are the criteria for each of these categories of thematic material:

Regression: The hero returns to an earlier stage of development to find a solution for frustrating situations. This return may be mental as when he retraces childhood innocence in daydreams; or it may be behavioral, as when the hero tries to discourage his parents from wanting a musician in the family by playing the violin discordantly and incessantly.

Projection: Having made a mistake, the hero tries to shift the blame to another. For instance, a boy accidentally shoots his father and complains that his father had the gun in the house where he could get it.

Ignoring: The hero disregards the feelings of another, his own responsibilities, or the moral implications of his actions in the solution of a problem.

Stories of failure may also represent anxiety about success. It is to be expected that a boy who sets a high value on a goal, who is mindful of competition, who does not dream of success without effort, who realizes that success depends in large part upon himself and comes at a cost—all factors presumably characteristic of the high achievers in this study—will be tempted to question his own ability at times and perhaps be vexed by fears and feelings of inferiority. Moreover, since he sets a high value on the objective good of successful accomplishment, he will likewise attach importance to its opposite, failure. Thus he is likely to give more thought to failure than does the low achiever, much as the Saints give thought to Satan.

Whatever may be the true meaning of the thematic material expressed in stories of failure in an individual instance, it seems apparent that high achievers attack frustrating situations reasonably, despite possible feelings of inferiority, emotions of fear, threat of sacrifice, danger of failure. They seem to be more realistic than their fellow low achievers in the face of frustrating situations.

Stories of cooperation suggest that the high achiever is ready to lay aside his individual interests and to join forces with others because he is not motivated so strongly by selfish interests. He is willing to share a project and its fruits. For him the important thing is that the project be successful. In an academic environment, this spirit of cooperation is an asset. It is associated with a readiness to learn, making the student an apt recipient of knowledge. It may serve to reduce the tension of interpersonal competition, directing rivalry away from individuals and allowing the high achiever to work for more altruistic goals such as the school's reputation for scholarship. Thus the high achiever does not see the striving of another as a threat to his own recognition as an individual, to his own achievement, his own acceptance and status, his own security. Rather, he sees that he can enlist with others harmoniously, and that the combined forces may overcome obstacles which he alone cannot surmount.

High achievers narrated more stories than low achievers of a hero who succeeded in overcoming a frustrating situation by turning to a father figure for help in time of frustration. The difference between groups is statistically significant. Thematic material of this kind seems to indicate more than habitual reliance on a father figure in time of frustration. It may be suggested, in line with our previous analyses of self-reliance, that high achievers are more aware of their readiness to assume an adult male role in society. Thus they can turn with more grace and greater ease to an adult male for help.

Low achievers narrate stories in which frustrating situations are met by regression, projection, ignoring, avoiding, and fantasy—all escape reactions—without any penalty for the hero. They tend to shift the blame for their mistakes to someone else, to disregard the feelings of another, or to resort to some childish subterfuge to extricate the hero from an unpleasant situation. The emotional element involved in reactions such as these seems to indicate real frustration. Perhaps there is a veiled admission by the low achiever that he is unable to cope adequately with frustrating situations.

Role of Basic Assumptions in Research Methodology

The chief justification for the inclusion of this report in the present volume lies in the new and distinctive approach it offers for research methodology in the study of human personality. The method proposed needs to be perfected. In its present form it is little more than a crude outline of how research on personality may be conducted by those who see man as differing in kind, and not merely in degree, from the brute animal.

Like all research methods, the present one is based on a conceptualization which seeks to embrace the *whole* subject matter. It is this effort of the human mind that leads the scientist willy-nilly into the domain of philosophy. He needs the truths expressed in the ultimates, in order to interpret the facts which he finds. Thus his interpretations will be stamped by his "frame of reference," his "conceptualization," his "theoretical framework," or whatever else he chooses to call his *philosophy*. In the final reckoning, the truth of his interpretation will be proportional to the truth of his philosophy.

In modern psychology it is a widely accepted tenet that man is essentially kin to the rest of nature. Psychologists taking this position set the "ultimates" of man only on the basis of matter. Thus human behavior is viewed as ineluctably determined in all men by the organism modified by the impact of previous experiences, and personality is basically an organic development at the mercy of the environment.

In the philosophy of the present research method, man's actions are not wholly at the mercy of the environment. Man is self-activating and self-directive. The direction which his actions take is purposeful, according to known and self-evaluated goals, or goals which were formerly known and evaluated but now have become "unconscious." Therefore, relying on his knowledge and his evaluation of goals, the normal man determines his own behavior. He is influenced, it is true, but he is not determined by his material organism with all its physical variations when he is healthy and acts with full consciousness. Man, fully understood, has the capacity to act and to direct his actions in accord with a reasoned plan which is not wholly imposed upon him by his environment.

Our study of the differences between high and low achievers was focused on this capacity of self-determination. It is this capacity in the human being which effects the unique organization of human powers that is the core of "normal" personality. Since the relative degree of development of this capacity indicates the degree of intellectual and emotional maturity in man, the empirical data of the present study strongly suggest that high achievers in the sample tested are more mature intellectually and emotionally than low achievers. The outstanding characteristic of high achievers is their ability to determine their own behavior in accordance with reason and not to follow the inclinations of their naturally determined appetites as low achievers do.

Summary and Conclusion

TAT stories of twenty high achievers and twenty low achievers, matched for intelligence and age, all male high school seniors, were analyzed to answer the question: "What is the difference between the personality of high achievers and low achievers in high school?"

Thematic material, selected on the basis of the complete stories with particular attention to outcome, formed the basis for an analysis of the difference between the groups. When the 5 per cent level of confidence was taken as the criterion of significance of the difference between groups, high and low academic achievers were differentiated by the following thematic material:

Thematic Material Given Mainly by High Achievers

1. After the death of a parent, the son adjusts successfully, shows self-reliance ($P = .01$).

2. Though a mother tries to restrain her son by an emotional demonstration, he succeeds independently without repercussions ($P = .04$).

3. The hero is dissuaded from crime, violence, or asocial behavior by a female character. Should he reject the advice, he suffers evil consequences ($P = .01$).

4. When stories in which a female character advises or persuades to some acceptable course of action are added to the thematic material mentioned under 3, the difference between groups increases ($P = .001$).

5. Story characters have clear, objective goals and choose means which are adequate for success ($P = .003$).

6. If the decision to strive toward a goal entails some sacrifice the hero readily and willingly accepts it as part of the price he must pay for achievement ($P = .002$).

7. When circumstances cannot be controlled, the characters in the stories modify their plans to fit circumstances ($P = .01$).

8. The hero manages frustrating situations reasonably, is adequately motivated, and succeeds in overcoming the obstacle ($P = .0001$).

9. The hero cooperates with another to the mutual benefit of both ($P = .01$).

10. The hero succeeds in overcoming a frustrating situation by turning to a father figure for help in time of frustration ($P = .004$).

Thematic Material Given Mainly by Low Achievers

1. After the death of a parent, the son shows emotional dependence ($P = .0001$).
2. A mother tries to restrain her son by an emotional demonstration. The son either accedes to her emotions or suffers because of his desire for emancipation ($P = .02$).
3. Motivation of the hero emphasizes subjective evaluation rather than objective values ($P = .01$).
4. Despite change of circumstances, the hero struggles on in a headstrong pursuit of his previously determined goal ($P = .02$).
5. Stories of daydreams of all kinds ($P = .01$).
6. Stories of daydreams about a suffering hero ($P = .01$).
7. Stories of daydreams of achievement not followed by successful action ($P = .04$).
8. Stories in which success is won through chance, luck, a *deus ex machina*, or through unexpected aid from another ($P = .002$).
9. The hero meets frustrationg situations by regression, projection, or ignoring ($P = .01$).

In interpretation, it has been suggested that high achievers exercise self-discipline to a greater extent than low achievers, see goals clearly and objectively and direct their energies prudently toward attainment, are willing to sacrifice immediate gratification for delayed but more important goals, yield more readily to the reasons of others, accept catastrophe as a challenge to be met, and possess greater self-confidence, though they acknowledge their real limitations. Guided by reason, high achievers are less affected by the emotions of others, show higher regard for reasons proposed by women, curb ambition to conform to reality, meet frustrating conditions successfully, and therefore probably suffer less from feelings of frustration, and apparently feel more secure in the adult male group.

Low achievers, on the other hand, are inclined to seek personal gratification; may see their goals clearly but want immediate results and cannot tolerate delay, stress the emotional value of goals more than the objective value, readily yield to the emotional needs of others, expect to fail when catastrophe strikes, feel emotionally dependent on the love of others, are unsure of their own ability, rigidly hold to a previous decision despite adverse circumstances which make execution impossible, act impulsively in the face of frustrating conditions, and seek to overcome frustration or escape from it by fantasy.

These interpretations seem to support the three hypotheses consonant with self-determination which were proposed for investigation:

1. ACADEMIC SUCCESS DEPENDS UPON THE CLEAR PERCEPTION OF A RATIONAL GOAL.

By an analysis of goal-striving it was found that high achievers evaluate their goals objectively and strive for their attainment because of the value which they perceive in the thing itself. This outlook is associated with greater realism, shown in a willingness to cooperate with others for a common end, and a readiness to accept an alternative plan when the original ambition proves to be beyond reach. For this group, obstacles and catastrophes are challenges to be met. If they can reason their way through the problem, high achievers feel confident of success; yet they seem to recognize their own limitations and are willing to admit the possibility of failure, another indication of their realism.

2. ACADEMIC SUCCESS ALSO DEPENDS ON STRENGTH OF MOTIVATION. IT WILL, THEREFORE, BE ASSOCIATED WITH A STRONG DESIRE TO ACHIEVE RATIONAL GOALS.

If strong motivation is indicated by the willingness to sacrifice, then this hypothesis is indeed confirmed by the present investigation. Our material shows that high achievers are willing to give up immediate gratification to obtain a more important goal. It has also been suggested that high achievers tend to express misgivings about their own ability, recognizing perhaps that one cannot expect to have all one's desires fulfilled perfectly.

Low achievers, on the contrary, do not seem to accept their own limitations so easily. They find it difficult to modify their plans. Functioning mainly on the subjective level, they resort to daydreams and wishes. Emotion rather than reason constitutes their chief driving force. Therefore, sacrifice is less acceptable. Moreover, their impetuosity hinders them from patiently stepping from one goal to another in slow progress to the final goal, and so they may be expected to have difficulty with the third hypothesis:

3. ACADEMIC SUCCESS DEPENDS NOT ONLY ON THE CLEAR PERCEPTION OF A RATIONAL GOAL AND THE DESIRE TO REACH IT; IT IS ALSO NECESSARY TO PERCEIVE AND SELECT THE APPROPRIATE MEANS TO THE CHOSEN GOAL.

This hypothesis is an expression of the virtue of prudence which governs the selection of means to an end. In the thematic material analyzed, the presence of this virtue would seem to follow as a corollary of the other two hypotheses. The man who controls himself reasonably, who directs his actions according to a clearly perceived goal, who willingly sacrifices incompatible gratifications, will also be inclined to choose carefully those steppingstones which lead to the desired success. Our data clearly show the high achiever to be a man who determines his own choices.

Finally, we might point to the fact that a subsidiary study of the same data analyzed in the traditional mode of setting up variables derived from attitudes or situations in the stories yielded results which were not significant statistically. Thus it might be argued from a purely pragmatic stand that the research methodology here presented promises more fruitful harvests for personality study.

COMMENT

In our opinion, this study is an empirical verification of one of the hypotheses proposed in Chapter 6, that human beings establish for themselves a self-ideal which governs their action, that they choose their goals deliberately, and that the hierarchy of goals they establish will allow a prediction as to their course of action in a given area of life.

This study is also an example of a correct method of quantification of qualities, as discussed in Chapter 2. Further empirical verification of the hypotheses of our theory will follow this method.

REFERENCES

1. ARNOLD, MAGDA B. 1949. A demonstration analysis of the Thematic Apperception Test in a clinical setting. *J. abnorm. soc. Psychol.*, 1949, **44**, 97–111.
2. ARON, BETTY. 1949. *A manual for analysis of the Thematic Apperception Test.* Berkeley: Willis E. Berg.
3. COX, BEVERLY, and SARGENT, HELEN. 1950. TAT responses of emotionally disturbed and emotionally stable children: Clinical judgment versus normative data. *J. proj. Tech.*, 1950, **14**, 61–74.
4. ERON, LEONARD D. 1950. A normative study of the Thematic Apperception Test. *Psychol. Monogr.*, 1950, **64**, No. 315.
5. FISHER, R. A. 1938. *Statistical methods for research workers.* London: Oliver & Boyd.
6. HARTMAN, A. A. 1949. An experimental examination of the Thematic Apperception Technique in clinical diagnosis. *Psychol. Monogr.*, 1949, **63**, No. 8.
7. LINDZEY, GARDNER. 1952. Thematic Apperception Test: Interpretive assumptions and related empirical evidence. *Psychol. Bull.*, 1952, **49**, 1–25.
8. MURRAY, HENRY A. 1943. *Thematic Apperception Test Manual.* Cambridge: Harvard University Press.
9. ROSENZWEIG, SAUL. 1949. Apperceptive norms for the Thematic Apperception Test; I. The problem of norms in projective methods. *J. Pers.*, 1949, **17**, 475–82.
10. ROSENZWEIG, SAUL, and FLEMING, E. E. 1949. Apperceptive norms for the Thematic Apperception Test; II. An empirical investigation. *J. Pers.*, 1949, **17**, 483–503.
11. SHNEIDMAN, EDWIN S., *et al.* 1951. *Thematic Test Analysis.* New York: Grune & Stratton, Inc.
12. STEIN, MORRIS I. 1948. *The Thematic Apperception Test; An introductory manual for its clinical use with adult males.* Cambridge: Addison-Wesley Press, Inc.
13. WHITEHOUSE, ELIZABETH. 1949. Norms for certain aspects of the Thematic Apperception Test on a group of nine and ten year old children. *Persona*, 1949, **1**, 12–15.

Chapter 8

PSYCHIC DETERMINISM, FREEDOM, AND PERSONALITY DEVELOPMENT

By Noël Mailloux, O. P.

Among the numerous problems encountered in the borderland of psychology, none is more difficult to approach dispassionately than the problem of human freedom. However, for scholars who are genuinely interested in elaborating a scientific synthesis and in furthering the advancement of human knowledge, a modest attempt at a more precise formulation is far more attractive than a noisy and too often sterile controversy. In our search for truth, is not the wisest attitude the one proposed by Thomas Aquinas? —who recommended that one consider *what* is said rather than the individual who is speaking, and who felt that so much time is needed to collect data for constructive thinking that none should be lost in futile discussion? Truth alone will stand the test of time, and, when it is manifested, errors are quickly abandoned.

A clear-cut definition of the various angles from which the problem of freedom can be envisaged will give us an orientation.

First, there is the metaphysician's viewpoint which may be qualified as *structural*. Regarding freedom as an essential element of human nature, he is not preoccupied with its proper use or functioning, leaving the consideration of these aspects to the moralist or the psychologist, as it were. To him, of course, the individual is immaterial; he does not care whether he is a child or an adult, whether he is normal or psychotic, whether he has a mature personality or an unstable one. In the human will, he discovers a universal appetite, which happens to be at the same time determined and free: determined toward Good as an appetite, even determined toward unlimited Good as a universal appetite; but also, however, undetermined, indifferent, free toward any particular sensible good with which it is confronted in the course of earthly existence, this second prerogative being the inevitable counterpart of the first one. Moreover, such determinism and indifference mean neither automatism nor passivity, but domination.

Being endowed with intelligence, man is aware that his appetite is made for the pursuit of good, and hence derives the concept of obligation and responsibility. Also, he is aware that, amid the multitude of particular goods, he remains the master of his decision; hence arises the necessity of a science proposing the art of deciding well, that is, according to the exigencies implied in the universality of the human appetite. Then freedom appears as a human prerogative, upon which the whole of moral science rests as upon an immediate foundation, playing in its turn the role of an indispensable guide. If we are to avoid missing the end of human life, the end most deeply embedded in our willing, it is absolutely necessary for us to overcome our initial indeterminacy or indifference and to conform to a rule. As we shall see later, such necessity has tremendous repercussions on the psychological level as well.

Freedom, then, is the basis of moral science. But the moralist's point of view being essentially normative, we must say (to be precise) that the subject matter of his consideration is rather the use, the exercise, or the acts of free will, and not free will itself. From the start, the moralist makes a clear distinction between the acts over which man has complete control, since they proceed from a deliberate decision and conform to the dictates of reason—*human acts*—and the acts which escape such control and the causes and motives of which do not submit to any rational influence—*the acts of man*.

Of course, the moralist has long since been aware of the fact that immaturity, insanity, intoxication, or emotional confusion is apt to deprive someone of his capacity for deliberate willing, temporarily or definitively, through the blunting of his rational judgment. Also, he knows very well that human behavior then becomes more or less rigidly geared to the deterministic functioning of fantasy and impulses. Aquinas goes so far as to say

that the great mass of human individuals remain immature to
the point of never finding in themselves sufficient courage and
insight to overcome this determinism of sensuality and continue
to let most of their behavior be dominated by it.

The moralist, however, whose main task consists in elaborating the norms of man's rational, deliberate, and free activity
cannot be blamed, as he too often is, for neglecting these insuffi-
ciencies or deficiencies of the will beyond the circumstances
where man remains responsible for them. Would any one blame
the logician, busy with formulating the norms of right thinking,
for not taking account of the delusional reasoning of the insane,
or of the distorted logic of the man in the street, as he expounds
his racial prejudices or his political convictions? Today, we
notice an unfortunate tendency to forget that our Christian moral
science constitutes undoubtedly the most fascinating scientific
synthesis ever elaborated. Any one who is familiar with the
extremely refined description of the efficacious functioning of
free will, either in the actual exercising of a specific choice or
in the habitual exercising of moral virtues, as it is proposed in
the *Summa* of Aquinas, can only deplore that such a wealth
of knowledge about the possible developments of human nature
is so frequently and lightly ignored. Many have come to think
that the study of "depth psychology," that is, the study of the
most primitive or archaic strata of personality, now buried in the
unconscious, is far more important than a deep comprehension
of the creative processes taking place at the highest level of our
rational consciousness.

This, of course, does not mean that whatever knowledge has
been accumulated by psychology can be discarded without great
loss. This would be equivalent to sinning against a cardinal
virtue so highly praised by the moralist himself: prudence. Precisely because the moral scientist aims at offering to men of all
ages and of all conditions the guidance necessary to make the best
of their rational resources, he will eagerly turn to psychology as
an indispensable source of information. As is well known, the
psychologist's viewpoint is predominantly *dynamic*. Having to
unravel and explain the interplay of a whole group of forces in
action, he needs to build up for himself a developmental or ge-

netic picture of this functional organization as well as an economical evaluation of the intervening energies.

Now, let us take the time necessary here to consider such a viewpoint as constructively as possible, with the hope that our effort will prove profitable to the psychologist, to the moralist, and to all of us who are interested in a deeper knowledge of human nature.

To say that, in its early phase, the new science of psychoanalysis was almost entirely preoccupied with the exploration of the unconscious realm of personality, with describing the vicissitudes of the instincts of the id, and with visualizing the various constellations of forces which characterize each step of infantile development, has become a commonplace. This means that we are increasingly aware of the importance of further tasks still confronting us. Through the patient and successful analysis of neurotic conflicts, much insight has been gained concerning the defensive functioning of the ego, but we are left with a very inadequate understanding of the latter's more normal and essential functions of synthesis and integration. Unfortunately, as French has remarked,

. . . a picture of the ego obtained by a study of its defense mechanisms might be compared to a description of the functioning of a government at a moment when its energies are absorbed in putting down an insurrection. Obviously we see here not the normal activity of the government, but its emergency activity when its existence is being threatened. Similarly in studying the defense mechanisms we are able to observe the activity of the ego only at a moment when its synthetic activity is struggling against the threat of imminent disintegration (5, p. 545).

It is self-evident that a science which emerged from an original and fresh attempt at understanding and resolving various symptomatic reactions could at first envisage psychic functioning from that particular angle only. Recently, however, the necessity of a new and broader approach (foreseen and even outlined by Freud himself and his early followers) has become more and more acutely felt in various circles where cultural interests have kept their importance along with therapeutic practice. The "conflict-free sphere of the ego," which Hartmann described so well some ten years ago, is only now under consideration as a focal point of observation. We have come to realize that conflicts, frequent as they are, are nothing but the accidents of the route. What is happening to the peaceful area of the mind is much more important from the point of view of human development. Many are inclined to forget it, because to them peace is equivalent to a condition of passivity or to the tranquillity of death, while in reality it must be conceived as the condition of normal creative activity. If it implies a relative absence of conflicts, it favors the strenuous efforts of a personality which is in the process of creating itself as well as the powerful striving toward a strongly organized mental synthesis and to an endogenous and dominating adaptation to reality. What I intend to describe, with the hope of stimulating further interest and research, is such a positive achievement of the peaceful mind which culminates in the acquisition of freedom.

No one who contemplates a thorough reconsideration of the problem of freedom, at least on the psychological level, can escape the confusion surrounding the whole question. In this field we are just beginning today to overcome the common temptation to fall into doubt where there is only a difficulty to solve or to neglect a real difficulty whenever the issue is certain. So it happens that the ground on which the problem of freedom had to be posed and studied dispassionately soon became the battlefield where the pseudo-scientific, mechanistic, and moralistic dogmatisms met to fight each other without mercy.

The moralistic attitude, on the one hand, was extremely simple. The close contact which existed between the psychological and moral sciences in their early phases of development had been lost and, slowly, the legalistic conception of morality had prevailed. Of course, as moral science became more or less a province of jurisprudence, it is clear that responsibility tended to be defined almost exclusively in objective terms. The only condition on the part of the subject which kept its importance was the intellectual capacity to discriminate between good and evil, the awareness of what one was doing and the consent given to such behavior. Certainly there were *casus conscientiae* and practical moral science was taking care of them. Unfortunately, we must state that the subjective conditions of the individual conscience remained almost entirely foreign to its consideration. It is a fact that practical moral science was mainly concerned with the objective determinations of the moral law, with the existence or nonexistence of a certain obligation, or with its grievousness. The psychology of the theologian was just as simple as that of the jurist. To both of them clear self-awareness, personal moral conscience, freedom, and responsibility were primary data. That the many conditions of moral behavior were realized at any time, when man is awake and mentally sound, was a matter of evidence; at all hours of the day a man, once he had attained the age of reason, was supposed to enjoy freedom and to behave in a moral and responsible way. So long as such an attitude was maintained the moralistic jurist had no use for psychology and could not avoid considering it as an unwelcome complication.

On the other hand, the mechanistic explanations upon which scientific dogmatism relies to maintain its assumptions that mind is brain and that freedom is a myth are no less naïve and unsatisfactory. It contends that all psychic events and all behavior are the effects of causes functioning at the level of physical necessity. Recently Juliette Boutonier, a French analyst, has shown convincingly the futility of the mechanistic attempt to reduce the acquisition of habits and of free behavior to nothing but a process of conditioning.[1]

What seems particularly important for us to mention at this point is that analytic psychology itself, at least if we refer to its most advanced representatives, has finally found a way out of this dilemma on a realistic basis. For the old postulate that all psychic events or reactions are the effects of a necessary cause it has substituted the postulate that all psychic events or activities necessarily have a cause, even if at first glance they appear to be mere products of chance. As to the attitude of the psychoanalytically minded psychologists in this matter, it can hardly be better formulated than in this passage from Zilboorg:

[1] Since this aspect of the problem cannot be dealt with fully in this context, the interested reader is referred to her inspiring little book, *Les défaillances de la volonté* (2).

There is a characteristic story about Freud. He was asked once whether a man could be held responsible for his dreams, and he answered: "Whom else would you hold responsible?" There is also Freud's profound sense of respect for reason, which he sought all his life to liberate from the fetters of the infantile, nonrealistic fog of a malfunctioning psychic apparatus. He wishes to secure for man the true ability of free choice, which he thought impossible when the psychic apparatus is not fully integrated and harmonized, even as it is impossible to make the free choice to take part in a race if one is legless, or paralyzed, or ataxic. This striving for the opportunity of free choice is inherent in psychoanalysis. If psychoanalysis does not explicitly accept the postulate of free will, it does not deny it; if anything, it supports it by its striving to liberate man's reason and will from the frailties which his biological, and therefore psychological, imperfections impose upon him in his daily life (19, pp. 333–34).

On this point indeed one can hardly remain in doubt, since Freud himself has expressed his own view clearly when he wrote: "After all, analysis does not set out to abolish the possibility of morbid reactions [in patients], but to give the patient's ego freedom to choose one way or the other" (7, p. 72).

These preliminary remarks, I hope, will at the same time permit us to see the problem in a more clearly defined perspective and open new ways for empirical research and progressive thinking. Analytic psychologists have investigated in detail the development of human thinking from its early prelogical to its mature rational manifestations, and their observations have been supplemented by the many more specific and more refined descriptions and interpretations furnished by the Swiss school of genetic psychology headed by Piaget. As yet, we see much less clearly how free will develops from the archaic stages of indeterminacy, ambivalence, and automatism. Certainly we are as well aware of the possible threats to freedom by such infantile characteristics as we are aware of the disturbances of rational thinking by symbolic representations. But, through Odier's recent contribution to the literature on the subject (17), new and abundant light has been shed on this difficult problem which involves the whole genesis of moral life. At this moment, then, an attempt to describe in some detail the various conditions implied in the emergence and the functioning of freedom would seem to be rather important.

To clear the ground from the start, we must say that the formulation of the question of the relationship between determinism and freedom has been entirely misleading. In fact, as long as the thesis of physicalism was triumphant in psychology, either under the form of behaviorism or of operationism, physical determinism was accepted as a scientific dogma. Moreover, such determinism was regarded as the alternative of free will. It is rather amazing that such a gross confusion could persist so long in the mind of many a scientist and philosopher. Here, let us remember that the real alternative of determinism, as Knight expresses it with lapidary precision, "is not free will, but indeterminism, which implied chaos, unpredictability, and a denial of cause and effect relationships in human affairs" (13, p. 262).

Now it appears that the first stage of development in this direction consists in the overcoming of primitive indeterminacy which is a constant source of painful anxiety. And during this early period this can be achieved only through the mechanization or automatization of psychic processes, which is equivalent to the establishment of the regime of psychic determinism. Long ago, Alexander had not only recognized in this mechanization one of the primal characteristics of the psychic apparatus but he had also clearly seen its advantage for the psychic apparatus. "Consciousness," he said, "is relieved of the task of the psychic elaboration of instinct, it is spared the development of anxiety with which the recall of the painful memory is associated, and is thus freed of the conflict between temptation and anxiety" (1, pp. 10–11). To be sure, at this level habitual human behavior, being deprived of the ideal preconditions of conscious motivation and of adequate reality testing, will inevitably present the characteristics of extreme rigidity and of schematic adaptability. Nevertheless, since it is oriented, structured, and organized, it can be exercised with a feeling of relative security.

But the stage is soon reached where this rigidly deterministic functioning appears to be a too narrow basis for adequately adaptive behavior. Once the child is challenged by his personal discovery of values, he makes the thrilling discovery of freedom for the first time, and he feels that he can now control his own autonomy. He realizes that freedom, being an instrument and an end, has to master itself also. At the same time his painfully acquired security is shattered, and he finds himself again compelled to face complete indeterminacy. It is no wonder then if anxiety—rightly called the emotion of the possible—reappears, and is felt more acutely than ever, and even threatens a still unstable equilibrium. Hence it is an important fact that anxiety is present with particular intensity prior to the infantile mechanization of the psychic processes, prior to the final crystallization of neurotic symptoms, and prior to acquiring the ability of mature free activity. As Juliette Boutonier (3) rightly affirmed, anxiety finds its fundamental root in indeterminacy or possibility, and it can be overcome only through the alternative of the rigorous determination of necessity or of the autonomous determination of freedom. As we all know, man will experience anxiety particularly when, more or less liberated from the grip of necessity, he still has to struggle for the acquisition of freedom, simply because he is taking the risk of losing what he has without obtaining what he wants. I am not intending to suggest, however, that no unconscious elements will remain in the newly elaborated function of free will. Even though that function represents the highest level of human activity, it must be regarded as the *completion* of a whole hierarchy of functions, which it does not suppress but integrate, which are still used even if surpassed.

It is now becoming clear enough that psychic determinism, far from being opposed to freedom, is a necessary step or condition for its acquisition. Moreover, it cannot be surpassed without being integrated, since freedom can no more be exercised without using psychic automatisms than without using biological mechanisms. It is only in the case of a neurotic condition that, on account of the lack of integration, these two levels of functioning will appear as conflicting, the lower one maintaining its autonomy. After what has been said already, it seems easier to introduce here a few other considerations about the psychological nature and the development of free activity, which have important clinical implications.

Free activity, corresponding to the most perfect activity of which man is capable, is certainly the activity in which least is left to indeterminacy and unpredictability. In other words, such behavior is fully controlled precisely because it is fully determined, because it constitutes the most adequate and accurate answer one can give to the more or less complicated set of demands imposed by reality at a given moment. It is easy to see that the more one has developed some skill and can master a situation, the more he takes account of even its minutest details. Each aspect of his activity corresponds to a definite element of reality, and finds in it its ultimate determination. The more complex the situation to which we have to adapt, the more necessary it is to surpass the gross and rigid determination achieved through mechanization or automatization. The extremely precise adaptability of the artist, of the craftsman, of the professional player, requires nothing less than the plasticity of free determination—free because it has to be complete.

But as free determination implies self-determination, what we call free activity is nothing else than self-determined activity. This means that such activity, far from losing the advantages gained through determination, namely, intentionality, structuralization, and organization, possesses the additional property of extreme flexibility, which makes it possible for it to respond in an integrated way to situations which are as varied as they are unique. Again, this point of view has been quoted by Knight, who writes: "That man is free who is conscious of being the author of the law that he obeys" (13, p. 256). This man, of course, instead of being determined by any particular motivation, is himself actively determining that particular motivation which will be the spring of his individual action. Moreover, he remains capable of changing it at any time.

Obviously self-determination implies the highest level of consciousness, that is, the only level at which deliberation and choice can occur. In fact, any free activity is one which proceeds from deliberate willing, or one in which the motivation has been rationally elaborated. It presupposes, therefore, a clear perception of the relationship existing between ends and means, and the ability to explore, invent, or create the means leading to the desired end. In brief, as science facilitates inventiveness and originality of vision, freedom facilitates creativeness and originality of action. And here we reach the root of an old misunderstanding which has been a serious obstacle to the development of psychology. Because creativeness and originality (which are the characteristics of free activity) were confused with indeterminacy, freedom came to be synonymous with unpredictability, and was discarded from the realm of science. It took the work of such men as Bergson and Scheler to rehabilitate freedom in the eyes of science. Now, however, it is more and more clearly understood that free behavior, far from being unpredictable, is the most predictable behavior, though it is not predictable in the same way as behavior which is the result of a deterministic process or of a repetition compulsion. Confronted with a difficult and problematic situation, the man who is really free is the only one who is entirely reliable, the only one whose behavior remains predictable, because he is the only one capable of making the right choice and of executing it. On the one hand, we always know that this man is going to do the only thing which ought to be done, namely, the right thing; but on the other hand, we also know that such an achievement, like any genuine discovery, escapes all our prevision.

We are now in a position to present an empirical description of the various attitudes toward freedom and the responsibility which are encountered in clinical practice. First, let us consider the case of the neurotic individual. Here we have to do with someone who is obviously overwhelmed by the fear of responsibility. Rather than face the risk of free choice, he tends to fall back on passivity and insists that he be told what to do. Actually he lives with the uncomfortable feeling of being locked within the grip of some unknown necessity, and his experience of freedom is painfully limited. Almost continuously he is complaining about actions or gestures over which he recognizes with more or less insight that he has practically no control. Let us recall here the reactions of the scrupulous man. His immense fear of responsibility reveals to us clearly how much he wants to be reassured about his incapacity to behave otherwise than he actually does. He spends most of his time persuading us that his will is not the determining factor of his behavior, that his consent has nothing to do with gestures escaping his control, that his conduct more or less resembles a series of reflexes. *His fear of being responsible for a sinful act inhibits his decision to achieve something good.* In other words, the risk of freedom appears to him so full of danger that he shies away from it. His increasing inferiority induces him to deny if not to destroy his most effective potentialities so that he will not have to use them any more and so that he can seclude himself in a fairly complete passivity.

On the other hand, it is easy to observe that the case of the man who does not make the effort to develop a strong personality but abandons his behavior to what might be called the regime of characterological automatism is far less serious. Faced with good and evil he feels free and essentially accepts responsibility. But if we compare him to a man who has acquired full-fledged freedom, he appears like a student repeating mechanically the half assimilated content of his textbooks beside an original thinker, who is ready for autonomous undertakings and personal discoveries. His freedom still shows evident shortcomings and hardly embraces the minimum essentials. Its influence does not make itself felt to the point of introducing a delicate tint of rationality into the circumstances of the human act, thus contributing to its full perfection. On the moral level, we are dealing with an individual who is satisfied with exerting only half of his capacity for free will and whose behavior remains characterized by the lack of precision and adaptability which is the hallmark of a conventional and formal gesture. At best, this individual may usually do *what* he ought to do; but he will seldom do it *how* it ought to be done. From the point of view of the moralist, he will appear rude and still unskilled in the art of autonomously determining for himself the ways of virtue—the art in which freedom finds its highest manifestation, and which is called prudence.

Let us conclude now with a brief clinical description of the person who has reached the heights of freedom and who has acquired what is usually called a strong and mature personality. As the scientist whose intelligence has mastered a whole sphere of knowledge does not claim infallibility but assumes the full responsibility of his formulated hypotheses, the free man whose will has mastered the art of autonomous choice does not claim impeccability but is the only one to face the total responsibility of his acts. If he becomes aware of a slight deviation from the dictates of reason in his behavior, he will not try to minimize it or to excuse it even for a moment. As the only way to the acquisition of knowledge consists in continuously recognizing one's errors and in modestly attempting to correct them, the only way to the acquisition of freedom consists in the courageous humility of the Saints, a humility which makes them capable of facing the reality of sin in themselves.

The psychologist feels frequently at a loss when he tries to pierce a strong armor of narcissism in his patients and invites them to drop the fetters of infantilism, so that they can acquire the mere capacity to choose one way or the other. The task of the priest, in a world which praises above all else earthly success and domination of the weak, is incredibly harder; he must break through this terrific armor of pharisaic pride—"Thank You, Lord, that I am not like this man!"—which even Christ has at least temporarily failed to pierce; he must invite men to drop the fetters of their sinful propensities, desires, and ambitions, so that they can acquire not only the mere capacity to choose one way or the other, but the capacity to choose the way leading to the highest good, to choose the way of perfect freedom. And perfect freedom, St. Augustine says, is found in perfect love, in Christian charity: *"Ama, et fac quod vis! . . . "*

COMMENT

The preceding paper raises the question whether Freud intended to leave open the possibility of self-determination in his system. As a matter of historical fact, he was a strict determinist, as numerous passages show (Cf. 4, pp. 161–62, and 6, p. 31 and p. 84).

If, then, Freud's system as proposed by himself does not allow for self-determination, how can it be developed so as to allow for rational judgment and real freedom? Freud's system exemplifies thinking according to the dialectical method. For the dialectically trained clinician, the interplay between theory and practice is more important than the structure of the theoretical system. Using Freud's dialectical system, the clinician then finds that he can interpret the system itself dialectically. On the principle that each action results in an equal and opposite reaction, not only can the action of the id bring about the development of the ego, but internal determination (self-determination) can be conceived as the result of a dialectical reaction to external determination. Since the focus of attention is on action and reaction, the mechanism by which the reaction is brought about is of minor importance, and conflicting opinions concerning it can be left to be resolved by time and the accumulation of more clinical material. Thus the clinician feels free to interpret the facts which Freud reports and which he finds duplicated in his clinical experience, on the basis of his own philosophical assumptions. Though these may be theistic instead of atheistic, realistic instead of materialistic, he uses Freud's terms to label his own findings. In that case, psychoanalytic terminology and psychoanalytic categories are used with the expanded meaning required by the change in basic assumptions; such an expansion is conceived not only as permissible but as a dialectical necessity resulting in the advance of knowledge. To illustrate our point we shall try to isolate the basic assumptions in Dr. Mailloux's paper and compare them with those of Freud. It will be seen that only a dialectical system can embrace such contrasts.

1. (a) N. Mailloux: The human person has various powers (cognitive and appetitive) which go through various stages of organization. The first organization (the id) is determined by pleasure; that is *organic* determination. Then develops an organization determined by external injunctions (the superego); this is a *socially* determined organization. Finally, rational organization (the ego) is imposed by the person; this is *self*-determination, culminating in human freedom. Reason (the specifically human form of cognition) and will (the specifically human form of appetition)

are potentially present at birth but become actual during development.

(*b*) For Freud: The superego is gradually split off or developed from the id because of parental demands; development is forced by environmental impact. In a similar manner, the ego is split off from the id because of the impact of external reality. The ego becomes the mediator between id, superego, and reality; the means of mediation is reasoning which itself is derived from instinctual roots.

2. (*a*) N. Mailloux's first assumption implies that the human being is designed to reach his perfection by supplementing the natural and social determination of his powers by self-determination; it also implies that development is a *natural but self-directed process* in which obstacles act as a challenge for personal effort. Hence the condition for development and normal activity is internal peace (p. 268).

(*b*) For Freud, only biological growth is a natural process; *psychological* development is *forced* by frustration, therefore conflict is the condition of development and the sign of normal activity; peace is a state of psychological near-death. Self-determination is a feeling which refers to unconscious determination, but is not an objective fact.

3. (*a*) For N. Mailloux, the person is a unit and acts as one. Id, ego, superego are not different factions but merely different stages of development, the remnants remaining throughout life as the unassimilable or unassimilated id or superego residue. Conflict represents the attempt of the person to establish the primacy of self-determination against the inertia of a previous organization based on pleasure and parental identification.

(*b*) For Freud, id, ego, and superego represent warring factions, though the individual acts as a biological unit. Conflict is normal between these factions and the victory goes to the strongest, which normally should be the ego. (The system provides no explanation as to why the ego should become the strongest or how a psychological unit could come of three warring factions.)

4. (*a*) For N. Mailloux, the final end of man is his free choice (and ultimate possession) of the highest good, which expresses itself in Christian charity (p. 276).

(*b*) For Freud, the end of man is the greatest possible biological satisfaction obtainable in his social environment. Freud deplores the wounds civilization has inflicted upon man's instinctual life, though he admits that full instinctual satisfaction never seems possible even under the most favorable circumstances (9, p. 77). He concludes, therefore, that man's quest for happiness is bound to end in disappointment.

With such different notions of the nature, development, and destiny of the human being, it is obvious that every term will have a different meaning. For Mailloux, for instance, the term "adequate ego functioning" or "a strong ego" would mean that the human being so described has achieved self-determination, has established the primacy of his highest goal, and is actively striving for it, even if he has to sacrifice id satisfaction in its pursuit. For Freud, it would mean that the ego is able to do justice to the demands of reality without sacrificing the demands of the id, so that the individual can hold the balance between instinctual satisfaction and fulfilment of his social obligations. For Freud, the sacrifice of instinctual satisfaction for a higher goal would indicate a dangerously dominant superego.

We do not deny that within a dialectical system Freudian terms can be used with an expanded meaning such as Mailloux is giving them. If today's psychoanalysts are more tolerant than their master, such an attempt at enriching and expanding the body of psychoanalytic tenets may be very successful. However, such an expansion of meaning will eventually lead to a major change in the Freudian system as a whole. If such an attempt is successful, then psychoanalysis will be understood as a theory of neurosis and not of the normal personality, and will be applied to man's irrational but not to his rational motives. Its method of free association will then be properly used to reveal the sources of "failed" or symptomatic acts, but not of scientific or other object-directed thinking. Even in the analysis of neurotic manifestations, the value of a therapeutic *resynthesis* of personality will then depend not on the method of psychoanalysis but on the validity of the philosophical assumptions as to the nature of human personality professed by the individual analyst.

280 THE HUMAN PERSON

REFERENCES

1. ALEXANDER, FRANZ. 1935. *Psychoanalysis of the total personality.* New York: Nervous and Mental Disease Monographs.
2. BOUTONIER, JULIETTE. 1945. *Les défaillances de la volonté.* Paris: Presses Universitaires de France.
3. ———. 1949. *L'angoisse.* Paris: Presses Universitaires de France.
4. BRILL, A. A., (ed.). 1938. *The basic writings of Sigmund Freud.* New York: Modern Library, Inc.
5. FRENCH, THOMAS M. 1938. Defense and synthesis in the function of the ego. *Psychoanal. Quart.,* 1938, **7**, 537–53.
6. FREUD, SIGMUND. 1920. *A general introduction to psychoanalysis.* London: Boni & Liveright.
7. ———. 1927. *The ego and the id.* London: Hogarth Press.
8. ———. 1928. *The future of an illusion.* London: Liveright Publishing Corporation.
9. ———. 1930. *Civilization and its discontents.* London: Hogarth Press.
10. ———. 1934. Psychogenesis of a case of homosexuality in a woman. In: *Collected papers.* Vol. II, No. 18 (1920). London: Hogarth Press.
11. ———. 1945. Negation. In: *Collected papers.* Vol. V, No. 16 (1925). London: Hogarth Press.
12. HARTMANN, HEINZ. 1939. Ich-Psychologie und Anpassungsproblem. *Int. Z. Psychoanal. u. Imago,* **24**, 62–135.
13. KNIGHT, ROBERT P. 1946. Determinism, "freedom," and psychotherapy. *Psychiatry,* 1946, **9**, 251–62.
14. KRIS, ERNST. 1951. Psychoanalytic propositions. In: *Psychological theory. Contemporary readings.* (Ed.) MELVIN H. MARX. New York: The Macmillan Co.
15. LOTTIN, D. ODON. 1942 Psychologie et morale aux XIIe et XIIIe siècles. Tome I: *Problèmes de psychologie.* Louvain: Abbaye de Mont-César.
16. MCKEON, RICHARD. 1951. Philosophy and method. *J. Phil.,* **48**, 653–82.
17. ODIER, CHARLES. 1947. *Les deux sources consciente et inconsciente de la vie morale.* Neuchâtel: Editions de la Baconnière.
18. RIMAUD, JEAN. 1949. Les psychologues contre la morale. *Etudes,* 1949, **263**, 3–22.
19. ZILBOORG, GREGORY. 1943. *Mind, medicine and man.* New York: Harcourt, Brace & Co., Inc.
20. ———. 1951. *Freud: His exploration of the mind of man.* New York: Chas. Scribner's Sons.

PART III

PERSONALITY INTEGRATION

Chapter 9

INTEGRATION AND THE SELF-IDEAL

By VINCENT V. HERR, S. J.

IT HAS been clearly demonstrated by able persons that in every emotion there is an evaluation process, as, for example, asking one's self the question : "How does this affect me?" The question may owe its origin psychologically to a fusion of expectancy and sensation of a stimulus object. The resulting emotional attitude probably initiates nerve impulses from the cortex to centers in the thalamus-hypothalamus, which activate the appropriate pattern of emotional expression as well as the corresponding peripheral changes. The "bodily changes" are probably reported back to the cortex, and this cortical perception of organic changes may again be evaluated—"How does this affect me?" The complete emotional experience would include a twofold judgment process or evaluation, and bodily resonance and expression. It would necessarily include a "self-reference" of some kind. This reference of the quality of the stimulus to the "self" seems to me to be the characteristic of emotional experience, which differentiates it from cognitive processes on the one hand, and from the appetitive processes on the other. In the former this evaluation of the stimulus is not necessary; there is rather an assimilation of the object-quality to the mind. In the latter there is an attraction or repulsion consequent upon evaluation, but the direct awareness of the fact that "something peculiar is happening to me" is not necessarily present.

This empirical description of emotions is more fully elaborated in the article by Magda Arnold in (1). Its theoretical advantages are there amply related. Its similarity to the description given by St. Thomas as well as to those of such modern scholastics as Joseph Froebes is well known.

283

We might digress at this point and ask whether emotions are disorganizing or motivating (Leeper, 6), or whether they are organically localized (Cannon, 3, Bard, 2), or whether they are integrated into the complex individual experience or prior matrices of experience (Kruger, 5) and if so, how. Since it is agreed that the process of learning and unlearning emotional experience forms the crux of the problem of emotional adjustment, we propose to take up only the last question concerning the integration of emotional experience. Moreover, the problem of emotional adjustment occupies most of the space in recent discussions of personality. This is to be expected, since the definition of personality which is most commonly used is the one formulated by Allport—namely, "personality is the sum total of psychophysical systems which constitute the individual's unique adjustment." If we include in the definition (as is often done) the notion that this "unique adjustment" cannot be fully understood without some knowledge of its core, man's "ego-value," if we include his beliefs and expectancies regarding himself in his social environment (Stagner, 9), or finally "his rationally planned and self-determining efforts" to maintain a healthy status (Symonds, 10), we see at once how important the notion of "self-regard" becomes for any discussion of emotions. Also, if we maintain, as do good authorities from Raimy onward, that "psychotherapy is a process of changing the concept of self," or that successful therapy includes the acceptance of the self as perceived by the self, we see the practical value of a theory of emotions which includes the "self-reference" aspect.

We are all aware of the new impetus given the study of ego and self by psychoanalysts. We also remember that the self-regarding attitude or sentiment was one of McDougall's favorite conceptual tools. We may or may not remember that the distinction between the objective and subjective selves was one of the most bitterly disputed topics in the whole history of philosophy. The ancient seekers after wisdom told us that we must know ourselves, and that it would require serious study in order to know ourselves as we really are. With a return to a more common-sense philosophy in dealing with personality problems in recent times, there is clearly a re-emphasis upon the

"rational and reflective" life of man. And there is an openly
declared admission that man not only can know himself,
but that he *must* do so in order that he may be healthy and adjusted.

To resume our previous line of thought, we stated that emotions are always organized in some way, and integrated into
each person's unique experience, and that in each emotional
experience there is the element of self-reference.

In paging through the Mooseheart Symposium (7), I was able
to find only ten authors out of the forty-seven who were explicit in
mentioning the self- or ego-element in emotion. Some of these
writers give the self only a passing mention. Elmgren in Swe-
den, for instance, when discussing love and hate, says these are
integrated with the total personality through self-regard. Harms
thinks that when we experience ego control we have feeling,
but when there is ego uncontrol we have emotion. Jenkins, a
psychiatrist from the University of Illinois, brings the concept
of ego into his explanation of guilt feelings. Van der Horst, a
psychiatrist from Amsterdam, stresses the study of ego development as learned from children's drawings. Gardner Murphy
thinks that the self is the primary element in social perception.
Likert creates a special class of dynamics called ego-derived
motivation. The only authors who build their whole discussion
of emotions around the notion of the self are Rogers, French,
Michotte, and Buytendijk. Their speculations and elaborations
will be of great value to us in giving an account of the role of
self-regard in emotional experience and the integration of emotions into the total pattern of personality.

In a recent presidential address given by Rogers to the members of the APA, he declared that the client's "perception of himself" goes through significant changes during the process of
therapy, and that this change is reflected in the client's attitude
toward himself. When the client comes to accept himself thus
changed as the real agent capable of solving his own problems
and of facing the consequences of his own solutions, he has made
good progress toward recovery. All these statements were docu-
mented from interviews over periods of time varying from a
few to over a dozen weeks.

In this brief resumé of the concept which Rogers had at that time of the nature of the therapeutic process, we notice that he placed a good deal of emphasis upon the role of self-evaluation in bringing about and maintaining a healthy adjustment. The author of these statements was not ostensibly concerned with the subtler problems connected with the problem of self-knowledge and self-direction. Psychologists from other schools who heard this lecture declared outright to me that he was bringing concepts which had no scientific foundation into psychology. But Rogers was only being true to the facts of the case; it is not unscientific to take the verbal statements of the client for real descriptions of what was going on during the counseling sessions. A therapist of this school does not seem to need a very elaborate concept of personality or of the self to describe the processes of change which take place in the client. I would suggest that their approach to the larger question of personality structure and integration is more on the common-sense level, and that it comes up to our expectations in so far as it does not actually hinder the progress of personality study. It does not, of course, attempt to establish any laws nor does it give us a complete picture of the "ultimates" of personality or of the emotional life.

This common-sense view sometimes crops up in classes where the instructor has done his best to expound his pet theory of personality structure. There is, for example, the student who described his view of himself and of his place in society thus :

There are certainly some spiritual values which guide me during life; these are the result of my impact with society over a period of years, and these give goals and incentives to my strivings; and these aid me in maintaining a healthy and useful form of existence. I am thus made capable of guiding my own destiny by means of the image which I have of myself (which is probably deeply rooted in my nervous system), and it is this image which carries value; when my self-image both represents what I am and what I would like to be, I am satisfied.

It will not be out of place here to compare these common-sense views with those of textbook writers, as for example

Stagner (9) and Symonds (10). For Stagner, the personality is not only the sum of the psychophysical systems which make up the individual's unique adjustment but it must also include the beliefs and expectancies which each one has for himself in his own particular environment. These beliefs and expectancies can be reduced eventually to one's sense of values or to one's image of his ideal self. Symonds has made serious efforts to go further than Stagner in clarifying this notion of the ego and the self. When we read his comments on the views of other writers we get the impression that no other view is satisfactory, for the other writers, according to Symonds, have not stressed the role of rational planning sufficiently in their attempts to introduce the "self" as an integrating principle. The ego, for Symonds, is the thinking, perceiving, and acting (expanding) subject, whereas the self is the "awareness of this growing capacity for control and adjustment . . . " (p. 86); "the self-concept may be good or bad . . . it becomes of value . . . it may be a system of activities in response to these values . . . " (p. 4). That makes hard reading, yet this interpretation seems to be a step forward to a more comprehensive framework, as well as a clarification of the concept of the ego, id, and superego, for it deals specifically with the "rational and self-determining side of man."

In orthodox psychoanalytic circles, too, there are signs of a new emphasis on the integration of the self. French, for instance, denies that neurotic symptions are simply wish fulfilments; they are rather *unsuccessful attempts* at wish fulfilments. The real problem for him is to find out *why* the neurotic does not integrate his behavior in such a way that he achieves his twofold goal, namely, avoiding what is painful and injurious, and securing the hoped-for satisfaction. Now it is true that this double striving belongs to rational and purposive behavior, for man strives to relieve the tension of needs and obtain the hoped-for good. But irrational dream behavior shows this double striving too. Even in dreams the "integrative mechanism" searches for satisfying memories and reassuring opportunities in the present situation, upon which to base its hallucinations of wish fulfilment. In the case of rational goal-directed behavior, increase of tension may disintegrate into diffuse and poorly directed motor discharge, as, for example, when one "loses one's head." To achieve a goal, then, it is necessary to *know what to do*, not merely to do something, no matter what. For French, "this leads to a new approach to the study of behavior." [1]

But how much does the client himself know about the way to achieve his purposes, and how effectively is his behavior guided by such knowledge? His knowledge must be inferred from his behavior because his subjective report is apt to be misleading. Now if his "integrative span" (which is taken to designate his practically effective knowledge of how to gain his ends) is too small, he will not attain his ends. His integrative capacity will be enhanced if he is confident of his ability to achieve his goal, and confidence is an important factor in keeping his span broad. The positive *hope* of being able to solve the problem will be complementary to the release of the tensions caused by needs. Such confidence in the self (an emotion, of course) will give motivation to striving. This "new conception" of behavior, French thinks, should guide the formulation of new problems in psychoanalysis.

Perhaps the phenomenologists and the existentialists have stressed more than any other school the necessity of basing our concepts of reality upon the concept of the self. Buytendijk,* for example, stresses the fact that consciousness is always consciousness *of something*, some object other than the self. The ego is *subject*, or subjected to a situation; that is to say, consciousness implies that we, the observer,

. . . find ourselves as subject . . . viewing ourselves in the situations in which we are involved (7, p. 130).

He goes on to say:

. . . feeling and emotion are the affirmations of our attitudes toward situations, and the pure phenomenon of feeling reveals the human being as always *projecting* it and projecting the world (7, p. 130. Italics mine).

[1] New for French, no doubt, to come back to some notion of self-direction.

* Quotations from *Feelings and emotions. The Mooseheart Symposium*, edited by M. L. Reymert, copyright 1950. By permission of McGraw-Hill Book Company, Inc.

The progress of phenomenological analysis of feeling and emotion depends on the discovery of the invariance which occurs during the continual experience concerning a feeling in various situations in relation to the modes of existence of normal and also of neurotic individuals. . . . The implicit conception of human reality . . . must become explicit during such a research through the evidence of insight into the signification of every intentional act of a concrete mode of feeling (7, p. 141).

It would seem that for Buytendijk a self is necessary to any explanation of emotion, and therefore also for the integration of the emotions and the self.

Michotte,* by means of a simple little experiment in perception, demonstrates the need for a self-concept in studies of emotion. The subject of emotional experience *knows* that he is attracted or repelled. An emotion, therefore, is the modification of the subject with regard to the object. The adjustment must, then, also concern itself with the knowledge of the ego. In fact, it is the self "who acts in such a way toward such and such a person or thing or who feels this affective reaction for this person or thing" (7, p. 124). He continues,

Finally, there is the inmost ego [besides the superficial and bodily egos]; and it is precisely this one which is lived in action and passion; it is the ego of our thoughts, of our mental attitudes, of our desires; and these latter also intervene as factors of integration when there is community of aspiration or as factors of segregation when there is divergency of opinion or sentiment.

The ego, however, constitutes only one of the poles of emotion. Since emotion is considered as a "functional connection," it must link this ego to something else (7, p. 125).

Man . . . not merely . . . "feels" . . . but also "thinks" and "knows." . . . Onto the *felt connection* there is superimposed the knowledge of the *abstract relation* implied in that connection. A man "feels" himself attracted or repelled by an object, and at the same time he "is aware" of the attraction or repulsion, he "knows" it is happening (7, p. 126).

* Quotations from *Feelings and emotions. The Mooseheart Symposium,* edited by M. L. Reymert, copyright 1950. By permission of McGraw-Hill Book Company, Inc.

Michotte here follows an analysis of emotional behavior which clearly demands an "ego," and this concept of the ego appears to be the result of the abstract consideration of self as an invariant for the changing modifications of the self.

Common sense has consistently attributed to the person two kinds of acts: those which he himself directs and those which he is not aware of regulating or controlling. Common sense is never totally unreliable or totally reliable; it may be in error about those acts over which the individual does have control and those over which he does not, but it recognizes the distinction. Moreover, it is incapable of being totally in error when it attributes a value to the self; the person actually knows he is a being, actually thinks he is such and such a being, desires to be (and to be considered as) such and such a being. Bits of conversation culled from any gathering will confirm the fact of such an attribution of value. All these ways of thinking about himself are contained in the person's attitude to the self—what he thinks he is, what he thinks others think he is, what he wishes to be and to be thought.

But the psychologist thinks otherwise. In his theorizing he must, he thinks, categorize each of these ways of thinking about the self before he can admit them to the dignity of facts or seek an explanation of them. The psychologist who attempts a personality theory acts somewhat like the "general psychologist" who used to claim that he needed no "faculties," particularly no "will," while the expert in abnormal psychology realized that he had to treat the abnormalities of the will before he could consider that his treatment was complete. Only recently have the personality theorists recognized their need of a concept of the self in order to give a complete description of human behavior. Symonds, who is a fair representative, goes so far as to say that his objective ego is the same as that of the behaviorists, and that his subjective ego is as good as that of the phenomenologists, since it allows for introspection.

In scholastic psychology we recognize a twofold act of the self with regard to the self. There is the act whereby we understand that we understand, by the very act of understanding. This gives us immediately a self-knowledge of the singular self. This knowledge *that we are* seems to be neglected by modern theorists. It needs no further elaboration except for the statement that we know we are a being which understands, an understanding self.

The second kind of knowledge of the self is of the self as a species, that is, as a particular *kind* of thing. This is a much more complicated process, and presupposes, it would seem, that we have known other things, and presupposes also that they are like us in some respect. The way in which this specific knowledge arises in us cannot be treated here, though we might mention that recent child psychologists, notably Piaget, have thrown some light on the subject.

In connection with the knowledge that "I am an individual, a single self," there is also the enigma which arises from the fact that "I the individual remain the same throughout change." The ability to abstract "same-ness" from the changes gives us the sense of the self's continuity in time (Cf. Symonds, 10). All the acts of any one individual over a period of time constitute a universe of traits, which Hilgard claims can be made the subject of a science of the individual. The universe of traits which we possess as a species makes possible the science of the class *homo sapiens*.

Now let us try to draw some conclusions from these considerations.

1. Knowledge of the self as a singular, *always changing*, may lead to the development of tendencies to inferiority, smallness, or nothingness. Knowledge of the self-singular as permanent through change need not result in the same tendency.

2. Knowledge of the self as species always changing and being changed, therefore always dependent, may also foster attitudes of inferiority. But knowledge of the communality of rational beings, far from fostering attitudes of weakness, ought to and does develop ego strength. If this sounds like Adler in reverse, we should remember that in Adler's system "compensation" is the explanatory principle whereby the ego-weak person becomes strong, and that the "will to power" has to be harmonized with the "will to community."

3. The belief that the self is singular and supreme may give rise to a feeling of grandeur, of pride in the self and hatred for others who may not acknowledge that supremacy. But the belief that the self is one with all rational beings will lead to a willingness to share, will lead to love.

There are some advantages to be derived from such a concept of the "self" and the "idea of the self" for a theory of emotions, even without theorizing about the conformity between the self-concept and the "others-concept," and without moralizing about the real value of the self. With such a concept of the self, we would avoid falling into mere description of behavior or enumeration of changes in the person. Once we have a basic frame of reference for the emergent synthesis which we call personality, which is the product of the self-determined activity of the person, we would be able to explain why "consistency in change" is desirable and why the harmonious interplay and control of human functions will lead to the desirable integration.

COMMENT

The place of emotion in the organization of personality, an issue raised in this chapter, requires extended treatment. Instead of a brief editorial comment, the next chapter will take up this matter in greater detail.

REFERENCES

1. ARNOLD, MAGDA B. 1950. An excitatory theory of emotion. In: *Feelings and emotions. The Mooseheart Symposium.* (Ed.) MARTIN L. REYMERT. New York: McGraw-Hill Book Co., Inc.
2. BARD, PHILIP. 1934. The neuro-humoral basis of emotional reactions. In: *A handbook of general experimental psychology.* (Ed.) C. MURCHISON. Worcester: Clark University Press.
3. CANNON, WALTER B. 1927. The James-Lange theory of emotions: a critical examination and an alternative theory. *Amer. J. Psychol.,* 1927, **39**, 106–24.
4. FRENCH, THOMAS M. 1938. Defense and synthesis in the function of the ego. *Psychoanal. Quart.,* 1938, **7**, 537–53.
5. KRUGER, FELIX. 1928. The essence of feeling. In: *Feelings and emotions. The Wittenberg Symposium.* (Ed.) MARTIN L. REYMERT. Worcester: Clark University Press.

6. LEEPER, R. W. 1948. A motivational theory of emotion to replace 'emotion as disorganized response.' *Psychol. Rev.*, 1948, **55**, 5–21.
7. REYMERT, MARTIN L. (Ed.). 1950. *Feelings and emotions. The Mooseheart Symposium.* New York: McGraw-Hill Book Co., Inc.
8. ROGERS, CARL R. 1947. Some observations on the organization of personality. (Presidential address.) *Amer. Psychol.*, 1947, **2**, 358–68.
9. STAGNER, ROSS. 1948. *Psychology of personality.* (2d ed.) New York: McGraw-Hill Book Co., Inc.
10. SYMONDS, PERCIVAL M. 1951. *The ego and the self.* New York: Appleton-Century-Crofts, Inc.

Chapter 10

FEELINGS AND EMOTIONS AS DYNAMIC FACTORS IN PERSONALITY INTEGRATION

By Magda B. Arnold *and* John A. Gasson, S. J.

THE PRECEDING chapter raises several problems: First, if emotions involve a double reference, both to the object and to the self experiencing the object, how can that functional relationship be formulated? And since that relationship represents the emotion, how can we define the term, how can we come to an adequate concept of emotion? In other words, what is an emotion? What is the difference between feelings and emotions? And what is the purpose or function of feeling and emotion in the economy of the living being, especially the human being? And finally, what is the role of emotion in relation to the self? How does it serve self-actuation and personality integration?

What Is an Emotion?

We suggest that an emotion or an affect can be considered *as the felt tendency toward an object judged suitable, or away from an object judged unsuitable, reinforced by specific bodily changes according to the type of emotion.*

The felt tendency. This tendency is a vital response impelling toward suitable objects. We are *aware* of the attraction that draws us to the thing or situation which we have judged suitable for us. Moreover, the natural goal of that seeking tendency is something actually perceived or imagined. Therefore, an emotion will always occur when something is recognized as attractive or repulsive.

Judged. The individual must perceive and judge the object in relation to himself (as suitable or unsuitable, good or bad for himself) before an emotion can arise. The emotion will follow this judgment, whether or not it is correct. In the animal, such judgment will be an estimate based upon sense knowledge and sense memory; in the human being, the present estimate always includes rational elements which have entered into the situation in the past and are recalled in the present. While it is obvious that this emotional response cannot occur at all unless the situation has been perceived and evaluated as to its effect on the individual, such evaluation is immediate, based upon a perceived similarity of this situation with situations in the past (Cf. page 344 f.). In practice, there is no perceptible time interval between grasping the meaning of the situation and feeling the emotion appropriate to it, though there may be a perceptible interval between receiving a stimulus and grasping its meaning. That the emotion does depend on the evaluation of the situation, on its meaning for the individual, can be observed in a person's reaction to a sudden sharp noise: the startle reflex comes first, without any emotion; if the noise is recognized as that of a car backfiring, there is no further disturbance, but if the person discovers that it was a shot aimed at him, there will come fear with its accompanying physical sensations, which are very different from the sensations connected with the startle reflex.

Reinforced by bodily changes. The simple felt tendency toward or away from something has a physiological accompaniment, consisting of organic changes. These changes are perceived in their turn and so continue to reinforce that tendency.

Specific changes according to type of emotion. There is considerable evidence (Arnold, 1) that there are specific organic changes in fear, anger, and love.

An emotion is complete when there is the whole sequence described above, including the practical estimate of the situation, the reaction of wanting or dislike, the somatic expression and organic changes, and the awareness of these changes. An emotion is incomplete when there is an evaluation of the situation and resulting from it wanting or dislike, but no appropriate emotional expression or organic changes. This may happen if the neural pathways between cortex and thalamic centers are interrupted (by surgery, disease, or accident). Because we have defined emotion as the felt tendency toward or away from something which is merely reinforced by the appropriate bodily changes, it is possible in these cases to speak of emotion even though such emotion is not complete and the person neither shows nor is aware of emotional *expression* or organic changes. On the other hand, there may be the same organic changes as are ordinarily experienced during an emotion and the person may become aware of them—as happens, for instance, after adrenalin injection or in states of disturbed endocrine balance; the simple awareness of such a changed physiological state, however, cannot be called an emotion but should be called a feeling, indicating the response to changed functioning (see our discussion of feelings on page 301 ff.).

Types of Emotion

To discover the diverse types of emotion, we shall have to examine the objects toward or away from which the tendency is directed. The simple partiality toward that which is suitable could be called simple *love* (St. Thomas' term, "simplex amor"), and the simple repugnance to something judged unsuitable or harmful, *hate*. Since the tendency away from something harmful is secondary to the tendency toward something suitable (for the harmful object threatens the possession of something suitable), love must be basic in all subject-object relationships, and hate and other avoidance emotions can only be a reaction to the actual or threatened deprivation of things loved (see page 201, Footnote 8).

This tendency to respond emotionally has the same characteristics which we found in every other action tendency, namely, that it acts when conditions are favorable, and that it seeks an opportunity for action when none is given or when there are obstacles to its exercise. When conditions are favorable, the person simply *tends* toward the object or away from it; when they are unfavorable, he *contends* for or against it. In the first case, he acts from an emotional *impulse*, in the second from an emotional *urge* or a *contending emotion*. There will be a simple tending toward, when the loved object is present, at least in imagination, or is easily accessible; a simple tending away from, when the repellent object is present at least in imagination, and easily avoidable. There will be contending when the loved object is attainable only with difficulty and the repellent object can be endured or evaded only with pain.

If the loved object is not present, that is, not possessed, but is easily accessible, simple love will become a *want* or *desire*. But if the loved object is neither present nor easily accessible, we feel the urge to overcome the obstacles to its possession, we *aspire* to it, we *hope* and *strive* for it. If the obstacles are judged to be insuperable, the urge to *despair* will overcome us. But if we gain the object we love, we rest and delight in its possession, we feel the impulse of *joy*.

On the other hand, if there is a threat of something harmful which can easily be evaded, we tend away from it, we feel *aversion* and *dislike*. If this threat is immediate and difficult to avoid, we turn away from it actively, we have the urge to flee, we feel *fear*. But if we judge that we can overcome that which threatens us, we contend with it, we show *daring*, we have *courage*. If something harmful is actually present and is frustrating and obstructing us, we have the urge to turn against it, we feel *anger*.

In this way, we can order emotions according to their aim as directed toward a suitable object and away from a harmful one, into *positive* and *negative* emotions; and according to their operation, their degree of impulsion, into *impulse emotions* and *contending emotions*.

The accompanying schematic table will show this twofold analysis of emotions according to the degree of impulsion, while the above analysis has been according to the object of emotion.

Polarities in Emotion

From a consideration of this scheme we come to see that opposite emotional attitudes can develop from one and the same emotion. Love is basic if understood as the tendency of all organisms to tend toward something suitable, to love it, want it, possess it. But when we cannot attain that object, or when its possession involves some attractive, some repulsive aspects, we

Basic Emotions

1. Emotions differ according to their *object* (as it is suitable or harmful to the self). Therefore we distinguish

   positive emotions (tending toward suitable objects)
   and **negative emotions** (tending away from harmful objects)

2. Emotions differ according to their *operation,* the degree of impulsion. Therefore we distinguish

   impulse emotions (tending toward or away from an object when conditions are favorable)
   and **contending emotions** (contending for or against something when conditions are unfavorable)

	A. Impulse Emotions	Emotion Toward Object as Such: (Whether Present or Absent)	Object Not Present (Tendency Toward or Away From)	Object Present (Rest in Possession)
positive	Object Suitable (*good*)	love	wanting, desire	delight, joy
negative	Object Unsuitable (*evil*)	hate	aversion, dislike	sorrow, sadness

	B. Contending Emotions	Degree of Difficulty	Object Not Present (Tendency Toward or Away From)	Object Present
positive	Object Suitable (*good*)	if judged attainable	hope	
		if judged unattainable	despair	
negative	Object Unsuitable (*evil*)	if to be overcome	daring	anger
		if to be avoided	fear	

feel a different emotion according to the conditions which we judge to be attractive or repulsive, to be overcome or to be avoided. There is a polarity of emotions, either because they refer to different objects, suitable or unsuitable, or because they refer to the same object under different conditions, favorable or unfavorable, or because unfavorable conditions are either judged as yielding to attack, therefore to be mastered, or as insuperable, therefore to be avoided. We either love or hate, we either wish for something or strive to attain it, we either fight for it or give it up altogether. Therefore the emotion will differ according to precisely defined conditions which depend on the way in which the individual judges the situation.

This is a very different emotional polarity from the polarities discussed by Freud which occupy so important a role in the psychoanalytic system. Freud deals with such phenomena as the reversal of one emotion into its opposite (love into hostility); a transformation of a passive aim (to be looked at) into an active aim (to look at); or the reversal of a content (night into day). He assumes that these polarities are an inherent factor of the instinctual life; in particular, that our mental life is governed by three basic polarities—subject-object, pleasure-pain, activity-passivity. In each of these, one opposite pole may be replaced by another. Because the polarities are inherent in instincts, there is an implicit assumption that the reversal may occur at any time, may be set off by any chance occurrence, and is therefore unpredictable.

Our usage of the term "polarity" approaches contemporary usage much more closely than does Freud's. For Freud, polarity in an emotion, for instance, implies two poles in the same thing, after the manner of a north and south pole in a bar magnet. For us, polarity means orientation in one direction rather than in another, after the manner of "polarized light," which vibrates in only one plane.

That there are polarities we do not deny: What is good for us we love, what is bad for us we avoid. But one and the same object cannot at one and the same time and under the same aspects be both loved and hated by the same person. If we love something, we love it for its attractive, its lovable aspects. If we hate it, we hate it for its repulsive and unattractive aspects.

It is quite possible, of course, that one object has many aspects which are significant for us. One person may love another —but it would be more accurate to say he loves those features in another which give him pleasure, which enhance his personality, and which are in harmony with his own goals. He may also hate in him the things which repel him, which frustrate his goals, and which are a threat to his love of possession, his psychological stability, and his self-actuation. We never love another person's good looks and hate them at the same time. If his good looks attract us, the comparison with our own lack of attractiveness may displease us, but that is another aspect entirely. The more a human relationship depends on sensory appeal, the more ambivalent will it be; for on the sensory level many characteristics of the other person may be attractive, but some are bound to be repellent. Not only will there be a conflict between different sensory aspects; the sensory appeal may also come in conflict with other goals—for instance, the tendency toward stability and self-actuation. Similarly, if the relationship is not based on sensory appeal but on the satisfaction of one of the three basic tendencies, there will be a possibility of conflict and therefore ambivalence so long as these tendencies are isolated and not ordered in their proper hierarchy. Another person considered as a possession, or even as a means to self-actuation, is bound to disappoint us. While we love him for his promise, we shall hate him for his defection.

In general, the more a human relationship is based on sensory appeal, or appeal to isolated tendencies, the more ambivalent will it be. Only when it is based upon a common striving toward a common goal which is in harmony with man's final end, to which all other aspects of that relationship are subordinated, will there be love properly so called, love which is integrated, and undisturbed by hate, jealousy, or envy. Only on that level will it be love of a person rather than love of his physical or intellectual attractions. On that level, love becomes a sharing of the Good, and that sharing is the natural overflow of goodness which is inherent in the Good itself.

Feelings, Moods, and Emotions

In discussing the difference between feelings, moods, and emotions, we are well aware that this topic has been a vexing problem for psychologists. That feelings, moods, and emotions do not belong in the same class seems clear, but it is extremely difficult to distinguish them in such a way that their differences become definable. There are some feelings, for instance, which are called emotions when they become intense, and there are some emotions which are called moods when they last for a considerable length of time.

As a tentative scheme for distinguishing the three we shall classify feelings as *those affective states where the psychological reference is principally to the subject*. Pleasure and displeasure, then, would be the simple elements of sensory feelings, or, more precisely, they would be affective reactions to sensations. Gemelli, in a recent article (3), calls such feelings "affective sensations," but we prefer the term "sensory feelings" because this term makes it clear that we are dealing with feelings and not with sensations. Sensory feelings are different from sensations because one and the same sensation can be either pleasant or unpleasant for different persons; moreover, for the same person, that sensation may be sometimes pleasant, sometimes unpleasant; or the same sensation, judged pleasant at first, may become decidedly unpleasant if it is much prolonged.

We call these feelings *sensory* feelings because they are always the reaction not to an object as an object but to sense perceptions connected with the object. When we say that a color or an odor is pleasant, that a walk is pleasant, or dancing, or painting, the judgment we make is always a judgment of sensations, and the psychological reference is to the inner state of the individual. The feeling of pleasantness or unpleasantness is the result of a preceding awareness in the same way that an emotion is. But in the case of feelings, the question, "How does it affect me?" is answered by being aware how the particular object affects the individual's sensory and motor functioning and not how it affects him as a person. When a color is pleasant, it is really the sensation, or more accurately the *sensing* that is pleasant. When a walk is pleasant, it is the walking and breathing and looking connected with it that is pleasant. But since the walking and breathing and looking can be known as pleasant only because of the diverse sensations that inform us of the fact, it is correct even in this case to speak of pleasantness as a *sensory feeling* or an *affective reaction to sensation*. Thinking, imagining, and reasoning can also be smooth or difficult in their functioning, and will correspondingly be felt as pleasant or unpleasant.

The practical judgment preceding an emotion also answers the question: "How does it affect me?" but the "me" in this case is not my functioning but my person. When I say the fragrance or taste of wine is *pleasant*, I do not necessarily want the wine; in fact, I may never take it. In tasting its fragrance, I possess the pleasant sensation and no possession of the object is asked for. But when I say I *like* wine, it means that I *do* want it when the occasion is given. The aim of the *emotion* (liking or simple love in this case) is possession of the object, while the *feeling* of pleasantness simply indicates smooth functioning in the subject. Hence, emotion aims at the object, feeling reflects the state of the subject.

For a sensory feeling to become an emotion it is necessary that the preceding judgment—how this sensation affects my functioning—should be followed by a judgment how the object which occasions the sensation affects me *as a person*. As an illustration, we quote a passage from Gemelli's above-mentioned article, which is an introspective report from one of his subjects in an experiment on pleasantness/unpleasantness.

The odor was disagreeable in itself, but the disagreeable sensation quickly disappeared when the stimulus ceased; immediately in my mind there arose a much greater repugnance, and different because it was not physical, causing an aversion to the source of the odor. I saw that this repugnance was caused in me by the memory of certain parasites, the smell of which had actually been presented to me as a stimulus. I also felt a strong movement of nausea, disgust, and repulsion (3, p. 211).

Here we see very clearly that first the *odor* was judged, then the *object* which possesses this odor. As soon as the object was judged as it affected the person, there came the tendency away from it which we have called emotion.

When there is a feeling state which is not ascribed to a particular sensation, but which reflects the total inner state, the total functioning, and this feeling state is protracted, we call it a *mood*. If we wake up in the morning feeling in a cheerful mood because all our powers are functioning smoothly, we find it easy to get up, to dress, to drive, and to work. Often, of course, the morning's cheerful or despondent mood may be the result of a dream, whether we remember the dream and the dream emotion or not. In that case, a disturbing dream, which provokes an emotion of sadness, will result in the physiological changes appropriate to the emotion which (in the case of sadness) will inhibit smooth functioning. Then the despondent mood next morning will be an indication of such hampered functioning. But a mood can also be the result of a *physiological* acceleration or retardation of functioning, as, for instance, in the euphoric mood of patients suffering from slightly febrile states such as occur in tuberculosis or the depression observable in some persons after taking massive doses of sulfa drugs which prevent cell nutrition.

Feelings and moods, then, are indicators of the smooth or difficult functioning of the organism. As such, they can act as danger signals to induce the individual to take steps toward reestablishment of effective physiological and psychological functioning.

The Purpose of Emotion

We have seen that feelings and moods serve as indicators of the inner state of functioning of the individual. He can, but need not, make use of them to correct unfavorable conditions of functioning.

Emotions, on the other hand, aim at the possession of suitable objects. They could be considered as instruments not only to reach particular objects but also to help us reach the perfection of our personality, the actuation of our potentialities in the possession of these objects. From even a cursory reflection upon our own experience it is evident that emotion can move us to action and can facilitate action. We pursue and achieve something we want very strongly without any feeling of effort; but we feel burdened by the effort we must expend to reach a goal we *ought* to reach, for which we do not care. The same thing is found in the speedup of action which comes with the exhilaration of daring or the impetus of anger and fear. Impulse emotions as well as contending emotions can be such instruments in the pursuit of our purposes. The possession of an object begins in desire, is achieved in action, and perpetuated by our joy in it. If ill befall us, we try to work clear of it, looking for something better.

It is an intricate matter to make clear how the negative emotions and the states brought on by them can facilitate action toward a goal. We must bear in mind that a "negative" emotion and the "negative" movement involved in it are in fact positive states—there is actually something going on. The movement is called negative because it is away from whatever provokes it. But this movement is not simply away from the undesirable object or state. It is reasonable to argue that this movement is as much positive (toward something) as it is negative (away from the undesirable), because even on the principle of sheer mechanical evolution of the organism, survival is the function of avoidance reactions. Thus the negative movement is always toward something better, not simply away from a present evil. It is true, of course, that the "something better" is only dimly and confusedly known, while the object evoking the emotion is very clearly in the forefront of awareness. But what makes for survival is not the clarity of perception nor the fact of avoidance; it is rather the value of the movement for reaching its positive aim. "Out of the frying pan into the fire" situations are exceptional and rare.

Moreover, the emotional reaction in negative emotional states is seldom the result of simply a single object or an uncomplicated state of mind. Sadness, which at first glance seems to be wholly depressing, has a positive bearing: a heading toward something—anything—constructive and elating. The case is somewhat more complex when the sadness comes from loss. Here we have a negative emotion reinforced and perpetuated by a contending emotion. We *desire* the lost good now unattainable, and are depressed by its *absence* now unavoidable. It is the contending emotion that keeps us *bound*, as it were, to the cause of our sadness. The whole problem of anxiety, sadness, and the negative emotions in general needs reinvestigation from this point of vantage. There is, however, a way of managing these negative emotions so as to facilitate action. There is a rational way of dealing with evil suffered which is called patience, just as there is a rational way of reacting to good denied or lost which is called longanimity or long-suffering.

This gives us some answer to the question whether the emotion, though a proper instrument for achieving the object toward which it tends, is necessarily a means for the integration of personality and for actuation of the person. The contending emotion coupled with sadness, as we said, keeps us bound to the good we have lost; in that sense, one purpose of the emotion is achieved. But the wellbeing of the person would require that he detach himself from the lost object which causes his sadness, and focus his attention on something else. Like every function, emotion is drawn toward its own objects. But also, like every other function, emotion can be organized so that it will tend toward the integration of the personality, provided that the person actively directs it toward rational ends.

Emotions, we have said, are aroused as the result of a value judgment, made primarily on the basis of sensory appeal or repulsion. But what is good for the human being cannot be judged solely on such a basis. It must be judged also on the basis of a rational evaluation. An object may be judged to afford bodily pleasure and satisfaction but be known as harmful from rational considerations. A chocolate bar may be very attractive to the diabetic, but he knows he will suffer if he takes it. Similarly, spring air and sunshine may arouse an intense desire in the student to skip lectures, but if he gives in to it he will defeat his hope of passing his examinations.

If, then, emotion is to be instrumental in self-actuation, the objects of emotion must be harmonized with the person's larger goal as a human being. If these objects are seen in their real value, if they are seen in the proper perspective of man's final end, then the judgment that they are suitable will be objective and well ordered.

We can discuss now in detail how emotions aid in personality integration and self-actuation. When the impulse-emotions simply tend toward objects, they will work as means for achieving possession, just as the impulse-emotions which tend away from harm work as means for retaining possession. Impulse-emotions, therefore, could be identified with the tendency toward possession which we have discussed earlier as one of the human being's three basic tendencies (see Chapter 6). The contending emotions or urges, on the other hand, act as means for establishing and stabilizing possessions, and also for establishing the self in its possessions, that is, for self-actuation. Contending emotions could be identified with the basic tendencies of the human being toward psychological stabilization (or security) and toward self-actuation.

Effects of Emotion on the Person

Every emotion is preceded by knowledge, evaluation, judgment, not on the speculative or intellectual level but on the practical level. This particular situation has been judged: What does it mean to me and what am I going to do about it? Following this judgment, there will be the emotional state accompanied by the appropriate muscular and glandular changes which are an integral part of emotional activity. Furthermore, emotion leads to motor action to achieve the desired object or to move away from impending danger.

The evaluative judgment requires sensation, imagination, and memory; it involves the intellect, too, because the factor of meaning is always present on the human level. Now we saw in our discussion of the personality structure that the meaning of any particular situation is gradually built up, is the result of innumerable experiences of the person with similar objects or in similar situations. Since the emotional situation involves the activity of many powers, often of all the powers of the human being as they have been organized and ordered up to the time the emotional situation occurs, we find that not only are all the functions working simultaneously, but the total person, as he is here and now, is actively ordering and integrating the present situation into the total pattern of the personality as he progresses toward the self-ideal.

We can see now why the emotions play such an important part in the integration of personality. They are found in a setting which involves the whole person because an emotional state involves all his physiological and psychological activities.

Emotions as Factors Disturbing Personality Integration

In most of the literature, emotion is assumed to be a disorganizing factor in personality. True, Cannon insisted that emotions had an emergency function, so they could not be said to be disorganizing altogether, but he pointed out at the same time that a state of emergency puts a burden on the organism which cannot be sustained for very long.

To correct this view, Leeper has recently suggested that emotions cannot adequately be explained outside a motivational framework. Though extremes of emotions may be disorganizing, he holds that normally emotions act "primarily to arouse, sustain, and direct activity" (4). This view is in agreement with our discussion in so far as we have stressed that emotion in its very nature is a tending toward or away from something, and will therefore lead to motor action and to the possession or avoidance of the object aimed at.

But it ought to be pointed out that emotion can act as a disorganizing factor as well, first when it is so intense as to overwhelm the individual, and secondly when its object is not in harmony with the person's rational goal. There is no doubt that extremely intense emotions are disorganizing, as Leeper himself admits. But perhaps it would be more adequate to call such emotions disabling rather than disorganizing, for they are disabling in the same way as response to excess stimulation is disabling. If an individual has an epileptic fit, his motor activity is excessive and disabling. If he is blinded by a strong light, he is temporarily disabled.

But the very intensity of emotional stimulation depends on our judgment how this particular object or this particular situation affects us. If it is judged dangerous, we are afraid, and this fear is a spur to escape. But if we judge that this danger situation is so threatening that flight is useless, we shall be overwhelmed by extreme fear, feel terror, and become incapacitated for flight. Whether or not fear becomes excessive will therefore depend on how dangerous we judge the situation to be.

But that judgment depends on other factors too. We may see that the danger is overwhelming, and yet not be overwhelmed by fear, provided only that the evil we fear is not the worst thing for us, no matter how important it may be in itself. Men have faced a firing squad with a smile on their lips, and martyrs have died with a shout of joy.

The intensity of an emotion, then, depends not only on how attractive or repulsive or dangerous we judge this situation to be, but also on how important this attraction is for us, how much we would mind having to put up with that repulsion, or how fatal for our real self this particular defeat would be. In other words, we can order and regulate the intensity of an emotion if we consider the emotional situation in its relation to our rational goal and to our final end. This will result in a proportional reduction in the degree of its affective appeal or repulsion. If we are successful, the danger will be judged less threatening, the attraction less compelling than formerly, because now it is seen only as important to part of us and not so important to our real self.

If, on the other hand, the object or situation is habitually judged as pleasurable or attractive regardless of its harmfulness to the person as a whole or its incompatibility with his properly organized life pattern, then desire may become intense and force action. In that case, emotion will not be so intense as to disable the person. He will go in the direction his emotion impels him, but doing so will prevent the achievement of wider and more important aims.

Moreover, emotion acts as disturbing factor not only when it seemingly functions as a separate power pursuing its own aim. Personality integration can also be disturbed if emotions serve one of the three basic tendencies when these tendencies are not properly ordered.

A man may intend to remain an honest upright businessman. But he makes a lucky deal, becomes fascinated by easy money, gives in to his tendency to possession and finds before long that his taste for money makes him less careful to avoid shady deals. Or a father may intend to be a good companion to his children, but he is attached to his own stable way of doing things, and the children always interfere. As a result he gives in to his anger on every occasion and before long the children tremble when he tries to be kind to them.

Emotion may disturb personality integration even when it serves self-actuation. If a man becomes inordinately attached to his self-ideal, he will become fearful of anything that may threaten it, and will judge himself frustrated by every trifling incident. He will be fearful and aggressive in turn, and will worry and fret and spend his energy in emotions that will bring him no nearer to his goal. In such a case self is in the center of attention and the end result will be self-glorification rather than self-actuation. Only if the self-ideal is what it ought to be, and *influences the person as a motive rather than as a blueprint*, will emotion be saved from excessive self-reference and be an integrating rather than a disturbing factor.

Emotions urge a man toward particular goals and enable him to satisfy present-moment demands. But unless these demands are in harmony with the wider requirements of the total personality working toward self-actuation, their satisfaction will disintegrate rather than unify, will lead to inner conflict rather than healthy growth. If emotions are allowed free play, tempting a man toward any and every goal, they will first disturb and then prevent personality integration. For this reason, there has to be some emotional control.

Control of Emotions

Though emotion normally leads to action appropriate to it, it is possible to go counter to the emotion, whatever it may be. But it is possible only when the goal we want to achieve is so important that we are willing to suffer to achieve it. Since emotions are instruments for attaining something beneficial and avoiding something harmful, their physiological components are so arranged that motor action will follow under pain of discomfort. Fear is intensely unpleasant; to act as fear prompts us to act, namely to flee, means to escape not only the external danger but the internal discomfort. Hope or longing for something difficult to attain is a torment when intense; to act as hope prompts us to act so that we achieve what we long for brings not only the possession of the longed-for object but also relief from emotional suffering. But to act counter to any emotion, to suffer fear, to deny ourselves the relief of attack, or the striving for something we long for, means not only giving up the object of the emotion but also enduring subjective discomfort. For this reason, acting counter to emotion is difficult; it is also unintelligent if the control of emotions can be achieved in some other way, for going against emotion means turning a help into a hindrance.

In animals, this possibility of going counter to emotion does not exist, nor is there any possibility of reducing the intensity of the emotion, or rather its persistence, by evaluating the immediate situation in the light of a more important goal. In animals, the estimate of the emotional situation is invariant because it is a sensory judgment depending merely upon the strength of the sensory appeal or repugnance. Of course, the strength of the affective appeal will be influenced by the animal's past experience, but the animal himself cannot do anything to change it. True, animals sometimes seem to act as if they could go counter to emotion. A dog has braved fire to save his master—but he does not quake with fear while he does it. His emotion is directed *toward* his master and *contends with* an obstacle in the way. His emotion always coincides with his action and nothing but a contrary emotion can interfere with it. That is why we have to train a dog for hunting in such a way that we counteract by his fear of punishment his tendency to tear and devour his prey; even the most intelligent dog will not train himself. A man may judge, for instance, that flying in a superannuated plane is dangerous and will feel fear with all its symptoms: cold feet, trembling knees, racing heart; but he knows that the only way to save a badly injured man is to be flown to his assistance, so he will decide on flying in spite of his emotion.

The very characteristics which make emotion a fit instrument to achieve our object also make it difficult to control—namely, the fact that the whole organism is engaged in tending toward or away from a thing. There is not only a psychological *tendency toward*, or *wanting*, there is a physiological urge as well. The physiological changes which constitute that organismic wanting will continue, once started, and will become cumulative. That is the reason why a decision to act against an emotion becomes more difficult as the emotion progresses.

Nevertheless, control is possible because reasonable decisions have a chance to intervene. We do not have to be forced by emotion, for most emotional situations have aspects which good sense rather than passion can assess. Now reasonable decisions follow good sense, not sheer emotional appeal, but to make the intervention of good sense effective it is easier to exercise it in the beginning rather than later on. Making a reasonable decision early in the situation will not eliminate emotional inclinations against the course of action decided upon, but it will lessen the attraction for the opposite course and reduce the pressure which emotion uncontrolled can generate.

A decision may be made and carried out either *accompanied by* an emotional tending toward the goal, or *without* any emotion, or *against* an emotion. Only when we decide to do something which also attracts us will the action be felt as easy and pleasant. In the human being the decision to act is ordinarily based on rational judgment, but the emotion follows the prior evaluation which has revealed what satisfaction this may bring here and now. The object of an emotion may be anything which gives physical pleasure, intellectual satisfaction, or spiritual fulfilment. But the more intense the satisfaction which the object affords us here and now, the more intense will be the emotion.

If the desired object is judged rationally suitable but has sensory aspects which are undesirable, either there will be no felt emotion or the felt emotion will pull in the opposite direction. In deciding, for instance, to attack in battle, there is not only danger but also the appeal of physical combat and mastery. If the latter aspect is focused on, there will be the emotion of daring or courage which will make action easy and effective. But in deciding to stand up for one's convictions in writing or speaking to a large audience the element of combat is absent while the hostility of the audience or the disapproval of friends contains a powerful deterrent which makes such a course of action highly distasteful. In both cases we speak of courage, but only in the first case will it be an emotion in the strict sense of the term. Accordingly, action in the first case is easy, in the second it may be extremely difficult.

The only way, then, to have emotion as a help in achieving our aim is, first, to reach a certain detachment from appeals directed to the senses, and secondly, to discover in the rationally chosen objects whatever appeals to the whole man here and now. Then they will become important enough so that physical aspects become ancillary.

Suppose a student decides to become a physician. If he wants to achieve his end easily and quickly, he will first have to order all his other goals (especially those that have a strong sensory appeal) with reference to this end. He may play baseball or any other game, he may go to the theater, to concerts, the movies, but unless he comes to see that all these activities are less important than his profession, unless he comes to the point where he gladly gives up coveted pleasures in favor of a professional demand, he will find it extremely difficult to make progress in his profession. Only when he comes to develop genuine interest in medicine, when he comes to concentrate on it in such a way that he will find satisfaction and even exhilaration in overcoming difficulties, when he is able to feel the joy that comes from sharing his knowledge with others or helping them by his skill, only then will studying cease to be drudgery, only then will it be easy for him to succeed.

REFERENCES

1. ARNOLD, MAGDA B. 1945. Physiological differentiation of emotional states. *Psychol. Rev.*, 1945, 52, 35–48.
2. CANNON, WALTER B. 1927. *Bodily changes in pain, hunger, fear and rage* (2d ed.). New York: Appleton-Century-Crofts, Inc.
3. GEMELLI, AGOSTINO. 1949. Orienting concepts in the study of affective states. *J. nerv. ment. Dis.*, 1949, 110, Part I, pp. 198–214; Part II, pp. 299–314.
4. LEEPER, R. W. 1948. A motivational theory of emotion to replace 'emotion as disorganized response.' *Psychol. Rev.*, 1948, 55, 5–21.

Chapter 11

CONTEMPORARY LEARNING THEORY AND HUMAN LEARNING

By Frank J. Kobler

THE IMPORTANCE of learning and the closely allied psychology of motivation in contemporary psychology can be gauged by Boring's statement in the second edition of his classic *History of Experimental Psychology* (3) that these topics now have the right to stand as companion topics in experimental psychology with sensation and perception.

Learning is gradually taking the center of the stage in American psychology. It is the factor through which we can hope to come to an understanding of nongenetic, nonmaturational changes in man. It is the area in psychology through which we can hope to understand that aspect of man that offers the greatest and currently the only prospect of working realistically with him.

The importance of learning in relation to the understanding of man can readily be gauged by a consideration of the following questions: "How is the human personality formed?" "What leads to its malformation, as for example in the appearance of a neurosis?" "How are ideas acquired?" "How are habits formed?" "The attitudes and opinions of men—how are they crystallized?" "How are walking, talking, reading, thinking, good manners, and feeling acquired and perfected?"

The influence and importance of learning in American psychology can likewise be gauged from the marked increase in learning articles published in the professional journals, and particularly in the *Journal of Experimental Psychology*, as well as from an examination of the roster of presidents of the American Psychological Association, many if not most of whom in the past two decades have had a great interest in learning and learning theory. Learning theory is likewise of major importance for the more general theory of psychology, and in the past ten years it has assumed an increasing importance for clinical psychology. Learning appears to hold the key to the future solution of many complex problems in psychology.

The difficulty that arises as one reads the literature on learning theory is to find a theory that adequately encompasses the known facts, that synthesizes the various interpretations, and that offers a suitable experimental framework in which to attack the unsolved problems of human nature. The need is for a theory sufficiently broad to encompass all the kinds of learning found in man. The major criticism that can be leveled at contemporary learning theory is that, in segmentalizing human learning and in concentrating upon significant aspects of learning, it has neglected equally important aspects, or it has set up a system of parts that has made it impossible to entertain in the theory other more crucial elements of human personality. That this has been done in the interest of a justifiable scientific parsimony is known and is commendable. Such a restriction has made for intense scientific activity and for considerable progress. A simple monistic interpretation of the facts of learning is useful in the interests of rigor and clarity. It is particularly useful if it is not a closed system that precludes the erection of a sound psychology of learning. That the limits of such a systematic structure have been reached, that dissatisfaction with it is being expressed, particularly in the light of the crucially important new clinical interests and experiences that are coming to dominate American psychology, is evident on many sides in the attempts to reconstruct, to resynthesize the systems that have dominated the American scene in the past two decades.

It is useful to examine the current learning theories in the light of their historical development, in the light of their limitations and suggested inadequacies, and in relation to a substitute theory that proposes to function in the stream of psychological tradition, and yet proposes to offer a more satisfactory set of principles for an explanation of the perplexing problems posed by experience with the human person.

The systematic discussion of learning is a relatively new event in psychology, having its inception in the twentieth century. Learning theory in any formal sense is still more recent, having developed largely within the past two decades. The earlier concern with learning was largely experimental and methodological, finding its characteristic expression in the work on memory by Ebbinghaus, the work on the acquisition of skill by Bryan and Harter, and the work on problem solving in animals by Thorndike. Prior to these experimentalists and in line with the tradition in which they worked, learning was discussed under the topic of remembering, and particularly under the topic of association. For the associationists of the nineteenth century, learning was a process of acquiring sensory experiences called "ideas" from the sensory experiences called "sensations."

There is no question about the legitimacy of identifying contemporary learning theory with the associationistic tradition because the bulk of present-day learning theorists are avowed associationists of one type or another. The major exception to this are the field theorists whose tradition stems from Plato through Leibnitz and Kant to the modern *Gestalt* psychologists.

Aristotle in his brief essay on memory (Boring, 3, p. 159) outlined the basic principles of association which dominate learning theory today. For some obscure reason his specific doctrine languished, or was interpreted differently until it was refurbished in the seventeenth century and flowered in the nineteenth century, where in modified form it was regarded as the sole basis for all mental operations.

It was the mechanism, the dualism, and the artificial interactionism of Descartes that were instrumental in the inauguration of associationism as we see it expressed in learning theory today. His thought made possible the work of subsequent writers whose theories we have with us today. All modern learning theory stems from Descartes' theory of knowledge. It is the gap that he created between mind and body that must in some way be bridged in an adequate comprehensive theory today.

Hobbes begins the more pertinent associationistic tradition with his attempt to explain mind by motion. For Hobbes, internal motion or imagination was started by external motion or sensation. Once begun, these imaginal activities continue by an automatic process. Sensations succeed one another in a definite temporal sequence and this sequence of continuity is impressed upon the imagination and accounts principally, if not exclusively, for the association of ideas. Control is exercised over these freely wandering images by desire. Thus, Hobbes solved Descartes' parallelism by eliminating the rational mind and contending that images are dominated by the emotions.

Locke had a much more decisive influence on modern learning theory with his emphasis on experience as the basis for all ideas. For him it was the imagination that provided the complexity of the ideas which were initially simple in experience. These ideas, or more correctly, these images have a natural logic or a natural associative power that accounts for the essential unity of experience.

Berkeley in his brilliant *Essay on a New Theory of Vision* exemplified the new doctrine of associationism by applying it to the psychological perception of distance as this develops in man. Berkeley contended that to account for this new dimension in experience there must be an interaction or association of the visual processes with the body movements involved in contacting a seen object. His use of the doctrine of associationism, however, was somewhat unusual because he felt that ideas are experienced as ordered by virtue of the activity of the Eternal Spirit.

Hume, a critical empiricist, who denied substance, maintained that the mind *was* its contents. The memory, the image, the idea, are all sensations for Hume. While he appeared to see the need for an "ego" to associate ideas he was unable to accept this concept in his system. His emphasis was on association by contiguity and by similarity. His famous notion of causality was merely a type of association called succession. In Hume we find associationism utilized as the only basis for explaining the mind.

Hartley combined the previously entertained notions of association by succession and by simultaneity to which he added the principle of nearness. He maintained that things were learned or remembered if they succeeded one another, if they occurred at the same time, and if they were closely juxtaposed in space or time. Thomas Brown, one hundred years later, transformed this associationism into the newer ideas of mental chemistry, without making any essential changes in the doctrine. Brown was among the first who furnished the basis for the later connection-istic learning theory when he developed the notion of the so-called secondary laws of learning: namely, frequency, recency, and vividness. These were used by Brown, just as by Thorn-dike, to buttress the law of contiguity which even then could not stand critical analysis as a single law to explain all of learn-ing. Perhaps the most literate and technically able of all the expositions of the doctrine of associationism is given by James Mill in his *Analysis of Mind*. The essential emphasis here is that ideas are complex sensations linked by the process of asso-ciation.

It was Bain, however, operating in this tradition of associ-ationism, who had a direct influence on contemporary American systematic learning theory. While he held to the two funda-mental laws of contiguity and similarity he introduced and used accessory principles such as contrast and utility. He modi-fied the more superficial and intellectualized type of associa-tionism by introducing a hereditary and specifically a reflex component as important in complementing the experience factor.

We see from the foregoing discussion that associationism was characteristically a product of British thought. It had its counterpart, however, on the continent, crystallizing in the im-portant accomplishments of Ebbinghaus and Wundt, who de-veloped a broad avenue through which this tradition found entrance into America. These systems, together with concur-rently developing doctrines of hedonism and evolutionism, led to the development of the modern theories of Thorndike, Pav-lov, and Watson.

In contrast, however, with the associationistic tradition that has ended in our own time with the current theories of Thorn-dike, Guthrie, Hull, and Skinner, we have another tradition that reaches back to Plato and Leibnitz through Kant and down to *Gestalt* psychology and to Brentano and Külpe and eventually to

Freud. We should emphasize in passing that it is certain theories of Freud which are gradually becoming an integral part of some contemporary learning theories.

The opposition that crystallized against associationism centered largely in Germany, where it took many forms. Its most exuberant and enduring forms were *Gestalt* psychology and psychoanalysis, both of which developed on the continent and then migrated to America to achieve their greatest success. The one, *Gestalt* psychology, already appears pretty thoroughly accepted and meshed with the more typical American behaviorism. It is represented in the contemporary field theories of learning. The other, psychoanalysis, has proved much more difficult to digest, and its assimilation by the typically American psychologies of function and behavior has been correspondingly slower. Its importance for contemporary learning theory will become apparent later.

The opposition to associationism centered around the notions of function, of act, of power, in contrast to the content or images of the mind emphasized by the associationist. The implications of this opposition between content and act psychologies are crucial for learning theories. Such opposition represents an expressed need for something to unify experience—for something to bring together the separate experiences. Associationism had tried repeatedly to do this in one way or another. The limitations of the system had been clearly set forth in the able expositions of a long line of philosophical psychologists. Unity was an experience that was not found in the separate elements of consciousness—an experienced fact for which the associationist had no answer.

Wundt and Titchener had worked extensively to furnish the experimental proof for a content of mind that the philosophical psychologists had outlined. Now, however, it was felt in many quarters that there must be an emphasis on the activity or the function of the mind. Perhaps this would be the means of establishing its unity since the notion of substance had been eliminated. But the emphasis on function as an additional element in mind might conceivably be the way of reintroducing substance. The reason for this is that if mind is not "content" alone, it might also be more than matter alone. To add function was typically to add another element in the structural approach, but it nevertheless represents an approximation to a more realistic evaluation of mind since it reflects a dissatisfaction with the contentual emphasis of the associationist. It is an easier transition from an act or a power to a soul than it is from an image to a soul. Von Ehrenfels' "Gestaltqualität," for example, emphasizes the existence of a synthesizing element superior to and beyond the sum total of elements resident in the mind. In like manner under Külpe, the experimental emphasis was on thought and volition, elements that associationists neglected, and that the functionalists in America developed extensively. Typical of the new psychology of learning which protested the oversimplification of the associationistic hypothesis were the new experimental approaches of such workers as Marbe on thought, Ach on determining tendencies, Binet on problem solving, Judd on transfer of training, and Fernald on memory.

From this historical development two major trends have emerged in learning theory. One trend is reflected in the several contemporary variations and revisions of the associationistic hypothesis which in greater or lesser degree have taken into account the criticisms that have been leveled in our own time. The other trend is reflected in the field theories that have proliferated by way of rebellion against the shortcomings of structuralism, behaviorism, and associationism. One writer (Hilgard, 5) points out that the modern associationists prefer to emphasize the influence of the environment, to consider wholes according to their composition from constituent elements, to concentrate on response behavior rather than introspection. They have a preference for mechanical models and historically oriented causation. The field theorists, on the other hand, are nativists and consider wholes according to their unique pattern and organization. They gravitate toward perception and ideas (rather than responses) as materials to analyze, and as a consequence utilize introspection. Their models are dynamic and their emphasis is on contemporary causation. They account for the present by the present and not by the past. The differences and similarities between the associationistic and the field theories of learning can be illustrated by a consideration of the theories of Thorndike, Hull, Tolman, and Mowrer.

Thorndike defines his theory of connectionism as the "doctrine that all mental processes consist of the functioning of native and acquired connections between the situations and the responses." He is an associationist whose system is fundamentally but vaguely physiological, since he postulates a one-to-one connection in the neurons between the stimulus and the response. Learning for him is the end product of all one's experiences added together. Thorndike uses reflexes and instincts in addition to habits to explain learning. Basic to an understanding of Thorndike's theory of learning are his so-called laws of learning. These are of two types: the primary laws of effect, exercise and frequency; and the secondary laws such as belongingness, associative shifting, and set. The most fundamental of these laws in Thorndike's system is that of effect. He states it as follows: "a modifiable bond is strengthened or weakened as satisfiers or annoyers attend its exercise." This law of effect has become the basic issue around the acceptance or rejection of which theories of learning have been built (Postman, 14). Thorndike may be called a psychological hedonist, since the pleasure-pain principle is essential to the functioning of his law of effect. For many years Thorndike thought that pleasure and pain or reward and punishment had similar effects on learning. During the third decade of this century, however, as the result of further experimentation, he modified his views to emphasize reward and to minimize punishment. He also discarded the law of exercise, for he discovered that practice is effective only in so far as it permits other factors to operate. It is these factors which really determine whether or not learning will occur. Connections are made stronger by being rewarded, not alone by being repeated.

A phenomenon called the spread of effect was discovered by Thorndike about 1933. This refers to the strengthening of connections adjacent to the one directly related to the reward. It works backwards and forwards in time, and diminishes gradually as it leaves the point of origin. This was an important experimental finding for connectionism because it supports the law of effect and this law's mechanical influence on connections. With it, there is no need of a symbol or an idea to account for learning. Later experimenters, however, have shown that principles of organization other than the spread of effect must operate to explain learning. Thorndike's learning theory excludes ideas or any element of consciousness. His is an automatic sort of behaviorism that has little or nothing to do with such human activities as meaning or understanding. This theory is adequate for the explanation of most of the learning processes of children, and it is in the field of educational psychology that it has had an enormous but not altogether favorable influence. It does not explain adult learning except on the most rudimentary levels.

Hull places his emphasis on logical behaviorism mathematically analyzed. His basic attempt is to reduce all learning of even the most complex type to simple rote learning. The fundamental laws of the latter are then sought in the hope that these will be applicable or importantly related to all learning. The basic principle in Hull's system is simply association reinforced by tension-reduction. Activity of the organism is brought about by a need for tension-reduction which stresses object goals. This reinforcement theory has been summed up in this way: to learn an organism must want something, notice something, do something, and get something (Miller and Dollard, 9). Hull clearly emphasizes the external or the behavioral factors and he seeks to found this realistically on a physiological basis. He relates goals to the organism by way of gradients. In other words, the closer the activity to the goal, the more effective is the learning. This is simply a sophisticated restatement of the law of contiguity. For Hull, goal attainment and tension reduction are similar to the classical reward or pleasure, and hence, we have a refined hedonism. Hull has devised a set of extremely complex postulates which he sets out to test and which revolve around a series of so-called intervening variables or factors within the organism that will effectively anchor the stimulus and the response.

Hull's theory of reinforcement through tension reduction is crucial in his system, and in the sense that it is a rigorously scientific statement of hedonism, it has a relation to what is true in learning. However, Hull uses it as a single principle to explain all learning, even that of the most complex type. There is no experimental evidence to support such a claim and common sense disavows it. Some learning takes place because of contiguity; more learning—or more exactly, more performance— takes place as a result of need reduction. However, learning is also something perceptual and cognitive that occurs at several levels of organization and that must be mediated by several principles of organization. The experiments on latent learning, for example, which are related to these ideas, tend to undermine the entire complicated and elaborate system devised by Hull.

Tolman's sign-significate theory of learning approximates more closely a system that incorporates a sufficient and adequate set of principles to explain the complexities of human learning. It appears that by a blend of nativism and behaviorism spiced with a touch of a slightly transmogrified unconsciousness we shall arrive at a palatable learning theory. There is an approach to this in the system of Tolman and the persuasiveness of this system demonstrates the relationship between eclecticism and common sense. Tolman's system combines associationism and field ideas. He uses purpose, objective observation, cognition, and intervening variables as essential ingredients in his system. Tolman maintains that organisms respond to a sign-gestalt, and not to stimuli. Learning for Tolman is not a process of conditioning, but one of setting up expectations and of inventing solutions which may eventuate in performance. Tolman, however, is not "mentalistic," since the ends that regulate behavior are "objectively determined." He thinks of behavior as molar rather than molecular, which reflects an emphasis on the observable rather than the physiological or the mentalistic. In this respect his system aims toward a science of psychology rather than a physiology or a philosophy.

One of the most challenging and interesting aspects of Tolman's learning theory is his development of the doctrine of intervening variables. It is here that he touches on cognition and on purpose and thereby gets closer to a workable system. A further challenging aspect of his system is the notion of sign-gestalt learning introduced as a substitute for the more usual response learning. The essence of this suggests that the organism learns meanings and not responses or movements. It goes away from the mechanical and toward a purposive explanation of learning. A large amount of experimental evidence on latent learning, on place learning, and on expectancy has been collected to support this point of view.

To explain how cognitive structure activates behavior without resorting to the principle of reinforcement or to the law of effect, Tolman has recourse to a special brand of motivation. In this system the learner acquires a knowledge of a means-end relationship largely through the influence of emphasis or interest. We learn those things to which we attend, which we emphasize, or in which we have an interest.

Tolman's system, as we have noted, has distinct advantages over other systems previously proposed. However, a theory based on the psychology of rats, no matter how sophisticated and adequate for rats, will suffer from certain limitations when applied to human beings. Tolman himself recognizes this in his rather sweeping explanations of clincal and cultural data on the basis of rat psychology. His writings here are a good illustration of a beautifully trained technician who is engagingly ingenuous in recognizing the limitations of his procedure but because of his apparent lack of expert knowledge in related areas of human behavior is in no position to do more than make delightfully irrelevant and humorously inapt remarks.

Writers who have tried to compare these systems of learning or who have tried to reconcile them or mediate between them have faced a difficult problem (Dashiell, 4, and McConnell, 7). Too often, the various learning theorists attack different problems, or they attack the same problem at different levels. Hence, comparisons become difficult or impossible. Perhaps the most telling criticism that can be leveled is that all these systems are part systems. They explain a segment of the total learning process, and then tend to generalize from this to an explanation of all human learning. The importance of this can be illustrated indirectly when we compare the experimental evidence in those areas where the theorists have worked on comparable and crucial problems. For example, in the areas of latent learning, of continuity versus discontinuity in discrimination learning, and in place versus response learning, we find different results and different conclusions by different investigators on essentially similar problems. Some results favor one theory, others favor another theory, and some results could lend support to any theory.

One would hope that as a minimum an adequate learning theory would incorporate the processes experimentally established by the different theorists. It seems possible, also, that an entirely different theory will be necessary to explain human learning. However, it is more reasonable to suppose that learning is a matter of levels, and that the current learning theories have operated at the lowest possible levels in the interest of a parsimonious science. It seems improbable that there is only one learning process. If they have taught us anything, the *Gestalt* theorists have shown that there are learning processes qualitatively distinct from conditioning and trial-and-error learning.

Munn (13) emphasizes that none of these theories gives a satisfactory account of how new responses are learned. If a response must occur before it can be reinforced or learned, how can it be learned when it is new? A new set of responses, such as a new learning theory, for instance, can only be accounted for in terms of perceptual and ideational processes aroused by a stimulus. The *Gestalt* psychologists solve this by suggesting that the stimuli arouse innately organized perceptual processes. This seems reasonable on a perceptual level and it could form a groundwork for ideational functioning. However, to explain such phenomena as insight and intention and hypotheses, we have to postulate a third order of events to which we may now address ourselves.

A very recent theory of learning that holds considerable promise because it appears to be working in the right direction of encompassing all the relevant aspects of human nature is the two-factor theory proposed by Mowrer (10). One reason why this theory is particularly challenging is that it begins to build a bridge between learning, personality, and the problems of clinical psychology. In this way it humanizes American learning theory that has been and is a rat psychology. Such a theory reflects the currently appearing limitations felt by an increasing number of observers in reinforcement and association theories generally. Mowrer's two-factor theory restricts the term "conditioning" to the learning of emotional or autonomically determined responses which are explicable by the principle of contiguity. He uses problem solving behavior to explain the learning by reinforcement mediated by the central nervous system. This abandonment of a single principle to explain learning is much more in accordance with the facts of human learning despite the violence that a multiple principle might do to the widely held principle of parsimony. In Mowrer's theory this departure from the principle of parsimony appears defensible to him because the two factors that are suggested are grounded in two distinct physiological systems—the skeletal muscular system and the viscero-vascular system. The acceptance of two basic learning processes, one problem solving and the other conditioning, is a much more tenable hypothesis regarding learning. Its greatest limitation is its failure to articulate these levels of learning organization, that is, the viscerogenic and the sensory perceptual processes, with insight or the activity of the ego.

Two major problems that confront the theorist unwilling to make such an extension are the factors of human conflict and the fact that the human animal works characteristically in terms of the future rather than in terms of the past. It is this reaching out into time, which is done with the characteristic mark of humans, namely, symbolic speech, that represents the greatest challenge to the contemporary truncated learning theories. It is in the concern with the psychology of ego involvement that we shall be able to come to grips with the role and importance of thought and volition in systematic learning theory.

In the area of mature, normal adult human relations we find evidence for the repudiation of the law of effect, of the principle of reinforcement, and of the doctrine of hedonism (Allport, 2).

For it appears that the distinguishing mark of mature adulthood is *renunciation*. It is this that exposes the limitations inherent in a one- or even a two-factor theory of human learning. To act symbolically—to act with the ego involved—is to go counter to the principles used to explain learning on the lower levels. When I feel obligated, when I act from sentiments of honor, when I sacrifice, when I succeed at being virtuous, I thereby do violence to all that is associationistic, hedonistic, and evolutionary in myself. In doing this I stand above conditioning, above trial and error or perceptual problem solving—and my ego demands a principle to explain that which is so peculiarly human, and often distinctly uncomfortable, in me. Learning and behavior are biological, hedonistic, *and ethical* (Mowrer and Kluckhohn, 12).

It is important to recognize, in this connection, that while learning theory could be based on associationism (conditioning), hedonism (problem solving), and rational ego processes, the last is based upon and derived from the other two while simultaneously maintaining an essential distinction. The "functional autonomy" notion is an illustration of the possibility of this in the scientific context lending itself to experimental determination (Allport, 1).

The problem of meaning and the notion of conscience, particularly the latter, are good illustrations of the need for a learning theory which recognizes these three levels. Since both conditioning and trial-and-error learning work mechanically, a third factor must be postulated to account for the complex nature of conscience. Conscience as an act or a habit of making moral judgments is essentially a product of learning and consequently requires integration into learning theory. In the evaluation of the conscience factor we see the limitations of the effect theory. The self-reward of conscience can easily overcome the most severe internal or external punishment, and the disapproval of conscience, as shown for example in guilt feelings, can torpedo the most objectively effective strategem of rewards that can be devised by any therapist.

Learned behavior that is integrated at these higher or specifically human levels requires an essential harmony between the actions of the self or the ego and the conscience. To acquire such an integration of learning, a rational power is essential. The paramount function of this power operating in the interests of integration is to deal on an abstract or symbolic level with remote and present consequences and to organize them into an effective unity. The function of the ego is to deal with conscience, which is learned act or habit inclining to good, and of integrating this within the total personality.

Nonintegrative or neurotic behavior is learned behavior in which remote and present consequences have been inadequately integrated. It is what we have done and would that we had not, rather than what we would do but cannot permit ourselves to do, that is the core of the neurosis (Mowrer, 11). It is this interplay between the ego and the conscience which can lead to adjustment or a failure in adjustment that illustrates the need for a third principle of learning. This principle is peculiarly human and therefore rational.

It is the neurotic individual, then, who illustrates all too clearly the need for including a third factor in an adequate learning theory. The conscious repudiation of conscience by the ego dissipates conscious guilt and substitutes for it the neurotic signals of anxiety and self-condemnation. The ego cannot deal effectively with these feelings because they have no "real" relation to the events that make for conscious guilt. When we have learned to have rational insight into this relationship, we have learned adjustment. When our conscience gives us pleasure rather than anxiety, we have learned to be in the best possible condition for lasting human happiness. This is directly contrary to the Freudian notion which states that happiness is a function of properly liberating the instinctual and aggressive life from an "overlearned conscience." When we have learned to be no longer neurotically anxious or guilty about what we have done or about how we have repudiated our moral urgings (and not when we have "learned" to liberate our repressed impulses— this leads to neurosis and psychopathy), then we can think of ourselves as adjusted. Adjusted means distinguishing adequately between normal anxiety and guilt and the neurotic anxiety that disables the human organism. Conditioning and trial-and-error learning cannot do this for us. Only a third factor of rational insight permits the ultimate adjustment on the human level.

It seems clear from all this that a comprehensive learning theory must include the three factors of contiguity, reward, and freedom. It is the last—the feeling of obligation, of conscience, of oughtness that is crucial to uniquely human learning. Whether one learns to become a mature adult or a neurotic depends upon the set of habits, the set of attitudes, and the set of ideals that one has learned to integrate into a consistent or inconsistent pattern of personality. To ask the question of how one learns to behave in terms of "I ought" is to see the neglected crucial factors of learning theory. In the area of conscience, specifically as related to other characteristics of man, we require a factor of rationality to explain man's adjustment.

The importance of these statements about learning theory is minimal in present-day psychology unless they afford an opportunity for scientific or experimental verification. Unless these principles can be introduced into an experimental design that will make their objective verification possible, they will have little value for science, however useful and valid they may be in terms of common sense.

If experimentation is to concern itself with the crucial third or rational factor of systematic learning theory, it must perforce use human beings and not rats as subjects. Human beings learn by conditioning or association, and they learn by problem solving or reinforcement, but their peculiarly human learning is rational or ego-involved. To state this points the direction of research without specifying its details. There is no reason why some programmatic research on reasoning, on willing, and on conscience could not be systematically instituted along lines similar to that suggested by low-level theorists on rats, or on man's lower learning activities. Let us devise experimental situations that will not control out these elements in man that are most useful in understanding his unique human learning and adjustment.

COMMENT

The obvious comment to this chapter is: Work out a theory of learning which avoids the defects of the theories criticized. Chapter 12 proposes a general theory of learning along just these lines.

REFERENCES

1. ALLPORT, GORDON W. 1937. *Personality: a psychological interpretation.* New York: Henry Holt & Co.
2. ———. 1946. Effect: a secondary principle of learning. *Psychol. Rev.,* 1946, **53,** 335–47.
3. BORING, E. 1950. *History of experimental psychology* (2d ed.). New York: Appleton-Century-Crofts, Inc.
4. DASHIELL, J. F. 1935. A survey and synthesis of learning theories. *Psychol. Bull.,* 1935, **32,** 261–75.
5. HILGARD, E. R. 1948. *Theories of learning.* New York: Appleton-Century-Crofts, Inc.
6. HULL, CLARK L., HOVLAND, C. I., ROSS, R. T., HALL, M., PERKINS, D. T., and FITCH, F. B. 1940. *Mathematico-deductive theory of rote learning.* New Haven: Yale University Press.
7. McCONNELL, T. R. 1942. Reconciliation of learning theories. National Society for the Study of Education, 41st Yearbook. Part II.
8. MAIER, N. R. F. 1939. The specific processes constituting the learning function. *Psychol. Rev.,* 1939, **46,** 241–52.
9. MILLER, N. E., and DOLLARD, J. 1941. *Social learning and imitation.* New Haven: Yale University Press.
10. MOWRER, O. H. 1947. On the dual nature of learning. A reinterpretation of "conditioning" and "problem-solving." *Harvard Educ. Rev.,* 1947, **17,** 102–48.
11. ———. 1948. Learning theory and the neurotic paradox. *Amer. J. Orthopsychiat.,* 1948, **18,** 571–610.
12. MOWRER, O. H., and KLUCKHOHN, C. A. 1944. A dynamic theory of personality. In: *Personality and the behavior disorders.* (Ed.) J. McV. HUNT. New York: The Ronald Press Co.
13. MUNN, N. L. 1950. *Handbook of psychological research on the rat.* Boston: Houghton Mifflin Co.
14. POSTMAN, L. 1947. History and present status of the law of effect. *Psychol. Bull.,* 1947, **44,** 489–563.
15. SKINNER, B. F. 1938. *The behavior of organisms.* New York: Appleton-Century-Crofts, Inc.
16. THORNDIKE, E. L. 1932. *The fundamentals of learning.* New York: Teachers College, Columbia University.
17. TOLMAN, E. C. 1932. *Purposive behavior in animals and men.* New York: Appleton-Century-Crofts, Inc.

Chapter 12

A THEORY
OF HUMAN AND ANIMAL LEARNING

By Magda B. Arnold

If the characteristically human way of learning is to learn by understanding, let us explore the possibility that the human being will operate in this characteristic way whenever conditions are favorable. Conditions will be favorable when, first of all, the situation is such that it can be intellectually grasped, that it can be understood. Secondly, conditions will be favorable when the human subject is in such a psychological state that he can use his understanding, and that he himself will decide to use it. If he is delirious, or in the grip of an overwhelming emotion, or coerced from the outside, or if he does not want to make the effort, he will not use his reason and therefore will not learn by understanding.

Granted that he is in a favorable psychological state for exercising his proper human function, and that he himself decides to use it, let us see what the situation could be which would make it difficult or impossible for him to do so.

Trial-and-Error Learning. First of all, learning situations can be physically restricted. If the experimenter sets up a blind maze, the human being has no opportunity to work his way out except by exploring every opening, trying every blind alley, in exactly the same way as the rat does. But even in this situation the human being does not learn by random trial and accidental success as does the rat. If he is properly functioning, he will try to form an imaginative picture or a map of the maze. Depending on his ability to do that, his progress in making an errorless run will be greatly accelerated. The rat has to depend on a gradual acquisition of an action pattern and the memory of sense impressions, where the human being learns the maze by reflecting on its plan, by using memory and imagination deliberately, therefore by reasoning and understanding as far as they are possible.

Memorizing. The human being can also be restricted by materials and instructions. If he is given lists of nonsense syllables and told to memorize them, he is prevented from using his reason, for understanding is made impossible by emptying the material of all intelligible meaning. In this way, he is reduced to the necessity of acquiring a meaningless (or next to meaningless) visual and sound pattern. But even here he tries to understand and organize the material in the only way left to him; he will remember the first and the last word, the words next to them, he will remember words in bold type or in different colors. He will even try to find arbitrary meanings by connecting the nonsense syllables with a similarly sounding meaningful word. Even in this restricted situation, where he is confined to a minimal structure, he uses visual memory where he must, but tries to provide nonsense syllables with private meanings unless he is explicitly prevented by the experimental instructions.

Conditioning. In conditioned response experiments, the situation is likewise seriously restricting for the human being. There are either no instructions or irrelevant instructions, and the subject is left to understand the situation in any way he can. Ordinarily, most adults do try to understand the conditioning situation, that is, they try to judge what the sequence of conditioned and unconditioned stimulus could mean. They judge whether the conditioned stimulus is a signal for the unconditioned stimulus (the light a signal for the pretzel) or whether they have no connection; whether they are *meant* to take the one as a signal for the other, or whether the experimenter wants to deceive them. In Razran's terms, they develop an attitude to the experiment. According to their judgment or attitude, they will develop a positive or a negative conditioned response, or they will not become conditioned at all.

Because the human being always tries to understand the conditioning situation in some way, human conditioning is markedly different from animal conditioning; most adults become conditioned in one or two trials, some do not become conditioned at all, and only a minority needs several trials as do animals. Razran, who has done a great deal of work with human subjects as well as with animals and children, says that

. . . pure conditioning is only the "animal" and the "casual" form of human learning, which manifests itself best only when the symbolic and attitudinal behavior experiences of the human subjects are either underdeveloped or lowered or decomposed or elsewhere preoccupied (young children and subnormal adults; fatigue, hypnosis, emotional stress, absorption in some other activity), and that to say that one's learning is no more than mere conditioning is more of an insult than a theory (13, p. 335).

In other words, to obtain the same kind of conditioning in adult human beings as is regularly obtained in animals, their human powers of functioning have to be severely restricted.

Insight Learning. In situations which show insight learning the properly human mode of learning can be fully applied. Though the term "insight" is often defined by *Gestalt* psychologists as "understanding, or an appropriate transformation of the field" (Koffka, 8, p. 224), or "organization" (Katona, 7), and in that formulation applies without difficulty to animal learning as well as to human learning, Köhler's definition is more explicit. For him,

. . . the concept is used in a strictly descriptive fashion. I . . . have tried to make it quite clear that, taken in its basic sense, the term insight refers to experienced dynamics in the emotional and motivational fields no less than to experienced determination in intellectual situations (9, p. 342).

According to this definition, then, insight would require the *experience* of means-ends relationships in motivation, and cause-effect relationships in emotional and intellectual situations. We shall attempt to show that the human being not only *experiences* such relationships (as do animals) but also *recognizes them as*

such. This recognition of means-ends and cause-effect relationships adds the properly human note to insight learning, and
distinguishes it sharply from analogous insight-learning in
animals.

Human Learning. The most important factor in human
learning, then, is properly human functioning, rational functioning, which includes understanding and deliberate choice. Once
we assume that this factor is operative, we must next see
whether it operates only in learning situations; if so, then it
could be called *the* principle of learning which might be restricted in certain situations (trial-and-error learning, conditioning) but never completely abolished.

Here we touch upon a problem that demands our attention:
do we understand and learn only when we deliberately set out
to learn or do we learn by understanding also in an incidental
nondeliberate way? When we see something moving in the
fog, and we gradually recognize it as a man and not an animal,
and then as a well-known public figure whom so far we had
known only from pictures, have we learned anything? We certainly have, in the sense of having acquired knowledge which we
did not have before. Therefore, if we define learning as *acquisition* (either of knowledge or of performance) as is often done, we
should have to include many if not all cases of perception as instances of learning. Knowing and understanding do occur in
perceptual situations, whether that knowledge remains on the
sense level or whether it is a knowledge of the significant feature distinguishing this thing from anything else together with
a knowledge of its relation to other things. Moreover, as we
shall see, knowledge or understanding is also necessary for acquiring a motor skill; the more complicated the skill, the greater
will be the role played by understanding as against sheer kinaesthetic memory. Yet complicated actions, like applying the
combination which will open a safe, can be executed immediately
on the basis of written instructions—which is not usually considered a case of learning but of understanding. Thus understanding seems to be involved in other human acts, not only in

learning. If that is so, then understanding cannot be the sole principle of learning.

But neither can association by contiguity in time or space be the sole explanatory principle, nor can it be reinforcement or reward. Association is necessary for all learning; recognition of the present situation as requiring the same response as a similar one in the past would be impossible without it. And reinforcement or reward as a principle of learning simply states the empirical fact that a learning situation must have a goal for which the human being or animal will strive. A tendency or drive always implies a goal toward which that tendency is aimed. Therefore drive reduction or tension reduction (which follows upon reward or reinforcement) implies that the goal has been reached (the rat in the maze has reached the food box and has fed). As a matter of fact, the importance of a goal (motivation) is conceded even by theorists who explain learning by contiguity, just as the importance of association or contiguity is conceded by reinforcement theorists.

The solution seems to be that both a goal and associative memory are *necessary* for learning, but that neither alone nor even both together are a *sufficient* condition of learning. Without memory the learner would not be able to learn, without goal the learner would not learn this particular thing. Both are indispensable, both occur in every learning situation. However, both also occur in other situations, therefore neither can be a sufficient explanation of learning. Associative memory occurs in free association, but free association is not learning. Goals can be present in situations where no learning occurs, for instance in driving to town every day. In fact, in that situation there is a goal and there are also memory associations (of the right turn to take, the houses along the road) which shows that even taken together these two factors can occur in other than learning situations, and are therefore insufficient to explain learning singly or combined.

It would seem, then, that there is no one factor responsible for learning, that learning is neither a unitary function nor does it depend on one or several exclusive principles. We shall come closest to a valid definition of learning if we assume that the understanding of the situation, the goal to be achieved in it, and the deliberate choice of the means to that goal belong to proper human functioning in learning; but that all the other capacities of the human being are engaged as well. In learning, the individual will use sensation, memory, imagination, emotions, and motor functions, but he will use them in knowing and choosing the goal and understanding the means to be used to achieve it. In some situations, the use of rational thinking (understanding) will be minimal—as, for example, in a conditioning experiment where the subject's attention is otherwise engaged. But even in such restricted conditions he will try to understand as best he can—and it is this understanding which makes human trial and error learning or human conditioning different from that of animals. Even though in these situations the human being exhibits a lower level of functioning, it is still human functioning and not animal functioning. Precisely as the human being can function on a vegetative level in digesting his food, without being confined to that level as is the vegetable, so he can function on a level of sense memory in learning as does the animal, without being confined to the animal level.

We shall attempt, then, to delimit the *area* to which the term "learning" will properly apply, both for the human and for the animal, rather than describe it as a special process governed by one or the other principle. In favor of such a definition would be the persistent reports that there is no "general learning ability" or at least that it cannot be isolated in spite of persistent efforts. Factor analysis has failed to uncover it and intercorrelations between various learning tasks have consistently been low. But if all human functions are used as the particular learning situation requires, we would not expect them all to be equally efficient —thus we would not expect a general learning factor. In particular, we would not expect a high correlation between understanding, memory, sensory acuity, or speed of movement. If the learning situation favors one of these functions for one task and an unrelated function for a second learning task (learning a simple motor skill versus making a scientific discovery) the correlation between the achievement in the two tasks will be as low as the correlation between the main functions used in them.[1]

Definition of Human Learning

To clarify the issue, we propose a definition which will delimit learning so as to distinguish it from other situations in which there is a new acquisition either of knowledge or performance. It must also bring out the differences between human learning and animal learning which follow from the differences in human and animal functions. *Human learning consists in setting up a new goal of knowing or doing, and finding rationally appropriate means to achieve it.* This definition implies that human learning is rational, based upon a recognition of means-ends relations, and deliberate choice of means and ends.

A new goal. If I decide to go to town I set up a goal. But I have been there dozens of times before so that this is not a new goal and there is no learning.

A new goal of knowing or doing. This distinguishes learning from emotion, which we have defined as a tendency toward something suitable. If boy meets girl and falls in love, the new goal is to marry. Though rationally appropriate means may be found to achieve this end, it is not a case of learning.

Setting up a new goal. Human beings typically set up goals for themselves. Even if the goal is proposed by the experimenter (learning a poem, solving a problem) the person has to make it his own before he will learn. This fact has always been recognized; witness the emphasis on proper "motivation" in the learner. Recently, the concept of a "set" for the learner has acquired more and more importance; and set is merely another name for "proposing a point of arrival" or "setting up a goal."

---

[1] Madison Bentley has recognized the difficulties involved in defining learning as a unitary process when he says in his review of E. Newman's chapter on learning in Harry Helson (ed.), *Foundations of psychology:*

"Now it seems reasonable—at least to one reviewer—that the general label "learning" should be either specifically defined to apply to a smaller and more homogeneous area within psychology or discarded for a half-dozen terms to be judiciously applied to a like number of subjects for investigation and theory" (*Amer. J. Psychol.*, 1951, **64**, p. 616).

Animals have goals but they hardly ever are said to have a set. While a given "set" can be acquired by learning, some kind of "set" is prior to any learning at all. Unless the human being is set to learn this particular thing, there will be no learning; with a wrong set (that is, a set not intended by the experimenter), something will be learned which is irrelevant to the experiment.

Finding means to achieve the goal. This implies a recognition that the goal can be reached in various ways, that there are several means to the chosen end. In the human being, there typically is such a recognition of means-ends relations.

Using rationally appropriate means. This phrase emphasizes the fact that there must be an understanding of the fitness of the means used for the end in view, not merely the experience of such fitness. Understanding is a special form of experiencing the connection between means and ends. These means comprise whatever tools and activities are employed in reaching the goal.

This definition allows us to judge or measure three aspects of learning where the usual definitions allow us to measure only one.

The first aspect is the *degree* to which the goal has been achieved, or the *length of time* needed to achieve it. This is the aspect of learning which is usually measured. Most theories imply that it is the only measurable aspect.

The second aspect is the *effectiveness of the means.* Were the means used the most appropriate or most effective means to the desired end? If a student wants to master the physiology of the nervous system, memorizing the relevant chapter in his textbook would not be the most appropriate means to his end. This is an aspect of learning which is usually not formally taken into account, in fact, associationistic or connectionistic theories deny by implication that it exists. Yet to any educator this aspect must be the most important one in learning, for we only begin to discuss methods of teaching and methods of learning when we become concerned about the most effective means to our desired end, the proper education of the young.

The last aspect of learning is the *relevance of the goal of learning* to the self-ideal as it is and to the self-ideal as it ought to be. We can judge and therefore eventually measure whether the newly set up goal is relevant or irrelevant to the person's larger and more inclusive goals, and finally, whether it will help him or hinder him to establish a harmonized pattern of life. I may want to crack a safe—I set up a new goal. But safe cracking itself may be the means to a further goal, either to become a burglar or to manufacture safes which cannot be cracked. In either case, a process of learning occurs which can be judged according to its effectiveness as means to my end (second aspect) and according to the degree of skill I have achieved (first aspect). But the goal itself can be judged also to see whether it will divert me from my proper self-ideal (as becoming a burglar would do) or whether it will allow me to achieve it (third aspect). This third aspect of learning connects learning theory with personality theory.

Such a definition of learning emphasizes that human learning is not a separate function but rather self-directed progress using every human function. To decide upon a new goal and find appropriate means of reaching it, the individual has to know, judge, evaluate, and want the goal; he has to use memory, imagination, and motor functions to achieve it. The definition also emphasizes human self-determination in learning without denying that man can take over goals current in his culture or goals suggested by others, though in every case it is he who has to perceive, to judge, to decide for himself.

It can be shown that this definition covers adequately the whole gamut of human learning, from invention to emotional habit formation.

Invention. The genius of the inventor consists in finding a means-ends relationship where it had never been discovered before. The invention of the sewing machine, for instance, depended on the realization that two interlocking threads could make a seam as efficiently as one continuous thread; and the additional realization that the needle carrying the locking thread could have the eye at the point so that the interlocking could be done by a reciprocating motion.

Learning a Science. The new goal in this case is the knowledge of a new area of learning. If a student decides to study psychology, for instance, he wants to acquire a knowledge of the principles of human activity. To achieve his end, he must select one of several rationally appropriate ways: he can go to college or medical school, or he can embark on a course of reading. In either case, he will have to learn by understanding the available material and by testing his understanding in experimentation and practical work. The better he grasps the principles involved in every aspect of the science, and the better he can apply them, the more adequately will his aim be achieved.

Motor skills. The goal in this case is to acquire mastery over a tool, or over one's motor functions. The way in which he can achieve mastery varies: A man can learn to play tennis by watching others and imitate as best he can the way they use the racket. He can take instruction from a coach, or let one of the players explain the game to him. Finally, he can try to learn the rules and motions from a book. But whatever the choice, his most effective course will be to use the means which will give him the best understanding of the essentials of the game and of the way in which he has to handle the racket and himself.

It is sometimes said that motor learning does not require understanding. Hilgard, for instance, remarks: "We can form vowels satisfactorily without knowing how we place our tongues, and we can read without being aware of our eye movements" (6, p. 8). But that statement is a misunderstanding of the proper object of motor learning. We do not have to understand (or even to be aware of) the mechanism of our movements; to understand in that sense, by concentrating our attention on the mechanics of muscular action, is actually a hindrance rather than a help. The learner must know the object of movement, he must know that he is to produce a specific sound, or that in reading he has to look for a visual pattern in sequence from left to right. We may not know how the means we use comes to be a means to our end but we must understand that it is such a means and we must know how to use it. Analogously, we may not know how the dictaphone records the human voice and reproduces it; but we must know that it does and must know how to use it if we want to transcribe dictation.

Motor learning can occur, of course, without understanding, on the level of sense memory and imitation, but that will be successful only in simple actions—the baby waving bye-bye, the ape imitating sewing motions or shaking hands. Such learning is totally ineffective for a complicated set of actions like mixing a cake or frying a steak.

Sensory Discrimination. The newly set up goal is, for example, to improve pitch discrimination. The various means available range from practicing the scale to practice in recognizing tones sung and played on various instruments. The most successful method will be the one which gives the best understanding of the means-end relationship, in this case, of the way in which a given tone produced and heard is related to the tonal scale.

Memorizing. The goal here is to learn an exact sequence of sounds which either mean something or which are a meaningless visual or sound pattern (nonsense syllables). It is well known that it takes far less time to memorize poems or meaningful material than it does to memorize nonsense syllables. The reason is not the one originally given by Ebbinghaus (and repeated since) that nonsense syllables exclude prior associations, for many word sequences in poems are completely unfamiliar. Moreover, we do not learn a foreign language, for example, by *associating* one word with another; all we learn that way is a vocabulary, but not the free use of the language. We learn a foreign language by using words in continually changing contexts and ever varying associations until their differing grammatical usage has become familiar, and their meaning has been thoroughly understood. Meaningful material is memorized more quickly because it refers to situations which we can reconstruct imaginatively, that is, precisely because it can be understood. Therefore, in memorizing the most effective method will be the one which allows for the best understanding of the material within the limits inherent in it.

Mechanical Puzzles. The goal is to take the puzzle apart, then fit it together again. The means, to isolate the structure of the component parts. Because of the construction of the puzzle (which was designed to mislead) there is no rational way in which the structure of the individual parts can be detected when the puzzle is complete. Therefore, the only appropriate solution is to make a series of guesses and try one after another. But in taking the puzzle apart, its structure can be understood, the means can be related to the end, namely, the pieces to the completed puzzle. The person who does this will have no difficulty in fitting the pieces together again.

Conditioned Response Learning. In animal conditioning, whether it is of the classical or instrumental type, there is always a naturally determined goal (food or escape from pain). The difference in the two types of conditioning lies in the aspect of learning which is measured, whether perception or performance or, in Tolman's terms, learning and performance. Classical conditioning focuses on the animal's awareness or expectancy of the goal object, instrumental conditioning on the performance necessary to obtain it. In classical conditioning, the animal learns that a given *perception*, something he sees or hears (the conditioned stimulus), is followed by food (the unconditioned stimulus). Salivation to the conditioned stimulus is merely an indicator (which can be measured) that perceptual learning has occurred. Similarly, the animal learns that another *perception* is followed by pain (electric shock); the withdrawal of the foreleg to the conditioned stimulus is merely a measurable indicator that such learning has occurred. In instrumental conditioning, on the other hand, the animal learns that something *he does* (lever pressing) is followed by food, and this action is the indicator required by the experimenter that motor learning has occurred.

In human (classical) conditioning, the subject also has a goal, but a goal he has set for himself, namely to do what is demanded in the experimental situation. Since instructions are either lacking or irrelevant, his goal becomes simply to observe. But in observing, each individual will judge what the situation means. And because several judgments are possible in the situation (for the human being, not for the animal), namely, that the conditioned stimulus announces the unconditioned stimulus (the flashing light announces the pretzel) or that the sequence of conditioned and unconditioned stimulus is arbitrary, or that the sequence is a ruse of the experimenter, the reaction or expectation of each individual will differ according to his judgment. If he has judged that the conditioned stimulus announces the unconditioned stimulus, he will develop the conditioned reflex immediately, for salivation accompanies the expectation of food. If he took the sequence of conditioned and unconditioned stimulus to be arbitrary, he will not become conditioned at all, for if he does not expect food there will be no occasion for salivation. Finally, if he thinks the experimenter is trying to dupe him, he will develop a negative conditioned response, for in that case he will expect something unknown and possibly unpleasant, and unpleasantness decreases salivation. Alternatively, of course, it may take him several trials to arrive at the conclusion that the conditioned stimulus is followed by the unconditioned stimulus, in which case his conditioning resembles animal conditioning, for he begins to salivate in response to the conditioned stimulus as soon as he has learned to expect that food follows after it. In every case, however, the way in which the human subject sets up his goal and judges the goal situation will determine his expectation and therefore the physiological reaction which goes with it. The reaction itself is no more than an indicator of his expectation or attitude in the situation; the conditioned response is not learned but is merely the physical concomitant of perceptual learning. This holds good for all varieties of classical conditioning, whether the unconditioned stimulus is food, acid, or electric shock.

Emotional Learning. Emotional learning is usually said to include any emotional habit which can be acquired. What is learned is conceded to be not the emotion but a new object of emotional response. A fear of snakes is not present from birth or from the first appearance of fear, but is acquired some time later in the individual's life, therefore is said to be learned. But fear itself is not learned; neither is weeping or smiling or being angry. These are all responses which belong to our human heritage, like our ability to see, or feel pain, or to have a sense of repletion after a meal. Emotional learning is said to occur either gradually (the child learns to be afraid of lightning because he sees that his mother is afraid of it) or suddenly, sometimes in one traumatic experience ("emotional conditioning"). If a child is suddenly frightened by a dog, he may have a pronounced and continuing fear reaction which may develop into a phobia. Are these cases of acquired fear an instance of learning in our sense of the term? If not, how do we account for their occurrence, and particularly, how do we account for the persistence of the emotional reaction?

In the first place, neither gradual emotional learning nor the cases of sudden "emotional conditioning" seem to be included in our definition of learning. It is true that the experience of sudden danger from the dog has resulted in a new way of acting toward dogs. Also, there has been an acquisition of knowledge, namely, that this dog is dangerous (generalized later to all dogs and perhaps even all animals). But this is merely the kind of knowledge that can result from any perception, whether or not there is an emotion. (The child could be *told*, for instance, that dogs are dangerous; this would be an acquisition of knowledge without any appreciable emotion, let alone a phobia.) Since we have agreed that perceptual knowledge should not be called learning, is perception accompanied by emotion to be called learning only because it is retained so long? If not, why is the knowledge acquired in an intense emotional experience (that dogs are dangerous) remembered so well, never to be forgotten? Only closer analysis will answer this question.

When we examine the process of evaluation which arouses the emotion, any emotion, we find that our estimate that this is good for us, or dangerous, also includes the expectation that this thing we love or fear will remain desirable or dangerous. There is a constancy in the value of a thing for us which corresponds to the constancy which we expect in all sense experience. When we see something and recognize it as an apple, we expect it to remain an apple as long as it appears as it does. When we say we like apples we expect that they will go on having the qualities we like, and that we shall go on liking them. And if the child is hurt by a dog he will expect that the dog will remain dangerous.

More than that, just as we expect all apples to have the same apple qualities, so the child will expect all dogs to be dangerous; and when he gradually realizes that other animals are like dogs in some way, he may expect them to be dangerous like dogs, too.

Emotional conditioning, then, is the inevitable result of the expectation that the object which we have experienced as dangerous will keep its dangerous qualities. No repetition of the fear-producing situation is needed because the experience had maximum intensity in the first place. The expectation is never disappointed because fear effectively keeps us away from the feared object, therefore we go on expecting the danger to remain or recur. Even in experiences which have no emotional overtones, our knowledge of objects and our expectation of their constancy remains for good. Once a child knows what a table is, or a doll, or the color "red" he is not likely to forget it. Only when we see too many things at once will our attention span as well as our memory span become inadequate to the task. Then we have to set about deliberately to remember words or nonsense syllables, or the sequence of a set of stimuli. Ordinarily, in our sense experience with things, our expectation of their constancy if not our memory of their individual existence, remains indefinitely. What should be explained, therefore, is not why our judgment of a situation (and therefore our emotion) remain the same, but why they ever change. The realization of change is a rational process in which we compare the thing as it is at present with its appearance or effects in the past. In the case of fear, however, our very avoidance of like situations makes it unlikely that we will recognize the fact of change, hence fear is self-perpetuating.

The same reasoning can be applied to the acquisition of an emotional craving. The craving for reading or for sweets or for drink is a habit which has developed from an initial pleasurable experience. An initially neutral or even displeasing experience is sought for other reasons (e.g., smoking and drinking for social reasons) until its pleasure-giving qualities are discovered. From then on, the potentialities for addiction are present precisely because of our expectation of constancy, which is confirmed with every indulgence. It requires a rational decision to keep from indulging and the willingness to suffer the discomfort of thwarted desire. Such a habit is not learned, properly speaking, but *given in to*. It is acquired in the first experience of pleasure with our expectation of its constancy. A rational decision is required to break it; failing that, an emotional craving also is self-perpetuating.

There is one important difference between our perception of the physical world and of other living beings. Our expectation of constancy in the physical world makes it possible for us to act with assurance, confident that things will be as we expect them to be. Whatever our expectancy, it does not change the qualities of the physical world, though it may affect our perception of them. But in our relations to other individuals what we expect of them influences our attitude toward them and our behavior in turn influences their attitude toward us, so that we often provoke what we expect. When a boy is bullied by an older brother, he expects that the brother will go on bullying him, and that he will go on resenting it. He will also expect that every boy and later every man who is in some way like his brother will try to bully him. And if that is what he expects, he will at first be aggressive toward this pseudo-brother and later, when the other's anger is provoked, the boy will give in because he expects his adversary's victory. Thus our expectation will lead us to provoke what we fear, and no special "need for punishment" needs to be invoked.

Similarly, a traumatic experience does not need to be "repressed" to affect our attitude on a similar future occasion. Whenever there is excessive or inappropriate emotion it will be found that the present situation is perceived as similar in some way to an intense emotional experience in the past which is sometimes forgotten but just as frequently remembered, though the connection between the traumatic experience and the present emotion may not be recognized. The present situation is evaluated at first glance as if it were a repetition of the earlier traumatic one. The emotion, though generated right here and now (and not repressed in the past) is excessive or inappropriate because it is not a response to the present situation but is a re-living of a previous intense emotional pattern. What has remained in the interval is not the "repressed" emotion but the tendency to expect that we shall experience in every future situation of like type what we have experienced in the traumatic situation. And the more intense and important the original experience, the more firmly established will our expectation be.

To sum up: Emotional learning, whether it be sudden or gradual, should not be called "learning" in our sense of the term but can be compared to the acquisition of knowledge in perception. The evaluation that this is suitable or dangerous or hateful is immediate, based on sensory appeal or repulsion, and does not constitute "setting up a new goal of knowing or doing." The emotion which follows the judgment is not learned but naturally determined; positive emotion arises when something is judged suitable, negative emotion when it is judged unsuitable. The expectation that the situation will go on having suitable or unsuitable qualities is not learned either but is present in every perception. The knowledge that this is suitable or unsuitable is acquired in evaluating the perception, not in the later emotion or action which merely follows that evaluation.

In learning properly so called (in formal learning) there also may be emotion. Because there is a goal intended by the learner, that goal may be not only rationally chosen as something that is good for the person as a whole, it may also have a sensory appeal. On the other hand, the new goal may have aspects that are decidedly displeasing. In the first case, learning will be accelerated, in the latter retarded. I may decide to learn French, which means that I must have judged that French is good for me. But learning it is not pleasant. I shall have to work when I want to rest or enjoy myself. Therefore, the judgment that learning French is good for me does not call out a positive emotional response; in fact, it may arouse a more or less intense dislike of the work which will retard it. We have seen that emotion is a means which helps us to reach our goal. If we have that means at our disposal, as in the desire for an object which represents our new goal, then learning will be considerably accelerated.

If we have set up a goal, however, which in some aspect arouses intense dislike or even fear, learning will be seriously disturbed. Emotion, then, is present in learning many things, perhaps in all learning. But it becomes noticeable only when there is a physical dislike connected with the new goal which interferes with achieving it, or when there is a physical appeal which noticeably accelerates learning.

Animal Learning

If we now turn from human learning to animal learning, we can use the same scheme for definition which implies that there must be a goal which is reached in various ways. But we shall see immediately that our definition allows us to establish the differences between human and animal learning clearly and unambiguously.

Animal learning consists in going toward a naturally determined goal in naturally available but newly found or newly prescribed ways. This definition implies that animal learning is nonrational, without any *recognition* of means-ends relationships.

A naturally determined goal. The goal is never set by the animal, nor is it set by the experimenter. The animal's goals are inherent in his animal nature and the experimenter merely makes use of them for his own purposes. Therefore, the number of goals an animal has is stricty limited (food, water, mate, freedom from pain) and learning experiments have to be adjusted to this limitation.

Going toward a naturally determined goal. Only when the animal has a specific need and is therefore attracted toward a particular goal-object (food, mate) can he be induced to learn. The degree of such physiological need becomes important for experimentation. If the animal is too hungry, his hunger will interfere with learning an intricate path; if he is not hungry enough, his learning will be inconveniently retarded. It could be said with some justice that all animal learning is emotional learning.

In naturally available ways. The ways which are available to an animal for reaching his goals are determined by nature and merely utilized by the experimenter. Every animal species has its distinctive ways of acting, and learning is possible only within the available range. The seal, for instance, nuzzles his young and uses his mouth for investigating; he can be taught to play ball with his snout or balance things on it. The cat hits and catches mice with his paws; he can be taught to play ball with his paw, or to pull strings with it, while the seal would use his mouth for the same purpose. Apes have an amazingly large natural repertory of motions in climbing and reaching for food, so they can learn easily a great many human actions. They can imitate sewing with needle and thread, hammering, sawing, and shaving. But they are not able to imitate voice sounds or melodies. Birds, on the other hand, who burst into song naturally as a preliminary to mating, can be taught to reproduce melodies (the roller canary is the most famous example) or even whole spoken sentences as does the parrot.

In newly found ways. The new way of going toward his natural goal may be inherent in the animal's nature but newly discovered when the function matures, as in the case of the young bird learning to fly. Learning is involved because the newly found way of functioning has to be used before it is perfected. The matured function is available but until the bird exercises it he cannot achieve his goal in flying.

The new way toward his natural goal may be found accidentally and used by memory association. This seems to be the case in the famous "insight" experiments with apes: the bamboo poles are fitted together accidentally and now form a long stick like those the ape had used before; the ladder he had climbed before is found leaning against the wall and the ape uses it to reach for a banana hung from the ceiling.

In newly prescribed ways. The maze, the puzzle box, the Skinner box, are new ways prescribed by the experimenter to reach the animal's natural goal, food. In the same way, the innumerable tricks we can teach animals are ways prescribed by us to the animal to get food or avoid pain.

Differences Between Human and Animal Learning

The most conspicuous difference between learning in humans and in animals lies in the fact that the human being can set up goals for himself (over and above the goals naturally determined for him), and can recognize and use means-ends relations. The animal, on the contrary, goes toward naturally determined goals in ways which are possible to him according to his animal nature. Even when he uses what we would call a tool (a stick or ladder to reach food) he does not recognize it as a *means* toward an *end*.

It is true that most psychologists working in the field of animal learning would dispute this point today, though not so long ago they would have hailed it as a platitude and would only have contended that what was true for the animal was true for the human being as well. But fashions change in a curious way. The revolt against animism produced a sense-impulse and stimulus-bound theory of animal learning according to which the responses depended completely on the stimulus. At present we are in the midst of a counterrevolution in which the animal is again credited with the perception of relations, the ability to form hypotheses, with reasoning and the use of symbols. True, these terms are used only in an approximate sense; they are either not defined at all or, even more commonly, given a definition which is patently at variance with common usage. Perhaps such practice could be defended in the interest of scientific rigor if the terms were not used again with their common meaning for human beings and if it were not assumed that the preceding animal experiments had revealed the same processes in animals that are known to occur in human beings. Using the same terms, the conclusion is taken to be proved that there is only a quantitative but not a qualitative difference between animal and man.

Perhaps our meaning could be made clearer by an examination of the experimental evidence on the basis of which the animal is credited with a semblance of rationality, to see whether such inferences can be defended. Before we do so, it is well to emphasize that our definition of animal learning recognizes implicitly the capacity of the animal to *know* his natural goal object (as a thing, not as a bundle of sensations), to *want* it, that is, to recognize that it is good for him, and to have sensory memory images of past situations, that is, to *remember*. These assumptions are in no way different from those generally made by animal experimenters: the animal's awareness of the goal-object is implied in providing food, or water, or mate; the wanting is implied by the experimental practice of letting the animal become hungry or thirsty before he is used for a learning experiment; memory is implied by the common assumption that the animal can learn from experience.

Psychologically speaking, memory must imply some kind of representation of past situations, visual, auditory, tactual, or kinaesthetic, and that is all we mean here by "sensory memory images." And why should we not be willing to grant memory images to animals (particularly the ones we use in experiments) when we know that their processes of sensation are very similar to our own? It is only the stimulus-response psychologist who has to deny memory images or even sensations to animals because his systematic position does not allow him to acknowledge them in men (in spite of the fact that he must use them in making his own observations). On the face of it, the inference of memory images is at least as legitimate as the inference of memory traces or a stimulus reserve. Lashley seems to voice a similar opinion when he says:

In discussing this work [on visual discrimination in rats] I have not hesitated to use an anthropomorphic terminology. There is little choice between the Scylla of reflexological dogma and the Charybdis of mentalistic implications. . . . For the present it is more important to recognize that the same sensory problems are common to the lower animals and to man than to try and rephrase these problems in a deceptively objective language (10, p. 125).

Taking for granted, then, that the animal has sense knowledge and memory, drives, or appetites, let us see whether we can find any evidence that he possesses also what used to be called "higher mental processes."

Do Animals Perceive Relations? According to Yerkes, the answer is an unqualified yes. He says:

> . . . I include here as the fifth type of learning process one which I suspect must depend upon processes in the chimpanzee which are either identical with or function instead of human perception of relations, images and ideas. . . . It is my working hypothesis that, under favorable conditions, the ape is capable of perceiving various sorts of relations; that it has also a limited capacity for abstraction or the isolation of elements in a perceptual complex; and for generalization, as exemplified in its response to relative instead of absolute brightness, or to the relation of middleness in differing arrays of objects (20, p. 134).

Now let us see first of all what happens when the animal responds to relative brightness, or to middleness, or to triangularity, and then we can decide whether this is an instance of generalization and of perception of relations.

That both rat and ape can be trained to respond to the "middlemost object" or to a triangle rather than a square or to the brighter of two things has been demonstrated over and over again. In fact, the ape can discriminate a triangle from a circle even when it is a white figure on black ground instead of a black figure on white ground, while the rat's discrimination is completely disrupted by such reversal. Even in the ape, however, we need not assume that he generalized from the shape *presented* to him to the *concept* "triangularity." All that is necessary is a discrimination between this shape and that shape—for such a discrimination neither a concept nor a generalization is required. The fact that animals perceive shape and that such perception needs no training has been affirmed by Hebb:

> . . . an area thus sensorily limited (as figure on ground, made up of a homogeneous zone of color surrounded by another color and having a sharply defined boundary) is seen as one, unified and distinct from its surroundings, by any normal person, by the congenitally blind on the first occurrence of vision following operation for cataract, by the normal rat, and apparently also at first vision by the rat that has been reared in darkness. The unity and distinctiveness of such figures from their background, then, is independent of experience, or "primitive" (5, p. 19).

If Hebb is right, then an animal as low in the scale of life as the rat has not only a primitive perception of shape but also can discriminate between two different shapes without prior learning; for only by finding such discrimination could the experimenter have inferred that the rat has a native perception of shape. Now a judgment of relationship (side-by-sideness, middleness, or triangularity) which requires generalization of the *essential* feature in one object to every related object, cannot be formed without experience, cannot therefore be "primitive" in Hebb's sense, and certainly would not be expected at first occurrence of vision in a rat reared in darkness. In fact, it has been reported that in human beings, after cataract operations, the *discrimination* between a triangle and a circle, a sphere and a cube, is possible immediately, but the triangle or cube *could not be recognized as such* until the patient counted the corners—and that in spite of the fact that he obviously had the concept of triangularity or cube-ness (Hebb, 5, p. 28). What happened in the case of this patient was that his concept had to be applied to a *visual* situation where so far it had only been derived from experiences of touch and movement. The abstraction of the essential feature of an unfamiliar perception evidently requires a special kind of learning, while the discrimination between two objects as similar or different is present as soon as the object is reacted to at all. This is easily explained by pointing to the fact that discrimination is possible on the basis of a *sensory* perception (Hebb's primitive perception of shape), but the concept of triangularity only on the basis of singling out the *essential* feature, the feature common to a class of objects—and none of our senses, neither vision nor hearing nor touch, is designed to do that.

In the same way, it is easy enough to explain the fact that animals can learn to react to the middlemost object or to the larger of two objects. All we have to assume is that animals can discriminate between two objects and that they have not only a sensory impression but a memory image of shape and location.

Do Animals Form Hypotheses? Tolman and his followers speak of rats forming "hypotheses" at choice points. A preference for turning left rather than right, or of alternating between left and right, would be called a hypothesis which is "checked" and changed when it is not confirmed. But in common parlance a hypothesis means an informed guess. There can be no information before the first run, even if animals were capable of surveying alternatives rationally and choosing the more appropriate one. Positional alternation can be explained much more simply by assuming that animals have a repertory of preferential habits which can be used one after another as the situation requires.

Do Animals Perceive Cause-Effect or Means-Ends Relations—i.e., Do They Reason? Tolman not only credits the rat with hypotheses but with practically every other human function as well. He writes:

[The chimpanzee] engages in a few fights and establishes a high dominance status in his group. He therewith discovers (that is, learns) the *instrumental fact* that this establishing of high dominance status is *a means* to obtaining practically all of a limited food supply. . . . On the other hand, in some other quite different situations he may learn the *instrumental value* of using *collective techniques* instead. . . . Learning is thus a "reasonable" activity which tends to keep the individual well adjusted to the actual environmental realities (18, pp. 59–60. Italics mine).

Now there really is no evidence that the chimpanzee discovers at any time that he has a high dominance status or that this status is a means of obtaining more food. The chimpanzee fought every other animal because he wanted the food; he learned that he could defeat them all and he knows that now he has all the food he wants. He did not learn that defeating other animals results in high dominance status nor that this is a means of obtaining food. To say that the animal came to such conclusions is to credit him (without any evidence) with the ability to form concepts and to reason syllogistically. To think that a psychologist can escape the reproach of anthropomorphism if he ascribes reasoning to animals but protests at the same time that human reasoning is not really syllogistic reasoning either is to presume on the objective status of his brand of psychology.

That even "insight" experiments are not evidence for the perception of means-ends relations is implied by Spence, who comments that the suddenness of the solution is no argument in favor of genuine insight, for

Incorrect responses are also adopted abruptly . . . there were many instances in which the subject, having previously suddenly adopted the correct response, subsequently dropped it and shifted abruptly to an incorrect response. The fact that this latter shift was sudden must logically be interpreted to mean that the subject was insightfully abandoning a correct response for an erroneous one. If such behavior is insightful, it certainly is not intelligent (16, pp. 49–50).

In addition it could be said that once the relation of action to success is really understood, this action would not be dropped, either suddenly or gradually. Furthermore, in apes as well as in lower animals, irrelevant motions seem to persist (one of Guthrie and Horton's cats always turned around before touching the pole in the puzzle box), which would be inconceivable if the connection between one particular action (touching the pole) and the opening of the door had been understood. Neither can such persistence of irrelevant actions be explained on the basis of the law of effect, for it was not the irrelevant action that was rewarded but the relevant movement which followed it. But the dropping of correct responses can be explained if we assume that the response was accidental or based upon sense memory; and the persistence of irrelevant action can be explained on the assumption that the cat learned that the whole action sequence of turning and touching the pole was followed by finding its way to food unbarred. The memory of what the cat did while the door opened is reproduced in action on the expectation that the door will be found open now as it was previously.

Do Animals Use Symbols? Several psychologists have recently insisted that animals use symbols. Seward, for instance, in a reply to Allport's article on *Scientific models and human morals*, has insisted that animals can be said to use symbols, which would confirm his premise that the basic behavioral mechanisms of rats and men are homologous. He defines a symbol as

. . . a sign produced by its interpreter that causes a disposition to respond under certain conditions as to some other sign, even when the latter is absent (15, p. 281).

This definition is so wide that it allows the use of the term for memory images as well as for symbols so called.[2] A symbol as used by human beings, for instance, has no natural likeness to the thing symbolized, while the image has (the sound or visual pattern for "lamp" has no natural likeness to the object, the reflection in a mirror has). The symbol has independent existence apart from the thing symbolized, the image does not: the word "lamp" is visible or audible, while the memory image of the lamp has no existence apart from the person who remembers, nor has the mirror image any existence apart from the mirror. Finally, the symbol may (and usually does) refer to a class of things (animal, basket, clay, etc.) or to abstract notions (cf. the statue of liberty, or the symbol of the cross for Christianity), while the image always depicts individual objects or individual situations.

Seward's examples, from which he infers symbolic behavior in animals, never go beyond the animal's use of memory images. Two examples will suffice.

In the experimental room the objective hung from the roof out of reach. The chimpanzees had already learned to climb on boxes and ladders but there were none in the room on this occasion. Before the door to the room was opened the chimpanzees were allowed to play in an adjacent corridor where, around a corner, stood a ladder. For a long time their efforts to secure the objective were futile. Even leading Sultan past the ladder had no immediate effect. But eventually the ape disappeared and returned dragging the ladder (15, p. 290).

Seward remarks that any diagram of this feat of intelligence would have to include a "ladder-surrogate, i.e., a symbol, as an

[2] Oxford Dictionary definition of "symbol": Something that stands for, represents, or denotes something else (not by exact resemblance, but by vague suggestion, or by some accidental or conventional relation); especially a material object representing or taken to represent something immaterial or abstract, as a being, idea, quality, or condition; a representative or typical figure, sign, or token.

essential factor in Sultan's insight." But this "ladder-surrogate" need not be a symbol at all, merely a memory image of himself standing on a ladder high up, near the ceiling. This memory image in conjunction with the present situation would give rise to the action and Sultan would repeat a past action in new surroundings. And another quotation from Seward:

> Blodgett demonstrated latent learning. . . . on one maze, Maze C, consisting of two paths to food, one long and one short . . . Blodgett's experimental group was given 15 unrewarded trials, one a day. On the 16th day, with food in the end-box, 11 out of 21 rats took the long path. On the 17th day all but four rats took the short path. What caused seven rats to shift away from the reinforced path? . . . Without inferring a symbol (as intervening variable) I am unable to account for this phenomenon (15, p. 292).

Again, Seward's "intervening variable" is a memory image, not a symbol in the usual sense of the term. The rats are allowed to become thoroughly familiar with the maze on fifteen separate occasions; it can be assumed, therefore, that they will have memory images of the end box and of *both paths* leading to it. Once the rat is aware that there is food in the end box (sixteenth day) the rat can make use of its memory image to travel along the shorter path. The situation is puzzling only when we assume that there is no learning (or only "latent" learning) unless we can measure it. The rat has learned to find its way in the maze, therefore the learning has actually occurred. It is not at all latent for the rat, though not measurable by the experimenter. To call such learning latent only because it cannot by measured in units of time taken during the first fifteen days is to make learning depend on its being measured. If a different method of measuring were used, for instance, the time saved in learning to use the shorter path after food had been introduced as inducement, and rats unfamiliar with the maze were used as controls, learning could be demonstrated to have occurred. [3]

The explanation of Blodgett's result is not difficult once we concede that the rats did learn in the first fifteen days. Sense

---

[3] To measure learning by this method, the long path would, of course, have to be made considerably longer than the short path.

memory would account for the fact that the rats knew that both paths terminated in the food box; since the rat has learned on the sixteenth day to expect food, there is an urgency in getting to the end box on the second reward trial which was not there before, hence the shortest path will be taken.

But perhaps in discussing the use of symbols in animals we should concentrate on the ape rather than the rat. Indeed, it is in connection with learning in the great apes that the most outspoken statements have been made. Nissen, Riesen, and Nowlis (12) say, for instance:

Comparison of the facts of delayed response and discrimination learning in chimpanzees and human subjects, with spatial and non-spatial cues, led to the suggestion, (a) that delayed response requires an available symbolic mechanism, and (b) that in chimpanzees (and probably in many other animals) such a mechanism for spatial cues is highly developed, but is either absent or poorly developed for visual stimuli until acquired or brought to expression by training (12, pp. 384–85).

Let us see, then, what experiments lead to these conclusions and what the suggested "symbolic mechanism" could be. Yerkes had noticed that the chimpanzee can find food hidden in a box even after considerable delay. But if the box in which the food is hidden is moved elsewhere in the room and another box is substituted in the delay interval, the ape will go to the place where he saw the food hidden and search for it in the wrong box. In this situation, the ape evidently never learned to find the food, in spite of long continued training. It is instructive to quote Yerkes' conclusions at some length:

Reluctant to believe our subjects incapable of responding correctly to visual cues such as color, brightness, or form, after an interval of delay during which the situation had disappeared from view, we made thousands of observations with different forms of box test, and later with a turntable apparatus, in an effort to discover conditions under which correct response from memory should be possible. Evidently enough it was not simply a matter of forgetting what had been seen, for the subject responded readily enough to the positional cues which were provided, and that in spite of long delays. We finally were forced to admit that our subjects either *failed to perceive the essential visual cue,* or were unable to hold it in mind because they lacked a symbol or representative process comparable with our word "green." On the other hand, it seemed clear that they were able to hold in mind, and therefore ready for immediate use at the end of the period of delay, the spatial relation or configuration of the object to be selected. Whether this is possible by reason of a symbolic process, or a memory process which suffices for recognition of the object as a given position, has not been determined (20, p. 179. Italics mine).

In other words, as long as the ape was expected to find the correct box in the room or on the turntable, the training was unsuccessful. As Yerkes says:

To us it seems almost incredible that with both boxes before it, but interchanged in position, the animal should go where the food had been concealed, in spite of the altered appearance of the box (different color and shape) and there search persistently for its expected reward (20, p. 178).

Such "almost incredible" performance can be explained, however, if we remember that there is a vast difference between having a memory picture of the total situation with the food hidden in a particular place, and acting according to that memory picture, or *isolating* one particular feature, the *essential* feature, namely the shape and color of the box, and then connecting the food with this particular feature. Such selection of the essential feature is not a sensory discrimination, therefore could not be expected of animals on our hypothesis.

Later experiments, especially those by Nissen, Riesen, and Nowlis, simplified the experimental situation considerably. Either a white or a black box had to be chosen after a delay up to fifteen seconds. The ape saw the experimenter hide a banana in the box when the boxes were shown *one above the other.* During the delay, the position of the boxes was changed so that the ape had to choose the correctly colored box, which was now either to the *left* or to the *right* of the empty box. One ape failed to solve the problem after 1,217 trials, another reached a level of 70 per cent correct after 1,440 trials. Such performance does not indicate an *understanding* of the essential feature of the problem but a laborious *association* of a part of the memory image with the requirements of the present situation. The fact that there was success at all when there had been failure in Yerkes' experiments can again be explained by referring to the peculiarities of the later experimental situation.

In the Nissen, Riesen, and Nowlis experiment, the ape stood in front of a 33.8-cm² backdrop with sides shielded, so that nothing was visible except the two boxes, which were conspicuously in the center of his field of vision, whereas in the earlier experiment the ape had been in the middle of the room, with a different box in each corner. However, in the whole series of experiments conducted by Nissen *et al.*, in which there was better than chance success, there still is no indication that the ape used a symbol instead of a memory image. In fact, if a symbol had been used (to designate "white" or "black," for instance), it would indicate an understanding of the essential means-ends relation (white-food) and therefore would have resulted in sure and permanent success, not in a 70 per cent correct performance. While a sudden new response, even a sudden correct response, is not a sufficient indication of understanding, as Spence said, the fact that the correct response was made only in 70 per cent of the trials, and that such partial success was reached only after hundreds of trials, is a sufficient indication that understanding or "insight" has *not* occurred. In still later experiments, Riesen found that:

. . . the (prior) establishment of a reliable and persistent color discrimination habit made possible single trial learning of color discrimination on the delayed reward apparatus. . . . This suggests that, if given the proper previous experience, animals can achieve sudden solutions characteristic of problem solving by means of symbols (14, pp. 50–51).

But this is not really color *discrimination*; rather it is a habit of color association, in which the ape had learned to associate the white box (or black box) with food. The ape did not *discover* the *essential* feature in the situation but had been trained beforehand to respond to this *particular* feature. There is no more need to assume a symbolic process here than in any of the previous learning situations, and only the lack· of any distinction between symbol and memory image would incline anyone to suggest that a symbol was used.

If, then, the feats of animal learning which we have discussed here can be explained by a memory process which we know the animal possesses, why explain them by symbolic processes for which we have no independent evidence? The difference between apes which are capable of delayed response learning and lower animals which are not would then be a difference in the quality of the memory process. There may be an additional difference in the persistence of attention which, however, may be the result of the greater vividness and longer persistence of memory images in higher animals. That apes can remember location easily, even after long delay, but color and shape only with the greatest difficulty, could be explained by the fact that location requires simply the persistence or reinstatement of the total memory image while the memory of color or shape requires the isolation of a particular feature (the significant feature) out of the total memory picture. If that isolation is made easy for the animal (as in Riesen's apparatus, or by previous training in color association) then the animal will succeed, though not invariably, and only after considerable training. Where, however, such an isolation of a special feature is made difficult, the ape will fail even after many trials—because he never recognizes this special feature as the essential feature, as the means toward his desired end.

Why Do Spatial Cues Dominate Animal Learning? Yerkes seems to be willing to concede the possibility of a "memory process" in the case of response to spatial cues (Cf. page 358 f.) ; and all investigators comment on the fact that learning to respond to positional cues is easier than learning to respond to color, size, or shape. But let us see why spatial cues have such a preferential position. If we ask ourselves, How does the animal perceive spatial cues? we realize at once that the perception of spatial characteristics (location or position) depends mainly on vision, and only secondarily on the other senses. The ape, who saw the experimenter hide the banana in a box and after a delay went back to the right location but the wrong box, surely depended exclusively on vision; in the same way, the rat which develops a positional response (jumping to the card on the right) more easily than a response to shape (jumping to the triangle, whether it is on the right or the left side) has to depend on vision.

When Nissen *et al.* say, therefore, that "a mechanism for *spatial* cues is highly developed but is either absent or poorly developed for *visual* stimuli" (*op. cit.*, p. 25), their objective language betrays them into distinguishing two things which are not distinguishable in that way, for both are perceived by vision. And if both location and color are perceived visually, why should a "symbolic mechanism" be developed for one kind of visual stimuli and not for the other, on their premises? The difference between the two kinds of perception is to be found in the fact that location or position is represented by the total memory picture while color or shape is an isolated feature of that total image. Only when size or shape or color is specially emphasized in the experimental situation, only when the objects to be discriminated fill the total visual field (as in a discrimination apparatus for rats, or in Nissen's *et al.*, delayed reward apparatus described on page 359 f.) will it be possible for the animal to single out the emphasized feature and to associate it with the reward.

This preference on the part of the animal for location as against other cues has puzzled many experimenters. Hebb has tried to explain it recently by suggesting that the animal's response is dominated by visual cues from remote objects rather than by cues from near ones. He explains this preference for remote objects by pointing out that "remote objects provide the most stable and constant stimulation of the animal's environment" (5, p. 92).

But is it true that the animal's response is dominated by cues from remote objects? Any kind of visual cue will influence the animal's response only if seen in conjunction with the memory image of a past situation. If a rat has learned that jumping for a circle leads to food while jumping for a square is followed by a bump on the nose, then presenting a circle and a square will call out a response—but only if the rat compares the two shapes with a memory image of previous situations. The rat's action in the present is dictated by its memory of the past. In this particular case, there are no remote objects which could dominate the response, so Hebb's hypothesis cannot be tested. But Hebb provides a better illustration:

> Teach a rat to jump from a small platform to another one near by. The second platform is just large enough for him to land on safely, and holds food. After he has made ten jumps, move the second platform through 90°. The rat hesitates, shows disturbance, but finally jumps—into space, in the former direction of food (5, p. 93).

Now the present visual cues in themselves could not possibly occasion the jump into space, for right here and now there is nothing there which could attract the rat, neither food, nor platform, and the background itself offers no incentive. But *past* visual cues and a *past* habit of action pointed in that direction; thus the visual-kinaesthetic *image* of the *past* won out against the *present* visual *sensation*. To say that cues from remote objects instead of cues from near ones dominate the response is an unwarranted inference; it would be true only if they did so when the rat makes its first jump. But in the first response, no matter what the remote objects, the rat headed toward food, which was a *near* object; it heads away from food now only because it acts according to its memory image of the past total situation in which food was in the direction of its present jump. Thus it is the memory image of the past situation and the motor habit acquired on this basis which determines the present action, and not the present visual perception of either near or remote objects.

Do Animals Have Language? In any controversy concerning the use of symbols, this question will obviously play the deciding role. If it could be shown that animals have a symbol language, then it could be presumed that they use symbols in learning situations. We shall simplify our discussion by restricting it to the great apes, the animals most likely to have a language similar to that of humans. Yerkes, who has worked with apes for many years, claims that chimpanzees, for instance, have not only a language but racial tradition and culture, though in their most rudimentary form. He says:

> Certainly chimpanzees communicate affectively with one another by sounds, gestures, facial and bodily expression, postures, and visible attitudes which function as meaningful signs. *Symbols probably are rare* and play a subordinate, *if significant,* role in their linguistic expression. Therefore, the composite language of the chimpanzee differs greatly from our own. They, e.g., have no system, or even assemblage of sounds which may properly be termed speech, and nothing remotely like a written language. Chiefly because these sign processes readily observed in the daily behavior of these apes profoundly affect their social activities and relations, it seems reasonable to say that they constitute a simple language (20, p. 190. Italics mine).

Thus Yerkes seems to think that chimpanzees not only communicate feelings but use a symbol language as well, though in a rudimentary form. No wonder that in that case he finds it

> . . . surprising that the animals neither speak nor even in slight degree learn to imitate our vocal expressions. No indication of linguistic inventiveness has been observed and never yet has a chimpanzee been taught to talk (20, p. 192).

No doubt it is true that as soon as symbols are used there should be no obstacle to using symbol language or learning *human* symbol language. But as we have seen, the evidence from which Yerkes infers "symbolic processes" allows us to infer images but not symbols as they are required in human language. If we use the Webster definition of language: "any means, vocal or other, of expressing or communicating feeling or thought," then we can concede that animals, especially apes, communicate feelings; but there is no evidence that they communicate thought, for that would require both concepts and symbols, and not merely memory images. There is another specific usage of the term "language," however, also given by Webster, connoting (a) the faculty of verbal expression and the use of words in human intercourse, and (b) the inarticulate sounds by which animals express their feelings. In that usage, the term is used analogously for human beings and animals, and explicitly denies to animals the use of symbols.

The opinion is sometimes voiced (even by psychologists) that apes cannot learn human language because they can imitate only gestures, not sounds. Yerkes,* for instance, says:

Perhaps the chief reason for the ape's failure to develop speech is the absence of a tendency to imitate sounds. Seeing strongly stimulates to imitation; but hearing seems to have no such effect. . . . Perhaps they can be taught to use their fingers, somehow as does the deaf and dumb person, and thus helped to acquire a simple, non-vocal, "sign language" (19, pp. 179–80).

One hates to think how much time would be required to teach the chimpanzee a sign for the color green, for instance. when it took an intelligent specimen almost 1,500 trials to choose the correct box after fifteen seconds' delay when it was put in a different position!

While there is no doubt that the ape does not naturally imitate sounds (as was pointed out earlier, page 349), the main obstacle to his acquiring human language is that he does not understand that a sound is a means to an end, that it is intended to refer to the object symbolized, or that it stands for a class of objects. Where the child will try to produce the correct sound because he knows it refers to things or people or actions, and will spontaneously apply a particular sound (a word) to many different objects which have an essential feature in common, the ape must be taught to make a sound artificially, even though that sound may be present in his vocal repertory. Furness graphically describes the procedure:

By getting [the orang-utan] to stick out her tongue and then by holding the tip of it up against her teeth and at the same time forcing her to breathe through her mouth I finally got her to make the sound *th* (2, p. 285).

This certainly is a different procedure from the one used with a human child after the babbling stage is over. Garner, one of the staunchest defenders of the idea that apes not only have a symbol language of their own but can be taught human language,

* Yerkes, Robert M., *Almost Human*. New York, copyright 1925, The Century Co. Used by permission of Appleton-Century-Crofts, Inc.

makes this curious admission in trying to explain why the ape cannot imitate speech sounds:

[The ape in his own language] speaks precisely as the human does, with his vocal organs used humanly and with the air ejected through the glottis. But in attempts to utter human speech by imitation, apes are predisposed to inhale instead of exhale. This, however, is purely because, in attempting to move the lips as they see the teacher move his, *they do not quite grasp the modus operandi* of what they do naturally when talking on their own account. . . . (21, p. 305, quoted from Garner, 3. Italics mine).

In other words, they do not grasp that they are doing the same thing as the teacher does when they are vocalizing naturally—and no wonder: for them the sounds they make naturally express their internal feeling state (as do laughter and tears in humans) but do not refer to objects or concepts, nor are they produced deliberately, apart from the feeling state of the moment.

Finally, it should be pointed out that there is a difference between the use of sounds as expressions of feeling, as signals for action, as indicating a particular thing, and the use of sounds which represents a class of things. The first three uses of sounds really treat them as signals and only the last use of sound is symbolic in the proper sense of the term. The whine of a dog when he wants to go out is an expression of feeling; the command of his master, "down!" is a signal of action; the master's name refers to this particular individual; but the sound "table" is a symbol denoting a class of objects. There is enough evidence even without experimental observation that animals can *use* sounds as expression of feelings, that they can *respond* to such sounds, and that they can *respond* to sounds that are signals of action.

There is evidence also that animals may learn to respond to sounds that refer to one particular individual—the dog may cock his ears when his master's name is mentioned. There are even reports that apes can be trained to *produce* sounds that refer to one particular individual or one particular object. So Furness reports that he taught an orang-utan to say "Papa," referring to himself, and "cup" when the ape saw his own drinking cup. The training took six months, by the above mentioned tedious method of artificial sound production. The same feat can be accomplished by parrots and other talking birds in a considerably shorter time.[4]

These reports justify the conclusion that we are dealing here with memory associations of sounds with the desired object, which seem to be produced in the auditory sphere in the same way as in the visual sphere (Cf. our discussion on page 351). The production of a sound from an auditory memory image requires even more careful training in emphasizing and isolating the desired sound than is required for the recognition of color and shape apart from location. In addition, the ape, at least, requires help in the production of sound.

There is a vast difference, however, between the association of a remembered and reproduced sound with the reward object and the connection of such a sound with a concept, which is what is required for human language. Concepts are formed by abstracting the essential feature of an object and discovering this feature in a whole class of related objects. When the sound is connected with the concept, it can at once be applied to the whole class of objects to which the concept refers. When a child, for instance, learns a new word, "door," he will immediately point to every door he sees, whether it be large or small, of wood or metal, whether it belongs to the doll's wardrobe or to the kitchen stove. Once the essential feature is isolated and the concept formed, it is never forgotten, though the sound connected with it may be (for instance in a foreign language). Once the child has learned to form concepts, there is no limit to the number of objects which can be related by discovering the same essential feature, to which the same sound can be applied.

Neither is there any limit to the number of concepts that can be formed, nor any difficulty about connecting several conventional sounds with one and the same concept (*bread*, *pain*, *Brot*, all refer to the same class of objects). In animals there is no evidence which would indicate such concept formation. Their

[4] Mowrer says in connection with bird "language": "The first thing we can say with any certainty is that birds can be taught to indicate their wants by means of words, i.e., to say the name of whatever it is they want to eat or drink. It is also clear that birds can 'associate' certain words or phrases with particular events" (12, p. 694).

mechanism of "talking" is one of associating one particular sound with one particular object or situation, and every new object requires a new sound association, even though it should belong in the same class. To put it differently, animals can learn at best the names of individuals but not the names of a class of individuals.

Summing up our discussion thus far, we should like to point out that the performance of animals can be explained in every case by their use of sense knowledge and sense memory. There is no evidence that animals can reason, that they can make hypotheses or understand means-ends relations, or that they can use symbols properly so called. The animal can estimate that one thing is different from or similar to another, but cannot form the abstract concept of relation, size, shape, or any other concept. Since symbol language requires concepts, such language is impossible even for the animals highest in the scale of life, the great apes.

Capacity for Learning in Humans and Animals. Comparing human and animal learning on the basis of our definition, we find that human beings learn differently from animals because they have different powers or capacities. The human being can

1. set up new goals for himself,
2. recognize that he must find means to achieve his end,
3. devise, choose, and use such means.

Therefore, he will use sensation, memory (sensory and rational), motor functions, and understanding in judging the situation, and uses in addition creative imagination and deliberate choice in selecting means and ends. The animal, on the other hand, can

1. follow naturally determined goals,
2. in naturally determined ways.

Therefore, he uses sensation, sense memory, motor functions in estimating the situation and will follow the ways which are possible for him toward his natural goals. In human learning, all the capacities of the human being are used unless the situation restricts him or he restricts himself, wittingly or unwittingly. In animal learning, all the animal's capacities are used as far as the situation allows. Considering the different capacities available in human and animal learning, the term "learning" should be considered analogous because it refers to analogous but not identical activities in humans and animals.

REFERENCES

1. ALLPORT, GORDON W. 1947. Scientific models and human morals. *Psychol. Rev.,* 1947, **54**, 182–92.
2. FURNESS, WILLIAM H. 1916. Observations on the mentality of chimpanzees and orang-utans. *Proc. Amer. Phil. Soc., Philadelphia,* 1916, **55**, 281–90.
3. GARNER, R. L. 1892. *The speech of monkeys.* London: William Heinemann, Ltd.
4. GUTHRIE, E. R., and HORTON, G. P. 1946. *Cats in a puzzle box.* New York: Rinehart & Co., Inc.
5. HEBB, D. O. 1949. *Organization of behavior. A neuropsychological theory.* New York: John Wiley & Sons.
6. HILGARD, E. R. 1948. *Theories of learning.* New York: Appleton-Century-Crofts, Inc.
7. KATONA, G. 1940. *Organizing and memorizing.* New York: Columbia University Press.
8. KOFFKA, KURT. 1924. *Growth of the mind; an introduction to child psychology.* Tr. R. M. OGDEN. New York: Harcourt, Brace & Co., Inc.
9. KÖHLER, WOLFGANG. 1947. *Gestalt Psychology.* New York: Liveright Publishing Corporation.
10. LASHLEY, K. S. 1938. The mechanism of vision. XV. Preliminary studies of the rat's capacity for detail vision. *J. genet. Psychol.,* 1938, **18**, 123–93.
11. MOWRER, O. HOBART. 1947. On the dual nature of learning. A reinterpretation of 'conditioning' and 'problem solving.' *Harvard Educ. Rev.,* 1947, **17**, 102–48.
11a. ———. 1950. *Learning theory and personality dynamics.* New York: The Ronald Press Co.
12. NISSEN, H. W., RIESEN, A. H., and NOWLIS, V. 1938. Delayed response and discrimination learning by chimpanzees. *J. comp. Psychol.,* 1938, **26**, 361–86.
13. RAZRAN, G. H. S. 1936. Attitudinal control of human conditioning. *J. Psychol.,* 1936, **2**, 327–37.
14. RIESEN, A. H. 1940. Delayed reward in discrimination learning by chimpanzees. *Comp. Psychol. Monogr.,* 1940, **15**, No. 5, 54 pp.
15. SEWARD, JOHN P. 1948. The sign as a symbol: a reply to Professor Allport. *Psychol. Rev.,* 1948, **55**, 277–96.
16. SPENCE, K. W. 1939. The solution of multiple choice problems by chimpanzees. *Comp. Psychol. Monogr.,* 1939, **15**, No. 3, 54 pp.

17. TOLMAN, E. C. 1938. The determiners of behavior at a choice point. *Psychol. Rev.,* 1938, **45**, 1–41.
18. ———. 1942. *Drives toward war.* New York: Appleton-Century-Crofts, Inc.
19. YERKES, ROBERT M. 1925. *Almost human.* New York: Appleton-Century-Crofts, Inc.
20. ———. 1943. *Chimpanzees. A laboratory colony.* New Haven: Yale University Press.
21. YERKES, ROBERT M., and YERKES, ADA W. 1929. *The great apes. A study of anthropoid life.* New Haven: Yale University Press.

PART IV

PSYCHOTHERAPY AND SELF-INTEGRATION

Chapter 13

PSYCHOLOGY AS A NORMATIVE SCIENCE

By ALEXANDER A. SCHNEIDERS

EVERYONE IS aware of a growing tendency in modern psychology to establish norms and criteria by which to evaluate the adequacy of human behavior and conduct. This phase of development in psychology has several roots, and we shall take occasion later on to discuss the background in more detail. Here we should note at once certain important implications in this development. First of all, there is the obligation of psychology to itself as an empirical science. Can psychology afford to run the risk of becoming normative? The history of psychology as an empirical science is a very short one. In fact, it has barely reached the point of fulfilling all the criteria of a true science. Is it, then, ready to embark on the hazardous mission of setting up rules for effective living? There are many gaps in our knowledge of human personality and behavior. Since knowledge of human nature is the basis for the formulation of normative standards, should not these gaps be filled in before we attempt to establish criteria for wholesome personality development and adjustment?

Related to this problem is the very real danger of developing inadequate or even harmful criteria for the regulation of conduct. We need only mention the deterministic theorizing of much of modern psychology, and the completely inadequate statistical concept of normality, to indicate how real the danger is. We need not go very far for some striking examples. Thus, Thorpe writes:

> . . . the mental hygiene point of view stresses the value of the individual in a democracy and indicates that human freedom is contingent upon respect for the dignity of man. It emphasizes the impor-

tance of satisfying human needs and assisting the individual in feeling adequate rather than depreciating him and deflating his ego. *It has dispensed with the concept of blame* and has supplanted it with that of understanding human dynamics, i.e., the cause of behavior "good" or "bad."

The objectives of mental hygiene include the fullest possible development of personality, as well as harmonious interpersonal relationships. . . . Mental hygiene practice is intended to make possible the building of personalities sufficiently well adjusted to withstand the cross currents of stress and frustration incidental to a competitive society (10, p. 6. Italics mine).

In this statement we see an implicit rejection of an important aspect of morality, as well as a tendency to replace ethical norms with norms of a psychological nature. A great deal of what the author says is sound psychology, but some of his statements make it necessary to determine specifically the role of psychology as a normative science. Shaffer deals with the same problem:

The problem of defining what constitutes a good adjustment is a very difficult one. . . . Good and bad are essentially ethical concepts and have no place in the realm of science. . . . As a scientist, the psychologist can ignore any consideration of good and bad and can think of a so-called maladjustment as a certain kind of behavior. . . . To the psychiatrist or clinical psychologist, however, a maladjustment is an ailment to be remedied. Like the physician, he is called upon not only to investigate but also to judge and to modify behavior (9, pp. 136–37).

Following this, Shaffer then sets about determining a *psychological* criterion for good adjustment. Rejecting satisfaction of needs and motives as a wholly adequate criterion, he says,

For a person to satisfy all his motives with regard for their functioning as an interrelated system, is good adjustment. To achieve this requires *unified and integrated behavior,* the presence or absence of which provides what is perhaps the clearest distinction between good or poor adjustments (9, p. 138).

This concept of unified and integrated behavior is not enough, because it does not take into account the relation of the individual to society. Thus:

. . . the concept of individual integration must, however, be supplemented with one of integration in society. When the interrelated motives of a person are satisfied without undue emphasis or slighting of any one motive, and when this is achieved with consideration for the adjustments of other persons, then a state of good adjustment may be said to exist (9, p. 138).

In this statement, too, the problem of the relation between psychology and ethics stands out very clearly. If good and bad are essentially ethical concepts, then certainly good and bad adjustments have some relation to morality. Yet it is obvious that the criterion which Shaffer finally evolves is not an ethical one. It is essentially, as he himself says, psychological.

So too are the criteria set forth by Louttit in his analysis:

In order to define deviating behavior it is necessary to accept some description of average normal behavior. This can be formulated only in terms of social adaptability and acceptance. Evidently, a definition in social terms will depend upon the society that sets the standards. . . .

Most simply stated, the requirements for average normal behavior in our culture include: (1) a physical organism physiologically and anatomically adequate to maintain its own living processes and to carry out necessary receptor, coordinating, and response functions; (2) abilities, both in the nature of so-called general intelligence and in specific aptitudes, sufficient to enable the individual to acquire the knowledge and skills necessary to secure and retain a position significant to the broad socio-economic needs; (3) maturity, which involves control and direction of "emotion" and physiological drives to the end of the efficient functioning of the person within the group; and (4) the operation of all the foregoing in a stable, integrated total individual personality (7, pp. 16–17).

In this concept, too, although the criteria by which to judge normal or adequate behavior are psychological, there are serious implications for the relation between psychology and ethics. The author implies that deviant behavior is determined by reference to social mores, which vary from one society to another. If deviant behavior includes moral misconduct, then morality would be interpreted as stemming from society rather than from moral law or principles. All of these notions point up the necessity of developing adequate criteria of good adjustive behavior.

They indicate too the importance of defining the relation between psychology as an applied science and moral science. While there are numerous problems which the psychologist faces that have little or no ethical import, there are many others that are as much ethical in nature as they are psychological. Hence, before the psychologist can know what stand to take with respect to problems of this kind, he must determine the extent to which the problem is psychological in nature, and what criteria can be applied to it. He must also know what aspects of the problem are more precisely ethical, and thus require the application of moral criteria.

In similar vein, but more specifically, this problem of psychology as a normative discipline imposes the necessity of defining the relation between normative psychology and Christian thought, as it is expressed in philosophy, religion, and ethics. The concept of man as a rational substance, the idea of self-determination, man's relation to God, the notion of sinfulness, and like concepts have to be considered in defining the principles of normative psychology. Man is not a segmented group of moral, religious, philosophical, and psychological aspects which can be kept apart when human problems are dealt with. The concept of man in his entirety must constitute the basis for working out practical principles for the development of personality or the achievement of adjustment. For much the same reason, the relation between normative psychology and the fields of psychiatry and mental hygiene must be clearly defined. Both of these latter disciplines are normative in character and are largely concerned with the same kinds of problems with which normative psychology deals. The relation here is very obscure, and a great deal of confused thinking could be eliminated if it were more clearly defined.

Tendencies Toward Normative Thinking in Psychology. In the early history of psychology, when it was still a philosophical discipline, the problem of psychological norms did not exist. As a part of philosophy, psychology was closely related to ethics, but the differences were clear-cut. Psychology was assigned the task of explaining human conduct, and ethics was given the responsibility of determining rules and norms for the rightness and wrongness of conduct. Similarly, logic established rules for right and wrong thinking. Thus the division of labor was neatly drawn; psychology was philosophical and partly empirical in character, whereas ethics and logic were normative and disciplinary.

This distinction carried over into the field of empirical and experimental psychology in its earliest stages. In this phase of its growth, psychology was regarded as purely scientific, and all problems of an ethical or philosophical nature were rigidly excluded. The business of psychology was analysis and description of the mind. But this phase was short-lived, and it was not long before the advancements in abnormal psychology and the development of the field of mental hygiene led to a great deal of normative thinking. In fact, once the direction of interest shifts to questions of mental health, abnormality, and personality development, some norms become inevitable. Problems like the distinction between normal and abnormal, adjustment and maladjustment, mental health and mental disorder, enforce a consideration of norms by which such distinctions become meaningful. Allers * points up this necessity when, in discussing psychoanalysis, he says:

> This basis of the psychoanalytical views on values—or rather, the view implied by the psychoanalytical conception of human nature—is overlooked by H. Hartmann in his plea for maintaining the notion of the objectivity of values and combining it with psychoanalytical ideas. He points out that psychoanalysis in its practical endeavors has to start from some definite value-ideas, e.g., that of health. The analyst in attempting to restore health to his patient has acknowledged health as a value. He does not create or posit this value, but accepts it (1, p. 105).

Here we have a clear statement of the necessity and inevitability of determining norms or criteria for conduct and personality. Values may be regarded as the basis for such criteria. The clinical psychologist, the mental hygienist, the psychotherapist

* Quotations by permission from Rudolf Allers, *The Successful Error.* Copyright 1940 by Sheed & Ward.

must decide for themselves and for their patients what is good or bad, what is valuable and what is not, whenever they are dealing with questions of health, adjustment, or wholesome living. This requirement has become more and more prominent with the advances in clinical psychology and psychotherapy, in which practical principles of good living are indispensable. This responsibility had already been faced by medical science and physical hygiene, and by psychiatry in its treatment of mental disorders. These disciplines were forerunners of the development of psychology as a normative science, setting the pattern in many important respects for this development.

The Nature of the Problem

Is Psychology a Normative Science? To answer this question in any definitive sense, we must determine first of all what a normative science is, and secondly, the nature of psychological phenomena, that is, the manner in which and the extent to which they differ from those with which the science of ethics is concerned. Needless to say, if psychology is purely empirical—and some writers contend that it is—then it has no business with norms and criteria. A normative science is one that investigates and develops standards (of good and bad, of right and wrong) for the regulation and control of behavior, adjustment, personality development, health, and the like. It is clear, from what we have already pointed out, that there are several normative sciences that seek to regulate human conduct—ethics, psychiatry, and mental hygiene; and it will be argued by some that there is neither need nor justification for psychological norms. But the fact is that psychology is concerned with a psychological and psychosocial order of phenomena which are regulated by their own laws and principles independently of other normative disciplines. It is this fact which, in the writer's opinion, justifies the development of a normative psychology.

A clearer perspective of this problem can be gained by considering the nature of ethics which, of all disciplines, is the one most likely to conflict with normative psychology. According to Allers:

. . . ethics is viewed, by whatever philosophical school, as being essentially normative. It deals not with human conduct as it actually is, but as it ought to be if it is to be commensurate to man's ends and the fulfillment of his destiny. The note of "oughtness" is characteristic of all systems of ethics, including those of a strictly relativistic nature. . . .

No statement on what man ought to do, no commandment, law, or rule, can be significant, unless account be taken of the capacities of human nature. . . . Ethics needs to know what are human nature and its abilities in general and how the latter are modified by personal or environmental conditions. Ethics requires a "moral psychology" of which we, unfortunately, as yet know not enough (2, p. 239).

In this statement we have a precise indication of the nature of ethics as a normative science; but let us note the idea that ethics deals with human conduct as it *ought to be* from the standpoint of *man's ends and destiny,* and not from the standpoint of efficiency or adjustment. As Dr. Allers expressed it in a personal communication to the writer:

I agree with you that there are what you call psychological norms. That is, human nature requires a certain conduct of life to permit the actualization of its potencies within the given conditions of reality or the human situation.

This viewpoint, however, is qualified in the next sentence:

However, it seems to me still an open question whether these norms can be considered as norms in the same sense as those of ethics. To be sure, there is a definite interrelation. But many of the psychological norms might be of the same kind as those of hygiene . . .

To this statement the present author would simply say "Amen." The following discussion will show why.

Ethics as normative begins from the standpoint of morality, of what is good or bad for the individual from a strictly moral point of view, of the moral rightness of some acts and the moral wrongness of others. Its starting point is the moral order, and the acts which it approves are morally good and those which it condemns are morally bad or sinful. In the analysis of a sinful act, the difference between psychology and ethics as normative sciences stands out clearly. According to O'Brien:

Speaking of his definition of sin as an evil human act, Saint Thomas explained that a human act is evil if it does not measure up to the norm or the standard for human acts. Thomas taught that this standard was twofold, and that one part of it was our own right human reason, and the other the eternal law of God. . . . The fact that a human act is by definition *free and voluntary* brings in the element of fault and consequent imputability to the agent who is the *master of an act* done contrary to reason and God's law (8, p. 85. Italics mine).

Thus, if any act is to be considered objectively sinful in any degree it must fulfill three conditions: (1) the act must contain malice to some degree; (2) there must be in the agent some advertence to the malice of the act; (3) there must be consent of the will, either direct or indirect, because every sin is a human act.

It is here that the difference between normative psychology and ethics stands out. Morality is concerned with distinctively human acts, acts that are free and voluntary and under the mastery of the individual. But there are numerous responses which do not come within the scope of morality, and are certainly not sinful, even though they are "bad" for the welfare of the organism. These are the responses that are interpreted as abnormal and maladjustive, such as compulsions, hypochondria, enuresis, stuttering, nail-biting, truancy, and many others. Thus, normative psychology has its starting point in the psychological order, and considers what is good or bad for the human being from the standpoint of adjustment, mental health, normality, or personality integration. It does not operate under an immutable set of principles in the way that ethics does, unless the behavior in question is moral as well as psychological in nature. There is not the force of "ought" governing psychological behavior that exists with respect to moral conduct. Ethics can condemn lying, stealing, or murder in a way that psychology cannot condemn neurotic or symptomatic behavior.

The two fields must not be confused from the normative point of view. What is psychologically bad may also be ethically wrong, *but for a different reason*. The norms of the one do not contain the norms of the other. Thus the psychotherapist, listening to the difficulties and complaints of his patient, is not a confessor; he may not evaluate the behavior morally as long as he maintains his position as a psychologist. It is for this reason that he can effectively employ the principles of acceptance and permissiveness in the therapeutic relationship. His evaluations, as contrasted with those of the moralist, are based on standards or criteria of efficiency, adjustment, mental health, social effectiveness, level of integration, or normality. We may conclude, therefore, that psychology is normative to the extent that it establishes and applies norms for "good" behavior; and it promises to become increasingly more normative as it continues to enter the clinical field in which human problems are the central issue.

The Norms of Psychology. A fuller meaning can be given to this discussion by a consideration of the principal norms that are available to psychology for the evaluation of behavior. It is these norms, in turn, that lead to a better understanding of what is meant by "normality" and "adjustment" as these terms are used in psychology. Among the primary and general norms or criteria of good behavior are (1) personality integration, (2) reasonably good achievement and efficiency, (3) happiness, (4) mental health and emotional stability, and (5) freedom from disabling personality characteristics and symptoms. In terms of these criteria, then, it is not difficult to define what is meant by normality or adjustment. The normal well-adjusted person is one who is integrated, mentally healthy, happy, emotionally stable, and capable of a certain level of achievement and efficiency in whatever he undertakes to do.

But this is not quite enough, because there are many secondary characteristics of the normal person which are important. In addition, then, normality requires (6) intellectual and emotional insight, (7) an adequate, dynamic philosophy of life or scale of values, (8) resiliency and adaptability, (9) proper orientation to time, (10) vocational satisfaction, (11) an adequate social, moral, and religious orientation, and (12) a wholesome sense of humor. It is obvious, of course, that if the first group of criteria are fulfilled it is likely that all the other characteristics will be present. From the standpoint of clinical practice or psychotherapy, however, it is helpful to identify specifically the characteristics of normality and adjustment.

The Bases of Psychological Norms

Human Nature as a Basis. The nature of ethics as a normative science makes it clear that ethical norms are definitely related to the nature of man. Morality is inconceivable in the absence of a rational nature. By the same rule, the norms which psychology uses to judge the goodness or badness, the normality or the abnormality of some response must be drawn from the nature of man. Kelley makes this clear when he writes:

> The treatment of the psychoneuroses, I think, is of main interest, and in order to treat psychoneuroses intelligently, it seems to me that we need some standard toward which we are aiming, and toward which the patient is or should be aiming. . . . psychiatry, like any other field of activity that deals with human beings, must necessarily be based upon a concept of human nature; and a correct concept of what a human being is, where he came from, and what he is for, what the purpose of his existence is, must be found in psychology. . . . And so we go to the science of psychology to get some clear conception of what we are dealing with when we deal with human beings (6, pp. 18, 19).

Much the same idea is expressed by Allers in referring to the basis of morality:

> Morality starts with the recognition of the particular dignity of the human person. It is perfectly nonsensical on the infrahuman level to talk of categories belonging to ethics . . . a conception of man which does away with morals, not by replacing it by "immoral" ideas but by rendering the use of ethical categories quite impossible, is no longer a theory of man. The capacity of moral behavior is as fundamental to human nature as rationality is; the former is indeed but a particular manifestation of the latter (1, pp. 111–12).

This analysis makes it clear that the norms of psychology, like those of ethics, must be developed in relation to man's nature. Neurosis, psychopathy, or psychosis, like sin and immorality, are contrary to the well-being of man. They stand in the way of his achieving the goals of mental health, integration, or adjustment, in the same way that immoral acts stand in the way of man's achievement of his final end. To know what man *should* be, from the standpoint of mental health or adjustment, we must know what man *is*. We must, in other words, take into account his physical and psychological needs, his capacity for high-level integration and self-improvement, his moral and religious capabilities, and his characteristics as a social being. On this basis only can we evaluate behavior and personality disturbances properly, and also evolve norms for the achievement of wholesome adjustment.

Man's Relation to Reality and Objectivity. In the development of these norms, we must also consider man's relation to reality. Man necessarily exists in and constantly reacts to an objective world of people and events; and if this relation is disturbed in a serious way, adjustment becomes very difficult. It is well known that neurotic and psychotic personalities are often characterized by their inadequate relation to reality. The "flight from reality" of the schizophrenic patient is the most typical example, but there are many other instances where the relation between the individual and objective reality is seriously impaired. Normality and adjustment, therefore, require of individuals the ability to react adequately to reality and to cope successfully with its demands: thus, normative psychology must be based in part on this relationship. In his personal communication to the author, Dr. Allers remarked:

. . . to become fully himself man must turn away from himself towards that kind of actuality which corresponds to the particular capacity to be developed. It seems to me . . . that man serves his personal interests most by moving away, as it were, from himself.

This movement away from himself exists in two main forms. One is that by which man comes to terms with reality in complying with the objective demands of his concrete situation; and herein is rooted the moral and psychological significance of work. The second is the way of love, that is, the self-abandonment of true love "not seeking its own."

Hence, the relation of man to his environment and to other persons in his environment is of paramount significance to wholesome adjustment.

Man's Relation to God. A third source of adequate psychological norms is man's relation to God. God is a special part of man's reality; and just as, in the interest of adjustment, man must acquire the capacity to cope with his natural environment, so must he develop wholesome and satisfying relations with his Creator. As Allport * points out:

> . . . psychotherapy knows the healing power of love, but finds itself unable to do much about it. On the side of theory . . . it lacks an adequate concept of the nature of tenderness. On the side of practice, the psychotherapist finds himself unable to supply the love his patient needs, nor to receive the love the patient wants to give. . . . As for mental hospitals, they seem equipped to give their inmates almost everything they require excepting love.
>
> By contrast, religion—especially the Christian religion—offers an interpretation of life and a rule of life based wholly upon love. It calls attention again and again to this fundamental groundwork. On love for God and for man "hang all the Law and the Prophets." The emphasis is insistent: "Beloved, let us love one another; for love is of God; and everyone that loveth is born of God, and knoweth God. He that loveth not knoweth not God; for God is love" (3, p. 81).

Thus religion, which is another name for man's relation to God, is fundamental to wholesome living. It is not the whole of adjustment, nor can it guarantee peace of soul or mental tranquillity; but it stands out as one of the most important factors in man's attempts to live the good life.

Psychology and Ethics

From the foregoing analysis of normative sciences in relation to human conduct and adjustment, it has become more and more apparent that psychology and ethics have common boundaries, in much the same way that hygiene and physiology have. Both

* Quotations from Gordon W. Allport, *The Individual and His Religion.* Copyright 1950. By permission of The Macmillan Company.

ethics and normative psychology are oriented toward the good life, toward the achievement of happiness, peace of soul, and wholesomeness in living. Yet there is the difference that we pointed out, that the one is concerned with regulating deliberate self-determined conduct which always comes within the scope of morality, whereas the other is concerned with behavior which, often indeliberate and nonmoral in character, is significantly related to normality and adjustment. Because of these similarities and differences, the two disciplines are complementary to each other; and both are indispensable to the welfare of man. Allport points up this relationship when discussing the respective roles of the clergyman and the psychiatrist in the treatment of human problems. He writes:

Returning to the relation of the clergyman and psychiatrist, this conclusion seems in order: in so far as the clergy is the better able to deal with issues of basic belief, values, and orientation toward life, he has an inescapable role to play in the conservation and advancement of mental health. His role seems complementary to that of the psychoanalyst who, by professional training, is ordinarily more skillful in plowing than in planting. But in so far as modern psychotherapeutic techniques have become medically oriented, or otherwise specialized, the clergyman, of course, must give ground. No longer does the cure of souls fall entirely to his office. The growth of psychological science does not mean, however, that he is relieved of responsibility. Quite the contrary: it means that now for the first time he can embrace his ministry to the individual with some degree of confidence, for he no longer stands alone in the face of a task too great for his skill and training. He can make psychological science his ally, and share with its practitioners the solution of a problem of joint concern. Furthermore, he can and should become familiar with many of the psychological procedures that may fortify his own skills (3, p. 85).

Father Ford, S. J., professor of moral theology, is somewhat less certain that present-day psychology can be entrusted with the role of a normative science, but he is equally aware of the complementary relation of psychology and ethics. In a personal letter to the author, Father Ford carefully analyzes the relations among psychology, mental hygiene, and ethics, and concludes that, while they are complementary to each other in securing the good life, psychology has a long way to go before it can be considered adequate as a normative science. We may as well use Father Ford's statements as a conclusion to this discussion, for he says:

> I think the following difficulties are encountered when we speak of psychological norms of human conduct. First, these norms are apt to be more nebulous, or more subject to controversy among psychologists themselves, than the norms laid down by physical medicine, for example, for the care of the body. People cannot be expected to live by norms that are vague or which are not firmly and scientifically established. Secondly, Christians believe that they have, in the system of the Christian virtues, properly understood, a way of wholesome living which is both practical and psychologically sound. In addition it has the authority of the Church and of the revealed doctrine of Our Lord behind it. . . .
>
> Who is going to teach me how to live a wholesome and well-adjusted life? The mental hygienist, or a spiritual director who applies to my soul the principles of Christ, who is the Way, the Truth, and the Life? If the mental hygienist happens to be a Freudian he will grossly exaggerate the animal part of man, and will interpret everything without sufficient regard for man's spiritual nature, free will, and essentially *rational* make-up. If the spiritual director is inexperienced or not well educated, he will neglect the emotional and instinctive side of man, and may not be aware of the psychological implications of his consultant's difficulties. I do not believe there is any real conflict between sound psychology and the practice of Christian virtue. But I believe there is or sometimes would be a sharp conflict between what certain psychologists would advise a client to do in practice in the name of 'scientific' psychology, and what Christian virtue would require or advise him to do in the name of his religious profession. . . .
>
> From all this you can see that I do believe that psychology is normative and should be more normative of human conduct. But it should play its role within Christian ethics and not apart from it. . . .

COMMENT

As Dr. Schneiders points out, the criterion of the "normal personality" has not been adequately discussed or established. Commonly three definitions have been suggested.

The Statistical Norm. Psychologists have often equated the "normal" with the statistical average. For example, according to Foley, "it is obvious that deviation implies relative variability of behavior; the responses of the individual must be considered in relation to the responses of other individuals" (4, p. 289). This interpretation of the term "normal" is borrowed from the measurement of various personality traits, such as intelligence, and applied to the evaluation of the personality as a whole. But there is an important difference. The various traits can be arranged on a continuum from an arbitrary zero point to the limit of the possible test responses. In that continuum there will be a subnormal (below average), a normal (statistical average), and supernormal (above average). The trait itself, however, may well be "abnormal" in the sense that it is not necessary or desirable for normal functioning. It is possible, for instance, to measure the extent to which a given population exhibits paranoid ideas, which would constitute a "paranoid" trait. Any individual could possess this trait to a degree that is below average, average, or above average. Only the person who possesses this trait to a degree considerably above average might be called "paranoid" or "abnormal" while the fortunate possessor of a minimum of paranoid ideas surely would have to be called normal in the sense of healthy or nonparanoid.

In evaluating personality traits, therefore, an extraneous criterion is required to decide whether in any given trait the high or low end of the range is desirable for normal personality development. It cannot be assumed a priori that the average is necessarily the optimum. Every psychologist would agree, for instance, that a minimum of such a paranoid trait is optimal for personality development, while he would demand a maximum of the trait of "emotional stability." Thus a trait must itself be evaluated as normal or abnormal, desirable or undesirable for normal personality development, rather than serving as a statistical norm for evaluating personality.

In practice, this difference is well understood. No clinician, for instance, would take as the goal of his therapeutic effort "average" adjustment for the client. Rather, he would try to aim for the best possible psychological functioning obtainable for this particular person, given his life situation, his endowment, his opportunities. To reach personality integration, the clinician must aim for better-than-average freedom from prejudices, fears, and worries.

The Normal as Socially Accepted Behavior. Moreover, the statistical average obviously depends on the group which provides the sampling range. If that is taken separately for every cultural group we might find such wide variations that the members of one group might be "abnormal" according to the standard provided by another group. If the range is taken as humanity as a whole, then actual measurement, no matter how crude, is not feasible and the norm remains an individual hypothesis. In practice, therefore, a statistical concept of normality amounts to accepting a social norm which is different in every society : that person will be normal who is accepted as normal by his social group. Then the question arises how large a social group must be before it can be allowed to set up its own standards of normality. It obviously cannot be a subgroup in a culture. A gang of criminals or homosexuals would not provide a standard of normal behavior for their own members. But it may not even be possible to grant such a privilege to a national group. In Hitler Germany, for instance, aggressive and sadistic actions toward political prisoners were not only permitted but required, therefore were considered normal in that society. If we are seriously considering the socially acceptable as the normal, then these actions could be called neither criminal nor abnormal. Obviously, the trial of war criminals proves that the world considered such actions neither as socially acceptable for humanity at large nor as statistically normal.

Finally, the socially acceptable cannot be the norm because psychiatrically abnormal individuals are often accepted and tolerated by their family or community group unless they show grossly disturbed behavior. Conversely, there is at least the possibility that any given group may itself be abnormal in the psychiatric sense. In the latter case, the acceptance of a social norm would force us to consider a healthy individual living in a paranoid community as decidedly abnormal. (Every anthropologist living among a people like the Dobu would perforce become "abnormal" during his stay.)

But there is one interesting feature about the socially acceptable as a standard of normal behavior which is worthy of our attention.

The basis of social acceptability will be found on analysis to be rational behavior. If we judge another's actions as queer or deviant in the sense that they do not conform to the accepted mode of behavior, we assume that he could act as we do but is unwilling to do so for reasons of his own. If a man's action deviates in nonessentials, such as wearing feathers instead of hats, we merely call him queer. If he deviates in important areas of conduct such as marriage, and marries two women at once, we call him a criminal. But if his action is such that we cannot conceive of any reason at all for it, therefore his action is not rational, we call him abnormal (for instance, when we see a man fighting a nonexistent enemy). In every instance the underlying assumption is that there are rational principles of conduct, that they are *universal*, therefore binding on everyone, but also that the principles *we* have are rational and universal and that everyone who is not ill or incapacitated should obey them. Hence the indignation when a foreigner seems to flout our conventions wilfully.

Anthropologists have shown us that many of our own rules of conduct do not hold in other societies, but they have drawn the unwarranted conclusion that therefore all existing rules of conduct are not rational but arbitrary or conventional. Analogously, much of our scientific knowledge of the external world is unknown in many other societies which seem to operate by rule of thumb and superstition; yet no one has suggested as yet that therefore our science is invalid and sacrifice to the local gods is as effective in producing a good crop as are fertilizer and irrigation.

Normal behavior is equated in every society with "rational" behavior, that is, with actions which have a reasonable motive and will serve mutual cooperation and individual perfection. Social disapproval is meted out to the nonconformist because it is assumed that he can but will not be rational. Punishment is inflicted upon him when his actions go against the interest of the community because it is assumed that the pain he suffers will make him willing to conform. Finally, *incapacity* for rational behavior is assumed only when neither disapproval nor punishment has the slightest effect, as in the case of the mentally ill or mentally deficient. To conclude that the notion of "rational conduct" has no meaning because it is interpreted differently in different cultural groups is no more reasonable than to conclude that the external world does not exist because different societies differ in the degree to which they know it or can manipulate it.

Thus the notion of the normal as the socially acceptable has a core of truth in it in so far as socially acceptable conduct is also rationally determined conduct. It is inadequate only because it depends on casual untrained judgment as to what is rational conduct, and because it depends in addition on the untenable assumption that everything considered right in a given society is also according to right reason.

The Normal as Freedom from Symptoms. Would it be possible, then, to adopt a medical norm and define the normal personality negatively as the personality which is free from pathological symptoms? Such a definition implies that we know enough to recognize symptoms as symptoms. And how can we distinguish symptoms from normal functioning except by first knowing what normal functioning is! In other words, we must know how the human being ought to function before we can recognize the disturbance represented by a symptom.

Normal Functioning. Medically speaking, normal functioning, like health, has no superlative. If every organ and organ system in the body functions according to its design, and the various systems function in smoothly harmonious coordination, then the organism functions normally, the person is healthy. Any interference with normal functioning will be an interference with health, will lead to various degrees of *ill*-health. The fact that in a given society the majority may suffer from slight or serious ill-health will not deter the physician from holding to an unchanging, that is, absolute, standard of health, which is represented by unimpeded normal functioning. Nothing better than that can be envisaged, though there may be many degrees or kinds of *abnormality*, that is, *ill*-health.

The concept of normal personality would seem to demand the same treatment. Psychologically speaking, the person will be normal if he functions according to his nature, according to the way in which he was designed to function. The only difference between physiological and psychological normality lies in the fact that physiological functioning is strictly determined while normal psychological functioning requires that the basic determination should be implemented by deliberate rational goal-setting. Therefore we must first distinguish between a disturbance in the activities which are strictly determined, which are the product of the single human powers, and a disturbance in the deliberate ordering of these activities. If there is a disturbance of functioning in the single human powers such as occurs in delirium tremens or opium intoxication, then the deliberate organized activities of the human being will be disturbed, too. Behavior cannot be rational when the nervous system, mediating organized deliberate action, is attacked by a toxic agent and ceases to function normally.

Secondly, there may be a disturbance in the *organization* of the single functions while the functions themselves remain normal. This disturbance will necessarily affect smooth functioning of the person as a whole because the single functions are not properly coordinated and will seem to conflict with one another. But the various powers mediating sense knowledge (vision, hearing, imagination, memory) cannot be the disturbing elements. Disturbance comes with conflicting tendencies and alternatives of *action*, not with *knowledge* in itself. Therefore, the disturbing elements must be the emotional tendencies connected with our goals.

As we have seen in Chapter 10, these emotional tendencies are designed to be the means for self-actuation. But genuine self-actuation can come about only when the person has established the proper hierarchy of goals, that is, when he has established a rational self-ideal. If such a hierarchy of goals is not successfully established or not consistently adhered to, emotions will hinder self-integration instead of aiding it. Such a state of affairs will reveal itself as unconscious conflict and may become a chronic state of indecisiveness or anxiety or focalized fears or emotional compulsions. Here the single powers are functioning normally but their integration is disturbed, "abnormal." The person acknowledges the necessity of rational action but is unable to organize himself in such a way that such action becomes easy or even possible without excruciating emotional suffering.

Finally, psychological functioning may be abnormal when there is not even an attempt to establish a hierarchy of goals. This lack of concern may result superficially in an absence of emotional conflict because disturbances of organization or emotional control cannot appear when no organization or control has been attempted. When every impulse is given in to, provided only that it is physically possible to do so, then difficulty or frustration in the pursuit of goals will come only from outside, from other persons or things. Such a person will be free from anxiety, for he does not see the necessity of controlling his impulses. He will appear frank and likable, very different from the inhibited, introspective, and restrained neurotic, because his attention and energy are not taken up with the attempt to restrain his appetites.

At the same time such a person must be considered abnormal because he does not act in a properly human way, subordinating sensory satisfactions to rational goals. Any time his inclination conflicts with the interests of others (and even with his own ultimate interest) his inclination of the moment will win out; without rational restraint, his impulses will demand satisfaction in ways that become increasingly antisocial. Punishment will have the immediate effect of inducing him to promise reform, but where punishment is the only motive, reform cannot be permanent. On this level of personality disturbance, there is no experience of "drivenness" or emotional compulsion, as there is on the second level; there is rather an inability to give a rational reason for any specific impulsive action. The impulse was reason enough for the action but is not credible afterwards when the consequences have to be faced. It is not so much that the individual could not have left undone what he did as that he could see no reason for restraining himself from an action to which his impulse urged him.

On the other hand, on this level we must distinguish between a person who is normal (because he has a self-ideal and therefore a rational hierarchy of goals) but whose self-ideal is seriously at variance with the self-ideal as it ought to be, and a person who not only is normal in the sense of having a self-ideal but who has the right self-ideal, a self-ideal as it ought to be. A person is normal whether or not he strives for the goal he was meant to achieve, as long as he acknowledges rational goals at all and strives for them, whether his actions are right or wrong. If his self-ideal does not correspond to his self-ideal as it ought to be because of ignorance of the proper goal, he will have to pay the price in unconscious conflict—just as a man disregarding any natural law will suffer the natural consequences.

As long as he strives for the highest rational goal he knows, or strives for ever closer approximation to objective truth, he is normal and an asset to his fellow-men. If the rational goal for which he strives is deliberately egocentric, he will be at best a parasite, at worst a criminal in his society. But if he refuses to follow any rational goal at all, if he refuses to set up even a wrong self-ideal and follows the impulses of the moment, then he does not function as a human being is designed to function. He is therefore abnormal, even though every one of his single functions be normal and even though he should show no emotional tension or anxiety. At the same time, this abnormality is not a disease he has contracted, but a result of his refusal to organize himself.

Normal functioning, then, must be established on three levels. To be normal a person must (1) have a self-ideal, (2) he must properly articulate his powers in striving toward it, and (3) all his powers must function in such a way that they reach their proper aim.

Ethics and Psychology

Psychology, then, can establish a norm of proper human functioning. It can establish whether a given person functions according to his proper nature on all three levels of functioning. If a man's single powers function normally and he is able to integrate and control them, he will be in a position to exercise his self-determination, to choose his goals and his self-ideal. He will be responsible for his conduct because he can choose actions which will either help or hinder his progress toward his ultimate goal. While the psychotic, for instance, is not responsible for his actions, and the neurotic may not be responsible in the area influenced by his neurosis, the psychopath is responsible because his single powers function correctly; his control over them is intact but he does not exercise it because he is unwilling to deny himself the desired satisfaction.

While psychology establishes the proper functioning of the person which will help him to achieve his final end, ethics determines

394 THE HUMAN PERSON

what specific actions will help or hinder the human being to achieve his quest. Thus psychology and ethics deal with the same human actions, but the one asks whether they are indications of his proper human functioning, the other, how they affect man's direction toward his final end. The two disciplines are necessarily coordinated though they use different terms and have a different aim. The science of psychology decides whether a man is functioning according to his proper nature, that is, whether he is normal or abnormal, whether he is well or poorly integrated. Moral science, on the other hand, has to decide whether any given action was done voluntarily or not, regardless of the fact that the person as a whole may be functioning normally or abnormally. Whenever the moral theologian decides that any action was done involuntarily and the person has lost control over such actions, it becomes the task of the psychologist to help him regain voluntary control. Conversely, whenever the integration of the person is made impossible by the gross divergence of his self-ideal from what it ought to be, it may take not only a therapist but a moral theologian to provide the necessary conditions which will enable the person to correct his self-ideal.

REFERENCES

1. ALLERS, R. 1940. *The successful error.* New York: Sheed & Ward, Inc.
2. ———. 1950. Ethics and anthropology. *The New Scholasticism,* 1950, **24**, 237–62.
3. ALLPORT, GORDON W. 1950. *The individual and his religion.* New York: The Macmillan Co.
4. FOLEY, J. P. 1935. The criterion of abnormality. *J. abnorm. soc. Psychol.,* 1935, **30**, 279–90.
5. FORD, JOHN C. 1951. *Depth psychology, morality and alcoholism.* Weston, Mass.: Weston College.
6. KELLEY, OTIS F. 1948. Is there danger of substituting psychiatry for religion? In: *Psychiatry and Religion.* (Ed.) JOSHUA LIEBMAN. Boston: The Beacon Press.
7. LOUTTIT, C. M. 1947. *Clinical psychology of children's behavior problems* (Rev. ed.). New York: Harper & Bros.
8. O'BRIEN, PATRICK. 1950. *Emotions and morals. Their place and purpose in harmonious living.* New York: Grune & Stratton, Inc.
9. SHAFFER, L. F. 1936. *The psychology of adjustment.* Boston: Houghton Mifflin Co.
10. THORPE, L. P. 1950. *The psychology of mental health.* New York: The Ronald Press Co.

Chapter 14

FREE ASSOCIATION AND
FREE IMAGINATION

By Magda B. Arnold

PSYCHOANALYSIS HAS aroused violent championship as well as violent opposition. Now that it has been with us for a good many years it is perhaps appropriate to raise the question : what has psychoanalysis to offer as a *technique*, which could be used independently of the conception of man which was its foundation in the Freudian system?

To answer this question, we shall first have to investigate the technique of psychoanalysis in its nature and its effects; and afterwards we shall be in a position to decide whether this technique is the best one available for personality reconstruction.

Now what does psychoanalytic technique consist in ? It consists first of all in a method of investigation which is designed to uncover the roots of the patient's difficulties, namely the method of *free association*. If it is true, as Kubie says in his latest book, that "this dependence upon free association is the basis of all that is new and scientific in psychoanalytic technique" (8, p. 46), then an investigation of the way in which this method discovers the roots of an emotional difficulty must be our first concern. The second step in psychoanalytic therapy is the *interpretation*, which results in *insight*. Interpretation consists in illuminating for the patient the connection between his early memories, recovered by free association, and his present symptoms and difficulties, while insight is the realization by the patient that such a connection exists.

And what do psychoanalysts themselves think of the process of free association, with what psychological function do they identify it, and how do they explain its action? For Dalbiez, for instance, free association is "a process which brings about internal inhibition of the higher psychism as a result of suspending self-criticism and self-guidance" (2, Vol. I, 92). But Kubie goes much farther than that. For him, free association is

. . . that simple and naïve form of undirected musing which everyone uses in the solitude of his own chambers, and which is at the same time the most spontaneous and creative of all forms of thought.

It is not always realized that free association is the natural process by which the mind of the scientist and the artist creates. Free associations enable the psychological processes to roam through the mental highways and byways, unhampered by conscious restrictions, gathering up ideas and impressions, putting them together in various combinations, until new relationships and new patterns come into view. Both in science and in the arts, free association is an essential tool in the process of creative search. Subsequent logical scrutiny subjects the new patterns to a necessary secondary process of retrospective checking and testing. In analysis the free associations are provided by the patient, the logical scrutiny by the analyst (8, p. 46).

Not all analysts may be as explicit as Kubie, but most of them incline to his view that every relaxation of deliberate control in thinking results in a spontaneous creative process guided by unconscious forces, which is identical with the process of free association. If psychoanalysts are right and the method of free association really releases the same creative process which is active in artistic or scientific creation and synthesis, then it certainly seems as if such a method would be the method of choice for bringing about the resynthesis of a personality. As the artist is at his artistic best in creation rather than in routine work, so the human being may have a clearer and more integrated vision in his creative moments. But can free association really be identified with artistic imagination? Does it of itself lead to a creative synthesis? Or is it perhaps the analyst who provides not only the retrospective rechecking but also the blueprint for the new synthesis?

To discover what types of associations are possible in an associative chain, we tried an exploratory experiment with a group of subjects who received the following instructions:

When you hear the stimulus word, put down the first word that occurs to you. Then let your mind run on and put down everything that comes to your mind.

The associations were carried on for five minutes which, we discovered, was far too little time. However, even in such short association chains, several types of associations could be distinguished.

1. *Stimulus associations.* Some subjects associated consistently to the stimulus word itself:

Deep: sea, deep love, deep love for Christ, deep penetration, water is deep, deep sea fishing, deep eyes, deep well, watery eyes, deep in Christ's heart, deep in the heart of Texas, deep in the bosom of the Father, deep insight.

2. *Thought associations.* Other subjects let the association lead them from one thought to another:

Deep: water. Green water with blue fish, small island in middle of ocean, one palm tree, bushes on island with berries, red berries, brown berries, Lillian has brown shoes on and white socks, snow is white and cold, the wind is howling, it is cold, my sweater keeps me warm, sweater is black, black is also color of death, after death is heaven and God and three persons.

3. *Memory associations.* In most cases, associations to the stimulus word lead to straight memory pictures:

Pepper: hot. I once knew a girl named Pepper—wonder where she is now. She had a hot temper. Pepper grinders are nice to have, sort of rustic. Pepper's getting scarce now. San Pedro's have pepper grinders. It's a nice place for atmosphere but the food's terrible! Saw "Kim" that night, excellent movie. Dean Stockwell is really a fine little actor. Carroll Flynn was no good as usual. Wonder what he's been doing lately—never hear anything about him. Back to subject—was chased with a pepper gun once. . . .

4. *Picture associations.* Sometimes, associations to the stimulus word produce imaginative pictures:

Deep: deepness could be heavy thought, an abyss of the mind, a deep well, darkness is all I see, there might be water at the bottom or mud, it seems endless. I look to the height to counteract it—underground there is no light, only coldness.

5. *Hypnagogic associations.* Associations to the stimulus word in rare cases lead to hypnagogic pictures:

Shallow: water. A horse trough, with flies on top of it, in a hot summer sun. On the main street of a weather-beaten little town, board houses cracked and brown, and dust in the street. There are no people, nor anything moving. Even the flies are quiet.

The town runs away like water, charging ahead strongly, but there is no noise. There are no banks to the river. The river cracked like a whip and shot up into the sky. Floating in blue-black darkness with stars around and a cool moist breeze. . . .

If we examine these examples, we find that they differ first in the degree of control exhibited, but also in the type of mental function used. In the first type of associations which we have called stimulus associations, there is the highest degree of control, the stimulus word dominates the associative process throughout, whereas in the last type of associations, hypnagogic associations, deliberate control is immediately abandoned. Types 1 to 5 are arranged in descending order, from highest to lowest degree of control.

Apart from the degree of control, we can also distinguish two different types of mental function. In Types 1 to 3, the associations given represent memories. According to the degree of control, these memories are either things thought or read or seen. When there is least control in this type of association (in Type 3), the memories are of personal experiences. Even in Type 2, however, later investigation verified the fact that every association given is a memory of something experienced either in the present or in the past.

In some cases, however, we get associations of Types 4 and 5, though they are very rare. Type 5 was quoted from a subject who gave only types 4 and 5 productions, but only in this one person did Type 5 productions occur. Type 4 occurs a little more often, but usually only to one or at most two stimulus words (out of five) in any one subject. Thus the large majority of subjects in associations to most of the stimulus words produce

Types 1–3 associative chains. The distinctive feature about Types 4 and 5 productions is the fact that the subjects saw or rather experienced in imagination a series of events which had never happened in the past. In most cases, they themselves were part of the ongoing action, they were in the middle of the picture (e.g., Type 4) though in some cases they were merely observers. That the two examples given (Types 4 and 5) are genuine imaginative productions, nobody will doubt. The reason why they are so vivid and so different from imaginative productions with which we are familiar in waking life (stories) can be found in the directions which expressly asked the subject to "let his mind run on" and therefore precludes the degree of control (the intention) which would produce a story. But it will be noticed that these productions have the same autonomous quality that is characteristic of dreams, with the added vividness that comes with waking consciousness.

To clarify the difference between such imaginative productions and stories, we used an equated series of stimulus words with these directions:

When you hear the stimulus word, put down the first word that comes to mind. Then tell a story suggested by the word.

The following example will illustrate the difference:

Salt: mines. A young man wished to marry a Catholic girl in Russia. They were to be married secretly by a priest. When the authorities found out, they shot the girl and the priest. The man, because he wasn't a Catholic himself, was spared his life, but even worse than death was his sentence. He was sent to work in the salt mines. He of course hated this but in a few years after seeing salt day in and out he went blind. From then on he didn't mind his work because he could imagine he was doing other things. He lived in a delightful imaginary world. The salt between his fingers became sand and he could almost feel the cool sea breezes across his cheeks.

This is the same student who gave the memory associations to *pepper* quoted before. We see that in the waking state a very definite intention or set is required to produce a story (which is not a memory). There are other cases where the story given is the memory of some actual incident or of some story remembered from a book or a film. Moreover, it seems that a greater effort or higher intelligence is required for creating a story than for remembering and retelling it. We find, then, that a special set is required for producing a story, and greater control (in the sense of better focus or greater effort) for an original than a remembered story. It requires a different set to produce an imaginative sequence and still another set to produce memory images; again we find imaginative sequences of Types 4 and 5 only rarely, and in very intelligent subjects. In most cases and with less intelligent subjects, the instructions "let your mind run on" seem to produce exclusively memory images. Here, however, it is not a higher degree of control which will produce imaginative sequence as against memory sequences but merely a different focus or set. With our instructions (let your mind run on) the most commonly assumed set is that toward recall of memory images, while among 34 subjects only one produced hypnagogic imagery.

Psychoanalytic free association, as far as I have been able to ascertain, consists of memories of situations previously experienced or at least thought about, with occasional interspersion of comments, very similar to our Example 3. The resemblance of the associative chains which have been reported in the literature to this type is unmistakable. This resemblance becomes particularly pronounced when such associative chains, starting from our stimulus words, were carried on for a longer time (half an hour) as I have done with some subjects. Nowhere in the literature is there any indication that psychoanalytic free association includes productions of Type 4 or 5. This is understandable from a consideration of the psychoanalytic situation. The patient wants help with urgent personal problems and therefore is not detached enough for the play of imagination to happen spontaneously. His emotional preoccupation takes over as soon as deliberate control is relaxed and produces memory images connected with it. In fact, it is because he observed that nothing but memory images were produced during free association that Freud could suggest this technique for the recovery of repressed memories. To make comparison possible, I shall give the association reported by Frink* to the name *Pond*, which he kept forgetting. I have abbreviated the report, but have not left out anything essential.

1. Dr. Pond, a pitcher on a baseball team.
2. Indian pond, visited as a child when fishing. He saw himself throwing the big stone into the water which he used as anchor.
3. A man called Fischer, who played as pitcher in another team.

. . . . .

4. Pond's extract, contains witch hazel.
5. As a child, while pitcher in a baseball team, he rubbed his arm with witch hazel.
6. Fat boy, member of same team. This boy had fallen head foremost into a puddle once, looked like a pig.
7. Another young man, nicknamed Piggy.
8. Recalled he himself had been nicknamed Pig (5, pp. 84–87).

These associations are obviously of the same type as those obtained by us, of which Type 3 is an example. Freud himself has reported many similar association chains, as have other analysts. In none of them have I ever found evidence of imaginative sequences, as exemplified by Types 4 and 5. Throughout psychoanalytic literature, the association chains reported consist of memory images, though these may be extraordinarily vivid.

But if the method of free association produces only memory pictures, can it be said that it is "the natural process by which the mind of the scientist and the artist creates," as Kubie says? In answer, I would like to quote a rather striking report of scientific inspiration. According to Pfister,

The great chemist Kekulé was dozing on the top of an omnibus, and atoms were dancing before his eyes, first two by two and then in groups of threes or fours. He spent most of the night working out on paper the hypnagogic images which had thus appeared to him, and in the morning he had the answer to the problem which had occupied him. Another time the process was even more definitive. Atoms were again dancing before his eyes; they executed a snakelike movement, then the snake bit its own tail. Kekulé awoke with the impres-

* Quotations from H. W. Frink, *Morbid Fears and Compulsions,* reprinted by permission of Dodd, Mead & Company. Copyright 1918 by Dodd, Mead & Company, Inc. Copyright renewed 1946 by H. W. Frink.

sion of illumination and spent the rest of the night in perfecting his idea of atomic structure (9, pp. 240–41).

The dance of atoms in this quotation is a product of creative imagination and not a chain of remembered experiences; it bears an unmistakable resemblance to the river "which cracked like a whip and shot up into the sky" (Type 5).

It seems that we are dealing with two totally different processes, the one a sequence of reminiscences (Freudian free association), the other a free play of the imagination; in the one we *remember*, in the other we *create*. Creative imagination, whether in science or in art, represents a new organization, a pattern, a structure. Innumerable well-known instances could be cited, from Archimedes' sudden illumination to Poincaré's lucid description of the process of scientific inspiration. In artistic creation the process is similar. Schoenberg says:

It often happens to a composer that he writes down a melody in one uninterrupted draft and with a perfection that requires no change nor offers any possibility of improvement. It occurred often enough to myself. For instance, in the melody from my String Quartet No. 2, I certainly did not make the slightest change. . . . I had a perfect vision of the whole work—of course not in all its details but in its main character (10, p. 72).

Wherever we see creative imagination at work, there is a sense of completion, of finality, of wholeness; whether the inspiration is artistic or scientific, whether it is restricted to a small area or comprises the structure of a whole symphony, we always find an articulated structure, never a chain of scenes. Imagination uses the materials of sensation, therefore uses memory images, but is not bound by the pattern in which they were received. Neither is it bound to any particular sense modality, though vision and hearing seem dominant.

Imagining, no less than thinking, has an intrinsic direction. In thinking, we think so as to arrive at a conclusion; the end or goal of thinking is truth. In imagining, we imagine so as to produce a story, a picture, a melody. The individual elements will have their source in past experience, but the imaginative production is something novel. Any definition of creative imagination, then, will have to take this factor of directedness and novelty into account. In Example 5 in our experiment, there seems to have been a set to see, to observe what is going on, rather than a simple musing, that is, running along accustomed grooves. When the subject is thus set to see, imagination seems to take over and images, producing again a story, or at least the beginnings of one. According to our criterion of directedness and novelty, then, artistic production, scientific inspiration, dreams, and hallucinatory experiences as well as these instances of waking spontaneous imagination would be products of creative imagination. Free association as used by Freudian psychoanalysis, on the other hand, is a chain of memory images which have no discernible new structure, show no new action, tell no new story. The factors of intrinsic direction and novelty are completely lacking in them.

But, it may be objected, is not there some directedness in free association? There is, of course, and Freud is rightly given credit for having discovered this directedness where before the laws of association were thought to be sufficient explanation of the associative chain. The laws of association only provide an explanation of the linkage of one association with another—by similarity, by contrast, by contiguity. A great many images could be so linked with the preceding one—why was this particular one chosen? Over and above the determination by the laws of association, there is a tendency toward emotion-laden memories, a thematic undercurrent which seems to determine which one of many similar words and images will be admitted. This becomes clear when we consider Frink's associations once more. After an interruption, he went on to associate to the word *Pond*:

1. Pond, ponder.
2. Think, sicklied o'er with the pale cast of thought,
3. Hamlet—hamlet, a small village he knew,
4. Farmer in that village who told him that a neighbor had out of malice killed two pigs and thrown them into his well.

At that point, a memory of his seventh year arose:

As a boy, Frink and his brother used to play together at a pond. His dog Gip, of which he was very fond, used to try and retrieve stones the boys threw into the water, much to their amusement. Finally young Frink threw a big stone, thinking he would frighten the dog. He aimed badly and the stone struck the dog's nose. Gip sank and never came up again. Young Frink was heartbroken and could not be consoled. It was the greatest sorrow of his childhood (5, pp. 84–87).

This example gives us three different lines of association, all starting out from the name *Pond* and leading to the traumatic memory of Frink's boyhood over different routes. The first route (Dr. Pond, Indian pond, Fischer) leads to a pond in his childhood, to himself throwing in the big stone and to a boy who pitched; the second, to himself as pitcher, to himself nicknamed Pig; the third, to pigs thrown into water and finally to Gip in the water killed by him with a stone thrown. Thus the same starting point (Pond) is connected with the same traumatic experience over various memory routes.

Freud himself and innumerable analysts after him have reported similar associative chains, in all of which there is an unmistakable connection of the starting point with an emotion-laden memory. It can thus be taken for granted that such connections exist and that there is a direction guiding the choice of associations toward focal points of emotion. This direction is not the result of the laws of association. That a particular memory is chosen which is connected with a traumatic memory, that this emotional focal point is gradually approached more and more closely until the forgotten experience is actually recalled, is the effect of a factor extraneous to the associative process, namely emotion, and not of the associative process itself.

But why does free association lead through many seemingly indifferent memories to a memory charged with emotion? What accounts for the thematic undercurrent taking hold and directing the associative linkages? Freud answers that free association leads to the traumatic memory because conscious control is relaxed which would keep the memory repressed. As soon as conscious direction is abandoned, the repressed emotion guides the associative process to the traumatic event without being noticed, as it were, by the repressing force. Kretschmer describes the mental state of the analysand very well:

The more completely we relax into passivity, the more nearly does free association approximate to the psychic mechanisms of dream and hypnosis. Linkage by sentences begins to loosen, the verbal formulation of thought yields noticeably to concrete imagery, to the direct contemplation of living figures as scenes which rise to the mind's eye (7, p. 112).

Leaving aside Kretschmer's comparison with the dream and with hypnosis, we notice that in the process of free association the images become vivid—but they nevertheless remain memory images.

Free association, then, seems to represent a liberation of reminiscence from deliberate interference, and also from interference by the patient's desire to appear in a favorable light, though the latter is achieved but slowly. In the beginning, there is considerable resistance; first memory images are deliberately not reported. Later on they are prevented from arising. Gradually, various interferences with the emotion-guided memory process are abolished until this process becomes almost automatic, following its emotional determination.

But why does the repressed emotion activate and direct the memory process? This second question Freud answers by saying that the associative process represents a retracing of a causal link from repressed emotion to the present symptom or dream. According to him, the repressed emotion keeps on acting and expresses itself finally in symptomatic acts (such as meaningless gestures), disturbed acts (such as slips of the tongue), inhibitions (such as forgetting of names), and dreams. The same emotion which produces these activities also forces the thematic associations. Free association, then, only retraces the steps by which the repressed emotion expressed itself in action.

But it is a fact, pointed out by R. Allers and checked in our experiments, that free associations from neutral stimulus words will also lead to emotion-laden memories. Here the starting point was given from the outside, not produced by the patient; therefore the mere fact that free association will lead to traumatic memories is no proof that the evocation of associations occurs because emotion has produced the linkages which are now merely retraced. All that can be maintained is that the repressed emotion determines the *associations*, but not necessarily that the repressed emotion *produced the starting point* of such associations. Whether it did or not must therefore be decided on other grounds.

Some psychoanalysts, notably Dalbiez, admit the impossibility of strict proof that the associative linkage indicates a causal connection, but insist that causal connection can be demonstrated when the associations recover a memory which shows decided similarity with the starting point, let us say the dream. Saussure, for instance, says: "Associations often lead to recent events which are so analogous to the dream image that the most probable hypothesis is that they are causally related" (Dalbiez, 2, Vol. 2, p. 111). According to Freud, they are causally related to the emotion as the symptom is related to the disease which gives rise to it. Therefore Freud can say that the meaning of the dream is the cause of the dream. This is valid in exactly the same way for all symptomatic actions. When a girl develops an automatic gesture, for instance, raising her right arm above her head, and it is later discovered that this gesture had developed shortly after an occasion on which she raised her arm to ward off her stepmother's blow, it is reasonable to assume that the gesture is a result of the emotion felt during that incident which is expressed over and over again.

But if the repressed emotion is the cause of symptomatic actions, does it mean that therefore such emotion is the cause of all actions? Surely not, nor would any psychoanalyst seriously maintain the contrary. Dalbiez, for instance, would restrict such emotional causality to expressive actions, that is, actions which have no real object. Therefore all action which has such an object (driving to work, mixing a cake), including logical thinking which has as object the discovery of truth, cannot be explained causally. Neither can religious experience if we believe that it represents an activity directed toward God, that is, a reality outside ourselves. Other analysts, needless to say, do not restrain their scientific zeal to such an extent. For them, every human activity can be subjected to the psychoanalytic scalpel, whether it is expressive or directed toward an object. Literary products, religious experience, and scientific theories have been impartially subjected to the same reductive treatment, treated as if they were purely expressive, object-less activities.

The very fact that the majority of psychoanalysts consider every human activity as valid object for reductive analysis forces us to examine Dalbiez' distinction more carefully : if only expressive activities show true psychic determinism, are all the activities really expressive that he admits as legitimate objects of analysis, or are some of them purposive, that is, object-determined ? We can agree that symptomatic acts have no object, and the same is true for disturbed acts or inhibitions : the mistake was not intended, is not object-determined. But when we come to dreams, the case is somewhat different. The dream, like other products of the imagination, has an intention, it tells a story, it has a plot. Though all the raw materials may be, in fact must be, connected with past experience, there is an element of novelty in the dream which disappears as soon as free association reduces it to memory elements. With the *Gestalt* school, one is tempted to say that in the dream the whole is greater than the sum of its parts. The only reason why that escapes the analyst's attention is the fact that his very method of reductive analysis destroys the total structure. In the same way, analysis by free association will destroy the structure of every purposive activity : mixing a cake for supper could be traced to a repressed aggressive impulse, working out a scientific theory could be shown to be the result of a repressed Oedipal attachment.

Helene Deutsch provides an instructive example of such reductive analysis applied to scientific theories. She says :

The subjectivity of scientific theories can be experimentally demonstrated when the psychic life of a scientist honestly trying to achieve objectivity is subjected to psychoanalytic observation. Fortunately several members of a small scientific circle [anthropologists] studying the problems [of the matriarchal or patriarchal form of original society] became accessible to such observation. . . . It was revealed that the enthusiastic partisans of the matriarchal theory, men as well as women, were influenced in their scientific views by deeply unconscious motives. However, they did not all belong to the same psychological type, and identical views in different individuals often derived from diametrically opposed psychic tendencies. Thus, one anthropologist believed in the matriarchal theory because in his neurotically inhibited hatred he was fighting in vain against the patriarchal power of his own father. Another wanted to replace his strong, domineering mother, whom he had worshipped as a child but later devaluated because she was unequal to his ideal demands, with the "great mother" of the primitive past. He did not realize that actually he hoped that this mythical figure would help him rediscover his own once powerful mother whom he had long since lost emotionally. Another young anthropologist's numerous "objective" arguments in favor of masculine superiority and the patriarchal theory proved to be based upon his passive attitude towards his own father by transferring it to the fathers of the past, to whose rule he wanted to submit as to an ever recurring principle. My aim in pointing out the subjective influences in objective science is not to diminish the objective value of the latter, but rather to emphasize the caution imposed by such direct psychologic observations (3, Vol. II, p. 9.)

Despite the disclaimer, such an analysis does throw doubt upon the objective value of science. If every scientist chooses one theory or another according to emotional determinants, then the question of scientific truth is irrelevant and a science which provides true explanations of observed phenomena becomes impossible. Conversely, if a scientist can arrive at a true explanation, can formulate a true theory so that science becomes a body of knowledge rather than a mass of opinions, his emotional conflicts could never be the determining cause of his conclusions. On the contrary, he should be able to go counter to the emotional determinants influencing him. If Deutsch finds (as she does) that every scientist in her study acted in accordance with his emotional bias, then we must conclude that the scientist's rational purpose, to discover objective truth, is illusory and his irrational wishes are victorious every time.

Reductive analysis, then, if applied to science, will destroy the very foundation psychoanalysis itself is based on. If all scientific interpretation is determined by emotional factors and has no truth value, neither has the science of psychoanalysis. To avoid such a calamitous conclusion, psychoanalysts will have to admit that reductive analysis is inappropriate if applied to human activities which have an object outside themselves—in other words, which are purposive.

Let us see now whether the dream can be said to have such a purpose and how the method of free associations deals with it. Freud's conception of the dream as expressive or symptomatic action forces him to insist that release from waking control will immediately produce a dream expression of repressed impulses. But if an impulse has been repressed, therefore remains unsatisfied, its expression would be renewed *desire,* not wish *fulfilment.* To explain wish fulfilment dreams, Freud has to make another assumption, namely, that the dream is the guardian of sleep, and unfulfilled desire would arouse the dreamer. As the guardian of sleep, the dream must not only fulfill the aroused desire, it must also disguise any impulse that could be perceived as dangerous. So Freud has to assume a "censor" and "dreamwork" which transform the real latent content into the disguised manifest content. In this way he can explain a manifest frustration dream as a latent wish fulfilment dream. Finally, to explain nightmare dreams which awaken the sleeper, Freud has to assume that in such cases the dream disguise is wearing thin, the raw impulse comes dangerously near the surface, and the dreamer is awakened by the fear that it may break through into consciousness. For those anxiety dreams which repeat a real traumatic event, Freud later finds another explanation, namely that they are the result of a repetition compulsion. Freud's explanation of the cause and meaning of dreams thus needs one hypothesis after another. In any other field such a procedure would have earned a deserved reproach.

But let us take an example to see how wish fulfilment is diagnosed. One of Freud's patients, the youngest of five children, reported a dream she had had as a little girl of four, and many times afterwards, throughout her life. She dreamed that she was with a group of children, her brothers and sisters and her cousins, romping in a meadow. Suddenly they all had wings and flew away. Freud * comments:

She had no idea of the significance of the dream; but it will not be difficult for us to recognize it as a dream of the death of all the

* By permission from Sigmund Freud, *The Interpretation of Dreams.* Copyright 1915, The Macmillan Company.

brothers and sisters, in its original form, and little influenced by the censor (4, p. 214).

He imagines that the little girl must have asked previously what became of children when they die and must have received the answer : They grow wings and become angels. In the dream, the children have wings like angels and fly away and the little girl is left in sole possession of the parents' affection. Freud says : "Our little angel-maker is left alone, just think, the only one out of such a crowd!"

If we start with the assumption that every dream must be a wish fulfilment, all appearances to the contrary, we do arrive at Freud's interpretation. But if we remember that the very hypothesis of wish fulfilment was necessary only because the psychoanalytic method of free association led to traumatic memories, which resulted in the hypothesis of repressed emotion, then we may be willing to consider the dream before psychoanalysis has dissected it. If we pay attention to the dream story, a very different meaning appears : "Suddenly all the others grew wings, flew up, and were gone." That is what the dream says. If the little girl knew that children become angels when they die, she must have known also that only *good* children get wings and fly to heaven. She is the only one who does not. When children romp about in the meadow, they have fun; if suddenly all the others are gone, that is the end of her fun. So the dream story suggests loneliness and isolation for a bad little girl much more than a child gloating in the parents' affection. Freud can disregard the mood of the dream only because of his assurance that the dream does not tell a story but is merely an aggregate of various associations produced by a repressed wish.

Freud's treatment of dreams and literary productions amounts to a denial of creative imagination as a special function. Kubie, therefore, is following the spirit of the master when he equates free association (which, as we have seen, is pure recall) with creative imagination, and claims for the one the advantages of the other. It is true, of course, that the dream as well as any other product of imagination (or thinking, as we have seen) can be subjected to the reductive method. But what the method

of free association will do is to break up the organization of the
dream and resolve it into the memory images which constitute
its raw material. If we want to *preserve* the structure of dream
or story, a different kind of analysis is needed, which will reveal
what the dream is saying, which will reveal the plot of the
dream and refer it to the dreamer's life situation, rather than
work out the associative linkages with the past.

We are dealing here with two kinds of order. The one is the
order imposed upon the scenes and images by the design of the
dream, by the rationale of the story itself; the other is the order
imposed on the same images by the emotion which directs the
dreamer's associations to them. The associative order reaches
from the present into the past and represents the continuity of
the dreamer's emotions, the same continuity we can observe in
his waking life. Dr. Frink avoided a word which had a connection with a traumatic situation in his childhood, and it was pure
recall which made the connection. The imaginative order utilizes the past but has an intention in the present. As a function
of man, creative imagination (no less than recall) must have
relevance for him, must serve his purposes, must be designed to
help him reach his perfection as a human being. But while recall
starts with the present and links it up with the past and allows
him to see the present as it has developed from the past, creative
imagination will picture or illustrate the present and will allow
him to see it objectively as it will affect the future.

To show that these two kinds of order can be followed in
dream interpretation, I shall quote a dream with the interpretation given by Dalbiez as based on psychoanalytic investigation,
and an alternative interpretation which preserves the integrity of
the story. Dalbiez, who quotes the dream, mentions that the
dreamer, a young man, had accepted a role of adviser to a young
woman faced with a sexual crisis. He felt himself ill equipped
for the task and thought it dangerous. The night before he
consulted Dalbiez, the young man had the following dream
which he thought quite unrelated to the problem:

Dream: I was dealing with a religious who seemed to me to be
dressed in a brown fustian habit like that of the Capuchins. I found

that I had entered into some kind of engagement with him to look after lepers. I think this obligation distressed me, but believed I could not get out of it.

Associations: (a monk) A Capuchin I once knew, Fr. Anselm. Idea of austerity. A priest who once directed me in all my difficulties, the Abbé Etienne. (Bind myself) I have accepted an attitude of intimate friendship toward a woman who is passing through a moral crisis. (Lepers) Rémy de Gourmont, who was supposed to be one. One of this writer's novels, *Un coeur virginal.*

Dalbiez' interpretation: The dream can be regarded "either as a wish to hand over his role of moral adviser to someone else, or as the intention of adopting a more reserved, less sentimental attitude towards the lady in question. The second interpretation seemed to him more plausible."

Additional detail: (Letter written to Dalbiez by the dreamer.)
I am struck by another no less significant detail. Leprosy is a disease which infects those who tend it. The symbolism is clear enough. I wonder why it did not occur to you? But now the moral implication of my dream becomes strangely involved! Now it seems much rather to symbolize the thought that, through fidelity to an undertaking approved by a man in holy orders, I am going to tend a disease which I have every chance of contracting myself. An event now comes to my mind which might clearly have inspired this thought: the Abbé Pierre declaring that I was performing for Louise an indispensable service which no one could perform in my stead. It is even true that later the thought occurred to me: How can he be unaware of the danger which such a position holds for me? Here, I think, is the very root of my dreams laid bare. Note that I have discovered the thought symbolized more or less indisputably. *Now is this dream based upon fear, or desire, or the need of excuse?* I don't think we have any grounds for deciding between these hypotheses.
P.S. I see I have left out a detail. The first image which my dream religious evoked in me (even before that of Fr. Anselm, I think) had been that of the monk in "Thaïs," as I had seen it played in the theater at Toulon. The role of this character, who wants to save the sinner Thaïs and succumbs to her charms, presents a very clear analogy with the risk I am running. This seems so fundamental (note that the image of the actor is the only one that physically resembles the religious in my dream: dressed in fustian like him, and also, I think, tall like him—but as regards this last point I am not sure I am not

rendering the dream image more precisely than it was) that one might be tempted to seek the true source of the dream in this direction. Might there not have taken place a sort of fusion between the image of the monk in "Thais" and the thought of the Abbé Pierre binding me to play the part of a healer? (2, Vol. II, pp. 128–30. Italics mine).

In a dream interpretation in which the dream is considered as wish fulfilment, it is indeed difficult to answer the dreamer's question and to decide between two or three possible hypotheses. Just what wish is it that is fulfilled here? The wish to get out of a difficult situation, the wish to have the sanction of his conscience (and outward authority) to carry on? Or the wish to be more reserved, more monklike? Of course, there is still another possibility which Dalbiez does not mention, namely, that the dreamer really wants to go on from confidences to intimacies and uses his obligation as an excuse. The decision between those alternatives is necessarily arbitrary and has to be based upon the analyst's knowledge of the dreamer, is therefore extrinsic to the dream.

If, however, we treat the dream as an integral whole in which the meaning of the dream is expressed by the story itself, then the interpretation will reveal itself just as soon as we have ascertained the meaning of each image for the dreamer: We start, then, with a summary of:

The dream story: The dreamer entered into an obligation to look after lepers together with a monk.

Next, we investigate the significance of the dream figures:

The monk: An austere figure whose office it is to direct people who are in difficulties.
Even a man like that has (in "Thais") succumbed to the charms of the sinner he wants to help.

Lepers: Afflicted with a disease which infects those who tend them.
Even a leper can possess "un coeur virginal."
It may become a duty to tend them.

The dreamer: He is associated with a monk in this work, yet he is no monk, has neither a monk's discipline nor his grace of state.

Interpretation: The dreamer has undertaken to help someone who is in grave difficulties, though innocent at heart. His task holds such dangers that even one who is completely dedicated and disciplined has succumbed to it.

Interpreted integrally, the dream states the dreamer's life situation fully and concisely. Full weight is given to the physical resemblance of the dream figure of the monk and the monk in "Thais" which the dreamer himself recognizes as the central feature of his dream. Once the story of the dream is applied to the dreamer's life situation, there is no room for alternative interpretations; the dream story itself provides a precise diagnosis. It remains for the dreamer to draw the inference that to go on with such a task under the circumstances stated by the dream is foolhardiness, and to refuse to be drawn into it any farther.

Often a dream occurring in the beginning of therapy will not only state the dreamer's problem but will foreshadow some of his attitudes that will become overt later during treatment. A case from my own records will serve as an example: An artist consulted me about his personal difficulties because they began to stultify his artistic activity. He was happily married but he had for years had intimate relationships with various girl friends. At this point, his latest girl friend was a very attractive and accomplished professional woman and he decided that this relationship ought to be stabilized. He could give up neither his wife nor the other woman because he considered they were both necessary to him. So he had worked out a "new design for living" according to which the two women would share him and in this way they would all live happily ever after. His wife, however, categorically objected and threatened to leave him. He considered her attitude irrational and complained that he had always found her reasonable before.

In the first week I was working with him, he had a waking dream in which he saw himself leading a handsome tigress on a leash, and giving the leash to a beautiful Japanese girl. She had been a statue on a pedestal but had stepped down to him when he gave her his hand. After a while he wanted to leave both of them behind in the cave where he had found them, but neither the lady nor the tigress wanted to be left. So he asked them to get into his canoe and paddled down a subterranean stream with them, the tigress at his feet, the Japanese girl in the bow facing him. Eventually the stream brought them out into broad daylight, and he found himself paddling his canoe down a peaceful stream through a sunlit familiar landscape, with cows grazing, farmers working, crickets chirping—and he with a tigress and a Japanese girl! The humor of the situation struck him and he broke into laughter.

In this case we again have a perfect dramatization of the dreamer's life situation. The Japanese girl meant for him somebody serene and beautiful but remote—a woman who could be guide, philosopher, and friend: and that was exactly what his wife was for him. She had come alive when he married her (asked for her hand) but had always remained friend rather than mate. The girl friend provided the animal attraction his wife did not possess (and, incidentally, the girl complained bitterly that he treated her as a plaything rather than a friend). The dream sums up the situation so accurately that it seems almost incredible that the dreamer could not see it equally well in his waking life. In the dream, his "new design for living" is impossible, not because of opposition from any of the dramatis personae, but because of its inherent incongruity. In reality, the artist insisted if only his wife would be reasonable, the problem would be solved. In parenthesis it may be mentioned that it took him several months—about fifteen sessions—really to accept the diagnosis the dream had presented to him during the first week.

In fact, it was not until a whole series of sleeping dreams had illustrated his course of action and the inevitable consequences in the most unflattering way that he began to doubt the wisdom of his "rational" design. In those later dreams, he was flying in an airplane just above the heads of people until something went wrong with the motor. He jumped in time and landed in a garbage can. Another time, he dreamed he was flying a plane with his girl friend as passenger when the motor went dead and his girl friend disappeared. He made a parachute jump only to discover that his parachute was a huge circus umbrella full of holes, which landed him safely but ignominiously in a large mud puddle, amid laughter and jeers from the crowd. The dreams say, almost in so many words, that he believes that his new design for living will allow him to move above the heads of the common crowd; but his vehicle will not carry him. His attempt is bound to come to grief and he will end by making a fool of himself.

These dreams could have been analyzed also by the method of free association, and there is no doubt that they would have revealed many connections between the dream images and his emotional and sexual history. From my later work with him in which many forgotten memories were recovered spontaneously as soon as his attitudes changed (without the use of free association), it is fairly safe to guess that free associations would have connected the Japanese girl with memories not only of his wife but of a beloved older sister who forced him to a complete and painful sexual renunciation when he was a boy. That this experience was connected with the fact that his wife lacked any particular sexual attraction for him can hardly be doubted. Nor can it be doubted that as a result of these early experiences, sex and friendship were fundamentally incompatible for him. In a similar way, memory connections could have been traced from the tigress, the canoe, the landscape—but none of these connections would have thrown any light on his situation here and now. If such exploration had been undertaken, the story of the dreams themselves, giving such a concise and convincing illustration of his life situation, would have been lost sight of completely.

The two types of dream interpretation could be compared to two different attempts to explain the White House to a visitor from Mars. One way might be to use flashbacks to show scenes of bricklayers and masons putting stone upon stone, their petty quarrels, their casual chat during rest periods. We could show quarries which supplied the building materials, and the trucks and trains that hauled it—and no doubt our visitor would have an entertaining and instructive day. But would he know very much more about the building itself than he did before? Alternatively, we could show him the plan of the building, explain what it was designed for, and how it served its function. Surely, at the end of the day our visitor would know something about the building and its purpose, even though he might not know its detailed history.

From the scientific point of view it must be said that Freudian dream interpretation rests upon a doubtful theoretical foundation which needs a host of auxiliary hypotheses to maintain itself. The alternative suggested here has at least the advantage of economy of hypotheses : the dream can be explained as a product of creative imagination, freed from its daytime rational restraints. These restraints occur because imagination ordinarily is put into the service of planning for action. As soon as we have to formulate a plan of action, imagination is used to picture the action as well as its consequences—and our liking for one alternative and dislike of another will distort the picture. Only where the necessity for action in the real world is excluded, as in storytelling, doll play, and other forms of imaginative expression which have been utilized for projective tests, will imagination be able to work without interference. When it works freely, it always illustrates problems with which the person is preoccupied, and illustrates them accurately.

If the dream is a pictorial representation of the dreamer's life situation, the various kinds of dream can be categorized with remarkable ease. The wish fulfilment dreams of children and hungry explorers come about because of their intense and pleasurable preoccupation with the object of their desire, which the dream pictures for them. The frustration dream indicates a life situation that really is frustrating and that can be discovered by investigating the significance of the dream figures for the dreamer. Anxiety dreams are produced when the dreamer is in some danger or difficulty which he may or may not acknowledge in waking life. When this danger continues because the dreamer persistently refuses to deal with it, the anxiety dream becomes repetitive.

So-called "big" dreams occur when the dreamer is beginning to face the question of the meaning of his life, his relation to God, and his eternal destiny. This explanation also holds for the examples of artistic and scientific inspiration we have discussed previously (pp. 401–403). Kekulé, preoccupied during his waking hours with atomic structure, had his imagination illustrate it for him when his attention was relaxed. The illustration was accurate, undisturbed by the false leads which he had followed in his deliberate reasoning.

Such an explanation is so obvious that it is almost platitudinous, yet it needs to be said because it is an alternative to Freud's theory of dreams as wish fulfilment or Jung's explanation that the dream is a compensation or a complement to waking life. The dream can be compensation at times, just as it can be wish fulfilment; but if it is a compensation, if the dream does picture features of the life situation which are utterly at variance with the waking judgment of the dreamer, it is an indication that he must have departed rather radically from an objective estimate of his problem. There are other dreams dreamed by other dreamers which are so transparent that no interpretation is needed and the dreamer immediately and amusedly recognizes them as an illustration of his problem which at the same time contains the solution. There is, for instance, the dream of an older professional man who was refused by a religious order he wanted to enter: He dreamed that he tried to join the army as a buck private after he had been refused in his professional capacity. After standing in line for a long time at the recruiting center, he finally decided (still in the dream) that he could help his country as well by serving as a civilian consultant.

Psychoanalysis as a Method for Personality Integration

And now we can come back to the second aim of our discussion and can ask whether psychoanalysis with its method of free association is the best method of personality integration.

We have seen that free association cannot uncover the *present* significance of dream images, nor can it reveal to the patient the present pattern of his life. What it can do (and that is all it can do) is to trace back the origin of his present emotional attitudes to their roots and ramifications in the past. Reductive analysis can isolate the raw emotions but cannot synthesize them. Hence interpretation, and with it resynthesis of the personality, must be extrinsic to the method of investigation. Since it is extrinsic, it must follow in substance Freud's theoretical scheme, for no other scheme has been made available. If the dream fulfills a wish, then the wish must be identified. According to Freud, it will be an id impulse, though recently some psychoanalysts have contended that there could be repressed superego impulses as well. At any rate, the wish is identified on extrinsic grounds, recognized as infantile because traceable to its infantile roots. Thus insight is achieved and a change of attitude and behavior can follow. This sequence holds not only for dream analysis but for analysis of all material obtained by free association.

I am not concerned here with other features of psychoanalytic therapy, such as transference and its effects on the patient. My only concern is to show that psychoanalytic interpretation is necessarily extrinsic to the method and will depend on the theoretical orientation of the analyst. Personality synthesis has to be achieved according to the analyst's concept of the normal man, his existential situation, and his destiny. A Freudian who has taken over not only the master's method but his philosophy will have a model of man in mind which calls for a compromise between libidinal drives and the demands of society—no more than that. According to this model, he will interpret and aid in reconstruction. A Christian analyst, on the other hand, will picture man as a child of God, redeemed and living the life of grace. What one will consider an escape into infantilism, the other will see as a necessary religious activity. The only instance in which the analyst's interpretation and resynthesis will not be questioned by the patient is the case in which patient and analyst share the same philosophical convictions. In every other case, the patient will rightly feel that the analyst uses his superior psychological skill to persuade where only reason can convince.

Moreover, even in the most favorable case we are permitted to question whether the method of free association and extrinsic interpretation is really the best method to use in personality reconstruction. In Freud's time, it was an enormous advance to insist that man is not an aggregate of mental elements different in every moment of experience, but is the dynamic product of isolable traumatic experiences in the past; but today the one view seems as atomistic as the other.

It is a laudable undertaking to free the memory function of an individual from interference, as is done in psychoanalysis. But if it were possible to free other functions which are more directly concerned with the adjustment of the human being and his perfection, would it not be preferable to use these for personality reconstruction? One of these functions is reasoning— and it seems that nondirective counseling is the technique which specifically frees man's judgment so it can function without undue influence from his prejudices, desires, and appetites. But it is not my purpose here to discuss this technique.

Another one of these functions is creative imagination. If imagination can be freed from the direction our desires impose upon it, it will picture our life situation as it is, objectively and accurately. Such freeing of creative imagination occurs in the dream and also in "free fantasy," a technique of inducing a waking dream developed by Jung. Integral interpretation of such dreams will supply a blueprint of the dreamer's problems upon which he later can act. His action or his failure to act will again be pictured in its proper setting by subsequent (night or waking) dreams. In this way, it is possible to see a personality unfolding according to its own laws before our very eyes.

There has never been a single case in my experience where this process of inner growth did not at some time or other confront the person with his God. At that point his dreams become profoundly moving and he feels them to be of extraordinary significance. Since he is the author of his dreams, and the dream story contains its own interpretation which he himself discovers, he cannot reasonably complain that he is given an arbitrary interpretation and persuaded against his better knowledge. Furthermore, every new dream insight becomes immediately available for personality reconstruction. As he sees himself and his situation ever more clearly, he will gradually orient himself more and more toward his true goal and his self-ideal will become more and more his self-ideal as it ought to be.

COMMENT

This chapter as well as the following two (Chapters 15 and 16) discuss various methods of psychotherapy. Chapter 17 will attempt a general commentary on these methods as they would fit into a general theory of therapy.

REFERENCES

1. ALLERS, RUDOLF. 1940. *The successful error.* New York: Sheed & Ward, Inc.
2. DALBIEZ, ROLAND. 1941. *Psychoanalytical method and the doctrine of Freud.* 2 Vols. New York: Longmans, Green & Co.
3. DEUTSCH, HELENE. 1944. *The psychology of women.* 2 Vols. New York: Grune & Stratton, Inc.
4. FREUD, SIGMUND. 1915. *The interpretaion of dreams.* (Tr.) A. A. BRILL. London and New York: The Macmillan Company.
5. FRINK, H. W. 1918. *Morbid fears and compulsions. Their psychology and psychoanalytic treatment.* Introduction by JAMES J. PUTNAM. New York: Moffat, Yard & Co.
6. JUNG, C. G. 1934. *Wirklichkeit der Seele.* Zürich: Rascher et Cie.
7. KRETSCHMER, T. M. P. 1934. *A textbook of medical psychology.* (Tr.) E. B. STRAUSS. New York: Oxford University Press.
8. KUBIE, LAWRENCE S. 1950. *Practical and theoretical aspects of psychoanalysis.* New York: International Universities Press.
9. PFISTER, OSKAR. 1917. *The psychoanalytic method.* (Tr.) CHAS. R. PAYNE. London: Routledge & Kegan Paul, Ltd.
10. SCHOENBERG, ARNOLD. 1947. The musician. In: *The works of the mind.* (Ed.) ROBERT B. HEYWOOD. Chicago: University of Chicago Press.

Chapter 15

COUNSELING AS THERAPY AND SELF-INTEGRATION *

By Charles A. Curran

Good counseling is important to all human relations because its purpose is to increase a person's self-understanding and reasonable self-control. The final measure of good counseling is the degree to which it produces reasonable and successful daily action and, as a result, makes a person happier, more at peace with himself, and more able to grow in virtuous living. To accomplish this, the counselor's role must be precisely structured and defined. *Counseling is, therefore, a definite relationship where, through the counselor's sensitive understanding and skillful responses, a person objectively surveys the past and present factors which enter into his personal confusions and conflicts, while at the same time reorganizing his emotional reactions so that he not only chooses better ways to reach his reasonable goals but has sufficient confidence, courage, and moderation to act on these choices.*

A child or adult may know in principle what he ought to do. Yet he may be so overwhelmed and confused by the flood of conflicting urges, feelings, and goals in his own surroundings and immediate day-by-day activities that he cannot see his way clearly to take the right path to the things he knows he should do. Often, he chooses wrongly on the emotional impulse of the moment. Because of this, he needs the aid of a process by which, with God's help, he can integrate his uncontrolled instincts and

* The material of this chapter includes summarized excerpts from the author's recent book, *Counseling in Catholic Life and Education,* published by The Macmillan Company, New York, 1952, and is used by permission of the publishers.

emotions so that they follow the insights of his reason. In this way he can formulate and carry out more consistently those reasonable daily actions that make a man of principle. In proportion, therefore, as a person can, with the aid of grace, control and direct his emotions by his reason and will, his actions will be in conformity with natural and supernatural laws.

Counseling, then, can be an important factor in helping both children and adults to grow in reasonable understanding and responsible choices in their daily living and in the integration and co-ordination of their emotions so that they carry out these choices in their major life activities. This, in turn, will result in happier and more virtuous lives.

Recent research in counseling has resulted in a much more detailed analysis of the counseling process than was previously possible. The careful study of the contents of counseling interviews has been found to be one of the most valuable means of understanding the factors which enter into personal difficulties and of improving counseling skill. From this research on counseling which has been done particularly during the war years, there is now available a mass of recorded counseling interviews. These word-for-word records afford us an opportunity to enter into the actual interview with an accuracy which was not possible heretofore. Previously, we had to depend on the counselor's memory or, at best, on the degree of accuracy of the counselor's notes.

This detailed interview material is primarily important for research. For successful counseling, the skilled counselor does not necessarily need notes or any other record of the interviews, since the effectiveness of counseling is determined mainly by the changes which take place in the person. But since such research material is available to us, it will aid us to get a better grasp of the factors which enter into personal needs.

Since success is the final measure of counseling skill, we do not wish to imply the rejection of any methods that are effective in helping people with personal problems. Nor do we intend in any way to suggest that we have said the final word on counseling. Much more research and study are needed on all the questions treated here. Particular techniques are recommended because they have been verified in the experience and research of many counselors and because they appear to us in accord with the Thomistic concepts of counsel and prudence. Since Thomistic psychology is founded on the close observation of human action, research on counseling can provide added confirmation and can validly be integrated into the Thomistic synthesis.

Our plan is to present the data which the interviews themselves reveal and to reason about these data. If, as often happens, St. Thomas has come to similar conclusions from his own observations, so much the better, since he and others have already related many of these psychological conclusions to the broader fields of philosophy and theology. Moreover, many of these concepts, such as the dignity of man and the necessity of personal freedom and responsibility, are at the heart of our Western civilization. Especially significant for us in the modern contribution, however, are the skill of counseling and the refinement of technique which recent advances in psychology have uncovered for us, particularly through the study of recorded interviews. This in itself is a field so significant and so filled with promise as to challenge and stimulate the ingenuity of any investigator.

Finally, counseling and the virtue of counsel are part of the whole field of virtue, particularly of the moral virtues. We have, therefore, attempted to show how psychological adjustment is ultimately measured by the degree to which such adjustment reaches reality and produces that humility which in St. Thomas is "the reasonable pursuit of one's own excellence." This, then, and prudent living will, with God's grace, be the final measure of good counseling.

Counsel and Personal Difficulties

Personal difficulties usually arise from two sources: either we lack sufficient knowledge to find a solution, or, knowing the general direction of the solution, we still somehow are not taking the particular steps to reach our basic life goals. Consequently, there is a general and a particular aspect to every personal difficulty. We require norms and principles to point us in the general direction of our ultimate goals, and we must have the capacity and possibility to keep moving in the direction of these goals in our day-by-day activities.

We are all seeking permanent happiness. We want peace, certitude, security, and order. Yet, we live in the midst of constant change which can leave us restless, uncertain, insecure, and disordered. We need to know in what ultimate direction to guide ourselves if we are to escape final disillusionment. All our actions must, therefore, be centered on the permanent values of truth and reality which Divine Revelation and human reason have given us. This is the foundation upon which we can stand as we survey the moving stream of changing events. (See diagram.)

On the wide end of the triangle opening out into universal principles which are permanent and certain is the area of *general education*. Founded on theology and philosophy, this broad area also includes the field of the particular sciences as they are related to laws and principles, and the various arts which form the cultural, social, and material world in which we live. Without the foundation of a valid general education, a person's life will not be oriented to ultimate reality. Particular choices based on special sciences or expediency may appear to work for a time. If life is looked at as a whole, however, and a man's purpose is seen in its entirety, then without adequate basis in ultimate principles of living, particular choices must eventually prove shortsighted and ephemeral.

As we move down the triangle, we consider the more immediate application of knowledge to each person according to his particular needs. While general education ordinarily applies to everyone, the second area usually applies to particular groups. Since we live in a contingent world, we must be able in a limited way to find some security and achievement in the framework of the particular state of life, aptitudes, skills, and vocation which God has given us. Consequently, we need also a détailed kind of knowledge and understanding of our own abilities and capacities, as well as of the responsibilities, privileges, and obligations of the different temporary or permanent situations in which we find ourselves. This kind of knowledge is more personal. Information on marriage, for example, has little meaning for children,

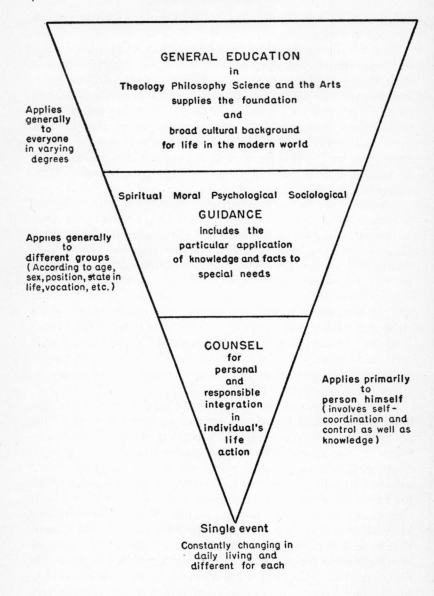

Applies
generally
to
everyone
in varying
degrees

GENERAL EDUCATION
in
Theology Philosophy Science and the Arts
supplies the foundation
and
broad cultural background
for life in the modern world

Appnes generally
to
different groups
(According to age,
sex, position, state in
life, vocation, etc.)

Spiritual Moral Psychological Sociological
GUIDANCE
includes the
particular application
of knowledge and facts to
special needs

COUNSEL
for
personal
and
responsible
integration
in
individual's
life
action

Applies primarily
to
person himself
(involves self-
coordination and
control as well as
knowledge)

Single event
Constantly changing in
daily living and
different for each

but grows increasingly important as the young adult approaches marriage. Many intense personal problems can arise in courtship and marriage because of the lack of this special knowledge which at other periods in life might be comparatively unimportant. In some way, a more complete understanding of one's own psychological aptitudes and vocational abilities might help a person to know better what particular life achievements he could reasonably seek. To use another example, application of general moral principles to the question of labor and management would enable one man to take a more intelligent and active part in his labor union, and another to have a better grasp of the responsibilities and rights of management. Moreover, for souls specially advanced in the spiritual life, more detailed and personal spiritual information and guidance are usually necessary. These and similar ways of understanding are more applicable to immediate life problems than the knowledge acquired from general religious, scientific, and cultural education and training. Consequently, we might call this the field of spiritual, moral, and psychological *guidance,* to distinguish it from the more general area of education in theology, philosophy, and the other sciences and arts.

In our daily lives there is still the final problem of the choice of ways to fulfill the tasks to which education and guidance direct us. This means coping with and controlling the personal disorder within us as our particular instincts and emotional impulses tend to reach for satisfactions not in conformity with the reasonable needs of our whole person, the rights of others, and the demands of reality. Daily living involves particular events which are unique for each individual and are always changing. Here we are at the heart of the human personality where each individual person acquires, in a greater or less degree, the integration necessary to fulfill all the needs, obligations, and tasks of his life. The individual on his own personal responsibility must be able to carry out the principles and practical information he has received. He must have acquired individual integration both in his ability to cope with the disorder within himself, the unreasonable impulses of his emotions and instincts, and the disorder of the world—in other personalities and in reality itself.

Knowledge must become activated in each individual's life as he copes with the single events in his daily actions. This is the function of *counsel,* as a part of each man's prudential judgment and action. We have put this at the point of the triangle.

Consequently, when St. Thomas discusses the various virtues necessary for a good and happy life, he includes both the ultimate and the immediate aspects of human action. To be normally happy and virtuous, according to St. Thomas, we must not only know the reasonable goal of any particular action as it relates to the ultimate goal of our life, but our emotional and instinctive tendencies must be pointed in the direction of this goal, and we must choose from the various necessary intermediate actions those which actually lead us to the goal. In the Thomistic synthesis, the theological virtues of faith, hope, and charity give us the capacity to know and love God. The intellectual virtues of wisdom, knowledge, and understanding give the broad direction in principle to guide us to the right goals. But these virtues of themselves will not give us happiness and a good life. We must constantly take responsible, self-reliant action in the changing material world. Consequently, we also must develop virtues of *action*: prudence, and the virtues of fortitude, temperance, and justice.

While the other intellectual virtues give us norms, they remain speculative and abstract. Prudence, however, is the understanding of the immediate steps in our daily life to reach any desired goal. Fortitude is the courage to be persevering and patient in situations where our path towards a particularly difficult goal meets with discouragement and frustrations. In things comparatively easy, temperance is the ability to restrain ourselves when our appetites tend to unreasonable excess. Finally, justice is the power which safeguards the right of our neighbor against our own exaggerated self-interest and protects us against the same abuse from our neighbor and the community.

We need both to know the right way to live and to grow in the ability to understand and control our highly complex instinctive and emotional reactions. Then, in any particular choice, we need to survey all the immediate personal factors in our own past and present life so that we do all the minute acts which lead to the particular things we seek. Failure in even one small act can sometimes throw us off the path. In this sense, good action is similar to any other good work. An artist or craftsman must not only know what he wants but have instruments at hand and take the right steps to get it done. Knowledge of an art or craft will not of itself produce the completed work. So, in the work of virtue, a man acts with his whole person, not simply with his intellect. In addition to right understanding, he needs the proper instrumentation of his emotions and instincts tending him towards the good work rather than making him hostile and resistant to it. At the same time, he needs the careful survey of all possible means at hand so that he takes the right steps to accomplish it.

Many difficulties of present-day living arise not so much because men do not know what they should do as because they are so disturbed emotionally they fail to do it. Their problems are in the realm of *how* rather than *what*. Mankind has always recognized that to know may be easier than to do, as Shakespeare's famous quotation indicates: "If to do were as easy as to know what were good to do, chapels had been churches and poor men's cottages princes' palaces." Catholic people, particularly those educated in Catholic schools and colleges, are often well informed. They are supplied not only with general information, but also with detailed knowledge of the rights, privileges, and responsibilities of different states in life. Special emphasis, for example, has been placed on the question of labor and industry and, more recently, on matters of marriage and the family. In this way, many people know what to do. But in various contingencies, in the particular, unique, and personal events of their own lives, they may fail to carry out what they know. With all the information given them, they can be living in a state of unhappiness, guilt, and personal confusion because they lack virtue to act on what they know.

Personal problems, then, while they may involve information and knowledge, are perhaps more often due to confusion about the right steps to take. This is usually accompanied by discouragement and a tendency to compensate by immoderate and unreasonable satisfaction in some other way. A man may drink

excessively because he is not succeeding in his work or getting
along with his wife. He knows his drinking is wrong and he has
seen its sad consequences, but he does not see how to overcome
his failure at work or at home. He relieves the pain of his failure
by alcohol. A young woman may rush into marriage with an
unsuitable partner, not because she could not recognize her
partner's inadequacies, but because of her inability to find in her
own family the love she needs. Problems of this sort call not so
much for information as understanding. We cannot help these
people simply by giving them more knowledge. They need,
rather, a way to coordinate and control their disordered emotions and, at the same time, to make more prudent choices in
their immediate daily actions.

Counsel and Prudence

A man's emotions are not under his control in the swift sure
way he moves his hand or foot. While they participate in reason
because it belongs to their nature to obey reason, yet, continues
St. Thomas, "they do not obey reason instantly. On the contrary they have their own proper movements by which, at times,
they go against reason." Our emotions must be managed, then,
with methods similar to those "by which free men are ruled
who have in some respects a will of their own." I, II, Q. 56, a. 4
(1, vol. 2, p. 425).

Personal difficulties usually come from the disorder of our
emotions at war and in conflict with our reason. Either we
guide our emotions or we are guided by them. The details of
life are apt at times to overwhelm us and leave us confused and
disorganized. We need to reorganize ourselves. The core of
this self-organization is prudence. But because of the individual
character of each of our actions, prudence as such cannot be
taught. Every action and event is different for each of us. We
must face that action on our own responsibility. Prudence is, as
St. Thomas points out, a very personal virtue. It consists in
(1) a survey of the best means and methods to reach our goals,
(2) a choice of the means, and (3) action on the means.

The first step in prudence, the survey process, which St. Thomas calls *counsel,* is most important because of the almost infinite variety of possible conditions, circumstances, situations, and personalities that can in one way or another affect our choice of various methods and means.

"Choice," says St. Thomas, "follows the judgment of the reason in matters of action. Now there is much uncertainty in matters of action, because actions are concerned with contingent singulars which, by reason of their variability, are uncertain. Now in things doubtful and uncertain, the reason does not pronounce judgment without previous inquiry. Therefore the reason must of necessity institute an inquiry before deciding on what is to be chosen; and this inquiry is called counsel." I, II, Q. 14, a. 1 (1, vol. 2, p. 286). This uncertainty of judgment, from the very nature of the world of contingent singulars in which we live, is one of the reasons from which we can conclude to man's basic freedom, since "particular operations are contingent, and therefore in such matters the judgment of reason may follow opposite courses, and is not determinate to one. And in that man is rational it is necessary that he have free choice." I, Q. 83, a. 1 (1, vol. 1, p. 787).

In discussing counsel St. Thomas points out that it involves two types of goal-seeking. In one, the goal is not impeded. Here the person uses the survey evaluation of counsel to choose means which will lead him to what he wants. Since there are so many means among which it is possible to choose, some of them will not bring him to the desired object or achievement. In the other type of goal-seeking, the path is blocked by obstacles which must be overcome, avoided, or circumvented. While difficulties may arise in the first situation, especially when the path to the goal is made complex by including a number of involved stages, it is primarily in the second obstacle type where personal conflicts most commonly occur.

If, over a period of time, we find that we are not reaching a solution to our problems, we can grow increasingly discouraged and gradually lose self-confidence and hope. We may realize that we are compensating by going to excess in other ways. In addition to the courage and the ability necessary to reorganize ourselves and set out again for our real goals, we must moderate these excesses. Popular psychology has made us aware of many of these compensation mechanisms which go all the way from exaggerated forms of self-justification and rationalizations down to numerous kinds of inferiority complexes. In this state of conflict we generally need help. While we may be able to rethink a problem alone and counsel ourselves, it is usually a longer process with greater disorder and personal suffering than if we had the aid of a skilled counselor. It is possible to reach such a state that each attempt makes us more confused. By this time we may even have lost sight of what we are seeking.

When we are failing, we need to resurvey the past and the present to discover other steps to our goal. For this stage of counsel, we often need another person to aid us in objectifying and clarifying our conflicts. Such objective self-clarification we call *counseling.*

Counseling and the Art of Living

Evaluation in Action. From this point of view, a good counseling process can also be said to improve a person's attainments in the art of living, for

. . . Prudence stands in the same relation to such human actions, consisting in the use of powers and habits, as art does to external makings; since each is the perfect reason about the things with which it is concerned. I, II, Q. 57, a. 4 (1, vol. 2, p. 435).

To perform any work of art well it takes more than abstract knowledge; it takes a complex process of organized activity that can only be learned by repeatedly performing that particular art and, at the same time, carefully evaluating one's successes or errors in each action. More knowledge of the particular art alone will not do this. The immediate evaluation in action is essential. Without such evaluation, one may never improve performance but continue at the same level.

If we apply these demands of a particular art to the whole field of living well, it helps us understand how any improvement of one's performance in the art of living requires, in addition to knowledge, the peculiar virtues which center around prudence. St. Thomas quotes St. Augustine on this:

Augustine usually applies the term *art* to any form of right reason; in which sense art includes prudence which is the right reason about things to be done. . . . Accordingly, when he says that *virtue is the art of right conduct,* this applies to prudence essentially; but to the other virtues, by participation, in so far as they are directed by prudence. I, II, Q. 58, a. 2, ad 1 (1, vol. 2, p. 443).

Stages of Practical Learning. If by way of illustration we were to analyze the process a young girl might undergo in learning the art of cooking, it might be said to involve four stages. First, the girl would have to study and memorize the recipes if she wants both to understand the purpose of the various combinations of foods and to have norms to guide her in the use of different ingredients and portions. Then, in the second stage, the girl might watch her mother cook, observing how her mother carried out in practice the things she saw in the recipe book. In the third stage, she might cook under her mother's direction, doing what she was told. Even here, although she may have produced an appetizing meal, she would not as yet have acquired the art of cooking. The actual art was in her mother who directed her, and not in the girl herself, since the girl's main function was to be passively acquiescent to what she was told to do. She will be a good cook herself only after she has undergone a rather long series of experiences in which she takes the direct responsibility for each judgment and action that goes into the meal. At the same time she will have to evaluate each result to make sure she continues to do the things that produce success while she corrects the causes of particular failures. Gradually, from this experience and evaluation, she will acquire the combined qualities and abilities that make up the complete process of the culinary art. As she does, evaluation and correction will become less necessary except perhaps when she wishes to learn a new recipe.

So, in a similar way, the art of living well and virtuously cannot be learned simply by studying the rules of moral science and memorizing and understanding them, although this may be an important first stage. Nor is it sufficient either merely to observe another's acting out these moral principles or even to act them out one's self under immediate direction from someone else. For while the action itself may be prudent—as the young girl may cook a good meal under her mother's direction—yet the prudence is in the one directing. For virtue to complete itself in a good life, it must, like the final stage of a particular art, proceed by way of responsible action and repeated experience. It is, therefore, often a slow growth in the ability to coordinate impulses and urges around the reasonable determination of what we should do. In this sense, then, we can see how this final stage of the art of living agrees with Rank's contention that the important thing in counseling is not the theory or the interpretation of the counselor but the experience a person undergoes in his own process of willing and feeling. Assuming that counseling can, as we have seen, objectify and clarify these feelings so that they can be more readily controlled and understood by the person's growing self-insight, we see how counseling and the art of virtuous living go together.

Exploring Childhood Influences

As people talk about themselves in an interview, their self-examination usually carries them into the past. Many personal conflicts which show themselves in later life seem rooted in a person's early experiences, particularly those of childhood. At the time these conflicts take place, the child is at least partially aware of them. As the years go by, the actual situations are often forgotten but the disturbing and confusing attitudes they engendered still remain. Because these attitudes do not meet the demands of a person's present life, they generate insecurities and fears. Such attitudes can produce increased conflict through the years. The home, the school, and other early influences are sources of stability and strength, provided the values they represent are permanently effective. When any of these values are unsound, it causes disturbance. As the child grows into adult life, he must face reality and assume responsibilities. Somewhere in a person's process of development, the needs for responsible self-determined decisions assert themselves. Then these conflicting values begin to take their toll and produce the kind of unhappiness that is characteristic of the opening interview in counseling.

Examining Conflicting Emotions

Those with personal problems not only have to deal with the confusing reactions carried over from the past. They are unable here and now to choose the right means for achieving their goals. Significant achievements usually involve a complex series of steps, extending over a long period of time. The person coming for counseling generally feels that he is not reaching or moving towards his desired goals because somehow he is not taking the right steps. As a result, he is caught between his desires to reach and possess various things he wants and the frustrations and disappointments which result when these desires are not realized.

Behind each of these frustrating and conflicting emotions is the strong urge towards reasonable, independent achievement. This urge increases as a person passes from infancy to adult life. In the small child, dependency, fear, insecurity, and frustration are obvious and understandable. The world is beyond him. It is a fearful unknown where he is a dwarf in the midst of giants. He must seek security in the loving acceptance and guidance of others, especially his parents. But at the same time, implanted in each child is a resistance to complete dependency and attachment. He wants some independent achievement. Even the very young child, as he learns to walk and talk, gets extreme delight in demonstrating what he can do. He has conquered two basic functional tasks which, until then, had been frustrations and barriers.

A child's early achievements, such as walking and talking, reveal the intrinsic dynamism in each person. A man needs to assert himself by controlling his impulses and by finding reasonable self-expression in his own actions and in things around him. If he cannot grow in reasonable fulfilment, he will experience conflicts. In proportion as he is unable to solve these conflicts, he becomes increasingly unhappy, fearful, and insecure. It gets harder for him to make the effort necessary to cope with his problems. As a result, people sometimes grow more passive. They may again desire the reassurance and affection which childhood dependency brought them, and so seek these from parents or from new attachments. But they are unhappy, because passive dependency for all its immediate security blocks and stifles their fundamental urge to independent reasonable choice and action.

Acquiring Self-Understanding and Integration

Accompanying these conflicting states of negative and positive emotion, there exists an almost continual state of confusion, as can be demonstrated from many excerpts of counseling interviews. This confusion has more of an intellectual than an emotional connotation. In the beginning of counseling, as the individual talks about the emotional turmoil he feels, he also expresses his inability to understand himself and why he acts as he did. He lacks both self-knowledge and self-integration.

Insight, therefore, involves both an increase in self-understanding and the ability to act on the knowledge one has acquired. In the counseling process, when insights become significant, it is not simply that people acquire new knowledge of themselves and others. Counseling may make them realize their lack of certain information and, as a result, they set out to get it. But this is not the most significant effect of insight. The possession of knowledge does not of itself imply the ability to act on that knowledge. There must also be the practical integration of knowledge in the here and now of each one's life. It is this latter aspect to which the term "insight" is especially applied. As we examine the interviews, we notice that, in this insight stage, the person either takes the knowledge he already had or new knowledge which he has acquired, and filters it through himself, so to speak, so that it becomes an integral part of his whole plan of action. His perceptions are now impregnated with this knowledge. To help the person achieve such active integrative insight is the main function of counseling.

Ideally, a man should be able to hold his reasonable judgments through any series of personal concrete experiences, but it is very difficult to maintain this consistency. As unreasonable actions mount, they produce a state of dissatisfaction, unrest, and unhappiness. A person needs counseling in proportion as he is failing to apply reasonable principles to his individual actions. Insight enables him to judge objectively the particular concrete issues in which he is involved. As the person, through the responses of the counselor, is able to penetrate his emotions and discover the basic issues and values motivating his conduct, he can begin to plan more realistic solutions. The counseling process, therefore, helps a person to be reasonable about concrete issues that were previously emotionally confused. His judgments are now made in relation to principles of conduct which he already knew but somehow was not applying to these individual situations.

Insight, then, includes both impersonal knowledge and the singular concrete event which is highly personal. Insight brings these two together and enables a man to act in a personal issue with the same objective judgment and integration he would have were he judging the conduct of someone else. This gives us a clue as to why the counselor, even though he does not offer advice or information in the counseling interview, is an essential part of the objectifying and impersonalizing process which produces insight. The counselor's responses mirror a person's problems for him and enable him to survey them with the same impersonal perception that he might have of the problems of someone far removed. The counseling interview, then, has some similarity to the slow perusal of one's self in a mirror. A person can slowly change himself as he sees with increasingly less distortion why and how he has been acting. The reasonable judgments he holds up to himself are the models to which he slowly conforms as he sees himself more clearly. This change is not immediate nor easy, but he is stimulated and encouraged as his actions better meet these reasonable norms. He grows more satisfied with what he sees as he surveys himself in the interview. This explains the increase in expressions of satisfaction, hope, and courage, which begin to show themselves. These positive expressions accompany new insights and resultant choices, which more completely fulfill what a person wants to be.

The Skill of the Counselor

The person's feeling that he is accepted and understood by the counselor and, at the same time, that he is going to be helped to work out his own solutions on his own responsibility are two factors which appear to be essential to the process of counseling. Somehow, a person does not generally unfold and think out complex personal problems except in an atmosphere of acceptance. But if this acceptance is such that it makes him dependent on the counselor for solutions and decisions, it will not further his own self-initiated judgments and actions. An important part of the skill of a good counselor, then, is his ability to promote responsible and reasonable evaluation and action by establishing a climate of acceptance and understanding which, at the same time, does not foster dependency.

The major contribution of the counselor, however, consists in his consistently penetrating responses during the flow of the interview. As the person uncovers his feelings or deeper attitudes or gains new self-awareness, the counselor must follow his statements carefully and accurately "reflect" them in his responses. These responses should hold up before a person an objective view of his feelings and attitudes towards himself and others. This enables him slowly to piece these attitudes together and get a more integrated and more profound understanding of himself. As we have seen, this broadening self-perception leads him finally to more positive and more successful life choices.

Since the counselor's role is one of mirroring the attitudes and feelings which here and now are contained in the person's expressions, he functions best when he reflects the person's attitudes most exactly. He should not speak too rapidly. His voice and manner should be calm and sincere. The person will recognize that the counselor is choosing his words carefully but this is not disturbing. If anything, it helps the relationship. In this, a typescript can be misleading, for the responses that appear wooden and flat when read may actually have *sounded* warm and accepting. Such a skill is not easily learned. Good counselor responses have a deceptive simplicity when we see them in an excerpt from a successful interview. Usually we must try such counseling ourselves before we recognize how difficult it is to make consistently clarifying responses that do not block or impede a person's self-investigation.

Conversational Responses

One of the main difficulties for the beginning counselor is the great difference between various counseling responses and the kind of statements he is accustomed to make in his ordinary relations with people. Responses made in everyday conversation fall into a number of categories. When a person states facts and draws a conclusion from these facts, we might agree or disagree with the facts, the conclusion, or both. We might consider the statement untrue because the facts are inaccurate. We might judge it illogical because the conclusion drawn does not follow from the facts. We might continue the reasoning by filling it out with our own ideas. We might disagree and challenge a particular point. This disagreement could be cautious and hesitant or it could be abrupt and even vehement. These different types of responses would be aimed primarily at the *factual* and *intellectual* content of what was said.

Another common type of response is one that mainly intends *to give acceptance*. It may be a noncommittal agreement such as nodding one's head. It might go further and commit a person to the same logical position by saying "I agree with you." With more enthusiasm one might say: "I completely agree with you! That's exactly the way I think and I have always held the same view!" These kinds of responses are not so much concerned with ideas as with conveying a sense of *agreement* with and *approval* of the other person.

Twofold Need. The problem here is that the person speaking has a twofold need. He apparently wants understanding and agreement with his ideas. But often his deepest need is to be accepted by the other person. Unfortunately, any disagreement with ideas may also appear to be personal rejection. Consequently, it is difficult for people to disagree without giving the impression of rejecting each other, and of a lack of sympathy and understanding. This seems to be the main reason why many discussions end in arguments and personal hurt. This subtle transition from discussion to offense seems to hinge on this confusion between intellectual disagreement and personal rejection. For this reason, any statement of intellectual disagreement runs the risk of carrying with it the sting of personal rejection by implying a lack of understanding and appreciation of the other person.

This difference between the intellectual content and the personal need contained in statements is very common and yet it is seldom recognized. Individuals may agree or disagree with one another not because of the truth or falsehood of the ideas expressed but because they are expressed in a tone of acceptance or hostility. If we observe a discussion carefully, we can notice consistent opposition between certain persons on any series of ideas. We may notice, too, that others usually group together. This is often due to their resistance to someone holding the other position or to their feeling of being accepted by the group which represents this opposition. They may actually have little real conviction about the ideas expressed.

Counseling Responses

Agreement Not Always Helpful. In the area of personal difficulties, however, a counselor does not necessarily help people by agreeing with them because they may not agree with themselves. A person's ultimate realistic attitude about himself is not always the one he expresses. If the counselor puts himself behind the attitude first expressed, he crystallizes that attitude. If the other person later wishes to express an opposite view, he cannot do so without feeling that he is now disagreeing with the counselor. This delicate balance between the changing statements of the person coming for help, as he expresses different views of himself and his problems, and the necessity of the counselor's remaining uninvolved, is one of the things that makes the counseling process so difficult. If the counselor takes a definite stand on one view, he may force the person to accept that view and work on it. But the counselor has no way of knowing that this will be the final attitude which the person has towards himself or that it is his deepest and most significant insight. In order to be productive of increasingly new insights and deeper understanding on the part of the one coming for help, the counseling relationship must keep flowing. It cannot fix or freeze the person on any set attitude until he himself has reached that conviction and has proved it to himself by adequate new choices in the world of reality.

Acceptance Responses. The counselor, therefore, must learn to give an indication of *acceptance* and *understanding* of the person's problems, while neither agreeing nor disagreeing with the logic or the intellectual content of the statement. This is no easy matter, and the skill involved is one that can only be learned through concentration and effort.

The simplest forms of this skill are the elemental responses, which give acceptance without any commitment. Such responses are "uh, huh," and/or nodding, as well as slow statements of "ye-e-es-s-s." These responses have a slight tone of a question mark, which keeps the responsibility on the other person and encourages him to speak on. The person can get the feeling that he is "flowing through" the counselor and being accepted by him. Yet there is, at the same time, no crystallizing attitude of agreement and no effort to take over and give the person a solution to his problems.

Another variation of this neutral accepting response is a simple restatement of what the person said in somewhat different words. If it is brief, such an "echoing" response at least gives the person a feeling that he is being listened to and accepted. But if the counselor's responses consistently go no deeper than this mere repetition of the same content, they will eventually be resisted.

A further development of this kind of acceptance is in the form of a question in which the counselor asks the person to explain the problem. The counselor may say: "Would you care to expand that a little more?" or : "It is not just too clear to me. Could you explain it further?" Such questions offer no agreement or disagreement with the position the person has taken, yet they convey an interested concern in the details of his problem.

These types of statements are not difficult. For this reason, they are usually the first thing a person learns about a self-directive counseling skill. But while there is some value in these neutral accepting statements, they are not generally the responses that bring about deep insights. To understand this, we must go a step further in the analysis of types of counselor responses.

Responses to Basic Attitude, or Recognition of Feeling. There is a significant kind of response that is entirely different from these. This has been called responding to feeling, emotional tone, or basic attitude. This is one of the most important counselor responses. There is a difference between the verbal form a person's emotional release may take—for example, the series of incidents he may recite to illustrate how he feels—and the basic emotion or attitude at the heart of this release. The counselor's response must go beneath the verbal form of a person's expression. This is a delicate distinction and one not readily understood. A skilled response involves a sensitivity to the fundamental tone of such a statement. Such a response must reach the attitude or feeling which motivates the actions the person has described. Sometimes the phrase, "you feel . . . ," followed by the underlying emotion, may touch it. This phrase, however, may become a habit and be used so much that it causes irritation. A better response catches the attitude or emotion directly. For example : "you are angry because . . ." or "you are hostile to . . ." may do it.

This skill of responding to basic attitudes is also called the recognition of feeling. This implies that a person's recognition of an emotion in himself through the counselor's response is something different from the feeling itself. To put it another way, *it is one thing for a person to feel and act on a strong emotion, and another to understand the feeling that is motivating his action.* When a person understands even one such emotional motive, he has gained in self-insight.

As various counselor responses uncover these motives, the person becomes better able to understand the different ways in which his emotions are moving him. As we mentioned in our earlier discussion of insight, this aspect of self-knowledge has some similarity to the process of seeing a picture or landscape in an integrated way, or solving a jig-saw puzzle. First, there is a consistent and concentrated examination of each motive and a survey of the forming patterns. Then, gradually, the person sees how one action fits into another to make different patterns. Like solving a puzzle, the first stages are the most difficult. As the general outlines of motive patterns are recognized and understood, it is easier to fit them together.

Integrating Responses. Whenever two or more factors are related together in a statement, the counselor makes an *integrating* response. Here, he not only reflects the feelings expressed but he precisely states whatever factors the person has disclosed which appear to relate these feelings to each other or to more fundamental causes.

The counselor's calm, cautious reflection of the basic motives behind a series of disturbing incidents which a person relates enables him to see himself objectively in action. This revelation is not simply a reproduction of his actions but a penetration into the feelings and attitudes that are behind these actions. The person, lost in the recitation and emotion of the incidents themselves, cannot see this clearly without the counselor's skilled help.[1]

Different Types of Responses Illustrated

To illustrate the difference between these kinds of responses and those that merely stay at the level of factual content, we can consider the following: A woman speaks of difficulties with her in-laws living in the home. She explains these difficulties in detail. She is irritated at the mother-in-law's interference when she has visitors. She recounts how the mother-in-law takes over

[1] This is not a complete treatment of the various responses that occur in counseling but only provides some typical examples. For a more complete discussion see Curran (5), Part III, "The skill of the counselor."

the kitchen and tells her how to cook, how she continually comments that the house needs cleaning, that the wife does not know how to iron clothes, does not dress well, nor prepare her husband's shirts as she should. If we analyze this series of statements, we notice that they all flow from one basic feeling. It is a resentment of the mother-in-law's taking over the wife's role. This is behind the recitation of the incidents. Each incident illustrates the wife's resistance and resentment at the mother-in-law's tendency to absorb what the wife feels is her position.

Agreement. A person might respond to this statement in a number of ways. He might, for example, agree by citing a similar irritation and perhaps give details of some other difficulties he has encountered. If he did this, the discussion might go further into the problems of cooking, ironing, or mothers-in-law. It would, consequently, stay on the same level as it began.

Disagreement. The counselor might disagree and defend the mother-in-law with some excuse, such as: "Well, she is old and you shouldn't pay any attention to her," or "Well, after all, she had the boy before you did and you should be able to put up with and understand those things." Here, too, the response remains on the plane of the incidents recited. In this disagreement, the wife might feel a personal rejection. One could guess that she might likely respond by further insisting on her grievance, especially if she felt it strongly. She might even begin to show some resentment toward the other person for taking the mother-in-law's part. Probably, rather than accepting the response, she would only become more negative because of it.

Noncommittal. A counselor might avoid this by a noncommittal "yes," or by nodding his head, or he might ask: "Would you care to talk a little more about those difficulties?" This would give acceptance but it would not unfold any deeper insight.

Responses to Basic Attitude. A more significant response would reach the core of the feelings at the center of this resentment. It would uncover and hold up to the person the basic attitude which has made these incidents so disturbing to her. The mother-in-law is resented because she takes over the wife's role and is critical of her. The counselor must be alert to catch this feeling as she talks. When she stops, he responds quietly: "You resent your mother-in-law for taking over and being critical of everything you do in the house." Such a response will invariably be accepted. It will often even elicit an enthusiastic "Yes, that's it exactly," or "That's right!" or "That's just the way I feel!" The person's tone here is evidence that she has expressed something significant for herself, that she was helped by the way the counselor understood and responded.

When one person disagrees with another, it seldom produces this feeling. Rather, there is an increased resistance and irritation. The disturbed person generally keeps insisting on his point. Moreover, even in agreement, there is usually no really deep sense of being understood. This difference is fundamental and is a major factor in promoting or impeding the dynamics of counseling. This is a delicate and subtle distinction that is hard for the beginning counselor to catch consistently.

Counselor's Response Does Not Soften a Person's Difficulties. We may wonder why the counselor responds the way he does instead of attempting to soften the person's difficulties or talk him out of them. It has been found that an effective aid in promoting positive growth is the person's realization of the unhappiness of his present situation. If the counselor tries to persuade him that his problems are not so great, the person is apt to feel that the counselor does not understand. This will prevent his revealing any deeper feelings. He may become either hostile or silent. To lessen a person's concentration on the unhappy aspects of his present situation is often to destroy his most effective motivation. It may be necessary for a person to become sharply aware of this unhappiness to make the effort to change. As he gets "fed up" with the effects of his present life, he is often strongly urged to a different way of living.

Counselor's Response Does Not Emphasize Difficulties. On the other hand, it seems unwise for the counselor to place greater emphasis on the person's difficulties than he himself feels. This, too, may cause a person to feel he is not understood. It might make him reply with a more positive statement such as "Well, things aren't quite that bad." This would not be his real feeling but simply an expression of resistance to the counselor.

Responses Should Further the Person's Self-Concentration. There seems to be a significant difference between a statement that comes from the depth of a person's growing awareness and conviction and one that is made in response to the counselor's suggestions. When a person answers that things could be worse simply because the counselor overstated how bad they are, or when he says that things are better because he does not want to disappoint the counselor, he is not speaking from personal insight. His attention is centered on the counselor. A good response never takes the person's attention away from himself. Rather, it keeps the focus directly on the state the person feels himself to be in at that moment. This is one of the reasons why he can unfold and understand his feelings in a way that is not possible in a conversation or when he simply mulls his problems over in his own mind.

Study of Actual Excerpts Can Improve Skill. This phase of counselor sensitivity can be improved by continued study of recorded excerpts and by experience in counseling. One may compare counseling to the skill of mastering the piano. Fingering out the theme of a particular classic is not difficult. Anyone can recognize the notes. So, it is not hard to give elemental acceptance to a person's statements in an interview. With a little more effort, one can also learn to recognize commonly expressed negations, such as hostility, confusion, fear, and certain positive attitudes, such as being hopeful and feeling encouraged. But the skill of counseling is subject to the same progressive advancement as the skill of the pianist. The musician must gain a high sensitivity to reproduce all the subtleties and complexities of a composition. So counselors may vary in skill from the simple elemental reproduction of one feeling or attitude to delicate and sensitive kinds of responses which contain nearly all the intricate combinations of feelings and insights of a particular statement.

The counselor cannot dictate the prudent decisions which a person must make about the contingent singular events of that person's life. If, however, the person seeks it and the counselor has the skill, he can create a situation where the "conflicting duties and multiple rules which crisscross in a context of circumstance," as Maritain says, can be talked out, objectified, and reorganized. Through the unfolding of the counseling process, a person's "deepest attractions and inclinations" can gradually become duly orientated to his reason. The conflicting rights and duties then fall into their immediate relationship of reasonable priority. The new choices made to meet each unique event flow now from the recognition of the "urgent demand of his most highly individualized, most personal desire," and are at the same time in more consistent conformity with the universal rules of reasonable conduct. Seen from the over-all and broad view of growing insight, the long-time reasonable goals are also the happiest and best. In this way the objective norms of morality can, through counseling, become "embodied in the ends which actually attract my desire and in the actual movement of my will" (7, pp. 50–53).

The process of counseling, as we have described it, is not coextensive with the virtue of counsel which is larger and may or may not involve the aid of a counseling interview. It is also distinct from guidance and general education. Taken by itself, too, the counseling process is distinct from the gift of counsel, even though, in individual instances, the choices a person makes as a result of the interviews, such as accepting a religious vocation, may show the influence of the gift as well as the virtue of counsel. People obviously can make prudent judgments without feeling any need to undergo interviews. However, in particular circumstances, especially where emotional confusions and an extremely complex series of persons and events are involved, the counseling process seems to be a great aid in objectifying, separating, and integrating all the factors and in helping a person to come to a more reasonable judgment about them. In this way, the steps of prudence and the associated virtues may be helped by skilled counseling.

COMMENT

In the preceding paper it is suggested that there are situations in life when the person is confused in his feelings and his rational goals, and lets himself be influenced by his emotions. What is amiss is not so much that the right principles of conduct are not known but that the person is uncertain about the right steps to take in the present predicament. Examples given are the case of the man who takes to drink to escape from marital unhappiness, and the girl who marries an unsuitable partner because she wants to escape from her parents' nagging. Thus people create difficulties for themselves because they are confused, but they also find themselves in difficulties if they are unable to reach a goal because of some insuperable obstacle.

On the basis of our previous analysis of conflict (pages 198–217) we could subsume these conflicts under "inconsistency of choice" when conscious, and under "incompatibility of goal with the order of things" when unconscious. The man who is frustrated because he cannot achieve a goal knows that there is a conflict, but he lays the blame for his unhappiness on the impossibility of achieving his goal, rather than on his sustained longing for the thing he cannot have. The man who takes to drink to escape from marital unhappiness recognizes that he must take some action, but will not face the fact that escape into temporary oblivion is incompatible with his aim.

Function of Counseling

In all these cases, the counseling situation makes it possible for the person to understand the connection between his choice of goal and action, and his present unhappiness. Not only that, it provides him with the necessary conditions for making the right decision and carrying it out. Of course, even though insight is achieved, it still requires determination to carry out the new decision. Freedom from conflict is to be had at a price, the price of temporary discomfort and suffering.

Counseling, then, produces favorable conditions for insight and action. The means used is "reflecting the client's feelings"; and the counselor's acceptance and permissiveness seem to be additional factors. Now let us see what psychological processes these three factors could represent. According to Curran, in ordinary conversation a person has a twofold need, intellectual and personal (5, p. 21). He wants understanding and agreement, but also he wants to be accepted by the other person. But are these two needs really distinct in therapy?

Understanding and Agreement. In ordinary discussion, disagreement implies that the other's reasoning is incorrect. Provided the evidence is clear and available to both, only one conclusion is possible, the right one. If the right conclusion can be demonstrated and one person's conclusion was wrong, he will have to admit that he made a mistake, an admission which is not easy for everyone. In most disagreements, however, the evidence is not clear, so that such incontestable demonstration of the right conclusion is rarely possible. Far more frequently, one or the other discussant realizes that he must provide more evidence, or more unambiguous evidence, to make a correct conclusion possible. In the counseling situation, all the evidence there is has to be provided by the client. If he tries to explain the situation and his own feelings as clearly as he can, and the counselor disagrees and tries to persuade him that his conclusion is wrong, his emotion inappropriate, then he either feels rejected because by implication the counselor accuses him of being in the wrong and making a fuss about it, or more likely, he thinks that he has not presented sufficient evidence for the counselor to come to the same conclusion as he did himself. In the first case, he will be hostile, in the second case he will try again to expound the situation. In both cases, there will be no progress in insight.

Agreement likewise has different effects in the counseling situation from its effects in ordinary discussion. Ordinarily, agreement in a discussion means that both discussants draw the same conclusion from the evidence provided so far, and either of them is free to use the conclusion as a new premiss, or supply additional evidence which will allow further development of the argument. But in the counseling situation agreement has none of these effects; it simply stops the discussion. If the client is right and the counselor agrees after a few words, the attempt to supply more evidence is unnecessary. The counselor will not develop the discussion and the client cannot: If he is right on the evidence produced so far, what need is there to risk being wrong by giving more explanations?

Thus the necessary condition for helping the client to develop his understanding of himself is the assurance that the counselor understands what the client is saying as he himself understands it, instead of agreeing or disagreeing. Agreement in the counseling situation means jumping to conclusions; disagreement, jumping to a *hostile* conclusion. But a response which indicates understanding permits the client to go on with his self-exploration. To respond to a recital of grievances by saying "You are resentful because your mother-in-law always interferes" is the best proof that the counselor has understood not only what was said but also what was implied, hence the quick agreement: "yes, that's it exactly." Not that the client is under any illusion as to his feelings for the mother-in-law, but he wants the counselor's confirmation that resentment is the obvious reaction to interference. Such a response is not only a recognition of feeling but a recognition that this feeling is the necessary result of the situation in which the client finds himself. On the other hand, if the counselor mentions an emotion which the client actually has not yet recognized in himself, the results will be unfortunate. In that case, the client will have to deny the imputation and insight will inevitably be retarded. In the counseling situation, understanding means personal agreement in the sense that the counselor is willing to understand the client in the way in which the client understands himself, without taking issue with him on facts which only the client has experienced.

Acceptance. And now let us examine the other two factors, acceptance and permissiveness, and see what is accepted and what permitted, in nondirective counseling. Carl Rogers, for instance, says that acceptance implies accepting hostile feelings, comments, decisions, actions (9, p. 355). He quotes with approval from Meister and Miller, who say: "The client's report of his behavior, his actual behavior, and his need to behave as he does—all are 'accepted'" (9, p. 50).[2] But just what is implied in this acceptance? Rogers

[2] Curran (5), Bixler (4), and Axline (3), however, do not agree that acceptance has to go this far.

recognizes the moral issues involved in acceptance of actions and asks these question:

Does the counselor have the right, professionally or morally, to permit a client seriously to consider psychosis or suicide as a way out, without making a positive effort to prevent these choices? Is it a part of our general social responsibility that we may not tolerate such thinking or such action on the part of another? (9, p. 48).

From his own clinical experience and research and that of others, Rogers is convinced—

. . . that when the counselor perceives and accepts the client as he is, when he lays aside all evaluation and enters into the perceptual frame of reference of the client, he frees the client to explore his life and experiences anew, frees him to perceive in that experience new meanings and new goals. But is the therapist willing to give the client full freedom as to outcomes? Is he genuinely willing for the client to organize and direct his life? Is he willing for him to choose goals that are social or antisocial, moral or immoral? If not, it seems doubtful that therapy will be a profound experience for the client. Even more difficult, is he willing for the client to choose regression rather than growth or maturity? to choose neuroticism rather than mental health? to choose to reject help rather than accept it? to choose death rather than life? To me it appears that only as the therapist is completely willing that *any* outcome, *any* direction, may be chosen—only then does he realize the vital strength of the capacity and potentiality of the individual for constructive action. It is as he is willing for death to be the choice, that life is chosen; for neuroticism to be the choice, that a healthy normality is chosen (9, pp. 48–49; Rogers' italics).

The kind of acceptance which will bring the client to "choose life" must imply a very special kind of indifference as to the outcome. True, the client must be accepted as he is, without censure or condemnation. But more important than this negative aspect, the counselor must have the firm and evident confidence that regardless of anything that has happened in the past, the client now not only *wants* to do better (choose life) but will actually come to do so on his own. Counseling is successful if the client comes to share the counselor's firm confidence that the better choice is not only possible but practically imminent. Thus the counselor's acceptance is not indifference to the client's eventual choice. He is willing to trust the client's decision because of his conviction that his trust is well founded in the client's good will and integrity.

Permissiveness. Similarly, permissiveness in the counseling situation implies a special kind of permission. The counselor cannot "permit" anything which natural or human law forbids—he has no authority to do so. This is confirmed in practice by the common agreement to "set limits" in the counseling situation. But what *is* permitted is to *think over* and *talk over* any kind of situation which might have induced the client to contemplate antisocial actions. Such permission is founded on the counselor's willingness to leave the ultimate choice of action to the client. There is a difference, however, between a refusal to influence such choice by using force or persuasion, and a total unconcern as to which alternative will be chosen. Total unconcern is neither required nor even allowed in the counseling situation—for one thing, because it would defeat the aim of counseling to *help* the client, which implies concern about his fate; for another, because the client has come to enlist the counselor's aid in problems he cannot manage alone. Once he would realize the counselor's lack of concern, there would be no reason to continue therapy.

Thus acceptance and permissiveness in the counseling situation cannot mean unconcern for anything the client does. Acceptance primarily means that the counselor has confidence in the client's good will. And permissiveness primarily means that the counselor will not use force or persuasion to ensure the right choice.

Since the counseling situation automatically excludes force, we are left with persuasion as an alternative to permissiveness. Now if it were certain that persuasion or advice would prevent the wrong choice or even make it less likely, a case could be made out for using these means, out of our very concern for the client. If, however, persuasion or advice is not likely to lead to the right choice, we have the right to use an approach that promises better.

If the counselor tried to dissuade the client, what would actually happen? Suppose a man declares that his situation is so desperate that suicide is the only way out. If I now say to him: "Suicide is wrong, you must not do that," or words to that effect, I imply that no matter how bad his situation is he must not allow himself to feel that way. The obvious reaction on his part will be to explain to me that his situation is even worse than he had led me to believe, and that no one could feel differently. In other words, he will "defend" his attitude and may even maintain it by actually committing suicide. Observationally, however, he is trying to supply the reasons for his feeling to convince me that it is the only possible feeling, which could lead to only one possible action. On the other hand, if I say to him: "Sure, the problem is so hopeless that suicide is your only solution," then I am saying that I doubt his ability to find another way out, nor can I see one. If he is deeply discouraged, that will be the last straw. If he has only played with the thought, he will conclude that I didn't understand his real meaning and so am incapable of helping him. But if I manage to make him see that I understand his predicament, if I acknowledge that in his circumstances his reaction is reasonable, then he will feel free to explore the possible alternatives.

"Acceptance" in that case is not accepting his decision as the *right* decision; it is merely acknowledging that he has the right to *feel* as he does under the circumstances. If that right is admitted, then he can go on exploring the reasons for his feeling and perhaps will discover that there are other factors which he has neglected up to now. Permissiveness, then, does not mean giving permission to *act* as the client proposes but permitting him to *discuss* both the proposed action and the feeling that led to it. Thus acceptance and permissiveness turn out to be terms used to describe a situation in which the client's *explanations* are accepted, where he is permitted to develop his survey of the problem unhindered by disagreement or censure, and sustained by the counselor's sympathetic understanding and unflinching hope. Acceptance and permissiveness are conditions of understanding, or rather signs that the counselor is really following the client's explanations and that his understanding is accompanying further explorations.

Primacy of Understanding. There is, however, one condition that has to be fulfilled before understanding as discussed here can be used to help people who voice an intention to commit suicide or any other criminal act: there must be at least some assurance that the person's ability to reason is unimpaired and that he fully recognizes his responsibility for his action. When a man is suffering from a severe psychosis and his basic sensory experience is abnormal, then the basis for his judgment and his judgment itself are so changed that he may see grounds for his actions which the normal would not experience at all. Therefore, he may have to be protected from the consequences of this abnormal functioning by force (sedation or restraint in a mental hospital) just as the man at the height of a fever delirium has to be protected from himself. This proviso is usually not made in nondirective therapy because mental illness of such severity is not found among the clients of a counselor or therapist outside the mental hospital.

That understanding is really primary in every therapeutic relationship has been brought out nicely in a recent study (Fred E. Fiedler, 6). Fiedler finds that experts of all schools of psychotherapy can readily be distinguished from nonexperts by their success in understanding the patient's account of his problem, following his line of thought, participating in his communication. Only two statements which were checked as holding true for experts but not for beginners seem to fall outside this category. One of these statements reads: "The therapist's feelings do not seem to be swayed by the patient's remarks," and the other: "the therapist gives and takes in the situation" (6, p. 491). It is obvious that when there is real understanding there is also participation, that is, give and take; and when there is understanding, the therapist will not be swayed from his attitude of friendly interest. Thus both these statements support the central position of understanding in therapy.

There is another point that deserves attention. Nondirective therapy with its careful evaluation of nuances of communication and understanding has eschewed every attempt to give any kind of "dynamic" interpretation to the client. This raises the question whether it is understanding alone which allows the client to help himself; in other words, it raises the question what effect such understanding has on another and whether it suffices to help him solve his problem. The answer is perhaps contained in a quotation from Rogers who, trying to describe the counselor's attitude toward the client, puts these words in the counselor's mouth:

To be of assistance to you I will put aside myself—the self of ordinary interaction—and enter into your world of perception as completely as I am able. I will become, in a sense, another self for you —an alter ego of your own attitudes and feelings—a safe opportunity for you to discern yourself more clearly, to experience yourself more truly and deeply, to choose more significantly (9, p. 35).

Thus the understanding involved in counseling is understanding of the client's situation from the client's point of view. This is clearly recognized by the client himself. For instance, an eight-year-old boy, during nondirective play therapy, says to the counselor:

Why do you just say what I say and think only what I think? I guess I can guess why you do. I'm the little me and you are the big me. I'm all of myselves and you're all of the other people in the world. You're my big shadow that I can move this way and that and *I can see just what I'm being* (3, p. 55. Italics added).

And the same experience as expressed by an adult:

. . . sometimes I would hardly know just what I was saying. This one may easily do if one talks for long periods to oneself—becoming so involved in verbalization that one is not keenly aware of just what one is saying and very definitely not aware of what the words actually mean to one. It was the role of the counselor *to bring me to myself*, to help me by being with me *to realize what I was saying*. I was never conscious that he was reflecting or restating things I had said but only that he was right along with me in my thinking because he would say to me things which I had stated but he would clear them for me, bring me back to earth, help me to see what I had said and what it meant to me (9, p. 37. Italics added).

One would be tempted to say that what happens is a clarification and objectification of the client's thinking. In fact, Rogers considered it at first as part of the counselor's role "to clarify and objectify the client's feelings." However, in his most recent presentation, he considers this concept "too intellectualistic" and continues: "If taken too literally, [it] may focus the process in the counselor. It can mean that only the counselor knows what the feelings are, and if it acquires this meaning it becomes a subtle lack of respect for the client" (9, p. 27). We agree that it leads to misunderstanding to say that it is *the counselor's task* to clarify and objectify the client's feelings. Such a misunderstanding could be avoided, however, by recognizing that it is the counselor's task to *understand* how the client experiences his situation; such understanding will help *the client* to clarify for himself (and for the counselor) what the situation is and what he feels about it, and so see it objectively. Thus clarification is the *result* of the counselor's understanding as shown by his responses; it is not the counselor's task.

Such a formulation avoids ambiguity though it does not escape the reproach of being "intellectual." But after all, how is one to understand, if not intellectually? First, the counselor must grasp the situation conceptually as the client presents it, or he cannot grasp it at all. But once he understands what the situation is, the counselor puts himself in the client's place, sees with his eyes, judges from the other's point of view. Such understanding from the other's point of view implies fellow-feeling, sympathy. Where such fellow-feeling (in Rogers' terms, acceptance) is not present, it is a sure sign that understanding is defective. To put one's self in the other's place, to see the situation as he sees it, and judge its importance as he judges it, means to feel as he does, for the time being. Fellow-feeling, which is an affect, follows such evaluation of the situation from the client's point of view; it does not occur before it. Such evaluation necessarily follows upon the intellectual grasp of the situation; it cannot precede it.

We could say, then, that real understanding of the client, as demanded in client-centered therapy, implies both an intellectual grasp of the situation and a fellow-feeling in it. The counselor's response makes clear to the client how he himself looks at his problem and how it affects him. The client then sees the effect of his own situation on his alter ego, on someone who for the time being has no concern of his own but merely reflects the effects of the client's situation, namely the client's emotions, in such a way that they can easily be recognized. This does represent an objectification and clarification of the way he feels about his problem and about himself; recognizing himself more clearly, the client can now go on exploring his feelings more deeply. The clarification is provided by the way in which he sees his own description of his situation summed up and the situation itself re-presented by the counselor. It is the client who does the exploring, the client who recognizes the image of his own emotions, but it is the counselor who focuses the image for him.

Nondirective or client-centered therapy, then, allows the client both to direct himself and discover himself; he is in the center of the picture in the sense that he paints it, he discovers its meaning, he decides on the action to follow. He recognizes the inconsistency between many of his choices, the incompatibility of others with the order of things. He also recognizes (and is cheered by the discovery) that his emotions were the necessary result of his confused evaluation, but that he can bring order into his goals and thus order his emotions so that they will serve as helps rather than as hindrances to him. In this way the client gains a clear picture of himself, his goals and strivings, the convictions he lives by. Now he is able to establish a hierarchy of goals and work out a consistent pattern of life. The goal he establishes, the decision he makes, will be his own goal, his own decision in a way that is impossible to achieve by other therapeutic methods.

Limitations of Nondirective Methods

Individual Counseling. There are, however, limitations inherent in the nondirective method. The client can reason only about what he has experienced, or the insights he is experiencing during therapy. His understanding of himself and the world around him is necessarily limited by his fund of information to which nondirective therapy itself can add nothing. As he comes to choose rational goals he finds that he can always achieve consistency if he is willing to sacrifice an attractive alternative. But in choosing an ultimate rational goal, in forming his self-ideal and conforming it to the self-ideal as it ought to be, he must know what the ideal ought to be for all men; and next, how that ideal applies to himself in his own particular circumstances of life. Here he may need information which he does not as yet possess. If at this point the counselor can refer him to competent advisers, as Curran suggests, the client can go on without hindrance; otherwise progress will be limited by his present resources of knowledge or information.

There is another point which deserves mention: If the client is confused in an area which the counselor has never explored for himself, the client may leave that area unexplored altogether, to his loss. That happens, for instance, when the client is deeply religious and the counselor is an agnostic or atheist. In the area of his religious problems, the client will soon realize that the counselor is out of his depth, as evidenced by badly worded and superficial responses, and with the best will in the world the counselor will be unable to help.

The opposite effect is not likely to happen, namely that a client is restricted or limited by the fact that the counselor has definite religious convictions while the client has not. Here the only difficulty will be to ask for help in the first place, because of the client's fear that the counselor may force the issue beyond the point which he is willing to explore. But a truly nondirective counselor will soon dispel the client's fears. The client will discover that the counselor merely lights up his confusion, focuses his understanding, but does not go beyond the import of the statements actually made. This again represents a limitation of the strictly nondirective method: that even in cases where the client obviously shirks facing an important problem the counselor who takes the technique seriously cannot even make a suggestion, let alone, as some clients might fear, force the issue.

Thus the nondirective or client-centered method provides a means for self-understanding and self-direction in which the counselor is no more than a sympathetic partner helping the client to reorganize himself. If self-understanding or self-direction is sought, the counseling situation will provide it. If the aim of the client should be to understand others rather than himself, or to understand natural laws or principles of science, that is, phenomena which have no bearing on his personal life, then there is no particular advantage to be gained from a nondirective approach.

Group therapy. It was perhaps inevitable that an approach which yielded such brilliant results in the therapeutic situation should have been tried also in situations that involve a group rather than an individual. It came to be used in group therapy and finally in classroom teaching, on the supposition that the same release of individual reasoning and decision which occurs so dramatically in individual counseling would appear also in group situations. But it was overlooked that group therapy sessions (not to mention a classroom situation) present an entirely different problem: If every member of the group or class is granted the freedom of the counseling situation, then he will talk not only about his own problems, but also about the problems of the other members as he understands them. When he talks about himself, the counselor can reflect his feelings in the usual way, with the usual results. But when he responds to the remarks of his fellows, he has neither the counselor's skill nor the counselor's intention of understanding without interfering. As he reacts to others, so they will react to him, so that each member of the group will have to defend himself against the misinterpretations of others.

Moreover, since the counselor cannot direct the group, the most aggressive members will take the lead and they are the ones who are least able to keep from interfering with another's understanding of himself. While they agree and disagree with one another and violate every rule of the counseling situation, everyone's understanding of himself will be delayed until the mischiefmakers gain enough insight into their own behavior to subside. Anyone who has had experience with nondirective groups will agree that this can be a very protracted process. The other members of the group learn patience and forbearance in the meantime—if they do not, they drop out.

Classroom Teaching. The situation is worse in a classroom.[3] When the class is left to its own devices by a nondirective leader, there is first surprise, then discontent, then resentment. Now that may be an inadequate reaction to an unusual but constructive situation—and the nondirective enthusiast usually takes it as such and waits for the resentment to subside. But discontent and resentment may also be reactions to an intolerable situation—intolerable because objectively inappropriate.

To decide whether the students' objections are justified or not (and they occur with monotonous regularity in nondirective teaching) we must first discover what is the aim of teaching as compared

---

[3] Perhaps it should be emphasized that we are concerned here with the attempt to introduce nondirective methods as a teaching or classroom technique. It is obvious that counseling employed as an *adjunct* to teaching and discussion will facilitate the educative process.

with the aim of therapy. In counseling, the client gains self-understanding. In learning, the student also gains (or ought to gain) understanding, but not primarily of himself or of his classmates but of the subject matter which is being taught; more broadly speaking, he gains an understanding of the world he lives in. This world includes human beings, true. But the student does not want or need to understand the particular reactions of the particular people who share the same classroom with him, *in the way they understand themselves*. If he studies physics, he wants to understand the actions of physical bodies. If he studies psychology, he wants to understand the actions of human beings in many situations, not in the one situation he happens to be involved in at the present time.

We discussed (page 92 f.) the two levels of knowledge which seem to be confused in a nondirective teaching situation: the student seeks primarily to know the reality of things as they are in themselves, apart from any immediate relationship to himself; the client in need of therapy seeks experiential knowledge, seeks to understand himself as he is related to others. There is no doubt that the one kind of knowledge has to be supplemented by the other. The client may need more information, more knowledge about things; the student may also need experiential knowledge. But to turn a teaching situation into an ineffective counseling situation is even more harmful than to use the counseling situation for giving advice or instruction. In practice, the nondirective teaching situation eventually forces the student to take the initiative and read (on the basis of a reading list, but without guidance from the instructor) to gain some information.

Books must be directive; they argue a thesis or at least present authoritative information. Unless it be gratuitously assumed that a man is entitled to a hearing only after he has published a book, there is no reason why books should be allowed to be directive and not the instructor. Class discussion on such reading may be carefully reflected by the leader, but in our experience the grossest mistakes in logic in some of the students' remarks pass unnoticed in spite of the leader's reflection. Thus the class ends by getting to know each other rather well and the books they have read rather vaguely. It is to be doubted whether they know even as much about their reading as they would by discussing it in bull sessions without a nondirective leader, because they would at least have no distraction from the topic under discussion by having their feelings reflected by the leader.

Thus the attempt to apply nondirective methods to teaching because they are effective in clinical counseling is based on a misunderstanding of the aims of education as compared to the aims of counseling. True, the learner must be active in learning and the best education is self-education; yet such education is not confined to self-understanding or understanding of others as they understand themselves. As is clearly shown in Dr. Curran's diagram, the two areas of education and counseling do not overlap—in fact they do not even touch. Only in a case where there is a real difficulty in a teaching situation, where for instance the whole group is upset about a particular practice of grading or of discipline, would it be appropriate and advisable to have some nondirective counseling sessions until the difficulty is resolved. Even in this case it is conceivable that the students' complaint is justified, in which case counseling alone will not serve to resolve the difficulty and administrative action will have to be taken to give them redress.

REFERENCES

1. AQUINAS, THOMAS. *Summa Theologica.* In: *Basic writings of St. Thomas Aquinas.* (Tr.) ANTON PEGIS. 2 Vols. New York: Random House, 1945.
2. AQUINAS, THOMAS. *Summa Theologica.* (Tr.) Fathers of the English Dominican Province. 3 Vols. New York: Benziger Bros., 1947.
3. AXLINE, VIRGINIA M. 1947. *Play Therapy.* Boston: Houghton Mifflin Co., Inc.
4. BIXLER, R. H. 1949. Limits are therapy. *J. consult. Psychol.,* 1949, **13,** 1–11.
5. CURRAN, CHARLES A. 1952. *Counseling in Catholic life and education.* New York: The Macmillan Co.
6. FIEDLER, FRED E. 1950. A comparison of therapeutic relationships in psychoanalytic, nondirective and Adlerian therapy. *J. consult. Psychol.,* 1950, **14,** 436–45.
7. MARITAIN, JACQUES. 1948. *Existence and the existent.* New York: Pantheon Books, Inc.
8. ROGERS, CARL R. 1942. *Counseling and psychotherapy.* Boston: Houghton Mifflin Co., Inc.
9. ———. 1951. *Client-centered therapy.* Boston: Houghton Mifflin Co., Inc.

Chapter 16

LOGOTHERAPY AND EXISTENTIAL ANALYSIS

By Magda B. Arnold *and* John A. Gasson, S. J.

Existentialism presents a challenge not only to philosophy but to psychology as well. Sartre himself has applied his philosophical postulates to the psychology of emotion and the psychology of imagination without, however, arriving at a consistent psychology of personality. Viktor Frankl, a practicing psychiatrist in Vienna, has tried to supply the omission, thus adding one more name to the illustrious group of medical psychologists who made Vienna famous. Freud's psychoanalysis and Adler's individual psychology both come from Vienna and perhaps this fact as much as anything has centered Frankl's attention on these two rival explanations of human personality.

He conceives his own system as completing both and therefore logically supplanting them.

Since existentialism is arousing considerable attention and has been thought to offer an acceptable alternative to the mechanistic and objectivistic view of the human person so fashionable in psychology until comparatively recently, we thought it advisable to include a discussion of Frankl's *existential analysis*. His books have not been translated so far and are comparatively inaccessible to the American reader. Therefore we are including a rather detailed exposition of Frankl's thought which summarizes his main theoretical work, *Ärztliche Seelsorge* (1), in his own words, suitably simplified. All page references refer to this work unless otherwise stated. The translation of quotations is our own.

Summary of Frankl's Existential Analysis

Psycho-therapy, so-called, is really affect-therapy, at least in the Freudian and Adlerian system. Its main concern is either the Oedipus complex or the inferiority complex. In both cases, it deals with the complex emotions aroused which are considered decisive for personality development. But emotions are not the deciding factors in human life. What is deciding is the way in which the human being deals with his emotions, what convictions he has acquired, what principles of action he acknowledges, what philosophy of life he has built for himself.

This philosophy of life may be either adequate or inadequate, but such adequacy or inadequacy is not the result of his neurosis, though his neurosis may incline him toward one rather than another view of life. When psychotherapy has eliminated the patient's emotional drivenness and so restored his objectivity, he will have to be convinced that his philosophy of life is inadequate before he will change it and so complete his cure. The human spirit (*das Geistige*) [1] has its own laws which go beyond psychology. A philosophical system or an artistic creation must be judged on its own merits, not reduced to conditions which influence its creation but have no bearing on its logical validity or artistic value.

Such reduction of the life of the spirit to psychological causation must be considered an interesting psychological phenomenon. Its roots are to be found in the attempt to escape from the *content* of reasoning or art or religion into the realm of psycho-

[1] The German *Geist, Geistesleben, das Geistige,* etc., is not amenable to proper rendering into English. In the present instance, it becomes doubly difficult because Frankl attaches his own special meaning to the whole family of terms. In a letter written to the editors (dated July 7, 1953) he comments: "*Rational* seems to me to mean the contrary to *emotional*; but, at least in my opinion, the spiritual (axis or nucleus of the personality) is rooted just in an emotional ground!" He suggested either *spiritual* or *noölogical* instead of *rational*. But *spiritual* will not do for the obvious reason that it is a fighting word among psychologists because it is redolent of the supernatural, and *noölogical* is too suggestive of the trichotomy *soma, psyche, nous,* which had great vogue in the second century A.D. but is not current in American psychological literature. We shall do what we can with simpler words or paraphrases.

logical action. Because psychologists do not want to face the question what rational systems of philosophy or art or religion mean for the human being, they have to look for irrelevant because extraneous causes of their production, whether in the individual or in society. Such psychologism is an escape from the reality of human life which contains ideal, artistic, and religious values. Though Adler's individual psychology preaches courage, it does not bear the mark of courage, which is a certain humility before facts, before the reality of human ideals, of art, and of religion. As a result, both in psychoanalysis and individual psychology, human activity is explained as dependent on and caused by biological, sociological, and psychological factors. Yet properly human activity means to come to terms with such influences, to be free to give in to them or to control them and bend them to our uses. Existential philosophy has reacted decisively against such causal explanations of human activity and human existence and has insisted that the human being is essentially characterized by his responsibility in the face of such biological, psychological, and social influences. Once the responsibilty of the human being is recognized it will become apparent that psychotherapy must be complemented by logotherapy, that the analysis of the psychological influences to which an individual is subjected must be complemented by an analysis of his ideal aspirations and deliberate choices.

Psychotherapy, then, consists in the analysis of psychological, particularly emotional, influences. In its particular form as psychoanalysis its emphasis is on unconscious emotions and its method consists in making such unconscious emotions conscious. Logotherapy, on the other hand, aims at making the person conscious of his human aspirations. In its special form as existential therapy, it concentrates on his consciousness of responsibility and aims at making the person aware of his responsibility as the foundation of his existence. While logotherapy in general is "a therapy based on reason and motives," existential analysis in particular is "a therapy based on the consciousness of responsibility."

Since responsibility is always responsibility toward an obligation, and an obligation can only be understood when there is a meaning or purpose in human life, the question of the purpose or meaning of life is necessarily central. The normal human being has a direction in life, a consistency of purpose which transcends the demands of the moment. If he tries to forget his obligation to adhere to such a purpose and tries to live in the present (the alcoholic, the playboy), he perverts human life. That the question, "What is the meaning of life?" is of central importance has been shown by a recent survey. In their search for the causes of longevity the investigators noticed that every one of their "long-living" subjects had a serene and thoroughly positive attitude toward life. For them life was worth while; it had a meaning.

The meaning of life can be taken as equivalent to the meaning of the universe. If, then, we ask for the meaning of the universe, we shall have to admit that we, as part of the universe, cannot possibly grasp the meaning of the whole, just as domestic animals do not know the purpose of their existence for their owner.

But at the same time, the fact that there is meaning in *parts* of the universe (which is all we can know) refers us to some kind of meaning for the totality, a supermeaning, which expresses the fact that that meaning cannot be grasped, but also that it is *more* than can be grasped.

This is expressed in a passage from Schleich:

Gott sass vor der Orgel der Möglichkeiten und improvisierte die Welt. Wir armen Menschen hören immer nur die Vox Humana heraus. Ist sie schon schön, wie herrlich muss das Ganze sein! (Quoted by Frankl, 1, p. 26).

(God, sitting at the keyboard of the organ of possibilities, improvised the world. We, poor humans, only distinguish the Vox Humana. If it is beautiful, what splendor in the whole!)

Faith in such a supermeaning is creative and of the greatest significance for psychological health. Rooted in inner strength, faith makes man strong. With such a faith, there is nothing that is meaningless, nothing in vain. Seen in this light, no human effort can disappear without some effect, everything is recorded, everything preserved. Time, change, the impermanence of

human life, cannot take the meaning out of it. What has been
still is in some sense—past existence still is *existence*.

When the meaning of personal life is sought, it becomes obvious that it cannot be pleasure. We all know that there is more
displeasure than pleasure in every human life. And according
to experimental evidence, the normal human being feels displeasure far more frequently than pleasure during each day.
But joy can make life meaningful, provided only that joy itself
has meaning. That meaning is in its content, in its intention,
whether its object is a symphony, a beautiful sunset, or human
love. Only when objective values are aimed at can there be real
joy. Therefore, the meaning of life must be in the realm of
value, which is a realm of objectively real goals. When we intend a goal, then its existence as well as its objective value is
given, whether we achieve it or not. Even though our picture
of the world and therefore of values necessarily is partial, we
know that both are there, objectively given, absolute—though
in every particular case what we ought to do to achieve this value
is bound to be relative and depends on concrete circumstances.
We see the realm of values in perspective, as it were, but from
any given point of vantage only one perspective, the right
one, is adequate. There is absolute rightness or accuracy, not
in spite of but because of the relativity of individual perspectives.

In the realm of human values, there are some which are
realized in deliberate action, *creative values*. These depend not
on the significance of each action but on our manner of acting
responsibly. There are also *experiential values* (realized in
the enjoyment of a symphony, a painting, or the joy of friendship) ; both these values give meaning to human life, a meaning
that is judged by the heights reached in moments of intense experience, not by the number of experiences compressed into a
lifetime. Finally, there are *attitudinal values*, which can be realized even in situations where neither creative nor experiential
values are present. They are measured by the degree of courage
and patience exhibited under restrictive and adverse conditions.
Every man has an obligation to actualize values as long as he
lives, and attitudinal values can always be achieved. From this

point of view we cannot have the right to prevent anyone from realizing the attitudinal values inherent in suffering and rob him of the chance to die "his death." For this reason, euthanasia of the unfit, the incurable (whether in physical or mental illness), cannot be defended; in fact, the physician has not only the right but the duty to restrain the would-be suicide, so defending the person against himself.

In many cases of threatened suicide, there is no psychological reason for it. True, there is a feeling of distaste for life, but in responsible human action a feeling of distaste has never been considered a reason for omitting a right action or committing a wrong one. Therefore not psychotherapy but logotherapy is needed to convince the person of his obligation to realize the meaning of his life. An example is given to illustrate the point: A patient was committed to a psychiatric institute because of suicide tendencies. But he was not suffering from any psychiatric disability, was seemingly perfectly rational, and insisted on his right as a rational human being to choose the time and manner of his death. The director of the institute, much impressed, ordered his discharge with the diagnosis, "sine morbo psychico." But one of the psychiatrists, convinced that the man needed not psychotherapy but help in his thinking, that is, logotherapy, asked him to step into his office on the way out. In a surprisingly short time he convinced the former patient that the freedom of a rational being was not a "freedom from" but a "freedom to"—the freedom to accept his responsibility. Suicide does not *solve* any problem and that is the point on which the would-be suicide must be corrected. He must realize that he is like a chess player who is faced with a difficult problem and "solves" it by upsetting the chess men. If he once realizes that life represents a task, the task to actualize values, then he will be forced to the conclusion that it acquires the more meaning the more difficult it proves to be.

Thus the aim of existential analysis is to show the person that every man's life has a unique goal to which he must find his uniquely fitting way. And if the patient objects that he knows neither goal nor way, it must be pointed out to him that his task is to know both. As Goethe says:

Wie kann man sich selbst kennen lernen? Durch Betrachten niemals, wohl aber durch Handeln. Versuche, deine Pflicht zu tun und Du weisst gleich, was an dir ist. Was aber ist deine Pflicht? Die Forderung des Tages (1, p. 45).

(How can we come to know ourselves? Never by reflection but by action. Try to do your duty and you will know what you are. But what is your duty? The demands of each day.)

The task with which life confronts a man is always there and never impossible to fulfill. The more he experiences life as a task, the more will he realize the meaning of life. Some men go a step further: they experience not only the task but the task master—which could be called a definition of *homo religiosus*.

To perceive the task character of life and his own personal task is difficult for the neurotic because he has lost his instinctive sureness in recognizing tasks. A task that is generally valid, a life goal that is universal, is impossible. To demand one is to act like the reporter who asked the famous chess champion: "And now tell me, maestro, which is the best move in chess?" The question, "What is the meaning of life in general?" has no answer because it is wrongly put. It should be, "What is the meaning of *my* life?" "of *your* life?" etc. Man cannot question or interrogate life, he is interrogated by life; his role is merely to respond, to be responsible. Only because man is conscious of being confronted by life is he led to ask for its meaning. The same intuition which leads him to recognize his own task leads him to undertake the fulfilment of his obligation. "This moral intuition is conscience" (p. 49). Everyone hears the voice of conscience but the religious man has better hearing, he also hears the speaker.

The Meaning of Death. Death sets limits to activity and forces the human being to make use of his opportunities. In existential analysis such observations are put into easily remembered formulae which the patient can use in his thinking—for instance: "Live as if you were living the second time and had acted as wrongly the first time as you are about to act now." If the patient succeeds in realizing the implications of this statement he will become aware of the weight of responsibility which he carries in every moment of his life, for the way in which the next moment shall be lived. Man must finish his task in time and within time's limitations—in finitude. He must risk the end. And as the end belongs to the story, so death belongs to life. If life is meaningful, then it is so whether it is long or short, whether a man can live in his children or dies childless. If the meaning of life consisted in reproduction, then every generation would find its meaning only in the next generation. Hence the problem of meaning would be postponed from one generation to another but never solved. If the life of each generation of men has no meaning, is it not likewise meaningless to perpetuate something that has no meaning?

Human freedom, like human responsibility, is self-evident for the unprejudiced. To doubt seriously that he can act as he chooses is possible only for a man who is caught in a deterministic philosophy and therefore will not accept self-evidence, or for the schizophrenic who experiences his acts as compelled and unfree. Stories that deal with human beings seemingly unaware of their freedom of choice strike us as so incongruous that they are the object of wit—like the story of the man lamenting the lack of moral fibre in the present generation, who said to his wife, "For instance, I found a purse today. Do you think it would have occurred to me to take it to the police?" Biological determinism is no more than the material for human freedom, a fact which is illustrated by many examples. Psychological determinism has been emphasized especially by psychoanalysts who see man as driven and controlled not only by the id but by the superego. ⌐In contrast, Existential Analysis repudiates any conception which would make the self the plaything or the product of *any* kind of forces.⌐

But the id and superego only make demands; it is the self that decides whether to grant or refuse them. Freud admits that, but accounts for the ego's power by deriving it genetically from the id. Such a situation is the kind of paradox that could be compared with a court hearing in which the defendant is asked to take the place of the prosecutor and enter a charge against himself. The danger inherent in the psychoanalytic system is that the neurotic finds it devastatingly easy to believe in the determination of his actions. He must be led to see that a strong will is not a character trait but the result of clear goal perception, honest decision, and a certain training in following through.[2]

The person remains free to choose his attitude even under psychological or biological compulsion. There is the example of a woman patient in a psychiatric ward who had been suffering for years from intense auditory hallucinations. She incessantly heard strident voices accusing her and making scornful remarks. One of the other patients asked her how she could be so happy in spite of it and she said, "I say to myself, 'after all, I'd rather hear voices than not hear at all.'"

The Meaning of Suffering. Lack of success in one's chosen work or in any particular aspect of life is not synonymous with lack of meaning or significance in life. Even lack of joy is not absence of meaning. Suffering makes possible the realization of attitudinal values and with it an inner growth which may be of far more significance than outer success or pleasure. But beyond such realization of attitudinal values, suffering has a value of its own. When we grieve over someone we have loved and lost, our sorrow perpetuates our affection. Repentance purifies the guilty, the sinner, and changes him into a new man. In suffering and through suffering we remain active, we are preserved from routine and rigidity. Emotions have meaning, namely, to enable us to deal with their object. If we try to escape into oblivion, the problem remains unsolved. Suffering and death both belong to life; they could not be eliminated without destroying the meaning of life. Under the blows of fate, in the white heat of suffering, life is hammered and formed.

The Meaning of Work. Work provides an opportunity for actualizing creative values, but it is not the work or profession which is meaningful; rather, it is the unique manner in which each person tackles it. Any kind of work can provide such opportunity if only we are willing to grasp it. Of course, division

---

[2] As Frankl says: "Man sagt, wo ein Wille, dort ist auch ein Weg; ich ergänze dies und sage: wo ein Ziel ist, dort ist auch ein Wille." (It is said: where there is a will, there is a way; I add: where there is an aim, there is a will.) (From Frankl's letter to the editors, dated July 7, 1953.)

of labor has reduced some types of work to repetitious motions. In that case, any creative effort will have to be made in the worker's time off. Sometimes also, work is so exhausting that there is no "time off," only time to rest. In such a life, only attitudinal values can be realized. But work is often felt as meaningful in itself, and life as meaningful as long as there is work.

When work stops, there is often malaise, apathy, indifference, either temporarily (Sunday neurosis) or for long stretches of time (unemployment neurosis). Work in itself is not decisive for the formation and perfection of the human being—or an invalid would necessarily have to become psychologically crippled. And lack of work, correspondingly, is not necessarily fatal for man's psychological development. Here as elsewhere, the human being can give in to fate or he can act constructively as far as conditions allow. While many that are unemployed suffer from apathy and indifference, there are some who keep themselves occupied, as volunteers in charitable institutions, public libraries, and the like. They may suffer from economic deprivations but they keep a balanced and even serene outlook upon life without falling into neurosis. As long as the human being remains conscious that his life is a task, that he is responsible for the way in which he acquits himself of it, so long will he see meaning in it and will remain psychologically healthy. For those who have developed a neurosis (and unemployment is no more than a precipitating occasion) psychotherapy will hardly be helpful. But logotherapy can make it possible for a man to find meaning in his life even though he is not working. Only the man whose life had no meaning, though he was working, will suddenly discover that his life lacks meaning when his work is gone. ⌈For that man work was no more than an escape and a self-deception, very similar to the escape of others into voracious reading or the movies or into the ranks of onlookers at boxing matches or ball games. People who continually must be entertained, who must have one sensation after another, merely achieve a kind of dulling of their conscience which accuses them that they are not fulfilling their obligation, that they evade the task with which life is confronting them.⌋

The Meaning of Love. The meaning of personal life is in the uniqueness and singularity of the person. It is actualized in his achievement which he shares with others. If self-actualization is seen with reference to *one other*, we enter the realm of love in the narrower sense of the word. In such a mutual relationship self-actualization comes as a gift from the other rather than as an achievement. To be loved means a realization of the person's uniqueness without any effort on his part—by grace, as it were. In love, the beloved is seen as being this person and no other, a Thou who becomes impossible to exchange or replace. Love is not only grace but magic. It gives a new value to the world which enriches the lover. Love is not blind but far-seeing. And finally, out of mutual love comes the miracle of a new existence, the child.

There are three kinds of attitudes to the other which are possible to the lover: love can either be directed toward another's body, in sexual love, or it may be directed toward the other's charm of manner or his temperament in what may be called erotic love or romantic infatuation. But the other can also be loved as he is in the core of his being. As a person, the other becomes the *carrier* of his physical and psychological character-istics in which he himself is revealed. Love which is such related-ness to the other as a person, which realizes the uniqueness of this other being, does not suffer the impermanence of sexual attrac-tion or romantic infatuation. Since the other's being is intended, his actuality becomes secondary. Such love will fear neither death nor separation:

Echte Liebe an und für sich bedarf des Körperlichen weder zu ihrer Erweckung noch zu ihrer Erfüllung; aber sie bedient sich des Körperlichen in Hinsicht auf beide (1, p. 108).
(Real love needs the body neither for its arousal nor its fulfilment; but love uses the body for both.)

Therefore the modern emphasis on physical appearance, as expressed in the overvaluation of cosmetics, betrays the fact that love is mistaken for sexual attraction or at most a romantic emo-tion. This represents a devaluation of men and women as per-sons in favor of external characteristics. Real love intends the other as what he is in his uniqueness (his *haecceitas*) but also as what he can be or will be (in his *entelechy*).

Since love brings vision and makes far-sighted, since love results in a realization of new values, love is always enriching—even if unrequited. But requited love is creative. ⌈Love helps the beloved to actualize those values which the lover sees as potentiality. Wanting to resemble the picture the beloved has of him, the lover in turn will strive to become more and more "what God intended and wanted him to be." In mutual love there is a dialectical action and reaction in which lover and beloved grow for and with each other.⌋

Sexual activity offers pleasure, infatuation brings joy, but love is happiness. This progression indicates an increasing intentionality. Pleasure is connected with momentary functioning, joy intends something outside the self. But happiness has a unique direction—the actualizing of the self of lover and beloved. Thus happiness is not only intentional, it is also productive, self-actualizing.

The development of love as it actually occurs in the growing human being is very different from Freud's description of what he calls "psycho-sexual development." Even in Freud's system, infantile sexuality is different from adult genitality. Because of this difference, Freud used an extended meaning of the term sexuality. But the difference is so far-reaching that it is doubtful whether infantile sexuality is sexuality at all in the proper meaning of the term. Therefore, the discussion of the development of love should start from the time of puberty when the three attitudes to another (sexual desire, romantic infatuation, and love properly so called) become possible for the first time.

At puberty there is a break-through of the organic into the psychological realm, often accompanied by a shock reaction. Sexuality, rooted in physiological changes, has to be integrated into the psychological and personal life of the human being. At first, sexuality merely represents a physiological tension without concrete goal or direction. Gradually it acquires a goal, detumescence, for which any member of the opposite sex can become a sufficient opportunity. Still later, the sexual impulse is directed toward a *particular* member of the opposite sex; it has now become a striving toward a *specific* goal. Thus sexual *tension*, sexual *impulse*, and striving toward a *particular person* are the stages of psychosexual development and represent an increasing directedness and intentionality, so that sexuality gradually achieves its character as expression of the ideally ordered self. What is it that gives direction to sexuality? It cannot come from sexuality itself for sexuality as such intends at most a member of the opposite sex. It must come from outside, must stem from an intention toward another *person*, an intention which could be called "erotic" but is definitely not sexual. It is directed toward another not as a member of the opposite sex but as a person, toward mutual understanding, a being together in soul and body. Such an intention toward sociality or intimacy is primary and not derived, for it often comes in opposition to the sexual striving and can be repressed or suppressed as often as sexuality. In the mature human being, the sexual impulse is fully integrated into the properly human erotic intention which is directed toward another as a properly human person in his uniqueness and singularity. Therefore, fidelity is a necessary result of love—the other becomes irreplaceable because he is literally the only one. Monogamy is the end station of sexual development as well as the goal of sexual education and the ideal of sexual ethics. Of course, in practice this ideal may be reached by only a few, just as only a few will become fully mature and capable of mature love. This end station is more easily reached by women than by men. For a woman, to be sexually attracted only where sex is felt as the expression of a truly human relationship is nothing unusual. A man has to be ideally mature to reach the same integration.

The development from sex to love, or rather the developing integration of sexual and human attraction, may be disturbed in various ways. It may proceed normally until the last stage is reached where the sexual impulse becomes integrated into the erotic intention, that is, the young person falls in love. If he is then disappointed, rejected, he may become so discouraged that he reacts to it by regression. He may no longer believe that it is possible to combine the sexual and erotic goal and so he begins to seek isolated sexual satisfaction. This is the *resentment type* of maldevelopment. Or there may be a disturbance in the development of integration. The young man may feel himself driven toward sexual satisfaction and may not believe that a properly human relationship can be combined with this drive. This is the *resignation type*. To such a man, all love is sexuality, there can be nothing beyond it, neither can there be any love without sexuality. The Don Juan type is only one of the forms of this disturbance in psychosexual development. Finally, there is the *inactive type*. The two preceding types are unable to go beyond the purely sexual relationship to another. But the inactive type is incapable of even this type of relationship. Sexuality is experienced without an object, as it were, primarily in the form of self-gratification. Such a form of sexuality signifies a retreat from even the most primitive form of human relatedness.

A temporary absence of such human relatedness produces the "sexual conflict" [3] from which many adolescents and young adults seem to suffer. Sexual conflict, so called, occurs only in young people whose attention is focused on sex instead of on the human relationship to another. It is not the inevitable result of sexual abstinence and cannot be cured by sexual indulgence. This is shown by the fact that such difficulties disappear as soon as the young man falls in love, that is, as soon as he establishes a properly human relationship. This therapeutic effect of the restored or established dominance of love over sex has been confirmed in thousands of cases. Once the proper hierarchy is established, sex can be integrated into the affectionate human relationship so that it becomes what it ought to be, the expression of love. When love is dominant, there will also be the proper sense of responsibility without which a sexual relationship cannot endure.

Therefore, the psychotherapist will have to insist that sexual relations between young people who are sexually but not psycho-

[3] "Sexual conflict" is an inadequate translation of the German term "Sexualnot," which is almost a specific noun. "Sexualnot" means literally "sexual need" and refers in this context to the frustration and despair of adolescents and postadolescents who are sexually mature but find no acceptable opportunity for sexual activity.

sexually mature are harmful for their further development. But the therapist has no right to advise either for or against a sexual relationship when love is dominant because it is the essence of man's responsibility to make such a decision for himself. The therapist can point out, however, that abstinence has no ill effects provided only that the person freely decides for it. There is just as little reason why the boy or girl should enter sexual relations immediately after puberty as there is for both to become independent economically and start working immediately they have reached the proper muscular development. If they are forced to work at that time, they will never have a chance to prepare themselves for a profession for which their abilities might enable them; and if they indulge in sexual activity before they are psychologically mature, they will never have a chance to prepare themselves for a truly human love.

Special Existential Analysis. While existential analysis in general is the analysis of *human existence* from the point of view of responsibility, special existential analysis is the analysis of *psychological illness* from this point of view.

Psychological illness, whether neurotic or psychotic, is primarily a special mode of existence. It should be interpreted primarily as the expression of a psychological state and only secondarily as means to some particular end. Adler to the contrary, neurosis or psychosis never has a purpose of its own (such as to prevent the patient from achieving his aspirations). It is not the neurosis but the human being who has purposes, and existential analysis helps him to recognize the place of illness and neurosis in his scheme of life. When he has found his proper task, his goal in life, he will free himself from his neurosis. Therefore he must exercise his *freedom to* decide on his positive goal before he can achieve *freedom from* his neurosis. Every form of neurotic anxiety is basically an existential anxiety; every neurotic obsession-compulsion state is a deflection of the normal striving for perfection into one narrow channel, intensifying it to perfectionism. Existential analysis, considering anxiety as a mode of existence, enables the patient to correct the root of his fear by finding the meaning and task of his life, so that the patient can take means to reduce the habitual physical symptoms of anxiety. For obsessive-compulsives, existential analysis uses a suitable formula for retraining, helps build "golden bridges" for the neurotic perfectionism, to reduce it to the normal striving for perfection. Such a formula could be, for instance, this sentence:

Irgendwie ist es wohl gewissenlos, so oder so zu handeln; am gewissenlosesten wäre es aber—überhaupt nicht zu handeln (1, p. 166).
(It may be wrong to act in this or that way; but it is wicked not to act at all.)

Psychosis also, being primarily a mode of existence, can be treated by existential analysis. Manic-depressive psychosis represents essentially a reaction of the person to a physiological change (a speeding up or slowing down), while the schizophrenic suffers from an insufficiency of self-directed activity; he experiences his behavior as something done to him. Therefore the schizophrenic experiences himself as an object instead of as a responsible subject and so is affected in his very existence as a human being. However, the schizophrenic as well as the manic-depressive has a remnant of freedom with which he can confront his illness and realize himself not only in spite of it but because of it.

From Secular Confession to the Medical Cure of Souls. Since existential analysis is designed to help the patient to realize and acknowledge his existential responsiblity, it will have to move in the borderland between the psychological and ideal rather than in the borderland between the psychological and the somatic sphere. Since logotherapy examines man's human aspirations, it becomes important to decide whether or not the therapist is competent to deal with problems of value. Psychotherapy simply frees the patient from psychological or even physiological obstacles to proper functioning, and extends the self toward the soma by bringing unconscious processes into awareness. Logotherapy wants to free the person in a wider sense, wants to transform the "freedom from" into a "freedom to" self-actualization

and self-determination. Existential analysis aims at helping
the person to assume his responsiblity; but this means that
existential analysis borders on philosophy and the therapist
might be in danger of exceeding his competence. Does the therapist have the right to make value judgments? Every therapist,
physician or psychotherapist, has values and acts accordingly;
health is the primary value, and secondarily every physician has
to make value judgments in special cases—whether to risk a
dangerous operation, what to do in the problem of euthanasia,
whether to take drastic means to prevent a possible suicide. But
though all therapy is based on value judgments, the psychotherapist is facing a peculiar dilemma: on the one hand he is faced
with the necessity of making value judgments, on the other with
the necessity of avoiding any interference with the patient's own
values. To discuss a patient's philosophy of life might seem to
imply the preference of a particular philosophy over any other.
But that is not the case. Existential therapy merely brings the
patient to the realization that being human means being conscious and being responsible. As soon as the patient becomes
aware of his responsibility he will make his own independent
decision as to what his goal is and what his life task requires.
Existential therapy does not determine which hierarchy of values
should be chosen—it merely tries to make the patient conscious
of the fact that he must choose. Once he accepts his responsibility he will spontaneously look for a way to his own particular
goal. For existential analysis it is sufficient to lead the patient
to the univocal experience of his responsiblity for choosing;
to help toward concrete decisions or advise him is not permissible. The only exception is the case where interference or immediate decision is demanded in the patient's own interest, for
instance, in suicidal depression. Though ordinarily the therapist
must neither decide nor persuade, he should help the patient see
the implications of the decisions he might make.

Finally, what are the indications for logotherapy? There is
no one "right" therapy; the individuality of patient and therapist
will always have to be the deciding factor. Intuition and tact
will determine the specific therapy to be used in each specific

case. Logotherapy is not specific or causal therapy, but neither is psychotherapy. Not every difficulty successfully treated by psychotherapy is necessarily of psychogenic origin, and not every neurotic conflict yielding to logotherapy is necessarily rooted in an inadequate philosophy of life. Psychological causation is not the only indication for psychotherapy; on the contrary, psychotherapy is often effective though the cause is physical. Similarly with logotherapy: logotherapy may be indicated and adequate even though it does not treat the cause of the disorder. It is sometimes preferable to start the reorganization of personality from the top, to start with a man's ideals, even though the disturbance has started on a psychological or even physiological level. With a thorough reorganization of the patient's philosophy of life and therefore of his attitude, the neurosis is undercut, as it were, and made harmless. But existential therapy is not meant to be primarily a treatment of neuroses or psychoses and is not confined to psychological disturbances. It is needed also in general medical practice. Every physician needs to make sure that his patient achieves the right attitude to his illness as a mode of existence, so that he can grow in it instead of experiencing it as a frustration. And that always amounts to existential therapy in one way or another, for the patient's philosophy of life will have to be examined to help him become aware of his responsibility so that he can take a constructive attitude toward his illness.

Existential analytic logotherapy is indicated particularly whenever the patient is oppressed by problems of living. At other times, emotional difficulties have forced him to philosophical convictions which reinforce his very problems and necessitate a logotherapeutic approach. Finally, existential analysis, what might be called the medical cure of souls, is indicated when conditions exist which make life extremely difficult and which cannot be changed (unemployment, invalidism, incurable disease, etc.). It is in these cases that the greatest values can be actualized provided the patient can be made aware of the challenge.

Thus far Frankl.

COMMENT

Evaluation of Existential Analysis

It is not easy to give full appreciation to Frankl's conception of Existential Analysis because one can never be quite sure that one has penetrated to the core of his thought. One reason is that he is writing about the medical cure of souls and his remarks must be interpreted against a background of more or less serious illness. Secondly, it is well to remember that Frankl is principally concerned with setting down the minimum essentials in mental outlook, emotional response, and conduct that are required of the patient for successful therapy and complete rehabilitation. Finally, Frankl's dialectical mode of expression and paradoxical literary style hide a thought as often as they embellish it.

But what is most provocative in Frankl's exposition is the fact that one may follow his train of thought for long stretches with complete agreement and acquiescence only to be thrown into confusion by the example he uses to illustrate his principle. Thus (p. 32) Frankl argues defending the existence of absolute and objective values. He illustrates his point with the example of a man who finds his sex partner beautiful only when his sex instinct is aroused. The man concludes that the passion *produces* the beauty he sees. Frankl, however, tells us that the man's conclusion is a mistake. The beauty is there all the time; what the passion does is render the man capable of seeing it. And this relativity of beauty to the situation proves its absolute existence. "Es gibt demnach eine absolute Richtigkeit nicht trotz sondern gerade wegen perspektivischer Relativität." (There is absolute rightness or accuracy, not in spite of but because of the relativity of individual perspectives. p. 33.) Perhaps this example is too bound up with Frankl's dialectical mode of reasoning to be used as a fair sample. There is another (p. 54). There, Frankl recounts the case of a patient who suffered from a transmissible disease which contraindicated his having children, yet he strongly desired to have a son. He had decided to break off an engagement to marry but Frankl persuaded him that having children is not the sole purpose of marriage, any more than having children is the purpose of life. Frankl then proceeds to advise marriage without generation. It can be prudently surmised that it was not virginal marriage which was advised. But the example leaves the reader completely confused as to how Frankl meant his words to be understood. Did he suggest marriage without sex or sex without children?

Again, (p. 66) he recounts the story of a badly crippled young man who made a success of his life in spite of the most severe handicaps. He became the center of an intellectual set and had a bevy of beautiful women competing for his sexual favors. It is hard to resist the implication that this was really the badge of success in the man's life. But to aim for a goal like that belies the tenor of Frankl's theory.

No matter how obscure or exasperating Frankl may be at times, the general effect of reading him is refreshing and heartening. His outlook is kindred to our own. In him we find a psychiatrist who in his writings portrays the human being as a rational creature— not as an animal whose natural condition is neurosis. In him we find a clinician who is willing to believe that his patient is capable of self-control and direction—not the complete and abject victim of THE UNCONSCIOUS. In him we find a professional scientific worker who is convinced that the proper perfection of the human being is to be found in the realm of the spirit, not within the confines of instinct or reflex muscle twitches. Not everyone, perhaps, will consider these ideas progressive—we do; it is only in this direction that progress can be made in perfecting the human spirit. That has been our emphasis throughout; and there are more and more people in this troubled world who are beginning to realize (what Frankl says more than once) that a man becomes properly human in proportion to the liveliness of his religious faith and the goodness of his works.

Psychology is rediscovering the dignity of man, and Frankl makes it the cornerstone for his structure of thought. Clinical psychology has been too often swayed by the cosmic concept of the last decades that considered man a small, unimportant, and not very successful part of the evolutionary process. The old conception of man as lord of creation was laughed out of the schools. Frankl does not restore man's lordship over creation (quite to the contrary) but he does restore man's lordship over himself. Let us hope that Frankl's example will again make it possible in academic circles to speak of the human being with respect. Psychology will advance in the direction toward which so many psychologists seem to tend when consciousness, responsibility, freedom, life, and human love become familiar and pregnant concepts; and reflexes, social demands, indeterminacy, mechanisms, and genitality remain in the areas where they belong. To recognize human aspirations as something more than gland secretions and instinctual strivings will at least have the flavor of untried adventure and give room for discovery and originality. Frankl's venture into the realm of human values does not always lead him to conclusions which command our wholehearted acceptance, just as it does not always move along a path where we can follow him. If we map the doubtful spots along the way we do so only to show where we lost him and where we think we should have found him.

Because of Frankl's dialectical mode of thinking, and the difficulty of reconciling his theory and his examples, our agreement or disagreement with his statements can only be hesitant and tentative, lest we disagree out of lack of proper understanding, and praise without full comprehension. Nevertheless, we think his ideas merit an extended comment, especially since a suitable discussion of his position is not as yet available to American readers. For our evaluation, we shall single out three of his fundamental concepts: Responsibility, Freedom, Existence. These concepts are not clearly defined by Frankl nor are they systematically explored but they are the cornerstone of existential analysis as he expounds it.

Responsibility. For Frankl, man is faced with life and is conscious of his responsibility toward it. This implies that he has an obligation to carry out the task life imposes on him. Each man must shoulder his responsibility and fulfill his obligation if his life is to be wholesome and meaningful. This is the very minimum upon which a wholesomely normal life can be built. As a statement of basic principles this seems clear enough, but doubts begin to creep in upon closer examination. It is true, of course, that the most distinctive characteristics of man can be summed up under the rubrics "consciousness and responsibility," but these terms are none too clear in Frankl's use of them. It is hard to decide how often "consciousness" means simply "conscience," just as it is difficult to tell whether responsibility means moral accountability or simply physical responsiveness. To resolve the doubt it is hardly helpful to be offered an engaging play on words:

Er hat nicht zu fragen, er ist vielmehr der vom Leben her Befragte, der dem Leben zu antworten—das Leben zu ver-antworten hat (1, p. 48).

(Not for him to question, it is he who is questioned by life, he who has to answer—to answer for life.)

We confess that here literary style (or Frankl's personal dialectics) has clouded the meaning, for us at least.

Frankl takes for granted that the fact of the individual's responsibility to life is self-evident. But is it as evident as Frankl makes it? No man has ever asked to be born. No man has ever chosen his parents or the time and place of his birth. No man has determined from the very beginning in what environment he is to live or under what conditions his life is to begin. In this sense at least, no man can be said to be responsible for his existence. If, then, no man is responsible for life, how can he be said to be responsible *to* life? Would anyone say that the child is responsible to the parents for life? Would we not rather say that the parents are responsible to the child for life? If life gives existence to the human being as Frankl's whole exposition seems to imply, then the responsibility is not the human being's, the responsibility is life's. Life has no business asking a man any questions or imposing upon him any tasks. Man can ask of life: Why am I here, and by whose authority am I subject to these tasks you impose? The only basis for the power of life's imposing obligations is suggested by Frankl's remark that an animal does not know the purpose of its master (page 465). But man is not the slave of life. Here we are thrown off the track by an exasperating example.

That man is responsible for what he does with himself and to himself, when he has once reached the age of discretion, is something that nobody will deny, and this is something for which he has to answer. But that he should do something to himself or with himself follows not from the fact that he is living or that he has existence or that he is a being, it comes from the fact that he was created for a purpose which involves the highest and the truest perfection that man can achieve.

The primary thought which the fact of existence should arouse in a man's mind is not that existence imposes a task, but rather that it affords an opportunity. The primary question is not the one Frankl imagines life puts to man, but rather the question which man puts to life: "What is there in life for me? Why am I here? Why am I living?" Surely the fact of life, no matter in what sense it may be taken, can give me no adequate answer to that. To answer that question, not only must there be a purpose assigned for my being here and my living, but also a sufficient reason for its being the purpose of *my* living.

There is no doubt that Frankl avoids all these questions because he wants to find the common and minimum basis for the religious, irreligious, and nonreligious alike. He hopes to have found it in man's subjective experience of existence, rationality, and especially responsibility. But Frankl might find that his professional colleagues would either deny the fact of such subjective experience or would doubt its validity—and so would convinced skeptics and agnostics. Even if he could convince others that these assumptions are better than their own, there is reason to believe that this minimum is not enough. To face responsibility, we must understand what is implied in it. Thus the understanding and the experience of being responsible are primary data of life. Responsibility, however, implies not only an obligation and someone to discharge it; it also implies someone or something to which one is bound.[4] Obligation always implies a reciprocal relationship, a return for value received. Where is the reciprocal relationship in my responsibility to life?

[4] It could be objected that a sufficient explanation of moral obligation could be found in the requirements of rational human nature: "Human nature, because it is human, strives by its own natural tendency after the good and the true. To fail in its human dignity, to disregard the requirements of justice towards our fellow men, is self-degradation and a falling short of its own law" (4, p. 56). But this objection only postpones the question. As McCormick says: "The whole question of obligation resolves itself to this: Why must a being come up to the requirements of its nature when it is possible for it not to do so? There does not seem to be any answer to that question except this: Because the creator of that nature requires that it should. The will of the creator, then, and not rational nature itself, is the sufficient and only sufficient reason for the existence of moral obligation" (3, p. 92).

The value received is life, on Frankl's or anyone's premises, but life is the gift, not the giver, and our obligation is not to the gift but to the giver. True, we have to fulfill the purpose of life, use the gift rightly, but the gift is not its own purpose or meaning.

Frankl hopes that his basis is adequate because of the universality of the subjective experience of self-possession and responsibility. But such a hope acknowledges rationality only to frustrate it. It is the part of intelligence to ask the why of facts, the why of values, the why of their ordering. If the question is avoided or considered irrelevant, or answered by sheer recourse to existence and experience, rationality is not taken seriously. In a *logo*therapy which is based on reasons and motives and aims at the patient's reasoned conviction, a philosophy of life that is offered him must stand on the solid ground of reality, not on the shifting sands of existentialist subjectivism. The patient may be *persuaded* to accept such minimum ration, but unless the persuasion is based on a *conviction* that is sustained by reason, the last state of the man can become worse than the first. If there are values, they must be grounded in human nature and human nature itself grounded in the reality which originates and sustains it.

Frankl tries to build "golden bridges" not only to tempt the patient out of his neurosis, but also to tempt him to accept his responsibility, live his life task. But even golden bridges must lead to something and not stop short in the fog of subjectivism. Unless the therapist as well as the patient is willing to follow the logic of their enterprise to the end, there will be not the security of objective conviction but the bleak uncertainty of mere contingency. If "golden bridges" are to be built let them go from solid ground to solid ground; from the human creature, dependent upon God his maker and responsible to Him for every thought, word, and deed, to the need of the present moment and the opportunity it provides for living one's life. They are not to be raised on the neutral ground of a vague responsibility to a nebulous life of which full many a man these days has said: Je m'en fiche!

Freedom. It is true, of course, that the patient has come to the psychiatrist because he is being overwhelmed by the consequences of just this sort of declaration of independence. But he will be loath to accept the kind of freedom Frankl offers him in place of the freedom of death ("Freitod," i.e., suicide), unless something more substantial is given him than a persuasion that freedom means not a freedom *from* but a freedom *for*. Freedom, says Frankl, is the freedom to realize values. But why are creative, experiential, and attitudinal values preferable to other values that have been held dear by human beings, such as power, prestige, and pleasure?

Pleasure as a goal is inadequate, according to Frankl, because pleasure is a subjective state that is cut short by death and therefore is devalued even before death, while joy has an object outside the self. Furthermore, says Frankl, if every action were done for pleasure, any distinction between ethical and unethical actions would disappear because either action would be done only to escape feelings of displeasure. Thus moral action would be devalued. Again, there is a hidden assumption that moral action is on a higher level—but according to what criterion? Responsibility could mean merely the responsibility to act, not necessarily a responsibility to act morally. Actually, Frankl's stand presupposes not only responsibility to life but to a moral law, otherwise there would be no necessity for ethical action.

Frankl's preference for objective rather than subjective values similarly presupposes such a design of human living that the self is truly enhanced only when it is directed away from itself, when it creates (in work), when it actualizes itself by sharing with another (in love), when it conquers even suffering. Even in realizing experiential values the self must be focused on an object. In contrast, power, prestige, pleasure, mean concentrating on one's self, preferring subjective to objective values. A philosophy which not only assumes a hierarchy of values but also assumes the supremacy of objective over subjective values must answer the question how that supremacy is founded. If values are not only objective but absolute, as Frankl further contends, they must be given to us, discovered by us, but cannot have their origin in us. In that case, the question is legitimate: What has created them? What has established the hierarchy? What has given us the disposition to realize objective values and asks that we do? Why should we realize objective values, unless a work of art created and enjoyed, a life that is lived bravely in the midst of pain and sorrow, *is* somehow precious, to be preserved and cherished? And cherished not by the doubtful memory of a superorganism but by Someone who has created man in his image and given him beauty and the ability to enjoy and achieve it, who has put him in the midst of pain or sorrow but also given him the courage to welcome it.

Existence. The noteworthy qualities of Frankl's thought: the inspiring, the disconcerting, the impalpable, stem very largely from the existentialist outlook that Frankl has and the existentialist dialectic he uses. It is beyond the scope of this chapter to enter into any discussion of the existentialist frame of mind. Something has been said of that in Chapter 3. Moreover, there seem to be as many existentialist philosophies as there are individuals who think they are existentialists (which is as it should be, according to the existentialist point of view), and there is no guarantee that even the term "existence" means the same for any two of them. Obviously, the term does not mean the same to the existentialist and the nonexistentialist (the objectivist). Similarly, Frankl interprets the term in his own way.

Nevertheless, from the context the general idea seems to be that existence somehow comprehends the individual, the objective "situation," and the challenge the situation flings to the individual. The challenge is inescapable—it must be taken up—and to it the individual must respond correctly under pain of annihilation or disintegration. These are fundamental facts, primary and self-evident: first principles, so the existentialists say. But this is simply an assertion, unproved. No one denies that there is a challenge in life—but one can be mildly skeptical that challenge is the stuff out of which existence is made. In the same way one can be skeptical about the ineluctability of the demands made by this challenge. It is quite true that each individual is unique in himself and in the life situation that confronts him. It is true that the task of making an ideal person of himself is his and his alone. It is true that each man must solve his own problems for himself in his own way, individually and uniquely. Each problem's solution will be relative to the situation wherein it arises. But to jump from that judgment to the proposition that the meaning of the whole of life is unattainable though there is such an absolute meaning—nay to assert that *because* each life task is relative, the challenge is absolute, requires a kind of thinking that comes hard to most of us.

The existentialist will reply to all comments upon his position with the sad admission that he is defenseless against any objectivist assault because he is completely open only to subjectivist understanding. We must respect the plea and have recourse, in the case of Frankl at least, to watching the application of his principles and discover if not their truth, at the very least their value.

Evaluation of Existential Analysis As a Method. If the philosophy of existential analysis is not adequate for its goal, namely to give an answer to the existential doubts of the patient, what of its method? As far as can be gathered from Frankl's exposition, the method of logotherapy, as used by him, seems to be discussion and dream interpretation. Since he aims to clarify the patient's convictions and make him conscious of his responsibility, the method of rational discussion is adequate. In this case the patient has no more factual evidence than the therapist. What is required of the patient is that he state his convictions; he does not have to explain a particular personal situation in which his feelings are involved.

Therefore, discussion becomes a mutual search for the truth, for a right conception of reality, rather than a search for clarification of emotional tangles. Agreement and disagreement will be taken to mean that either the one or the other of the discussants is not in possession of enough evidence; and mutual discussion will eventually provide both with the relevant facts. The only doubt that remains is a doubt not of the technique but of its use when the philosophical foundations are not well and truly laid. The restriction apparent in the refusal of existential analysts to make inferences from existential facts is liable to lead to a misinterpretation of facts.

As an example we quote an actual case given by Frankl (2, p. 55) : A woman patient who wanted to discover why she had such a dislike for Christianity (she had not practiced her religion since childhood) was given the posthypnotic suggestion to dream the solution of her difficulty. This is the dream (our translation) :

	I am in Y. where I used to live as a child. I am waiting for
1.	the train to Vienna. *Dr. X* is living here. I want to visit him.
	I don't know what his address is; I ask a woman and she says:
2, 3,	*"Near the church."* I think I shall *remember the way* to the
4,	church. But *everything is different* from what it used to be. I
5,	wonder *which street* to take. I have been walking a long time.
6, 7,	*I feel doubtful.* . . . *A little girl* is standing in front of me and
	tells me: "Near the church! But you have taken the wrong way,
8. 9,	*you must go back!" I am thirsty.* The child draws clear water
	from a spring, and now I am actually going back. Now there
10,	are poplars across the street. But then the road is clear again
	and in the distance there is the church—a resplendent *cathedral,*
11.	*milky white,* like the one in Z.

And the interpretation by Frankl:

1. *Dr. X* is a psychotherapist, therefore, according to the dream, the dreamer realizes she needs psychotherapy.
2. She knows that her recovery, though started during therapy, must be perfected through religion.
3. She is optimistic.
4. To go back is not so simple for an adult, after she has been through life's doubts and difficulties.
5. She is wondering which way she has to take to come back to religion.
6. The doubt refers to God—his existence, his care.
7. The patient said later the little girl was herself as she had been. Interpretation: "Unless you become like little children."
8. She must go back to her naïve faith.
9. She is thirsting for God.
10. The way back means psychotherapy, existential analysis. The poplars mean the difficulties and relapses during therapy.
11. The cathedral refers to the cathedral in a city far from her home. When driving through on a trip in the past, she had looked forward to seeing the cathedral because she had long known and loved it from pictures. But when their party arrived at the cathedral it was dark and foggy so she never actually saw it. Interpretation: The transformation of the actual experience, where the cathedral was invisible, to the shining visibility of the dream church, means the transformation in the patient's concept of God during therapy, from the *Deus absconditus* to the *Deus revelatus.*

The method of dream interpretation seems to be that of Jung rather than Freud, though stripped of archetypal implications. It is very like the "integral analysis" described in Chapter 14. Up to No. 9 there is very little difference in interpretation, but with No. 10 Frankl brings in an extraneous interpretation: the "way back" means existential analysis. When we remember that the dream was the result of a posthypnotic suggestion that the patient should dream the solution of her difficulties with Christianity, then Frankl's interpretation makes the dream a rather roundabout performance. The patient has been in analysis all the time—then why the dream request that she go back to something she had forgotten? If her concept of God had already changed and that change was the solution to her problem, why was it necessary to give her the suggestion to dream the solution in the first place?

If we keep to the dream content a little more rigorously, as integral analysis requires, another interpretation becomes possible which offers a solution still to be achieved:

1. The patient realizes she needs healing and looks for it in existential analysis (Dr. X).
2. Analysis leads close to religion.
3. She thinks now that she will find her way.
4. But everything is different now that she is a child no longer.
5. She is wondering what is the way back to religion.
6. She does not know where to start, which way to take.
7. When she was a child she knew the way.
8. Knowing that, she knows suddenly that she must go back to the church she knew as a child.
9. She is thirsting for the living water of faith which was hers as a child.
10. So she is going back to the Church. There are difficulties in the way but as she keeps going the road clears again.
11. And now the Church, long ago known and loved, is visible in all her splendor, still in the distance, but our patient is on her way.

If the dream did provide a solution to her difficulties with Christianity, it means that the answer is to go back to the Church of her childhood. The dream suggests going back to religion, not to analysis, for after the initial mention of Dr. X it is the church which is in the center of the dream, not the therapist. And existential an-

alysis may be close to religion, but what the dreamer is really looking for, according to the dream, is the Church of her childhood.

We see, then, that the logic of the dream requires an interpretation different from Frankl's. To consider as he does that the solution of the patient's difficulties lies in her *experience during therapy*
in which the *Deus absconditus* was transformed into the *Deus revelatus* is possible only if the *experience* is considered the important
factor and not the *object* of that experience. If the experience of
God becomes important, not His objective existence, then therapy
can easily substitute for religion. But for the individual human
being, God as a psychological experience is a shaky foundation. Unless He really exists, the experience can be an illusion. And what
happens if our feelings fail us and we do not experience Him any
longer?

Thus it seems that in its application existential analysis suffers
from the same defects apparent in its philosophical assumptions:
there is a basic unwillingness to follow through the implications
of the primary data of existential analysis, *consciousness* (or self-
awareness) and *responsibility*. If this awareness is taken seriously,
then the truth it discovers must take precedence over any feeling-
experience. We are conscious (i.e., we know reflectively) that we
are responsible; if we go on reflecting, we find that a task must have
a task master, whether we "experience" him or not. Only where
sensory and emotional experience is valued above rationality will
religious *experience* be allowed to decide the issue. But that is
precisely what Frankl presupposes when he says that the religious
man hears not only the voice of conscience but also hears the speaker.
(Surely, to hear voices without a speaker is to have hallucinations?)
In the dream interpretation, he takes a reference to something "beside" or "close to" existential analysis, as a reference to analysis; in
his system, he takes the experience of responsibility for an explanation of it. In both cases, he takes subjective truth to be objective
truth—but one need not be the other.

Existential analysis has philosophical foundations which are
more acceptable than are the foundations of Freud's or Adler's system, because here the human being is considered in his basically
human functions. But a near-truth still is not truth. It will help
people to strive for a self-ideal but cuts short that striving before

it can discover the self-ideal as it ought to be. Since existential therapy is *logo*therapy, it stands and falls with the logic of its philosophical assumptions. While logotherapy could be used with any philosophical assumptions, its value will never be independent of these assumptions

REFERENCES

1. FRANKL, VIKTOR E. 1948. *Ärztliche Seelsorge.* (Fünfte Auflage.) Vienna: Franz Deuticke Verlag. (Published 1946. Quotations are from reprint of 1948.)
2. ———. 1947. *Zeit und Verantwortung.* Vienna: Franz Deuticke Verlag.
3. McCORMICK, JOHN F., S.J. 1931. *Scholastic metaphysics.* Part II. Chicago: Loyola University Press.
4. MERCIER, DÉSIRÉ CARDINAL. 1922. *Manual of modern scholastic philosophy.* London: Kegan Paul, Trench, Trubner & Co.

Chapter 17

THE THEORY OF PSYCHOTHERAPY

By Magda B. Arnold

At the present time, there are many well-defined methods of psychotherapy. They all show results but none of them is successful all the time or with every therapist. If there were only one method, failure could be ascribed to lack of skill in application. Since there are many methods, the usual practice is to try various methods and therapists until one succeeds or the case is abandoned as intractable. Historically, it has happened that a lucky guess has developed into a successful therapeutic method.

It is certain that apparently successful techniques have led to elaborate theories of personality. But success in therapy is not its own explanation, for it may be that it works for reasons quite different from those assigned for its success.

Until now there has been no systematic study of therapeutic methods to establish their nature or laws. Unless some attempt is made to examine what it is each system does do to the patient and how it achieves its results, we shall be hindered in our scientific approach to psychotherapy. While psychotherapy remains a purely empirical procedure, its practitioners are forced either to adhere rigidly to the system in which they have been trained or to become sheer eclectics. In neither case can they give an objective account of the reason for therapeutic success or failure in any given case or with any given type of disturbance. Their individual clinical experience will not become fruitful for psychology as a whole but will remain purely an art. It is for lack of a theory of psychotherapy that schools are increasing in this field while they are gradually becoming obsolete in general psychology.

Our discussion is offered merely as a preliminary and very tentative formulation. It is not comprehensive nor does it pretend to be definitive. It is hoped, however, that such an attempt will stimulate others to more extensive efforts.

If a theory of personality deals with the organization of personality, then a theory of therapy must offer some explanation of the way in which such organization can be disturbed and the means by which it can be restored. Since we have discussed the various levels of function and their disturbances in a previous chapter (Chapter 13) we will merely summarize our findings as they apply to therapy.

Nature of Disturbance

Disturbance of Naturally Determined Function. Personality organization can be disturbed on the level of naturally determined functions as they work together to form our experience of the world around us. The simplest examples are toxic psychoses, for instance those produced by opium, alcohol, or other drugs, in which sensory experience is disturbed in a variety of ways. The various single sensory functions may be normal but the integrated perception of things and people is disturbed. There may be an altered perception of time, of object size, or a distortion in shape. There may be outright visual and auditory hallucinations. The world is perceived differently; it becomes unreal and threatening. This is strikingly illustrated in recent experiments with lysergic acid (Rinkel *et al.*, 16). Experimental subjects report that the world looks strange to them, so strange that they cannot find words to describe it nor words to convey their feelings. No wonder they cannot find words, for all our concepts, and therefore words, are based on normally integrated perception. A disturbance in the integration of our sensory experience would need new concepts and a new language.

Obviously, such disturbances in the way in which the world is perceived will also affect the way in which things or people are imagined and evaluated. Imagination, judgment, emotion, reasoning, will all be disturbed as well. So it comes about that the well-known feelings of strangeness and depersonalization are usually considered merely one symptom of psychosis among many. And the disturbances of judgment, reasoning, imagination, as well as feelings of depersonalization, hallucinations, delusions, are usually ascribed to a loss of control over imaginative processes so that internal conflicts are projected in external hallucinatory images. Theoretically speaking, it is at least unlikely that an entirely normal perceptual experience could go with a striking disorder of imagination, for surely perception is the basis of imaginative productions. In acute disorders, such as fever delirium, perception is distorted together with imagination.

If perception is distorted, then the extraordinary stubbornness of the psychotic in the face of reasonable explanation or interpretation becomes intelligible. Even the psychotic knows the difference between imagination (which is something he does) and perceptual experience (which is something that happens without his volition). When the psychotic complains that an influencing machine is working on him, or that he is made of glass, then he really has the experience which he interprets in this way—just as the neurotic really feels the pain that disables him. In both cases it is not "imaginary" perception or "imaginary" pain; it is a real sensory experience. In the case of the neurotic, we know that the pain is the physiological result of his emotion; in the case of the psychotic we do not know how the changes in perception are produced, but that does not mean that they are exclusively the product of a disordered imagination. The elaborate delusional system which the psychotic gradually develops is an attempt to *account* for his experiences; it cannot be disproved as long as his perception is disturbed.

In psychosis, the disturbance seems to be on a biological rather than on a psychological level. This is well recognized in toxic and in organic psychoses. But even in such a so-called "functional" psychosis as schizophrenia there is a growing opinion that the predisposing cause is a disturbance in brain function or a change in cell metabolism rather than psychological conflicts. Even when psychological stress seems to occasion a psychotic break, similar stresses in other people do not result in a psychosis but in various forms of neurosis. The break with reality which distinguishes psychosis from neurosis is explained much more consistently by a basic disturbance in integrated perception, the function that mediates our experience of the external world as well as of our body. Hence a psychosis seems to be a true disease in the medical sense of the term which may be precipitated by stress, like any other disease, but is not caused by it.

This does not mean that there is no room for psychotherapy in psychosis. After all, the psychotic remains a human person even though his disease falsifies his perception and robs him of rational communication with his fellow-men. But psychotherapy in psychosis must be content to help the patient regain his contact with reality rather than help him reorganize his life. Hence the notable success of methods which simply seek to provide some human contact, as against the failure of conventional methods of psychotherapy.

Disturbance in Self-Organization. Next, there may be a disturbance not in the integrated functioning of human capacities in perception but in the deliberate choice of human goals. Here the disturbance is not physiological but psychological. What interferes in self-organization is the emotional conflict which results from a man's inconsistency in choosing a goal or his unwillingness to choose the right one. (Cf. Chapter 6, and Chapter 13, Comment.) Such attitudes create conflicts and prolong them, thus producing emotional disturbance.

It is true that there may be physiological factors which may influence a person's choice: His constitution may be such that his emotions affect him more than they do others, or a severe traumatic experience as well as habitual indulgence may result in more violent or more prolonged emotional reactions. But even here it depends basically on his choice of goals whether he will or will not resolve his conflicts. If he does not he will fall prey to continual disturbance.[1] Thus the neurotic can hardly be said to suffer from a disease in the usual sense of the term. However disabling such a state of chronic emotional disturbance

[1] Cf. Hoch: "The conflict is a prerequisite to the development of a neurosis, but the inability to handle the conflict is really the essence of a neurotic disturbance" (6, p. 109).

may be, it is the result of his mismanagement or lack of management rather than its cause. (It should not need emphasis that such mismanagement can come from ignorance as much as from self-will.) The resulting emotional disturbance may show a host of symptoms, both psychological and physiological, but these accompany the emotion and may reinforce it, they do not produce it. Any neurosis is really a psychosomatic effect, the result of attitudes toward things to be sought and things to be avoided, which produce both emotional disturbances (a psychological state) and their organic expressions (somatic symptoms).

There is no doubt that a chronic emotional disturbance may lower resistance to any kind of disease—whether a psychosis or a physical disease. The symptoms of emotional disturbance may also be so severe or so prolonged that they become incapacitating or irreversible. Hence neurosis may result in disease even though it is not a disease in itself. In the long run, a man's psychological state is bound to influence his total functioning. It is hardly conceivable that he could be suffering from severe and prolonged conflict, no matter in what area, and at the same time enjoy radiant health. Conversely, adverse circumstances will affect even a man whose life is well ordered, whose mind is serene. He cannot help suffering in mind and body when he is bombed out, starved, fatigued, exhausted, or seriously ill. But such suffering need not necessarily disturb the rational ordering of his life, his self-organization. It need not result in neurosis.

If a man's life is not properly ordered and he is in a state of chronic conflict and internal difficulty, his emotions will get the better of him and he will be unhappy, disturbed, and anxious. Every unresolved conflict will disturb integration on three levels : integration of appetitive (emotional) tendencies will be disturbed when goals conflict and a person's choice is inconsistent; the integration of the basic tendencies to possession, stabilization, and self-actuation will be disturbed if they become ends instead of means; there will be a disturbance that is even more basic when the self-ideal as it is diverges from the self-ideal as it ought to be. The disturbance is most obvious on the appetitive level. The patient always brings definite emotional problems into therapy, goals he cannot reach, fears he cannot master. But it is the task of therapy to go beyond his immediate problems to the more important problem of how he can manage his life according to the self-ideal as it ought to be.

For the man who simply drifts, whose self-ideal is the whim of the moment, who follows all his impulses and inclinations, there may be no obvious emotional disturbance. The psychopath does not suffer from conscious conflicts, but he does run into every kind of difficulty with his fellow-men. In such a case it is even more obvious that the disturbance is not confined to the level of isolated emotional indulgences, no matter how severe the clash with the rights and expectations of other people. Such a man has never seriously tried to set a goal for himself that goes beyond the whims of the hour. Since it is hardly credible that his impulses should be so much stronger than anyone else's, the root of his troubles must also be his failure to manage himself.

In these cases, there is a disturbance of self-organization, but no disease. And the disturbance is produced by every man's decisions, his own actions, even though he cannot see the connection. It is never an isolated problem to which he cannot find the answer which disturbs his normal living, it is his whole life pattern that is disturbed and must be reorganized—and this pattern, as we have seen, is formed and implemented by himself and must be changed by himself. Wolberg puts it concisely:

> The patient always comes to therapy with a problem for which he wants active help. He assumes that, as in other contacts with doctors, he merely has to present his problem to the physician and the latter will either remove his problem or tell him how he can get well. . . . What we most desire as a goal is to get the patient to a point where he can function through his own resources as a strong, capable, assertive person, making his own choices and decisions in his effort to lead a productive life (in: Hoch, 6, p. 47).

Such a patient, then, does not have an isolated problem; neither does he have a disease.[2] But he does need help, not help

---

[2] When he has a mental *disease* (e.g., a toxic psychosis) he is usually in no condition to ask for help or cooperate when it is given; he has no "insight."

to cure a disease but aid in regulating his life. Once he can "make his own choices and decisions in his effort to lead a productive life" he will succeed in regulating his emotions. Thus the help given him cannot be "specific therapy" but must be general, in fact more so than is usually admitted. The choice of goals implies values, even a hierarchy of values. Anyone who wants to help such a patient should be an expert in this area. In addition, he needs special knowledge to understand the connection between goals and emotions, as well as the physiological effects of emotions and their interplay.

Control, Prevention, and Correction of Mental Disturbance

Control: Counsel and Therapy. The study of values and goals and their application to the individual's self-ideal has not traditionally been the domain of medicine. Perhaps we have been mistaken in placing our emphasis on disease and comparing every kind of "mental disturbance" with physical disease. If we do we are in fact asking the medical profession to assume a burden which it may well reject. Frankl asks the question whether a physician is competent to make value judgments. He says he is because he must make them every day in medicine. But it is in his own field that his expert knowledge makes it possible for him to make value judgments : he takes the responsibility for his decision to operate, for the techniques he decides to use, for the precautions he will employ. In psychotherapy he is asked to help others to make value judgments in another field altogether.

Traditionally, the field of value judgment has belonged to the practical moralist, the spiritual guide. When anyone became confused about his goals and values and the conflict and inner turbulence they aroused, he used to discuss his problems with parents, older friends, teachers, priests, or clergymen. The psychiatrist and psychologist have been added to the list comparatively recently, under the influence of a growing conviction fostered by scientists and diffused among the public that man is an "organism" and not a person. If something goes wrong with an organism, the physician is summoned just as a technician is called when something goes wrong with a machine. Neither organism nor machine can be held responsible when its functioning is disturbed.

If all psychological difficulties are considered to be the result of strictly determined internal and external factors which disturb smooth functioning, then, of course, the analogy between physical and psychological disturbance is well founded. In that case even medically applied psychotherapy is inappropriate, for it appeals to "insight" and depends on a person's deliberate reorganization of his attitudes and his behavior. Psychotherapy should really be replaced by psychosurgery, chemotherapy, and situational therapy if we want to have effects without the patient's deliberate activity.

How prevalent is the conception of neurosis as a disease, and how obvious it seems when its implications are not examined, is shown by the following two excerpts from letters of psychiatrists who take a strong stand against psychotherapists without degrees in medicine:

The whole subject bores me. I first encountered it in Europe in connection with lay analysis and now again in this country in the form of clinical psychology. Anyone who wishes to treat sick people should get a medical degree (7, p. 193).

Unfortunately, a medical degree does not provide for any expert knowledge of the worthwhileness of human goals, nor for any special competence in value judgments. A similar stand is taken by another psychiatrist:

This whole problem is not related only to psychologists—there are others in the so-called ancillary services who have been taking on more and more responsibilities which are clearly in the realm of treatment. Perhaps we have erred in not defining limits so that the training of ancillary workers will include such limits just as it does in the training of the nurse in her relationship to the doctor and to the patient in terms of her role in treatment (7, p. 193).

Such limits obviously could not have been devised because the medical profession has never had the supervision of the training of various types of counselors, of those who in the past have given help and counsel to individuals overwhelmed and confused by indecision, guilt, fear, or remorse. Perhaps Rogers has taken the right step when he insisted that such people need counseling and not therapy; that they come for aid in a course of action which they have to implement and initiate themselves—hence they are clients, not patients.

It will be objected that there must have been a reason why counsel as discussed here has gradually become the province of medical therapists. There is a reason, and a very good one.—It has always been recognized that right living, that is, living according to right principles, is necessary if a man is to have peace of mind. But it has not always been recognized that hankering after what his conscience forbids, or disciplining himself reluctantly and rebelliously, will not result in peace of mind but in emotional disturbance, no matter how blameless a man's actions. It is the great contribution of Freud and medical psychologists after him to have pointed out the connection between a man's inner conflicts and their symptomatic expression. But while it is true that in times past moralists did not pay attention to the havoc wrought by inner rebellion to accepted ethical principles, psychotherapists today are inclined to forget that a right ordering of life which is fully accepted and acted upon *prevents conflicts and therefore neurosis* instead of creating them.

Thus the psychiatrist is qualified to deal with emotional problems because of his special knowledge of the connection between a man's wants, his emotions, and his physical state, a knowledge which he has not acquired as part of his study of medicine but in his study (or practice) of medical psychology. Since such emotional problems and conflicts are not disease, though they may lead to disease, the psychiatrist's special knowledge of the effects of emotion should really be supplemented by a knowledge of the normal goals of normal people, and by some experience of that ordering of life which holds out promise for personality integration. Here the nonmedical therapist is not at any disadvantage. The psychologist particularly, whose special study is not only emotion but personality integration, could be expected to aid someone who has failed to manage his life and is confused about his goals.

But neither psychiatrist nor psychologist has any professional knowledge of the norms of human behavior at its best, and is therefore hampered in his activity unless he uses the norms made available by the discipline which discusses them, namely ethics (Cf. page 123).

Prevention. At what point a troubled and confused human being becomes a neurotic is difficult to decide. But to conclude, therefore, that everybody is neurotic, some more, some less, is like saying that there are no white flowers because there is no certain transition point between white and yellow or pink. At any rate, it is certain that the first symptoms of a neurosis are not noticed by the man who has them in the same way as he notices symptoms of physical disease. If he has a recurring stomach-ache, he will soon consult a physician; but if he has a persistent personal problem which he cannot solve alone, he will turn not to a psychotherapist but to someone whose wisdom and experience he trusts. Only when the *effects* of unsolved problems become noticeable and interfere with his everyday living and working will he consult a therapist.

Since the cause of neurosis is not a medical problem, prevention also falls outside the medical domain. There is no doubt that a human being needs a knowledge of the right way to manage his life. He often needs even more some guidance in applying such general knowledge to his own particular circumstances. In the nature of the case, such counsel will be given by individuals whose age or wisdom qualifies them, or by professional men specially trained in pointing the way to ultimate human goals, namely, priests and clergymen. At this stage it is relatively unimportant that the counselor have a precise and detailed knowledge of the interrelation of goals, emotions, and psychophysical functioning. Only when the wrong decisions have been made and the wrong habits developed, when conflicts have become chronic and emotions begin to disturb the even tenor of life, only then may a knowledge of the connection between unhappiness, emotional tension, and various somatic symptoms be of advantage. Theoretically it is quite possible that such counsel could prevent serious disturbance or restore emotional balance, merely by helping to restore the right hierarchy of goals, even though the counselor should have no knowledge of these connections or should not elect to make use of his knowledge for interpretation (as in nondirective counseling).

Thus the process of taking counsel is basic in managing one's life. In his discussion of counseling (Chapter 15) Dr. Curran rightly applies the term to the nondirective approach, for it concentrates on the person's goals and the means of reaching them. But the term "counsel" should not be restricted to this approach. It is applicable in any situation where a person seeks aid in clarifying his goals and the means to them.

Correction. *Therapy,* on the other hand, would apply to the much more restricted cases in which help is sought because emotional disturbance threatens to become disabling. Frankl uses the term "psychotherapy" in much the same sense as therapy of emotional disturbances. Once a man is disturbed and the disturbance has spread to a large area of living, so that he seeks counsel not only in a particular decision but in reorganizing his life, he enters a therapeutic relationship. No longer is he merely seeking help in organizing his life; now he is looking for help in retracing his mistakes and recouping his losses. We can, therefore, call psychological *therapy* any situation which helps a human being to reorganize himself, as distinct from *counsel* which helps him in mapping out his course in the first place or deciding an individual issue. The art of healing in medicine consists of helping nature in restoring health; in psychological therapy, in helping the person to reorganize himself.[3]

---

[3] Subsequently, we shall treat nondirective counseling also as a form of therapy. The only objection to this usage could be the implication that the client is someone who is ill, and therefore needs a remedy to make him well again without having any responsibility himself. This implication is excluded by the tenor of the whole discussion and particularly by the definition of psychological healing as the art of *helping the person to reorganize himself.*

If we define therapy in this way, then we can distinguish sharply between the counselor (or spiritual guide) who is primarily concerned with aiding another to find the right goals in life (though the man who is seeking such aid may often be disturbed), and the therapist who is primarily concerned with the reorganization of a disturbed personality (though such reorganization cannot be done without finding the right goals).

It might be of considerable advantage if the man who gives counsel (whoever he is) also had some knowledge of the effects of emotions and their interplay. Such knowledge is not absolutely necessary, however, because his main role is helping another to achieve the right ordering of his life, and only incidentally does he prevent emotional disturbance. For the therapist it is indispensable to have a clear conception of human goals and their relative importance. No matter what system of therapy he uses, he must necessarily aim for the reorganization of the person's goals as well as his emotions. This is recognized by every system of therapy. There is not one which is content to remove the symptoms of disturbance or tackle only superficial problems. The various systems differ principally in their view of man and his goal in life, in the choice of the level at which they will treat the disturbance, and in their method of approach. This will become clear if we attempt a theoretical appraisal of their aims and methods. Such an appraisal might make it possible to relate the various systems to one another and combine them, if need be, on the basis of our theory of personality.

First of all, we will examine each theory to discover what is the professed goal of therapy because that can indicate, at least by inference, what each system takes to be the goal of human life. Whatever the therapist holds to be the norm toward which he will help the patient, that is at the same time the most important feature of human striving for him. If the goal of therapy is adjustment, for instance, then the well-adjusted man is the ideal man for the therapist, and adjustment becomes the criterion of human development, the goal of man's striving. We examine the levels of organization because that can indicate the *chief* goal implicit in the system of therapy.

Psychoanalysis as a therapy tries to achieve a working compromise between an individual's inner drives, the societal taboos, and external reality. Individual psychology (Adler) tries to reduce a man's striving for superiority to the level justified by his capacities, which can be harmonized with social feeling. Analytical or complex psychology (Jung) tries to make the individual conscious of his complementary personal and racial unconscious, helps him integrate the two, and so aids him in achieving individuation. Nondirective counseling (Rogers) helps a man to understand himself, to clarify his goals, and make his own decisions. And existential analysis (Frankl) has the avowed aim of making the human being conscious of his responsibility and willing to fulfill his obligation.

These goals of therapy exactly correspond to the goals of human life pictured by these different systems. According to Freud, a man's happiness lies in having the greatest possible biological satisfaction consonant with his social milieu and the circumstances of his life. For Adler, a man's goal is to achieve the success his capacities warrant without losing contact with his fellow-men. Jung sees human perfection in full individuation. Rogers sees the goal of human living in self-understanding and responsible decision; Frankl in acknowledging life as a task and a responsibility.

Biological satisfaction (through compromise with reality), personal success, individuation, independence, and finally responsibility: there is no doubt that human life contains all these purposes and in one way or another demands them all. But that does not mean that all are equally important or that each and every one of them could be made the end of all human striving.

They cannot all be valid as the *chief* human goal; they cannot all be invalid because they are all goals which are found among human beings. The only way to reconcile their claims is to order them according to importance, to establish an order of importance. To establish such an order psychologically among these different systems, we must examine the level of personality organization to which each system applies.

Systems of Therapy

Psychoanalysis. Psychoanalysis can be considered as dealing with the appetitive level of human life. It is concerned with the "dynamics" of human action, with inner motive forces which are conceived as drives or impulses moving the person actually and emotionally in a polarity of love and aggression

(Eros/Thanatos). Psychoanalytic *free association* traces back the pattern of impulses (the emphasis is on impulses, not on the pattern, even in character analysis) to its roots in the past, reduces the present emotional overreaction to its appropriate size, and tries to obtain a balance in favor of constructive (Eros) drives. Within our scheme of personality organization, psychoanalysis would deal with the genetic development of man's appetitive tendencies and what arouses them. But our discussion in Chapter 10 has shown that the intensity of emotional impulses depends only partly on their genetic development, the person's traumatic history, and his habits of restraint or indulgence. It also depends on the proper ordering of these impulses, or rather, on the proper ordering of the person's rational goals to which these impulses will be subordinated. Habits of restraint or indulgence will be established according to these goals.

If the intensity of such impulses is the result of traumatic experiences, psychoanalytic free association may correct excessive or inappropriate reactions by discovering their roots in the past and freeing the individual from his emotional hangovers; [4] but emotional difficulties which are created or intensified by inconsistency of choice and improper ordering of goals cannot be solved by discovering the first occasion for the conflict. Such conflicts may be shelved and their discomfort alleviated by "freeing the id from an unduly strict superego"; they can be solved only when the person is helped to establish the right hierarchy of goals.

Mowrer takes the latter alternative and speaks of a "repression of conscience" rather than the repression of id impulses. He conceives the role of the therapist as finishing the work which the parents left undone. Mowrer's solution does imply a reordering of the patient's goals, but such reordering has

---

[4] In some cases the person is well aware of the first occasion on which he experienced similarly intense emotional reaction. If so, all that is needed for him is to understand the connection between the original (traumatic) reaction and his present excessive emotion. In other cases, there is no memory of any relevant incident. In that case, the method of *free association,* used in psychoanalysis, is necessary to trace back the traumatic incident. As a tool for discovering the forgotten roots of excessive emotional reactions, this method is a permanent contribution to the analysis of emotion.

to be attempted on the individual therapist's own responsibility, on the basis of his own philosophy of life. Freud's view of man sees the goal of human life in his greatest possible biological satisfaction, restricted only by expediency. To discipline id impulses beyond expediency can be defended only on the basis of some more important goal—but that is not Freud's philosophy.

Individual Psychology. Adler seems to deal not with the appetites but with human striving organized by the basic tendency to self-establishment, that is, toward achievement. Subjectively, Adler points out, it is a striving toward superiority growing out of the painful feeling engendered by infantile inferiority. This striving for superiority intends to achieve the dominance over things and persons that is necessary for self-actuation. What possessions or what achievements a man strives for in particular depends on his interests; hence he develops an individual "life style." The core of this striving for superiority is the striving for self-actuation, for excellence. It becomes excessive and develops into a striving for superiority only because the tendency is allowed free play instead of being subordinated to a rational goal, the self-ideal as it ought to be.

Individual psychology analyzes that striving for superiority by examining together with the patient his attitudes to his family, his friends, his subordinates and superiors, and the therapist himself. Therapy is successful when the patient gains an objective estimate of himself and his achievements, when he can approach others with affection instead of trying to dominate them or resentfully submit to them. Thus the striving for superiority is reduced to the normal striving for excellence, justified by the patient's abilities and balanced by his social feeling. There is no doubt that there is merit in reducing the intensity of the human tendency for self-actuation through possession, by means of rational analysis, but such analysis presupposes that the patient recognizes the desirability of rational control and that he has a positive goal, the self-ideal as it ought to be, which will dominate the striving for self-establishment and thus reduce its intensity. Here again, the usefulness of the therapy will depend on the goal-centeredness of the patient and the therapist, or rather, it will depend on the possibility of establishing the proper hierarchy of goals during therapy.

If we compare individual psychology with psychoanalysis we notice that the former taps a higher level of organization. If successful, it should include also a therapy on the appetitive level, for the higher includes the lower level of organization. Hence Adler correctly insists that emotional and particularly sexual difficulties are part and parcel of the disorder in the tendency toward superiority (or self-establishment, as we have called it).

Complex Psychology. Jung seems to work on the level of self-integration, and to assist in the formation of the self-ideal. The distinctive method used is active imagination combined with dream analysis.[5] According to Jung, the insight gained by the patient results first in a considerable extension of awareness, secondly reduces the dominating influence of the unconscious, and thirdly induces a change in personality (8, p. 171). The method itself is described by Jung * as follows:

[Active imagination] is a method of introspection, namely the observation of the stream of interior images: one concentrates one's attention on some impressive but unintelligible dream image, or on a spontaneous visual impression, and observes the changes taking place in it. Meanwhile, of course, all criticism must be suspended and the happenings observed and noted with absolute objectivity. . . . Under these conditions, long and often very dramatic series of fantasies ensue. The advantage of this method is that it brings a mass of unconscious material to light. Drawing, painting and modelling can be used to the same end. Once a visual series has become dramatic, it can easily pass over into the auditive or linguistic sphere and give rise to dialogues and the like. With slightly pathological individuals and particularly in the not infrequent case of latent schizophrenia the method may, in certain circumstances, prove extremely dangerous and therefore require medical control (9, p. 228).

---

[5] Our own method of integral analysis has developed out of this method and it would seem useful, therefore, to quote Jung's own explanation at some length.

* Quotations by permission from C. G. Jung and C. Kerenyi, *Essays on a Science of Mythology.* Copyright 1949, The Bollingen Foundation, Inc. Published by Pantheon Books, Inc.

Among Jung's examples is the following (part dream, part active imagination) :

A magician is demonstrating his tricks to an Indian prince. He produces a beautiful young girl from under a cloth. She is a dancer who has the power to change her shape or at least hold her audience spellbound by faultless illusion. During the dance she dissolves with the music into a swarm of bees. Then she changes into a leopard, then into a jet of water, then into a sea-polyp that has twined itself about a young pearl fisher.

Between times, she takes human form again at the dramatic moment. She appears as a she-ass bearing two baskets of wonderful fruits. Then she becomes a many-colored peacock. The prince is beside himself with delight and calls her to him. But she dances on, now naked, and even tears the skin from her body, and finally falls down—a naked skeleton. This is buried, but at night a lily grows out of the grave, and from its cup there rises the white lady, who floats slowly up to the sky (9, p. 238).

According to Jung,

This piece describes the successive tranformations of the illusionist (artistry in illusion being a specifically feminine capacity) until she becomes a transfigured personality. The fantasy was not invented as an allegory. It was part dream, part spontaneous imagery. . . .

The death of the dancer is . . . to be understood in this sense [of a sacrifice] for these maidens are always doomed to die, because their exclusive domination of the feminine psyche hinders the individuation process, that is, the maturation of personality. . . . As long as a woman is content to be a *femme à homme*, she has no feminine individuality. She is empty and merely glitters—a welcome vessel for masculine projections. Woman as a personality, however, is a very different thing: here illusion no longer works. So that when the question of personality arises, which is as a rule the painful fact of the second half of life, the childish form of the self disappears too (9, p. 239).

If active imagination as well as the dream picture the individual's reaction to his total life situation, or at any rate to the problem that preoccupies him (as many published reports and our own clinical observations amply confirm), then this method certainly represents a tool for exploring personality organization and the self-ideal. In Jung's hands, however, this tool becomes a means of exploring the unconscious and deriving from it guidance for individuation. While Freud's unconscious is a seething cauldron of instinctual forces and ought to be known only to be restrained, Jung's unconscious is peopled with gods and demons, heroes and villains which represent the collective even more than the personal forces of the unconscious and are so taken to be reliable guides to personality integration. No wonder that Jung's patients are in danger of "inflation," of developing a "mana-personality." If out of themselves they can create gods and demons, powers and principalities to guide them, why shouldn't they become first elated and then inflated?

Moreover, Jung's ideal personality is the four-square man or woman. Thinking/feeling, sensation/intuition are all on the same level; neither is subordinated in theory. In practice, every individual has his preference for one of these functions, and the others are correspondingly neglected. There is no integration needed or demanded; the ideal is the maximum exercise of each function. The ideally mature person should be able to use all his functions with equal facility. In justice to Jung it should be said that his "sensation function," for instance, is neither sensation as understood in psychology nor sensory knowledge. It is rather a deliberate preference for everything that can be experienced in a sensory way so that a man's whole life is oriented toward concrete experience, detailed observation. For Jung, individuation consists in developing all four functions equally, in being able to draw upon the wisdom of the unconscious to provide a balance for the conscious. In this way man is made whole, integrated, individuated, living with both his conscious and his unconscious resources. The integrated human being lives his self-ideal, so to speak, is master of the psychic forces which at first he projected into reality as gods or demons, and therefore can control them. Yet Jung protests that he is committed neither to agnosticism nor skepticism:

Wenn daher Gott oder das Tao eine Regung oder ein Zustand der Seele genannt wird, so ist damit nur über das Erkennbare etwas ausgesagt, nicht aber über das Unerkennbare, über welches schlechthin nichts ausgemacht werden kann (10, p. 64).

When God or Tao is called a psychic force or state, I am talking only about the knowable and not about the unknowable, about which nothing can be known or said at all. (Our translation).[6]

For Jung, personality develops according to the laws laid down in the unconscious—the conscious has to step aside and "let it happen" until the unconscious lives through the conscious, or rather until it is the unconscious that lives, not the conscious. That at any rate is how Jung interprets the words of St. Paul: Not I but Christ is living in me (10, p. 61). There is no real goal that can serve as focus for a man's striving; there is only a being, developing by an evolutionary force toward autarchy.

However, in the case of Jung's system of therapy the method seems to promise more than its originator has seen in it. While Jung has used it to explore the personal and collective unconscious to help the individual toward autarchic growth, it can also be used to increase man's self-knowledge for more effective self-determination. It is a moot question whether the personality changes because the person becomes aware of his unconscious striving for completion and perfection, or whether that awareness must first produce a change in self-direction before there can be any change in personality.

To quote but one example: a professional woman, who had never failed in an examination, dreamed repeatedly over a period of some twenty years that she was back at school, about to be examined in Religion, that she had had no time to study, and so failed miserably. It was not until she found her way back to religion that the familiar nightmare dream stopped for good. It stands to reason that sheer knowledge will not automatically produce either a change in behavior nor, therefore, a change in personality. We must first decide to act upon that knowledge in one way or another, must exercise our self-determination, before knowledge can change our goal or the direction of our striving.

[6] This passage very pointedly indicates one of Jung's epistemological assumptions. For Jung, "das Erkennbare" is always an act of consciousness. Throughout his works, he gives the impression that the direct and immediate object of knowledge is the act of awareness itself; the objectivity of the content of consciousness must always be inferred or assumed—it is not directly known. Jung's epistemology is Kantian in character if not in origin.

If, then, personality change does not happen automatically as soon as we cease to hinder it by our lack of awareness of our unconscious striving, as Jung says, then it seems reasonable to suppose that our awareness of the significance of imaginative productions gives us an opportunity for reorganizing our life, actively reshaping it toward the self-ideal as imagination has portrayed it. In the dream of the illusionist, for instance, the symbol of the buried skeleton and the white lady that rises from the grave and floats upward could be a pictorial representation of what ought to happen, that is, of the ideal as it should be, rather than an expression of what is actually and inevitably happening in the personality. In that case, the dreamer would have to act, become detached from being a *femme à homme*, and deliberately work toward a higher goal. When the dream figures are taken to represent the person's impression of the situation in which he finds himself, of the forces he experiences—both natural and supernatural—impressions which are not falsified by waking desires and waking rationalization, then the dreamer will recognize in them a picture of his self-ideal. When used in this way in integral analysis (Cf. Chapters 6 and 14) the method reveals the personality organization as directed by the self-ideal.

Nondirective Therapy. As we have seen in Chapter 15, Roger's counseling makes it possible for the person to understand himself, recognize his feelings, clarify his goals. It frees his practical judgment from emotional interference, allows him to develop the implications of his momentary insights. In Dr. Curran's terms, it fosters the virtue of counsel. Not only does the person become able to reason and judge freely; he also becomes practiced in making decisions for himself. He is, therefore, able to come to a reasonable view of his goals in life and can act accordingly. If he is serious-minded, he can develop a self-ideal; if he is intelligent enough or informed enough, he can come to see what that self-ideal ought to be. As the impetus comes from him under pressure of his practical problems, it is very possible that the larger problem of the meaning of his life, his ultimate goal, never enters into his considerations at all. It is different, of course, for anyone for whom this very problem is in the center of attention. Compared with the method of active imagination and integral interpretation in which these life problems inevitably arise, nondirective therapy seems restricted to the sphere of ad hoc decisions, though in its own field (in the field of the client's deliberate choice) it holds out the promise of real and lasting reorganization.

Nondirective therapy does not confine itself to any given level of organization. It aids the client in exercising self-determination and leaves it to him whether he will apply it to a comparatively restricted field or will exercise it in striving for a self-ideal. Even at best, the self-ideal remains strictly subjective. To bring this private self-ideal in harmony with the self-ideal as it ought to be objectively, it is necessary to go beyond the strictly nondirective counseling (Cf. page 457).

Existential Analysis. This system, finally, in its form of logotherapy, deliberately deals with the self-ideal as it ought to be. That is, it concentrates on the rational convictions of the person, his philosophy of life as it applies to his individual living. But because of the deficiency of its own philosophical position, its notion of the self-ideal as it ought to be is a minimum program which could be better expressed negatively: it shows the patient what his self-ideal ought not to be. As logotherapy, the technique could be used by any other therapist except the nondirective counselor, whose nondirectiveness excludes the deliberate concentration on anything, including the patient's philosophy of life.

Theoretically, logotherapy applies to other methods besides existential analysis. It is used to some extent in integral analysis of imaginative productions, for we have seen that these always incorporate the raw materials for a philosophy of life.

But logotherapy is not restricted to the usual discussion method either. In its concentration on the patient's philosophy of life it could use a method of question and answer, usually called the Socratic method. This method provides for a collaboration in working out the logical consequences of each statement and so avoids the undesirable results of disagreement. The philosophical basis of such a method would, of course, have to be chosen in such a way as to stand up to the rational questioning of the person.

And now the question arises : Is there any indication that a particular kind of therapy should be used or that one or the other therapy could be used advantageously in different kinds of disturbances or with different kinds of people?

Choice of Therapeutic Methods

First of all, let us look at the methods which are distinctive and perhaps mutually exclusive. Nondirective therapy, for instance, by definition excludes logotherapy, integral analysis of imaginative products, and psychoanalytic free association. It is perhaps the safest method to use in acute emotional disturbances because it does not focus on the emotions themselves, but on the problem of how they can be understood and handled in the person's own life situation. The limits of personality integration will be determined by the client's own concept of the meaning of human life.

Psychoanalysis also has a distinctive method, *free association*. Its material, however, has to be interpreted. It does not produce its effects directly, as does the nondirective approach. Interpretation can be either content analysis or attitudinal (character) analysis. In the first case, the content of the patient's associations will be examined and the meaning assigned according to psychoanalytic concepts (the dream that the little girl's playfellows fly away and leave her alone means she wishes their death. Cf. page 410). In attitudinal analysis, the content is secondary and serves only as illustration for the development of particular character traits : the oral, anal, genital character. In content analysis, impulses and emotions themselves are concentrated on, rather than the pattern they form in the patient's life; in character analysis, it is the persistent emotional pattern they form that becomes important. Whether psychoanalysis remains content analysis or becomes character analysis, if free association provides the material for interpretation it requires more time than any other therapeutic method. If brief analysis is substituted for the Freudian type of therapy, as has been done recently by many analysts, the distinctive method of psychoanalysis (free association) is abandoned and "psychoanalysis" now means exclusively *interpretation* according to the Freudian system.

Though the technique of free association is used at present only when combined with interpretation according to the Freudian system, it could be used theoretically by any therapist for the purpose of resolving particularly intensive emotions which overwhelm the patient, when there is no memory of a traumatic situation. Therefore this method could be used in dealing with various neurotic manifestations, phobias, compulsions, and the like. Since, however, emotions are always affected by a person's rational goals, since neuroses are always anchored in the patient's philosophy of life, it should be supplemented by logotherapy in some form. In practice, of course, this is done whenever the analyst's own philosophy of life permits him to acknowledge the necessity of a rational ordering of life. Since such complementary logotherapy reflects the therapist's own often unvoiced and unacknowledged philosophical assumptions, it is impossible to judge its value.

Even without such a complement, or a complement that is based on a philosophy of life like Freud's, emotional hangovers may be resolved. In that case, conflicts will be resolved only by reducing the person's aspirations and reconciling them with the demands of his appetites, rather than by ordering the appetites toward a rational goal. Adjustment will be possible, but on a lower level of functioning. When the patient ceases to demand of himself that he come up to an ideal, then the discomfort which comes from his lagging efforts toward the goal or from his dependence on sensory pleasure will disappear, too. Guilt feelings can be resolved by persuading the patient that human acts are determined and therefore no guilt is attached to them—that may make a man more comfortable, rid him of his neurosis, which is the symptom of his inconsistency of choice and the incompatibility of his goals, but it will not make him a better man.

Neither individual psychology nor existential analysis offers a specific method. In both cases, the ordinary discussion method is used, in individual psychology for the discussion of personal problems, in existential analysis for the discussion of the patient's rational convictions. From our analysis of agreement and disagreement (Chapter 15, Comment) we would expect that the discussion method would generate considerable emotion when personal problems are dealt with. This is actually what happens in individual psychology where the central problem is the patient's attempt to be superior in the therapeutic situation and he experiences frustration and resentment at the fact of his inferiority.

If the discussion method is used, it would seem preferable to use it for the patient's rational convictions. In that case, he is able to concentrate on the facts of the case instead of having to defend himself against a misunderstanding of his own feelings or actions. Furthermore, the analysis of the person's striving for superiority as it is organized in his tendency toward self-establishment is really not possible at all without touching upon his attitude to things and people, that is, upon his philosophy of life. Therefore Adlerian analysis sooner or later develops into some form of logotherapy. The therapist devises maxims and formulae for the patient's use which embody a general truth important for his daily life. That is true of Adler as well as his orthodox followers, but also, for instance, of Fritz Künkel, who has started from an Adlerian position and gradually approached a form of therapy which has considerable similarity to that of Frankl.

Jung's method of active imagination, as mentioned before, can be used to let the person find his self-ideal as it ought to be. Since the self-ideal is the focus of man's self-determination, and self-determination is inherent in his nature, it is of central importance for psychotherapy. Integral interpretation of imaginative productions (including active imagination) will portray the self-ideal of the person according to his particular gifts and talents, and his particular position in life, but it will also portray the basic determination of his nature, that is, the self-ideal as it ought to be. When the self-ideal presented in the dream or in active imagination is recognized not only as *his* self-ideal but also as the self-ideal *as it ought to be,* and the person sets about attaining it, then the aim of therapy has been achieved.

The purpose of therapy, in our meaning of the term, is self-integration through aiming for the self-ideal as it ought to be. To use imagination rather than rational discussion has the advantage that the area of discussion is not prescribed by the therapist, that the patient always is taking the lead. At the same time, imagination does not suffer from the same restrictions as are apparent in the rational judgment freed in nondirective therapy. Once imagination acts without the direct control of reason and emotion (thus excluding rationalization) the situation will be portrayed as it really is. Moreover, that portrayal will show not only the momentary practical conditions of life in which the patient finds himself, but his total life situation, his relation to the world around him, to other people, and to God.

Active imagination is particularly indicated when the patient is suffering from discouragement or has lost his zest for living, when his old goals have become stale and uninteresting. In short, it is indicated particularly in problems of living, where none of the other methods has a chance of success—not logotherapy because there may be a satisfactory philosophy of life; not psychoanalysis because there may be no neurotic symptoms. In addition, active imagination (and integral interpretation) can be used in every case where logotherapy or free association or Adlerian therapy might be useful.

The only clear contraindication to its use is schizophrenia or a preschizophrenic state, as Jung has pointed out. Its use is doubtful with patients who are highly imaginative and confused and who may take this opportunity to indulge in fantasy as a substitute for practical action. True, even in such cases, the excessive flowering of imagination will eventually be reduced to the portrayal of the factual life situation in which action will be demanded. But it is possible that with such patients therapy might be cut short and better results achieved by using nondirective therapy in the beginning until the confusion has cleared and they have learned to decide upon action. Because active imagination in integral interpretation reveals the self-ideal as it ought to be, emotional difficulties are also resolved secondarily. During therapy, the patient's attitude to the objects that attract him will show a marked change. His emotions will change accordingly; imagination will again reflect these changes and show what still needs to be done. Such therapy does not mean reliving old emotional situations in the patient-therapist relationship but seeing them with new eyes in their imaginative portrayal.

Finally it ought to be emphasized that all methods of therapy have in common that they are attempting to help the patient to understand himself. They differ only in what it is the patient is led to understand or how much he is led to understand: his impulses and emotions, what he has made of them, the decisions and actions required, the meaning of his life, his ultimate goal.

To help the patient understand himself, the therapist must first show him that he is understood: that is the meaning of Fiedler's finding that experts of all schools show better understanding and better rapport than nonexperts. To help the patient to direct himself, there must be a goal toward which he is striving. For that reason, every kind of therapy has to assume some goal of human living, therefore a philosophy of life. Hence every therapy must in some way, no matter how restricted, also be logotherapy.

Success and Failure in Therapy

Not only does every system of therapy have a definite conception of the nature of the human being and his goal in life— this view will determine the criterion of success and failure. To decide when therapy has failed, it is necessary to know the criterion of success. And the criterion of success corresponds to the implicit but nevertheless real goal of human perfection which each therapeutic school and each individual therapist has assumed. The exception to this rule would seem to be the case in which the patient breaks off treatment prematurely. Apart from the rare instances in which that is done after the first two or three interviews, however, it is the therapist and not the patient who decides that the ending was premature. This very judgment, surely, depends on the therapist's goal in therapy, on his criterion of success.

In a recent book, De Grazia points out that success may be judged according to different standards:

One man, formerly impotent, may be considered cured now because he can cohabit with a prostitute, though with no one else. His therapist did not think to remember that prostitution was illegal . . .

Another man, formerly impotent, may be considered cured now because he divorced his wife and married another woman with whom he could be potent. His therapist was not a Catholic . . .

A woman, wanting a career but worried about its conflict with woman's duty, established by God, to bear children, may be deemed cured if she gains the insight that not God but her superego established that duty . . .

Another woman, doing well at a responsible office job, may be considered cured when she comes to the conclusion that a tailored job and a tailored suit are not woman's true lot, that women should glory in their femininity . . .

Still another woman may be considered cured after it is clarified for her that the unconscious notion that her love affair with a married man was sinful was causing her needless guilt and anxiety. Her therapist, too, was unmindful that adultery happened to be illegal in that community . . . (3, p. 153).

It is clear that such "insights" are strictly private. They reflect the ethical principles acceptable to the therapist but hardly the human values and principles of conduct accepted by the patient before his disturbance, or current among the members of his community.

Now it is quite true that this particular change in values and therefore in the patient's self-ideal was not the primary or the only criterion of success for any of the therapists whose cases are quoted by De Grazia. There were emotional disturbances which were resolved together with such a change, from vague anxiety, compulsions, phobias, to various somatic symptoms. But the fact that the self-ideal did change and the fact that the change was accompanied by improvement and is so interpreted by the therapist surely show that the conflict between self-ideal and subsidiary goals is primary, the various symptoms secondary. As soon as one alternative was chosen and the self-ideal was rectified accordingly, the conflict and the symptoms were resolved; the patient's "insight" merely justified the change of self-ideal.

The choice could have been different and the insight different. If the choice had been equally wholehearted, if it had been in accord with the self-ideal, then the conflict would have been resolved, too, and with it the symptoms of emotional disturbance. In many of the examples quoted from De Grazia, conscious inner conflicts and their disturbing emotional expressions have been exchanged for a crop of external difficulties. The new choice, permitted by the changed self-ideal, may result in disease, ostracism by family and friends, family disagreements, divorce; the respite is only temporary, for all these problems will have to be solved again with new possibilities of conflict.

There is universal agreement among therapists that the disappearance of a symptom is not the guarantee of a cure. If one symptom is suppressed, another will take its place as long as the original object of the emotion retains its power and the disturbance continues. But if the symptom is eradicated by changing the import of the object which arouses the emotion, then treatment is successful. A radical change in the importance of such emotional objective means to establish a self-ideal and bring other wants and objectives in harmony with it. If that means a change of self-ideal as well, such change should approximate the self-ideal as it ought to be. Then it will have objective validity and not be merely private and subjective. A private self-ideal would mean a truce in the conflict, not real peace. Soon new protagonists would renew the conflict, with the outcome as doubtful as before, but if the self-ideal is established as it ought to be there will be an integration of individual and community in a commonly accepted ideal.

Just as opinions are divided as to what constitutes success, so they are divided as to what are the causes of failure. Obviously, failure of treatment may be the fault of the therapist or the fault of the patient, whatever factors account for either. Rogers and his school characteristically see the therapist at fault, for they assume that the client can and will grow if only the conditions are favorable. Other schools and other therapists see reasons for failure on both sides. Muncie, for instance, says:

Failure or success in treatment depends on the nature of the problem under treatment; the type of treatment; the personality of the physician, his grasp of the problem, and his technical equipment (in: Hoch, 6, p. 22).

Even the failures of the therapist are ascribed to different factors. Rogers thinks that counseling fails whenever the counselor interprets or directs; yet interpretive and directive treatments can show many successes. Muncie (in: Hoch, 6) and Koren and his associates insist that treatment often fails because the therapist does not have a sufficient grasp of the psychodynamics involved in the problem; but therapists who do not interpret a problem in psychodynamic terms, either for themselves or for the patient, are successful, too.

There are other therapists who emphasize the fact that the patient bears the primary responsibility for success, that no treatment will succeed unless the patient is willing to do his part. Wolberg, for instance, says:

One of the chief reasons for failure is that the individual has no adequate motivation, sees no need for working out his problems, is satisfied with an inadequate adjustment to life or to people, or is unwilling to work with the type of technique that would make it possible for him to achieve these goals (in: Hoch, 6, p. 47).

Not only adults but children, too, must have this willingness to work on themselves if therapy is to succeed. Levy reports:

Various forms of psychotherapy were utilized by the different therapists [in a clinic]. The attitude of the child for whom no problem existed according to his own lights, resisted any of the forms, or any of the therapists, regardless of skill (in: Hoch, 6, p. 104).

The one indispensable factor seems to be that the individual must realize he needs help, that he is willing to accept it, and is willing to take the necesary steps which will lead to a reorganization of his goals and therefore to a reorganization of his personality.

The Relationship Between Helper and Helped

Authority. De Grazia insists that the help-giving relationship is one in which the helper has authority to give moral direction:

> Moral authority . . . is the crux of psychotherapy. . . . Neurosis is a moral disorder, the psychotherapeutic relationship is one of authority, the therapist gives moral direction. . . . So though the trappings and language of authority never stay the same, the seat and the word are always present. The seat of authority may be no seat: authority resides in the eye of the beholder. The word of authority may be no word: the moral may never be worded but suggested and brought slowly by repeated images before the patient until it stays in all clarity, complete. Of these two things, the seat and the word, no psychotherapy can divest itself, now or ever, and yet be a therapy (3, p. 104).

For De Grazia, authority means rightful power vested in a person devoted to the common good. He insists that the therapist's authority is not only like the parents' authority over the child but derives from it. Granted that the therapist has authority (which is merely restating the fact that he is the one who can help, therefore has resources the patient does not have), authority admits of differences in range and degree. The child is absolutely dependent on the parents; only when they abuse their authority will the community step in. The teacher has authority, too, but it is restricted to the communication of academic knowledge. The teacher's authority is delegated to him by the parents and the community; but it is not derived from the parents.

Whenever a man on request exercises any special skill or capacity for his neighbor's benefit, by that very fact he takes on a kind of power over his neighbor, but his power is restricted to the area in which help is needed. His authority will be commensurate with its object. Thus the different types of counsel and therapy, ranging from a friendly discussion of a knotty personal problem to deep analysis, will result in types of relationship and types of authority which will vary with the breadth of the problem and with the approach that is used.

Transference and Resistance. Counsel as distinct from therapy concentrates on principles of conduct and human values, rather than on emotions and their effect on the individual. Since every person has to clarify such principles and values and apply them to his own life he is a collaborator in the counseling relationship. In every case where help in personal problems is sought and gladly given, there is bound to be a person-to-person relationship which is intimate and warm. To the extent that help is given as expected, the person seeking help will feel affection for his helper; to the extent that his expectation is disappointed, he will feel resentment and even hostility. Though an emotional relationship is thus presupposed, this cannot be called *transference* unless it can be shown or assumed on theoretical grounds that the emotions felt in this relationship are not newly aroused but *transferred* from their original objects (parents) to the therapist.

In *psychoanalysis* such a transference relationship is assumed. Lagache gives the definition current in psychoanalytic literature:

Transference is generally defined as a repetition in present-day life, and particularly in the relationship to the analyst, of unconscious emotional attitudes developed during childhood wtihin the family group and especially toward the parents; . . . the transference may be friendly, hostile or ambivalent (14, p. 2).

Lagache claims, however, that this definition is incomplete because transference also has a functional significance:

For instance, for a woman whose brother was preferred to her and whose husband neglected her, the functional significance of transference consists in giving her a sense of her personal value and in allowing her to realize herself to be a woman; for a man brought up by an authoritarian father, the import of the analytical experience is to escape from the analyst and to show him that he is much more wicked (14, p. 3).

Thus the transference is not only a repetition of emotions but also of the patient's purposes in childhood, which were then thwarted and are now perhaps to be fulfilled. That such a repetition of early patterns of emotion and defense is not only assumed on theoretical grounds but is actually found in psychoanalytic practice cannot be doubted. It is possible, however, that this repetition is produced by the particular situation in which the patient finds himself during analysis. This situation is different in other forms of therapy; hence the therapeutic relationship is bound to be different, also.

The rule of psychoanalytic free association is to say whatever comes to mind. Ordinarily, such reckless baring of one's dreams and fantasies, one's failures and miseries, is only possible in the most intimate love relationship, for only love can cast out fear. Until the analyst has convinced the patient that such frankness is safe, there is bound to be resistance. Such resistance is not always unconscious, either. Many an analyst has found that a patient concealed a traumatic experience for months and years of therapy, not because he had forgotten but because he was loath to reveal it. Since sexual and aggressive impulses and their developmental expression are in the center of discussion, there will be resistance to the sheer recital of emotional experiences, at least as long as the patient sees them as good or bad, deserving approval or condemnation. Only gradually, in the course of the therapeutic relationship, can the patient come to realize that such frankness is not only safe but required, and rewarded by unconditional acceptance.[4] Assured of such acceptance (which only the infant, but not even the child, receives from its mother) the patient inevitably comes to have an infant's dependence and makes an infant's emotional demands.

In this relationship it is not important that the therapist is superior to the patient, for inferiority has no meaning for someone who is loved and cherished unconditionally. Hence the therapist's interest, approval, and love become the main prize; if they show any signs of changing, of becoming conditional on the

---

[4] The quality of such unconditional acceptance is very different in psychoanalysis from its nominal counterpart in nondirective therapy. The counselor accepts the client's *feelings* as *necessary under the circumstances* (Cf. page 453). The analyst accepts the patient's libidinal and aggressive impulses as the *central facts of human life*.

patient's insight or right choice, the patient's "positive trans-ference" is liable to turn into violent hostility. This is not the transference of an infant's hostility, either, but the savage hos-tility of an adult who is threatened in his infantile indulgence.

In psychoanalysis, a forced change from one therapist to an-other is often disastrous, for love—whatever its quality—does not accept substitutes. For the same reason, the patient will re-sist maturing in such a relationship. Still more will he resist ending it, for he would have to face the sharp contrast of adult give-and-take for which this uniquely sheltered relationship has ill prepared him.

In *individual psychology* (Adler) the therapeutic relationship reflects the differences in goal and method. Since inferiority feelings are in the center of attention, this aspect of the patient-therapist relationship will be intensified. The therapist is the master, the patient the disciple. This master not only points the way to self-improvement, this master is also an enemy to be conquered. In a true master-disciple relationship the disciple acknowledges an insufficiency of knowledge or information or even of self-management, but he is eager to improve. In this relationship, however, the patient is shown that he not only wants to improve but that he wants to be better than the master. To acknowledge one's imperfection is one thing; to be shown that one is envious of somebody else's greater perfection is quite another. This is a double humiliation and will be correspond-ingly resisted. Hence resistance is the rule rather than the ex-ception in this type of therapy. It can be called "negative trans-ference" because it is assumed that this resistance is a repetition of earlier resistance to authority. As treatment proceeds and the patient gains an objective estimate of his aims and his capaci-ties, his resistance will be replaced by confidence in the therapist's good will.

Nondirective counseling, which attempts to help the client to clarify his objectives and make his own decisions, tends to develop a counselor-client relationship that is rather unique. The counselor becomes an "alter ego" in a mutual communion which makes feelings understandable and eventually manageable. The client is neither playing the role of an indulged infant nor of a rebellious adolescent. Typically, the counselor-client relationship is one of warmth and mutual respect but has an almost impersonal tinge. Apparently, a new counselor can take over without disrupting the progress of the client.

As there is no "transference," so there is no "resistance" as understood in psychoanalysis. There may be resentment, but it is directed against the therapist's unexpected handling of the situation. When a man comes to a therapist, he expects help in a situation which he cannot manage unaided. But the help that is given here comes in an unexpected guise. The very fact that the counselor refuses to answer questions and give advice, but instead "structures" the situation to make the client understand that it is his opportunity and his task to bring order out of the chaos of his feelings, may arouse confusion and resentment. Perry and Estes say:

> In view of the very deviance of Rogerian non-directive behavior from our client's preconceptions, it is in its impact far from "passive" or "accepting"; it is the most violent attack that can be made upon these preconceptions. In its unrelieved contrast, it cuts the ground from under the client's expectations by offering these no sensory support whatever. The counselor offers instead the elements of a role unassimilable to the client's prototypes of authority. Only such consistent behavior can force the client rapidly to reorganize the field, and only great compensating warmth from the counselor can keep him from leaving it before he does (in: Mowrer, 15, p. 13).

Once the client has reconciled himself to his unexpected role, the occasion for resistance has passed and nondirective counseling may take its course. There is a possibility that resentment may appear again when the client expects the counselor to join with him in a search for the solution, after he has made his problem sufficiently clear, yet the counselor goes on reflecting feelings. Perry and Estes themselves advocate a more active role for the counselor at this point, so that client and counselor become collaborators in a common search. Then the counselor is at liberty to mention aspects of the problem which the client had not considered, just as the client sees points which have escaped the counselor. Here it seems that the client's "resistance" has

pointed the way to a change in technique which has proved fruitful. Not always, evidently, must resistance be conquered. Sometimes it ought to be heeded.

The *complex psychology* of Jung requires a different kind
of relationship again. The closest analogy is the collaboration
between a senior and a junior colleague. The aim of investigation, this individual's goal of individuation, is unknown both to
patient and therapist. For Jung, this goal is an "objective psychic" reality which must be discovered from archetypal images
in the unconscious. Since it is the patient who produces the
guiding symbols and he who endows them with meaning, the
therapist becomes merely a fellow-explorer who is familiar with
the maps of the country but is as surprised and pleased as the
patient when he finds his own particular path. According to
Jung, such a collaborative relationship of patient and therapist
is the rule rather than the exception. It may happen, he adds,
that the anima of the patient is projected unto the therapist,
which constitutes a transference neurosis in Freud's sense. In
such a case, the transference must be worked through in a
lengthy analysis of archetypal images until the projection is with-
drawn.

In such an exploration of archetypal images to find his individual goal, the patient often goes through a period of elation
when he finds himself the author of profoundly significant discoveries. As his self-knowledge increases, his elation gives way
to a realization that constructive action is demanded—not by
the therapist but by the logic of his own unfolding life pattern.
At this point, he may experience a sense of pressure, of coercion,
and it may seem to him that the therapist who has helped him
discover himself is allied with the forces that coerce him. In this
time of stress the patient is fighting himself in fighting the therapist. A refusal to reorganize his own life may take the form of
finding fault with the therapist, or even breaking off therapy.

Such resistance is different from that encountered comparatively early in psychoanalysis or individual psychology where it
is a refusal to reveal one's self or to acknowledge motives im-
puted by the analyst. It is different also from the resistance that
occurs at the beginning of nondirective counseling, where the

client objects to the counselor's nondirective attitude. Here the patient resists the necessity of committing himself, of deciding on an unpalatable course of action which a further self-discovery will demand. This resistance is quite comparable to the resistance noted by many therapists of other schools under similar circumstances, whenever the necessity of action is seen as a threat. Perry and Estes point out that it also occurs in learning situations:

> Resistance is also noticeable when a learner is moving too rapidly under his own power. It is attributable to the fact that he is exposing himself to involvement with ego-relevant stimuli faster than he can assess their safety (i.e., the nature of the integrations they will demand (in: Mowrer, 15, p. 100, footnote).

Essentially, the patient is afraid of the effort that will be demanded, the pain that is waiting for him. Fear turns into resistance when it is acted out.

Existential analysis is too recent to have produced any discussion of the patient-therapist relationship. On the face of it, it would seem that existential analysis also implies a master-disciple relationship. The therapist helps the patient to discover himself in discovering his life goals and freely acknowledging his responsibility. Here, as in Jung's Complex Psychology, therapy will arouse a growing sense of obligation, of responsibility, but here as there it is possible for the patient to refuse facing deeper issues, so shutting his eyes to his potentialities.

Resistance may develop with any method, and usually does, at one point or another during therapy. But there are several kinds of resistance. The patient may oppose the therapist's demands (e.g., to say everything that comes to mind, or to carry the burden of the discussion) by blocking or hostility; but this opposition may be either the result of a secret wish to keep his neurosis, or the result of a reasonable conviction that he is entitled to the privacy of his thoughts in the presence of a stranger, that he should keep secrets entrusted to him or secrets he has discovered, or that he has come to hear the therapist's opinion rather than engage in a monologue. In the nature of the case, every system of therapy presupposes that its method is especially designed to remove the roots of a man's conflicts. Hence resistance, be it ever so reasonable, must give way to the demands of the method.

There is another kind of resistance which is treated just as cursorily: the patient's opposition to an interpretation which threatens his conviction of self-determination or which favors a self-ideal lower than he is willing to accept. There is also the patient's resistance to a violation of his conscience which may occur, for instance, with a method in which there is danger of giving away important secrets. This matter is of particular urgency in the case of professional people (e.g., atomic scientists) who come for therapy. In such cases, it would almost seem that a therapeutic method is preferable which allows the patient to select the topics of discussion.

The whole problem whether and when resistance is justified patently hinges on the question whether the therapist can correctly evaluate the resistance of a patient with whose philosophy of life he cannot agree. If the therapist is convinced that any self-ideal is acceptable as long as it avoids conflict, while the patient is striving, though confusedly and far from wholeheartedly, for the self-ideal as it ought to be, there will be resistance and conflict arising out of the therapeutic situation itself.

Since every therapist uses the method he deems the best, and has the philosophy of life he deems the most adequate, every type of resistance will seem to him the natural evasion of someone who is threatened in his accustomed pattern of living which yet has clearly proved to be inadequate. Hence resistance is always considered something to be overcome at all costs. Yet some of these resistances the therapist would do well to heed, for they will retard the work of self-organization not only if they persist but even more so if they are conquered.

Use of Interpretation. Therapists of various schools are still debating whether or not to use "interpretation." By "interpretation" is meant making the patient aware of the "real" motives underlying his actions and his expressed thoughts. The difficulty is that there are as many interpretations possible for one and the same set of events as there are schools of therapy. The orthodox

Freudian will interpret the transference relationship as the repetition of the Oedipal situation. In every action he will look for the underlying wish which on the surface is either denied or cleverly disguised. Thus actions, thoughts, dreams, are interpreted as flowing from defense mechanisms or being disguised wish fulfilments no matter what the apparent motive. Obviously, such dynamic interpretations are explanatory only if the psychoanalytic systematic premises are accepted from the beginning. Needless to say, even dynamic interpretations may and do differ from one another, depending on the individual variations in systematic outlook.

At the same time, no therapy can do without interpretation or explanation, for it is this clarification which will give the patient the necessary impetus for changing his attitudes. Only when he realizes that his attitudes have been confused and led him into conflict, that his values somehow are contradictory, will he face the prospect of having to reorganize his pattern of thinking. That does not mean that interpretation and the insight it provides are in itself the motive; but interpretation helps in making the right choice.

The therapist's interpretation may be direct: he simply tells the patient what his "real" motive is. In that case, there is bound to be resistance, the more intense the more disreputable the motive is in the patient's eyes. Or the interpretation, though direct, may deal with the universal significance of the motive, as in Jung's type of analysis. Here the import of dream or artistic production is given on the basis of the meaning of the dramatis personae in the patient's personal life and supplemented by an archetypal interpretation. Since such interpretation does not reduce motives to appetites but rather elevates even appetites to cosmic significance, there is no danger of resistance though there may be danger of inflation.

In integral analysis, the danger of inflation as well as resentment is avoided because the therapist restricts himself to helping the patient recognize the import of the dream figures in his own life.

Here, as in Jungian analysis, resistance may come later when action is required for the reorganization of personality.

Interpretation may also be indirect, subtly guided but never explicit, indicated only by the choice of feelings which are reflected. In this case, the patient does not show resistance either; indeed, he never realizes he has been guided. At the same time, the subtle guidance is as surely a factor in the client's choice of further discussion or future action as is the most explicit interpretation. An example will illustrate what is meant. Rogers describes a case in which a deeply disturbed young woman develops a close attachment to the counselor:

In the course of the interviews, this woman has wrestled with deep guilt feelings, many of which center around possible incest with her father. She cannot be entirely sure whether the events really occurred or whether they exist only in her own mind (17, p. 210).

In the ninth interview, her attachment to the counselor is openly expressed:

S (*Client*) : This morning I hung my coat out there instead of here in your office. I've told you I like you, and I was afraid if you helped me on with the coat, I might turn around and kiss you.

C. (*Counselor*) : You thought those feelings of affection might make you kiss me unless you protected yourself from them.

.   .   .   .   .

S (*later in interview*) : I've never told anyone they were the most wonderful person I've ever known, but I've told you that. *It's not just sex. It's more than that.*

C. You really feel very deeply attached to me (17, p. 211. Italics mine).

Mowrer discusses this excerpt and points out:

If an orthodox analyst were to respond to productions of this kind, he would probably do so in terms of an interpretation that stressed the Oedipus complex and libidinal fixation upon the patient's father; and the stage would be set for the kind of interminable "negative transference" previously discussed. Although the nondirective therapist in the present case avoided such an interpretation he appears to have made the equally serious error of "accepting" the patient's intimation that she was sexually attracted to him. On the basis of the very considerable information which the therapist probably had at this point—including the patient's fantasies, and possible experiences, with respect to *incest*—we believe it was incumbent upon him to make, not a reflection, but an interpretation, one which would have stressed the essentially *nonsexual* nature and objectives of what the patient had done and said. In many similar situations, we have found that if the patient's attention is drawn to the possibility that she is trying to get the therapist sexually interested in her, not because of her own sexual needs, but in order to neutralize and discredit him as a proper father figure and therefore as an effective therapist, this kind of behavior can be quickly liquidated, new material released, and a great positive step taken toward the patient's self-understanding and recovery (in: Mowrer, 15, p. 569).

Curiously, Mowrer does not see that the counselor's "reflection" is an interpretation, too, for the counselor reflects the expressed attraction the patient feels, but not her equally decisive statement that "It's not just sex. It's more than that."

Every explicit interpretation depends on the systematic premises inherent in the method of therapy. This is illustrated by Mowrer's interpretation which deviates from the orthodox Freudian interpretation just as Mowrer's system deviates from Freud's. Almost like Adler, Mowrer sees the neurotic attempting to dominate the therapist by her sexual advances as she had earlier used sex to gain preferential treatment from her father.

Naturally, such an interpretation must be timed properly, or the patient's resistance would prevent any favorable effect. It will only be accepted either when the patient has ceased to regard such a motive as disreputable or when she has begun to suspect that her actions in the past and in the present have often been designed to mislead others as well as herself. Even when such an interpretation has been accepted and is acted upon, that does not mean that the motive which is now admitted was either the only one or the decisive one. It does mean that this particular possibility, that she might use sex for ulterior ends, is now admitted as something to be guarded against, or something to be overcome.

In the nondirective situation, the indirect interpretation used by the counselor is also an important factor in subsequent thoughts and actions. In the case quoted, the next interview following upon the counselor's selective response brought renewed expressions of the client's affection. This time the sexual aspect was stressed, culminating in a proposal of sexual intercourse which was gently refused by the counselor. Thus the nondirective approach also uses interpretation, albeit subtly, by selection of the feelings which will be reflected.

When the systematic premises are implicit rather than explicit (as in nondirective counseling) or when there is a plethora of dynamisms to choose from (according to Freud, every action is "overdetermined") then it is up to the individual therapist to select the *important* factor, interpret that, and bring it to the patient's attention. But what is the criterion of importance? There is no doubt that in the case quoted above the young woman had thoughts and feelings which would give good grounds for the orthodox Freudian interpretation. It is quite possible also that she had enjoyed the feeling of power which comes from the knowledge of being sexually attractive, in the relationship with her father as much as in that with the counselor— which would justify Mowrer's interpretation.

There is still another factor, that "more than sex" which she expressed but which was acknowledged neither by the counselor nor by Mowrer. Granted that she expressed what she really felt, is it not possible that this "more" is her admiration or even adoration of the helper who is kind yet firm, who will make it possible for her to become the person she wants to be? Now the question is : Which of the three factors, all present, will be the most important for the client in reorganizing her life? Acknowledging her infatuation to be a "transference neurosis" will help, but she might linger in the enjoyment of the emotion as it is analyzed before taking the next step. Acknowledging her feeling to be a ruse will help, but such an insight will not immediately counteract the attraction, and the resulting humiliation might make her distrust herself. Realizing that the sexual attraction is merely one element (though potentially disturbing) in an important and constructive relationship would make it possible for her to renounce it and free herself from it gradually for the sake of the assured gain. Thus she would neither be tempted to indulge herself nor to despise herself; her attention would be centered on the task in hand, and the hope it arouses.

Since no one motive is decisive, no one interpretation can be right in a causal sense. No interpretation will isolate *the* cause of any action, real or symbolic, simply because the decisive factor is that the patient has *yielded* to her desires (whether for gratification or power) which are motives but not decisive. If causal interpretation cannot isolate the cause, it also cannot eradicate it. Its only remaining function is to induce the patient to yield no more to this particular desire by emphasizing that it is infantile or implying that it is dishonest : therefore the infantile attachment should be outgrown ; the use of sex appeal for ulterior purposes should be renounced ; the femme à homme should become a real person. Thus causal interpretation is effective, not because it uncovers the cause and neutralizes it but because it implicitly appeals to the patient's self-ideal and so encourages him to exercise self-determination. He should renounce infantile desires because he wants to become mature, because he wants to become a real person. If that is so, then we are justified in insisting that the most effective interpretation will be one which emphasizes the person's self-determination and encourages his striving toward a self-ideal that will be worth while and all-absorbing.

The alternatives are not *interpretation* versus *no interpretation.* The problem is rather : *What kind of interpretation?* and : *What form of interpretation?* As to the form, an interpretation made by the patient rather than the therapist has much to recommend it, for it avoids opposition. As to the kind of interpretation, we have seen that it must allow for self-determination and must encourage the patient to attempt it, in striving for the right kind of self-ideal. Since causal explanations appeal to the self-ideal only incidentally and are not concerned about the kind of self-ideal the patient has as long as it is held without conflict, causal interpretations should be used with caution. If they are too successful in their primary purpose, to convince the patient of the cause of his action, he might be tempted to use such an explanation as a convenient excuse for continued indulgence. We have all met the man, veteran of a thousand analytic hours, who still dwells on his infantile loves and frustrations and recounts them at length to explain his foibles and idiosyncrasies—completely forgetting that analysis should have freed him from such shackles long ago.

Conclusion

Effective reorganization of the personality must aim for the same goal as the organization of the developing personality: the successful establishment of an individual's self-ideal as it ought to be. The oughtness of this self-ideal is developed in community and affects the community, but it is not exclusively a social enterprise. It has more than a social sanction.

To establish such a self-ideal and make it effective as the term of the person's striving may require an indirect approach. Counsel, in fact, is distinguished from therapy by the very fact that the man who needs therapy has lost the ability to move toward his self-ideal without conflict and disturbance. He has lost the ability either to decide on objectives or to act unaided without discomfort. Therefore all psychotherapy has to clarify the confusion of objectives before the patient develops enough detachment from his emotions to choose prudently. The central factor in psychotherapy, then, is the support provided by the therapist, the affectionate relationship which aids him in clarifying goals and undertaking the work of reorganization.

The *psychotic* needs affective support to establish sheer contact with reality. The *neurotic* needs it to clarify the connection between his objectives and his emotions, and to understand the effects of emotions. He must understand himself and develop an accurate self-concept before he can begin to establish his self-ideal as it ought to be. The *psychopath* really needs conversion rather than therapy or counsel; he must be set on fire with the conviction that there is something that is important beyond all petty personal indulgence. He needs a motive to acknowledge the self-ideal as it ought to be and strive for it. Depending on these varying needs of the patient, the therapeutic relationship should vary from the completely supportive parent-child relationship (for the psychotic) to friendly collaboration and enthusiastic leadership. Since this relationship provides the climate in which the patient can become independent and self-determining, he should be granted at every point as much responsibility as he can bear without endangering himself or others. If the neurotic receives too much support, he will have no incentive to take the initiative; if too little, fear will prevent him from making an all-out effort. If the psychopath is allowed too much responsibility before his self-ideal becomes firmly established, he is bound to harm others.

The best therapeutic method will be one which can provide affective support as the patient needs it and on the level he needs it; which recognizes the need to establish his self-ideal as it ought to be, but does not force him to it; which encourages him to change inadequate attitudes by appealing to the highest ideal he acknowledges; which treats repeated failures of the patient by encouraging him to wholehearted commitment to his self-ideal as it ought to be, rather than by inducing him to lower his sights; which heeds the patient's resistance lest it retard reorganization, and so does not force undue intimacy or refuse due collaboration.

But when all is said and done, when the therapist has done his best, when both his proximate and his ultimate aim are in line with the patient's self-ideal as it ought to be, it is still possible for the patient to draw back in fear, preferring his known discomfort to the unknown pain and effort of steady self-discipline which a pursuit of his true self-ideal would demand. If we grant him self-determination at all, we must also admit that he may use it against his best interests and so miss the self-integration that would ensure his peace of mind, heart, and soul.

Summary of Theoretical Principles

1. Mental disturbance is not synonymous with disease. While psychosis does seem to be primarily a disturbance in physiological function (a disease), neurosis seems to be the effect of a disturbance in self-organization.

2. Such disturbances in self-organization are the product of unresolved conflicts. Conflicts may be resolved and disturbances prevented by counsel (as distinct from therapy).

3. When conflict is unresolved, the disturbance may be corrected by various therapeutic techniques which differ in relevance and effectiveness.

4. To be relevant, psychotherapy must act on the level of personality organization which is disturbed. To be effective, it must produce a personality reorganization which is guided by the self-ideal as it ought to be.

5. Freudian psychoanalysis applies to the appetitive level of human life. Adler's system deals with the striving for self-establishment. Jung's therapy works on the level of self-actuation. Frankl's logotherapy deals with the minimum ideal for a human being. Rogers' counseling frees the practical judgment from emotional interference so that a self-ideal can be established more effectively.—None of these systems provides in principle the means to discover *the self-ideal as it ought to be*.

6. Integral analysis can be used as a method to establish and confirm the self-ideal as it ought to be.

7. The therapist's authority and skill, the affective relationship between helper and helped, the patient's resistance, are all factors in therapy but none of them is decisive.

8. Even with the best method (both relevant and effective) and the best therapist, final success decisively depends on the patient's willingness to follow through on the reorganization of his life and the establishment of his self-ideal.

REFERENCES

1. ADLER, ALFRED. 1927. *Understanding human nature*. (Tr.) W. B. WOLFE. New York: Greenberg, Publisher.
2. BRILL, A. A. (Ed.). 1938. *The basic writings of Sigmund Freud*. New York: Modern Library, Inc.
3. DE GRAZIA, SEBASTIAN. 1952. *Errors of psychotherapy*. New York: Doubleday & Co., Inc.
4. FIEDLER, FRED E. 1950. A comparison of therapeutic relationships in psychoanalytic, nondirective and Adlerian therapy. *J. consult. Psychol.*, 1950, **14**, 436–45.
5. FRANKL, VIKTOR E. 1948. *Ärztliche Seelsorge*. Vienna: Franz Deuticke.
6. HOCH, PAUL H. (Ed.) 1948. *Failures in psychiatric treatment*. New York: Grune & Stratton, Inc.
7. HUSTON, PAUL E. 1953. Some observations on the orientation of clinical psychology. *Amer. Psychol.*, 1953, **5**, 191–96.

8. Jung, C. G. 1933. *Die Beziehungen zwischen dem Ich und dem Unbewussten.* Zürich: Rascher et Cie.
9. Jung, C. G., and Kerenyi, C. 1949. *Essays on a science of mythology.* New York: Pantheon Books, Inc.
10. Jung, C. G., and Wilhelm, R. 1944. *Das Geheimnis der goldenen Blüte.* Zürich: Rascher et Cie.
11. Koren, L., Goertzel, V., and Evans, M. 1951. The psychodynamics of failure in therapy. *Am. J. Psychiat.*, 1951, **108**, 37–41.
12. Künkel, Fritz. 1938. *Character, growth, education.* (Tr.) B. Keppel, C. and B. Druitt. Philadelphia: J. B. Lippincott Co.
13. ———. 1943. *In search of maturity.* New York: Chas. Scribner's Sons.
14. Lagache, Daniel. 1953. Some aspects of transference. *Int. J. Psychoanal., London*, 1953, **34**, 1–10.
15. Mowrer, O. H. (Ed.) 1953. *Psychotherapy: A symposium on theory and research.* New York: The Ronald Press Co.
16. Rinkel, Max, DeShon, H. Jackson, Hyde, Robert W., and Solomon, Harry C. 1952. Experimental schizophrenia-like symptoms. *Amer. J. Psychiat.*, 1952, **108**, 572–78.
17. Rogers, Carl R. 1951. *Client-centered therapy.* Boston: Houghton Mifflin Co.

PART V

SELF-INTEGRATION THROUGH RELIGION

Chapter 18

RELIGIOUS EXPERIENCE IN CLIENT-CENTERED THERAPY

By Walter Smet, S. J.

In this chapter I would like to discuss a problem that is of concern to all of us. We all agree, I think, that personal and emotional problems have their roots in a spiritual problem, and that every complete and lasting therapy depends in the last analysis upon the restoration of a right relationship with God; only when God is seen as the greatest good and the ultimate goal will man's relationship to Him be dynamic, that is, supply the motive and the power for his daily living. If that is so, then how can such a reorientation toward God be brought about in therapy?

With a directive and interpretative kind of therapy, there does not seem to be much of a problem, at least superficially: the therapist himself can orient the person toward the experience and acceptance of religious attitudes. But what happens in nondirective therapy? Have we excluded the religious aspect if we follow the principles and practice of client-centered therapy? There are some who seem to think so and who, in consequence, find the nondirective, client-centered approach inappropriate for pastoral counseling. But is the directive approach really the only way in which the religious aspect of a therapeutic reorientation can be achieved? And if it is not, in what way does any kind of religious experience enter into the nondirective therapeutic situation? For any therapist who is concerned about the client as a person, this problem must be solved before he can adopt the client-centered approach without reservation. I would like, therefore, to discuss this point by analyzing the process of nondirective counseling and its effects on the person.

First of all, let us follow the change of perception occurring in counseling. Suppose the client sees the counselor make a consistent effort to understand him fully; suppose he sees that the counselor accepts him sincerely, respects his freedom, trusts in his capacity for growth; he recognizes the counselor's disinterested sympathy and genuine concern; and finally, suppose he realizes that the counselor attempts to be perfectly honest and is staunchly loyal. What will happen?

The answer can be found in the various published analyses of the counseling process, especially in Rogers' works (1, 2). Briefly, first comes a period of emotional release in which the client uses the acceptance and understanding of the counselor to bring out all the aspects of his life problems. As he gradually discovers that this is a situation in which it is safe to express real feelings, deeper and deeper attitudes are revealed, even those which have been previously repressed and were never really faced. Following upon this period of emotional release (and to some extent intermingled with it) come insight and acceptance. In his very acceptance of the atmosphere created by the counselor, the client finds the strength to face himself and others objectively. In so doing he achieves self-integration, and this self-integration liberates energy which enables him to carry out the actions that will implement his reoriented striving toward his life goals.

In this process of changed perception of himself and the world around him, the client cannot exclude God. If therapy has gone deep enough so that he is freed from defenses, repressions, and conflicts, he will see God in a different light, or rather, God will come to have a new and deeper meaning for him. This is what actually happens in many cases. The following excerpt, quoted from the case of Mrs. Sar, may serve as illustration.[1]

S188 Have you ever been ashamed of yourself? Well, that is the way
      I have felt all my life. Just ashamed for I don't know what.

---

[1] Case material from the files of the Counseling Center of the University of Chicago, quoted by permission. Mrs. Sar came to the Counseling Center with a problem concerning herself and her daughter. The quotation is an excerpt from the third interview. S stands for the subject, C for the counselor.

Even as a little girl, I felt, mm, sort of ashamed. And that's a horrible feeling.

C188   Just ashamed of yourself, hm?

S189   M-hm. And then, of course, mother always taught me that God watched everything I did, and that gave me a sense of . . . (laughs) well, just having no privacy whatsoever. (C laughs) . . . and that he punished very severely, that . . . God is a wrathful God, and if I'd stub my toe, why I'd quick try to think, well now, what have I done bad? Oh, I must have done something bad, because God's punishing me. Well, that's another thing: being raised to fear God. As . . . whatever God is, I don't know. And . . . that's one thing she's teaching Carol. Well, I don't believe in that. And that's another thing I'm going to have to . . . to do, because . . . I think maybe God's a swell guy.

C189   M-hm. That is, really as you think it over, it changes your notion of God as well as changing your own feeling of . . .

S190   Yes. I've gone through something terrific the last couple of days. I don't know. My whole outlook seems to have changed. Now whether it'll last or not I don't know. We'll see.

C190   It's so new and so kind of striking that you don't really know whether you can believe in it or not, but . . . but you do feel as though something has happened inside of you.

Two weeks *after the ending* of the therapeutic sessions, the counselor in a follow-up interview asked the client for some clarification of the previous passage. Here is her answer.

S258   Well, that just comes back to the . . . as I don't exactly recall what I said, but . . . I was raised to fear God. I mean, I did and I thought that he was, as I said, spying on me all the time. That's the way I felt and . . . no sense of privacy at all. And feeling that he was quite a wrathful God, I guess that is what it says in the Bible. And . . . I just learned that . . . There was no mention as you say, of God, no one mentioned anything to me about anything really. And it came to me that . . . (pause) that in thinking for myself without any . . . I'm trying to make this clear; it's a little difficult . . . that in thinking for myself for the first time, I also thought about God in a different way. In the way that I'd always wanted to feel about God. So that . . . say if a minister said to me, why you can't treat your mother that way because God, so and so, you know, I would have thought, well, there's that old God again, you know. But well, people do have resentments about God. It's shoved down their throats you know, and God's either mean or he's awfully good or something. But my conception of God is just good. And that he's not going to punish me or anything for any mistakes that I might make. But it all goes back in being allowed to think for myself. Does that answer your question at all?

C258   Yes. That's fine.

S259   I don't remember what I said, but I know that that's the feeling that all my life I hadn't liked God very well, to be perfectly honest. I mean, I think, . . . you know, a wonderful thing and everything, but, you know, He seemed sort of a personal enemy of mine. And I don't think it should be that way. Do you?

C259   (Laughing) I remember one of the things you did say on that; that when you were expressing this newer notion, you said: "I've come to think that maybe God is a pretty swell guy."

S260   Yeah. That's it. (Laughter) Well, that . . . I don't mean to be sacrilegious or anything of that sort, but . . . I remember that I had to go to church and I went to church and I . . . well, I just, why, I feel I can just talk to Him now. Well, I mean, that He's just part of me. And that's the way actually that I've always wanted to feel and I think that that's the way everyone wants to feel. Down in their hearts, I think that they want to feel that . . . God is good and helpful and . . . that He will help you if you're sincere and ask for it rather than, well, you go ahead and do what's right; but if you do anything wrong you'll be punished? And that's the conception I have, now whether . . . whose fault that was, I don't know. And probably no fault at all, but simply that . . . it just, I just, started thinking for myself. That's the answer to it. It's a wonderful feeling. I mean, you feel a little safer. I was all wound up in all sorts of apprehensive fears of this and that. I mean, not actual punishment, like, oh, I'm going to burn in purgatory or whatever it is, but just a feeling, oh, I was all alone, you know. But I don't feel that way now.

But there is more, it seems, that goes on in therapy. In a chapter recently prepared by Rogers, he describes another aspect of client-centered therapy that has not been emphasized enough before. This is an aspect which has some importance for religious counseling, as I shall try to show.

Under the influence of the warmth and *communion* of understanding, of mutual trust and faith, the client comes to experience the unique quality of human relationships that are based upon respect for personal freedom—something he has perhaps never experienced before. He comes—often after long hesitation—"to let the counselor and his trust and care enter into his life, not only as counselor but on the basis of a feeling of communality, of brotherhood within." ". . . To discover," says Rogers, "that it is not devastating to accept the positive feelings of another, that it does not necessarily end in hurt, that it actually 'feels good' to have another person with you in your struggles to meet life, is one of the most profound learnings one may have" (2). Indeed, feeling liked by another, the client feels encouraged to draw the conclusion that he can esteem and actually like himself. Being loved, he must be lovable. He experiences the pleasure of being himself, and he knows with certainty that that is the way he should feel. This feeling finally restores his faith in his assets, awakes his confidence in his capacity to make decisions and changes. He discovers the positive side of himself, and feels a desire to expand it. Accepting himself, the client can then accept others as they are. Where there is no need to defend, there is no need to attack; and finally, he can now give without depriving himself.

Now it seems to me that this special kind of interpersonal relationship between counselor and client could serve as the model for a *mature* relationship of the human being with God considered in its psychological aspect. For someone who has never before had a warm human relationship based upon respect for his freedom, this experience seems to be the best preparation for a dynamic relationship with God and the religious growth such a relationship implies.

I have often tried to analyze the psychological development occurring in myself during my annual retreat. On reading Rogers' analysis (pp. 3–4) I was struck by the parallel between the client's changing conception of God during therapy and one of the lines of spiritual development which the Spiritual Exercises of St. Ignatius are intended to bring about in the retreatant. The core of these parallel experiences—as it appears to me—is the growing realization of being personally loved by God. Let me attempt to clarify this statement by analyzing this experience of being loved by God, which is an essential feature of all Christian religious experience.

In the first place, God *is* love. He is not an abstract love, but rather a deep personal love. Hence, He really cares for me and accepts me as I am, for He made me and knows that He has made me. He had me in His thoughts from all eternity. He chose to create me out of all the multitudes of those He could have created, and He decided to keep me in existence. He destined me to share in His own divine happiness and perfection. He could have damned me so many times, and instead He spared me. More than that, He died for me on the Cross. He is faithful and ever attentive, ever ready to help me. He never rejects me. He gave me freedom and always respects it, even though I should turn it against Him. He loves me and cares for me, even if I do not love Him and care for Him.

Secondly, this love of God is a *unique kind of love*. Human love often leaves man disappointed, frustrated, even devastated. Human love is often jealous, demanding, often limits our freedom. But the love of God never threatens, it always respects the freedom God Himself has given us. God is not demanding, He will not impose His will upon us. In the experience of His love, we learn to have faith in all love and in love's ability to free us. So we learn to love and to accept the love of others.

Much more than the love of a human being, God's love *assures me that I am lovable in the depths of my soul*. It may be difficult for me to esteem myself, but why should I hate and condemn myself continually when God Himself loves me and appreciates me? So, for the first time, I really feel able to accept myself and to be at peace with myself. But that is not all. Under the eye of God, filled with His love, I want to see myself as *He* sees me and as I *really* am. I see every part of myself, the good and the bad in me, in the right proportion. There is no longer any reason why I should hold back, why I should deny to myself and to God certain parts of myself that I like least. If I let myself be filled with the assurance that God loves me completely, with all my sins, with all my faults, I no longer have the slightest need to play a role, or wear a mask, or hide. This utter honesty and sincerity will bring about my full integration and with it an indescribable feeling of inner freedom in God Himself.

Encouraged by God's personal interest in me, stimulated by His merciful love, I discover that His work in me is good. I realize His great plans for me. I could be a masterpiece if only I collaborated with Him, if only I responded to His invitation.

Backed by His love and the assurance of His help, I start to work. I feel strong enough now to bring order into myself, and to build upon the good which I have discovered is present in me. Since God trusts me, I shall not betray Him; since He has faith in me, I shall show myself to be worthy of it. And since there is no limit to His love and mercy, I shall give myself generously. All in all, I try to measure up to His expectations, but also I am pleased *to be* what He *wants me to be*. Why should I accept any other standards than those of God, any other will than His? Ultimately, to be with myself and God will become the source of my greatest joy.

My attitude toward others is changing with the change of my attitude toward God and myself. Accepting God's will for me, I can let others be what they are. Filled with God, with nothing to lose but all to win, I can give without limit. Accepting others, they accept me; caring for others, they in turn care for me, and so I am given more than I gave. My security increases because I feel more and more belongingness, and feeling more belong-ingness, I am more aware of the love of God present in all.

It will have become clear by now that the counselor-client relationship bears some analogy (on the natural level) to a re-lationship between God and man such as we have described in psychological terms. It may well be that love and acceptance have to be experienced on the human level before love can be sought and found in God. If so, client-centered therapy might offer a good foundation for the establishment and growth of a mature relationship with God precisely because it does not *refer* the client to such a relationship but lets him *experience it on the human level*. We cannot expect to find a mature and personal love of God when such love has never been experienced and prac-ticed on the human level.

There may still be some who think that such indirect dealing with the problem is not sufficient, that the client should be helped to find God in a more direct and explicit way. In my opinion, such a direct way is not at all excluded. If we suppose that a mature and personal relationship has been established between client and counselor which resulted in therapeutic progress, a further development in that relationship will follow sooner or later, depending on the nature of the case. The client will become interested in the person of the counselor, he will start asking questions about his past and his future, about his family, about his personal concerns. These are signs that therapy proper has come to an end and the client feels that he is now able to carry on without the help of the counseling situation. One kind of relationship has fulfilled its purpose and now the client feels the desire to initiate another kind of relationship with the counselor.

For any one of several reasons the counselor may decide not to enter into such a new kind of relationship: he may wish, for instance, to keep himself available for possible future therapy. But if such a new relationship should be begun, then the non-directive interview will give way to discussion and the counselor's own religious motivation will spontaneously come to light. Without being told, the erstwhile client will feel the connection between the counselor's deep respect for human dignity, his loyalty and sincerity, and his personal religious life. He will want to know more about the source of the counselor's strength and will want to draw from it as well. There is no reason why the counselor should not reveal to his new friend at this point that the counseling relationship only represents a human analogy of another, much deeper relationship, which is his for the asking. He can explain now that the last goal of therapy is the meeting of the person with his God, his creator, his savior; and that he, the counselor, was merely an instrument used by God to draw him toward Himself. He could also point out that his real concern during therapy was never to interfere with God's work, and that he wished nothing better than to make way, one day, for God—according to the confession of St. John the Baptist: "He must increase, I must decrease."

At this point the counselor may want to refer the client for religious help to someone else, perhaps a priest. He may invite him to join some religious organization, or to make a retreat. Or he may, especially if he is a priest himself, carry on a new relationship with the client on the basis of a common quest for God.

Summing up, we may briefly indicate the stages in the religious development of the client during and after therapy:

First stage: Therapy proper. Strict client-centered relationship for the benefit of the client and as a prerequisite to a religious orientation.

Second (transitory) *stage*: End of therapy. The client becomes interested in the person of the counselor. Here the counselor may make explicit his deeper religious motivation. In discussing the counseling experience, the counselor may explain that there is another experience that will achieve and confirm the growth attained in therapy; that there is another relationship which is infinitely more valuable and infinitely deeper. The counselor may show that he was only the instrument of God and will now make way for Him.

Third stage: The client is related directly to God. The counselor may then function as confessor, as spiritual guide or as companion in the quest for God.

COMMENT

Instead of commenting on the issue raised in this chapter we proceed at once to a consideration of the role of religious ideas in personality organization, in Chapter 19.

REFERENCES

1. MOWRER, O. HOBART (Ed.). 1953. *Psychotherapy. Theory and research.* New York: The Ronald Press Co.
2. ROGERS, CARL R. 1951. *Counseling and psychotherapy.* Boston: Houghton Mifflin Co.

Chapter 19

RELIGION AND PERSONALITY INTEGRATION

By JOHN A. GASSON, S. J.

IN THE previous paper the question was discussed whether a particular form of therapy offered an effective preamble from which the religious life of a person might progress, grow, and become firmly established. The very putting of the question points to the wider problem of what is the reciprocal influence of religious ideals and practice upon personality integration. That each has an influence on the other is being recognized more and more by clinicians. We need only refer to the work of Frankl and the Existentialist school in Vienna (cf. Chapter 16) and the interest devoted to religious matters by Jungian analysts (Cf. Schaer, 8). Even the strict Freudian (as, for instance, Menninger, reported in *Time*, April 16, 1951) is beginning to recast Freud's notions of the psychological function of religious ideas. The clinician and the analyst, however, study religious thinking and practice as a therapeutic agent in the psychological reorganization of the disturbed person or an etiological factor in the precipitation, aggravation, or induration of disturbed behavior. The psychological significance of religion in the dynamic psychology of normal persons merits some attention also.

The limits set to the discussion of this question in the present context are perforce narrow. Within these narrow limits no discussion could be useful or enlightening unless it be narrowly defined and confined to a special and specialized subject matter. This very specialized subject must, nevertheless, not only be a special case of the broad field of religious living in general but, if possible, also an epitome of it. Thus whatever we may discover of the mutual influence of religion and personality could be validly extended to the whole field of religious living.

The Spiritual Exercises of St. Ignatius as Religious Activity

It has already been hinted in the previous paper that such a well-defined field could be found in the experiences of a person engaged upon the meditations of an eight-day retreat according to the Spiritual Exercises of St. Ignatius. What was there used merely as an illustration we will take as the explicit matter for study. More than thirty years of experience of making retreats of three, eight, and thirty days—some seventy retreats in all— and almost twenty years' experience in directing men and women, both lay and religious, in the making of them—to the number of two or three each year—together with a systematic study of the ascetical and psychological dynamics involved in the Spiritual Exercises of St. Ignatius, have made the present writer sufficiently acquainted with this area of religious living to write about it from the inside. I have observed the Exercises at work not only in myself (of that no mention need be made here) but particularly in a large variety of individual personalities. I have observed with a psychologist's eye the effectiveness of the Exercises in contributing to the cure of souls sick spiritually, some of them psychologically as well. But what has been by far the most frequent object of my observations is how efficacious the Exercises are in improving not only spiritual but psychological functioning in whole and well souls.

A psychological analysis of the Spiritual Exercises of St. Ignatius from the point of view of personality dynamics will serve admirably to define and clarify the function of religious ideas in the structure and growth of the total personality. Perhaps some qualification should be made to justify taking the Spiritual Exercises as a paradigm of religious ideas in general, since to one who has but slight acquaintance with them, it would hardly seem likely that even the germ of the religious thought of all mankind could be found in so small a book. However, when we examine the book more closely, we find that the ideas and motives expressed are no less than the common tenets of any sincere Christian (Cf. Dudon, 2, p. 451). It is not our purpose to argue the validity and scope of the religious ideas expressed but only to discover the psychological dynamism of such ideas and values in a culture which we know is based on Christian faith and morals. Hence what we find in the Spiritual Exercises will be of sufficient validity and scope, even if there be religious ideas and values contrary to the Christian faith that might be accepted as true in another time or place or culture.

Moreover, it should be made clear that what we propose to examine and analyze is not the *book* of the Exercises but the method contained in it which prescribes certain religious activities for a definite period of time under certain prescribed conditions for attaining certain definite results. We propose to examine the activities of a *retreat* that is made according to the method proposed in the Spiritual Exercises of St. Ignatius.

The term *retreat* is a technical expression from asceticism denoting a period of time of varying length (three, eight, ten, thirty days) during which a person in silence, solitude, and recollection of spirit ponders the truths of Revelation in a systematic way so as to shape his life in accordance with them and make his interior supernatural life more vigorous and effective. There are innumerable methods by which the exercises of a retreat are carried out and spiritual renovation is achieved. In general the exercises of a retreat consist in prayer, vocal and mental; self-examination; and some practice of penance. The various methods of making a retreat differ in the particular material taken for meditation; in the order in which it is taken up and the systematic approach or lack of it to the particular goal to be attained.

A retreat according to the method of the Spiritual Exercises of St. Ignatius takes at least eight days. Any smaller amount of time is not sufficient for the essential method of the Exercises to have its proper effect. It is true that the greater number of retreats for lay people last only three or four days but this is a matter of necessity, since ordinarily the people making these retreats cannot spare more time than that from their daily duties. These days are spent in a place away from home, or if at home, completely separated from the business of daily life. Silence and solitude is the optimum atmosphere and conversation even with the director of the retreat should be held to a minimum. The function of the director is not to provide a wealth of material for thought or a sum of alternatives for choice, still less to indoctrinate in some set idea or dragoon along to a set goal. His function is to provide material for meditation adapted to the capacity and needs of the retreatant; show him how to think things out for himself; answer questions and resolve doubts; help him to make his own decisions; bring him along in an ordered and progressive way so that the retreatant gets the most possible for himself out of the retreat.

The ideal condition, therefore, is that a single individual make a retreat by himself under an experienced director. This ideal situation is rare. Usually what happens is that a group of some thirty or forty listen together to the director proposing the matter for meditation for a half hour, four or five times a day, then each meditates by himself on this matter for half an hour or more; between times each occupies himself in vocal prayer, other private devotions, reading or resting, and in private consultation with the director for whatever advice or direction is required. In summary, a retreat is a retiring as much as is possible into the presence of God to consider the affairs of one's soul for a protracted period of time.

If the Spiritual Exercises are made for thirty days, the retreat is divided into four periods called Weeks. This division is not strictly according to the calendar but only roughly so, depending on the nature of the matter to be pondered and the capacity of the retreatant. In the first Week the retreatant meditates on the fact of Creation and its consequences for man's relationship to God; on Sin and its consequences; on Death, Hell, and the Mercy of God. This usually takes eight days. In the second Week the matter for meditation is the Hidden and the Public Life of Christ and the practical meaning of the Incarnation for the individual's spiritual life. During this time the retreatant determines for himself what readjustments must be made in his pattern of living. This usually occupies twelve days. In the third Week the Passion of Christ is meditated on with

a view to confirming the decisions and resolutions the retreatant has taken. This takes five days. The rest of the thirty days
is spent in meditating on the Risen Life of Christ and in strengthening the soul's union with God through love so as to make it
habitual and lasting. In an eight-day retreat there is a similar
division of matter so that two days are spent on the matter of the
first Week, four on the second Week, and one each on the third
and fourth Week.

What is distinctive of the Ignatian Exercises is the *progressive approach* to a decision, contained in the meditations that are
peculiar to the Spiritual Exercises as St. Ignatius wrote them.
These meditations, the content of which we shall study in detail
later on, are: The Foundation, in the beginning of the first
Week; the Kingdom of Christ, in the beginning of the second
Week; the Two Standards, Three Classes of Men, Three Kinds
of Humility, at the end of the second Week and immediately preceding the Election or decision made in retreat; and the Contemplation to Attain Love at the end of the fourth Week. The
framework provided by these meditations and the distribution of
matter outlined above constitute the *method* of the Spiritual
Exercises.

Psychology of the Exercises

It has long been a commonplace among retreat masters that
the Spiritual Exercises of St. Ignatius, when they are properly
given in a retreat, produce remarkable spiritual results, irrespective of the skill or lack of it in the retreat master. Skill in
the retreat director enhances the fruits, of course, but there
seems to be an efficacy peculiar to the Exercises themselves.
That this notion is not merely a part of the "family prejudice"
of the Jesuits is evidenced by the fact that Popes have voiced
this opinion to the universal Church (Mens Nostra, 4, p. 704).
Even psychologists have analyzed the Exercises and their psychology in order to find the secret of their efficacy. Thouless
(9, pp. 175–79) and Wright (10, pp. 292–95), for example,
whose work is classic in the field of the psychology of religion,
devote considerable space to a discussion of the Exercises as a

method of inducing what they call mysticism. Though their treatment is only of historical value now, the interesting thing is that they consider the Spiritual Exercises such an important "phenomenon." Perhaps the most famous of the psychological analyzers of the Exercises is Carl Gustav Jung. Some dozen years ago he devoted a full summer course to the analysis and discussion of the Spiritual Exercises as the most remarkable example in Western culture of the process he calls *individuation* (3).

Now it may be that the reports that were privately printed in Zurich are a distorted reflection of what Jung actually said in his lectures. Nevertheless, Jung's students receive them as genuine. In any case they contain a faulty conception of the Exercises. It might have been desirable (in conformity with the principle which analysts untiringly reiterate: that no one should presume to comment on depth psychology until he has been thoroughly analyzed) if he had made a closed retreat under a Jesuit before commenting on the Exercises.

But even in that case, Jung's comments would not be very instructive. They would stem from the theory of personality structure that is peculiar to him and would tell us much more about Jung than they would about the Exercises. We will not burden the discussion with a digest of Jung's psychology of personality. We presume it is well enough known. There is but one point that we might bring out to point up a little more sharply the fundamental inadequacy of Jung's "process of individuation" as a key concept to explain human personality growth. It would seem that the process of individuation would imply some sort of self-determination by the individual, either in the insight he acquires of the unconscious functions, or in the use he makes of them. If we look more closely, however, we shall see that the process of individuation as Jung describes it leaves no room for self-determination.

Intellectual development in man, according to Jung, is part of the intellectual evolution of the species; the individual development in the cognitive sphere from the sensory level to the intellectual, and from there to more and more abstract conceptions, is a perfect recapitulation of the evolution of the species—or even of the whole sweep of organic evolution! In like manner the development of individual freedom copies the growth of the freedom of the race. One must be careful to note that for Jung freedom and self-determination are equivalent to and synonymous with independence and immunity from external regulation. Jung seems not to be aware of what is fundamentally the essence of human freedom and self-determination. The basis of human freedom is not emancipation from rule or law as Jung seems to imply but immunity from physical compulsion in making a choice between alternatives. Hence for Jung the development of individual freedom is very much like the development of political freedom in the history of nations, and specifically the growth of national political autonomy in European history.

The process of individuation is the process by which the individual becomes fully autonomous. Though there seems to be some room for a striving for perfection, the striving that really counts is unconscious and complementary to conscious activity because no human being can get away from his natural bent. If he errs and misses the goal, it is for lack of awareness of the unconscious processes which would point the way when conscious deliberation fails. Because of the complementary nature of the personal conscious and unconscious, progress and development have a necessary direction which is imposed on man by the process of evolution. Evolution will ultimately lead to complete individuation, when the individual becomes not only autonomous but completely autarchic. At the contemporary stage of evolution this level has not been reached except by a few rare individuals. Freedom, as it now is in the individual, according to Jung, is something *like* self-determination. It can at most be a freedom of passive indifferentiation where to be this or that is *absolutely* contingent on something other than the activity of the individual, though it *looks* like active indifferentiation, that is, true self-determination. The ideal of individuality, for Jung, is the freedom of absolute independence, where the individual is subject to no law but his own will. Toward this goal it is nature that impels him. All he can do is put obstacles in the way.

How Jung with this concept of the ideal human person as the completely autarchic individual could ever expect to come to a proper appreciation of the psychological meaning of religion and God is a mystery. By the same token, it was psychologically impossible for him to understand the Spiritual Exercises. The whole orientation of the Spiritual Exercises points in a direction almost diametrically opposite. Far from developing the individual in the freedom of independence, their whole aim is to establish him in the freedom of the children of God (Cf. Chapter 8). Other "dynamic" theories of personality would succeed no better in uncovering the psychological dynamics of the Exercises (just as they miss the point when they attempt to account for religious experience in their description of human activity). The inadequacy of current "dynamic" theories has been discussed in a previous chapter. The goals they set for human personality growth are a far cry from the real goal of human self-actuation. The modes whereby the organization of human personality is supposed to be achieved are purely mechanical and atomistic, even when they strive to take into account the spiritual constituents and aspirations of man.

In a previous chapter we sketched the theoretical foundation for an adequate dynamic explanation of the psychological structure and development of human personality. We propose now to indicate how the Spiritual Exercises make use of the motive forces of human action to achieve that integrated personality organization that is effective in the spiritual and supernatural life of the soul. Since we are making a psychological analysis of the Exercises, our primary concern will be with the basic driving forces of human nature on the *psychological* level. Let us remember, nevertheless, that the Exercises are not merely a psychological device employed by St. Ignatius to achieve a certain psychological state in those who go through them. Personality integration in a purely psychological sense was not St. Ignatius' primary aim, even though the Exercises do in fact produce it. St. Ignatius was not a professional psychologist nor was he concerned with the construction of devices to produce psychological effects. He was concerned with the salvation of a man's soul and the progress a man is expected to make in the way of God. The Spiritual Exercises were devised as an instrument to help a man to establish himself in the way of Christian perfection and strengthen his efforts to achieve it. We must keep in mind also the economy of man's elevation to the supernatural order by sanctifying grace and its consequences for human action.

The fact is that man is not simply a natural thing, working out for himself a natural happiness within the narrow boundaries of this life. Man has been raised to the supernatural plane by sanctifying grace. Whether the individual accepts the fact or not, it remains true. The life of grace, the inner supernatural life demands that man surpass himself in a way that requires effort and discipline. The ideals which grace holds out are far beyond anything that man could imagine for himself without the knowledge that comes from what God has revealed about them. Man must pursue these ideals not only to reach his ultimate destiny but even to achieve the inner concord and peace of mind that he looks for in this life. It will be objected, of course, that grace and revelation have no place in a serious discussion of psychological matters. There have even been psychologists who have said that "it has been scientifically proved" that the supernatural life is a delusion and revelation is a snare. But to believe that God's grace is a delusion and that science is salvation is worse than a delusion; it is superstition.

Divine revelation is not a source from which we can draw psychological truth. But it can and should be used to test basic assumptions lest these lead us astray in our interpretation of the facts we find in psychological research. A *valid* assumption in science will not contradict a truth in *any* other field. In psychology we use other sciences as negative norms, we shun errors in physics or history or jurisprudence. Why shouldn't we be as docile with respect to revelation?

We mention this point mainly to make clear that the Spiritual Exercises of St. Ignatius are not just a psychological tour de force. We do say that the Spiritual Exercises make use of the basic dynamisms of human action in a remarkable manner and achieve an effective integration of human personality, on both the natural and the supernatural planes. St. Ignatius drew the Exercises not out of texts either in psychology or asceticism, but out of his own inner spiritual experience: at Loyola, at Manresa, in Paris, and later on (Dudon, 2, pp. 203–28). His personality certainly was adequate and effective. By means of the Exercises he formed not merely finely integrated men but even exceptional saints. It can be said that the Spiritual Exercises of St. Ignatius are the grammar of the soul's integration toward Christian perfection, accomplished by grace but founded on nature.

Dynamic Approach to a Self-Ideal

The very title St. Ignatius gave his book foreshadows the dynamic approach to the matter in hand. [21] [1] "Spiritual Exercises which have as their purpose the conquest of self and the regulation of one's life in such a way that no decision is made under the influence of any inordinate attachment." The first Annotation defines what St. Ignatius means by Exercises:

[1] By the term "Spiritual Exercises" is meant every method of examination of conscience, of meditation, of contemplation, of vocal and mental prayer, and of other spiritual activities that will be mentioned later. For just as taking a walk, journeying on foot, and running are bodily exercises, so we call spiritual exercises every way of preparing and disposing the soul to rid itself of all inordinate attachments, and, after their removal, of seeking and finding the will of God in the disposition of our life for the salvation of our soul.

St. Ignatius thought of the ordering of one's life as accomplished in activity and through activity. This ordering was to be done not by doing violence to any activity or even to any affection but by establishing the proper motive to the right goal. Thus in the Colloquy at the end of the meditation on Three Classes of Men, he says:

[157] It should be noted that when we feel an attachment opposed to actual poverty . . . it will be very helpful in order to overcome

[1] The numeral prefixed to any quotation from the text of the Exercises and the numeral given for any reference to the text denote the number assigned to the paragraph in the critical edition of the text in *Monumenta Historica S.J.* (5). It is now the general practice to make references to the text in this way. Puhl in his translation (7) numbers his paragraphs in this way. In the main our citations will be from Puhl's translation, except for certain few instances in which we will retain the traditional rendering. Thus, instead of the clumsy "Introductory Observations" we will continue to use "Annotations," as in the citation above.

the inordinate attachment . . . to beg our Lord in the colloquies *to choose us* to serve him in actual poverty. We should *insist that we desire it . . . provided, of course, that it be for the service . . . of the Divine Goodness.*

And in the sixteenth Annotation:

[16] Hence, *that the Creator and Lord may work with greater certainty* in His creature, if the soul chance to be inordinately attached or inclined to anything, it is very proper that it rouse itself by the exertion of all its powers to desire the opposite of that to which it is wrongly attached. *As a result, the reason he wants to retain anything will be solely the service of the Divine majesty.*

The effective motive for such detachment will be established when the individual is made aware of the general goal of human life and its particular application to himself. To put it into the frame of the theory of personality previously sketched: the proximate aim of the Exercises is to prepare the individual to eliminate any deviations from the self-ideal as it ought to be, as soon as he becomes aware of them; the ultimate aim is to come to know the self-ideal as it ought to be and to bring the self-ideal as it actually is to correspond to it.

As the whole course of the Spiritual Exercises makes clear, the central point is the Election, or Choice of a Way of Life, as Puhl translates the original. Puhl's translation is better, but Election has a centuries-old tradition of usage in this context. The Election, as we mentioned before, is a definite decision with respect to the pattern of life of the Exercitant. In the thirty-day retreat that is particularized in the book of the Exercises, this decision is a choice of a stable way of life that the retreatant has found to be the will of God for him.

In a wider field, however, the Election is the effective and active choice of the self-ideal as it ought to be. This ideal is Christian perfection, adapted, however, to the individual case as to manner, mode, and detail, as the exercitant has discovered them in the course of the retreat. The dispositions necessary for choosing well are the same as those required for finding and recognizing what ought to be chosen. These same dispositions are needed in the continued arrangement of one's life, i.e., in the progressive integration of activity in accordance with the choice that has been made. Once the soul has been "prepared and disposed . . . to seek and find the will of God" [1] it will be disposed to choose it, and having chosen it, "to order its life" [1]. For the *active* choice of the Ideal as it ought to be contains also the choice of the means for attaining it. The goal, then, to be reached in the Exercises is the discovery and choice of the self-ideal as it ought to be (for this individual) and the effective orientation of the self to reach that ideal in the course of life.

The term of discovery and choice is reached, during the retreat, in a series of eight steps. Each step follows the other in a psychologically graduated way in such a manner that the goal might not be reached if one were omitted. These eight steps constitute, structurally, the essential method of the Spiritual Exercises of St. Ignatius. They consist of the six distinctively Ignatian meditations of the Exercises: The Foundation, The Kingdom of Christ, Two Standards, Three Classes of Men, Three Kinds of Humility, The Contemplation to Attain Love. These six bear an important relation to the seventh Ignatian feature, the Election. Since the Election will be different for different individuals, it will determine the extent to which meditation of Sin and Hell will be included in the retreat. But these meditations are to be included to some extent in every retreat. The progression runs therefore: (1) The Foundation; (2) Sin; (3) The Kingdom of Christ; (4) Two Standards; (5) Three Classes of Men; (6) Three Kinds of Humility; (7) The Election; (8) The Contemplation to Attain Love. Within the framework of these meditations, the life, passion, death, resurrection of Christ are proposed for meditation for the purpose of enlightening and strengthening the exercitant to seek and find God's will in his regard.

What we will attempt to do here is to unfold the psychological momentum of each and all of these steps as they affect personality integration. In the Annotations, St. Ignatius, after giving some idea of the mechanics of the Exercises [1, 2, 3], remarks [5] that large-hearted liberality towards God is a primary requisite for one who is to receive the Exercises. If they are to be given in full, it is supposed that the exercitant is "one desirous of making as much progress as possible" [20]. The exercitant is to begin with single-minded dedication of himself to his task "in solitude and silence, without distraction, as far as that can be arranged" [20]. From the very beginning the exercitant is put into an atmosphere of singleness of purpose, seriousness of intention, and willingness of mind. We need not point out how necessary these dispositions are for anyone who wishes not only to make something of himself but in the making to achieve an adequate personality. This generous offering of one's self to God in the beginning is as all-embracing as the offering of the Contemplation to Attain Love [234] at the end of the Exercises, but there the specific content will be more detailed.

Principle and Foundation. The first step in the preparation for finding and embracing one's proper self-ideal begins with the Foundation. This is a clear and convincing statement of what in general is the purpose of man's life, what are the general means available to attain that purpose, and the outlook a man must adopt towards these means if he is to be successful in reaching the goal.

[23] *First Principle and Foundation.* Man is created to praise, reverence and serve God, and by this means to save his soul. The other things on the face of the earth are created for man to help him in attaining the end for which he is created. Hence, man is to make use of them in as far as they help him in the attainment of his end, and he must rid himself of them in as far as they prove a hindrance to him. Therefore, we must make ourselves indifferent to all created things, as far as we are allowed free choice and are not under any prohibition. Consequently as far as we are concerned, we should not prefer health to sickness, riches to poverty, honor to dishonor, a long life to a short one. The same holds for all other things. Our one desire and choice should be what is more conducive to the end for which we are created.

Meditating on this the exercitant sees in a general way that "getting the most out of life" means coming to possess God. He becomes convinced of the "just as far as they help" rule and is disposed to "desiring and choosing only what is more conducive to the end for which we are created." This disposition is the first determination of the indeterminate orientation he had given himself in the beginning. In the course of his meditating on the Foundation, the exercitant has become aware in some more or less vague way that he has deviated from the goal he should reach—whether in some particular instance or in the general tenor of his life.

Self-Ideal As It Is. The next step is to bring to full consciousness the extent and significance of this deviation so that he be more effectively moved to whatever reorientation may be necessary. This is accomplished in the meditations of the first Week wherein the exercitant comes to know himself not only in his deviant conduct, which has been gravely sinful, but also in the deviating attractions and motivations that have been at the root of his sinful behavior and in the disintegrative principles ("worldly and vain things" [63]) which have been the source of deviating motives. It is precisely this knowledge that is the burden of the Triple Colloquy after the third exercise of the first Week.

[63] . . . grace for three favors: 1. A deep knowledge of my sins and a feeling of abhorrence for them. 2. An understanding of the disorder of my actions, that filled with horror of them, I may amend my life and put it in order. 3. A knowledge of the world, that filled with horror, I may put away from me all that is worldly and vain.

In the first exercise he had meditated on the dire consequences of sin in others. In the colloquy he had found himself before Christ on the cross, the victim of sin, to reflect in shame and confusion on why and how he had escaped the penalty of sin, and to ask himself what he is to do in the future. In the second exercise he had meditated more specifically on his own deviations from the goal set by God; coming to know the full extent of the malice of his sins, whatever their gravity might have been. This clear and objective self-concept, defining the extent by which his actual behavior had diverged from the goal to be reached, led to the Colloquy of Mercy [61] and an effective resolve to amendment. The third exercise then extends the content of the self-concept to include deviant motivation and the sources whence they flow. A hint is given that the ideals which the exercitant had actually set up for attainment—"worldly and vain things"—may be in fact disintegrating rather than integrating factors in the total "laying out of one's life." Other meditations in the first Week confirm the efficacious desire which the exercitant has conceived of responding to Christ's love and deepen his detestation for sin [65]. Until the exercitant comes this far, he is not ready for the next step in the process.

Up to this point he has been occupied mainly in considering general and abstract truths in an analytic way. He has come to some realization that the way he has lived is not bringing him to the goal he should attain. He has in a vague way come to a resolve to reorientate himself more effectively towards that goal. He knows now that the self-ideal he actually had does not quite correspond to the self-ideal as it should be. He feels that these ideals should be made to coincide. And to make them coincide, he knows he must divest himself of "all disorderly attachments to creatures" [1]. This difficult task will hardly be accomplished with the help only of abstract motives. The Exercises now take the first step in making the self-ideal as it ought to be, more concrete and personal.

Self-Ideal As It Ought To Be. In the meditation on the Kingdom of Christ, the person of Christ Our Lord is proposed as the exemplar of the offering of self to the service of God. St. Ignatius proposed a parable of an earthly king, calling for followers to join him in the conquest of the lands of the infidel. Such a parable would appeal to a sixteenth-century young man of parts and promise (the retreatant the book has in view) because he would appreciate and sympathize with its military and feudal character. The parable is not important. What is important is the attractive quality of Christ's personality and the worthwhileness of an enthusiastic response to His appeal. Stress is not laid upon the following of Christ in external actions; internal victories are specified:

[97] Those who wish to give greater proof of their love, and to distinguish themselves in the service of the eternal King and Lord of all,

will not only offer themselves for work, but will act against their sensuality and carnal and worldly love, and make offerings of greater value and of more importance.

These offerings are more fundamental and wider in scope. What the Kingdom is designed to do is to make a concrete person the motive for striving for the true self-ideal and to intensify the desire of the exercitant to seek and find it. It is a kind of second Foundation where the true self-ideal becomes better specified and the means of attaining it are outlined in a general way. The person of Christ and the work of Christ are proposed as the object for striving and attainment. An enthusiastic response is called for and the means are provided to assure this response. These means are sketched in the third point of the second part of the exercise quoted above. Those who wish to signalize themselves make offers of greater value in deciding to act against their love for creature comforts, their love for those connected with them by ties of blood, and their love of worldly things and principles.

These three loves are, for the most part, the motives for action found in the majority of men. They stem from the self-ideals men actually set themselves and they govern not only large segments of personality formation but often enough they determine the total pattern of living. These three loves, which to such a great extent manifest the self-ideal as it is actually set up for so many people, are the sources of the inordinate attachments that are responsible for the deviations from the true self-ideal. These three loves are nothing more than particular manifestations of the basic tendency inherent in every human being to actualize the self in psychologically stabilized and secure possession of what is attractive to human nature.

Creature comforts (sense pleasures of whatever kind), one's own "flesh and blood" (relatives, friends, social companions, the people who belong to us in some way), the world (its ways, requirements, rewards, renown, and approbation), are "the good things of this life" (Nonell, 6, pp. 206–09). These are the *satisfactions of human life*; these the goals, for the most part, of human striving. On the other hand, privation, discomfort, disapprobation, reproach, rejection, are the "evil things" from which human nature is so strongly repelled. These are the *frustrations of human "needs,"* the *obstacles and barriers* to self-realization. (Any psychologist will recognize the flavor of the emphasized words.)

Freeing the Self-Ideal; First Stage. It is to the management and coordination of these "good" and "evil" things that the second Week addresses itself, for the dynamic motivating force of each must be truly assessed if the exercitant is efficaciously to find and choose the true self-ideal. The scope of the second Week is to disencumber the self-ideal as it is, of all disintegrating elements and motives and to bring it into conformity with the true self-ideal. This is done in a graded series of stages leading to the summit of preparatory dispositions—the Third Degree of Humility (Nonell, 6, pp. 228, 229).

The first stage is the realization that the "good things" of this life are not absolutely necessary for true peace, modest happiness, and effective living. During this stage the Incarnation, the Nativity of our Lord, the Hidden Life, and the Finding in the Temple are contemplated. In these events in the life of Christ the exercitant learns how Christ manages and deals with the three loves. The contemplation on the Incarnation gives a broad and general summary; the Nativity follows, showing Christ's disregard for comfort and convenience; the Finding in the Temple shows the relative importance of love for one's parents and the demands of God's will; the Hidden Life, showing in what small regard Christ held the opinion and approbation of the "world."

Freeing the Self-Ideal; Second Stage. The second stage in the second Week is the realization that the "good things" are difficult to possess and use without disorder. This stage comprises the meditations on Two Standards and Three Classes of Men, the fourth and fifth steps towards the "Election." In the meditation of Two Standards—the Standard or Banner of Lucifer and the Standard of Christ—the exercitant comes to see how Lucifer uses the "good things" to deceive and ensnare mankind, while on the other hand Christ uses the "evil things" to bring man to his true perfection. This meditation is a thorough study of the artifices of the devil (and of our own natural inclinations, which so often are fellow-travellers with Satan and slick propagandizers of his party line).

This study is introduced by St. Ignatius for a rather special reason. The exercitant whom the book has in view is a young man of good worldly prospects and well endowed with human talents, who is seeking to decide his vocation in life. Such a young man will very likely make his decision by examining reasons for and against the various ways of life that lie open to him. The reasons that might be found for staying in the world and devoting one's self to secular pursuits are all appealing to the natural man and are very likely to exert an influence on the young man's decision out of proportion to their true weight in the balance of things. The amount of real good that a person of wealth and influence can do in secular life might obscure for the young man that the important factor is the will of God in the matter. Some means must be provided by which the exercitant can evaluate justly the appeal that humanly attractive things do have, because for all their attractiveness these things can be deceitful.

That the deceits of the devil are the cardinal point in this meditation seems to be clear from the text and context. St. Ignatius seems to want everything to subserve to this element and to bring out by contrast "what is the true life." In the third prelude, he reverses the order of the points proposed in the first and second; he makes the first grace asked a knowledge of the deceits of the rebel chief [139]. In the meditation itself he reverses the order of the considerations he proposed in the section immediately preceding the meditation [135]. In any case, the way in which St. Ignatius goes to the very roots of the motivation leading to the true life proposed by Christ on the one hand and the life proposed by the "enemy of our human nature" [136] on the other is psychologically so apt and penetrating that it deserves some study.

There is no need for any extended experiment to establish the fact that there is a twofold polarity in human activity. All history, all culture, all experience point to it. It goes by a myriad of names: Good and Evil; Yin and Yang; Progress and

Decline. It is characteristically human, for in no other class of beings do we find so pronouncedly that push toward surpassing the present conditions of affairs combined with a reluctance to disturb the status quo. No dray horse colt leaves home to seek his fortune, by becoming the champion dray—much less to beat Citation's record on the track. No human being is ever quite content to remain what he is where he is, but seeks always to better himself some way or other, yet is reluctant to pay the price of effort and privation that striving for the higher and the better necessarily exacts. Hence only in the human do we find inner states of tension that are never reduced to equilibrium —states of tension that are easily mistaken for conflict but which of themselves do not imply either hostility or destruction.

There is a striving for the increase of the life of mind; a craving to discover, to make one's own the hidden and the secret, the unannounced, and the unpublished. Some men spend their lives wresting the secrets of Nature from her bosom; measuring the immeasurable, pondering the imponderable—the vast majority reach no further than gossip and the newspaper. But withal the demands of the body and its senses are no less insistent and much more immediate. And strange to say, the lesser values exert the stronger pull. The human being finds himself urged in two directions at once and the consequent tension, unless it is somehow released, becomes intolerable. Some unification, some combination is necessary, for the human being cannot long go on being so pulled apart.

Some individuals take one direction, give in to the more immediate and more insistent demands of the flesh exclusively, and suppress or deny the higher life. They devote themselves to the demands of the body and refuse themselves the higher delights of mind. "A shady glade, a jug of wine and thou!" But even these find steadfastness in a single aim hard to achieve. Because of this, others try to live each kind of life alternately, while keeping them as mutually exclusive as possible. They give the higher things a whirl during the working season, then put their backs into the job of dissipation during vacation. They find that this may work for a time, but sooner or later their watertight compartments spring leaks, and the demands of neither life are ever adequately satisfied. Others there are, more reasonable and perhaps more honest with themselves, who try to split the difference and play both ends against the middle. They select features out of each life that suit them or are more easily combined and deem that the kind of life to live. They make a provisional parallelogram of forces and strike out along the diagonal, only to find to their disillusionment how crooked the diagonal gets to be because of the fickleness and inconstancy of the forces they seek to combine and the vagaries of their momentary wants and needs. The harmony of life that will temper sweetly the demands of the whole man is hard to come by. What is needed is a rational appreciation of all the factors that enter into making a rewarding life, together with a skill in fitting them all together in such a way that they complement one another.

When we consider man's supernatural state and destiny, how much more difficult the problem becomes! For the fact remains that man does not have merely a natural life to live but has been put on a higher and more exacting plane. This is not the place to expound at length the economy of grace. Suffice it to say that the coming of Christ and the gift of grace to man have made this difference—that man must somehow reach the summit of Christlikeness, with grace to help him, to be sure, but with only his human motive powers to use as tools in the ascent.

These motive powers are the basic tendencies to possession, social recognition, and self-actuation. And these by nature are inclined not to the arduous and spiritually rewarding but to the least resistant and effortless. If the impulse to possession is to work towards what even in the natural man is deemed perfection, then it must be a giving and not a taking, or at the very least a being content with less, without avidity for more. And how much more so on the supernatural level! The drive toward self-establishment and domination must be altered to conform to what John the Baptist announced to be his aim: "He must increase and I must decrease" (John 3:30). Self-actualization must become the realization of those nuances of Christlikeness that grace demands in different individuals. Much more than nature does grace require that each man's life be lived in the third person.

St. Ignatius had experienced in himself this bipolarity of human aspiration. In the long hours spent on his sickbed at Loyola he had experienced, reflected upon, and come to understand the spirit that moved him to opposite ambitions at various times. He had made such a resolution of the tensions that were pulling him apart psychologically that not only did it harmonize and unify the pattern of his life, it brought him in the course of his career to full integrity. In this light we must interpret what he proposes for consideration in the plan of campaign described as Lucifer's and the one described as Christ's. Riches, honors, pride, are the steps the devil uses in his plan to keep men from reaching the goal of life. We must not think that St. Ignatius believed that the devil works exactly that way with everyone in every case. But St. Ignatius knew that for the retreatant for whom the book was written, a young man with prospects in the world, the attack of the devil would take that direction. Nor must we imagine that St. Ignatius was unaware that the young man would be harried also in the same way by "the enemies of his own household"—his own emotional proclivities. To make the proper resolution of the tensions that the exercitant finds within himself, he must become convinced that detachment from riches and honors, and only detachment, will enable him to assess the value of these things objectively. But to attain this detachment more surely, he should aim higher and *ask* for actual poverty and humiliations. This disposition can be acquired only with the aid of prayer, hence a solemn triple colloquy is put at the end of the exercise and its use is prescribed throughout the rest of the Week.

St. Ignatius, however, saw the implications of the Two Standards more clearly than we can. He hints at a widening of the concept contained in the riches-honors-pride sequence, when he says that Christ wants the opposite doctrine to "spread among all men, no matter what their state or condition" [145]. Now not all men will be tempted to gain riches, not all men will be subject to the same wiles of the devil or be bedeviled by their own emotions in the same way. If we recognize that *spiritual* poverty [146] is the opposite of riches [142] we can safely enlarge the concept to mean cupidity or *acquisitiveness*. It becomes clear, then, that riches-honors-pride is a paradigm for a more fundamental sequence. We can then take the wider concept that includes honors to be *desire for credit or recognition,* and pride to be *inordinate esteem of self*. How close this is to saying that the devil, to gain his own ends, makes use of the basic motive tendencies of human action, is recognizable at a glance. What the meditation says is that the exercitant will be subject to deceit if he lets the basic tendencies to possession, psychological stabilization and self-actuation work themselves out in an unintegrated way.

Detachment, humiliation, humility, then, are a paradigm for these same tendencies in a properly oriented and integrated way. Detachment therefore is possession moderated and controlled by the will of God; humiliation, self-establishment with its foundation of security in dependence on God; humility, self-actuation according to the ideals that God sets up. The outcome of the meditation thus becomes the conviction that following the natural bent of the natural tendencies will render integral development precarious. To be secure one must follow the example of Christ and manage these tendencies as He did. The self-ideal as it ought to be now becomes much more clearly defined. It is the person of Christ, as it was proposed in the Kingdom, but now made more definite in detail and containing elements more narrowly applicable to the individual.

Immediately following upon the Two Standards, the meditation of the Three Classes is made. This is the last step in the second stage of the second Week. The meditation concerns three classes of men who have an inordinate attachment to a sum of money innocently acquired and wish to rid themselves of the attachment. The purpose of the meditation is not the actual choice of the more difficult or the less self-indulgent mode of going about it, but a consideration of different frames of mind that might be found in people in a situation similar to the exercitants, *so as to choose the best*. This may not seem to be much of a forward movement, since it does not appear to aid us in making a choice merely to evaluate what others may do in similar circumstances. Psychologically, however, it is a forward movement because what is made clear is the irrationality both of no real resoluteness at all and of escape by compromise. The exercitant is psychologically cut away from the self-ideal as he has had it, when following purely natural bents and "worldly" inclinations and is set free to turn toward the true self-ideal.

Freeing the Self-Ideal; Third and Fourth Stage. The third stage of the second Week is the realization that the "frustrating" things of life need not be feared by one who has turned to the true ideal. This is the burden of the meditations on the Public Life of Our Lord. In contemplating these, provision is made against the difficulties that will become apparent when the enthusiasm of the retreat has died down. The exercitant's reluctance in the face of privation and self-denial is diminished by the conviction, drawn from the example of Christ and his disciples, that God will provide what is needful and protect him should danger threaten his person. In the life of Christ, altruistic devotion to others was no obstacle but rather an effective means to progress in the work He set out to do. So too for the exercitant. And thus any remnant of negative bias against the true ideal is removed and the exercitant is freed of diverging factors.

The fourth and last stage of the second Week, and the final step in the preparation for making the effective choice of the true ideal is in the consideration of Three Kinds of Humility. In this meditation, an unconscious bias in favor of the "good things," which enables them to exert a stronger appeal upon a person than they should, is counteracted and eliminated. Given the case where the goal may be equally attained by the use of the easy things as of the hard, the exercitant is inclined to take the hard way because of a desire to be more like Christ, "who chose the cross, despising the shame." (Heb. 12:2.) This positive bias toward privation and abnegation is not for the sake of mere privation or pain but in order that the Christlike personality which is now proposed as the one and true Ideal, may have more room in the individual's life to grow and develop. In this meditation there is not proposed a motive or a method of avidly seeking sheer self-abasement but rather the true self-ideal is unfolded. This consists in complete and total dependence on God in the governing of one's life. It reaches its summit when Christ and His love so dominate the individual that, in the order of grace, the assimilation of the soul to the mystical Christ and its transformation into Him has become real at least in germ. Self-abnegation and humiliation are necessary only so that the personal characteristics that are not Christlike be eliminated from the motivation and behavior of the individual. Even on the natural level, to wish to be poor with Christ poor, lowly with Christ lowly, unknown with Christ unknown, rejected with Christ rejected, out of personal attachment to Him, will give the most rewarding direction to life and the greatest stability in all its vicissitudes.

Nevertheless, after the exercitant has put himself in the requisite dispositions for making a good choice and has made it, he has no assurance that he will remain constant in his decision. In Annotation 18, where there is reference to one who makes only the first Week, certain practices for the future are recommended "so as to retain what he has gained" [18]. So, for those who make the Exercises in full, the third and fourth Week are meant to preserve the excellent dispositions thus far inculcated and to give constancy to each one's plan of life. Moreover, if we remember that the thirty-day retreat, as it is written in the book, was given only once in a lifetime and was presumed to form the solid substructure upon which the subsequent life of perfection was to rest, it is to be expected that there would be some element in it to confirm the choice made in the Election and be of some avail for perseverance. This strengthening would not be brought about merely by holding on to what one has acquired in the retreat thus far; it requires rather a distinct forward movement, which results in the final attainment of the twofold aim of the Exercises, detachment from disordered affections and the ordering of life according to the will of God.

Confirming the Self-Ideal. The work of removing all disintegrating movements in one's basic motivating tendencies has not yet been finished. There still remains the natural inclination toward what is pleasant and the natural aversion from what is unpleasant. These natural impulses cannot, of course, be removed; to attempt that would be to attempt to destroy human nature itself. What can be removed, though, is disorder in the activities they set in motion. This disorder consists first in going counter to the known will of God and secondly acting without reference to the will of God. To translate this into the terms of our personality theory: disorder comes in going counter to the true self-ideal deliberately and with knowledge of it; and secondly, in organizing our behavior without reference to our true self-ideal.

Removal of disorder from our actions had been the aim of the first Week. After that effort had been directed toward removing disorder from the tendencies that lie at the root of action. In the second Week emphasis was put on removing disorder from our tendencies to the "good things" of human life. The aim had been to change an unreflecting drive to possess these things into a holding back lest we be led too far in the wrong direction. The third Week now aims at removing the disorder from the natural aversion from the unpleasant and frustrating things. This task is the more difficult one because man tends to avoid the unpleasant things more energetically than he seeks to enjoy the pleasant things. The third Week aims at changing this energetic avoidance into a positive movement toward embracing the painful things out of love for Christ suffering, a motive that has already been proposed in the Third Kind of Humility.

The mysteries of the Passion, with the personal note being struck continually, are calculated to do just this. The powerful psychological means employed are the continued use of the colloquy of the Two Standards and the Three Classes [199] which keeps before one's attention the reorientation of motives that must become habitual, and the "what I desire" of the third prelude to all the contemplations: "In the Passion it is proper to ask for sorrow with Christ in sorrow . . ." [203], that is to say, the *actual experience of suffering* (Nonell, 6, pp. 360–61). The transformation into Christ that the exercitant aims at will only be accomplished through love. Love is a transforming virtue and only love assures constancy. And whether it be of the nature of love or not, love in this life must always mean suffering. It is this love of *compassion*—in the strictest sense of the word—that will enable the person to do and suffer the great things entailed in reaching the perfection of his self-ideal (Ambruzzi, 1, p. 105).

Making the Self-Ideal Permanent. The process of making permanent the unity of the self-ideal as the exercitant now has conceived it and the true Ideal in the person of Christ is completed in the fourth Week, where any disorder, even in the attachment to spiritual and supernatural things, is removed by making the joy and triumph of Christ in His Resurrection the motive for any satisfaction felt in the integrated movement toward the true Ideal. Thus a complete detachment from self is achieved, and the person is set free to move without hindrance or deviation to the pinnacle of self-actuation which is found in thoroughgoing Christlikeness or, what amounts to the same thing, complete integrity, that is, sanctity.

The Exercises end with the Contemplation for attaining Divine Love. This is the crown and pinnacle of the retreat and the term toward which ultimately the integrated personality must move. How far the exercitant has moved in that direction during the retreat may be judged by examining the offering of self with which he began the retreat [5] and comparing it with the one he makes in the Contemplation: "Take, Lord, and receive all my liberty, my memory, my understanding, and all my will, all that I have and possess. Thou hast given all to me. To Thee, O Lord, I return it. Dispose of it wholly according to Thy will. Give me Thy love and Thy grace, for this is sufficient for me" [234]. At the start, he *offered*; now he makes a donation. In the beginning he submitted himself to whatever would occur; now he makes a mutual interchange of gifts. Before, the motive was liberality; now, it is strict justice and right reason. When he began, the "magnanimity" was come by with difficulty; now, the fervor of love makes the difficulties no obstacle. Before, the aim of the offering was to *serve God*; now, the object of the gift is to *love God for Himself alone*.

In the field of personality integration and development, the Exercises lead to the most perfect mode of self-actuation—the mode which consists in the *active* possession of the *adequate* object of *all* desire. All the tendencies and powers peculiar to the human being as such, which in so many instances work in conflict or at cross purposes, are brought into a harmonious active unity by active, actual, practised love of God. In the actual and active loving of God the person finds himself in the most suitable condition with respect to himself, with respect to his environment, with respect to his inner tendencies. "For them that love God, *all* things work together unto good."

The foregoing analysis has sketched in broad lines a single instance of the influence man's religious living has on personality integration. We trust that it has shown in a clearer light the function of man's relationship to God in the whole business of living. We trust, too, that a better understanding of the Spiritual Exercises of St. Ignatius has been the result of our analysis. We do not expect that everybody will agree either with our psychology or our interpretation of the Spiritual Exercises. But it is always possible to test our psychology and our interpretation by making a retreat.

REFERENCES

1. AMBRUZZI. 1939. *Spiritual Exercises of St. Ignatius.* Bangalore: St. Joseph.
2. DUDON, P. 1949. *St. Ignatius Loyola.* (Tr.) WM. J. YOUNG, S.J. Milwaukee: Bruce Publishing Co.
3. JUNG, CARL G. 1939–40. *The process of individuation—The Exercitia Spiritualia of St. Ignatius.* Lectures at the Eidgenössische Technische Hochschule, Zürich. English Reports, 1939–40, privately printed.
4. *Mens Nostra.* Encyclical Letter of Pius XI, Acta Apostolicae Sedis, xxi (1929) pp. 689–706.
5. MONUMENTA HISTORICA SOCIETATIS JESU. 1919. *Exercitia Spiritualia.* Madrid: Ribedineira.
6. NONELL, JAIME. 1896. *Los Ejercicios Espirituales.* Manresa: San Jose.
7. PUHL, LOUIS J. 1951. *The Spiritual Exercises of St. Ignatius. A New Translation.* Westminster, Md.: Newman Press.
8. SCHAER, HANS. 1950. *Religion and the cure of souls in Jung's psychology.* (Tr.) R. F. C. HULL. New York: Pantheon Books, Inc.
9. THOULESS, R. H. 1928. *An Introduction to the psychology of religion.* Cambridge: Cambridge University Press.
10. WRIGHT, W. K. 1935. *A student's philosophy of religion.* New York: The Macmillan Co.

INDEX OF NAMES

References to bibliographies are in italics

INDEX OF SUBJECTS

IMPRIMI POTEST
    Joseph M. Egan, S.J. Provincial. Chicago, Oct. 8, 1953.

NIHIL OBSTAT
    Austin G. Schmidt, S.J. Censor Deputatus. Oct. 30, 1953.

IMPRIMATUR
    ✠ Samuel Cardinal Stritch, Archbishop of Chicago. Nov. 4, 1953.